COMMUNICATION
AND PUBLIC RELATIONS

COMMUNICATION
AND PUBLIC RELATIONS

EDWARD J. ROBINSON
Chairman and Professor
Communication Research Division
School of Public Communication
Boston University

Charles E. Merrill Publishing Co.
Columbus, Ohio
A Bell & Howell Company

Library of Congress Catalog Card Number: 66-14409

3 4 5 6 7 8 9 10 11 12 13 14 15-76 75 74 73 72

Printed in the United States of America

To My Wife, Priscilla

PREFACE

"Public Relations: A Great Idea with a Bad Reputation." This title, given to a summary of a research report by a former graduate student of mine, in certain ways sums up my reasons for writing this book. The notion that an organization should be consciously concerned with earning acceptance and respect *is* a great idea. Furthermore, the concept that earning this acceptance requires a careful charting of goals and ascertaining that these goals are consistent with the best interests of the various individuals, organizations, and groups involved is a sophisticated idea. Finally, the realization that one needs a specialist to implement and guide the various actions required to reach an organization's goals is consistent with modern administrative practice. A specialized function requires a specially trained individual.

Why then does this good idea still suffer from a bad reputation? There are two reasons that stand out.

First, the functions of a public relations practitioner have not previously been properly identified. Some books on public relations tend to portray this field as a splintered, complicated, and unintegrated combination of many responsibilities, skills, and functions. These same books generally have either chapters or subheadings within chapters devoted to a discussion of public relations in banks, in hospitals, in higher education, in nonprofit agencies, in the military, etc. This approach suggests that each category of public relations functioning requires different knowledge and skills—that a public relations practitioner in one context operates according to different principles than one in another. This, in turn, prevents those interested in the future of this field from agreeing upon the training necessary for a public relations practitioner. It also stands in the way of arriving at a consensus about what related bodies of knowledge are essential for a public relations practitioner.

Secondly, there has been no conceptual framework developed into which to fit the functions of a public relations practitioner. This resistance to a theoretical analysis of public relations has had a number of effects. For one, public relations is seen as more of an "art" rather than as a potential science or discipline. There is the implicit, sometimes explicit, assumption that it can never become rigorous in practice. Another effect has been to impede the use of research in helping to solve public relations problems. Finally, the realization that public relations is undergoing an evolutionary change that borders on a revolution, *as is the case in most applied fields*, is obscured. The awareness that business administration, advertising, journalism, and television are all undergoing dramatic changes is difficult to appreciate if one remains wed to the notion that applied fields are, by definition, non-theoretical.

This book represents an effort to combat problems that obstruct the sound growth of the field of public relations. In the first three chapters, four completely different public relations cases are presented and then examined in order to find what *common* characteristics can be perceived. Whenever a public relations problem situation is analyzed, it almost inevitably boils down to some sort of attitude and behavior change or maintenance problem. That is, the practitioner in question is either trying to change or maintain someone's or some group's behavior and attitudes. All the activities that the practitioner undertakes to achieve these attitude and behavior changes or maintenance highlight *superficial differences* that tend to belie *fundamental similarities*. This is why I have defined the public relations practitioner as an applied social and behavioral scientist.

Also consistent with this definition is the emphasis on communication that is to be found in this book. Chapters 4 and 5 carefully develop a communication theory model *into which* public relations problems can be translated so that they can be more systematically analyzed and solved. This permits the development of a conceptual framework—in this case a communication theory model—which I feel has been missing in other books on public relations. The social and behavioral science definition and the communication model emphasis serve notice that public relations practice is *not* always to remain a non-rigorous "art." Chapters 6 through 16 relate the social and behavioral sciences to public relations practice and indicate how increased rigor can and should be forthcoming.

The communication model approach also permits the utilization of research by the public relations practitioner. This is a development that is long overdue. The last four chapters of this volume, Chapters 17 through 20, are devoted to explaining the relationship between research and public relations practice. These chapters convey to the reader the essentials of research and how the methods of the researcher apply to public relations practice. This is partly why I have emphasized what I call "do-it-yourself" research efforts, which are the main topic of Chapter 20.

As any author, I am indebted to many people who have contributed their talents to make this volume possible. I trust that I will be forgiven any oversights in acknowledgments inadvertently made. To begin with, I want to acknowledge the assistance of various members of the Public Relations Division (both past and present) of the School of Communication, Boston University. As a one-time member of that Division, I benefited greatly from the many discussions that took place with other faculty members. I would also like to recognize the many public relations practitioners, both in this country and abroad, who provided me with advice and encouragement to write this book and gave me additional opportunity to see public relations practitioners "in action." Others who deserve acknowledgment are Professor Albert J. Sullivan for his assistance and Professor David Manning White for the wisdom that only a successful author can impart. To Miss Linda Goldberg, my secretary, a sincere vote of thanks for patiently and expertly typing the entire manuscript.

I particularly wish to thank members of my Division, Dr. Ralph L. Rosnow and Dr. F. Earle Barcus, for the time that they devoted to a critical reading of my manuscript and for all their valuable insights and suggestions. Also, Dr. Fredric Powell, a former member of my Division, deserves much credit for his comments, which strengthened various portions of my work.

Finally, I wish to acknowledge the constant support and encouragement from my wife, Priscilla, whose presence made it all possible.

Edward J. Robinson

Westwood, Massachusetts
January, 1966

TABLE OF CONTENTS

About the Remainder of the Book, 55
    Questions for Discussion, 56

PART TWO   PUBLIC RELATIONS:
             A THEORETICAL ANALYSIS

Chapter 4   A COMMUNICATION THEORY MODEL, 61

               Introduction, 61
               Why Do We Need a Model? 63
               Communication Is a Process, 65
               Case Study No. 5—The Case of the Perishing Fish, 65
               The Sender Stage, 66
               The Message Stage, 78
               The Media Stage, 82
               The Recipient Stage, 86
               Visualizing Communication as a Process, 88
                   Questions for Discussion, 88

Chapter 5   THE COMMUNICATION MODEL IN A SOCIAL CONTEXT, 90

               Introduction, 90
               Five Observations Concerning the Communication Model
                   as a Whole, 90
               The Communication Process as Part of the Larger So-
                   cial Context, 105
                   Questions for Discussion, 123

Chapter 6   THE SENDER STAGE IN MORE DETAIL: ADOPTING THE
               PROBLEM-SOLVING ATTITUDE, 125

               Introduction, 125
               I. The Beginning Point: Self-Analysis, 126
               II. The Next Point: Adopting the Problem-Solving At-
                   titude, 130
               III. The Third Point: The Public Relations Process with
                   Additional Refinements, 138
                   Questions for Discussion, 140

LIST OF FIGURES

COMMUNICATION
AND PUBLIC RELATIONS

Part 1

PUBLIC RELATIONS:
A POINT OF VIEW

Chapter 1

INTRODUCTION

In a survey[1] conducted by the writer a few years ago, designed to ascertain the attitudes of a group of advertising men toward public relations practitioners and their activities, the following question was one of several asked with respect to public relations: "When you hear the expression *public relations*, what comes to your mind?" This question was followed by "Would you describe your impressions of the typical or 'average' public relations man?"

As a first step in reading this volume, it will be of significant value to the reader to answer those two questions before going on to the next paragraph. What do you think of when you hear the expression *public relations*? Is this a question that you find easy or difficult to answer? How certain are you that your answer is a "typical" one, or do you think that your views in this regard might be atypical? In answering the second question, how did you describe the typical or average public relations man? Did you avoid answering the question by claiming that there is no such thing as an "average" public relations man? If you did venture an opinion, were your impressions, on the whole, positive or negative?

Let's see how your answers compare with a brief summary of the responses of the advertising men to the same two questions. A small

---

[1] This survey was based on a 10% probability sample of the total membership of the Boston Advertising Club. It was conducted by graduate students in the School of Public Communication, Boston University, under the direction of the author, as part of a course on survey research methods. A summary, entitled "Public Relations: A Great Idea with a Bad Reputation," was written of the study by Michael Clifton, a research assistant to the author.

percentage of respondents, in response to the first question, said that their first thoughts were summed up by the following words or phrases: *crooks, con men, glad hands.* The largest percentage of respondents said that their first thoughts were of persons who "did publicity," "created images," or were responsible for "liaison between a company and the public."

With respect to the second question, the respondents summed up the typical or average public relations man as: "A personality boy—able to meet, impress, and work well with people." "A communicator—able to speak and write well, but one to watch—he may have great integrity or may be a 'con man'; he may be personable and mature or a shallow extrovert; he may succeed due to doing good work or through using people."

How did your replies to the two questions asked in the opening paragraph square with our brief summary of the advertising men? Were you among the group with rather negative attitudes or views about public relations practitioners? Or were your views closer to the much larger percentage of respondents who held rather ambivalent views about the field of public relations and its practitioners?

Obviously, we cannot be certain as to how these data, obtained from a comparatively homogeneous group of individuals engaged in an occupation that has some overlap with the field of public relations, would apply today to the same group. Even more uncertain is the question as to how much these data would be applicable to all advertising people in the United States, or to the "general public"—that is, all persons over 21 years of age who reside in the United States.

The writer would suggest two thoughts at this point: (1) these data appear to be consistent with the impression one gains from many sources in our society today that the field of public relations is often misunderstood, often badly practiced by a number of public relations practitioners, and often maligned by a variety of writers whose material has appeared in widely read publications; (2) these data are consistent with the views that many public relations practitioners themselves hold about how others view them. That is, most public relations practitioners whom the writer knows are quick to admit that the field has a long way to go before it becomes widely understood and respected as are a number of other professions, such as medicine, engineering, law, and teaching.

What is it, then, that we are attempting to examine in this volume entitled *Communication and Public Relations?* In short, what is our definition of the subject matter of this book—public relations? This is, as the old saw goes, "an extremely good question." What is our answer?

Certainly many definitions of public relations can be found, ranging from simple ones such as "doing good and getting credit for it" to the one in Webster's *New International Dictionary* that runs more than one hundred words. A definition that has obtained rather widespread acceptance is the one suggested by the *Public Relations News,*

> Public relations is the management function which evaluates public attitudes, identifies the policies and procedures of an individual or an organization with the public interest, and plans and executes a program of action to earn public understanding and acceptance.[2]

If one replaces the word *management* in the above quotation with "those responsible for the administration of an organization," it becomes apparent that this definition can embrace *any* operating organization in our society, be it a business, a nonprofit organization, or some unit of our governmental structure—local, state, or federal, or all three.

If, in addition, one makes the distinction between public relations as "an operating concept *of* management" and as "a specialized staff function *in* management," as Cutlip and Center suggest,[3] it becomes clear that public relations is (1) a point of view that is in a sense a philosophy or a set of operating principles and (2) a specialized staff function that is performed in an organization by persons with particular skills and education, utilizing a variety of specialized tools and techniques in the performance of that organizational function.

Since public relations can be defined in a perfectly respectable manner, why is it that this activity is so misunderstood and still viewed in a rather suspect fashion? The author would suggest several factors which partially account for this state of affairs:

1. Practitioners today must own up to some rather undesirable heritages or forerunners. For example, the work known as press-agentry has often embraced exploitation, untruthfulness, and ruthlessness, and this past is unquestionably a contributor to present-day negative thinking about public relations.[4]

---

[2] *Public Relations News,* October 27, 1947. Used by permission.

[3] Scott M. Cutlip and Allen H. Center, *Effective Public Relations* (3rd ed.; Englewood Cliffs, N.J.: Prentice-Hall, Inc., 1964), p. 5.

[4] The author is aware that not all of the undesirable practices that are associated with press-agentry are necessarily in the past. However, it is safe to say that present-day abuses of this sort are comparatively infrequent and, more important, are not practiced by reputable public relations practitioners esteemed by their colleagues.

2. There appears to be a rather prevalent suspicion that anyone who communicates with a purpose (what's even worse, for pay) is a propagandist. Although the word *propaganda* as used by social scientists is a neutral term, the most common interpretation of this word is a negative one. If you propagandize, ipso facto, you are "bad." The fact is that propaganda, in itself, is neither "good" nor "bad." It depends upon your point of view. Likewise, it is intimately related to the integrity of the persons responsible for implementing the propaganda. Nevertheless, the public relations practitioner has been tainted by the negative connotation attached to this word.

3. A third reason might be expressed by the saying, "a cobbler's children always have holes in their shoes." Thus, while one of the major functions of a public relations practitioner is to communicate an understanding of and attain a positive acceptance of his organization and its objectives and policies, he has failed to do the same thing for himself and his own occupation. In general, the public relations practitioners, either individually or collectively, have neglected their own public relations.

There are undoubtedly many other factors. Certainly the reader can generate additional reasons to add to the list. However, there is one additional factor which is the most important of all.

This last point, which accounts for most of the misunderstanding about just what public relations is and what a public relations practitioner does, is that, *as a group, the public relations practitioners do not know either!* To date, they have failed to generate a theoretical framework in which to insert their activities and they have not formed a consistent, integrated approach to problem solving in their own field. They have not developed a body of knowledge to be utilized in their problem-solving efforts. In fact, they have tended to resist codification and systematization with the belief that "public relations is an art" and therefore cannot be adequately defined, taught, and made more rigorous in application. In essence, all of the features that tend to make for professionalization, regardless of the field, have tended to be ignored and have not been actively pursued. Consequently, as of today we have the unfortunate situation wherein if one were to ask five different public relations practitioners to handle the same problem, one would very likely get five different plans for solutions, and for five different reasons. Everyone in public relations has his or her own theories. Naturally, if the practitioners are unable to agree, how can we possibly expect outsiders to understand and respect the practitioners?

This book is an effort to make some modest progress toward generating a consistent, integrated framework within which to insert the activities of a public relations practitioner. *The fundamental assumption behind this volume is that the public relations practitioner is an applied social and behavioral scientist*—that the activities of public relations practitioners, no matter how divergent they may appear on the surface, are, in fact, quite similar if translated into such things as attitude change or maintenance, or efforts to teach or induce learning. For this reason, this book is written with the avowed purpose of relating many concepts and theories from the social and behavioral sciences to public relations. In addition, the general orientation of this book is in terms of a communication theory model, primarily because the public relations practitioner is assumed to be functioning as a communicator so much of his professional life.

At this point we need to return to the question of definitions. Unfortunately, one is not able to put down immediately a definition that will be acceptable to all or nearly all practitioners in the field. This is not to say that there are no definitions available. As we saw earlier in this chapter, there are some to be found. However, the author feels that the present definitions do not suffice, mainly because they are not formulated from the point of view of the practitioner as an applied social and behavioral scientist. In addition, definitions in the area of public relations tend to presuppose a lot of information on the part of the reader. The author would prefer postponing the introduction of a formal definition until we have discussed some important concepts and arguments that pave the way to a definition of public relations.

For this reason, in Chapter 2 we will consider four different cases which describe problems facing practitioners in a deliberately wide range of different settings. From these cases we will derive a series of principles common to thcm all which will enable you to become familiar with the many assumptions and prejudices that the author has and that should be stated early in this volume. These cases and the principles and assumptions that they suggest will serve to illustrate our notion of the public relations practitioner as an applied social and behavioral scientist and develop a definition of public relations. This will be the subject matter of Chapter 3.

QUESTIONS FOR DISCUSSION

1. Develop your own definition of public relations. Compare your definition with the definition of at least one other person. Note par-

ticularly your points of agreement and disagreement and why each of you included the particular elements that you did in your respective definitions.

2. Make a list of your own reasons as to why the term *public relations* means different things to different people. After you have developed your list, indicate which reasons could be rather easily changed by an organized group speaking for the field of public relations (such as the Public Relations Society of America). After you have done this, indicate which reasons would be very difficult to change. Be sure to be prepared to give the reasons for your answers.

3. Although the concept has not been spelled out as yet, jot down your notions as to what the implications might be if one were to accept the thesis stated in this first chapter: that the public relations practitioner is an applied social and behavioral scientist. Be sure to save your answer and have a look at it again after you have finished reading Chapters 2 and 3.

Chapter 2

A FIRST STEP TOWARD
UNDERSTANDING PUBLIC RELATIONS

INTRODUCTION

The first portion of this chapter consists of brief descriptions of four problem situations faced by different public relations practitioners. These cases are excerpts from the real-life, day-to-day functioning of several public relations practitioners.

The four cases embrace a wide range of problem situations in completely different settings. The first one describes a public relations practitioner in the military (U.S. Air Force), the second in an industrial scientific research and engineering company, the third in a small college in New England, and the last in a nonprofit organization whose operations are national in scope. These cases were selected deliberately to give the reader a feeling for the tremendously different types of problem situations that public relations practitioners find themselves in. They were also selected because each embraces a set of particulars completely different from the others. On the surface, at least, these cases have nothing in common other than the fact that each represents problems to be solved by a public relations practitioner.

After the cases have been presented, we will use them as a means for noting some key generalizations that apply to all of them regardless of their differences. From these generalizations, we will derive some principles that will aid us in spelling out the critical areas of knowledge that public relations practitioners must possess if they are to function intelligently and effectively. In short, we hope to demonstrate that *the differences among the cases are not nearly so important as the underlying similarities in the functions that they highlight.*

CASE STUDY NO. I

Title: Modification of Activities at Bolling Air Force Base: Some Resulting Confusion[1]

Background

Bolling Air Force Base is located across the Potomac River from the Pentagon, within five miles of the United States Capitol and the center of our nation's capital city.

The base is under the command jurisdiction of Headquarters Command, USAF, and is operated by that command's 1100th Air Base Wing. The mission of the base is to provide "housekeeping support" (administration, housing, feeding, finance, and other military support functions) for all U.S. Air Force personnel and units assigned within the Washington, D.C., area. This includes personnel of Air Force Headquarters in the Pentagon, other Air Force units overseas and in downtown Washington, and personnel of nearby Andrews Air Force Base in addition to the personnel of Bolling Air Force Base.

The total units supported by the base number approximately fifty-six world-wide organizations, including a major air command headquaters (Headquarters Command, USAF), Air Force Headquarters itself, and seven specialized agencies.

In addition, Headquarters Command, USAF, is charged with the responsibility of providing aircraft for and supervising all administrative and proficiency flying for officers in the area. Since 1918, Bolling Air Force Base has been "in the flying business" and has been involved in all important Air Force developments.

Bolling Air Force Base covers approximately 624 acres in the southeastern portion of the city. There are approximately forty-six hundred military and civilian personnel assigned to the base. The base facilities include housing, exchanges, a large base commissary that serves hundreds of armed forces personnel each day, cafeterias, clubs, and a large dental clinic and a small medical facility. (There is a large USAF

---

[1] The author is indebted to Captain Bonnie O'Leary, USAF, Deputy Director of Information, Headquarters Command Office of Information, Bolling Air Force Base, Washington, D.C., 20332, for her kind permission to use this case.

medical center at Andrews Air Force Base, ten miles east of Bolling.) Like other military and naval bases in the Washington area, Bolling has approximately twenty sets of officers' quarters, the same for ranking noncommissioned officers, barracks for single airmen, and a large, modern trailer park for married airmen. The largest housing facilities are the barracks for several thousand airmen and the visiting officers' (and airmen) quarters for several hundred more. The Pentagon gets many official visitors and most of them stay at Bolling Air Force Base.

Problem Situation

In late 1957, the decision was made by the Federal Aviation Administration, the Civil Aeronautics Authority, and the Department of Defense, that it was no longer safe to have military aircraft flying from the Bolling-Anacostia area so near Washington's National Airport—one of the nation's busiest. The National Airport is just across the Potomac River from Bolling Air Force Base and the Naval Air Station at Anacostia.

The following memorandum was sent from the Secretary of the Air Force, the Honorable James Douglas, to the Deputy Secretary of Defense, 3 March 1958:

SUBJECT: TERMINATION OF FIXED WING FLYING OPERATIONS,
           BOLLING AIR FORCE BASE AND ANACOSTIA NAS.
1.   In accordance with the instructions contained in the memorandum from the Deputy Secretary of Defense, subject, JOINT USE OF ANDREWS AIR FORCE BASE BY THE NAVY AND AIR FORCE, dated 10 February 1958, discussions have been held with representatives of the Chief of Naval Operations. As a result of these discussions, the USAF and Navy have jointly agreed to recommend:

a.   The Air Force military flying units now based at Bolling Air Force Base and Washington National Airport and the approximately 145 Navy aircraft now based at Anacostia NAS be transferred to Andrews Air Force Base upon completion of adequate aviation facilities at Andrews Air Force Base, Maryland. The target date for the transfer is to be 1962.
b.   The Air Force is to allocate to the Navy space at Andrews Air Force Base sufficient for the Navy to construct aviation and support facilities to accommodate the units in paragraph "a" above.

Releases were made to news media when the decision was made to move the aircraft from Bolling Air Force Base to Andrews Air Force Base. The Secretary of Defense informed the Secretary of the Air

Force, who in turn notified the Chief of Staff of the Air Force. The Commander of Headquarters Command, USAF, met with the Commander, Potomac River Naval Command, to coordinate press releases for Washington media. The personnel of Bolling Air Force Base heard the news three ways: from the local press, from duty supervisors if their work was connected to aircraft duties, and from the stories in the base newspaper. The usual base grapevine method of communication also operated to spread the word.

In spite of all these efforts to communicate the fact that the base was closing down *only* the flying operations at Bolling and that, in addition, steps were going to be taken to make increased use of Bolling Air Force Base, the general public, aided at times by incorrect press releases, became convinced that Bolling was going to close down entirely. The following occurrences illustrate this misconception:

One article in the *Evening Star*, June 29, 1960, stated: "The Bolling site is tentative. The Air Force has announced that the field will be surplus next year." When the person who made this statement was asked where he got this information, he said, "Oh, we meant only the *flying* field part. Everyone knows the planes are leaving. We didn't mean to imply in our release that the base is closing." [Italics added.]

A lieutenant reported: "My landlady tells me the base is closing. I tried to tell her only the aircraft were moving to Andrews, but she can't understand how you can have an air base without planes."

A new colonel on base, when buying a house, had the builder reassure him: "Even though Bolling's closing soon, your house isn't far from Andrews. It'll be easy to sell when you leave."

The Bolling Air Force Base Director of Civilian Personnel complained: "I'm finding it real hard to replace people here at Bolling. No one wants to take a job here because they tell me they'll have to leave soon when Bolling closes. I'm about ready to throw in the towel!"

An airman's mother called long distance from Arizona and was told by the Washington operator: "I can't find a phone number for the base. Guess it's closed up. I know they've been planning to shut it down."

A major, stationed in Germany, received orders to report to Bolling in June, 1960. Early that spring, he wrote a friend at the Pentagon and asked, "Where do you think I'll be going from Bolling after it closes? I hear it'll be leveled and they're gonna have a World's Fair there in 1964."

Summary Statement of What the Public Relations Practitioner Faces

From these examples it is clear that the misconceptions concerning the future of Bolling Air Force Base are numerous and exceedingly widespread—even persons stationed in Germany had the wrong information! The information personnel (military term for public relations) of the offices at the wing and command levels were, for a time, continually besieged by base personnel: "Why don't you put out a release and tell 'em the base isn't closing?" As a matter of fact, it was reaching a stage where the military personnel were losing faith in the command and in the Pentagon. "What do you do all day? Why not work on some stories and kill these wild rumors?"—so asked a major at the officers' club.

CASE STUDY NO. 2

TITLE: Esso Research and Engineering Company: A Leader in the Field of Industrial Research Re-examines Its Reputation for Basic Research Within the Scientific Community[2]

Background

Esso Research and Engineering Company is the principal scientific and engineering affiliate of Standard Oil Company (New Jersey). It is America's largest oil research firm and one of the largest in the world. The company was established in 1919 as the development department of the parent firm, Jersey Standard, and is among the nation's oldest research organizations. It was organized as a separate affiliate with its own board of directors in 1927.

The company's research expenditures are on the order of seventy million dollars annually. The work engaged in by Esso Research and Engineering encompasses a variety of projects and programs ranging from advanced exploratory research to applied research and engineering. Approximately 25 per cent of the company's work is long range in nature. In recent years, a growing emphasis has been placed on chem-

[2] The author is indebted to Frank T. LeBart, Manager, Public Relations Division, Esso Research and Engineering Company, Linden, New Jersey, for his kind permission to use various materials produced by his company to develop this case.

icals derived from petroleum. The work is done on a world-wide basis for the benefit of other companies associated with Jersey Standard.

The nearly fourteen hundred professional employees have thirty-one hundred degrees in the technical sciences such as chemistry, engineering, and physics. One in four of these professional employees has a Ph.D.; one in three a master's degree. Many of the nontechnical personnel are also college graduates.

The main facilities of the company are at two locations in New Jersey. One is the Esso Research Center in Linden, and the other is the new Esso Research and Engineering Center in Florham Park. The total number of employees is about twenty-nine hundred, with approximately six hundred of these located at Florham Park. Affiliated scientific facilities are situated elsewhere in the United States and Europe.

Located on a fifty-seven-acre tract, the Esso Research Center in Linden was occupied in 1948. It originally consisted of one modern three-story building that housed both laboratories and offices. Today there are twenty-one buildings. The principal fields of research at Linden are the development of new and improved petroleum and chemical products and processes.

The Esso Research and Engineering Center in Florham Park was completed in the fall of 1959 on a 675-acre site. The largest of the three buildings at Florham Park is the three-story Engineering Building which serves as headquarters for the company's engineering divisions. The other two structures are the Process Research Building, where medium- and small-scale process experiments are conducted, and an engineering research laboratory. The engineering divisions are responsible for designing and supervising the construction of new refinery units built by affiliates located in nations throughout the free world.

The company has developed a number of processes and products of major importance over the years. These include fluid catalytic cracking, the most widely used method for producing high-quality gasolines and heating oils and also a source of petrochemicals; butyl rubber, one of the most versatile and widely used synthetic rubbers; the first synthetic lubricant approved by both the British and United States Air Forces for jet planes; fluid coking, in which tarlike materials of low value are converted into gasoline and other oil products; hydrofining for improving a variety of petroleum products by reacting them with hydrogen; and powerforming for producing high octane gasoline. Other technical achievements include the development and design of a new continuous process for the manufacture of polypropylene plastic and the successful development of a technique for the injection of fuel oil or natural gas into a blast furnace for smelting iron from iron ore.

Problem Situation

In its early years, Esso Research and Engineering was almost exclusively concerned with development work or applied research. That is, it did comparatively little fundamental research. In recent years, however, Esso Research and Engineering has shifted its research efforts so that more fundamental and chemical research is conducted. This has been true for more than five years.

The public relations people are acutely aware that a considerable lag exists between doing research, especially fundamental research, and being able to inform the scientific community about it. For example, it is not unusual for two years to elapse between completing a research project and having the results of this research published in a scientific journal. In addition, the public relations people are very conscious of the relationship between a company's research reputation and its ability to attract top research people who are essential if an organization is to continue to make contributions to fundamental knowledge in the area of the physical sciences.

Before attempting to implement specific public relations programs, the company hired an outside organization to do a survey of attitudes toward its standing and reputation in the scientific community. Specifically, the survey was designed to attain the following objectives:

1. To obtain a scientific evaluation of the status and reputation of the Esso Research and Engineering Company in the "scientific community."

2. To acquire guidance on how best to allocate money and manpower for the "scientific community" phase of the company's public relations program.

3. To provide base lines of opinion against which the effectiveness of the company's public relations program can be measured at regular intervals in the future.[3]

On the basis of the comprehensive report of Louis Harris and Associates, the public relations division was faced with both pleasant and unpleasant information. From one point of view, Esso Research was doing very well in competition with other petroleum research firms. Esso Research was known as the "largest," "biggest," and "best known." However, as more detailed replies were obtained from the respondents

---

[3] Taken from a summary report by Frank T. LeBart (September, 1960) of "A Study of Esso Research and Engineering Company's Standing and Reputation in the Scientific Community" by Louis Harris and Associates (July, 1960). Used by permission of Frank T. LeBart.

and analyzed (in this case there were 688 scientists interviewed in nineteen colleges and universities), some weaknesses in the reputation were
uncovered. Two quotes from the report submitted by the survey organization employed by Esso Research to conduct the survey illustrate
the problems that the public relations division faced:

> It is Esso's greatest assets which seem to stand most in the way of
> its reputation for basic research. It is precisely because Esso is con-
> sidered to be the giant of the petroleum industry that the scientific
> community expects the most of Esso in the field of basic research—
> including a broadening out from oil and chemical research.
>
> Rather than contradicting each other, the answers to the rating
> scale and to the free response questions indicate that Esso has been
> successful in reaching some scientists with its story of technical achieve-
> ment, fine laboratories and top-grade scientists—but not enough of the
> members of the scientific community have been reached or convinced.
> In other words, the scientific community is not fully aware, as yet, of
> the full strength of Esso's staff, facilities, achievements, and outlook."[4]

Summary Statement of What the Public Relations Practitioner Faces

From these data it is clear that more work is needed to be done to
strengthen the reputation of Esso Research and Engineering's research
work among people in the scientific community. Among other things,
the unavoidable lag in publication of basic and chemical research being done by the company is apparently contributing to the lack of
accurate information on the part of scientists in what might be called
the research community.

CASE STUDY NO. 3

TITLE: The "Image" Problem of Lesley College of Cambridge, Massa-
          chusetts[5]

Background

Lesley College began in September, 1909, as Lesley Normal School,
a private enterprise. It was, and primarily still is, a women's college.

---

[4] These two quotations are from "A Study of Esso Research and Engineering
Company's Standing and Reputation in the Scientific Community" by Louis Harris
and Associates (July, 1960). Used by permission of Frank T. LeBart, Manager,
Public Relations Division, Esso Research and Engineering Company.

[5] The author is indebted to John J. Canavan, Jr., President's Assistant for Development and Public Relations, Lesley College, Cambridge, Massachusetts, for
his kind permission to use this case.

The first entering class numbered ten. The first faculty was Miss Edith Lesley, her sister Olive, and a number of part-time instructors from Harvard College and elsewhere. All of the functions of the school were carried on in Miss Lesley's home on Everett Street and in three rented rooms in the Cambridge-Haskell School on Concord Avenue.

The history of the school during the twenties and thirties was one of modest growth and expansion. The campus grew; curriculum expanded to include a household arts major, a nursery school course, and eventually a third year to prepare students to teach in grades one through six. Changing educational demands, especially the requirement that teachers in the public schools have college degrees, and the unsettling influence of the war brought corresponding changes at Lesley. Mrs. Wolfard (Miss Lesley) began the transformation of the school to a college by giving control, in 1941, to a board of trustees, who made it a nonprofit corporation. The board began at once, in difficult wartime circumstances, to build up the school and especially to expand its offerings to college caliber. The legal change to a four-year college came in 1943, and the first five baccalaureate degrees were conferred in June of 1945.

The college achieved regional and national accreditation in 1952 and in 1954 was empowered to confer the master's degree.

Miss Lesley's home at 29 Everett Street, now called Founder's House, continues to be the administrative and spiritual center of the college. Physical properties have been expanded to twenty-six buildings, including a modern classroom unit and a new dormitory housing 146 students, with lounges and dining halls. The college now owns and operates three laboratory schools: the Lesley-Ellis School for gifted and normal children (average I.Q. is over 130); the Walter F. Dearborn School for children with emotional blocks to learning; the Carroll-Hall School for retarded children. With these three specialized laboratory schools, Lesley is in a truly unique position. There is no other college in the country with comparable facilities.

A great deal of research in education of normal as well as special children is carried on at the college and in the laboratory schools. The research has gained a degree of fame in very limited educational circles but little or no renown outside of these circles.

The college presently has an enrollment of 500 full-time undergraduate students and 150 graduate students. The full-time teaching faculty numbers 36.

Problem Situation

Lesley College has hired a person to handle their college public relations. Prior to the hiring of this individual, the college had no planned publicity, no planned community relations program, nor was there any semblance of the usual functions of a college public relations office. In addition, the college did not have an alumnae association and had never done any development or fund-raising work. The basic problem situation is that in a cultural environment (surrounded by Harvard, M.I.T., Radcliffe, etc.) where visibility is vital to viability, where public and, particularly, private support is imperative for sustenance and growth, Lesley College is virtually unknown. In Harvard Square, only two blocks away, most people have never even heard of the college, much less understood its reason for existence and the needs that must be met if it is to continue to grow, flourish, and serve its important function in a modern society.

Summary Statement of What the Public Relations Practitioner Faces

From the data supplied it is apparent that the public relations practitioner in this case has a complete building job to be done, ranging from generating statements of purpose for the continuing existence of this college to developing the many day-to-day functions of a college public relations office (*e.g.*, developing relationships with the press, developing a strong, active alumnae group, and establishing lines of communication with students, faculty, administration, and trustees).

CASE STUDY NO. 4

TITLE: Automobile Seat Belts: A Classic Case in Overcoming Resistance to Change Encountered by the National Safety Council[6]

Background

The seat belt is a personal-protective device designed for use in motor vehicles and airplanes. The most common form of the seat belt consists of two straps, each anchored at one end to the vehicle and fitted at the other end with a buckle coupling. When fastened in place, the belt encircles the passenger, holding him firmly in the seat. In case of collision or sudden stop, he is thus protected from being thrown

---

[6] The author is indebted to Arch McKinlay, Jr., Director of Public Information of the National Safety Council, and John Naisbitt, former Director of Public Information of the National Safety Council, for their kind permission to use various materials produced by the National Safety Council to develop this case.

severely against the windshield, interior, and fittings of the vehicle and prevented from being ejected from the vehicle.

The very first airplanes and automobiles made use of such devices, but only in the airplane was the seat belt developed, perfected, and made standard equipment as part of the seat itself.

As recently as World War II, seat belts were ignored by virtually everyone but a handful of safety specialists and a few visionaries who were considered crackpots. From time to time, one of the specialists or crackpots might gain the attention of a manufacturer or an organization interested in safety, but while the idea was deemed sound, at least two factors prevented a grand-scale professional acceptance in safety, health, and medical circles: (1) the absence of reliable, research-based proof of the value of seat belts and (2) an absence of engineering standards for manufacture and installation.

The general public, however, could not have cared less. It knew nothing about the belts, or at least did not indicate any knowledge through purchase, in spite of the fact that as early as 1947 the devices were marketed by Nash.

From what might be considered a low point of interest in seat belts in 1947, there gradually emerged a series of events that had considerable bearing on the two factors listed above. Briefly, some of the events were as follows:

1. In 1947, Cornell University's Aeronautical Laboratory studied the action of the human body during deceleration when held in place by a seat belt. It was demonstrated that the severity of head injuries would be appreciably reduced in collision if the body were held in place with a seat belt. The report of the study was filed in 1949.

2. In 1953, under a project sponsored by the Liberty Mutual Insurance Company, the Cornell Laboratory studied the action of the human body during automobile crashes, particularly front-end collisions. It was determined that seat belts would eliminate the most severe injuries caused by the unrestrained body colliding with the windshield or dashboard.

3. In 1955, the Society of Automobile Engineers, after several years of study, issued its first seat belt standard.

4. In 1955, a National Safety Council policy statement recommended the installation and use of seat belts in motor vehicles. The statement further recommended adherence to SAE stand-

ards and called for a continuation of research and development such as that done by Cornell, Minnesota, UCLA, Purdue, and several other universities, the Society of Automotive Engineers, and various manufacturers.

5. In 1957, Cornell's Transportation Safety Research Committee announced, after studying five thousand injury cases, that automobile seat safety belts save lives and reduce the frequency and severity of injuries to car occupants "beyond all reasonable doubt."

In spite of the fact that by 1957 substantial progress had been made in overcoming the lack of research on just how valuable seat belts were in reducing death and injury and establishing engineering standards for manufacture and installation, acceptance and use of seat belts remained at a very low level. For one thing, conflicting information concerning the value of seat belts was before the public. For example, Andrew J. White of Motor Vehicle Research, Inc., of Manchester, New Hampshire, issued releases and articles to a number of publications casting strong doubt on the value of seat belts. The tenor of the attacks ranged from calling seat belts "over-rated" to "lethal." The basis of the attacks included evidence that purported to demonstrate that "jack-knifing" of the torso would inflict serious abdominal and head injuries, depending on how the body reacted. Such articles certainly gave anyone opposed to seat belts—informed or otherwise—support for his particular point of view.

Further confusion resulted when *Consumer Reports*, published by the strongly pro-seat belt Consumers Union, was critical of (in its opinion) inferior products on the market and warned of the necessity for proper installation. This was further compounded by the fact that early in 1958 the General Services Administration of the United States Government established specifications for seat belt purchases which were more stringent and more limited than SAE standards. Although the GSA standards were developed as a guide to government purchases and, as such, were not strict standards of minimum acceptable quality, the effect was that there seemed to be two sets of "standards."

While the above attacks and confusion-producing events did not reach as wide an audience as the pro-seat belt material, it can safely be assumed that the opinion leaders and educated persons reached by it were affected somewhat and, as a result, blocked a more immediate and widespread acceptance.

Problem Situation

By virtue of the very nature of its organizational goals, the National Safety Council was vitally interested in the progress that had (or, more properly, had not) been made to gain widespread acceptance of seat belts by the motoring public. By the end of 1960, an estimated one million vehicles were equipped with one or more belts. The average installation was two belts in the front seat. This tiny fraction of the nation's more than seventy million vehicles was particularly disturbing to the National Safety Council. By this time, a considerable number of public promotions had been attempted. For example, *The Saturday Evening Post* carried a typical "personal" story of how belts saved an individual's life, then launched into the vital facts. *Woman's Day* ran a straightforward "how-to-protect-yourself" story written by a Cornell University specialist. Ford, with its 1956 models, promoted a "safety package" which included emphasis on seat belts as well as padded visors and dished steering wheels. In fact, the Ford advertisement probably constituted the first major national promotion of seat belts by a major advertiser.

In addition to these public promotions, there were many promotions of an "internal" nature—*i.e.*, attempts within certain organizations to promote the use of seat belts. For example, certain businesses, particularly motor vehicle fleet operators, encouraged seat belt usage. Police force adoption of seat belts is another example of what is meant by "internal" promotions. As a matter of fact, in 1959, the International Association of Chiefs of Police had adopted a resolution urging all law enforcement agencies to use belts, set an example for the public, and promote the use of belts wherever possible.

In spite of these various programs, a sizable task still confronted the National Safety Council to promote the use of seat belts. A distressingly small proportion of the driving public (estimated at one in seventy) made use of a device that was known to prevent injury and save lives.

Summary Statement of What the Public Relations Practitioner Faces

From the background data, it is clear that the public relations practitioner for the National Safety Council has a particularly complex problem with which to cope. Not only is the scope of the task large —with the entire motoring public as his audience—but it is clear that there are a multitude of conflicting forces, some helpful, some detrimental, to furthering the cause of seat belt usage. If this were not enough, it is also apparent that any program that the public relations practitioner develops must be constructed with an eye to taking advantage of the work of the many organizations which share the goals of the National Safety Council and at the same time avoid the conflicts and entanglements that the mere existence of so many organizations encourages.

SIX GENERALIZATIONS FROM THESE CASES

The cases selected for this chapter were deliberately taken from widely separate segments of our society. They represent some of the major subdivisions of our contemporary culture: the military, a private research company, a college, and a nonprofit organization. The very diversity of these organizations and their public relations problems provides a strong case for the following statement: In spite of the enormous *differences* among these organizations and their completely different *specific* communication objectives, there are several unifying generalizations that can be extracted from their public relations problems.

Some of the generalizations which follow, particularly the first, second, and sixth, are offshoots of the topics which make up the hard core of this volume: communication theory, research, psychology, and sociology. We will have much to say about these areas of study and how they relate to the practice of public relations. Our other generalizations have to do with ethics and with principles of organization and administration as they are found normally in sequences of study in business administration colleges. Because these topics fall outside of our main areas of specialization, we will have less to say about them in the remainder of this volume. Nevertheless, we have included the entire range of generalizations in order to spell out the breadth of activities that public relations practitioners engage in. We must think of the public relations practitioner as a "whole man," in spite of the fact that we may emphasize certain features of this man because of our own special areas of competence.

1. The Need for Communication

One of the most striking similarities among all of these public relations problem cases is the emphasis placed upon communication. In each one of the background sections of the cases, the role that communication has played—from face-to-face situations up to and including the mass media—is clear. In the Bolling Air Force Base case, one of the major factors that "triggered off" some of the more visible manifestations of their public relations problems resulted from stories that were printed in the various newspapers in and around Washington, D.C. Superimposed upon the confusion engendered by the misleading newspaper articles were all of the word-of-mouth rumors about what was going to happen to the base. Likewise, in the seat belt case, the mass media played a role in contributing to the confusion about whether seat belts were really safe when the various articles hostile to the use of seat belts were published. Although the evidence is not as explicit as it was in the military case, the face-to-face discussions that followed the articles hostile to seat belts undoubtedly contributed to the difficulty that the public relations practitioner would encounter later as he attempted to increase seat belt usage.

Our first principle: A theoretical as well as practical understanding of communication is required. The public relations practitioner is first and foremost a communicator. Every day he must shape and execute communications that are part and parcel of his public relations plans or programs for the organization with which he is associated. It would seem to follow from this observation that the public relations practitioner must understand communication thoroughly, from both a *theoretical* point of view and a *practical* one. Knowledge of communication from a practical point of view is rather obvious: The public relations practitioner must know *how* to write well, *where* to place what he has written, and in *what* appropriate form—*i.e.*, newspaper article, letter, brochure, etc. The importance of the spoken word (and the combination of the visual and the audible, as in television) cannot be overlooked either. Written communications, although very important, do not cover all of the means by which a public relations practitioner communicates. The public relations practitioner must be prepared to operate in whatever media are appropriate to his communication objective and be able to do so in a professional manner.

Knowledge of communication from a theoretical point of view may not be so obvious, but it is just as important as the practical knowledge. Theoretical knowledge will contribute to a better understanding of *why* he is communicating and help provide the public relations practitioner with guides as to what form his practical communications should take. Just as we believe that the practical side of being an engineer is enhanced by theoretical knowledge of physics, so it is that the practical side of being a public relations practitioner is enhanced by a

theoretical knowledge of communication. The reader is asked to accept
this relationship between the practical and theoretical on faith for the
time being. This relationship is the major point of this whole book.
There will be many opportunities for the reader to conclude for himself
whether the author has been able to substantiate this assumption that
the practical side of communication is enhanced by a theoretical understanding of the communication process.

2. The Need for Shaping Attitudes or Behavior

A second observation that can be made is that, in each case presented
earlier, the public relations practitioner was concerned with shaping
the attitudes or behavior of certain key individuals or groups. For
example, it is clear that the public relations practitioners associated
with Esso Research and Engineering Company are particularly interested in modifying the attitudes of the scientific community toward
their company's role in basic research. They want the scientific community to consider them an important contributor to new knowledge
derived from scientific research.

The seat belt case is an even better example of this second generalization. Clearly, the people responsible for the public relations programs of the National Safety Council are interested in changing the
attitudes of as many drivers as possible in the direction of viewing seat
belts as an indispensable accessory to their cars and one that they will
use regularly.

The Lesley College public relations practitioner has a slightly different attitude-shaping situation. It is more of a question of providing new
information in order to form the attitudes of a lot of people who have
never heard of Lesley College. For these people, his objective is that
the attitudes formed be favorable ones, based on the state of affairs
at Lesley as they now exist.

This preoccupation with shaping attitudes and behavior on the part
of most public relations practitioners is widespread enough that one
could redefine most public relations problems in terms of attitude
change. In fact, it is difficult to imagine a public relations problem
situation *without* some aspect of attitude and behavior change as the
ultimate objective of the public relations practitioner concerned.

One could go further and suggest that at least two types of attitude
change are the constant preoccupation of the public relations practitioner—what might be called Type A and Type B changes. Type A
involves change from misconceptions to accurate conceptions. This

is where the public in question has one particular set of negative attitudes concerning an organization, and the main objective of the public relations program is to change these negative attitudes to positive ones. Type B involves a change from a neutral attitude to a positive attitude.

The seat belt case is an example of Type A change. Persons who believed that seat belts were dangerous or only for "reckless drivers" constitute persons with negative attitudes that the public relations practitioner wishes to change to positive. The Lesley College case illustrates Type B change. Persons who know nothing about Lesley College (and happen to have neutral attitudes as well) are exactly those whose attitudes the public relations practitioner wants to change so that they will have positive attitudes about the college.

Our second principle: A theoretical as well as practical knowledge of attitude and behavior change is needed. Our preceding discussion points to the second principle involved in the practice of public relations: Because the public relations practitioner is concerned with attitude and behavior change, he is involved in having to understand human behavior. In order to modify attitudes and behavior, it is essential that one have as solid a working knowledge as possible of what are believed to be the key factors that affect human behavior. As a matter of fact, the terms that we have been utilizing in the past few paragraphs—*i.e.*, words such as *attitudes, behavior, communication*—are extensively used in the social and behavioral sciences. This suggests that public relations practitioners have something in common with the social and behavioral sciences. Social and behavioral scientists are concerned with understanding and predicting human behavior. In many ways, this describes the objectives of public relations practitioners. From this it would seem to follow that public relations practitioners must know something about behavior and attitudes from a theoretical point of view as well as from an empirical one. For precisely the same reasons that we argued earlier that the public relations practitioner needed to understand the theory behind communication, we also submit that the public relations practitioner needs to know the reasons behind his various efforts to modify attitudes and behavior. In addition to knowing *what* actions on his part will play a role in shaping behavior and attitudes, he needs to know *why* these actions are effective in changing behavior and attitudes.

Another way of expressing what has been written above is to say that in many ways the public relations practitioner functions as an *applied* social and behavioral scientist. By *applied* we mean that whereas the social scientist focuses on *discovering* knowledge that leads to an understanding of human behavior, the public relations practitioner focuses on *applying* this knowledge. (See Chapter 3 for further details.)

3. The Need for Planning

Another noteworthy common thread that can be found in all of the cases cited earlier is the pronounced implicit need for planning. That is, it is evident with even the minimum of details supplied in our brief case descriptions that, whatever the public relations practitioner decides to do, it can take place only after a lot of careful planning. All of the details of a public relations program have to be thought through carefully. There must be reasons, and good ones, for one particular action in one case and another particular action in some other instance. The seat belt case is a particularly good one to illustrate this need for planning.

Although the case was presented in an abbreviated form, it is clear that by now a tremendous variety of efforts have been made to increase seat belt use among the motoring public. In order for the public relations director of the National Safety Council to be able to justify additional expenditures of time and money to further the cause of seat belt use, he must be certain that his efforts are, in fact, doing some good. He has to sift all of the available knowledge of what has been done, make some appraisal of the effectiveness of these programs, and conclude what his organization should do.

Perhaps the most difficult working situation that the public relations practitioner can find himself in is one where a tremendous amount of previous work has been done on a particular problem. The reason: It places an even greater burden on the one who suggests that additional work be done to demonstrate just how this work will make a contribution toward solving the problem at hand.[7]

---

[7] The reader may be interested to know to what extent the seat belt case is particularly apropos to this generalization about the need for planning. John Naisbitt, former Director of Public Information of the National Safety Council, initiated some time ago a program of action that resulted in the Safety Communications Conference held in Chicago in September, 1963. "The purpose of this conference was to develop criteria (*i.e.*, guidelines and standards) for highway safety communications. This task has never been undertaken. The final conference report, to be published in book form, *Guidelines and Standards for Highway Safety Communications*, promises to be a landmark in highway safety." One especially important piece of work generated in connection with this conference was an eight-month critical survey of the public opinion literature relating to effective communication of safety messages. Admittedly, most public relations

Also implicit in all four of these cases is the fact that careful planning will be required to delineate the various target audiences that will be the objects of the public relations programing. The public relations practitioner must determine what persons he wants to reach and what particular communications steps are appropriate to reach the particular audience or audiences he has in mind. In the Esso Research and Engineering case, the public relations program must be geared to the fact that one target audience is the general scientific community made up of engineers and scientists. Special efforts are needed in order to reach this particular audience and persuade them about Esso's role in conducting basic research.

Our third principle: Some knowledge commonly found in a business administration background is needed. From this set of considerations we can generate our third principle of public relations: Public relations programing requires a high degree of ability to plan ahead in every detail. This means that the public relations practitioner must have training in certain management skills, particularly those requiring an understanding of organizational theory and structure, elements of supervision and coordination of others, and an understanding of how the organization relates to the larger society of which it is a part. Whereas in Principle No. 2 we were emphasizing the need for the knowledge of psychology and sociology, here we are stressing the need for the public relations practitioner to possess at least some of the knowledge that makes up a business administration background.

4. The Need for Relating Public Relations Programs to Management

A fourth thread that can be easily discerned in our cases is that the public relations practitioner is a part of the management function of the organization with which he is associated. The word *management* is employed here in its broadest sense. Every organization, industrial or otherwise, has people who run the organization, and they are known to be a part of management. Thus, people who are responsible for running a nonprofit foundation are a part of management just as are the people who direct an industrial organization.

It is clear from our cases that the public relations program of an organization has enormous implications for the operation of the entire

---

practitioners have neither the time nor the sophistication in the social sciences to engage in this much planning before taking action; however, it is an extremely good illustration of the type of preliminary work that one particular public relations practitioner deemed necessary *before* he did further work in his problem area.

organization. In the Esso case, for example, the reputation of the company as a whole is very much affected by the degree to which the public relations program is successful in informing the general scientific community about Esso's role in conducting basic scientific research. This in turn has implications for such things as the type of personnel that may or may not be attracted to Esso as prospective engineers and scientists. In a company such as Esso, whose whole existence is heavily dependent on the quality of the research they do, the type of engineers and scientists attached to it is of the utmost importance.

It is because of the intimate relationship between public relations programing and company policy that the public relations practitioner must be a part of the management function. This is one reason why, increasingly, one sees the director of public relations within an organization at the vice-president level or, if not an officer of the company, as a member of a top-level planning team.

Another observation that the example cases afford is that if a clear-cut policy is not in existence, the development of a public relations program tends to precipitate one. When those responsible for administrating the public relations functions of an organization begin to think through a public relations program—delineating target audiences to be reached, deciding what attitude and behavior changes are to be induced—it is almost inevitable that policy will be established.

The Lesley College case probably illustrates this point about precipitation of policy the best of the four cases because there had been no public relations practitioner associated with the college prior to the hiring of the individual mentioned in the case. As the public relations programs are developed, it will be necessary for the administrative personnel of the college to become involved. Certain policies will have to be established with respect to alumnae—broadly speaking, what will and will not be communicated to them, what will and will not be requested of them, how requests will be made, and other similar determinations. With respect to news releases and other materials that will start flowing from the college, there will have to be policy about how and when specific people are to be mentioned, what information will be released to the general public and what will not; how difficulties that students get into will be handled through the local press; what will be sent to home town newspapers about the students; and so on. In other words, time and time again, as different portions of the overall public relations program developed and implemented by this new public relations practitioner are put into effect, the question of whether particular parts of the program square with existing policy or whether new policies will have to be developed will come up.

Our fourth principle: The public relations practitioner must be an integral part of the management team. All the factors that have been examined in connection with our fourth generalization highlight the fact that it is impossible to have an effective public relations program without integrating it with the over-all management activities of any organization. Public relations programs implicate and, therefore, must reflect the top-level policies of any organization. Because this is true, it is impossible to intelligently separate public relations activities from top level management as a whole.

5. The Need for a Searching Examination of the Ethics of What Is Planned

Although this point is not nearly so evident in the example cases as some of the other generalizations we have listed, an integral part of any public relations program is that of the ethics of what is being planned. At the same time that a public relations program requires a thorough examination of the goals, the means toward the goals, and whether the program is consistent with company policies, it also requires those responsible to examine the ethics of what they are planning. In short, the public relations function of any organization is not only to set a particular goal but also to raise the question of the right to strive for that goal. Some writers have likened the public relations function of an organization to that of the conscience of an organization. Otto Lerbinger expresses this point when he writes,

> In addition to the general policies of an organization, a public relations man is concerned with three special ones: the public philosophy it follows; its sense of social responsibility; and its control of the truth.
> An organization's public philosophy determines how it will react to public opinion. One extreme is elitism, which assumes that a small group of managers, scientists, or other select people has the exclusive right to make decisions. The other extreme of a public philosophy is popularism, which assumes that public opinion is unfailingly the correct guide. Hence, a leader tries to conform to what public opinion wants. A public relations expert will seldom choose either extreme. Instead, he must be able to counsel management on the appropriate reaction to public opinion, and this reaction will usually consist of a compromise between the two approaches.
> The exercise of social responsibility—the second policy area—concerns the judicious balance between self-interest and public interest. The assumption made by some business men that profit maximization automatically enhances the general welfare is abandoned. In its place is a

conscious effort to consider the social consequences of business activities and to recognize social obligations to a variety of civic, educational, and charitable institutions.

The way in which an organization controls truth in its communications has a direct bearing on the social impact of communications.
Aside from obligations to provide the government, the stockholders,
employees, and other publics with information that is legally required,
an organization must decide whether to go further; whether the public's
appetite for more information should be satisfied. Such demands for
information must be balanced against the rights of privacy of organizations and individuals. Finally, there is the tendency to slant information in favor of an employer's or client's position. The question is how
far in this direction it is ethical to go.[8]

It should be clear by now that consideration of the ethical nature
of what is being planned as part of a public relations program is both
exceedingly important and a rather complicated affair. In fact, it is
important enough and complicated enough to deserve a more detailed
examination.

Public relations on an ethics continuum. One way of thinking
about the ethics involved in public re¹ .:ions is to visualize the effects
of public relations programs as lying on a continuum of mutual benefit
vs. self benefit (see Figure 1). The self-benefit end of the continuum
represents public relations activities whereby the individual or organization in question benefits from the public relations programing at
the expense of the public in some manner.

Figure 1

Ethics in Public Relations Continuum

---

[8] Otto Lerbinger, "Professional Formation of the Public Relations Expert," unpublished paper presented at the III Inter-American Conference of Public Relations, Santiago, Chile, October, 1962. Used by permission.

The mutual-benefit end of the continuum is depicted by public relations programing that is helpful to both the organization and the
public. That is, in achieving its ends, the organization works in such
a way that others, not associated directly with the organization, are
aided in some manner. Let's consider an example that illustrates the
mutual-benefit end of the continuum.

There has always been a problem with individuals who litter public
beaches, highways, and parks with papers, bottles, and other refuse,
and this situation becomes even more acute as our population continues to grow. In some areas, especially states with comparatively
large resort areas, there has been increasing public irritation with the
lack of litter control. One industrial group that is very aware of this
problem is the container industry—organizations that manufacture
bottles and paper containers for all sorts of purposes.

A few years ago, the Vermont legislature passed a bill eliminating
one-way bottles as containers. (The term "one-way" applied to glass
containers means that there is no deposit on the bottle required.)
Apparently, part of the reasoning behind the law was that the one-way
containers encourage people to throw them away because they have
no money invested in them. Regardless of the wisdom of the law and
of the arguments that could be put up about whether the presence or
absence of a deposit would have any effect on litter behavior, the fact
is that this was a problem to be faced by the container industry. One-
way containers represent an important segment of their container
production, to say nothing of the danger of a precedent being set in
one state that might be picked up by other states.

Several important public relations people in the container industry
got together to see what they could do to help solve this problem of
litter in public places. Out of this working together came the idea of
Keep America Beautiful, Incorporated, a nonprofit public service
organization dedicated to the elimination of all litter everywhere—not
just one-way containers in any one state. This nonprofit group came
into existence because of the support given to it by various industries
directly related to the container industry and also by industries only
indirectly related. This approach to a problem represents a sophisticated effort designed to benefit the organization or organizations that
are directly affected, in this case the manufacturers of one-way containers. To some extent, as the organization Keep America Beautiful makes
progress in licking the problem of litter in public places, the container
industry forestalls actions from any quarter that could adversely affect
their container-making business. This represents the self benefit. At

the other end of the continuum—mutual benefit—the public benefits
at the same time. That is, the people in the container industry, instead
of regarding the Vermont legislature as stupid or misguided, asked
themselves what their responsibilities were in this matter, then acted
accordingly and in a manner that couldn't help but benefit all concerned.

The line of thinking we have followed—that the effects of public
relations activities range along a continuum from self benefit to mutual benefit—suggests that there are many public relations programs
that fall somewhere in between the extremes depicted in Figure 1.
An illustration of the mid-point of the continuum, where the organization benefits but not necessarily at the expense of the public, is best
demonstrated by the old practice of paying employees in silver dollars
so that the community is made more acutely aware of the importance
of that company in the community. This technique is also used by
military public relations people in a region of the country where silver
dollars are rarely seen. In a very short time, the local community is
flooded with currency in a more obvious form than paper money, and
the degree to which the community is financially dependent on the
local base is very nicely highlighted ⹁ his particular public relations
action is one whereby the organization attains its communication objective—making their value to the community more salient—without
doing any injustice to the community. That is, the community is made
aware of the presence of a group by a technique that is neutral in
character.

A common variety of public relations activity that qualifies for
inclusion under the self-benefit end of the continuum is the withholding
of information from some particular public. If, for example, an organization is going to close its plant and move to a distant location, there are
many who would be tempted to withhold the information from the
employees and the community in the hopes that they could forestall
losing good employees or prevent a sagging morale. In such an instance, the organization benefits (at least on a short-term basis) at the
expense of the employee and community public.

Now that we have examined this ethics concept as applied to the
effects of public relations programing, let us see how the question of
ethics can apply to our example cases as we know them. In the Esso
case, there is the problem of balance in attempting to represent the
company as one that does a lot of basic research. No matter what
public relations program the public relations practitioner at Esso
develops, he must be certain that he does not mislead the scientific

community with respect to the amount of basic research done by his company as compared to applied research. In the seat belt case, one must resist the temptation to "oversell" seat belts—*i.e.*, to report or emphasize only that research which shows the value of seat belts and to avoid reporting the drawbacks of seat belts, whatever they might be. In the Lesley College case, the public relations practitioner must be certain that, among other things, the literature he develops to describe the college does not misrepresent the facts. This is particularly true today when the number seeking college education is rapidly exceeding the number of institutions capable of providing sound college education. Lastly, in the Bolling Air Force Base situation, the public relations practitioner must be certain of his ground that the base is, in fact, not closing. Likewise, he must be careful to not overstate the importance of this particular Air Force base when he tries to explain its mission and that recent changes in some of the operations at the base actually mean that the Air Force plans to make increased use of the field.

These examples drawn from the cases only scratch the surface of the situations that a public relations practitioner faces when an ethical consideration is involved in his programs. Because it represents one of the most important considerations that the public relations practitioner must face in his daily work, the question of ethics will be referred to in different ways throughout this book.

Our fifth principle: A strong sense of ethics must accompany all public relations programing. It was comparatively easy to spell out some of the dimensions of the ethical considerations that face all public relations practitioners in the execution of their programs. However, to derive a principle from this discussion, which is, of course, our major purpose in considering these cases, is another matter. Our fifth principle is, simply, that the public relations practitioner must consider what is ethical to do in a given situation and act accordingly. However, the implementation of this principle—*i.e.*, how to learn, acquire, establish, and practice ethics—is not so simple. In other words, to understand more fully the process of communication or the psychological or sociological bases for human behavior, one can recommend studying communication theory or books dealing with psychology or sociology, but no such neat recommendation can be made in the case of ethics. So as to not belabor this point, we will leave this fifth principle for now, with the realization that it is an essential yet, at the same time, difficult-to-attain component in the over-all training of the public relations practitioner.

6. The Need for Feedback of Information

The last observation that can and should be derived from these cases may be the least obvious of all to the reader. It's this: The public relations practitioner is constantly in need of feedback of information about the impact of his public relations programs. He needs this feedback of information so that he can intelligently shape—and modify when necessary—his public relations programs. He also needs this feedback in order to answer the fundamental question that is eventually asked by management of all of its operating subdivisions: What success are you having in coping with your problems and how efficiently are you solving them?

In all four of our cases the need for feedback of information will become evident sooner or later. In the military case, obtaining measures of effectiveness may not be so difficult: one measure of success could be newspaper releases that give the correct version of what is to happen at Bolling Field. Likewise, in the seat belt case the ultimate measure of success—i.e., that more and more people install and use seat belts—is a fairly direct one. Either more belts are made, sold, and used after the efforts of the public relations practitioner in question, or they are not.

The Esso case is not nearly so simple a measuring situation, however. Improving a particular company's reputation for basic research is not very simple to communicate (as, for example, the changes that are going on at Bolling Field); neither is it a simple matter to find out how many engineers and scientists in the scientific community have, in fact, changed their attitude toward Esso's involvement in basic research. In this respect, the Lesley College case is similar. The public relations practitioner at the college is always faced with the problem of how he is going to measure the fact that he has achieved increased recognition of the college; that he has achieved improved understanding among professors and administrators of other colleges of the fact that Lesley College has changed from the old days— in short, the problem of how he is going to know that his efforts have changed the "image" of Lesley College with the various publics he deems important to the college.

Our sixth principle: An understanding of social and behavioral science research methods is essential. Our last principle, derived from the preceding discussion, bears repeating: The public relations practitioner must have a solid working knowledge of social and behavioral science research methods. The reasons for this statement are as follows:

1. Feedback of information is obtained through research. It may be feedback of information in the form of a scientifically conducted opinion-attitude survey. It may be research with far more limited generalizations possible, based on a study of a sample of clippings from newspapers in your local area over a particular period of time. Regardless of the type of research involved (we will have much more to say about this in Chapters 17 through 20), feedback of information is obtained through research efforts.
2. Knowing how and what to measure, in order to ascertain what effects a particular public relations program has had, is dependent on understanding research. Measurement is one of the keystones of the research process.
3. An increasing body of knowledge in the social and behavioral sciences is developing with direct application to many of the problems facing the public relations practitioner. More often than not, however, this information is presented in technical form in professional journals. In order for the public relations practitioner to be able to use this information, he must have enough understanding of research to be able to read the reports and intelligently relate the material to his own public relations problem situation.

For these main reasons, and for a host of others, the public relations practitioner of the future must have a substantial grounding in social and behavioral science research methods.

SUMMARY OF PRINCIPLES DERIVED FROM OUR CASES

Let us attempt to summarize the principles that we have derived from our cases; then, with this summarization in hand, decide what implications they have for defining public relations.

First, we examined four cases, each describing a problem situation to be faced by a public relations practitioner. These cases were deliberately chosen to make them as heterogeneous as possible. One described a military situation; another, a situation plaguing a private research and development company; another, the dilemma of a small, relatively unknown but emerging college; and the fourth, the problem of a nonprofit organization faced with an unconcerned and unbelieving public. In spite of the diversity of these cases, several common denominators can be discerned clearly. These are:

1. All four situations revealed a tremendous emphasis on communication.
2. All four cases revealed concern with changing attitudes and behavior of certain key individuals or groups.
3. All four cases required a considerable degree of planning ability on the part of the public relations practitioner concerned. In order to solve his problem (or problems) he had to devise a plan that was an improvement over other, previously attempted approaches and that enabled him to ascertain accurately his target audiences.
4. All four problem situations revealed that public relations programs must coordinate with the over-all management of the organization in question. Some of the aspects of coordination discussed were:
   a. Public relations program must be consistent with management policies, and
   b. If no policies existed, the public relations function would precipitate them.
5. All four cases called for a searching examination of the ethics involved in the various public relations programs that might be implemented to solve the problems implied in the cases.
6. In all four cases, sooner or later the public relations practitioner would be called on to demonstrate his effectiveness in solving his problems. This suggested the need for assuring the feedback of information on the effectiveness of the public relations program, which in turn pointed to the need for research in public relations.

Second, on the basis of the various generalizations that could be made, based on the cases, a series of principles were derived. It was hoped that by spelling out these principles two things would happen: (1) a better understanding of public relations would emerge, and (2) a basis for defining public relations would be established along with an improved conception of the educational needs of the public relations practitioner of the future. The principles derived were as follows:

1. Because of his constant need to be an effective communicator, the public relations practitioner of the future must understand the process of communication from a theoretical as well as a practical point of view.
2. Because of his preoccupation with changing attitudes and behavior, the public relations practitioner must understand human behavior as an applied social and behavioral scientist. That is,

he must have enough knowledge of such disciplines as psychology and sociology to have a solid, working understanding of the factors that affect human behavior.

3. Because of the administrative and planning skills called for in implementing a public relations program, the public relations practitioner must have some management training, particularly in organizational structure and the elements of coordination and supervision of other people.

4. Because every action taken by a public relations practitioner on behalf of his organization reflects management's policies and decisions, the public relations practitioner must be a member of top management, regardless of the type of organization.

5. Because every action taken by a public relations practitioner on behalf of the organization with which he is associated has ethical implications, the public relations practitioner must have a strong, active ethical and moral code to guide him in his everyday work.

6. Because of his need for feedback of information to guide him in subsequent public relations action and to make him capable of demonstrating the effectiveness of his actions, the public relations practitioner of the future will need a thorough grounding in social science research methods.

QUESTIONS FOR DISCUSSION

1. What evidence, pro and con, can you generate concerning the degree to which present-day practitioners in public relations have theoretical as well as practical knowledge of the communication process?

2. Obtain a number of cases of public relations problem situations from any source available to you. Examine these cases from the point of view developed in the material supporting Generalization No. 2 (see particularly page 25), namely, that ". . . it is difficult to imagine a public relations problem situation *without* some aspect of attitude and behavior change as the ultimate objective of the public relations practitioner concerned." Are you able to dispute this contention with any one or more of the problem cases that you uncovered?

3. Using the Ethics in Public Relations Continuum depicted on page 30, try to find three different public relations programs, each of which illustrates one of the following points on the ethics continuum: self benefit, mutual benefit, mid-point.

4. Using any two of the cases that you obtained in order to prepare yourself to discuss the points raised in questions 2 and 3 above, try to find: (1) illustrations of where the public relations practitioner concerned had made some provision for obtaining feedback of information, and (2) places where additional feedback of information might have been obtained but was not.

Chapter 3

THE PUBLIC RELATIONS
PRACTITIONER AS AN APPLIED
SOCIAL AND BEHAVIORAL SCIENTIST

INTRODUCTION

As the second step toward understanding public relations, we considered four cases depicting four different problem situations facing four different public relations practitioners. Out of these cases we were able to derive several principles which revealed that, when the content differences of the problems were overlooked for a moment, there were fundamental similarities involved in the problems. They all proved to be problems in a communications context; all were problems with attitude- and behavior-shaping implications; all involved organizational and administrative skills; all had definite moral and ethical ramifications; and all required feedback of information about effectiveness of the public relations programs eventually implemented.

All of this adds up to the fact that the public relations practitioner must have a wide range of skills based on knowledge derived from the social and behavioral sciences in order to function successfully. In fact, the suggestion was made earlier that the public relations practitioner is, in effect, an applied social and behavioral scientist. The public relations practitioner as an applied social and behavioral scientist is one of the fundamental assumptions lying behind this whole book—one that has guided the writer as to what to include in this volume and what not to include. It is now necessary to examine this contention in more detail.

Examination of this argument that the public relations practitioner is an applied social and behavioral scientist is the last step required before an examination of a definition of public relations can fruitfully be undertaken.

HOW PEOPLE GOT INTO PUBLIC RELATIONS IN THE PAST

Many years ago, Ebbinghaus wrote "Psychology has a long past, but only a short history."[1] It seems to the writer that no more appropriate an expression to describe public relations could be found. The long past of public relations is easy to substantiate, as Cutlip and Center have effectively done:[2]

"Efforts to communicate information to influence actions likewise can be traced from the earliest civilizations. Archeologists found a farm bulletin in Iraq which told the farmers of 1800 B.C. how to sow their crops. This effort was not unlike today's distribution of farm bulletins by our U.S. Department of Agriculture. Much of what is known of ancient Egypt, Assyria, and Persia was recorded in efforts to publicize and glorify the rulers of that day. Much of the literature and art of antiquity was designed to build support for kings, priests, and other leaders. Vergil's *Georgics* represented a persuasive effort to get urban dwellers to move to the farms to produce food for the growing city. Demonsthenes used publicity to oppose the imperialist schemes of Philip of Macedon. The walls of Pompeii were inscribed with election appeals. Caesar carefully prepared the Romans for his crossing of the Rubicon in 50 B.C. by sending reports to Rome on his epic achievements as governor of Gaul. Historians believe *The Commentaries* were written by Caesar as propaganda for Caesar."

The short history of public relations is also easily demonstrated. For one thing, an exceedingly high proportion of present-day public relations practitioners came from a variety of other fields. Predominant among these fields are journalism, advertising, and publicity. In this sense, most public relations practitioners today have one thing in common: They really didn't intend to get into the field—at least when they

---

[1] Hermann Ebbinghaus, quoted in E. G. Boring, *A History of Experimental Psychology* (New York: Appleton-Century-Crofts, 1929), p. vii.

[2] Scott M. Cutlip and Allen H. Center, *Effective Public Relations* (3rd ed.; Englewood Cliffs, N.J.: Prentice-Hall, Inc., 1964), p. 17.

were young and obtaining their formal education. They couldn't. For most of them the option of planning and preparing for a career in public relations—in the sense that one would plan and prepare for a career in law or medicine—was not possible.

For this reason, the practitioners in the field, along with the whole discipline of public relations itself, just "grew like Topsy," without a common body of knowledge or without evolving any theory to guide their problem-solving efforts; hence the short history that public relations must contend with today. This situation is the fault of no one and was probably unavoidable.

In addition to the fact that most public relations practitioners today came from a variety of other fields, the educational backgrounds of today's public relations practitioners are quite varied. A great many have only high school education. Others have college education. A comparatively few have advanced degrees, and they are from a mixture of fields. The point to understand is that, unavoidably, their formal education, whatever the level, was not obtained with a career in public relations in mind. They couldn't; as was noted earlier, they had no opportunity to "plan" to go into the field of public relations.

Some Important Implications of This Heterogeneous Make-up

Because of the heterogeneous make-up of public relations practitioners from both the standpoint of previous work experiences and formal education, it is certainly understandable that there are so many interpretations as to what public relations is and is not.

For some, public relations is hardly distinguishable from straight publicity. This subgroup approaches every problem in public relations with essentially the same formula—get your story to the public by using every conceivable publicity-type stunt possible. For others, public relations is a management function, part and parcel of the total job of running a corporate body. This interpretation subsumes almost every conceivable activity that a company (or any other type of organization, for that matter) might engage in under the heading of public relations.

In addition to heterogeneity concerning what public relations is and is not, there are also widespread differences concerning how one learns to be a public relations practitioner. To many practitioners, public relations is strictly an art—what's more, an art that cannot become anything that faintly resembles a science, or at the very least one more rigorous in execution than is true at the present time. Furthermore, for these same public relations practitioners, public relations is something that you have to learn "by experience." If there is one thing they are sure of, it is that you can't *teach* public relations. It is too intuitive, too varied, too complicated.

The major implication that must be seen clearly at this point is that however understandable the reasons may be for the heterogeneity in training, definitions, and previous experiences, the bulk of present-day public relations practitioners are a species of vanishing Americans, a species that might be called *Homo in Publicus Relationibus Indoctus—* the untrained man of public relations. The demands that will be placed on the public relations practitioner in the future will be such that many present-day practitioners will not be able to measure up. The fact that their previous training and experiences are haphazard and were not obtained with a career in public relations in mind will render these people unable to cope with the demands that management will place on them. The public relations man of the future (one might even say the near future) will have to demonstrate increasingly what effects his programs are having. This one demand alone will presuppose a lot. It will require that the public relations practitioner be conversant with social and behavioral science research in a very broad sense. It will require that the public relations practitioner of the future be capable of executing some of the necessary research himself. For more complicated problems, it means that he will have to understand the research done by the outside consultant and be able to read lengthy, technically written research reports and relate the findings contained in them to organizational public relations programs.

Demands will also be placed on the public relations practitioner of the future that will require him to be conversant with communication theory as well as practice. He will be expected to interpret all developments in communication theory and research in the light of his organization's communication needs.

In short, the public relations practitioner of the future is going to be expected to be aware of all pertinent developments in the social and behavioral sciences that have relevance for solving public relations problems. At the same time, he will be expected to possess enough knowledge of social and behavioral science theory to be able to decide correctly whether this or that particular social science technique can be used by him to further his communication objectives.

The End Result of These Demands

It is because of these demands that the present untrained man of public relations will become extinct. What's more, he *should* become

extinct for the good of the discipline of public relations. As long as
any speciality can be engaged in by a broad spectrum of individuals
with a wide variety of backgrounds and training, then that speciality
is in danger of being replaced.

*This does not mean that there are no present-day public relations
practitioners who are going to survive.* On the contrary: a new species, now mostly in evolution, will mature, and very soon. Two main
streams of individuals will feed into the supply of this new species of
public relations practitioner. One stream will be a certain proportion
(what proportion no one could possibly predict) of present-day practitioners who will avail themselves, in a variety of ways, of specialized
education in the social and behavioral sciences and research. The other
main stream, and the most important from the standpoint of the long-
range future of public relations, will be the young individual desirous
of a career in public relations and who will have received training at
the college level designed for public relations.

Public Relations Is Not Alone in This Evolutionary Dilemma

This evolutionary chain of events is not peculiar to public relations
practitioners or to the field of public relations itself. Two specific examples of other fields are included here to support the above contention that an evolution is taking place in public relations and that it is
also taking place in other fields. One example is general: the field of
business administration; the other one is specific: the field of purchasing. Let us examine both of these illustrations briefly for the light
they shed on the evolution going on in public relations.

Preparation for a career in business administration, particularly in
graduate schools of business administration across the country, has
undergone dramatic changes in the past few years. One of the characteristics of these changes is that preparation for becoming a businessman is recognized as one in which the candidate must acquire a *broad*
appreciation of the social sciences as they apply to business. Likewise, business curricula across the country are increasingly introducing
courses in such areas as research, mathematics, and understanding the
application of computer systems to business problems.

One of the major guiding convictions behind such changes in business education is the realization that business management in the
future has to become increasingly rigorous. It is not enough to have
"business experience." It is not enough to make decisions on the basis
of personal experience, hunch, intuition, or any other subjective basis
one might name. Rather, business decisions are being based increas-

ingly upon all sorts of research data, mathematical projections, surveys, and so on. This is true regardless of whether one is speaking of sales, production, personnel management, or any other facet of business. Businessmen of the future will have to know a lot of specific information from the social and mathematical sciences, to say nothing of situations where a knowledge of the physical sciences will also be required. So much for the general example.

More specifically, one can look at one small segment of business and find that the same thing is true. Consider the purchasing agent and the revolutionary changes the field of purchasing has undergone during the past twenty years.[3] The time was when a person became a purchasing agent after having done a wide variety of other things. Like most public relations practitioners today, the purchasing agent did not take any particular training to become a purchasing agent—for the most part such training did not exist. He drifted into the field from sales, from personnel, or from a wide variety of other backgrounds. In time, however, the job of the purchasing agent became an increasingly critical one in an organization. Such questions as the flow of raw materials, how much to stockpile, how to predict shortages, how to relate purchasing behavior most advantageously to economic changes in the society at large became of vital importance. (Here again, the analogy to public relations fits. At first, public relations was not recognized as being vital to the normal operation of any company. Today, the public relations function is widely accepted.)

While the job of the purchasing agent became increasingly critical, another important event took place in a parallel sense, so to speak. During World War II and afterward, a number of engineers somewhat disenchanted with engineering and looking for different challenges began to become interested in the problems dealt with in purchasing. Naturally, they looked at the problems in the light of their own previous training (just as purchasing agents from sales or personnel had done) and found that one segment of their training was particularly suited for purchasing problems—their mathematical background. Almost overnight, the field of purchasing was revolutionized by such developments as the application of "operations analysis" to purchasing problems. Today the picture is clear for the old-time purchasing agent. He must learn these new techniques or suffer the consequences from the standpoint of being able to do an effective job. Likewise, the

---

[3] These observations are based partly on the results of a comprehensive survey conducted by Harbridge House, Inc., Boston, for the National Association of Purchasing Agents in 1957. The author was a consultant to Harbridge House at that time and directed the survey.

picture is clear for the young people desirous of entering the field of purchasing. Their training will become increasingly specific, rigorous, and designed for the field of their interest.

In both of the examples above, we see other fields undergoing revolutionary changes. The implications of these changes for the general field of business, and the specific field of purchasing, is precisely what the author is attempting to argue for in the field of public relations. Revolutionary changes in approach, in training, and in use of techniques are taking place; these changes are comparatively simple but have profound implications for all those in the field of public relations. Those established in the field must do what it is often said that "old dogs" cannot do: namely, learn new ways of behaving. Those interested in coming into the field must recognize these revolutionary changes and prepare themselves accordingly from an educational point of view.

Let's stop a minute and examine what we have said thus far in our efforts to argue for the case of considering the public relations practitioner as an applied social scientist.

1. We demonstrated that most of the present day practitioners did not have the option of planning to go into public relations. The field is too new, and only within the past fifteen years has the opportunity arisen to actually specialize, educationally speaking, in public relations.
2. We pointed out the heterogeneity of previous work experiences that the bulk of present-day practitioners have. It was contended that people from journalism, advertising, and publicity constitute the majority of public relations practitioners today.
3. We argued that the effects of this heterogeneity of make-up among most practitioners are that public relations is defined in many different ways, practiced in many different ways, and has encouraged conflicting views about how one prepares educationally for a career in public relations.
4. The premise was put forth that a revolutionary process is taking place in the field of public relations. In response to the changing demands of all types of organizations in our society on public relations practitioners, the older practitioner, unable to change his ways, will be practically forced out of the field. Those who remain will be the seasoned veterans who have "learned new tricks," so to speak. The young people coming into the field will have to be educationally prepared for public relations practice as it will occur in the near future.

5. Some discussion was put forth concerning the nature of the demands that will be placed on the public relations practitioner of the future. These included such things as the ability to understand how to utilize social and behavioral science research and relate it to the organization with which the public relations practitioner is associated.

6. We argued that this revolutionary chain of events is not limited to public relations. Two examples were used to make this point, one broad and one specific. The broad one was the general field of business administration. The point was made the demands of this field are such that the businessman is increasingly expected to replace intuition with precision—precision derived from all kinds of sources, such as mathematics, computers, and operations analysis. The specific example was that of the purchasing agent, who in a matter of a few short years (especially from World War II onward) has had to change his method of handling purchasing problems. Decisions based on experience, hunches, guessing, intuition have had to give way to decisions based on such aids as mathematics and statistics.

7. Lastly, the contention was put forth that the changes in operation facing the businessman in general and the purchasing agent in particular are almost identical to those facing the public relations practitioner. The future is going to belong to the practitioner with specialized training that includes a considerable amount of specific knowledge of the social and behavioral sciences and their respective research methods. The reason: The public relations practitioner is increasingly having to behave like an applied social and behavioral scientist.

Let us now continue with additional considerations that should be put forth to support the concept of the public relations practitioner as an applied social and behavioral scientist.

The Problem-Solving Continuum: A Means of Changing Our Thinking Toward Public Relations

The revolutionary change noted earlier in the demands that are being (and will be) placed on public relations and the changes in the background and training of public relations practitioners who are rising to meet these new demands can be better understood if public relations practice is viewed in a problem-solving context. That is, if public relations is thought of as a field with problems to be solved, then a conceptual schema can be developed to accommodate the revolutionary changes in approach and training that are taking place in public relations. Let us look at this schema in some detail and see how it helps us.

Historically speaking, almost any discipline was at one time unscientific or nonrigorous in application. The practice of medicine is an example. Not too long ago, medical practice was a combination of a little knowledge, a little luck, and a lot of highly individualistic, untested assumptions about the causes of both sickness and health. Medicine was learned not through books but by serving a kind of apprenticeship to another physician. As a matter of fact, the attempts to teach medicine in schools, and then later to lengthen the course of instruction, were met with considerable resistance. Medicine was an "art"; that sort of subject could not be taught in school. You needed "practical" experience!

These early days in medicine could be characterized as "individualistic," a phase that has occurred in many professions. One of the outstanding characteristics of the "individualistic" stage or phase in the development of a discipline is that solutions to problems are rather unique to the particular individual involved. Everyone has his or her own theory. The other noteworthy characteristic is that there is no unified body of knowledge that can be called on by the practitioner to aid in the solving of problems at hand.

To return to our illustration, gradually the practice of medicine became increasingly scientific in character. The individualistic stage gave way to what might be called a "scientifically derived knowledge" stage, a point at the opposite end of the continuum from the individualistic stage. Today, the practice of medicine is not based on an individual's untested assumptions. Rather, it is based on rigorously conducted experiments which provide information about the causes of sickness and about the opposite condition, health. In addition, the practice of medicine is now supported by the logically related fields of biology, physiology, chemistry, and others. Lastly, no one disputes that you must go to school to learn medicine and that this knowledge must be combined with "practical" knowledge.

This progression from the individualistic stage to the scientifically derived knowledge stage has taken place in many disciplines. Some of the social sciences are somewhere in between the two ends of the continuum described above.

In order to be able to visualize this concept more easily, let us look at Figure 2, which depicts the problem-solving continuum we have been talking about. The left-hand end of the continuum describes the

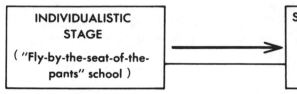

INDIVIDUALISTIC STAGE ("Fly-by-the-seat-of-the-pants" school)	SCIENTIFICALLY DERIVED KNOWLEDGE STAGE ("Best-obtainable-evidence" school)
Subjective, intuitive, personal, little use of theory or social and behavioral sciences	Objective, rigorous application of empirical knowledge, reliance on theory

Figure 2

Problem-Solving Continuum

means of problem solving called the individualistic. Essentially, this approach relies on intuition and/or practical experience. Practical experience is included at this end of the continuum because it is one of the oldest approaches that man has to problem solving. However, practical experience is a very personal thing, and we find it difficult at times to pass on to someone else what we have learned from past experience. The practical experience or individualistic approach to problem solving works surprisingly well. In time, however, the individualistic approach to problem solving becomes inadequate. For one thing, frequently we are confronted with a problem with which we have had no personal experience. For another, we tend to fall into habitual patterns of thinking and reasoning based on previous experiences. We do not readily revise our thinking in the face of new evidence. As a matter of fact, we tend to "forget" the instances when our previous experiences were not a particularly accurate guide and "remember" the ones when they were.

The scientifically derived knowledge stage is depicted in Figure 2 at the end opposite to the individualistic stage. When an applied field reaches the scientifically derived knowledge stage, its practitioners apply experimentally derived knowledge to solve their problems. Returning to our earlier example of physicians, we recall that today they solve their medical problems by utilizing knowledge from the logically related sciences. This means that their specialized training has supplanted practical experience almost entirely. Or, to express it more properly, specialized training is integrated with practical experience in order to produce the well-rounded physician.

In terms of Figure 2, public relations at the present time would be classified as being at the individualistic end of the problem-solving continuum. Everyone in public relations has his or her own theory. In addition, there is scarcely a unified body of knowledge that public relations people can call upon to aid in solving their problems. Theoretically, however, there is nothing to prevent public relations practitioners from reaching the scientifically derived knowledge stage in their problem-solving efforts. What is required is that they align themselves with the logically related sciences—the social and behavioral sciences, as we have argued earlier—and learn to apply this knowledge to their public relations problems. This is why in Figure 2 an arrow is drawn pointing to the right symbolizing the direction that public relations practitioners must strive for.

The assumption that public relations can never be anything but at the individualistic stage must be rejected. The state of a discipline at any time in its history in no way prejudices what it can be at some future time. The goal of public relations practitioners must be the scientifically derived knowledge stage. This means making use of the logically related disciplines of psychology, sociology, and economics in the same way that medicine related itself to biology, physiology, and other related disciplines. To do this, one must be trained to make use of the related knowledge as well as to know the practical side of public relations.

Naturally, we have no assurance that the scientifically derived knowledge stage will ever be achieved. There are a lot of factors that could prevent it from coming to pass and, incidentally, prevent public relations from becoming a true profession. In our analysis of the progression from the individualistic to the scientifically derived knowledge stage, we have implicitly outlined a way of defining a profession. One of the big stumbling blocks may be the slowness with which the logically related sciences of psychology and sociology develop. Just as the precision of medical practice was partly dependent on biology and physiology becoming more precise sciences, so will the precision of public relations practice be dependent partly on psychology and sociology (to name but two of the sciences that have relevance for public relations) becoming more precise sciences.

Other stumbling blocks exist potentially in the training that present, and future, public relations people obtain. If they are not academically trained along scientific lines so as to be conversant with the logically related disciplines, public relations itself will not evolve from the individualistic stage to the scientifically derived knowledge stage.

The main point is this: Regardless of the hurdles that lie ahead, arrival at the scientifically derived knowledge stage is at least theoretically possible. Being scientific is a question of method and application of methods to problem-solving efforts. It is not dependent on the subject matter involved. As a practical matter, public relations practice should be approached scientifically; this should happen in degrees and will vary from situation to situation.

The argument that has been put forth thus far, incidentally, could be made with respect to being a businessman or someone in government. The fact that a good deal of business practice is as yet at the individualistic stage does not preclude business from becoming more scientific. As we discussed earlier, much the same effort to make the execution of business more scientific or approaching the scientifically derived knowledge stage can be seen in many graduate schools of business administration across the country. What we have argued for here is not peculiar to public relations practice by any means.

We are now ready to combine the thinking contained in the two previous sections, both of which are in support of the general contention that public relations practitioners are, essentially, applied social and behavioral scientists. We have suggested the following:

1. It is useful to think of the work of a public relations practitioner in terms of problems to be solved. Essentially, these problems can be summarized as situations in which the behavior and/or attitudes of individuals need to be changed or maintained.
2. Translating public relations objectives into problems to be solved suggests that a public relations practitioner has a variety of means available to solve a particular problem. These means were summarized by a problem-solving continuum that demonstrated that problem-solving efforts can range from situations in which one is practically guessing or operating through sheer intuition to other situations in which the problem-solving action is based on research findings.
3. The primary objective of all public relations practitioners should be to attempt to solve more and more problems on the basis of some research evidence or more reliable knowledge and less and less on hunch, intuition, and guessing.
4. This change in approach indicates that the problem-solving attitude of the public relations practitioner should change from asking, "What do I think I should do in this case to solve my problem?" to stating, "In the light of available evidence from the social and behavioral sciences pertinent to this problem, I should do such and such to solve my problem."

5. The ability to be able to make this change in problem-solving attempts requires that the public relations practitioner obtain sufficient training to understand and use knowledge from the social and behavioral sciences. Such training suggests that one should think of the public relations practitioner as an applied social and behavioral scientist.

A DEFINITION OF PUBLIC RELATIONS

In Chapter 1, the question of a definition of public relations was raised and then postponed. The reason was simple. Because public relations is very complex and very misunderstood, no formal definition could be made until (1) some example cases had been studied and from them had been extracted the principles inherent in all public relations problems and (2) the conviction that public relations practice is an applied social and behavioral science had been given firm root. Now that these aspects of public relations have been examined, let us turn to a definition.[4]

Public relations as an applied social and behavioral science is that function which:

1. measures, evaluates, and interprets the attitudes of various relevant publics;[5]
2. assists management in defining objectives for increasing public understanding and acceptance of the organization's products, plans, policies, and personnel;
3. equates these objectives with the interests, needs, and goals of the various relevant publics; and

---

[4] Several of the notions contained in this definition (e.g., public relations seen as a management function) are also contained in the *Public Relations News* definition and, indeed, in the definitions of many other writers, such as John Marston, for example. The author acknowledges these many influences; where he was in agreement with the elements therein, they were incorporated into the present definition.

[5] The word *public* is used throughout this volume to refer to any group of people who share a common interest. The employees of a company are an example of a public—good pay, the company's stability and future, and the opportunity for advancement are a few of the common interests of members of a company. Some publics, such as employees, are part of an organization; these are called *internal* publics. In contrast, customers are an example of an *external* public. Other examples of external publics of a typical manufacturing company are suppliers, the community, and retail dealers. The internal and external publics will differ from one kind of organization to another.

4. develops, executes, and evaluates a program to earn public understanding and acceptance.

Major Implications of Our Definition

From this definition, it is clear that public relations is a management function. It should be stressed, however, that the term *management* should be thought of in its broadest sense. That is, every organization, whether it be industrial, nonprofit, or governmental, has people
who are responsible for running it. Regardless of the kind of organization, these people who are in charge are "management."

In addition, the term *management* should not be interpreted to refer only to organizations, corporate bodies, or governmental units. Individuals may utilize public relations services. What's more, public
relations planning and execution for individuals require precisely the
same ethical concerns as do the planning and execution for organizations. To be sure, far more money and effort are expended to achieve
public relations goals for organizations than for individuals. However,
recent events—particularly in politics—make it important for the reader
to realize that any segment of society, be it an individual or a group,
may utilize public relations programs to achieve increased understanding and acceptance.

One of the noteworthy developments in the field of public relations
during the past two decades is the realization that the persons responsible for running nonindustrial organizations—*e.g.*, schools, colleges,
universities, nonprofit health and welfare organizations of all descriptions—have public relations problems and responsibilities exactly like
those that industrial organizations learned they had to face—responsibilities, especially in the case of universities and nonprofit organizations
of all kinds, that were not being taken care of. This accounts, incidentally, for the fact that two of the most rapidly growing categories
of opportunities for persons interested in public relations are universities and health and welfare organizations.

Just as the public relations practitioner is a part of the management
team, the rest of the management team is an integral part of the planning and the policy making of its organization's public relations. To
put it another way, although management can delegate the *execution*
of its public relations programs, it cannot delegate its responsibilities
to review the planning and establish broad policies to guide the over-
all public relations actions. This point relates to the discussion that
was introduced earlier under the heading of *"Public relations on an
ethics continuum"* (page 30). There it was noted that any organization

has the responsibility of considering all public relations action both in the light of the interests of the organization and in the light of the interests of the general public. In addition, the point was made that public relations actions that serve only the interests of the organization at the expense of the public are to be rejected in favor of actions that serve the mutual goals of the organization and the public. Our definition reflects this by highlighting that public relations is a management function and that management must understand and take part in establishing policy to guide public relations action.

A second observation is also related to the ethics continuum. The definition, short as it is, is careful to point out that the public relations practitioner fulfills the function of defining objectives for increasing public understanding and acceptance of his organization's products, plans, policies, and personnel in terms of the *interests, needs, and goals of the various relevant publics.* As an integral part of the definition, we see that it is the responsibility of the public relations practitioner to see that the interests, needs and goals of various relevant publics are identified and *then* that programs of action are implemented that are *consistent* with the public interest while at the same time furthering the objectives of the organization.

The word *policies* (along with the word *plans*) in our definition suggests a third observation worthy of note. Essentially, the word *policy* highlights the question, "What do we stand for?" This means that in practice a public relations practitioner causes an organization to state what it stands for. In the process of developing a public relations function within the organization, some of the by-products, such as stating goals and considering what the public interest is, tend to induce a searching examination of the organization itself. In order to communicate about an organization, it is almost impossible to avoid these searching questions. Consequently, even though an organization has never before clearly thought out these important questions, with a public relations practitioner around they inevitably come to the fore.

The fourth observation is that, before executing a public relations program, an organization must know what it stands for and what it is trying to achieve. The word that sums this up is *planning*, and it was one of the principles that we earlier derived from the various cases that we examined in some detail. Planning requires that you know what goals you are trying to achieve, why you are trying to achieve them, and how these considerations relate to the ethics involved. The execution of a public relations program, although important in its own right and involving many skills and substantial amounts of creativity, can come only after plans have been clearly established.

The phrase *measures, evaluates, and interprets the attitudes of various relevant publics* in the definition highlights the fifth observation that should be made. This phrase clearly points to the applied social and behavioral scientist capability that was argued for earlier in this chapter. To be able to evaluate public attitudes, one must know something about attitude formation and attitude change. One must know how attitudes are measured and, if necessary, devise and execute the means for their measurement. Also, it calls for a background of socioeconomic and political information against which to evaluate attitudes and attitude change intelligently. In short, our definition embodies the requirement that the public relations practitioner be equipped to function as an applied social and behavioral scientist.

The sixth observation is this: The goal of the public relations practitioner is to earn public understanding and acceptance. To do this, the public relations practitioner must communicate; this highlights the very important role of communication in public relations, a principle that we extracted from all of our cases in Chapter 2. Why this emphasis on communication? The answer is simple: To change people's behavior—that is, to earn public understanding and acceptance—you have to communicate with them.

The seventh point is perhaps the most elusive and overlooked point of all, yet in some ways the most important. It's this: Contrary to common belief, even among many present-day practitioners, public relations actions can be evaluated in concrete terms. The end results of public relations action are not always something vague, obscure, and intangible. To be sure, there are many situations wherein one is not able to measure the effect of a public relations program. Or, more to the point, there are many side effects of public relations that cannot be isolated and determined. However, there are many times when one can determine if there has been any effect produced by a public relations program. The problem more often than not is that no systematic effort has been made to obtain the measurement. The thing to emphasize at this time is not the pros and cons of measurement, but to bring attention to the fact that our definition emphasizes that the objective of a public relations practitioner is to earn public understanding and acceptance. Understanding and accepting are things that are done by people and theoretically at least this implies that the effects of public relations programs can be measured.

Our last observation is tied up in the word *earn* that is a part of the definition. It is important that the word *earn* was used rather than a word such as *win*. This means that an organization or individual must be worthy of the public understanding and acceptance it seeks. This implies a lot of things, but in its simplest terms it means that an organization must behave in an ethical and responsible manner in the community, city, state, and nation of which it is a part in order to deserve acceptance by the public and to expect from it the interest necessary to understand its function and objectives.

So much for a formal examination of our definition and some of the more important observations that can be made of it. The reader should keep in mind that this is a *working* definition and one that should hold up regardless of the particular public relations situation under consideration. This definition and all that it implies will come up again and again in this book, and at those times we will add more refined interpretations to the function called public relations.

ABOUT THE REMAINDER OF THE BOOK

The remainder of this book is built around two main subjects: (1) a rather thorough exposition of one version of the communications process model (Part 2) and (2) a comparatively detailed examination of research (Part 3).

In Part 2, we will be breaking up the total communications process into several stages: the sender, the message, the media, and the recipient. In effect, this breakup of the total communication process serves as a model which facilitates an examination of communications. With the stages of the communication process as the basic outline, all of the principles of communication, generalizations concerning perception, motivation, learning, and sociology can be brought in where appropriate. For example, at the sender stage it is natural to talk about the topic of perception, as borrowed from the field of psychology, and illustrate how the public relations practitioner (*i.e.,* the sender in the communication process) must take the perceptions of his recipient (*i.e.,* the object of communication) into account in order to communicate more effectively.

In this way, the relevant material from the social sciences can be brought in, *but* in a context (*i.e.,* a communication context) that makes the most sense for the public relations practitioner. In addition, another purpose can be attained by this technique: the topic and practice of public relations can be redefined in social and behavioral science terms so that the practice of public relations can be demonstrated as a special case of applied social and behavioral science, and the public relations practitioner can readily be seen playing the role of the applied social and behavioral scientist.

Part 3 presents enough detail of social and behavioral science research that the reader, on completion of the material, will be able to understand the role of research in public relations. In addition, the reader should be able to do some research himself in the form of what the author calls "researchettes" and be fully equipped to understand how to utilize the research reports submitted to him (or his organization) and based on more complicated and sophisticated research that the public relations practitioner has had to have done for him by professional researchers. This second subject is particularly important because the public relations practitioner of the future will have to be fully conversant with research methods and must have the ability to use the reports produced by the outside consulting agencies that have been employed to help throw light on a particular public relations program.

QUESTIONS FOR DISCUSSION

1. At the end of Chapter 1 the suggestion was made that you jot down your notions of what the concept of the public relations practitioner as an applied social and behavioral scientist implied. Now that this thesis has been more fully discussed in this chapter, check the notes of your ideas with those put forth in this chapter. What implications did you anticipate? What implications did you develop that were not included in this chapter?

2. In this chapter, we have argued that the demands for increased rigor and precision in the problem-solving behavior of the public relations practitioner suggest that the public relations practitioner of the future be trained as an applied social and behavioral scientist. Take some other applied communication field—journalism, radio, TV, or advertising—and see whether the arguments put forth about the public relations practitioner apply to the practitioner in that field. In what ways do the arguments fit for these other practitioners? In what ways do they not fit?

3. Try to obtain one or two cases in public relations that illustrate the "fly by the seat of the pants" end of the problem-solving continuum developed in this chapter (Figure 2, page 48). Likewise, try to find a case or two that illustrates functioning at the "best obtainable evidence" end of the continuum.

4. Pretend that you are a public relations practitioner who is very successful and has been in the field about 20 years. In addition, let

us assume that you were previously a newspaperman and that you entered the field of public relations after several years of working on a newspaper. Lastly, let us assume that you have a B.S. degree from a school of journalism.

With this assumed role try to develop as many arguments as you can *against* the notions put forth in Chapter 3 (and Chapter 2 if you wish). For example: against the notion of defining a public relations practitioner as an applied social and behavioral scientist; against the notion that research ability or the understanding of research is of paramount importance for the public relations practitioner of the future.

After you have developed these arguments *against* the theses expounded in Chapters 2 and 3, change your role to that of the author's and answer these arguments as you would imagine he would do. What arguments were you able to successfully refute, in your opinion? In your opinion, which were you *not* able to refute successfully?

Part 2

PUBLIC RELATIONS:
A THEORETICAL
ANALYSIS

This section of the book embraces thirteen chapters devoted to a theoretical analysis of public relations. The major objective of these thirteen chapters is to provide for the reader a framework wherein public relations problems can be translated into social and behavioral science terms. The need for this translation stems from what we learned earlier—that public relations practitioners are faced invariably with the problem of communicating in order to modify or maintain attitudes and behavior. We put forth an argument that, because of this fact, public relations practitioners are, in effect, required to function as applied social and behavioral scientists. In order to function as an applied social and behavioral scientist, the public relations practitioner needs to have certain information from the social and behavioral sciences: theories about learning, motivation, perception, and the like.

Granted our objective, there is the problem of how to provide this framework. We have chosen a communication theory model, to be presented in detail in Chapters 4 and 5, to serve as a vehicle for this translation of public relations into social and behavioral science terms. After we have introduced our communication theory model, we will be in a position to do two things: (1) examine each "stage" of the communication model in detail sufficient to enable the reader to become moderately sophisticated in this type of approach to communication analysis; and (2) integrate into our model the pertinent concepts from psychology and sociology that public relations practitioners must have in order to make an intelligent analysis of their problems.

In other words, we will progress toward the right-hand end of the public relations problem-solving continuum introduced in Part 1 by way of a communication theory model by which public relations problems are translated into social and behavioral science terminology.

Chapter 4

A COMMUNICATION THEORY MODEL

INTRODUCTION

One process that can be observed as individuals attempt to understand something is their use of analogies or models—either two-dimensional models that can be drawn on paper or three-dimensional, as in the case of models depicting the molecular structure of a chemical compound. Employing analogies or models is so common that all sorts of examples come immediately to mind: some very simple; some rather complex.

At a simple level there is the analogy that is very often drawn between radio waves and water waves. A teacher, attempting to explain the action of radio waves, will occasionally ask his students to visualize a stone dropped in a calm pond of water. The waves produced by the stone and the ensuing patterns of wave following wave, are used by the teacher to explain radio waves. At some point in his lecture, he says to his students, "Now visualize the radio antenna of a transmitting station. The radio waves emanating from the antenna are very much like the waves produced by a stone dropped in a still pond of water."

A more complex example can be borrowed from the field of psychology, particularly that development known as field theory. The leader of this movement was Kurt Lewin. Lewin was influenced by the thinking of physical scientists in such a way that he began to conceive of psychological behavior in terms of events occurring in a sort of space that had a lot in common with physical space. However, he chose to think of this space as "psychological space." That is, the be-

61

havior of an individual could be thought of psychologically as progression from one point to another (here the analogy with physical space) in the "life space" of an individual. This "life space" was made up of the goals that an individual had, the barriers to achieving these goals, and so forth. To round out this model, Lewin borrowed from a branch of mathematics called topology. In topology one is concerned with regions and their boundaries and subdivisions, and the ways of progressing within these boundaries and subdivisions. With topology as his guide, Lewin then developed models depicting individuals in certain psychological situations.[1]

The use of this sort of model building, employing such concepts as "psychological space" and "life space" to help analyze behavior, is illustrated by Figure 3,[2] taken from one of Lewin's books.

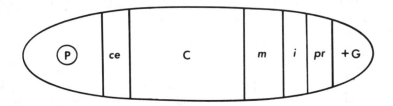

Figure 3

The vocational goal of a sixteen-year-old boy (p) is to become a physician. The "path" to this goal (G) leads through definite stages: college-entrance examinations (ce), college (c), medical school (m), internship (i), establishing a practice (pr). The boy may have a fairly clear idea of college. Medical school and the following stages may constitute a more or less undifferentiated region "beyond" which lies the goal of being a physician. Of this the boy may have a false but nevertheless a clear picture.

Obviously, the advantages of models are not limited to the examples cited above. There are as many opportunities to construct models to aid thinking as there are problem areas that receive the attention of man. The area of communication is no exception. There

---

[1] Kurt Lewin, *Principles of Topological Psychology* (New York: McGraw-Hill Book Co., Inc., 1936).

[2] *Ibid.*, p. 48. Used by permission of McGraw-Hill Book Co., Inc.

are numerous examples of the use of models to better understand the communication process. Among the better known are those developed by Wilbur Schramm,[3] George Gerbner,[4] and John W. Riley, Jr., and Matilda W. Riley.[5] Some of the treatments of communication models are more sophisticated than is required for our purposes. On the other hand, there are certain principles common to them all. Let us look at a communication model, developed by the author, that includes the amount of detail required for the public relations practitioner, and that will facilitate examination of public relations problems throughout the rest of this book.

WHY DO WE NEED A MODEL?

One difficulty in understanding communication is that as a process it can appear to be so deceptively simple. Every human being (and infrahumans as well) communicates in a variety of ways every day of his life. We talk, we write, we gesture, we frown, we laugh, we cry; in short, we communicate constantly. What's more, we are comparatively successful in achieving our objectives in a high proportion of our communicative efforts. Consequently, the fact that communication is something engaged in by everyone all of the time and with a reasonable amount of success contributes to the illusion that communication is a simple phenomenon. This contributes to the mistaken notion that we do not have to study communication in order to better understand it and thereby communicate more effectively. Nothing could be further from the truth. Communication is a complicated process, and public relations practitioners, more than most other groups in our society, must be aware of this fact. They must make communication a topic for study rather than something to be taken for granted. Schramm cites an example that is an excellent illustration of the complexity that lies behind what might otherwise appear to be a rather simple, straightforward communication situation. He discusses the difficulty of pre-

[3] Wilbur Schramm, "How Communications Works," in *The Process and Effects of Mass Communication*, ed. by Wilbur Schramm (Urbana: University of Illinois Press, 1961), pp. 4-10.

[4] George Gerbner, "Toward a General Model of Communications," *Audio Visual Communication Review*, IV, No. 2 (Summer, 1956), 171-179.

[5] John W. Riley, Jr., and Matilda W. Riley, "Mass Communications and the Social System," in *Sociology Today: Problems and Prospects* (New York: Basic Books, Inc., 1959), pp. 537-578.

dicting the effects of any particular message, then cites the following example:

". . . In Korea, in the first year of the war there, I was interviewing a North Korean prisoner of war who had recently surrendered with one of our surrender leaflets on his person. It looked like an open and shut case: the man had picked up the leaflet, thought it over, and decided to surrender. But I was interviewing him anyway, trying to see just how the leaflet had its effect. This is what he told me.

He said that when he picked up the leaflet, it actually made him fight harder. It rather irritated him, and he didn't like the idea of having to surrender. He wasn't exactly a warlike man; he had been a clerk, and was quiet and rather slow; but the message actually aroused a lot of aggression in him. Then the situation deteriorated. His division was hit hard and thrown back, and he lost contact with the command post. He had no food, except what he could find in the fields, and a little ammunition. What was left of his company was isolated by itself in a rocky valley. Even then, he said, the morale was good, and there was no talk of surrendering. As a matter of fact, he said, the others would have shot him if he had tried to surrender. But then a couple of our planes spotted them, shot up their hideout, and dropped some napalm. When it was over, he found himself alone, a half mile from where he had been, with half his jacket burned off, and no sign of any of his company. A couple of hours later some of our tanks came along. And only then did the leaflet have an effect. He remembered it had told him to surrender with his hands up, and he did so.

In other words, the communication had no effect (even had an opposite effect from the one intended) so long as the situation, the personality, and the group norms were not favorable. When the situation deteriorated, the group influence was removed, and the personality aggression was burned up, then finally the message had an effect. I tell you this story hoping it will teach you what it taught me: that it is dangerous to assume any simple and direct relationship between a message and its effect without knowing all the other elements in the process." [6]

It is clear from the example we have cited that communication is indeed a complicated affair. There was no simple relationship between the communication attempt (*i.e.*, the surrender leaflet) and how this particular North Korean soldier first reacted and how he eventually reacted to it. This illustration is cited here to highlight the fact that this phenomenon called communication, that all of us engage in con-

---

[6] Schramm, *op cit.*, pp. 17-18. Used by permission of the University of Illinois Press.

stantly, is a highly complicated affair, worthy of and in need of careful study.

COMMUNICATION IS A PROCESS

Some of the most extravagant claims have been made concerning the importance of communication. We hear many times that this or that problem is due to nothing more than "faulty communication." There is no question of the importance of communication. However, experience with problems in communication has taught us that a more useful way of thinking about this subject is (1) to avoid the tendency to lump many separate events into the all-too-broad category called "communication" and (2) to substitute in its place the term "communication process," which helps us to remember that communication is a complicated affair made up of many "parts" or "stages." Two of the parts normally identified are the person or persons initiating the communication and the one or ones receiving it. Also, we characteristically focus our attention on the nearly infinite number of conditions surrounding the sender and the recipient that can affect the communication. To better understand the communication process and at the same time begin to develop our version of a communication model, let us take a typical, comparatively simple public relations problem situation.

CASE STUDY NO. 5

TITLE: The Case of the Perishing Fish[7]

Background

The oil industry had undertaken a series of seismic surveys to search out oil-bearing areas off the coast of California. Shock waves, necessary to measure the subsurface geological formation, were created by submarine dynamite explosions.

Problem Situation

These explosions were felt in some homes along the coast. They also killed many fish. Coastal communities were aroused and joined sports-

---

[7] This case, modified only to the extent that it was made to fit a standard form for presenting cases, was borrowed from an article by Milton Fairman, "Public Relations Is Good Business," *Public Relations Journal*, XI, No. 2 (February, 1955), 5. Used by permission.

men and commercial fishing interests in bringing pressures to halt the seismic surveys.

Summary of What the Public Relations Practitioner Faces

Both the oil industry and the State Fish and Game Commission bore the brunt of the criticism. They combined to work out a solution. Experiments at the Scripps Institute of Oceanography eventually developed a method of using a slower burning black powder instead of dynamite. Thus, homes could be spared the annoyance of explosions, and the destruction of the marine population could be stopped.

Standard of California had mapped an extensive offshore seismic survey in an area that embraced many commercial fishing communities. The survey was scheduled for the height of the sports fishing season. Recalling past criticism, Standard feared that renewed public pressures might force the revocation of its survey permit.

The public relations department was called in. It reprinted the official report demonstrating the harmlessness of the black powder to be used in the surveys. It developed a basic press release highlighting the facts. Standard presented this information to the leaders of the commercial fishing industry. Fish and game editors throughout a broad area were similarly informed. Two public relations men moved through coastal communities in advance of the exploration crews. All editors were given the facts and invited to spend a day with the survey ships to satisfy themselves that the method was harmless.

Some Results

The basic cause of the community relations problem had been solved by the research that had developed the improved method. The secondary causes were removed through communication which forestalled criticism of the new survey. Editorials appeared hailing the improved method and complimenting Standard for adopting it and for developing new oil reserves. The search for oil continued.

THE SENDER STAGE

With this rather typical public relations problem, we have a basis for generating a communication model. First, there is the obvious statement that someone (either as an individual or as a person representing an organization) who has the desire to communicate is needed.

This initiator of a communication we shall call the *sender*. The sender, in this case, is the public relations department of Standard of California. The department, acting on behalf of the corporation, was most interested in communicating certain *facts* for certain reasons. The *facts* were that, through research, an improved means had been discovered for producing the shock waves necessary for subsurface geological analysis that were harmless to submarine life and undetectable by persons living in coastal communities. The *reasons* for communicating these facts were that this information would very likely play an important role in reducing or eliminating citizen objection to this geological survey work and that the company in question might even receive some favorable attention because this survey work and the development of a new technique for producing shock waves called attention to the company's continual efforts to discover new deposits of oil. Graphically, we can identify our first component in the model as in Figure 4.

Figure 4

Sender Stage

Before going on to the other components of our model, let us make some generalizations about this first stage.

1. Every communication requires a sender. This is an obvious statement, yet there are other concepts associated with this that are not so obvious. For example, there is the distinction between purposive and nonpurposive communication efforts as suggested by Westley and MacLean.[8] (We will return to this concept later when we take up the sender stage in more detail.)

2. The sender stage in the communication process can represent an individual (as in a face-to-face situation involving two persons), or it can stand for an organization. Thus, under certain circumstances the sender can be a company, The United States Government, The United Nations, or any other conceivable organization of any size or makeup. In addition, there can be a

[8] B. H. Westley and M. MacLean, Jr., "A Conceptual Model for Communications Research," *Journalism Quarterly*, XXXIV, No. 1 (Winter, 1957), 31-38.

personal-impersonal interchange at the sender stage that is worthy of attention. This phenomenon is nicely demonstrated in military life. When a sergeant is communicating to his men and giving them orders, he becomes the sender in our communication model. In addition, because of the close daily contact that he has with his men, he is reacted to as an individual—one whom the men like and respect or do not like nor respect depending upon the circumstances at the time. When, however, these same men are addressed by their commanding officer, an individual with whom they have had little or no personal contact, he is also a sender in our model, but one who can be, and unfortunately often is, reacted to as a symbol of office rather than as a person. The commanding officer can become a sender almost devoid of personality, reacted to in a highly stereotyped way as "one of the brass." In fact, one of the difficult problems in any organization is to induce subordinates to react to and think of superiors (especially those very high in the organization and not often seen) as people with likes and dislikes very much like their own. This "social distance" phenomenon, so well known among psychologists, accounts for the fact that it is a long time before the true personality of any leader can become known. It takes time to overcome the fact that followers can react to leaders in an institutional sense rather than a personal one. It accounts for the fact that it is often the public relations department that is called on to help devise ways to communicate the human qualities of management to such pertinent groups as employees, stockholders, and suppliers.

One further point. Although symbolically we may from time to time insert the name of a department, company, or even a government in the box reserved for the sender stage, the actual work involved in producing a communication is, of course, done by an individual or a comparatively small group of individuals. The advantage of identifying an "organizational sender," to coin a phrase, rather than an individual sender, arises from the fact that occasionally the sender is reacted to as a corporation rather than an individual. It is important to distinguish this fact in any communication analysis. Thus, in our perishing fish case, the aroused segments of the public were reacting to the oil company and the State Fish and Game Commission. In this instance, they were the senders in the eyes of the public in any subsequent communication effort.

The Encoding and Decoding Process

The sender must translate the thinking and planning that lies behind any communication effort into a form that is understandable to those with whom he is communicating and that is useful to his communication goals (*i.e.*, that achieves the behavior or attitude changes he desires.) Technically this is known as *encoding*. Encoding is the process of translating everything that lies behind a particular communication effort (the analysis of the problem, the planning of the public relations program, and so forth) into written or spoken (or both) versions that the one or the group with whom you are communicating can understand.

Encoding assumes two other important processes that are also performed by the sender: (1) *interpretation* or *assigning meaning* and (2) *making sense out of communications directed to the sender* from other sources. This latter process is technically known as *decoding* and is the other side of the coin, so to speak, of encoding. These two additional steps of interpreting and decoding are part and parcel of encoding and, as a matter of fact, they all take place simultaneously. The separation that is made here is for purposes of understanding. Much in the same sense that we break down a chemical reaction into many parts when in actuality they all function together in one inseparable whole, so it is with *encoding, interpreting*, and *decoding*. They are important processes associated with the sender stage.

By now we have introduced several rather complicated or potentially confusing concepts in a comparatively few words. Let us enlarge on our communication model, as started in Figure 4, to permit recognition of the more complicated processes that are associated with the sender stage. Figure 4 should be modified to give us Figure 5.

Let us return to our perishing fish case and relate the information there to our expanded sender stage as depicted in Figure 5. Earlier we noted that the public relations department of Standard of California was the sender in our public relations problem under consideration. As the public relations department gathered and analyzed all of the events that had taken place in connection with the unfavorable reaction to previous seismic surveys, they were *decoding* all of the information gathered from outside sources. Part and parcel with this decoding, or "making sense out of what they were exposed to," they were *assigning meaning* to the information. That is, they were attempting to make sense out of the reactions of the various groups and were making some estimate of the seriousness of the situation. This decoded

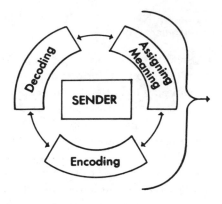

Figure 5

The sender stage with the processes associated with being a
sender added: decoding, encoding, and assigning meaning

and interpreted material was then used as a guide in the *encoding*
process. Remember that in order to solve their problem they needed
to communicate with the individuals and groups concerned, but *what*
they said and *how* they said it (*i.e.*, the encoding process, the step of
translating your thinking and planning into a form that can be understood by another individual or group) had to be carefully worked out.
Among other things, they came to the conclusion that *if* these various
individuals and groups learned about the research conducted with the
black powder and *if* they understood that it, unlike dynamite, had
none of the undesirable side effects of killing marine life and causing
tremors, substantial progress could be made toward having future
seismic surveys accepted.

The activities named decoding, assigning meaning, and encoding
are all parts of a never-ending, circular process. This is why they are
depicted in Figure 5 in a circular fashion. As individuals or as public
relations practitioners representing organizations, we are constantly
bombarded with signs or symbols (through all of our senses) to which
we react by the circular process of decoding, assigning meaning, and
encoding. *Any* person who functions as a sender in *any* communication situation engages in this circular process.[9]

---

[9] Two additional points should be made here. (1) This circular process of decoding, assigning meaning, and encoding is not restricted to the sender in any
communication situation. It is also true of the *recipient* of any communication, but
we will get to this point as our communications model enlarges to include the

Encoding, Decoding, and the Concept of Feedback

Much of what has been said can be summed up with the term *feedback*. In everything we do it is important and essential that we have the opportunity to learn something of the outcome of our actions. The outcome of our communication actions is merely one of a host of situations in which we need to know the effects of our actions. Take a simple example. If we are attempting to "sink a basket" with a basketball, we generally can do this successfully in a very few trials if we have any degree of eye-hand coordination at all. If, however, a barrier is placed between us and the basket, such that we can still shoot but cannot see the results of our shooting, then we take much longer to sink a basket. The reason: we have considerably reduced the available feedback. We can't see what we are doing and we now have to rely on hearing how well we are doing—something that we are not used to, as you can readily find out by closing your eyes and relying on hearing instead of sight. Take away any cues of sound, and we might never learn to sink a basket consistently. Only by chance would the ball go in now. This example illustrates the principle of feedback.

Let us now examine another simple example, this time emphasizing communication a little more. Let us assume that two gentlemen meet

---

recipient stage. (2) In one sense, we have described the total communication process by spelling out the decoding, assigning meaning, and encoding processes associated with the sender stage and noting at the same time that these same processes are used by the recipient as well. Thus, when a sender and a recipient *both* decode, assign meaning, and encode with respect to one another, this *is* the process of communication. This is what we are trying to build up to conceptually (and in detail) in this chapter and the next. However, because we are trying to spell out in a static model what goes on in a dynamic fashion, we sometimes touch upon concepts in advance of our model's being able to handle them fully. The present situation is a case in point. We have not, for example, discussed the concept of feedback, the message stage, the media stage, and the recipient stage. There are many important details associated with these concepts, and it is necessary to study them in order to understand the communication process more fully. To put it another way, the process of decoding, assigning meaning, and encoding contain within them details that must be made explicit but, in terms of our model building, will not be made explicit until later in this chapter and in the next. The reason that we have brought up this sort of discussion at this juncture is that there are some social scientists who would argue that the processes of decoding, assigning meaning, and encoding, along with the concept of feedback, *is* the total communication process. In one sense they are correct, except that these concepts leave unsaid many other details of importance concerning the communication process that can be more adequately brought out as additional portions of our communication theory model are unfolded.

for the first time at a cocktail party. Let's identify them as Mr. A and Mr. B. From the moment they meet and begin to talk, the process of feedback is operating for both of them. Mr. A may refer to a football game that was played that day. Mr. B may be completely uninterested in football and make only some polite, perhaps even trite reply. If he is halfway perceptive, Mr. A immediately detects the lack of interest in football on the part of Mr. B. This behavior of Mr. B now has served as feedback for Mr. A, and Mr. A may drop the subject, defend the sport, or what have you, depending upon his personality, the amount of spirits he has imbibed, and so on. In short, for both men, such things as gestures, facial expressions, explicit and implicit verbal statements all serve as feedback for both of them—feedback that they both will use to guide their subsequent behavior, particularly their communication behavior, which is our interest in this example.

What is true for an individual (our first example of trying to sink a basket) or two individuals interacting (Mr. A and Mr. B at a cocktail party) or any other possible combinations of individuals (such as an individual communicating to an audience in a lecture situation) is true for any communication situation. There will be feedback, however extensive or limited. In the perishing fish case, the protests of various groups that took place in a variety of forms (telephone calls, editorials, etc.) all served as feedback for the public relations department of Standard of California. This feedback was decoded, meaning was assigned, and both of these processes formed a basis for determining how subsequent communicative efforts by the public relations department back to the various groups would be structured and executed.

Some additional points concerning feedback. A few additional points might be made here concerning feedback. Although feedback occurs in most communication situations, the type and degree of feedback varies considerably from situation to situation. At the face-to-face level, we have a situation in which feedback is potentially the greatest. Not only can we hear what a person is saying, but we can view how he says it. The nuances in communication are potentially very great; we can assimilate at the same time the facial expressions, bodily stance, and a variety of other behaviors that add to total feedback. All of the major sensory inputs can operate to add (or detract, as the case may be) to what the person is saying. This richness in face-to-face communication can be dramatized by contrasting it to a telephone conversation where the feedback is immediately reduced. This reduction in feedback is often the reason why, in certain conditions, we postpone communicating with someone if it can be done only by telephone. There are times when we feel we must wait until we have the opportunity for the rich feedback that a face-to-face situation affords.

At the other extreme, we have communication through the electronic media, where the opportunity to obtain feedback is severely reduced—in some instances to a point where there is no feedback or where it is so delayed that one is not quite sure how to make use of it. Consider the situation where an individual has delivered a speech by radio. Days later he may receive a letter from a listener commenting upon something that was said. First of all, this feedback is far too late to have been used by the speaker at the time he gave the speech. (Skillful speakers, addressing live audiences, are constantly using feedback from their audience as a guide in their delivery. If a speaker appears to be losing his audience—quite a few of them begin to talk or squirm in their seats or look around and yawn—he may completely change his style of delivery, or he may ad lib material to try to regain its attention.) Secondly, there may be no opportunity to counter the letter with a reply (the writer may have forgotten to give his address). Lastly, the position in which the speaker now finds himself (he is busy with a hundred other things and is not in the mood to reply) may be different. All of these factors and many, many more render the feedback in this situation vastly different from feedback in the face-to-face situation.[10]

Secondly, feedback can be thought of as lying along a continuum of intentionality-unintentionality as depicted in Figure 6.[11]

To illustrate the left-hand end of the continuum, let us assume a situation in which an individual takes offense to something we say and goes so far as to try to punch us in the nose. Here the feedback is quite clear, and there is no question in our minds about the intentions of the person who is executing the feedback! Likewise, there is no question in our minds as to how we should react and interpret this feedback. Lastly, it is reasonably safe to try to speculate about the

---

[10] It should be noted in passing that this latter situation—that is, where feedback is severely delayed or almost nonexistent—is typical of the context in which most public relations practitioners operate. In fact, one of the major tasks of a public relations practitioner is to devise means for obtaining useful feedback that he can make use of in his subsequent public relations programing. We will return to this point several times in forthcoming chapters, particularly when we focus on research in Part 3.

[11] For another version of how intentional and unintentional feedback can be conceptualized in a communications model, see Westley and MacLean, op cit., XXXIV, No. 1 (Winter, 1957), 31-38.

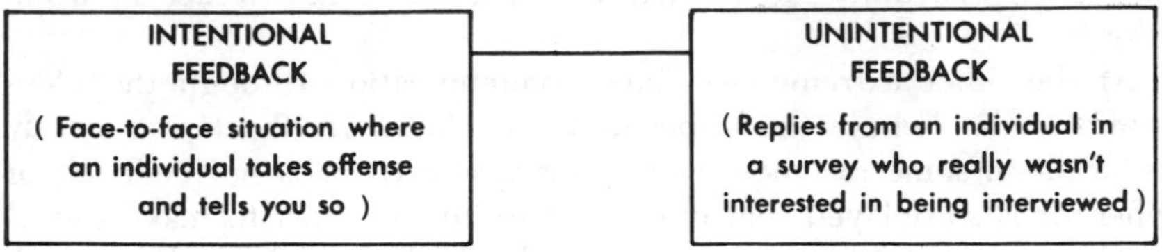

INTENTIONAL FEEDBACK	UNINTENTIONAL FEEDBACK
(Face-to-face situation where an individual takes offense and tells you so)	(Replies from an individual in a survey who really wasn't interested in being interviewed)

Figure 6

An Intentional-Unintentional Feedback Continuum

cause-and-effect relationship between our communication and the resulting feedback.

The classical opinion-attitude survey can be used to illustrate the other end of the continuum. Typically, the respondent is selected on some impartial sampling basis and questioned about a particular topic. In this situation, the individual is providing a form of feedback in that his answers are collated, along with the answers of others, and summaries are made that presumably describe the total sample of individuals interviewed. The respondent is providing unintentional feedback because he is not necessarily directing his views toward any particular person or organization. In fact, more often than not, the identity of the organization sponsoring the survey is kept confidential, at least until *after* the interview is completed. What's more, the identity of the respondent is not revealed to the organization paying for the survey. Contrast this situation with our previous example of one individual taking offense to another, and the potential differences in feedback become quite clear.

Feedback somewhere in between these extremes is depicted in another version of survey work—the use of questions to accompany the filing of a guarantee on a particular product just purchased. Very often the individual sending in his card to register for the guarantee is asked to answer several questions, such as in what type of store he purchased the product and through what media did he learn about the product. In this feedback situation, the respondent knows, at least in a general way, the object of his feedback, but he generally has a rather neutral feeling about providing it at all.

Unintentional feedback, unlike intentional feedback, poses greater difficulty in terms of assigning meaning and how to react to the feedback. In the case of the person who takes offense to what we have said, we can be more certain about the cause-and-effect relationship in the communication situation. In the case of survey data, it is exceedingly difficult, if not often impossible, to relate the results of the survey with any of our communications. In short, it is difficult to tell what caused the responses as recorded by the survey.

Public relations practitioners have good reason to be concerned with both of the additional dimensions of feedback that we have been discussing. Concerning the variation in degree and type of feedback, one of the major problems confronting the public relations practitioner is that there are so many situations in which he operates *without* feedback. Lack of feedback can be due to several factors: (1) it is not possible to obtain feedback, (2) it is not feasible to obtain feedback due to financial and other considerations, and (3) the public relations practitioner in question does not have the training or the sophistication to recognize the need for feedback. Let us consider each of these reasons in a little more detail.

Feedback is not possible. An example of a situation where it is not possible to obtain a measure of feedback is in the case of that elusive thing called "company image." The phrase *company image* means nothing more than a summary of a person's attitudes toward a company. Thus, if you have an image of a company that is characterized by such adjectives as friendly, efficient, progressive, and, in general, a "good place to have business dealings with," all of the various experiences you have had with that company, its employees, advertising, products, and so on are summarized by these adjectives. In short, the company has a very positive image as far as you are concerned. If a public relations practitioner were interested in sorting out the bases for your feelings, so that he could discern what role his various communications have had in shaping your image, he would be frustrated because such refined feedback is just not possible. Unlike the fellow who wants to punch you in the nose for something you have said, the public relations practitioner for an organization is not able to obtain such pin-pointed feedback.[12]

Feedback is not feasible. A situation in which it is not feasible to obtain feedback is a most common occurrence in public relations practice. Perhaps the main reason that feedback is not obtainable is that

---

[12] It should be pointed out that it is possible to get a measure of the image of a company in certain circumstances. It is even possible to obtain "trend" data— *i.e.*, changes in image over time. This is another dimension of feedback, however, in which the efforts of a company to project a particular image are being measured in general, and we are not trying to isolate any particular portion of the communication spectrum responsible for any particular aspect of an over-all image.

there just isn't time for it. The public relations practitioner operates
in situations which demand that a program of action be executed, and
generally before there is any time to assess the effectiveness of what
you have done, another crisis crops up, and attempts at obtaining
feedback have to be forgotten. Closely associated with the time factor
is the familiar question of budget. As a rule, efforts to obtain feedback
cost money: modest budgets in some situations, thousands of dollars
in others. There are many public relations practitioners who appreciate
the value of feedback but are unable to convince their management
that the expenditure of money for it is worthwhile. This is especially
true when things are going well. If a public relations operation is
successful, it may be even more difficult to obtain funds to gather
some feedback concerning the effectiveness of the public relations
program and just *why* it is effective. In this respect, public relations
practitioners have not been nearly so successful as their cousins in
advertising who have successfully sold their superiors (or clients) on
the need for feedback to assess the effectiveness of their advertising.

A public relations situation that typifies when feedback is not feasible is the occurrence of an explosion at, let us say, a chemical plant.
The public relations department must swing into action servicing the
press, providing news releases, notifying next-of-kin, and seeing to a
whole host of details that must be handled at such times. In such situations, there just isn't time to obtain any measures of feedback in connection with all (or any) of the various communication efforts that a
public relations department engages in during such emergencies. This
is unfortunately the general rule in spite of the fact that it would be
wonderful to have some information about the effectiveness of such
programs.[13]

The need for feedback is not recognized.   The lack of training on
the part of some public relations practitioners to either obtain feedback
or appreciate its importance is partly the reason that the author felt
impelled to write such a book as this. As was spelled out in detail
in Part 1, there are a number of reasons that a high proportion of
present-day public relations practitioners are not equipped to do or
to appreciate the need for research efforts that would provide them

---

[13] An interesting parallel between public relations and the social sciences is
worthy of mention here. There are many times when it would be wonderful if
research (*i.e.*, efforts to obtain feedback) could be conducted when important
social events are taking place, such as studying the conflicts that integrating schools
produces or the effect of panic on a large indoor gathering of individuals when a
fire breaks out. However, as a rule, there is not enough time to implement such
studies, no matter how desirable they may be.

with some feedback against which to analyze their actions. This point will be returned to in Part 3, when research is considered in some detail, particularly when we discuss research that is inexpensive and comparatively simple to execute. (See particularly Chapter 20.)

Summary of the sender stage

From our case of the perishing fish we evolved the first major component of our communication model—the sender stage. The sender stage was described as a device for symbolizing any *source* of a communication. Thus, the sender can be an individual (as in a face-to-face situation) or an *"institutionalized"* individual representing an organization (as in our case where the public relations department of Standard of California was speaking for the company to many different groups in our society). We also learned that the processes that go on at the sender stage are exceedingly complex, being made up of three major functions identified as decoding, assigning meaning, and encoding. With these terms, we synthesized the activities of any sender as that of receiving and collecting information (decoding), making sense out of this information (assigning meaning), and developing and executing a communications program consistent with this gathered and interpreted information (encoding). This process was described as a circular one, out of which one cannot really separate (except for analysis purposes) the three functions of decoding, assigning meaning, and encoding. Our communication model was enlarged to include this threefold circular process that is part of the sender stage in communication. Following this discussion, feedback was introduced as a concept that, in effect, summarized much that is involved in the circular process of decoding, assigning meaning, and encoding.

Feedback was seen to vary considerably in scope and type, depending on the particular communication situation. When the sender is an individual in a face-to-face situation, the feedback is potentially richest and made up of many factors. When the sender is an institutionalized individual—*i.e.*, a person communicating on behalf of an organization—the opportunities for feedback are usually limited and restricted in scope. Furthermore, a distinction was made between intentional feedback (when the source of the feedback is known and the intent to feedback information clear) and unintentional feedback (when the source of the feedback is much more diffuse and the intent to feedback information not present). Lastly, some discussion was devoted to the fact that public relations practitioners have a vital need for feedback. The degree of feedback they have to work with varies from situation to situation for three main reasons: (1) It is sometimes not possible to obtain feedback, (2) it is not often feasible to obtain feedback, and (3) many public relations practitioners do not have the training to obtain or appreciate the need for feedback.

THE MESSAGE STAGE

In our perishing fish case, it is safe to assume that many messages were developed and transmitted by the public relations department. The details that we have concerning them do not tell us about the various messages that were developed, but we have enough information to speculate about the format of some of these messages. This will be sufficient for our purposes. However, we first need to add another stage in our communication model and label it the *message stage*.

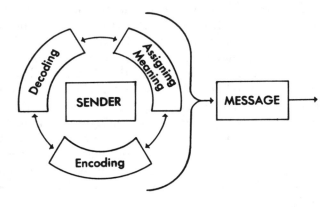

Figure 7

The sender and message stage of the total communication process

The message stage aids us in highlighting the message itself—its content, format, objectives, and so on. Messages may be in many different forms: the printed word, the spoken word, pictures, a series of dots and dashes forming some sort of a code, and many others. Literally, any sort of phenomenon that is capable of being interpreted meaningfully qualifies for inclusion as a message.

Returning to our case for a moment, the point was made earlier that we may assume that many different messages in a variety of forms were developed and transmitted by the public relations department. Let's consider one or two for illustrative purposes. First, there was the official report of the results of the research into using black powder in place of dynamite. This research was the outcome of the joint efforts of the oil industry and the State Fish and Game Commission. This particular message played a key role in the total communication efforts because it provided the basic rationale for Standard of California in its efforts to convert opponents to further seismic survey efforts. There were also the news releases based on this longer, more technical report. These messages were undoubtedly similar to the longer report. The format was probably shorter and tighter and contained less technical language so that the news release would achieve presumably wider reader attention. Lastly, there was the variety of messages that were verbally presented by the two public relations men who were moving through the coastal communities in advance of the exploration crews.

Overlapping of fields of experience of sender and recipient

Although we will return to this stage in much greater detail in a later chapter before going on to the next stage in the communication process, we will first touch briefly on a very important concept that is associated with the message stage and that is derived from the work of semanticists.

As different writers have pointed out, the word *communication* comes from the Latin *communis*, which means common. By overlooking (or being ignorant of) the origin of the word *communication*, we readily forget that the act of communicating is the act of making *common* to others something that we are thinking of or know about. As it becomes common, they, too, now understand or know about the same thing that we are aware of. This reminder of the Latin origin of the word *communication* leads us to an important point that should be made concerning the message stage. It is this: Messages, no matter what their form and how they are transmitted, must use symbols to which similar enough meanings are attached (remember the decoding and encoding process discussed earlier) so that the sender can make himself understood to the receiver.

Behind this seemingly simple statement lies an incredibly complicated process whereby men are able to use symbols for purposes of communicating with one another. Because this system of communication by symbols works so well in so many circumstances, we forget just how complicated the process really is. We will only scratch the

surface at this point, leaving for a later chapter a more detailed discussion of this topic. Suffice it to say that messages must be constructed
by the public relations practitioner so that there is sufficient overlap
between his world of experiences and the meaning that the recipient
of his message attaches to the same words. Figure 8 may help to
clarify this point. Depending upon the circumstances, the degree to
which there is overlap—hence experiences in common—between a
sender and a recipient will vary. For example, if a sender puts his

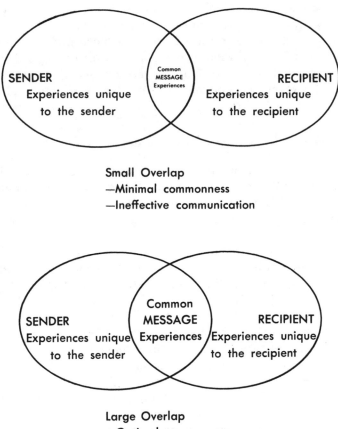

Figure 8

Two degrees of overlap of experience between sender and
recipient depicting ineffective and effective communication
situations

message into a language of which the recipient is ignorant, there will be little, if any, overlap between the two. Under these conditions, there would be no "commonness" between the two, the message would be virtually unintelligible, and little or no communication would take place. At the other extreme, if a message is written in a language common to both sender and recipient, there is maximum potential overlap and presumably a lot of commonness and communication.

One of the major difficulties facing every public relations practitioner each time he attempts to communicate is that of successfully achieving a sufficient degree of overlap between himself and his recipient(s), so that he effectively communicates. There are a host of barriers to overcome in order to achieve this overlap into commonness, barriers that the public relations practitioner must know how to deal with.

A brief return to our case will permit us to illustrate how Figure 8 relates to the messages that are implicit in that public relations problem situation. The official report was one type of message employed by the public relations department. This message was undoubtedly technical and probably written in a style uninteresting to the general public. This suggests that the number of people with technical or scientific experiences in common with the people who did the research was quite limited. Although this audience was a very important one and one that would play an influential role in paving the way for acceptance of future seismic surveys, revisions of this basic message had to be developed if other segments of the general public were to be reached by this message. This is why a basic press release that translated the scientific report into a form that would have more in common with a wider audience had to be prepared.

To some readers, the concept of the necessity of messages being couched in symbols that are common to both sender and recipient may appear almost childishly simple and obvious, particularly so when, presumably, most public relations practitioners are expert writers and face daily the task of couching messages in a form that achieves a commonness with their recipient(s). A recent study of how well employees understand company publications (a responsibility of the public relations department in most organizations) shows how easily the points made earlier can be overlooked even by experts. The survey was conducted by the Opinion Research Corporation, and the findings reported below were based on interviews with nearly five hundred workers.[14] Among other things the researchers found that:

---

[14] Opinion Research Corporation, "Word Impact for Management's Communications," *The Public Opinion Index for Industry* (Princeton, N.J.: Opinion Research Corporation, January, 1960). Used by permission.

Only 54% of those interviewed understood the meaning of the term "fringe benefits."

Only 54% of those interviewed knew the meaning of "mass production." (Ironically enough, one worker reported that mass production meant "producing more than buyers can absorb.")

Only 26% of those interviewed knew what "hidden salaries and wages" meant.

Only 12% of those interviewed read and subsequently understand the average article in a company publication.

55% of those interviewed were familiar with the word "capitalism," but only 26% could explain what it meant.

To the extent that these data are typical of all company publications, it is clear that there is sufficient room for improvement and a need for concern about the concept of overlapping fields of experience between senders and recipients.

Summary of the Message Stage

We have now briefly examined the second stage of our communication model—the message. Messages can be constructed out of any conceivable set of symbols that a sender wishes to use. The only limitation on symbol usage is that they make for common meaning between the sender and the recipient of the message—assuming, of course, that successful communication is the goal. An often overlooked fact about communication, namely, that the sender is trying to achieve a commonness on some topic or experience with a recipient, was discussed. This led to an examination of the concept of overlapping areas of experience between sender and recipient. When the experiences common to sender and recipient are extensive, the likelihood of achieving successful communication is high. When the experiences common to both are minimal or nonexistent, then communication is likely to be faulty or completely lacking. Lastly, it was pointed out—by some research data on the degree of employee understanding of company publications—that this seemingly fundamental and simple concept of overlapping experience is not always achieved, even by persons presumably experts in communication.

THE MEDIA STAGE

If the reader will substitute the phrase *means of transmission* for the word *media*, he will have the essence of this particular stage in the communication process. The media stage is designed to include any and all means by which messages are transmitted and represents the physical link between the one sending a message and the recipient of that message. The media stage highlights the need for a means of getting a message from one location to another, the need for an instrument to link one person with another, or one group with another through the modality of a message.

Our analysis of the media stage will not emphasize the technical details involved in the various electronic media and the kinds of the print media.[15] The reason is simple: The technical side of the media stage—*i.e.*, an examination of the electronic bases of television or radio, or a behind-the-scenes examination of the publication of a newspaper or a magazine—is not the subject matter that is of importance to us. It is not essential that the public relations practitioner know the technical details behind any of the more common media. Rather, he needs to know about the *use* of the media themselves. When it is desirable to use television and when is it not? Which communication goals can be achieved by radio and which cannot? Consequently, our analysis of the media stage will focus on *how* the media are utilized and *why*, and not on the technical problems associated with maintaining any particular medium. With the addition of this third stage our model now assumes the appearance of Figure 9.

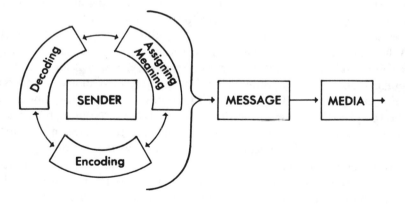

Figure 9

The sender, message, and media stages in the total communication process

---

[15] An electronics engineer has a different concern with the media stage. For him, the technical details concerning, for example, the functioning of a television station and how it is kept on the air are vitally important.

The "Seduction Quality" of the Media Stage

Unlike the other stages in the communication process, the media stage has the capacity to mislead the public relations practitioner more than any other. This is the reason why we speak of the "seduction quality" of the media stage. We use the term *mislead* in the sense that it is common for public relations practitioners to place excessive reliance on volume or frequency of messages transmitted in solving or coping with public relations problems. To put it another way, many public relations practitioners fall into the trap of thinking that even if one message transmitted is enough, two are better; or that if one form of mass medium does not do the job (say, for example, newspapers), then use another one—perhaps television. In short, it is very easy to begin to place an undue emphasis on the media stage of the communication process, especially from the standpoint of repeating messages and utilizing more than one medium for message transmission purposes.

Another factor in the "seduction quality" of the media stage is that, along with the message stage, the public relations practitioner feels most at home here. A large proportion of present-day public relations practitioners were formerly associated with the mass media; they were newspapermen, editors, writers for magazines, and the like. As a result, constructing a message and transmitting it are old hat to these former newspaper or magazine men turned public relations practitioners. What they are not at home with are the sender stage and the stage to be considered next, the recipient. Most present-day public relations practitioners are not prone to analyzing their own motives for communicating, nor are they likely to sort out and identify the motives of the recipient for paying attention to them. They are not at home with concepts such as learning and perception that are useful in anticipating how a person (or persons) will react to a particular message.

Another reason the media stage causes the public relations practitioner difficulty is that media exposure, particularly the mass media, is a common measure of the effectiveness of a public relations practitioner. Perhaps the most widespread means by which the public relations practitioner demonstrates his value (either to his employer or to his client) is in terms of volume of media placement. In newspapers, for example, there is the familiar "column inch." This is a measure of the inches of space in a standard newspaper column that a public relations practitioner managed to have placed in either national or local newspapers. The same measure can be applied to articles that are placed in national and regional magazines. Television and radio time are measured in a very similar way—*i.e.*, in terms of the number of minutes on radio or TV that the company (or client) was featured and thereby gained exposure to the listening or viewing audience.

This emphasis on media also extends into such things as the number of booklets produced and distributed; the number of speeches written and given; and the number of letters of inquiry received and subsequently answered. The particular content of any clipping book (the term used to describe the volume that contains samples of mass-media coverage achieved by the actions of the public relations practitioner on behalf of his company or client) will vary, naturally, from situation to situation. The one thing that they all have in common, however, is the emphasis placed on the *media*. These clippings are visible evidence of the efforts of the public relations practitioner on behalf of his company or client. With his effectiveness measured in this manner, it is little wonder that the public relations practitioner places such emphasis on the media stage in the total communication process.

It is commonly argued that the media placement is the most "visible" evidence of the public relations man in action. Yet, there is increasing evidence that the efficacy of the media, particularly the mass media, needs to be reassessed due to unique problems that he encounters. No one in his right mind would ever argue that public relations practitioners should not or need not make extensive use of the mass media. However, a legitimate question is this: Just *when* and *how* are the mass media (or any other media, for that matter) to be used? *When* and *how* do the mass media need to be supplemented, *by* what, and for what *kinds* of communication objectives? Some answers to these questions will have to wait until the media stage is considered in more detail.

Before going on to the last stage, it will be useful to return to our perishing fish case once more. Most noteworthy is the fact that a broad range of media was used. First, there was the research report itself, a very specialized use of the print medium. From this report, a press release was developed in order to gain reader acceptance of a popular version of this specialized material via the newspapers. More direct contact (presumably by telephone and mail) with fish and game editors and other key people was employed. Lastly, there was the transmission of still further communications through face-to-face contacts that the two public relations practitioners had as they moved through the coastal communities in advance of the exploration crews. In one simple, standard public relations case we see an exceedingly wide variety of means of transmission used, and all of these forms are embraced by the media stage in the communication process.

Summary of the Media Stage

The third major link in the communication process has been introduced—the media stage. The media stage is best translated by the phrase *means of transmission*. In short, this stage symbolizes the processes—whether they be the printed word, electronic devices, or films—by which the message is conveyed to the recipient.

The media stage was characterized as the most "visible" evidence of the activities of the public relations practitioner but not necessarily the most appropriate in all cases. The public relations practitioner was pictured as being most at home with the media stage in the total communication process, and for this reason the media stage was characterized as having a "seduction quality." By this phrase was meant the tendency for the public relations practitioner to place excessive reliance on the *volume* and *frequency* of messages transmitted to help solve public relations problems.

Two main reasons were suggested for this undue emphasis on the media stage by public relations practitioners. One was the fact that a great many present-day public relations practitioners were formerly associated with the mass media as newspapermen, editors, free-lance writers, or magazine writers. Experiences gained in these previous occupations make them very familiar with the means of transmission, generally much more so than with the other stages of the communication process. Another reason suggested was that the public relations practitioner's effectiveness (either for his company or for a client) is very often measured in terms of exposure through the media, particularly the mass media. Far too often, the worth of the public relations practitioner is measured in terms of the column inch in newspapers, minutes of radio and television broadcast time, and the number of feature articles placed in magazines.

THE RECIPIENT STAGE

In many ways, the recipient stage symbolizes the purpose of communication. Without some recipient in mind, either singular or plural, the whole point of communicating would be lacking.

As in the case of the sender stage, the definition of the recipient can be quite broad. The recipient stage can stand for such things as a single individual or the members of a group, a company, or a government. Any object of a communication capable of some degree of decoding and assigning meaning can be thought of as a recipient. With the addition of this final stage in our communication process, our model is now beginning to shape up as depicted in Figure 10. With this addition, we have enlarged it considerably.

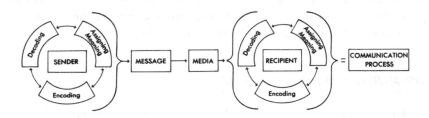

Figure 10

The sender, message, media, and recipient stages of the total communication process

Perhaps the most noticeable addition is the circular process of decoding, assigning meaning, and encoding attached to the recipient stage exactly as was done for the sender stage. This means that the recipient goes through the same processes as the sender in order to understand the messages sent to him. This generally means that the recipient must speak the same language as the sender. More particularly, the recipient must know any specialized vocabulary or slang expressions, if they are pertinent.

As we learned earlier, an inseparable part of the decoding process is that of assigning meaning. Inevitably, the recipient attaches some meaning to the messages he receives. Following this, the recipient very often communicates with the sender, necessitating the encoding process in order to do so. In the face-to-face situation, this circular process goes on continually, the sender and receiver constantly changing positions—i.e., one individual first receiving and then sending.

Naturally, all that has been said regarding the interchange that goes on at the face-to-face level goes on at the organization-to-organization level, individual-to-organization level, and in any other communication situation, regardless of the particular identities of the sender and recipient. In the context of our perishing fish case, the various groups that may have been upset by the survey work of

Standard of California are recipients. The most obvious were (1) the commercial fishing companies, (2) the fish and game editors of newspapers and magazines, (3) the homeowners living immediately along the shore, and (4) the various newspaper reporters and editors up and down the coast of California. Each one of these groups was a recipient of the appropriate communication effort of the public relations department of Standard of California; and, exactly as the model attempts to symbolize, each group was interacting with the public relations department with feedback taking place, based upon the never-ending processes of decoding, assigning meaning, and encoding.

VISUALIZING COMMUNICATION AS A PROCESS

One addition to our model in Figure 10 is labeled *communication process*. This addition, while not another "stage" in the same sense as the four stages we have been discussing so far, is, nevertheless, an important concept. It means that we are highlighting the fact that communication is not a *static* phenomenon but rather a most dynamic and complicated phenomenon. Also, it encourages the use of the model *as a whole*, recognizing that communication is made up of many, many parts, all of which must be operating at at least minimum efficiency for any communication at all to take place.

The addition of the concept of the communication process suggests a great many additional generalizations that should be made about the model, but we will do this in our next chapter. At this point, we have developed the basic elements of our communication theory model. It will prove useful to pause now and examine the discussion questions. This will enable you to consolidate all that we have considered in this chapter. In the next chapter, we will elaborate on our basic model, introducing many points that can and should be made about the implications of this model for public relations practice. Also, we are now in a position to take into account some sociological thinking, particularly the concept of the importance of the larger social context in which all communication, regardless of its content, necessarily takes place.

QUESTIONS FOR DISCUSSION

1. Take any model that you can think of, whether it be from physics, chemistry, biology, or psychology, and sketch it out on a piece of

paper. With this model, illustrate to a friend how it helps to explain certain phenomena or relationships that might otherwise be less clear.

2. Take any one of the cases that you have used to answer a discussion question in a previous chapter and "translate" it into our communication model. That is, identify the sender(s) involved, the various messages and media used, and the recipient(s).

3. Now that you have translated your case to a communication model, examine the case from the standpoint of the concept of *feedback*. That is, from what you can infer from the case, had the public relations practitioner in question obtained any feedback before he developed and implemented his public relations program? If there is no evidence that the public relations practitioner in question obtained feedback prior to implementing his program, do you think that it was because feedback was not possible, not feasible, or that the need for feedback was not recognized?

4. As was done when the concepts embodied in Figure 8 were presented, develop (*i.e.*, make up or obtain from case write-ups) two public relations problem situations, one in which the sender and the recipient have practically no overlapping fields of experience, and the other where there is considerable overlap. Which of the two situations poses the most difficulty from a standpoint of communicating? Why?

Chapter 5

THE COMMUNICATION MODEL
IN A SOCIAL CONTEXT

INTRODUCTION

The communication model articulated in Chapter 4 consisted of four stages: sender, message, media, and recipient. We developed our model stage by stage, defining each as it was introduced. Certain key concepts associated with the stages were examined, concepts such as the processes of encoding, assigning meaning, and decoding that are part of being either a sender or recipient.

In Figure 10 (page 87), the entire model is depicted, and it is stressed that all four stages are necessary to the communication process. Because the communication process is made up of many components, all of which must be operating at minimum efficiency at least, the only possible way to examine the process is by taking all four stages together. We are now ready to extend the analysis of our communication model by making a series of observations on the four stages taken together, then imbedding the whole model in a larger social context.

FIVE OBSERVATIONS CONCERNING THE COMMUNICATION MODEL AS A WHOLE

1. Comparison of the Communication Process to a Chain

One of the most obvious things noted in Figure 10 is that communicative effectiveness can be affected by any one or a combination of stages not operating at minimum efficiency. It is rather like the old saw about a chain being no stronger than its weakest link. This means that the public relations practitioner must think of his communication efforts as a whole, based on thorough analysis of the intended recipients. This analysis includes such things as his objectives, the plans for attaining those objectives, the behaviors he hopes those objectives will elicit, and the messages developed and transmitted through a variety of media—all must be efficient. Inadequate functioning at any one of these stages will cause his communicative effort to fail. The public relations practitioner's attention must be focused continually on the *total* situation within which he is operating.

At this point, it may be useful to borrow an engineer's term to further highlight the concept of considering communication as a whole. Engineers often speak of distortion at any one stage in a communication system. The distortion that they have in mind is generally a function of the various components in their system. For example, in the case of the telephone, research has established that certain frequencies of sound waves can be filtered out of a telephone receiver and yet not affect the intelligibility of the transmitted speaking voice. However, if a telephone is used to transmit music instead of the human voice in conversation, a great deal of the music is not transmitted, because there is considerable distortion (or, more properly, filtering) of the message—*i.e.*, the music being transmitted. In engineering terms, the frequencies of sound that a telephone receiver will or will not handle is a limiting factor in the efficiency of the total telephone system as a communication device. Typically, an engineer analyzes each component (or stage, to use our term) to understand the capabilities of the component itself and how the capabilities of one component or stage interacts with others. In this way, he is cognizant of the potential of the *total* communication system with which he is working.

Unfortunately, no such precise analysis of the communication stages in a typical public relations problem situation is possible. However, the analogy holds, and in spite of the fact that less precision is possible, this in no way obviates the necessity for an analysis of the total communication system by the public relations practitioner. Let us consider a concrete example. Several studies have indicated that stockholder communications (in the form of stockholder reports) often do not successfully link a company with its stockholders. One such study was made of a random sample of stockholder reports of large and small American businesses.[1] The emphasis of the analysis of these stockholder

---

[1] Dana J. Eastham, "Readability of Corporate Stockholder Communications" (unpublished Master's thesis, School of Public Communications, Boston University, 1954).

reports was on the level of difficulty of the writing. Among other things, the author reports that the level of reading difficulty of the material contained in the stockholder reports (as measured by the Flesch formula—see Chapter 9, p. 214) was well above the average reading comprehension of the intended audience. In addition, the style tended to be rather dull and uninteresting—at least as analyzed by the Flesch formula for reader interest as differentiated from reading level difficulty. To return to our "weakest link" analogy, this fact—*i.e.*, that the material was in general too difficult for the reader—made the message stage the weakest (or one of the weakest) links in the total communication process. In these circumstances, no amount of attention to the other stages in the communication process would necessarily correct this weakness. To put it in our engineering terms, the fact that the message is encoded at a level above the average reading comprehension of the group will produce distortion in the sense that the stockholder will not understand the message. He may understand parts of the report, but he will misinterpret other portions of it because he cannot fully grasp the meanings contained therein.

Our model lays out the *total* communications process in terms of stages that exist, regardless of the particular communication situation. This stockholder reports example touches on only *one* possibility in *one* particular communication situation, but it illustrates the point we want to make—that the public relations practitioner must train himself to think of the whole communication process and not become lost in any one stage, such as the message stage exemplified by the stockholder report.

2.   Feedback as an Important Element in the Total Communication Process

Although feedback is not considered a stage, it is of critical importance both in understanding communication theoretically and in being able to predict or anticipate problems of communication in a practical situation. Because the need to obtain feedback is so important to the public relations practitioner, further elaboration of the concept is called for at this time.

a. *Further considerations concerning the concept of feedback.*   To begin with, let us consider an average individual in his everyday environment from a communication standpoint. During every minute of every waking hour, this individual is observing other people and other aspects of the physical environment around him, including sights, sounds, smells, and so on. All of the sensory inputs to this individual enable him to interpret the world around him and permit him to achieve successfully comparatively simple things, such as dressing himself and walking across the street, and more complex behaviors, such as being able to get along with his co-workers at the office. Let's examine just one part of the simple act of dressing in a little more detail. At one point, our hypothetical individual reaches into his closet to select a suit to wear for that day. The very act of reaching for a suit on a hanger is actually a rather complicated feedback situation. As one extends his arm and hand toward the hanger, he is receiving feedback visually as well as kinesthetically as to how close his hand is coming to the hanger. Because of the feedback of information received, the successive muscular movements are altered to change the rate and direction of extension of the arm and fingers until finally the hanger is gently picked up. The fact that one can do this so effortlessly and smoothly should not cause us to overlook the importance of the various feedback cues that enable us to perform this act.

To realize how complicated this type of behavior is, one needs only to observe a young child learning to pick up a simple object such as a rattle or teething ring. The child extends the arm and hand with actions that are somewhat halting or jerky. In addition, he is very likely to miss by several inches the object he intends to pick up. He sometimes has to repeat the effort to pick up an object time and time again before he succeeds. Apparently, the seemingly pointless play of young infants and older children constitutes continuous practice situations wherein the infant or child is learning how to make use of feedback in all of its many forms.

Let us now turn to more complex acts of behavior. As adults, we are constantly making use of feedback in our relationship with others. What a person says, how he says it, what gestures he makes, his facial expressions—all are elements of feedback that we react to and use to interpret the actions and motives of another person. This interpretation, in turn, shapes our subsequent actions, verbalizations, gestures, and so on. This is feedback at the face-to-face level, and as we learned earlier in Chapter 4 (page 72) it is the communication situation with the richest potential for feedback.[2, 3]

---

[2] It might be added here that individuals naturally vary in the degree to which they are sensitive to the feedback available in face-to-face situations. Some people are practically insensitive to this sort of feedback, and only the most pointed remarks or insults will penetrate their rather dull perceptiveness to what is going on around them. As a matter of fact, the concept of personality is redefinable in feedback terms. More often than not when we speak of an individual with a desirable personality who is able to get along with and is well liked by others, we are describing one who is comparatively sensitive to the feedback he receives in face-to-face situations. This concept even plays a role in ascertaining effective

b. *Feedback related to public relations practice.* Let us now relate the concept of feedback more directly to public relations. In our discussion, we will ignore the face-to-face communication situations that the public relations practitioner encounters, because in these instances the availability of feedback to the individual practitioner is not a consideration. It is normally there for him to make use of.[4]

One way of summing up what we have stated about feedback is to say that by this process an individual is better able to assess his relationship with his environment. He is better able not only to determine how he should behave in the immediate and distant future but also to predict how others are likely to react to him. All of these potential by-products of feedback, so to speak, are certainly equally desirable sorts of information for a public relations practitioner to have to help solve his problems. It would be very useful to him if he could know how his readers are reacting to (1) his stockholder report; (2) his re-

---

leaders and persons who make good administrators, especially in situations requiring a high degree of cooperative effort.

[3] A related area of research that has received attention in recent years is called "sensory deprivation." (*See,* for example, `.v.` H. Bexton, W. Heron, and T. H. Scott, "Effects of Decreased Variation in the Sensory Environment," *Canadian Journal of Psychology,* VIII [1954], 70-76; T. I. Myers, D. B. Murphy, and S. Smith, "Progress Report on the Studies of Sensory Deprivation," Human Resources Research Office *res. memo.* [1961], v. 28; and Duane P. Schultz, *Sensory Restriction Effects on Behavior* [New York: Academic Press, 1965].) Although there have been some conflicting reports, it seems apparent that when an individual is completely cut off from the normal sensory inputs—sound, sight, and smell—it has the effect of interfering with even the simplest mental tasks that call for concentration. In specially constructed apparatus, which requires the subject to lie on a bed in a small, soundproof cubicle, or enclosed in a modified diving suit and immersed in a tank of water, certain subjects report rather strange reactions, some of which border on hallucination, or they evidence a strong desire to receive sensory stimulation regardless of its nature. These data seem to suggest that not only is feedback of a *specific* nature important—e.g., reaction to what another has said—but that *general* feedback such as minimal background noises, visual impressions, and the like are also necessary for normal mental functioning. To phrase it another way, feedback is important not only from person-to-person and person-to-group relationships but also from the general environment; we need it to function effectively alone as well as with others.

[4] Sensitivity to this type of feedback in a sense becomes part and parcel of the general human relations ability of the public relations practitioner. The utilization of this type of feedback is an important part of the daily work life of the practitioner. For this reason, human relations skills are an important part of the public relations practitioner's total repertoire of skills. However, at this point in our discussion we are focusing on communication situations other than face-to-face ones. In these other communication situations, the availability of feedback is reduced (see once again the discussion on pages 76 and 77 in Chapter 4), and the emphasis now becomes more one of how feedback is obtained rather than the skill of the public relations practitioner in using it.

cently distributed brochure describing retirement benefits; (3) the newspaper release that he gave out yesterday; and (4) his recent issue of the company newsletter. The list could be extended considerably, but in each instance the public relations practitioner would benefit markedly if he had some feedback from his recipients, just as he benefits from feedback in a face-to-face situation.

In most of the communication situations mentioned, there is, more than likely, feedback *potentially* available; the problem is obtaining it. Most of the readers of the variety of communications listed (stockholders' report, employees, etc.) would have some sort of reactions to what the public relations practitioner in question wrote. They probably have certain attitudes toward the topics discussed, and they are perhaps pleased or displeased by what they read. To repeat: normally the feedback is there to be obtained; the problem to be solved is *how* to obtain it.

As if the difficulty of obtaining the desired feedback were not enough of an obstacle, three other hurdles are likely to be present in contemporary public relations practice. One is that the average practitioner is not fully aware of his need for feedback. In line with the discussion of our problem solving continuum as applied to public relations (see Chapter 3, pages 46-51), he has operated at the "flying by the seat of his pants" end of the continuum for so long a time that he is literally unable to function in any other manner. Secondly, many practitioners are not aware that they must institute systematic (*not* sporadic) means of obtaining the feedback essential to sound practice. Lastly, those who assess their public relations activities in terms of the column inch have accepted this particular measure as the criterion of their performance and therefore have a vested interest in *not* obtaining measures of feedback.

c. *Feedback and the circular nature of the public relations process.* To help emphasize this point, let us examine Figure 11, "The Public Relations Process,"[5] in which the work of the public relations practitioner in coping with his daily public relations problems is symbolized in five basic steps as follows:

Step 1 consists of a thorough analysis of the problem situation. What are the goals of the organization? What are the policies (if any) relative to the problem situation? What are the problems that

---

[5] The author is indebted to Professor Carol Hills, Public Relations Division, School of Public Communication, Boston University, for permission to utilize in modified form, her Public Relations Programing Planning Cycle Schema as a basis for Figure 11.

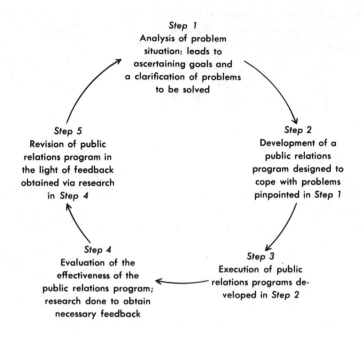

Figure 11

The Public Relations Process

have to be solved so that the public relations goals can continue
to be met?

Step 2 is the development of a public relations program that is
designed to cope with the problems spelled out in Step 1. This
means a *written* plan of action, one that has been carefully thought
out in as great detail as possible. This written plan also distinguishes between long- and short-range steps and includes financial
estimates so that the cost of the public relations program is consistent with budget available.

Step 3 represents the execution of the public relations program.
This is a self-evident step and needs no elaboration except to emphasize that the details of execution must be carefully followed so
that a thorough knowledge is available to permit a comparison
of what was planned *vs.* what was actually carried out. This is
essential in the event that certain portions of the program cannot
be implemented due to factors not foreseeable at the time of
planning.

Step 4 is the evaluation of the effectiveness of the public relations program. This is where implementation of research comes in in order to obtain the feedback deemed necessary for effective public relations functioning. It is at this step that the public relations practitioner must be aware of all of the ways in which he can conduct (or have conducted for him) the research that will provide him the necessary feedback in order for him to know how effective his public relations program has been.

Step 5 is a modification or revision of the public relations program in the light of the feedback of information obtained via the research conducted in Step 4. This is the step that is akin to the modification of our behavior that we make on the basis of the feedback we obtain in face-to-face situations. In exactly the same sense, the public relations practitioner must take this modification or revision step (if it is called for, of course) in his public relations programing.

The importance of systematically providing for feedback is brought out in the circle that we have entitled "The Public Relations Process." It is important enough to have received a full step, placing it on a par with developing and executing the public relations program. Contrary to the views of many public relations practitioners, *executing* the public relations program is *not* more important than *finding out what good the program has done.*

The public relations process is envisioned as circular in nature to emphasize some fundamental points not recognized often enough in public relations practice. These are as follows:

a) The process of identifying problems and developing programs to cope with these problems is a never-ending affair. The social environment within which all organizations operate is dynamic, fluid, changing. This means that the public relations analysis, planning and execution must be the same way: dynamic, fluid, and changing, whenever change is necessary.

b) The major weakness at the present time in public relations practice lies at Step 4. The research conducted by most (but not all) public relations practitioners is either nonexistent or very flimsy. All too seldom are they based on sound data collection methods which permit reliable generalizations. This point has been alluded to already in this volume and it is related to the concept that the public relations practitioner is *and must be* an applied social and behavioral scientist. As such, he must be conversant with the various techniques available to obtain feedback of information through research. Later (Chapters 17-20), the topic of research will be taken up in detail, and the reader will be provided with illustrations of a variety of research techniques that provide feedback for the public relations practitioner. Armed with these techniques, the practitioner can modify or revise his public relations program so as to operate at the maximum efficiency possible.

c) The public relations function, like any other function within an organization, must demonstrate its value to an organization. There must be ways of weighing the worth of public relations activities just as we weigh the value of advertising, personnel practices, accounting procedures, and all other functions within an organization. To be sure, there are aspects of an organization that are much more difficult to measure and assess (*e.g.*, executive ability) than others (*e.g.*, effectiveness of a particular new piece of equipment to increase production). The public relations function certainly is at the top of the list of those functions within an organization that are most difficult to evaluate. However, this does *not* mean that efforts should not be continually made (especially by the public relations practitioner himself) to determine the effectiveness of public relations programing. The vitality and increased acceptance of public relations as a necessary function within an organization is partly dependent on the degree to which public relations becomes more precise in execution and its effects on problems facing an organization become more specifically known. Research leading to increased availability of feedback for the public relations practitioner is of major importance in upgrading the public relations function within any organization.

3. Different Types of Problems Are Peculiar to Each Stage

Earlier we suggested an analogy between the communication process and a chain. In that context, we noted communication effectiveness could be no better than the functioning of any stage (*i.e.*, link) in the total process. Our third observation, that different types of problems are peculiar to each stage, is closely related to the chain analogy. Each stage has potentially many factors that can cause it to break down, that is, to operate in such a manner that it renders successful communication impossible. The factors that contribute to failure are unique to each stage and require different approaches to remedy their defects.

For example, let us assume that a university is engaged in a fund-raising drive. As part of the campaign, the public relations department develops a brochure outlining the various needs of the university. Let us also assume that this brochure is sent to all of the alumni of this university. In the process of outlining the needs, graphs are used (much in the same sense that they are used in stockholder reports) to show how operating costs are outstripping tuition income and the returns from investments belonging to the university. Let us say, for the sake of demonstrating our point, that the university's public relations department has obtained some data that demonstrate clearly that their brochure is perfectly understandable. That is, a sample of alumni that were interviewed to test the understandability of the brochure are able to give intelligent and accurate descriptions of the financial needs of the university. Let's make one further assumption, namely, that increased donations to the university do not materialize following the mailing of the brochure. (In view of current experiences of many universities, this would not be an unwarranted assumption.)

In this example, the problem does *not* lie at the message stage. It is fairly safe to assume that the recipients of the brochure understood the message. All we can really expect of the message stage is that the message be understandable.[6] It is probably safe to say that additional work needs to be done to obtain a more adequate understanding of the recipients—the alumni. For reasons unknown to the public relations department, it has not succeeded in inducing the alumni to give to their fund-raising campaign—at least no more than they gave *before* this latest brochure. Finding out more about the recipient is quite another matter from solving problems associated with the message stage. Had the message been unintelligible, correcting this defect would require remedial measures. However, finding out that the message is understandable but is ignored by the recipient is another kettle of fish altogether. Hence the generalization with which we began this section, that different types of problems are peculiar to different stages in the total communication process.

So it is with all of the stages in communication. A communication effort can fail because of problems at any one or a combination of the stages, and the steps that must be taken to cope with the problems at these different stages are vastly different. This third observation highlights the necessity for a public relations practitioner to be

___

[6] For the time being, we are ignoring the motivational aspects of the message. Admittedly, we rely heavily on messages to make people "get up and go." This is a complicated additional feature that we will return to in detail when the message stage is examined more fully in Chapters 8 and 9.

an extremely well-rounded individual in terms of formal and informal education. He must be an excellent writer to equip him to cope with some of the common problems associated with the message stage; and he must be an applied social and behavioral scientist as well, because understanding how to cope with problems associated with the sender and recipient stages requires completely different knowledge and skills. This point will become more apparent as we examine each stage more thoroughly in later chapters.

4.   Stress of One Stage to the Exclusion of Another

As one uses the communication model depicted in Figure 10 to analyze public relations problems, another observation that becomes very apparent is that public relations practitioners characteristically stress two stages to the exclusion of the others in their public relations programs. These two stages are almost invariably the message and media stage. In any discussion with a public relations practitioner or in any professional article that he writes, he tends to stress *what* he said or wrote and *how* he transmitted these messages. Seldom does he dwell on what he did at the sender or recipient stage as part of his total analysis of the problem. Let us examine briefly a case study as reported in the *Public Relations News* to substantiate this observation.

CASE STUDY No. 838   *How an Organization Wins Public Support for a Noted Christmas Program*[7]

This Christmas, more than 200,000 Americans will be getting food, children's gifts, and emergency help (clothing, bedding, personal services, etc.) from the *Salvation Army* (SA). Its bell ringing volunteers, standing beside bright red kettles, are a familiar sight throughout the U.S.A. But less well-known is the public relations effort that lies behind this annual Christmas Appeal.

The objectives of the program go far beyond seeking financial contributions from the public. To execute a "Service for People" policy, SA depends on the help of more than 100,000 volunteers who are enlisted through community service groups, clubs, churches, and the media.

A year-round PR program is conducted to gain strong public recognition and acceptance of SA's work, with stepped-up activities during the last quarter. Chief responsibility for implementing PR plans lies with its *local units,* but *important help comes from its National Infor-*

---

[7] *Public Relations News,* XVII, No. 49 (December 11, 1961), 3-4. Used by permission.

mation Service (NIS). Headquartered in New York, NIS is directed by *Major Andrew S. Miller.*

Step one in the Christmas Appeal campaign is the preparation by NIS of a *kit* (mailed in September) to guide each local unit. Included are tested materials used in previous years, such as: to-be-localized press releases (on formation of a committee of community leaders, opening of the Christmas Kettle Appeal, volunteer organizations which will help tend the kettles, and campaign results); suggested feature articles; ideas and background material for newspaper editorials; radio-TV scripts and outlets; fillers; and a spiritual message by SA's National Commander for church bulletins, calendars, and religious pages of newspapers. . . . *Also in the kit* are samples of additional materials available from NIS at low cost—greeting cards, posters, table cards and place mats for restaurants, window and envelope stickers, certificates of appreciation for cooperating organizations and individuals, newspaper mats (don't overlook the possibility that the newspaper's advertising department may be willing to drop some of the small mats into advertisements), pocket calendars, etc.

Step two is preparation of *Christmas recordings.* . . . One, produced by the Western territorial office located at San Francisco (*Sylvia Laurenti* is its Director of Public Information), is a *half-hour radio show.* Titled "Army of Stars," it features the voices of five top opera stars who donate their talents. Early in October, the New York office mails a descriptive leaflet to all commercial and FM radio station directors in the U.S.A. and Canada. They are given the record by a local SA officer, free, and donate time in turn. . . . Another, consisting of *Christmas music* rendered by the organization's New York Staff Band, gets similar local distribution, usually to disc jockeys.

Step three: 24-*sheet posters* (produced by the San Francisco office) are displayed across the country through the cooperation of the *National Outdoor Advertising Association*, which contributes the billboard space.

Step four: sets of *radio and TV spot announcements* (containing four or five varying lengths) are distributed early in October and in Mid-December.

Step five: efforts to line up *personnel to help man SA's red kettles* begin in the fall. A local Christmas Committee is appointed, members coming from such organizations as Rotary, Kiwanis, Lions, firemen, policemen, veterans, labor unions, and women's church, and student groups. On the day after Thanksgiving, representatives of these community groups begin tending the kettles and encouraging passers-by to toss coins and bills into them. This has proven to be one of the most effective fund-raising methods. Miller explains that it not only produces substantial funds but also brings SA's symbols and purposes to thousands of men, women, and children in an immediate and personal way.

Step six calls for *setting up*, in heavily trafficked areas in hundreds of cities, *giant evergreens*. The installation of each (dubbed "The Tree of Lights") is accompanied by a ceremony at which the Mayor and other *leading citizens offer endorsements of SA's Christmas Appeal*. Lighting of each bulb marks contributions towards a quota. When the goal is reached, an illuminated star at the top of the tree announces the good news to the community. (This newsmaking activity yields pictures and often daily stories and editorials).

Step seven is a series of *Special Events* which produce over 50% of the total amount collected. These include parades, auctions, and fashion shows. The popularity of coffee offers many opportunities, the beverage being given out free (to encourage contributions) at SA booths on the streets and through coffee breaks arranged in restaurants. With the cooperation of the *Retail Bakers' Association*, "Dollars-for-Donuts Days" are conducted (doughnuts are sold at a dollar apiece). Community organizations hold let-them-eat-beans luncheons (instead of regular meals), contributing the savings in cost to SA, and also make direct appeals to people at their homes. Counter boxes and cards asking donations are distributed to stores by Boy and Girl Scouts and Campfire Girls. Women's clubs dress dolls and put up "Sunshine Baskets" of gifts for shut-ins. Local musical talent—school bands, barbershop quartets, and school and church choral groups—serenade donors at collection locations.

Climax of the campaign is the actual distribution of gifts and services to the needy. This is followed up with *thank you letters and certificates* to community groups which have participated. Many SA offices hold *dinners in January to honor volunteers*.

All these diverse campaign activities produce a flow of newsworthy publicity at the local level. Media response to the program is always enthusiastic; it is a major contributor to SA's worthy work.

One of the most striking features of this case is that all of the copy can be inserted at the message and media stages of our communication model. Care is taken in the case description to spell out the use of both the written and the spoken word. The case description stresses publicity kits, which are packaged units totally concerned with the message stage. These kits also provide information concerning how the communication material can be most effectively fed into the various channels of available media. In sharp contrast by its omission is the fact that *at no time in the case description is there any material devoted to either the sender or the recipient in the communication problem situation*.

One could counter this remark that the recipient, at least, is implied all the way through the case: obviously all of these messages and the discussion concerning the means by which these messages can be transmitted were designed with the recipient in mind; some copy was discarded because it didn't seem to "fit" the recipient or was deemed inappropriate in some way for the communication task. All this can be granted cheerfully, and it still does not diminish the point being made here that the public relations practitioner is inordinately preoccupied with the message and media stages to the exclusion of other stages in the communication process.

As a matter of fact, this preoccupation is somewhat of a paradox if one recalls that the public relations practitioner is generally conceded (or is supposed to be) to be an expert in developing messages, regardless of the modality by which they are to be sent. Why does one need to explain in such detail the development of brochures, publicity kits, and the like to someone else who is presumably an expert at this already? It would be like one lawyer telling another the mundane details of preparing a case for trial. This expertise is assumed in the case of one lawyer communicating to another; the important features of a legal case are such things as the precedents or any insights that one lawyer may have for another. So it would appear to be for public relations practitioners. Why do they need to tell each other about how to get newspaper space, how to guide volunteer workers? The really important questions are such things as *why* brochures appeared to be called for, *why* certain message *content* was developed (in contrast to the nearly infinite range of themes available for copy purposes). Still other important questions are why it was assumed that a particular public relations program would be effective in communicating to the various recipients involved, or are *all* of the various portions of the public relations program equally important? If time or money did not allow it another year, what parts of the total program could be dropped without serious injury to the total effort? Basic questions such as these are not even touched on.

Some remarks are appropriate here in defense of the public relations practitioner. First of all, the case write-up itself is typical of most cases that one can read; it is representative of what is available to the serious student in public relations. Secondly, there is no disputing the fact that the activities described in the cases—which comprise a very high proportion of the daily work of a public relations practitioner—reflect what a public relations practitioner does. They are at least accurate in communicating the flavor of public relations work. For this reason, one would expect that the message and media stages of the communication model would receive greater attention. Lastly, there is no escaping the fact that many of the questions asked herein represent the most difficult types of research (or, more appropriately, feedback) questions that can be asked. Some of them can't even be answered in the light of current social science research techniques.

In spite of all of these good reasons for the preoccupation with the message and media stages, the fact remains that from the point of view of looking at our communication model as a whole a serious imbalance is apparent. The sophisticated public relations practitioner of the future must direct more of his attention to the other portions of the communications model if he is to communicate more effectively and solve his public relations problems more adequately. This point will come up again and again throughout this book, especially when we examine the sender and recipient stages in more detail. (See particularly Chapter 11, pp. 270-316).

5. Without Careful Analysis, Failures in Communication Can Be Wrongly Attributed

Preoccupation with the message and the media stages often encourages another related error, that of attributing communication failure to the wrong stage in the communication process. Let's explore how this type of error comes about.

Most public relations practitioners tend to summarize their problems in terms of "informing people." "If only the community understood the intentions of the company, then the problem with the zoning committee would disappear." "If only the employees understood what the company had in mind concerning new plant location, then they would be less concerned about losing their jobs or possibly having to move." "If only the public understood the wonderful work being done by Foundation X in combating certain children's diseases, then they would be more likely to contribute money." In each of these three hypothetical (but based on fact) public relations situations, if the goals of the public relations programs are not reached, the failure is generally attributed to the message or media stage or both.

In the first problem mentioned above, the trouble was that the company did not get enough articles published in the local paper or a brochure on the subject did not get written in time to be distributed to the townspeople. In the second problem, allegedly management did not publish a special edition of the plant newspaper devoted to the problem, as they should have done. In the last problem, allegedly Foundation X had not mounted a big enough communication campaign in order to inform the public about its work; more attention must be paid to news releases, pictures, tours of the facilities, and so on, in order for the foundation to become better known. In each instance, some aspect of the message and media stages is singled out for blame.

If one bulletin board doesn't work, put up two or three. If one publicity campaign is not sufficient, mount another. If one brochure hasn't done the job, develop another, ad infinitum. Seldom, if ever, does one hear the public relations practitioner speculating that perhaps the recipient has certain attitudes that will render *any* communication effort ineffective. It isn't that the message has failed or needs to be repeated, but that more fundamental questions have to be asked. What are the attitudes of the recipient, and do I understand them sufficiently well to be *able* to construct an effective communication?

Participation in voting, whether at the local, state, or national level, is an excellent case in point. Around election time, we dissipate an inordinate amount of energy concentrated at the message and media stages. We saturate the recipient with every conceivable type of message we can think of to tell him that he should vote, that it is his duty to vote, that it is his obligation to vote. Yet, the proportion of people who actually vote remains disappointingly low.

It would appear that this communication problem is *not* at the message stage—at least, not yet. What we need to know more about is the recipient and his attitudes toward voting and what presumably differentiates a voter from a nonvoter. Armed with this information, we may be able to devise more effective ways of attempting to change the individual citizen's voting behavior. For one thing, we may find that we need to use other techniques besides the mass media; perhaps we need to utilize face-to-face communication (with its richer feedback); maybe behavior such as voting is not readily induced by mass media.

To summarize this last point, the additional insight that our communication model provides us is that, as well as the fact that each stage has unique problems associated with it, the possibility looms that we can single out the wrong stage or stages to blame when communication attempts fail. Because most public relations practitioners are so much at home with the message and media stages and so comparatively unfamiliar with the factors that are important in the sender and recipient stages, the temptation is great to blame the message and media stages for failures in communication when they may not be at fault at all.

THE COMMUNICATION PROCESS AS PART OF THE LARGER SOCIAL CONTEXT

Up to now, our examination of the communication process and discussion of our communication model has not explicitly included any reference to the larger society in which communication must take place. In the perishing fish case, implicit in our discussion of the way in which the sender, message, media, and recipient stages could be identified was the fact that the *total* affair—*i.e.*, the actions of Standard of California and the reaction of the various directly affected groups— was part of a larger society including other people, institutions, and local, state, and federal governments. Any presentation of the communication process is incomplete without including provision for the impact of society on the communication process itself. We must now enlarge on our communication model to account for the fact that communication does not take place in a vacuum but rather occurs in a living, changing society, the effects of which must be included if there is to be any hope that we can come to understand the communication process.

Modifications Necessary at the Recipient Stage

Reference groups. As noted above, communication never takes place in a vacuum; there is always a larger society to be taken into consideration. This means that one never communicates to a single recipient or group only; rather, one communicates with a recipient *and* the total culture of which the recipient is a part.

It is difficult, obviously, to conceptualize the total society and then visualize how it has an impact on an individual or a single group. For this reason, sociologists and social psychologists have found it convenient to use a concept called "reference groups." Let us utilize two paragraphs from Sherif and Sherif[8] as a basis for defining this concept:

> A central portion of the individual's sense of personal identity, his ego-attitudes defining his status and role relations with others, his prestige concerns, the level of his future goals is derived from groups of which he is a part or aspires to be a part. In order that the concept have a distinct meaning, only such groups should be designated as 'reference groups' of the individual. When we speak of a *reference* group, we are specifying it from the point of view of given individuals.
>
> .   .   .   .   .
>
> A reference group of an individual is the group that provides his specific anchorings in attitude formation and attitude change. It is the position of these reference-group anchors that defines for that individual the relative positions (proximity or distance) of other groups. If the position of a given group along the social-distance scale prevailing in his reference group is low, this is reflected in his negative atti-

---

8 Muzafer Sherif and Carolyn W. Sherif, *An Outline of Social Psychology* (New York: Harper & Row, Publishers, 1956), p. 630. Used by permission.

tude toward that group. If the position represented in propaganda material is too far from the stand prevailing in his reference group on the issue, the individual reacts to it with irritation. If its position is close to the stand in his reference group, the individual may assimilate it.

The most important reference group for anyone is his own family, although the effect of one's family on behavior varies with the age of the individual. While we are growing up, particularly, our family has a powerful influence on behavior and attitudes toward the entire world. In our preschool years, the family is virtually our only reference group and consequently all but controls our thinking and actions. As we grow older, which in this context means that as we become members of other reference groups, the virtual monopoly that our family had on us starts to diminish. Gradually, our classroom peers, teachers, club members become very important in helping to shape our beliefs and attitudes and serve as guides and standards for our behavior. As a matter of fact, in the few short years that transpire between the first grade and high school, the family can change from a group with almost total control over a child to one that exerts comparatively very little control over that same child turned teenager.

Several important aspects of the reference group concept need to be highlighted. First, the need for such a concept. In our modern society, with all of the physical and social mobility that exists, there is a tremendous range of potential reference groups available to an individual. The so-called primitive society that the anthropologist calls to our attention is completely different in this respect, because the number and variety of reference groups in such a culture is much more circumscribed. For this reason, our ability to understand modern man (or, more particularly, to communicate with him more effectively) is heavily dependent on our understanding of his multiple group reference membership. Besides the availability of many different groups with which to identify, there is the necessary concomitant ability of man to be able to relate himself with an incredibly wide range of groups. Unlike primitives, modern man is not restricted by geographical or conceptual barriers, and for this reason, theoretically speaking, he can identify with any group he wishes.[9]

---

[9] This is one of the reasons that technological developments in communication, such as Telstar, whereby the whole world can be linked—electronically, at least—poses both exhilarating and frightening possibilities for the future. One frightening possibility among others is that the potential multiple group membership of man will be extended tremendously, thereby making even more difficult the communicator's task of figuring out a given individual's reference groups.

A second aspect of reference groups is that the term must never become confused with membership groups. A membership group is that group to which an individual belongs by virtue of kinship, by being an employee and having this fact in common with other employees, or by being physically present with other individuals in the same town, the same army unit, and so forth. Such factors as these and many, many more may cause individuals to belong to the same membership group.[10] However, an individual may be a member of a particular group, say, for example, a neighborhood, and yet not think of it as a reference group. The beliefs and attitudes of others in his neighborhood (including how his neighbors regard *him* as a neighbor) may have no effect on him. Thus, the concept of reference group is *psychological* by definition. For this reason, persons far away (or even dead, for that matter) can be a part of an individual's psychological existence and thereby function as a reference group. On the other hand, a group of which he is physically a part (*e.g.*, other workers in his office) may not exist psychologically for him.[11]

---

[10] Perhaps one of the most widely known and used variations of membership group classification systems (both academically and commercially) is that of socio-economic placement of individuals in terms of upper, middle, and lower classes. Hardly a study exists in which the analysis of data is not made in terms of this particular method of grouping individuals. (*See*, for example, W. L. Warner and P. S. Lunt, *The Social Life of a Modern Community* [New Haven, Conn.: Yale University Press, 1941]; *see also* our discussion of this topic in Chapter 16, pages 423-437.)

[11] The importance of the psychological relationship of an individual with others, as contrasted with his being in just physical proximity, is seen in the various distinctions that sociologists make when they try to classify human beings. The key terms used in this connection are *plurel, class, aggregate,* and *group*. A *plurel* designates any plural number of beings but does not specify any characteristics except that there are two or more individuals involved. In this sense, then, all groups are plurels but, of course, not all plurels are groups. The term *class* is used to identify any plurel with certain specified characteristics that all members have in common. Thus, all people with one blue eye and one green eye or all people who own sailboats make up a class. Note that classes of individuals may or may not be groups as well. *Aggregates* are persons in comparatively close physical proximity—such as individuals in a subway car—who do not exist psychologically for one another. This explains partly why one individual is relatively unaffected if another in the same subway car suddenly faints or experiences pain. In a very real sense, these individuals do not exist *psychologically* for one another. For this reason, reading about thousands dying of famine in China (or any other far-off place, *psychologically, that is*) commands only the passing attention of the average reader in the comfort of his home.

Psychological groups (or just *groups*) are plurels in which all individuals exist psychologically for one another. They identify with one another; share in the fortunes and misfortunes of the group as a whole. It is groups in this sense that the concept of *reference* groups embraces.

Primary reference groups. Certain reference groups are known as *primary*. Foremost among primary groups are the family, the neighborhood, and classmates at school. Several factors define what sociologists mean by primary groups. Among the more important are (1) degree of spatial proximity, (2) degree of interpersonal intimacy, (3) size, and (4) length of time in existence.[12] Primary groups are characterized as those with generally close physical proximity. That is, the individuals tend to live closely with one another and see each other very often, as in the usual family.[13] This is the reason that the second factor—close interpersonal intimacy—is required to describe primary groups. In a primary group, there is the feeling among the members that they may talk freely and often with one another, a feeling of being free to communicate at any time and do so in a most intimate fashion.

The third factor, size, helps to define primary groups in the following manner. All things being equal, primary groups tend to be small in number. Groups of three, four, six, or ten persons probably represent the usual number of members in each of the primary groups in existence. Naturally, this small size goes hand in hand with permitting frequent and intimate communication which in turn is related to close spatial proximity.

The last factor, length of time in existence as a group, is likewise consistent with the other three factors. In general, primary groups tend

---

One further point should be made here. Prior to the distinctions that now are made among these terms—*plurel, class, aggregate* and *group*—a collection of two or more individuals was called by the single term *group* whether it was a lynch mob or a Boy Scout troop. As the reader can readily understand, a classification so crude as to include various plurels that differ so drastically is very misleading. Although we still have an immensely long way to go before we understand the dynamics of the functioning of the various plurels, at least some improvement has been made in the classification system. (*See,* for example, George A. Lundberg, Clarence C. Schrag, and Otto N. Larsen, *Sociology* [New York: Harper & Row, Publishers, 1954], pp. 396-398.)

[12] The factors cited here as important to defining primary (and, later, secondary) groups—that is, spatial proximity, degree of intimacy, size, and time—are borrowed from Lundberg, Schrag, and Larsen, pp. 396-405. All passages from *Sociology* used by permission.

[13] Close physical proximity can be a misleading characteristic of primary groups. There are many instances where persons belonging to the same primary group are not in close physical proximity to one another for a variety of reasons. One of the most common is that of the family: the children tend to become separated from their parents and from one another as they grow older and establish their own homes and families. Even though they are separated, there are still close ties among them, and a person's family does influence his behavior. The factor of close physical proximity in this instance is a condition that occurred earlier in an individual's life, and the mere fact of geographical separation does not prevent his remaining a member of that primary group.

to be those that have been in existence for a long period of time. This is in contrast with groupings that are fleeting and consequently do not permit the other dimensions of a primary group to develop. To summarize what we have said thus far about primary groups, let us look at two passages from *The American Soldier: Combat and Its Aftermath*. These passages portray the spirit inherent in the relationships that exist in primary groups.

> Loyalty to one's buddies was founded on the fact of vital mutual dependence and supported by the cluster of sentiments grouped under the term "pride in outfit." In the words of a former infantry scout who was wounded at Salerno after fighting through Sicily,
>
>> You know the men in your outfit. You have to be loyal to them. The men get close-knit together. They like each other—quit their petty bickering and having enemies. They depend on each other—wouldn't do anything to let the rest of them down. They'd rather be killed than do that. They begin to think the world of each other. It's the main thing that keeps a guy from going haywire.
>
> In explaining why he would not want to leave his outfit, a soldier might express either thought: that he didn't want to let his buddies down, or that he felt safer with his own outfit. A wounded veteran of combat in North Africa stressed the aspect of security when he said:
>
>> The fellows don't want to leave when they're sick. They're afraid to leave their own men—the men they know. They don't want to get put in a different outfit. Your own outfit—they're the men you have confidence in. It gives you more guts to be with them.[14]

Secondary reference groups. Another major subcategory of reference groups that the sociologist distinguishes is *secondary groups*. The same four dimensions used to define primary groups can be used to define secondary groups. First, secondary groups tend to be those in which the individuals are *not* in close physical proximity with one another. A typical secondary group might be all of the policemen on the New York City police force. Or, they might be all the veterans of World War II, having returned to civilian life but still undergoing treatment in the various veterans' hospitals. In such groups, the individuals are widely separated. As a matter of fact, their very classification as a group is more imposed by someone else than by the individual participants themselves. Although a veteran still under treatment for wounds incurred during wartime may feel that he has more in common with all other veterans in the same circumstances, he is probably not

---

[14] Samuel A. Stouffer, S. J. R. Saunders, R. K. Merton, and P. F. Lazarsfeld, *The American Soldier* (2 vols.; Princeton, N.J.: Princeton University Press, 1949), Vol. II: *Combat and Its Aftermath*, 136, 143-144. Used by permission.

conscious of this group identification most of the time—at least not so conscious as he is of his membership in his immediate family.

The second dimension—degree of interpersonal intimacy—in secondary groups is low or nonexistent. As a rule, persons in secondary groups do not feel that they can communicate with others whenever they want to, and certainly not intimately. The communications tend to be more limited, dictated by external considerations such as their jobs or union contracts and are much more formal. The employee in any large company or government agency typifies the secondary group with respect to intimacy of interpersonal relationships. Most individuals in large organizations feel at one time or another that they are members of a large, confusing, impersonal group where they do not know the names of individuals who work across the hall from them.[15]

The third dimension, size, the reader has undoubtedly anticipated by now. Generally, secondary groups are large in size, ranging from just under a hundred to thousands of persons. The large size of secondary groups tends to fit in with the other dimensions (e.g., lack of interpersonal intimacy) in the sense that one factor contributes to the other. All things being equal, the larger the group, the less likely one will be in close spatial proximity with others and the less likely that the opportunity for communication will even arise let alone be intimate.

Lastly, with respect to the duration of secondary group contacts, they tend to be short. Lundberg, Schrag, and Larsen summarize this characteristic of secondary groups when they write,

> In person-to-person activity, a secondary relationship may be illustrated in the everyday touch-and-go contacts that one may have with the grocery clerk, the elevator operator, or the policeman on the beat. In a similar manner, numerous indirect interacts occur daily, e.g., when business transactions are entirely completed by wire, mail, and check. Such contacts, in contrast to a primary relationship, do not require that the parties know each other in any inclusive sense. Likewise, very little sentiment is attached to the relationship. It is viewed simply as a means of getting things done, and the relationship is dropped as soon as the goal is attained or the end changes.[16]

---

[15] This situation is all too true in many large organizations. More often than not, an employee feels less free to stop and talk to someone in the hall whom he knows only vaguely as "one of the bosses," and thereby part of the secondary group, than he would to strike up a conversation with a total stranger. The effects of being in a large organization with its accompanying feelings of impersonality and coldness can have quite adverse effects on individuals within it.

[16] Lundberg, Schrag, and Larsen, p. 426.

The relationships between primary and secondary groups are best depicted as being at opposite ends of a continuum of contact. There is no hard and fast dividing line between primary and secondary groups as a concept. The extremes are clear enough, as in a family compared to a large factory. However, there are other situations, such as the shading of difference between "friends and associates" and "persons that we meet occasionally." Here the distinction between the two groups is not nearly so clear.

Now that we have a better idea of what primary and secondary groups are, let us turn our attention to why this reference groups concept must be added to our communication model. The reason is simple to state, but far more difficult to understand and use in communication analysis: When we communicate to a recipient (either singular or plural), we are, in a sense, communicating with that recipient's reference groups as well. Understanding how a recipient will react to a communication is aided by knowing the reference groups of that particular individual. As we said earlier, no communication effort takes place in a vacuum; rather it takes place in a social setting. One of the key dimensions of any social setting is the reference groups of the recipients involved.

The influence of reference groups on the behavior of an individual is best known and undoubtedly strongest in primary group situations. Stouffer *et al.*, on the basis of their research of the *American Soldier*, suggest that the primary group relationship serves two main functions: (1) to set and emphasize group standards of behavior and (2) to support and sustain the individual in stress situations that he might not have been able to stand up under had this support not been supplied.[17] Other studies have indicated that the effects of primary group relationships range all the way from enabling individuals to endure more pain in the presence of others[18] to serving as a most effective method of controlling the behavior of others through the use of the group as a device for shunning the deviant member.[19]

The effects of secondary groups on individual behavior are in general

---

[17] Stouffer *et al.*, II, 130-131.

[18] W. Moede, *Experimentelle Masespsychologie* (Leipzig [1920]), pp. 133-136, as reported in Alfred R. Lindesmith and A. L. Strauss, *Social Psychology* (New York: Holt, Rinehart & Winston [The Dryden Press], 1956), p. 246.

[19] Lundberg, Schrag, and Larsen, p. 425. These authors write: "A news story from the Amish community in 1948 told of a member who used an automobile to take his sick child to a doctor. This act violated an Amish norm. The shunning penalty was applied. The effect on him was so severe that he went to court to attempt to force removal of the penalty."

not nearly so strong nor do we understand their effects on the individual himself so well. That is, we know that large organizations—those to
which the epithet "bureaucracy" applies—have all sorts of effects on
individuals, particularly undesirable ones. Likewise, we know that persons belonging to one organization—say the I.O.O.F.—are very likely,
as a group, to react differently to an issue than another organization—
say the V.F.W. The exact details of this reaction are very often fuzzy,
however.

Perhaps the least well understood category of secondary groups is
crowd behavior. We know clearly that mobs, lynching parties, looting
gangs, unruliness of people in queues at ticket windows have an effect
on participating individuals. However, the details of these effects are
exceedingly vague. We do not even have satisfactory labels and definitions of various types of crowd behavior, to say nothing of the fact
that to do research on such aggregates is practically impossible at the
present time.[20]

Regardless of the state of our knowledge, our communication model
should take cognizance of reference groups so that it is more fully
consistent with the real world. For this reason our model should be
modified as is depicted in Figure 12. In Figure 12, we have tried to
conceptualize the difference in impact between primary and secondary
groups by making the primary reference group affiliation circle closer
to the recipient than the secondary reference group affiliation circle.
With this addition to our model, we now have a conceptual means
for including, as part of our analysis of the total communication situation, the effect of reference groups on the recipient. This, in turn, provides us with a basis for predicting more effectively how the recipient
is likely to react to our communication effort. Although such detail
will be postponed until a more thorough discussion of the recipient
stage is taken up (Chapters 12 through 16), it may be useful to make
one adaption of the reference group concept to public relations practice to demonstrate the application of this type of thinking for the public relations practitioner.

Concept of reference groups applied to public relations. One of
the oldest industrial communication tools—dating back to the 1840's—
is the "house publication." There are various estimates as to the degree
to which companies have invested in various house publications, including such things as newspapers and magazines. One states they

---

[20] For an interesting book that attempts to cope directly with the problems inherent in understanding and studying the behavior of large plurels of individuals,
see R. H. Turner and L. M. Killian, *Collective Behavior* (Englewood Cliffs, N.J.:
Prentice-Hall, Inc., 1957).

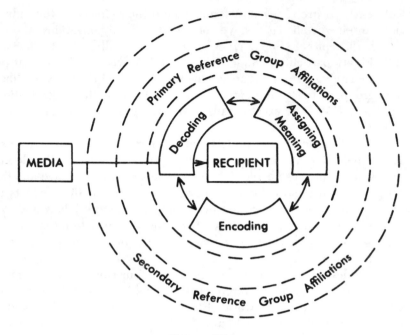

Figure 12

Reference Group Affiliations Added to Recipient Stage

run into millions of dollars per year with circulation of more than three hundred million per issue.[21] Company publications, especially those directed toward the rank and file employee, have become exceedingly important tools for management and take up an inordinate amount of the public relations practitioner's time. How might we interpret this important function in terms of our latest addition to our communication model?

First, let us examine why company publications came into being at all. When our industrial revolution was in its infancy and workers did their work in their own homes or in the homes of a neighbor or a relative, there were very few industrial communication problems in the sense that we know them today. The main reason was that the work situation could be characterized as a primary group. The work was done in a face-to-face, intimate setting, with a total of only a few people. However, as the industrial revolution began to grow, so did

---

[21] International Council of Industrial Editors, *Operation Tape-Measure* (1957). Summary of ICIE's 1956 survey.

the size of the work force necessary to keep up with the increased production. Today, we do not find employees in a primary group work situation as often as we might like. Rather, we find many work situations characteristic of the secondary group end of the primary-secondary group reference continuum. In a great many present-day companies, we find that the employee does not understand his role in the total organization. He does not understand where his company is going, what it hopes to do in the future, and his place in that future. In some instances, the employee has to go to a retail outlet store to be able to see the finished products that his company makes and that he had a hand in completing. In short, the employee can be a stranger in his own work situation.[22]

One remedy for this kind of situation is to set up a communication network linking employer with the employee. The major vehicle in this network has become the plant newspaper or magazine. This magazine has very often become linked with the public relations practitioner within the organization, and he develops magazine or newspaper content that will, hopefully, make the employee feel more a part of the organization.

The typical content of most company newspapers or magazines can be summed up with the words *information, identification,* and *feedback.* The public relations practitioner runs articles from time to time to inform the employee about company policy; to let him know about new developments in other parts of the company; to let him know about his future in the company and where he can expect to be financially and organizationally in the years to come. Identification with the company is engendered (or at least attempted to be engendered) by articles about the leaders in the company that stress their personalities and something about their personal lives. Such emphasis presumably will enable the employee to think of his leaders as individuals rather than as symbols of authority. In addition, sections of the publications are devoted to describing other employees, so that one can feel that he knows something about his co-workers, even though he does not spend any time with them. Feedback to the company and its leaders is provided through such devices as letters to the editors, gripe sessions in print, and the like, so that the publication serves as an outlet for communication of the employee to the employer but in a form that is sometimes more palatable since it is more (or entirely) anonymous.

What do all of these functions of the company publication have in common? What they share is, that to the degree that each of these de-

---

[22] In this connection, read footnote 15, page 111, once again.

vices is successful, *they tend, through communication, to produce among the employees a sense of primary group membership* to replace the secondary group membership characteristics that exist. A major objective of an employee publication, such as a plant newspaper, is to make the employee feel that he is on more intimate terms with the company, to make him feel as though he knows something about the people with whom he works. Instead of being a member of a large group with no intimacy, he is really part of a small group (reduced conceptually through communication) with a lot of intimacy. In short, company publications can be seen as an attempt to achieve and then maintain a primary group atmosphere in an organization for work, in spite of the fact that the organization may have grown very large and acquired secondary group characteristics almost entirely.

Modifications Necessary at the Sender Stage

The intimate relationship pictured earlier between the recipient and various reference groups (both primary and secondary) is also true of the sender. Therefore, our model must reflect this fact exactly in the same way that we modified it to take reference groups into account in relation to the recipient. Riley and Riley very nicely summarize this need to take into account reference groups at the sender stage when they write,

> Thus the communicator emerges as part of a larger pattern, sending his messages in accordance *with the expectations and actions of other persons and groups within the same system.* As a political communicator, he may act with reference to the other members of his party and the other citizens in his community; as a copy writer, he may act as an employee of an advertising agency sponsored by a particular manufacturing client.[23] [Italics added.]

Our model must be modified once again to account for the effect of reference groups on the sender. Figure 13 depicts this modification.

Let us relate this addition of our model to public relations practice in order to clarify our understanding of how the sender is affected by reference groups in his communication behavior.

---

[23] John W. Riley, Jr., and M. W. Riley, "Mass Communication and the Social System," in Robert K. Merton, Leonard Broom, and Leonard S. Cottrell, Jr. (eds.), *Sociology Today* (Basic Books, Inc., Publishers, 1959), p. 567. All passages from this work used by permission.

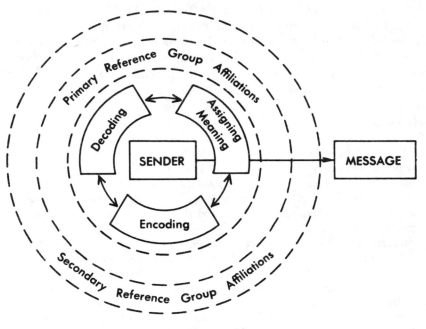

Figure 13

Reference Group Affiliations Added to Sender Stage

To begin with, people have more difficulty visualizing the "larger social impact" on the sender (*i.e.*, in this case, in terms of reference group relations) for two reasons. First, this type of analysis is very much akin to self-analysis. It requires the sender to introspect, to "look within." That is, for the sender to think about how he is affected by reference groups is not normally done. It is much easier to accept the statement that *recipients* are affected by their group identifications. Even the most unsophisticated communicator frequently engages in visualizing how a recipient might be affected by some particular reference group. By contrast, the *sender* seems to think of himself (if he thinks about it at all) as much more of a free agent, a great deal less affected by others than is the recipient. This type of analysis at the sender stage is somewhat clinical in nature: *why* he is communicating as he is; what the *reasons* are for his efforts to persuade; *how* he is influenced by others to communicate as he does.

The second reason is that, from a scientific point of view, we know comparatively less about the effect of others on the sender than on the recipient in any total communication process situation. (We shall return to this point in more detail in Chapter 16, pp. 449-457). Typically, research in this area of communication focuses on the recipient. We study the recipient in order to learn something about his reaction to propaganda efforts. In such studies, we make an analysis of the social structure as carefully as we can in order to determine the effect of the various reference groups. We particularly analyze the receptivity (*i.e.*, the persuasibility) of the recipient as a function of variations in the reference groups. Riley and Riley point this out well.

The prototype of studies of this type in the mass communication field is perhaps the evaluation by Shils and Janowitz of the impact of propaganda by the Western Allies on the fighting effectiveness of the German Army in World War II.* Contrary to earlier views of propaganda as a panacea, their findings did not reveal that the invocation of adverse political, ideological, and cultural symbols produced any sweeping disaffection or collapse in military morale. Nor did they reveal that the extraordinary tenacity of the Wehrmacht was due primarily to the political convictions of the German soldier—to his direct attachment to the Nazi system itself as a reference group, as it were. They showed, rather, that his resistance to Allied propaganda and his sustained motivation to fight rested upon the persistence of the primary-group structure of the component units of the army. These analysts concluded that only when the primary groups themselves start to dissolve does propaganda (and then only certain kinds of propaganda) facilitate disintegration.

This study merits careful attention, since it seems to illustrate an important, but little exploited, approach to the study of the social structure within which mass communications are received. In order to account for the stability of the Army and its resistance to propaganda against its norms, Shils and Janowitz began with an investigation of the basic military organization and its relationship to the system of primary groups. They examined the process by which the goals of the larger bureaucratic structure were met by the functioning of smaller groups of friends, suggesting a number of linkages between the Army and these smaller groups. For example, membership in the informal social group was seen to coincide roughly with membership in the military squad. Both the larger structure and the primary group are exposed to the same external danger and share the same ideal of soldierly honor. The small but hard core of Nazis, as well as the paternally protective NCO's and junior officers, served as mediators, or linking persons, between the primary group and the Army. Moreover, the

---

* Edward A. Shils and Morris Janowitz, "Cohesion and Disintegration in the Wehrmacht in World War II," *Public Opinion Quarterly*, XXII (1948), 280-315.

larger system was observed to exercise various controls over the smaller. Not only did the Wehrmacht exert authority throughout its officers, it also deliberately manipulated various factors affecting small-group solidarity. For example, it maintained in the same units men who had gone through a victory together and who shared the same recollections. It warned deserters of severe sanctions. It prevented family groups from weakening its own hold on the men by issuing strict injunctions against references to family deprivations in letters to the front. At the same time, it encouraged letters which would reduce the men's anxieties about their families and give the supplementary affection which the army unit could not provide.[24]

Enough detail is included in the quotation from the Rileys to illustrate the care that Janowitz and Shils gave in analyzing the relationship between communication in the form of Allied propaganda and the primary group structure of the German Army, that is, the three-way tie-in among the recipients, their reference groups, and the communications themselves. Unfortunately, we do not have as many studies that devote the same kind of careful analysis to the *sender* and the reference groups involved as we have for the recipients and their reference groups.[25]

To summarize briefly at this point, the addition of the reference group concept to our communication model (see Figure 14 again) is as necessary for the sender stage as it is for the recipient. What we have set forth in the past few paragraphs are two of the more important reasons why we ordinarily do not make this same group reference type of analysis with respect to the sender. One reason is that it is much like clinical self-analysis and this is always difficult to do. Another is that, from a scientific point of view, we do not have nearly so much research work to fall back on to help us in understanding this ramification of the total communication process.

Let us make a translation of this reference group concept as applied to the sender stage into public relations practice. One example that immediately comes to mind has to do with ethics in public relations.

---

[24] Riley and Riley, pp. 556-557.

[25] The reader can relate this last generalization to his own experiences in public relations study. It is very natural to try to understand why a group of stockholders or employees or citizens in a community (all recipients) did not respond to a particular public relations program in the manner expected. Part of this analysis may involve attempting to see if certain reference groups for these target groups held views contrary to those of the company. In each situation, however, seldom do we find ourselves utilizing the same step-by-step analysis of ourselves, the sender.

By its very nature, the practice of public relations can always be used potentially for the selfish ends of a few to the detriment of the general public. For this reason, the first principle in the Revised Public Relations Society of America Code of Ethics reads as follows: "To conduct ourselves both privately and professionally in accord with the public welfare."[26]

Our communication model implies that the public relations practitioner must be constantly aware that one very important reference group that has a direct and strong influence upon what he says and does is his employer or client. It takes a continuous effort to be aware of the influences of this particular reference group; it is very easy to accept readily the beliefs of others, especially if they are your superiors and in a position of power over you. It is the unusual public relations practitioner who can be even partially aware of how this reference group is influencing and shaping his communication efforts. This admonishment is made not because it is wrong for a public relations practitioner and the organization he represents to have similar or identical views, but because there is the ever-present danger that the public relations practitioner may come to have the same views and not even be aware of it. The danger here lies in his unconscious expounding of views that are contrary to his own or, more importantly, contrary to the public welfare, which is the first of a series of ethical standards that he is supposed to uphold.

One last thought in this connection. It is obvious that the limiting factor in the ability of a public relations practitioner to be cognizant of the many reference group influences on him is his ability to have insight into his own behavior. Some of us have a lot of insight; others have practically none. This fact is certainly recognized by the author. However, our model of communication takes such reference groups into account, and the fact that we are attempting to become more adept in using this model to guide our analysis of the total communication process should increase the *possibility*, at least, of greater insight in everyday public relations practice.

Modifications Necessary for the Entire Model

With the addition of the concept of reference groups to both the sender and recipient stages, we have brought into focus important

---

26 *Public Relations Register, Fourteenth Annual Edition, 1962/63* (375 Park Avenue, New York: Public Relations Society of America, Inc., July 1, 1962), pp. 20-21.

factors that affect the communication process. However, there are many, many more factors in a social structure within which all communications take place that have not been accounted for. In an introductory book such as this, we are limited as to how far we can carry this type of analysis. For this reason, we need to make one more modification of our model, one that will permit us to allow conceptually, at least, for the effect of the total social structure on communications. This has been achieved by placing our model, as it has been developed up to now, in a rectangle labeled "Total Social Structure."

With Figure 14, we have completed our working communication model. The added rectangle that encloses the four stages of the communication process as it was developed up to Figure 14 completes the effort to include conceptually the social context in which communication takes place. In the next few paragraphs, we will examine a specific illustration of how the social context itself must be taken into account when an analysis of communication is made. In many other portions of this book, particularly Chapters 12 through 16, we will bring in certain other concepts of the social context that are helpful and necessary for the public relations practitioner to keep in mind as he analyzes his communication problems. No one text could begin to include all of the possible social influences that can affect communication. However, armed with the completed model as depicted in Figure 14 and the various examples that are provided throughout the remainder of this book, the reader should be able to anticipate the impact of any other social context variable upon communication that he may wish to consider.

Let us take one specific example of how the social structure itself must be taken into account when trying to understand communication. In our illustration, let us assume the role of a public relations practitioner dealing with the same five hundred employees[27] in each of three different types of organizations: (1) an automobile manufacturing assembly line, (2) the administrative offices of a large company, spread over two or three floors of office space, and (3) a long-distance freight line whose truck drivers all operate out of the same home terminal.

In these three work situations, the problems associated with communicating with the employees would be different. In the assembly line context, all five hundred of them could be reached in a compara-

---

[27] In an actual situation, we might not find an organization with only five hundred employees having a full-time public relations practitioner. However, the five hundred can just as easily represent five thousand as far as the principle of relating the larger social structure to communication is concerned.

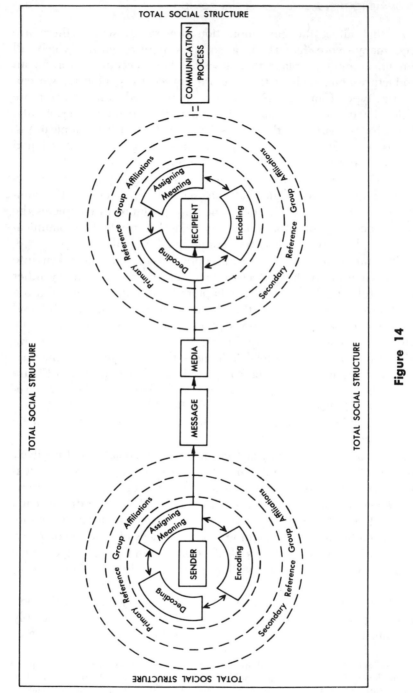

Figure 14

A Communication Model

tively short period of time, even on a face-to-face basis. The same is true in the office work context. It would not be true, however, in the trucking situation, because here the employees are *structurally* scattered over miles and miles in units of no more than two or three individuals. In this situation, face-to-face communication would require rather special arrangements. More than likely, other means of reaching the men would be used.

The interrelationships among the employees are likewise drastically changed as one goes from one work context to another. For this reason, the communication among the employees will be different; this, in turn, is bound to modify the type of communication feedback to the public relations practitioner, and so on.

One important thing to note is that we can make these assumptions about changes in communication patterns and the fact that there will be different problems in communication *without any reference to the personalities of the individuals in question*. Not that individual person-alities and their inevitable differences are unimportant in communica-tion. Rather, in this example we deliberately assumed the *same* five hundred employees to help focus our attention on the importance of the total social structure.

The examples that could be developed to illustrate the importance of the total social structure on communication are almost endless. As was mentioned earlier, we will be taking up numerous other examples in later chapters as we go into more detail in our communication model. We are now equipped to translate any public relations problem into our communications theory model as depicted in Figure 14, page 122. However, if we were to do so we would find that we lack many con-ceptual tools to help us visualize our communication problems and, more importantly, we would not have much to guide us in intelligently solving our problems. We need to relate the concepts from such social and behavioral sciences as psychology, sociology, and anthropology to communication. We can do this by imbedding these concepts in our communication model. The next eleven chapters are designed to do that for us.

QUESTIONS FOR DISCUSSION

1. Demonstrate the relationship between the concept of feedback and moving toward the right-hand end of the problem-solving con-tinuum introduced in Chapter 3 (page 48). That is, illustrate with ex-

amples how obtaining feedback enables the public relations practitioner to move away from the "fly by the seat of the pants" school toward the "best obtainable evidence" school.

2. Look for one or two public relations cases that demonstrate the assertion made on pages 100 to 105 that many public relations practitioners are preoccupied with the message and media stages of the total communication process. For contrast, try to find a case write-up that devotes a balanced amount of time to the sender and recipient stages as well as the message and media stages.

3. Develop an illustration of how not being aware of certain primary reference group affiliations would cause a public relations practitioner to handle a public relations problem inadequately. Be sure to specify in some detail the *type* or *nature* of the errors that could occur because primary group affiliations had been overlooked or were unknown.

4. On pages 113-116 of this chapter, the suggestion was put forth that company publications, as one form of communication, tend to produce among employees a sense of primary group membership. With this assertion in mind:

   a) Spell out in some detail what a public relations practitioner could do to supplement the effectiveness of his internal communication efforts to achieve this increased sense of primary group membership, and

   b) Speculate as to what sort of company communication efforts would appear to be the most effective in producing this sense of primary group membership. Why do you think whatever you have singled out would be most effective?

5. Although we will be taking this up in much more detail in later chapters, speculate at this point about what sort of phenomenon would qualify as "total social structure" as was spelled out in connection with Figure 15. Try to give some indication of how a public relations practitioner would be in error in solving some particular public relations problem if he did not take the total social structure into consideration.

Chapter 6

THE SENDER STAGE IN MORE DETAIL: ADOPTING THE PROBLEM-SOLVING ATTITUDE

INTRODUCTION

In this chapter we will engage in a more detailed analysis of a number of topics that belong at the sender stage of the communication process. As a public relations practitioner begins to analyze a particular public relations problem, there are certain considerations that crop up when he is examining the sender stage (*i.e.*, "his" role) in the total communication process that are distinct from those he sees when he is looking at the other stages.

The point of departure that we will take concerning problem solving in public relations is this: We will look at problems in public relations from the standpoint of what the *sender* should and must do. We will always assume that the *sender* has the responsibility of understanding and controlling as best he can the total communication process.[1] This means that for all of the stages the public relations practitioner must figure out what is appropriate and called for in order to assure successful communication.

---

[1] This view makes no distinction between the public relations practitioner who is employed by an organization as a member of its public relations department and one who is a consultant to a particular company but is an employee of a consulting agency.

125

There is a parallel between this assumption and one that exists in management or human relations training: in management training, we learn that management is supposed to take the initiative concerning its relationships with employees; in human relations training, the supervisor (*i.e.*, the one in charge) is responsible for demonstrating sound human relations practices to those under his supervision. It is not that the employee too should not be skilled in human relations; it would be very desirable if employees assumed more responsibility in making an organization function smoothly. The point is, however, we do not start with the assumption that they should; we do assume, on the other hand, that the managerial personnel must take this responsibility.

So it is with respect to the public relations practitioner in his role as an expert coming to grips with a particular public relations problem. We assume that it is his responsibility to assure effective communication, adequate feedback, and the like. As in human relations, it is a pleasant surprise when the recipient takes some responsibility to assure adequate communication between sender and recipient, but we operate from the assumption that he will not.

I. THE BEGINNING POINT: SELF-ANALYSIS

In Chapter 2 (pages 30-33), an ethics in public relations continuum was described which ranged from a self-interest end to a mutual-interest end. This concept was put forth as an aid to the public relations practitioner to remind him that any public relations program must be assessed as to whether it is strictly selfish, of mutual advantage, or somewhere in between. Consequently, one of the first things to be considered in a more detailed analysis of the sender stage is one's own ethical position. What are you trying to accomplish in this particular public relations effort, and can it be defended from an ethical standpoint? Who (or what groups) will benefit? Will they benefit at the expense of other individuals or groups? There is no escaping the responsibility of making as searching an analysis as is humanly possible of the motives behind any particular public relations action. It is at once one of the most difficult and conveniently overlooked steps of the total problem-solving effort undertaken by a public relations man.

One would be hard pressed to find other occupations that present a more trying context within which to operate and at the same time remain ethical. It is beyond the purview of this volume to engage in what might be interpreted as an attempt to develop a philosophy of public relations. The important thing about the self-analysis phase is that the public relations practitioner be aware of the following:

1. That he has made certain interpretations of his public relations problem and has taken a position as to what is "right" and "wrong."
2. That many of these interpretations of "right" and "wrong" are made unconsciously in the sense that he is hardly aware of (or is unaware of) the many factors that have led to his particular interpretations.
3. That it requires a conscious effort to be able to bring to light at least *some* of the bases for ethical judgments that are part and parcel of any problem-solving effort.

This calls for a careful examination of the ethics of any public relations program to be made with a full knowledge that there is no "right" or "wrong" public relations action in any absolute sense. The author is fully cognizant of the fact that whether one labels something as good or bad, right or wrong, depends upon his point of view. That is, what is true to you depends on your point of view—your motives or the vested interests you happen to have. Also it depends on what values you have as a result of all of your prior training and experiences. This means that we all approach a particular problem situation, take a position as to what we think is right and wrong, and behave accordingly. All of this is as it has to be; we can't help ourselves, if for no reason other than the fact that we are human beings. But the public relations practitioner, perhaps more than the practitioner in many other occupational groups, must be particularly conscious of the processes that influence how he interprets a particular problem; how he decides what is ethical to do and not to do. He must be more aware of these processes because his daily work places him in the position of having to achieve the objectives of the organization with which he is associated. The user of public relations, no matter how honest or sincere, is nonetheless interested in putting his best foot forward. This is true of corporate citizen and private citizen alike. A. J. Sullivan touches on this same concept when he writes,

> Partisan values are deeply human at their source. They flow from a belief in the essential rightness of some person or party or idea; and they underlie the willingness to champion the object of this belief, to further its cause, to defend it, to fight for it. Patriotism is a partisan value; so, in at least a certain sense, is the feeling a mother has for

her child, or a lover for his loved one. A lawyer, out of partisan values, defends a client with vigor and skill; a president promotes his program to the Congress; a supreme court justice writes a minority opinion.

The partisan values of public relations are well-known. When a public relations person, either counsel or employee, undertakes to win favorable public opinion for the institution he represents, his position is based on partisan values. All his skill in collecting and disseminating information, in analyzing target audiences and reaching and persuading them, is placed at the service of the institution. And because human values motivate him, he must bring to his assignment commitment to the ideas of the institution, a trust in the essential honesty of its directors, loyalty to their interests, obedience to their demands.[2]

With all of these forces, is it any wonder that we must strongly admonish the public relations practitioner to take the time to think through as carefully as possible the personal and organizational ethics involved in any attempt to solve a particular public relations problem.

The second point to be made at this time is that it appears useful to regard public relations in much the same way as social scientists view propaganda. Propaganda is essentially a neutral term, but the most common interpretation of this word is a negative one: If you propagandize, *ipso facto* you are bad. If we hark back to our definition of public relations (page 51, Chapter 3) it is clear that in the definition, and in the discussion accompanying the definition, public relations is "neutral" in the sense that it can be either good or bad, depending on the integrity of the persons responsible for the public relations policy and for implementation of the public relations program. In exactly the same sense that propaganda is neutral, communication programs used to attain certain public relations goals are neither black nor white, good nor bad.

One is reminded of Socrates, who warned his students to beware of the verbal trickery of the Sophists. They got paid for their performance and were thus more interested in winning arguments than in finding truth. All men who do business in the world of affairs suffer the same shortcoming, he added. Our point here is that the public relations practitioner cannot let himself become a Sophist even though he is being paid. Although he need not undertake the rather fruitless task of trying to identify what is "truth," he does need to identify the factors that enter into *his definition* of what the truth is and be as aware of these factors as it is humanly possible for him to be. While still on

---

[2] Albert J. Sullivan, "The Value Systems of Public Relations, II: Partisan Values," *Public Relations Quarterly*, VIII, No. 2 (1963), 15. Used by permission.

this topic, it is significant to note that Socrates did not forbid his students to listen to the Sophists nor did he suggest that they retire from
the world. Instead, he urged them to sharpen their critical faculties so
as to be able to recognize faulty reasoning wherever they found it.
This is still sound advice. We cannot legislate responsibility, nor can
we soften the danger or irresponsibility by instilling a greater concern
for public good in corporate management. The burden of protection
from manipulation and misuse of the techniques of mass persuasion
falls squarely on the shoulders of the educated individual. In spite of
this fundamental truth, however, it in no way absolves the public relations practitioner from doing his share to see to it that manipulation
and misuse are not perpetuated in the first place.

Sometimes Outside Help Is Needed

Up to now, we have been stressing self-analysis essentially from the
standpoint of the sender's "looking within" himself, so to speak, in
order to bring out more clearly such things as what he stands for and
the ethical implications of his intended (or existing) public relations
action. As necessary as this self-analysis is, there are times when an
outsider is needed to help fill in some of the details. The outsider can
potentially be any one of a number of individuals or organizations, but
a common one is a research organization skilled in such things as
opinion-attitude surveys. Its contribution to the self-analysis is to supply the public relations practitioner with information on how others
perceive his organization.[3] This independent, objective check in the
form of an opinion-attitude survey is very often a useful device to
check on your own assumptions about yourself or about the public
with which you are dealing. It sometimes turns up information that is
not expected and yet has a lot of bearing on the problem situation. The
case presented below provides some idea of how research (in this
case, in the form of an opinion-attitude survey) can be used to aid an
organization in clarifying its own position in a problem, and how it
helps to suggest what action should be taken to help solve the problem.
The case is from the Opinion Research Corporation's files on public
relations research.[4]

---

[3] We will return to this point in detail in later chapters when we discuss research and how the public relations practitioner uses all sorts of research to find
out more about what others (particularly the target audience or public that his
is concerned with) think of his organization.

[4] Opinion Research Corporation, "Case Histories in Public Relations and Employee Research," based on research done for clients by the Corporation (Princeton,
N.J.: the Corporation). Used by permission.

CASE NO. 11-741-W

PROBLEM AND APPROACH

Two non-profit health insurance plans had good reason for concern. In addition to increased competition from private insurance companies, they recently had found it necessary to raise their rates.

To obtain a clear sense of the public's attitudes toward their services, and guidance in promotional strategy, a survey was undertaken among members of the plans and non-members.

SOME OF THE FINDINGS

A large majority of members and a somewhat smaller majority of non-members had a favorable opinion of the plan operating in their area. Although rates had gone up, the feeling was that the increase was justified.

On the other hand, substantial minorities of both groups thought the plans were profit-making organizations. Persons in this category felt less favorably toward the plans than those who knew they were organized on a non-profit basis.

MANAGEMENT ACTION

An ambitious information program was undertaken to clear up misconceptions regarding the non-profit status of the plans and other misconceptions involving benefits and services.

Although this is only a brief description of the research project and of the problem situations that required the research, it is sufficient to make the point that through the services of an outsider information was obtained that permitted the sender (*i.e.,* public relations practitioner) to make a better analysis of the problems facing his organization. Also, we see that the sender obtained information that he was not aware of, information that was somewhat unexpected and required a revision of his thinking about his particular public relations problem situation.

II. THE NEXT POINT: ADOPTING THE PROBLEM-SOLVING ATTITUDE

The reader is undoubtedly familiar with the so-called case method used to train or teach potential business executives. Briefly, the case method consists of presenting to the students a thorough, well-written description of a problem situation that one would be likely to encounter in business (as a rule based on careful research of an actual business in order to make the case realistic). The students, either individually or collectively, or both, are required to solve the problems or to determine the problems to be solved in the case. In this way, the student presumably engages in behavior that is closely related to what he will encounter in the real world, yet he can enjoy the luxury of "making mistakes" since it is a classroom exercise.

Over the years, persons using the case method of instruction have evolved some principles of how to approach a case and of how others come to grips with the problems. When one combines these principles, there emerges what might be described as a "problem-solving attitude," which proves to be a useful one to adopt *regardless of the type of problem one is working on*. Because of the universal application of this approach, we will elaborate on it here as the next item at the sender stage following self-analysis.

A. There Is No Single or Obvious Problem

One of the hardest things to learn about coping with any case is the realization that there is no one problem to be solved. Different people studying the same case can arrive at completely different interpretations as to what the problem is (or problems are), and each one may be completely convinced that he is right. To illustrate this point, let us consider briefly an excerpt of a problem submitted by one of the students in a class taught by the author.

> Certain franchised auto dealers and all used-car dealers in a community adjacent to an Air Force Base were charging airmen excessive loan rates on car purchases. The entire bill presented to the airmen was unitemized and, therefore, legally unassailable. The airmen were usually young, impressionable and desirous of owning a car to the extent that they were easily bilked. After entering into legal agreement with the car dealers more often than not these airmen became disillusioned because of the excessive payments that they had to make. This in turn presented a severe morale problem not to mention the inherent moral question involved in these numerous transactions.
>
> The town is largely dependent upon the base economically and until this time there had existed an effective Base-Town Council for harmonious relations. This council was composed of Air Force officer personnel and influential town people.[5]

---

[5] A longer version of this case was submitted as a course requirement for Air Force Information Officers attending a USAF Information Officer Academic Program offered by the School of Public Communication, Boston University. The

Although this material is in abbreviated form, there is enough detail to give the reader a feeling for the situation that existed in one area of the relations between the air base and an adjacent town. The officers in the class were instructed to solve this case from the point of view of the base Information Officer. That is, what, if anything, should the base IO do in this situation? As members of the class began to discuss this case, it became readily apparent that there was more than one interpretation as to what the problem was in the first place. To some it was "obvious" that it was really a legal problem, and, as such, could be ducked entirely by merely referring the situation to the base legal unit. To others, who conceded that there were legal aspects to the case, the problem was one involving base-community relations, and, as such, could not be solved by turning things over to the legal unit. To still others, the problem was interpreted to be an "opportunity" to put the Base-Town Council to work on something that they could "put their teeth into." By so doing, the base personnel would come to better understand some of the leading townspeople and vice versa.

Anyone familiar with case work knows, of course, that there is no single way to interpret a problem situation. Rather, there are many problems, and which one you determine is "the" problem or is the most important problem depends on how you look at it. For those who have not undergone the experience of seeing how others can look at the same case and come up with an entirely different interpretation, it is a revelation indeed. The public relations practitioner must learn to approach every situation that he faces with the clear realization that there is no such thing as the "only" or the "obvious" problem; rather, the problems he identifies are a result of how he perceives the situation.

B. Identification of a Problem Largely a Result of Assumptions

Another factor in the isolation or identification of problems is the assumptions that one brings to the problem-solving situation. For example, in the case cited earlier concerning the excessive charges made by certain automobile dealers, it became clear from the discussion that some participants were assuming that most auto dealers (especially used-car dealers without new-car franchises) tended to be crooked. On the other hand, there were others who assumed that the auto dealers

---

author was one of several faculty members who taught this special course. This particular case was submitted in 1957, and it has been impossible for the author to identify either the Air Force officer who originally wrote the case or the individual who prepared the brief summary quoted here.

were basically honest and that the crooked dealer was definitely the exception. When the discussion turned to the possibility of going to the dealers themselves to ask them for their cooperation in getting rid of overcharging, those that made the former assumption were much less inclined to think that such a move would be successful than were those who made the latter, more favorable assumption.

This case serves to point out another important feature of the problem-solving attitude: The public relations practitioner must ask himself continually, "What are my assumptions? What have I assumed to be true (or false) in this particular situation?" Perhaps even more important, "What implicit assumptions have I made about the *human* elements"—*i.e.*, "What convenient generalization have I made about human behavior?" This last point is important enough to illustrate with one additional case obtained from another student in the same class mentioned earlier. Briefly, the highlights of this case are as follows:

> Serious physical conflicts between airmen of an Air Force Base and an adjacent city's teenagers occurred with alarming regularity. The situation was brought to the attention of the officers in charge of the base when two airmen were discovered leaving the base with carbine rifles and automatic pistols all fully loaded.
>
> These men disclosed that they had intended using the weapons on some youths who had twice attacked them and whom they had recognized. It was further disclosed that each night after dark the city youths cruised up and down the streets looking for airmen.
>
> The situation resulted in tension, poor community base relations, and damaged morale for the airmen. Later it was found that a disreputable family was the "nest" or source of these gangs. It seems as though they were extremely antagonistic toward anyone in uniform, and the things that these uniforms represented.[6]

In the discussion associated with this case, the individuals who assumed that juvenile delinquents were pretty much "born" rather than "made" were much less inclined to think that the gangs of kids who were "out to get" the airmen could be re-educated. Conversely, those individuals who assumed that the behavior of those kids was

---

[6] A longer version of this case was submitted as a course requirement for Air Force Information Officers attending a USAF Information Officer Academic Program offered by the School of Public Communication, Boston University. The author was one of several faculty members who taught this special course. This particular case was submitted in 1957, and it has been impossible for the author to identify either the Air Force officer who originally wrote the case or the individual who prepared the brief summary quoted here.

learned (*i.e.*, "made") suggested completely different courses of action to remedy the situation.

To illustrate a different pair of assumptions, those who took a retaliatory position toward the delinquents were much more inclined to argue that it was a "job for the Military Police," working, of course, in cooperation with the civilian police. Those who took the position that understanding rather than retaliation was called for were more likely to suggest that cooperation with such community agencies as the mental health centers and youth centers was called for.

We need not be concerned at this point with what we ourselves might think are the "right" and "wrong" actions to be taken in a case like this. The focus should be on the need for continual vigil concerning the assumptions that all of us bring to any problem-solving situation we are confronted by. One of the most important elements in the growth and sophistication of the problem-solving ability of a public relations practitioner is his ability to become increasingly aware of the assumptions that guide his thinking and decision making. It is a part of the problem-solving repertoire of the public relations practitioner that will *never* be outdated, regardless of future developments in the field of public relations.

C. There Is Not One, but Rather a Hierarchy of Problems

This third dimension of the problem-solving attitude should not come as any great surprise to anyone. However, a concept that is closely associated with multiplicity, namely, the importance of establishing a hierarchy, is not well known or very often adhered to. The concept of a hierarchy implies that another element of the problem-solving attitude is that one learns to establish priorities in his problem-solving efforts, priorities that distinguish between the short-term and the long-term portions of a problem situation. In both of the cases cited, concerning difficulties in the relationships between an air base and a nearby community, there are some things that can and should be done immediately and other things that are desirable to initiate, but can't be completed for a long period of time. In the second case, a desirable long-range goal should be improvement in the rapport between the young men of the community and the young men of the Air Force. Steps should be taken to bring this goal to pass. However, it generally turns out that the immediate steps are taken, and somehow the long-range plans fail to materialize. To put it into the parlance of the public relations practitioner, so much time is devoted to "putting out fires" that fire prevention steps get shoved into the background.

D. The Distinction Between Stating and Spelling Out the Means to Attain Goals

One of the most common gaps in the problem-solving attitude of the novice is his confusing of the stating of a goal with the attaining of that goal. For example, in the "crooked" auto dealer case the typical beginner tends to stress that the airman needs to be *informed* of the difficulties that he can get into when he buys a car. He feels that he has "solved" the problem since all that needs to be done is to implement some ways of informing the airman. It is not until much later in the discussion that he becomes aware of the facts that (1) just informing the airman doesn't necessarily do the trick—even with information he may still continue to get trapped; and (2), perhaps more frustrating, how one succeeds in informing the airman is not as simple as it sounds. It takes a surprisingly long time for a public relations practitioner to get over the tendency to state goals and behave as if this were the equivalent of spelling out explicit ways of attaining the goals.

E. The "I" Needs to Be Minimized in the Problem-Solving Attitude

This next-to-last element of the problem-solving attitude is one that the author adds to the more or less "standard" list that has been presented thus far in this section. Let's see what minimizing the "I" in problem solving means. If you listen to a person interpreting a problem, somewhere in his presentation he is very likely to say, "If I were in that situation, I would do such and such." Or, if he is directing his remarks to a particular individual, he might very well say, "If I were you, I would do this rather than that."[7] As a matter of fact, one is likely to hear the pronoun "I" throughout the entire discussion.

---

[7] He may very well go on to distinguish between what Chester I. Barnard calls "organization decisions" and "personal decisions." Barnard writes: "This distinction between two types of decision is frequently recognized in ordinary affairs. We very often say or hear sentences similar to this: 'If this were my business, I think I would decide the question this way—but it is not my personal affair'; or, 'I think the situation requires such and such an answer—but I am not in a position to determine what ought to be done'; or, 'The decision should be made by someone else.' This is in effect a restatement, with a different emphasis, of the suggestion . . . that a sort of dual personality is required of individuals contributing to organization—the private personality and the organization personality." (Chester I. Barnard, "Decision Making in Organizations," in *The Functions of the Executive* [Cambridge: Harvard University Press, 1938], p. 188; reprinted in Robert Dubin, *Human Relations in Administration* [Englewood Cliffs, N.J.: Prentice-Hall, Inc., 1951], pp. 199-200.) Used by permission of Harvard University Press.

To some extent, this point of view is quite understandable, since a great many people who employ the case method of teaching tend to do it in a context of "this case is designed to cause you to think about what *you* would do in this particular problem situation." The modification that the writer strongly presses for here is that the pronoun "I" should be used with a slightly different connotation. Instead of "what would *I* do in this situation," the approach should be *"What should I do in the light of certain principles of communication, perception, and motivation that are applicable to this problem."*

This change in emphasis does not lessen the need for the individual practitioner to think. Far from it. It merely stresses the importance of relating his practice (or practical behavior, if you will) to the appropriate social and behavioral science principles. (The presumption being, of course, that these principles will be helpful in suggesting sound practical steps to take.)

It should be apparent that this element in the problem-solving attitude is a more concrete translation of the concepts involved in the presentation of the problem-solving continuum discussed in Chapter 3 (see Figure 2, page 48). At that time, it was argued that the direction the public relations practitioner had to take in his problem solving was toward the "scientifically derived knowledge end." That meant that the public relations practitioner would employ whatever knowledge from the social and behavioral sciences that was useful and applicable to the public relations problem. We have now taken that concept and explicitly spelled out as an integral part of the problem-solving attitude that the public relations practitioner must adopt.

This particular element of the problem-solving attitude is not peculiar to public relations, by any means. It is being applied increasingly to many other fields—business being a particularly good example. As noted earlier, people identified with training executives in various capacities or specialties are continually striving to make their problem-solving efforts more precise and based on scientifically derived knowledge wherever possible. The use of mathematics to assist in making intelligent purchasing decisions is one example; the use of game theory to assist in higher order management decisions is another. The use of "operations analysis" as an aid to visualizing the entire operation of a particular organization is still another. In each and every one of these examples from business, this change in procedure is translating the previous businessman's approach of "what *I* would do" into "on the basis of this particular mathematical analysis of the problem, I think such and such a decision is now called for."

Making this fifth element of the problem-solving attitude a part of one's approach to solving public relations problems is no guarantee that the "scientifically derived end" of the problem-solving continuum will be reached, but it is only when it is applied that we have any hope of becoming more precise and rigorous in our problem-solving efforts.

F. A Problem Can Be Confused with a Symptom and Vice Versa

The last point that we must make with respect to adopting a problem-solving attitude is the warning that any one of us is susceptible to confusing problems with symptoms. That is, we can identify something as our "problem" when, in fact, it may be nothing more than a symptom of another problem not yet identified by us. Let us return to our case concerning the friction between young airmen and certain teenagers in the local community. The "problem" that came to the attention of the base Information Officer (because his commanding officer had had this incident called to his attention quite forcibly) concerning the friction between the airmen and local youths could conceivably be a "symptom" of any number of other problems not immediately apparent. This outbreak could be a symptom of (1) inadequate parental supervision, (2) chronic mental illness on the part of a limited number of youths, (3) a breakdown in neighborhood structure and control, or (4) the narcotics addiction of a handful of young individuals. In other words, the behavior of the youths that came to the attention of the base Information Officer (i.e., the public relations practitioner) could conceivably be a symptom of any number of hidden "problems."

Naturally, this last point about the problem-solving attitude is closely related to some of the other points that we have made, particularly the notion that there is no one or obvious problem but a hierarchy of problems to be solved in any given public relations situation. However, confusing symptoms with problems is a distinguishable, additional dimension of the ideal problem-solving attitude that we are advocating for all public relations practitioners.

One last point. There is no ready "cookbook" answer or guide as to how one can distinguish symptoms from problems. This particular stumbling block in solving problems confronts any practitioner in any applied field. It is an obstacle in scientific work as well. The history of medicine, psychiatry, and clinical psychology is full of examples of both scientist and practitioner alike confusing symptoms with problems. Fortunately, however, in spite of the fact that there is no easy guidebook available so that one can readily tell one from the other, there is evidence that *being aware of this pitfall* is enough to help the problem solver avoid this stumbling block more often than he might otherwise.

III.   THE THIRD POINT: THE PUBLIC RELATIONS PROCESS WITH ADDITIONAL REFINEMENTS

With a clear understanding of his own ethical position and equipped to approach his problem with the proper problem-solving attitude, the public relations practitioner is ready to turn to the particular problem situation at hand. This places him at Step 1 in the public relations process as depicted in Chapter 5, Figure 11, page 96. At that time, the public relations process was described in broad steps. In practice, however, there are also many smaller steps, and we are now ready to turn our attention to those between Step 1 and Step 2—that is, between "Analysis of problem situation" and "Development of public relations program."

Step 1a—Translation of Public Relations Problem into Communication Model

Part of the analysis of a public relations problem consists of translating the problem situation into the communication model developed in Chapters 4 and 5. Let us return to the case presented earlier involving the "crooked" auto dealers (page 131) to illustrate this process. For the sake of illustration, let us assume that the public relations practitioner concerned comes to the conclusion that one remedy for his "problem" is to bring this overcharging by some dealers to the attention of the local automobile dealers' association. One assumption behind this action is that if they become aware of and involved in the problem, they will either come up with an approach to controlling the undesirable behavior or will at least help the public relations practitioner arrive at a solution. In other words, the public relations practitioner has concluded that his "real problem" lies with the association. If he successfully involves them, then the issue that brought the whole matter to light in the first place will automatically take care of itself.[8]

---

[8] The reader is reminded at this point that, in the light of the six elements discussed concerning the problem-solving attitude, this is certainly not the only way this case can be interpreted. Even if one grants this particular interpretation, it

In the preceding paragraph we definitely identified two of the four stages of the communications process: the sender stage and the recipient stage. The sender is, in this instance, the public relations practitioner (representing, of course, the Air Force), and the recipient is now the automobile dealers' association (or, to be more specific, probably the executive secretary or the president of the association). The *media* stage is tentatively identified, at least at this stage of the analysis, as being personal communication originating with the public relations practitioner. That is, the public relations practitioner will probably visit the representatives of the automobile dealers' association personally. The *message* stage cannot be spelled out at this time, because further analysis is required of the public relations practitioner before he can be certain of what he wants to say and what approach he will use with the association representatives.[9, 10]

Step 1b—More Detailed Examination of Recipient

After the problem has been translated into the communication model in general terms, the sender must then make as detailed an analysis of the recipient as is possible, consistent with practical considerations. The reasons are simple: It is the recipient with whom the

---

does not mean that there may not be other steps that the public relations practitioner will take *simultaneously*. For example, with the cooperation of the legal unit on the base, he may institute for the airmen a lecture or two on what to watch for when making a substantial purchase such as a car or a home.

[9] The process of translating a public relations problem into a communication model implies, for the sake of expected gains in analysis, that any portion of a public relations problem which is dynamic and ever changing can be isolated and made static. It is similar to the chemist who assumes that he can translate a dynamic chemical process into a static, three dimensional model to aid him in his analysis efforts. He realizes all the time that this is a convenient fiction that enables him to solve his problems more effectively. So it is with our public relations problem. We are engaging in a convenient fiction of taking a particular slice of the total problem—one that we have deemed more important than a number of other slices that we might have taken—and translating it into our model for analysis purposes. The assumption is that we will be able to understand the problem situation more adequately after we have gone through this somewhat fictional procedure. One other point should be made. Because we are dealing with "time slices," this means that who (or whom) becomes the sender, or recipient, and what messages via what media are transmitted will vary from time slice to time slice.

[10] One other feature of the translation of the crooked auto dealer case into our communication model is that the first stage to be considered is the recipient stage. You must work backward by first identifying the recipient; after this has been done, the proper messages and the appropriate means of transmitting them can be determined.

sender is interested in communicating; and it is the recipient whom the sender wishes to persuade or change in some manner, either in his covert attitudes or his overt behavior, or in both.

As a part of *Step 1b* in the problem-solving approach, the public relations practitioner *as sender* must understand the recipient and must be able to predict how his own (the *sender's*) behavior is likely to be interpreted. In terms of the crooked automobile dealer case, this means that the public relations practitioner must have some understanding of how the representatives of the automobile dealers' association are (1) going to interpret the actions of the few dealers that are the concern of the public relations practitioner; (2) interpret the actions of the public relations practitioner himself; (3) interpret their responsibilities, if any, in this particular situation, and so on. The success of this particular phase of the public relations practitioner's efforts depends on his ability to anticipate how his actions appear to the recipient.

In addition to knowing how his recipients regard him and his actions, the public relations practitioner as sender must have a working knowledge of and an understanding of the principles of behavior. This is why the entire next chapter is devoted to highlighting *motivation, learning, and perception.* Our treatment is necessarily abbreviated; whole books have been written on each topic alone, to say nothing of all three combined. However, what is presented in Chapter 7 is a selective synthesis of this social and behavioral science material, designed to equip the public relations practitioner with the minimum number of the psychological concepts that he needs in order to better understand the recipient.

QUESTIONS FOR DISCUSSION

1. Take any one of the cases that you used to answer a discussion question associated with an earlier chapter and, assuming the role of *sender*, spell out some of the assumptions or interpretations of "right" and "wrong" that the public relations practitioner must have (or should have) made. To highlight the fact that what is "right" or "wrong" is a function of your point of view, try to contrast the recipients' probable interpretations of your assumptions.
2. Again using the case that you used to answer question No. 1, illustrate the generalization that there is no one "obvious" problem in a public relations problem-solving situation by developing at least two or three different "problems" involved in the case. If you have

trouble developing several, discuss the case with a fellow student; he should be able to point out "problems" that you are unable to see.

3. Demonstrate the generalization made in this chapter to the effect that it is easy to confuse symptoms with problems by taking any two cases that you have used for previous questions and abstracting the problems in them. After you have abstracted the problems, show how these problems could possibly be *symptoms of other problems*. Be sure that you spell out this revised symptom and new problem relationship in enough detail to be able to defend your interpretations.

4. Take still another case that you have used to answer a previous discussion question and use it to practice the process of translating a case into our communication model. Be sure you identify the sender and recipient(s) explicitly. To fill out the message and media stages, take one particular time-slice of a hypothetical public relations practitioner's activities.

Chapter 7

THE SENDER STAGE IN FURTHER DETAIL: MOTIVATION, LEARNING, AND PERCEPTION

INTRODUCTION

Chapter 6 ended on the note that if we are going to solve successfully our public relations problems, we must know and understand the recipient as fully as possible. To be able to do this, we need reasonable, detailed *psychological knowledge* of the recipient. This means that we need to know the basic principles of behavior obtainable from a study of three main topics—motivation, learning, and perception. (In later chapters, we will explore the *sociological knowledge* that will add even more to our ability to know and understand the recipient.)

MOTIVATION—SOME GENERAL PRINCIPLES

All Behavior Is Caused

As a starting point, it must be remembered that all psychologists make the very simple yet fundamental assumption that all behavior is caused. The behavior of an individual at work, at play, anywhere, anytime, is caused. Another statement that psychologists usually make in connection with motivation is that *all* behavior has "multiple causation." That is, it is highly unlikely that any behavior we observe in others or in ourselves is caused by a single factor. In all likelihood, it is caused by a multiplicity of factors. This sounds like a simple enough beginning—only two terms introduced: *cause* and *multiplicity of cause*.

It is because of the apparent "simplicity" of what was said in the above paragraph that we can be unaware of the fact that these two simple concepts render obsolete the approach that many individuals use when attempting to understand the motives of others. How many of us can think of times when we regarded the behavior of another in such a way that we were either implicitly or explicitly denying that his behavior had a cause—or, more accurately, causes? If we pay a little closer attention to our conversations, every once in a while we will hear ourselves say, "He flew off the handle for no reason at all." How many times we all have been guilty of summing up a situation with a statement such as, "The whole trouble with him is that he is just plain selfish"? The temptation is great to forget that behavior has causes at all or, conversely, to lump complicated behavior into a single explanatory system. So as not to overstate the point, we would readily grant that for "convenience" (another word for not knowing the whole story) we often talk and behave as if the behavior of another is due to only one cause, even when we know that such is not the case. However, the point being made here is that all too often we find ourselves taking advantage of convenience and falling into the error of thinking about causation in the singular rather than the plural.

The Question "Why?"

Making the assumption that all behavior is caused brings with it the almost immediate question, "Why?" Why did Johnnie strike his playmate? Why did Bob's boss fire him in a fit of anger? Why did a company with apparently good employee relations wind up with a strike on its hands? Asking the question "Why?" is essentially what psychology attempts to answer under the heading of motivation. Examination of the literature that normally is included under this heading reveals that a staggering amount of effort has gone into attempts to more adequately answer the why's behind human behavior. The major portion of this literature on motivation is much too detailed and complex for our purposes. A distillation of the literature, however, permits us to come up with some important generalizations that we should consider.

A Brief History of Motivation

Attempts to understand what makes man behave as he does are as old as the history of man himself. The earlier approaches tended to be all-inclusive: The theories put forth tried to account for all of man's behavior with only one or two principles. All of the early theorizing attempted to explain far too wide a spectrum of man's behavior. The vexing part about these theories was not so much that they proved worthless but rather that they all tended to contain a kernel of truth which made them irresistible for prolonged periods of time.

Hedonism. An excellent example of this type of theorizing is the so-called hedonistic theory. In brief, this approach sums up the motives of man by assuming that he tends to seek things that are pleasant or pleasing and avoids experiences which are unpleasant or painful. Armed with this twofold theory are writers attempting to explain all sorts of behavior. After all, anyone can think of many situations in which people seem to be guided by such a "pleasure principle."

As soon as this notion was put to experimental test or applied to a concrete problem situation, its inadequacies soon came to light. For example, the most troublesome observation about many people's behavior is that they seemed to function just opposite to the theory, at least on the surface. They seemed to seek constantly things or situations that brought them unhappiness or pain. Witness the gentleman who seems always to be stuck with the wrong kind of mate. He complains of being "henpecked." He wails, "Why is it that I am always getting the bad breaks when it comes to selecting wives?" Oftentimes this very same individual, after divorce and then remarriage, just "happens" to wind up with a second wife who is every bit as domineering as the first. In such cases, you find yourself coming to the conclusion that our mythical friend was in a real sense seeking out just such a mate. He would be terrified of one who would expect him to stand on his own two feet. Because of observations like this one, it became apparent that any such simple approach as hedonism was doomed to failure. It was not really very helpful in understanding behavior at all.

The hedonistic theory was neither the first nor the last attempt to account for the "why" of behavior in such an economical fashion. The history of psychology is filled with such efforts. Heredity *vs.* environment can legitimately be considered as another example. Under this system, behavior was thought to be due to either inborn factors (the hereditary side of the picture) or the influences of the world in which the individual lived (the environment). At other places in the literature, this same distinction is known as "nature" *vs.* "nurture" and "innate *vs.* acquired." Proponents of either one approach or the other expanded upon one portion of the dichotomy and attempted to attribute all human behavior to either inborn factors or environmental factors.

The instinct doctrine and the concept of habit. Two of the most widely known outgrowths of the dichotomy described above are the "instinct" doctrine and the "habit" doctrine. The instinct approach stressed the inborn factors in a person's make-up and, of course, fitted in on the hereditary side of the hereditary-environment argument. The habit doctrine accounted for an individual's behavior repertoire through the process of learning and therefore fitted into the environment side. The concepts of instinct and habit are recent enough developments in psychology to be heard commonly in everyday parlance even though they are no longer used in scientific psychology. If we follow the rise and fall of these two concepts, we should have a reasonably good grasp of some of the changes that have taken place in motivation theory within the past fifty years. In addition, we will have a foundation upon which to base present-day theorizing with respect to motivation.

The instinct doctrine. Around the turn of the century, the instinct doctrine had its heyday, which extended into the early 1930's. Just about any behavior that needed explaining was accounted for by an instinct. Thus we had the instinct of preservation, the instinct of gregariousness, and the like. In some textboks thirty to forty different instincts are presented to "explain" the motives behind behavior.

In the 1920's began a series of events that eventually led to the rejection of the instinct doctrine. First of all, the circularity of the doctrine invited and justified attack. Answering the question "why does a chicken peck?" with "it has a pecking instinct" does not produce a very satisfactory explanation. Secondly, when put to more rigorous test it became apparent that the instinct doctrine was a descriptive rather than an explanatory one. That is, lists of instincts (such as the one about pecking) merely highlighted the potential behavior of an organism. The real death blow to the approach came, however, from careful experimental work dealing with the very types of behavior the doctrine of instincts was supposed to "explain."

An excellent illustration of the inroads made by experimentation is afforded by the work done with the migration of wildlife.[1] Accounting

---

[1] *See,* for example, research work conducted by L. Roule as reported in "Migration and the 'Instinct' Problem," in L. W. Crafts, T. C. Schneirla, E. E. Robinson, and R. W. Gilbert, *Recent Experiments in Psychology* (1st ed.; New York and London: McGraw-Hill Book Company, 1938), chap. 2.

for the migration of fish, for example, was a stronghold of the instinct doctrine: The salmon went to the sea from mountain streams "because of instinct." More careful observation showed that at approximately one year of age changes occur in the pigmentation of the skin of salmon, and they become much more sensitive to sunlight. In shallow streams, however, it is not long before there is nowhere that the salmon can go to escape the sun. As a result, they need to seek out deeper water. One effect of their heightened sensitivity to the sun is that the fish actually become somewhat anesthetized, and careful observations revealed that many salmon were floating downstream toward the ocean tail first! They were not actually "seeking" the ocean, as the instinct doctrine would lead one to believe.

A tremendous amount of work ensued in attempting to understand the phenomena that the instinct doctrine supposedly explained. Studies were done on all sorts of animals, but, of course, the white rat was (and still is) one of the most popular experimental animals. More and more work was done to try to isolate the sorts of behaviors that were unlearned: that is, behavior which occurred on the part of the animal without any previous learning experience. This was a way of putting the instinct doctrine to a test, for in a vague way the instinct doctrine implied that a great deal of the causes of behavior were inborn and therefore did not have to be learned.

As research work went on, there was less and less that could be called unlearned behavior than was at first suspected. Of course, certain patterns of behavior, such as response to sexual stimulation and the effect of deprivation of certain basics such as food and water, did not need to be learned. In time, a list of behaviors which were instinctual or inborn (or true of all human beings and animals) began to emerge from the experimentation. Hence, the final outcome of what started with the instinct doctrine was a specification of factors which were considered to be universal and inborn in everyone. Shortly, we will see how these inborn factors are considered in contemporary thinking about motivation, but, before doing this, we must consider briefly what happened to the other half of the story, so to speak—the notion of habit.

The habit doctrine. The concept of habit as an aid to explaining behavior is, of course, logically related to the environment side of the heredity-environment dichotomy. The proponents of environment were fond of saying that the most important determinants of behavior did not emerge until after birth. From birth onward, the influences of the environment took on increasing importance. The term *habit* became one of the most popular terms to more or less embrace the effects of environment. Thus, for a time it became a way of accounting for a lot of behavior. "Why does one smoke? Because he has a smoking habit." Why does one stutter? Because he has a stuttering habit." And so on, ad infinitum.

The similarity between habit and instinct can be seen almost immediately. The habit doctrine proved to be circular in precisely the same way as that of instinct. It, too, was essentially a descriptive category rather than an explanatory one. Then habit as an explanatory concept fell into disfavor and was eventually dropped in the face of experimentation in precisely the same manner as the instinct doctrine. Thus, in spite of the fact that these two doctrines are at opposite poles so far as explaining behavior is concerned, they both went through essentially the same stages to rejection.

The outcome of experimental work in connection with the instinct doctrine resulted in less and less that could legitimately be considered inborn. In striking contrast to this, experimental work in conjunction with the concept of habit resulted in more and more that could be considered as being influenced by the environment or, more properly, considered as being acquired *after* birth rather than being inborn. Today we realize that a major proportion of human behavior and the causes which lie behind it are acquired and are the result of growing up in a particular cultural environment.

Terminology of Needs or Drives

The behavior that the two concepts, instinct and habit, presumably explained are today accounted for by the *concept of need* by most psychologists.[2] Needs are thought to be the pushes and pulls that motivate us. What was discussed earlier under the heading of instinct has now come to be regarded as the *primary needs*. The conventional primary needs are those that have specific physiological bases—*e.g.*, hunger, thirst, need for air, avoidance of pain.

What was treated earlier under habit has now come to be regarded as *secondary needs*. The secondary needs are needs (*i.e.*, motivations) which have a social basis in contrast to the physiologically based primary ones; that is, we acquire them in a cultural context. Which ones we have and how strongly they motivate us are a function of the particular culture into which we are born. Some of the secondary needs are the need for power, for security, and for social approval. The

---

[2] Terms such as *drives, urges,* and the like generally have essentially the same meaning as *needs* and can be considered synonyms for needs.

enumeration of secondary needs is made difficult by a number of factors. First of all, because they are the product of the environment in which we live, a particular list of secondary needs may hold true for one subculture but not apply very well to another. And if we move from one *culture* to another, the difference is even more apparent. Comparing an American to a Hindu in terms of primary needs is one thing—both Americans and Hindus become hungry in much the same fashion and according to the same rules—but comparing an American to a Hindu with respect to the need for power is another matter. In American culture, power may play an important role; among the Hindus, it may play a much less important role.

Secondary needs more important.   In spite of the fact that the secondary needs are much more difficult to specify, this part of motivation analysis tends to be more important for applied use in public relations problem situations. Although all behavior is a function of both primary and secondary needs, in general it is much more practical to think of the secondary needs when facing an applied problem. Most of the primary needs are somehow met for all of us, though many persons do not derive adequate satisfaction from them. But their connection to everyday behavior is usually too complex for an individual to handle well in the applied situation. For example, just what primary needs are related, and how they are related, to a person's extreme motivation for power or money is apt to be beyond the province of the applied practitioner.

Although secondary drives tend to receive greater consideration in the applied situation, this does not mean that primary drives are unimportant. Both types demand attention and understanding.

For example, following World War II, Americans were very desirous of Germany's becoming a democratic nation. To attain this end, one of the efforts of the occupation officials was that of helping the Germans set up a representative form of government. Although our goals were commendable, we overlooked the fact that the motivation we were attempting to bring about within the German people was very definitely a secondary need type of motivation. For a long time, our efforts appeared to be getting nowhere simply because the Germans were preoccupied with satisfying much more basic needs. They were concerned with where their next meal was coming from. Regardless of how worthwhile we regard a democratic form of government, it was very difficult for the Germans to become motivated in that direction when much more basic needs were not being met—namely, their need for food.

MOTIVATION—A FIRST SUMMARY

a) Attempts to answer the why of man's behavior have taken us from single, all-embracing principles to a reasonably well-established order of primary and secondary needs or drives that we employ today to account for behavior.

b) The primary needs are made up of a list of what might be considered "tissue" needs—that is, they result from the demands of our tissues. Thus, the need for food, water, air, and the like are among the primary needs. They are relatively few in number, universal among men, and have, of course, a physiological basis for their existence. Lastly, they are inborn, and although the *means* of satisfying them vary from culture to culture, they all must be satisfied for an organism to continue to exist.

c) The secondary needs include all those factors in man's behavior which we regard as having been learned. Thus, such things as the need for power, the need to relate ourselves in some way with other people, and the need for approval are called secondary needs. The secondary needs are sometimes thought of as "social needs" in the sense that it is the culture in which a person grows up that determines the kind and number of these social needs within him. Several other important summary statements need to be made about the secondary or social needs:

(1) Secondary needs are greater in number than the primary needs.

(2) The types and number of needs regarded as secondary are much more difficult to determine because they vary so much from one subgroup to another.

(3) The secondary needs are not so universally evident as the primary needs. All men have a need for water; not all of them need social approval in the same sense.

(4) Though they are not so urgent or universal, we *must not* make the incorrect assumption that secondary needs are less important than primary needs. Human behavior can be just as severely altered by lack of satisfaction of a need for social approval as by a lack of food.

d) The proper way to visualize the relationship between primary and secondary needs is as follows: Primary Needs × Secondary Needs = Behavior. That is, behavior is the *product* of the two major systems of needs interacting. It is more complex than just the *total* of primary needs plus secondary needs.

The material on motivation that has been presented thus far is summarized in Figure 15 (page 151). It will prove useful for the reader to review the material in this figure before going on to further generalizations concerning motivation.

MOTIVATION—SOME ADDITIONAL PRINCIPLES

The fact that much scientific research work needs to be done in the future in order to complete the psychologists' knowledge of what factors motivate each one of us does not prevent us from developing further principles as a guide to a better understanding of human behavior now. Although we cannot now give a final listing of needs and their interrelatedness, we can make a series of generalizations that are useful to public relations practitioners in their daily work.

The Variability of Needs

From our previous discussion of needs, it is easy to see that a given need is not as strong a determinant of behavior at one moment as it is at another. There is very definitely a continual ranking that exists, although the particular make-up of the ranking may change from moment to moment, day to day, or year to year. Thus, the need for success may be a very important determinant of an individual's behavior at one time and not very important at another.

This generalization is useful to bear in mind because most people tend to "sum up" somebody else rather quickly. Part of this summing up involves making assumptions about his motivations. We have to do this sort of thing, if for no other reason than that our time is too limited to be overly analytical about everyone we meet. On the other hand, our summaries of others have a way of becoming rigid. We behave as if the other fellow has a fixed hierarchy of motives. We need to remember that a degree of flexibility is needed which allows for the fact that at different times different needs may be operating to motivate an individual, and this change of importance of one need in relation to another will moderately or radically change his behavior.

This caution against rigidity in our thinking about need structure should not be applied only to individuals. We tend to react to groups in the same way. Thus, the public relations practitioner often sums up

Early formulations concerning motivation, or attempts to understand behavior, were generally single, simple statements or generalizations overextended to account for all behavior.

↓

Hedonism, or the notion that all behavior can be explained as merely the seeking of things which are pleasurable and avoiding all things that are painful is a good example of the single principle overextended.

↓

As attractive as hedonism was at first blush in explaining behavior, it did not go too well when subjected to test. Historically we can see that another phase in understanding motivation emerged in the form of dichotomies—between that which was invariant or universal among all men and that which was variant and found in men in differing degrees.

↓

Nature vs. nurture, innate vs. acquired were two of the better known descriptions for this dichotomy between heredity and the environment.

↓

The concept of instinct became one of the most popular "forms" of the hereditary or inborn side of the dichotomy. "Habit" became the term that embodied the effects of the environment upon man.

↓

When put to the test of experimentation both instinct and habit fell short of their objective as explanatory concepts.

↓

Out of this grew the present day accepted dichotomy of primary and secondary needs. They are assumed to account for all behavior when utilized together:
Primary Needs × Secondary Needs = Behavior

↓

The interrelationship between primary and secondary needs is still very imperfectly understood. However, several useful generalizations concerning motivation can be made and must be taken into consideration by the applied individual when dealing with people. Emphasis in the applied fields is on the secondary needs. Primary needs are still assumed to be of importance, but it is the secondary needs that can be manipulated more successfully by the applied individual.

The earliest efforts to account for motivation tended to be single "principles" that account for all behavior (e.g., Hedonism).

↓

This gave way to:
Popular dichotomies which were used to account for behavior.

↓

This gave way to:
The most widely discussed dichotomy of all: heredity vs. environment.

↓

This gave way to:
The most popular version of the heredity vs. environment dichotomy: instinct vs. habit.

↓

This gave way to:

Instinct	Habit
being	being
rejected	rejected

↓

This gave way to:

↓

Needs or drives distinguished in terms of:

Primary	Secondary
needs	needs

This gave way to:

↓

Emphasis on secondary needs—especially for applied social scientists.

---

* This review should be read by columns as the arrows indicate. However, the cross reference between columns will become apparent immediately to the reader.

Figure 15

A 60-second review of the history of attempts to explain man's motives.*

a particular public in terms of an assumed motivational hierarchy or structure. How often do we find ourselves slipping into complacency, convinced that we know what makes our employee public, stockholder public, or supplier public tick? How often do we assume we know what these particular groups want—the group action, of course, made up of a complex of individual motivations? Some very dramatic proxy fights involving the "unexpected" behavior of stockholders have resulted in part from the assumption that a relatively fixed hierarchy of motives was determining the action of the stockholders.

Cyclic Nature of Needs

Research on the effect of primary needs on behavior has highlighted, among other things, that *primary needs operate in cycles*. Thus, for example, the need for food in a dog can be seen to follow a pattern. Immediately after eating, the animal shows no interest in food whatsoever. After a couple of hours, food may be eaten if presented but it is not generally sought after. After five or six hours, concern for food increases until, after about eight hours, the animal is quite hungry and will eat immediately upon being presented with the food. The cycle then runs from satiation to satiation with gradually increasing need for food between satiation periods. The other primary drives also tend to show this cyclic nature but, of course, with different patterns. The cycle for the need for air is much more frequent than for water; for water, more frequent than for food; and so on.

It has often been assumed that the secondary needs operate in the same fashion—*i.e.*, being cyclic in nature. Actually, this way of thinking, which appears to fit the facts so well in the case of primary needs, does not seem applicable to secondary needs. For one thing, achieving a particular goal, which serves to satisfy a primary need, does not appear to operate in the same fashion for secondary needs. Thus, a man who is hungry gains a very definite satisfaction of that need when he eats; the relationship between the need and the act of eating food is a very direct one. In the case of a secondary need, the situation is more complex. For an individual who has a need for approval, receiving a commendation from his boss or a friend relates to his need, to be sure, but hardly in the same way that a good steak relates to a man's hunger need. As a consequence, we must be very careful in our thinking about secondary need satisfaction. Perhaps many of our so-called social needs do not have satiation peaks between which the satisfaction of the need can be ignored. Perhaps many of our secondary needs require almost continual satisfaction as though they operate, not in a cyclic fashion, but rather in a straight line.

The implications of this difference in need-satisfaction cycles for public relations are provocative. What we have been saying translates something like this: Making an employee aware of his worth to an organization (that is, satisfying his need for approval) may be something that needs to be continually in evidence—not something done on infrequent occasions with ceremony at five-, ten-, or twenty-five-year dinner awards. Frequent, positive evidences of approval extended to the employee in little ways throughout the work week may have much greater impact than infrequent but more elaborate and pronounced attempts to convey the same impression. The latter approach works on the assumption that secondary needs are noncyclic in nature and operate continually, hence need continual satisfaction. The former approach makes the cyclic-need assumption, which probably does not fit the situation very well.

Another factor should be raised in connection with the distinction in function between primary and secondary needs being made here— the *objects* of need satisfaction. The things that serve to satisfy the primary needs are generally fewer in number than those satisfying the secondary needs. Taking our need for food as an example once again, there is, comparatively speaking, a fairly narrow range of foods that will be acceptable to an individual to satisfy his hunger need. In the United States, for example, we prefer steaks and roasts, while many other cuts of beef, such as brains and sweetbread, will not be so readily accepted. Such things as toasted ants, snake steaks, and the like just will not do at all. Hence the statement that objects that will fulfill the need for food are comparatively few.

Such does not appear to be the case with many secondary needs. The need for self-expression (or self-actualization, as it has sometimes been called) within an individual can potentially be satisfied with a tremendous range of occurrences. Thus, any number of ways of achieving self-expression can satisfy this need, and all may operate equally well.

The applied aspects of this statement are worth keeping in mind. It suggests that we should be alert to the possibility of new ways of permitting self-expression of those persons under our control. Perhaps we have become rather fixed in the ways in which we permit them to express new ideas to us. Worse still, perhaps we have become rather fixed in our own mind as to *what* ideas we should permit to come to the fore. Thus, we may be too quick to stifle the expression of an idea with

"That won't work," or "We tried that before," or some such phrase! The *manner* in which we permit new freedom of expression is unimportant. The generalization which appears to be warranted here is that secondary needs apparently have a much wider range of events that will serve to satisfy them, and we must be vigilant in order to be sure that our behavior with others is permitting this expression.

Conflict Among Needs

We have observed thus far that (1) needs exist in a hierarchy; (2) needs are of different types, broadly divided into primary and secondary ones; (3) some needs are cyclic from the standpoint of satisfaction; and (4) some needs may continually need satisfaction. All this points to still another very important generalization concerning motivation: *Conflict among needs is inevitable.* As a matter of fact, one way of looking at personality development and optimum adjustment at maturity is to say that it hinges on the ability of the individual to learn to handle conflict so that he can live with it rather than be overwhelmed by it.

At one time, Freud had speculated that the fundamental cause of neurosis was due to the frustration an individual experienced in the satisfaction of his needs. For a while, this idea was interpreted by many clinical psychologists and psychiatrists that the proper way to rear a child was to see to it that he was not frustrated. One means of doing this was to permit the child to do anything he wanted to do, thus avoiding conflict in need satisfaction. Later Freud changed his thinking about the causes of neurosis. Unfortunately, however, many other therapists persisted for some time in advocating free expression on the part of the child. We still encounter traces of this thinking today, but it appears that a more fruitful approach begins with the realization that conflict among various needs is inevitable. Hence, what is needed in the early years of development of an individual is *not* removal of all conflict (which isn't possible anyway), but rather an environment in which conflict and frustration of need satisfaction are encountered *on a small scale* or *in easy stages*. It appears reasonable to conclude that childhood practice in coping with conflict or frustration of need satisfaction makes for more stable functioning in adulthood. Of course, this is only a tentative conclusion; we do not know for sure that this is the best way to rear a child. However we may theorize about the best way of rearing children or learning to cope with conflict among needs, one fact is certain: Conflict among needs and their consequent satisfaction or lack of satisfaction serves as a powerful factor in personality development in every one of us. A great deal of personality development hinges on just how we learn to cope with need conflict or frustration.

THE GOAL OF SATISFACTION

The statement that need-satisfaction conflict is inevitable need not cause us to despair. By the very nature of the motivational structure in people, conflict will result. In everyday behavior, however, there are many, many times in the lives of every one of us that the gratification that stems from need satisfaction far outweighs any conflicts that may exist. At such times, we are very happy human beings.

The more important question hinges mainly on establishing a *favorable ratio*, so to speak, between need satisfaction and dissatisfaction. The more the ratio leans toward satisfaction, the better. Translated into public relations application, this means that, in dealing with other individuals, effort should be exerted toward *facilitating* the existence of a favorable ratio. Many times we can bring attainment of more need satisfaction than dissatisfaction in other people with surprisingly little effort if we bring to bear some of the reasoning discussed above.

The first step—analysis. The first step toward establishing a favorable ratio of satisfaction should be analysis. We should ask ourselves what different and possibly conflicting needs are in existence. Let us consider an actual event, witnessed by the author, that illustrates the importance of making an analysis of the needs of others. During the business meeting of a local chapter of a professional organization, a Chamber of Commerce representative appeared with the objective of persuading these professional men to join the chamber. His whole approach was built on the theme that membership was reasonable and cost only a few dollars a year. The benefits to be gained through membership were mentioned only briefly. His appeal fell flat. The professional men actually responded rather negatively to his request and consequently did not join.

Although the representative of the Chamber of Commerce had undoubtedly given some thought to the type of approach he would make, he apparently had not speculated as to what contrary motivations might already exist within these people to stand in the way of their becoming members. Had he made a careful analysis (including some fact finding about the profession itself), he might well have anticipated a very powerful contrary motive. This motive was that the members of this profession wanted to be considered true professionals in the same light as are physicians and dentists; therefore, they were preoccupied with the concern lest they do anything unbecoming a

professional man. The doubt they had in their minds was simple: Was
it proper for a professional man to join the Chamber of Commerce,
or did it make him appear too commercial? Had he anticipated this
contrary motive (and a short talk with a few representatives of this
profession would have quickly imparted this concern of theirs to him),
unquestionably he could have brought in arguments that would have
helped to counteract this contrary motive. A passing mention of the
number of physicians and dentists who were members of the chamber
might well have been all that was necessary to dispel their concern,
but he had failed to analyze his audience in advance. Consequently,
he said nothing about an all-important question in the minds of his
audience: Were men who were members of the older, more respected
professions members of the Chamber of Commerce as well?

After the speaker left, the author, who had observed the whole
proceeding, took the trouble to ask the group about their reactions.
He discovered that to them the cost of membership was the least
important factor (as he predicted to himself while listening to the talk
by the Chamber of Commerce representative) and that the appropriateness of a professional man joining the Chamber of Commerce took
precedence over all other considerations. The low-cost approach had
been foredoomed. An analysis of the probable need structure of the
members of this profession could well have produced favorable
results.

The second step—facilitation. Once analysis has indicated the probable need structure of the individuals concerned, steps to facilitate
need satisfaction are called for. The most common pitfall to be avoided
is that of taking action which in and of itself is a contradiction in
motivational terms. An illustration of this point lies in relationships
with employees. For example, a company head complained that not
enough employees "have initiative these days." He said they tend to
hang back and work only when they are told. The type of employee
he would prefer, he said, is "the one who knows enough to go ahead
on his own." A closer examination of the work situation involving these
"lazy" people revealed that an inconsistent motivational structure had
been created by the very boss who was complaining. What workers
were rewarded for, in general, was doing what they were told. Taking
the initiative (when the boss didn't think *he* wanted it) resulted in being
criticized or punished. Hence, he really had motivated the workers
not to take the initiative, which is contrary to what he thought he
wanted. The "undesirable" employee behavior is understandable in
terms of conflicting motivational forces. For self-protection they had
resolved the conflict by engaging in behavior that avoided problems.

The problem of the employee who apparently "lacked initiative" was created as much by the boss as by any other influence. His unawareness of the conflicting motivations he had set up blocked the possibility of attaining a favorable ratio of need satisfaction for both the employee and himself.

The Results of the Conflict

In spite of all that we or others may do, it frequently happens that conflict occurs among the needs to be satisfied, and frustration results. The consequences of this state of affairs have caused therapists to generate what is now a classical portion of the theory about personality structure. Traditionally, it has been common to think of the behavior of an individual as directed toward integration, that a person tries to maintain personality organization in times of stress and that occasionally this personality organization is maintained by invoking certain "defense mechanisms." In the face of adversity, brought about primarily by need conflict and the frustration that ensues, the individual resorts to techniques which protect him from the possible pain that results when needs are not satisfied.

Because the defense mechanisms, as they are called, happen to be one of the most widely known interpretations or explanations of behavior, it is desirable to elaborate briefly upon a few of them.[3]

Rationalization. One of the most common defense mechanisms is rationalization. This is the process whereby an individual justifies or excuses his behavior in the face of disappointment. Thus, if you don't obtain the promotion you expected, you may tell everyone that you really didn't try for it; or you really did not want the job, and you would have turned it down if they offered it to you. The process of rationalization is, of course, not a new discovery of the contemporary psychologist. Aesop's fable concerning the fox and the grapes and the statement attributed to the fox that "the grapes were probably sour anyway" attests to an awareness of the process of rationalization by perceptive men centuries ago.

Projection. This term embraces the process whereby we attribute to other people the weaknesses or inadequacies which we ourselves have. Unable to admit to them and to accept them as our own to

---

[3] *See also,* for example, Anna Freud, *The Ego and the Mechanisms of Defense,* trans. Cecil Baines (2d printing; New York: International Universities Press, Inc., 1946).

cope with and correct, we "project" them onto someone else or some other group. Thus, frequently when an individual fails to attain some particular goal because of his own inadequacies, he blames someone else for his misfortune. Unlike rationalization, projection, in action, can have disastrous consequences for other people if the person or persons doing the projecting are in positions of power. This particular defense mechanism is commonly seen as related to prejudice of all kinds. It is very easy and convenient to project blame for your own inadequacies upon those against whom you are prejudiced.

Displacement.   On occasion, when a superior reprimands a subordinate, the latter is tempted to retaliate. This retaliation may be verbal or even with physical violence. However, very often he is afraid to do this and for many reasons refrains. He may be afraid of losing his job or afraid of precipitating further argument, or he may be dominated by the superior to such an extent that he cannot retaliate. Instead of dealing thusly with his boss, this man goes home and argues with his wife, spanks his children, or kicks his dog. In short, he displaces toward some other person or object the aggression appropriate for the person or object that provoked his anger in the first place. All of us have experienced the sight of an individual figuratively exploding over a small incident that ordinarily would not ruffle him. In many instances, this is the phenomenon of displacement in action.

Sublimation.   No one manages to achieve all the goals he has in life or satisfy all his needs, at least directly. However, we can at times find substitute need satisfaction. Thus an individual who desires children and never has any may obtain considerable substitute satisfaction by service work devoted to children; by teaching or finding other ways to bring him into intimate and satisfying contact with children. This process is commonly known as *sublimation.*

These defense mechanisms are only a few of the more common devices by which people insure personality integration. A few words ought to be added concerning the defense mechanisms in general. Whether a person behaves normally or abnormally is a matter of degree. The same perspective should be held concerning the defense mechanisms. All of us use all the defense mechanisms from time to time. Whether we use them to a pathological extent is a matter of frequency, how far out of touch with reality we are, how lacking we are in insight into the fact that we are using defense mechanisms.

Awareness of these processes contributes to our ability to understand the behavior of others more adequately, and that, as we have seen, is an important objective in public relations practice.

MOTIVATION—A SECOND SUMMARY

By now we have observed the following: (1) needs are variable; (2) needs are cyclic in nature with the probable exception of secondary needs; (3) conflict between and frustration of needs is inevitable to some extent; and (4) when conflict or frustration does occur with respect to need satisfaction, many possible results can take place to defend and maintain the psychological integrity of the individual. We have also examined some of the more common reactions to frustration.

A consideration of motivation is somewhat analogous to trying to find the sources of energy that cause an individual to behave as he does. However, accounting for the source of the "cause" of the energy is only part of the story. The directions that one takes in life in expending this energy are equally important. This is where the topic of learning comes in, because we have to *learn* how to satisfy our needs. Consequently, to understand human behavior we have to know something about how psychologists explain how we learn to behave as we do.

LEARNING

Any treatment dealing with human behavior necessarily must include the topic of learning. As a rule, when we think of another individual's behavior, we tend to interpret it in terms of some goal. Seldom do we describe someone's motives without supplying an objective to these motives as well. "He wants a better job"; "he is trying to forget an unpleasant experience"; "he is working for a higher degree"; and so on. It is almost impossible to speak of motivation without either implicitly or explicitly including the object or goal of the motivation. As a matter of fact, the fundamental dichotomy of motivation presented earlier is expressed in goal-oriented terms. Hence, we speak of a need *for* food, a need *for* success. Immediately upon identifying the need, we also supply the goal.

In spite of the fact that the goal is supplied, it is likely to be phrased in general terms. Thus, the need for food does not carry with it the identification of any particular food. Similarly, when speaking of secondary needs, the particular goal is not specified. There are a great many ways to achieve success or to satisfy one's need for acceptance. Thus, one important component of need satisfaction (hence motivation) is *learning*. Everyone has to learn what objects in his environment provide need satisfaction. For the primary needs, our very lives depend on it. In the case of secondary needs, successful adjustment and integration into our culture would not be possible unless we learned how to satisfy them. We take it entirely for granted; but when you stop to consider a typical adult in our culture, you realize that he has undergone a tremendous amount of learning about his need satisfaction with the net result that the objects of his motivations are the most subtle and complex imaginable.

Trial and Error: An Early Model for Learning

Around the turn of the century, Thorndike performed his now classical studies with the cat in the puzzle box, which led to some theorizing about learning that is still with us in modified form today.[4] Thorndike would place a hungry cat in a cage that contained a simple release mechanism. This release mechanism was activated when the cat touched it in any way. When placed in the cage for the first time, a cat would accidentally touch the mechanism and release itself. Thorndike would then put the cat back in the cage. During the earlier trials of the series, the cat's touching the release mechanism was entirely accidental and not at all "purposeful." The more times the cat was placed in the cage, the less varied its behavior became until, finally, the cat would touch the release mechanism almost immediately upon being placed in the cage and so gain its freedom and food. The cat *learned* how to free itself from the cage.

In watching the behavior of the cat, Thorndike made some observations which are important for us to consider. He noted that the initial behavior of the cat was exceedingly varied. The animal did all sorts of things to gain freedom. The behavior appeared to be "random" in the sense that almost anything was likely to happen. Another way of stating it—and this phraseology tended to stick—was to say that the animal *tried* a great many things. It underwent a lot of "trials" to solve the problem. Nearly all of these trials ended in failure—*i.e.*, release (and food) was not obtained. As the number of times that the animal was placed in the puzzle box increased, Thorndike noted, the random behavior tended to decrease. Gradually, the cat's behavior toward the release mechanism became more specific. There were fewer trials that met with failure prior to the one that met with success. Finally, the ran-

---

[4] E. L. Thorndike, *Animal Intelligence: Experimental Studies* (New York: The Macmillan Company, 1911).

dom behavior was reduced to almost zero, and only the behavior that was successful in obtaining release was followed.

The particular behavior that was learned and that obtained release for the cat was in no way different from hundreds of other behaviors exhibited by it during the "random" behavior period prior to learning. What was it that enabled this particular response to be learned and others to be excluded? Thorndike developed a principle having to do with the "effect" of the behavior and stated it in terms of reward and punishment (the Law of Effect).[5] With respect to the cat in the puzzle box, he postulated that all of the behaviors that *did not* obtain release (and subsequently food) were in effect punishing, and punishment tends to cause behavior *not* to occur. On the other hand, the one pattern of behavior that obtained freedom was rewarding (*i.e.*, it led to the food) and responses that lead to rewards tend to be maintained or learned by an organism. Thus, the combination of reward and punishment was a way of accounting for *how* the animal learned. This "model" of learning—trial and error coupled with reward and punishment, which argued that successful or rewarded trials were learned and unsuccessful ones were not—Thorndike felt, fit any type of learning situation and applied to any sort of organism. During the second decade of the twentieth century, this became a widely accepted theory of learning.

The Principle of Reinforcement

In time, Thorndike's position was modified to bring the principles of learning into a more intimate relationship with motivation. Hull was one of the best known psychologists to make this type of modification.[6] For one thing, Thorndike's formulation did not give any basis for being able to predict more carefully what behaviors would be considered rewarding and what behaviors would be considered punishing by the organism in question. In essence, Hull's position was that whenever an organism behaves, it is, by definition, motivated behavior. The motivational state at any time is the result of a combination of primary and secondary needs. Whenever any behavior tends to reduce or satisfy the needs that are operating at the time, this behavior is said to be *reinforced*. Behaviors that prove to be need-reducing are

---

[5] *Ibid.*, pp. 244-245.

[6] *See*, for example, Clark L. Hull, *Principles of Behavior* (New York: Appleton-Century-Crofts, 1943); or Clark L. Hull, *Essentials of Behavior* (New Haven, Conn.: Yale University Press, 1951).

reinforced and are more likely to be learned. Behaviors that are not re-inforcing—that is, which do not satisfy needs—are not learned.

This modification, so carefully spelled out by Hull with a great many other additions, enabled drives or needs to be related to learning—a most important step forward. One other very important change was offered by this reformulation and is of interest to us. This newer approach did not put learning solely in terms of success or failure, reward or punishment. This is very important because at times people do things or learn things that cannot easily be interpreted as rewarding.[7] Also, we know that people can learn when they are punished just as easily as when they are rewarded. (In all fairness to Thorndike, he did modify his thinking in order to account for the times when punishment enabled an organism to learn.) With the Hullian System, however, the ties between motivation and learning are much clearer, due to the direct linkage that was made between learning and the need structure of the individual. Lastly, the linkage is not dependent on someone's interpretation of what may be rewarding or punishing.

Motivation and Learning Brought Together

By way of summarizing, one of the most widely accepted formulations of learning that we described can be expressed in the following terms: The (1) *needs* or *drives* provide the "energy" within an organism that produces the (2) *behavior*, which has either need-reducing or non–need-reducing consequences, and leads to (3) *learning,* which is dependent on what served to be (4) *need reducing*. A four-part formula[8] may be used to put across these ideas. The formula is: $N \rightarrow B \rightarrow G \rightarrow DR$, where N equals the needs or drives which produce B, the behaviors exhibited by the organism, in order to reach G, the goal, which is related to the drive as, for example, food would be the goal of a hunger drive, while DR equals the need (or drive) reduction (which serves to reinforce behavior which successfully reduces the need in question).

Spelling out the relationship goes something like this. A particular combination of needs (N) tends to produce behavior (B) which, in general, is directed toward satisfaction of these needs. This behavior is

---

[7] A case in point is the masochist, one who seemingly derives great pleasure from being abused or hurt, often rather painfully.

[8] This formula was seen some years ago by the author, who subsequently made use of it, with minor modifications, in his work. Although every attempt has been made to identify the sources of the material, it has not been possible to trace its origin so that proper credit could be given.

directed toward some goal (G) which, if attained, permits some sort of consummatory response (in this case, eating) which provides drive reduction (DR). With this four-part formula, Thorndike's cat in the puzzle box would be explained as follows: For the hungry animal in a box, the need was, of course, hunger. The behavior evidenced in response to the hunger consisted of all of the exploratory activities in the box. In general, these activities were directed toward finding the food, which in this case is the goal (*i.e.*, after escape from the box). As food is repeatedly found, it permits a consummatory response of eating. This response tends to reinforce the behaviors which led to the food. Conversely, the behaviors that do not lead to food are extinguished or not learned and drop out of the behavior repertoire. Thus, in time, we say the animal has "learned" the puzzle—how to escape and obtain food. With one four-part formulation, we have brought together all we have said above about motivation *and* learning.

LEARNING—SOME FURTHER CONSIDERATIONS

When the topic of motivation was first discussed, the point was readily conceded that such a treatment did not do justice to all of the further problems and considerations due the topic of motivation. Also, we noted that there was still disagreement among psychologists as to the theorizing about motivation presented earlier. In spite of this, we went on to some generalizations concerning motivation which had definite applied value—*e.g.*, variability of needs, the results of conflict between needs, and so on. Precisely the same state of affairs exists for the topic of learning. What has been presented represents the barest outline of a very complicated topic. Here, too, there is disagreement among experts. But here, too, we can build on our brief presentation by considering series of generalizations which also have value for the public relations practitioner.

What Is Being Reinforced?—Conflict of Reinforcement

As mentioned earlier, it was thought at one time that learning was associated primarily with reward. This theory was modified to include the premise that learning also took place in conditions of punishment. (There were even arguments in the literature as to which was more important—punishment or reward—in terms of producing the most efficient learning.) This dichotomy gave way in turn to relating learning to motivation, so that now we speak of learning taking place when some particular need is reduced or reinforced. Thus, what used to be referred to in terms of punishment or reward is now handled with the single term *reinforcement*.

This brings up a very important applied feature of this way of thinking. The reinforcement principle highlights the importance of two questions: (1) Are we aware of just what behavior in others we are reinforcing? and (2) Is the behavior we are reinforcing the type of behavior we want? Let us take some illustrations that will serve to explain how these questions can be answered.

Very often executives stress to their subordinates or associates the need and importance of communication. They point out that it is important they be kept informed of what is going on. Thus, the behavior they would like for their subordinates to "learn" and frequently display is to communicate promptly. However, very often when a subordinate attempts to communicate a certain event or fact, they respond by saying, "Don't bother me with minor details," in a rather gruff manner that leaves no doubt in the mind of the subordinate that they are displeased or annoyed with his behavior. (The executive who behaves in this fashion is the very same executive who will complain again that he is "not being kept informed.")

When one does this, what sort of behavior is being reinforced—the tendency to communicate, or the tendency *not* to communicate? It is the tendency *not* to communicate because *not* communicating can become need reducing.[9] Going back to questions (1) and (2) above, it is very easy (1) to be unaware of precisely just what behavior we are reinforcing and (2) to *not* reinforce the behavior that we desire but, paradoxically, to reinforce the very behavior we do *not* desire.

To carry our example one step further, let us return to the illustration about a subordinate communicating with a superior; let us even concede that the information was minor and that the executive should not have been bothered with it. This points up the fact that what we may have is a problem within a problem. The additional learning that is required is to have the subordinates learn to *discriminate* effectively between what is relevant information and what is irrelevant information. (This next statement extends our example further than is needed at this time, but the approach here follows the same principles: You, as

---

[9] Although we did not go explicitly into this particular feature of reinforcement theory, it is important to point out that an organism can be motivated to *avoid* something just as well as it can be motivated to seek something. Thus, avoidance of pain or the absence of pain can serve to reduce needs, thereby enabling the organism to learn. In this way, we learn how to avoid experiences or situations that are *not* need reducing, just as we learn to seek out those that are.

the executive, *will have to learn how to reinforce the correct discrimination behavior* if it is to be learned.)

Let us take still another example to further demonstrate the importance of reinforcing the behavior we desire to elicit from others. Parents of teenagers continuously remark that they want to be "buddies" with their children, that they want their youngsters to confide in them and come to them with their problems rather than go to "strangers." Observing a parent-teenager relationship very often reveals the following typical pattern of events:

1. The teenager goes to a social affair.
2. Afterward, he (or she) may relate portions of what happened at the social event to his parents.
3. On hearing about what went on at the teenage affair, the parents embark on a series of comments of which the following are merely illustrative: "What will they think of next?" "How silly to do a thing like that." "In my day, youngsters didn't behave that way."
4. This is followed by decreasing amounts of "communication" from the teenager to his parents.

Whether or not the parent is justified or "right" in his observations is not important or relevant to this discussion. The fact of the matter is that the behavior of "telling Mommie and Daddy all" is *not* being reinforced. The exact *opposite* behavior is being reinforced—*not* telling their parents what they did. Many parents complain bitterly that their children are drifting away from them or not keeping them informed, without even being aware that, in spite of their good intentions, their behavior toward the children is reinforcing, hence producing, just exactly what they do not want to have happen.

Patterns of Behavior Accompanying Reinforcement

A second generalization of importance has to do with the so-called side effects which may accompany learning. No learning ever takes place in complete isolation. A parent teaching a child the alphabet or the multiplication tables may think that this is the only learning taking place at the time. However, along with the alphabet, the child may be learning something about how one person treats another and hence, indirectly, how to orient himself to the world and other people. If the parent uses threats to teach the alphabet, the child may be learning aggressiveness as a way of dealing with people at the very time the alphabet is being learned.

Thus, learning takes place in a context, and, rather than think of learning as being singular, we must remember that it is multiple. A lot of different learning can be going on at the same time in spite of the fact that we may be concentrating on one particular type of learning.

Along with multiple learning, we have generalization of learning, and the two operate simultaneously and very complexly. What we learn in one context may well spread (generalize) to other areas. An animal that is continually punished tends to crouch and cower before the individual who punishes him. Oftentimes, however, this submissive reaction extends to other individuals and even other animals, and we have an animal that is "afraid of his own shadow." The manner in which we react to a particular type of treatment received in one context can generalize, or spread, to another if there is similarity between the contexts.

This principle of learning is, of course, not restricted to animals. The illustration given above about a superior reinforcing incorrectly and thus causing a subordinate *not* to communicate can serve as an example. Not only may communication attempts tend to be inhibited, but spontaneity in other areas may be also affected. The employee may be less likely to "stick his neck out" (as he sees it) in any context which calls for his taking some initiative.

There are psychologists who have stressed the importance of the total context in which learning is taking place. Learning which takes place under positive conditions—*i.e.*, where *initiatory* behavior is reinforced, hence encouraged—produces positive side effects. The more desirable situation exists when someone is learning because he *wants* to learn, rather than because he is afraid of the consequences if he does not learn. The former is positive or outgoing; the latter tends to be negative and characterized by avoidance. The side effects accompanying avoidance behavior tend to be far more undesirable than those accompanying goal-seeking behavior.

Delay of Reinforcement

In the fourfold formulation of learning presented earlier, it was noted that on attainment of the goal (which is, of course, determined by the needs involved) need reduction takes place. It was also noted that when need reduction does take place, behavior that permits this need reduction to occur is reinforced by the reduction in need or, to put it another way, by this need satisfaction. Hence, the behavior was learned. Referring to our example of the hungry cat in the puzzle box, the series of behaviors which permitted attainment of freedom and food were reinforced and thereby learned.

This earlier presentation, however, neglected an important point which can now be handled. For a particular behavior to be reinforced and hence learned, the time between the execution of the behavior and the reinforcement attained by drive reduction must be reasonably short. Therefore, an animal trainer who is using hunger as the need to cause his animal to learn allows only a very short time to transpire between the occurrence of the desired behavior and the giving of food to the animal. If you are using food as the reinforcer in training a dog to sit up when a certain command is given, when the dog does sit up, this behavior must immediately be followed by the food; otherwise the animal does not learn. If the lapse of time is too great, the connection between the behavior and its function as a need reducer (*i.e.*, attaining food) is lost.

What is true with animals is equally true with human beings. When you attempt to train an individual under your jurisdiction, it is, in effect, the same situation as with the animal trainer and his pet above. The needs operating are different—in the human situation the secondary needs are much more important; however, the principle that the reinforcement should follow closely on the heels of the desired behavior is the same. Recognition, in the form of verbal commendation, greater responsibility offered, or whatever, must follow the behavior which you are trying to reinforce within a reasonably short period of time if the individual is to learn. If you delay your recognition too long, its value as a reinforcing agent is considerably reduced or possibly lost. Of course, this requires an alertness to everything that is going on around you; effecting change in others requires hard work and strict attention to the principles of learning that govern behavior.

LEARNING—A SUMMARY

Our development of basic principles has unfolded still more. By discussion and example we have briefly examined the topic of learning. Our short historical tracing—from trial and error to the principle of reinforcement—has enlarged our understanding of learning. Utilization of the principle of reinforcement as a means of theorizing about learning has permitted us to relate learning to motivation which is proper and necessary. We saw this interrelatedness between learning and motivation when we considered further generalizations under the topics of (1) conflict of reinforcement, (2) patterns of behavior accompanying reinforcement, and (3) delay of reinforcement.

We are now prepared to consider the last of the three major basic principles of behavior.

PERCEPTION—HOW WE ORGANIZE OUR WORLD[10]

Perception comes about by means of one of our physical senses or through a combination of two or several. It is the product of the senses, but it is more than that.

When we receive a stimulus through one of the senses, the effect is called a "sensation." Study of sensation leads to answers of some basic questions—for example, the limits of the range of light waves that the human eye can respond to or the range of sound vibrations that the human ear can accommodate.

Perception consists of the *organization* of these sensations into a total impression that is meaningful. Perception is the product, not only of sensation, but also of the memory of past experiences and of deep-lying motivations of which we may not even be conscious.

Perceptions Are Organized

Members of a group of people who are in the same place at the same time will notice the same thing in different ways or will notice different things. At a baseball game, most of the audience concentrates on the players—the crack of the bat engrosses them; they are absorbed in the fielder who waits for a high fly. But this is not all that is going on in the ball park. A woman spectator may perceive nothing but the cute hat three rows ahead, and a four-year-old junior is likely to have his attention riveted on the hot-dog merchant. There is nothing in the world "out there" that inherently commands universal interest and thus perception. Because most of the audience is reacting to the game itself, we look on this as the "natural" perception at a ball game, but the game itself does not completely govern. It can't entirely determine

---

[10] The material in this section was written previously and appeared as part of a chapter in a handbook devoted to public relations. It appears here in modified form. *See* Edward J. Robinson, "Applying Psychology," in Howard Stephenson (ed.), *Handbook of Public Relations* (New York: McGraw-Hill Book Company, 1960), pp. 143-151. Used by permission of McGraw-Hill Book Company.

what sensations plus memory plus motivation will be organized into perception by an individual spectator.

Figure and ground. A perception, regardless of which avenues of sensation are involved, is organized into figure and ground. "Figure" refers to that which stands out at the instant. In the ball game, the figure, to most spectators, is the fielder reaching for the high fly. Even the other players are "lost" for a split second. "Ground" refers to the remaining detail, the portion of the total perception that is not being given primary attention. What was the umpire doing at the tense moment when the fielder reached for the ball? Only vaguely can the spectator report on this. It fades out of focus with the crowd, the hot-dog man, the sights, sounds, and smells that together recede into the background, the ground.

What is the color of the draperies in your living room? What is the precise color of your sweetheart's eyes? How many stores, displaying what merchandise, are in the block you just drove by? We are limited in ability to perceive. The figure, the salient object of sight, sound, smell, taste, or touch, stands out against the fuzzy ground.

Perceptions Are Meaningful

As our senses combine with other factors to permit perception, this organized message has meaning. No matter how strange or bizarre the thing perceived, our grasp of it tends to be organized in such fashion as to make some kind of sense. To be sure, this meaning that one reads into his perception may be wrong. We shall come back to "correctness" of perception. But right or wrong, it tends to have meaning.

A woman telephoned police to report excitedly that a blind man was lost in the park opposite her home. She said it was pitiful to see him "poking his white stick here and there trying to find his way about." A squad car hastened to the scene where a park attendant, armed with a barbed white stick, was going about his normal duties picking up stray bits of paper.

The woman had received the sensations which made up her own perception of figure and ground. The man was the figure. All other details receded. She did not notice the bag slung over the man's shoulder—that would not have fitted into her perception of a blind man at all. The bag was part of ground—to her, it did not belong to the mental figure she formed. And her total perception had meaning, as she interpreted it. The fact that her interpretation was wrong did not affect the fact that she made it.

Our behavior and the behavior of a public relations client are always being perceived with meaning. Perception is strictly individual. The way our behavior is perceived by others may differ a great deal from the way we perceive it or want it to be perceived. Furthermore, even though we make no effort to communicate the meaning we intend, people will go right on perceiving, interpreting, and finding meanings. They don't wait for new facts or explanation.

Krech and Crutchfield give an account of a group of school children singing a Christmas carol, "O Tannenbaum."[11] Two tiny ones, heirs of the modern age, got a little mixed up on the words. The song came out, "Atomic Bomb." Here was sensation, perception, interpretation, meaning. And it isn't only children who sometimes don't get the message the way it was intended they should.

Perceptions can be highly stimulus-determined, influenced primarily by what is really "out there" and hence accurate. Or they can be highly subjective, influenced primarily by what the indivdual "wants" to see, hear, or perceive through some other channel.

Determinants of Meaning

How is the meaning of perception determined? This is a basic piece of psychological insight of great value to the public relations man, and hence we outline it in some detail. The reasoning of Krech and Crutchfield is followed here.[12]

Perception contains two sets of factors—structural and functional.

Structural factors. The structural factors comprise the contribution to the total perception that is made by the world "out there," all the physical aspects involved. The proportional effect of the structural factors varies. When they contribute heavily, the perception is said to be "stimulus-determined." The stimuli "out there" are so structured that it is difficult to get a different meaning from them than someone else would get.

In the Muller-Lyer illustration shown below it is difficult to overcome the impression that one line is longer than the other. Actually they are of the same length:

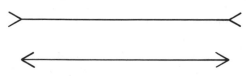

---

[11] D. Krech and R. S. Crutchfield, *Theory and Problems of Social Psychology* (New York: McGraw-Hill Book Company, 1948), p. 85.

[12] *Ibid.*, pp. 81-109.

There are also other types of structural factors that tend to determine what we perceive.

Similarity is one of these. A group of objects that are very similar tend to be seen as a unit. We see the lawn, not the blades of grass, or the driveway, not the individual pebbles.

Isolation is another. It does just the opposite. A pebble in your shoe is quickly noticed, much more so than an individual pebble in the driveway.

Distinctiveness can be a very powerful determinant in perception. A dandelion on the lawn is more dramatically perceived than any individual blade of grass. Put one old-fashioned on a tray of martinis, and it will not fail to attract attention. The very fact that an object is distinctive makes it difficult to organize the total perception without reference to it. Often we combine the three structural factors—similarity, isolation, and distinctiveness—to facilitate or bring about the type of perception we want. The advertising man presents the object on which he wants to focus attention, makes it distinctive, isolates it, and shows a context of other background items that are somewhat similar. This is a good way of compelling attention where it is wanted.

Functional factors. Functional factors comprise the contribution that is made to total perception by the individual himself. Thus whether one is happy or sad, contented or frustrated will have a great deal to do with how he perceives events going on around him. The functional factors, unquestionably the most difficult to predict, are nevertheless the most important elements in determining a total perception.

Though structural and functional factors in perception have been divided here for the purpose of discussion, they meld in actual perception (perception = structural × functional).

Functional factors can be divided into three additional categories—needs, temporary mood states, and previous experiences.

"Needs" are the pushes and pulls that motivate us. As we said before, some are primary, some secondary. All *primary needs* have some sort of physiological basis—hunger, thirst, need of air, avoidance of pain, etc. Secondary needs, on the other hand, have more social than physiological basis; that is, we acquire them in a cultural context. The *secondary needs* and their strength in motivation are a function of the particular culture within which one is born. In our society, the needs for social approval, for security, for power are among the important secondary needs.

Also by way of review, secondary needs are not inborn, they are learned, and they are influenced by the culture. One list of secondary needs might hold true for one subculture and not very well for another. In comparing one culture with another, this contrast is striking. For example, Englishmen and Eskimos alike get hungry, thirsty, etc. Their primary physiological needs are quite similar. But the set of cultural values possessed by the one is at odds in many respects with the values that satisfy the other, and hence their secondary needs are often dissimilar.

Under conditions of physiological stress, the primary needs are likely to come to the fore. Levine, Chein, and Murphy, for example, showed in an experiment a series of ambiguous drawings to two groups of college students—one hungry group and one that had just finished eating. The hungry group saw in the pictures food objects—sandwiches, salads, etc.—while the others did not.[13]

Secondary needs more important.   In applying what we know of human needs to practical purposes, it is the secondary needs that usually loom as more important. To be sure, all behavior depends on both physiological and psychic motivation, but the physiological needs somehow get met for those who are able to survive in any culture, because they must. But their relation to everyday behavior is frequently too complex to handle in the practical situation such as that which faces the public relations practitioner. (Cf. pages 147-148 for a comparison of primary needs with secondary needs.)

The secondary needs are not relegated to second place in public relations thinking but occupy most of the practitioner's attention. The relation between these needs and perception cannot be overemphasized. Understanding of human behavior has recently made great gains through recognition of this relationship. How people are motivated has a great deal to do with how they perceive and in their own minds organize the world about them.

Psychologists make extensive use of the relationship of needs, often of unconscious needs, with perception in the work of personality assessment. The projective techniques bring out these subjective needs. The Rorschach inkblot test, for example, presents shapeless blots of ink to the viewer who "reads into" them what he sees. His report reflects his need state. So it is with the variety of other projective tests. All have as their very basis the assumption that needs determine perception.

To give another illustration, a child is given a variety of dolls to play with, dolls made of clay or some plastic material. The dolls represent an adult male, an adult female, and several children. How the child arranges the dolls, what he does with them, and the stories he tells

---

[13] R. Levine, I. Chein, and G. Murphy, "The Relation of the Intensity of a Need to the Amount of Perceptual Distortion: A Preliminary Report," *Journal of Psychology*, XIII (1942), 283-293.

about them while absorbed in play reveal in striking fashion what problems the child is wrestling with, how he perceives adults in relation to himself—that is, what his psychic needs are as shown in his interpretation of relatively unstructured material.

Temporary mood states. When we are filled with anger, fright, frustration, apprehension, or elation, our mood states bear an easily recognizable influence on the nature of perception. An angry man perceives something in a social situation that he would not have focused upon so sharply had he been serene and calm. Late at night a noise in the basement is associated with a possible burglar.

The effect of frustration of perception and attitude was demonstrated by Miller and Bugelski in an experiment on a group of young men working at a camp.[14] First, the attitudes of individuals toward Japanese and Mexicans were measured. One group of camp workers was required to take tedious, uninteresting tests, so constructed that everyone was bound to do poorly. The tests were scheduled at a time when "Bank Night" at a local theater was going on, an event to which the youths had been looking forward. After the tests, the men were told they had done poorly. They were tested again as to their attitudes toward Mexicans and Japanese. These were definitely more unfavorable than the prior tests had shown.

The control group, the other workers in the camp, who had no examination and thus had not failed, and who had not been deprived of "Bank Night," were given a second test as to attitudes toward Japanese and Mexicans. Their attitudes had not changed for the worse, and some of them were slightly more favorable.

Perception thus was influenced by temporary events. But note that it is deemed unlikely that the increasingly unfavorable attitude on the part of the first group will be lasting after time has softened feelings of frustration and the mood is gone. Temporary states of need are not as crucial as more serious, deep-lying, longer-lasting ones, but they still deserve a place in calculation when we deal with perception.

Previous experience. Our previous experience is a sort of mental wastebasket into which anything and everything gets tossed, much of it "forgotten" promptly. But a traumatic or exciting past experience may well influence present perception. A person who has been frightened by an animal, for example, is likely to have his perception colored by this experience when at a later time his senses warn him of the presence of a similar animal.

---

[14] N. E. Miller and R. Bugelski, "Minor Studies of Aggression, II: The Influence of Frustration Imposed by the In-group on Attitudes Expressed Toward Out-groups," *Journal of Psychology*, XXV (1948), 437-440.

Education plays its part here. A trained geologist and a layman walk along a country road. Geological formations to the geologist are just a lot of rocks to the layman—the scientist differentiates between figure and ground in a manner that the layman does not.

Perceptions Are Functionally Selective

Each individual is unique with respect to those factors, structural and functional, that determine his perception. It is the relationship of needs within the individual that determines how he organizes his own world.

In an experiment reported by Doob, Marion Zillig asked a class of children to write the names of the five class members they liked most and the five they liked least.[15] They were not told anything that would relate this step to the later one. Then the five most popular and the five least popular were lined up alternately and told to perform a simple gymnastic exercise, following the commands "right arm up—arm down." The five popular children had been privately instructed to disobey the order and raise their left arms. So the popular children did the exercise wrong, and the unpopular ones did it right.

The class then was asked to write down the names of those who had done the exercise correctly and those who had not. Result: A greater percentage of the popular group was credited with having done it correctly—though all had done it wrong—than the unpopular children, all of whom had followed the instruction correctly. Clearly the class followed friendship ties, the functional factor. They had been so selective in their perceptions that it was impossible for them to report correctly what they had seen.

The public relations man is constantly confronted with the likelihood of dealing with the group whose perceptions are highly selective. Careful attention should be paid to an advance analysis of what functional factors could possibly distort communication to such a group. Otherwise, expensive attempts to communicate may be fruitless.

The Part and the Whole in Perception

A final generalization in the area of perception: Any part of the perception process may affect the whole, and the whole may affect any part. This two-way relationship operates constantly in perception and may involve either structural or functional factors, or both.

---

[15] Leonard W. Doob, *Social Psychology: An Analysis of Human Behavior* (New York: Holt, Rinehart & Winston, Inc., 1952), pp. 75-76.

Effect of part on whole. The way we perceive an individual or a social situation *in toto* often is determined by some of the parts. We speak of "first impressions"; we have a vague feeling that they are not always reliable, yet we know they do influence our future relationships. Well, on what do we base these snap judgments, these first impressions? It is likely to be upon semiconscious receipt of signals, such as a gesture, the turn of a head, necktie, the color of skin or hair. In his *Journal*, Arnold Bennett relates that H. G. Wells was inordinately attractive to many women because he smelled of honey to them. It is on trivia that the important first impression often is based.

To take a different kind of example, when the Russians launched their first Sputnik in 1957, this successful earth satellite came to form a part of our perception of the Russians. The whole was our concept of Russia, our negative and ambivalent feelings toward its government and its leaders. Official Amercian reaction was expressed in press releases full of double talk, hasty attempts to rationalize our tremendous surprise, a sorry demonstration of trying not to act like the fox who said, "The grapes were sour anyway." Our total perception of Russia was tremendously influenced by our perception of the part.

The temporal sequence, or order of events in which we reach judgment of a person, a cause, or a nation, has important bearing on our end perceptive result. If you first hear something favorable about a person, for example, you are more likely to reach a favorable over-all impression than if the reverse is true. After a good first impression it is harder to change to a bad lasting impression, despite later experiences, though the first impression had to be based on relatively minor part factors. But if your first impression was negative, later unfavorable impressions are likely to move you to think, "I knew it all the time."

Effect of whole on part. Conversely, the whole perception influences the partial impression. A friend may have a mannerism that we scarcely notice. Seen in a person we dislike, the very same mannerism stands out as offensive. It depends on our "frame of reference," the view we take of the over-all object or situation. Labor and management do not always get along well together because their frame of reference differs widely. Management may honestly think that thanks are due for many fringe benefits, including those to the families of employees. In precisely the same situation, the labor leader may think and say, with equal honesty and perhaps even more fervor, "It's the take-home pay that feeds the kids."

Prejudices, preconditioning that has led us to adopt "stereotypes" regarding persons and groups, illustrate the often massive effect the whole perception has on the part perception. Often, for example, it is difficult for Americans to distinguish clearly and at once the personal, individual characteristics of a person of another race with another color of skin. So overwhelming is the built-in prejudice that the real person is rendered invisible by the stereotype, which may be false.

PERCEPTION—A SUMMARY

Now to sum up what we have said about perception with respect to the communication process. (1) We stressed the need for the sender to anticipate how his attempts to change the recipient will be received by the recipient. (2) We said that this requires a knowledge of how the recipient perceives the sender, and for public relations people, this requires an understanding of perception. (3) We showed that perception is intimately related to motivation. (4) We explained that all perceptions are organized and meaningful. (5) We described the elements of perception as figure and ground. (6) We showed that the part of perception that is figure and the part that is ground can be understood as a combination of structural and functional factors, together determining the resultant perception.

STEP 1C—TRANSLATION OF PUBLIC RELATIONS OBJECTIVES INTO BEHAVIORAL TERMS

With some understanding of motivation, learning, and perception, the public relations practitioner is now ready to take another small step in the public relations problem-solving process. This consists of making a *first approximation* of translating his public relations goals into behavioral terms.[16] Translation of public relations goals into behavioral terms means that the public relations practitioner must specify what behavioral changes (from the standpoint of such things as motivation and perception, for example) he is trying to bring about in the recipients as he has identified them. To illustrate this process, let's return to our auto dealer case as we worked it out in *Step 1a* (Chapter 6 pages 138-139). At that time, we were interested in translating the main problem (as the public relations practitioner might interpret it) into our communication model. This meant that the real problem seemed to be that of bringing these unfair business practices to the attention

---

[16] The phrase "first approximation" is used here because the public relations practitioner may find it necessary to make changes in his translation of public relations goals into behavioral terms in the light of the additional considerations that we will take up when a more detailed discussion of the recipient stage is made.

of the local automobile dealers' association membership. In this context, the recipients were now the association members in general, and, at first at least, the officers of the association in particular. Translating public relations objectives into behavioral terms in this particular problem situation would mean spelling out what behavior (both verbal and nonverbal) of the association officers, and later of association members, is expected or desired. For example, the public relations practitioner concerned would expect the following list of behaviors on the part of the officers:

Verbal statements (in the first encounter with the public relations practitioner) to the effect that they agree there is a problem to be solved and that they (the association) have responsibilities to fulfill in helping to solve the problem.

Nonverbal behavior in the form of meeting with the public relations practitioner to discuss the problem in some detail.

Verbal behavior in the form of promises to take specific action to solve the problem on the basis of these personal conferences.

Nonverbal behavior in the form of initiating some action, such as the censure of the dealers behaving unethically.

This is, of course, only a partial list of the behaviors that one could imagine the public relations practitioner might expect from the auto association people. One could also list behaviors that he is expecting on the part of the dealers who are overcharging. Implicitly, at least, the public relations practitioner is assuming that these dealers are going to change their behavior when their fellow dealers (through the dealers' association) start to bring some action against them either in the form of verbal censure or expulsion from the membership or other such measures that they, as an association, are able to take.

Advantages of Translating Public Relations Problems into Behavioral Changes Desired

Our focus here should not be on the behaviors per se because many different and long lists could be made on the basis of this one interpretation of the auto dealers case alone. The important thing is the realization that it is necessary at some point to begin to envision what sort of behavior changes you are expecting to take place, assuming that your analysis of the problem is correct and that the steps that you take as a part of your public relations program are successful. There are several important reasons for making the translation from public relations problem language into behavioral changes.

Clarity of Thinking

Translating public relations objectives into behavioral terms tends to contribute to clarity of thinking about the problem itself. The author has all too often discussed public relations problem solving with public relations practitioners only to find out that they had never clearly spelled out what behavior they thought (or hoped) they were going to bring to pass through their public relations program. For example, we all too often speak of improving the "community relations" of a particular organization in such a vague way that it becomes a wastebasket expression. When you force yourself to visualize what is going on in the community in terms of the behavior of the individuals who comprise it, the attempt can be a disconcerting experience if you have never done it before. By "improved community relations" do you mean that every time the name of your company comes up in the conversation of two or more members of the community they will speak well of the company? And do you mean that the *number* of such incidents is going to increase substantially because of your public relations program? Do you mean that when the members of the community think of your company's products, they are going to think they are dependable, worth the money, desirable to purchase? Do you think that the proportion of the members of the community who think positively of the products is going to increase substantially because of your public relations program? The answer to any or all of these questions *could* be a resounding "no" coming from any particular public relations practitioner. He may protest that he means something entirely different by the expression "improved community relations," and that is perfectly all right. However, it is all right only if he is able to *supplement his definition* with the *behavior changes* that he expects to bring about in the community and then label it as "improved."

This point is important enough to take another example. Let us take the company newspaper as another example. What behavior changes can a public relations practitioner expect from the introduction (or continuation) of a company paper? Under what conditions is this newspaper successful? When it is read regularly? Or is it successful only when it is read *and* attitudes of the employees are changed (or in some way modified) by it so that they are consistent with management's views on some issue? Once again, the point is not to spell out what a newspaper *should* do in terms of changing the behavior of employees. An exceedingly long list of possibilities could be developed and still not include some that the reader might think of. What *is* important is that many public relations practitioners are either responsible for or directly produce the newspaper themselves without having spelled out what they think the effect of the newspaper is (or should be) on the behavior of the employees. Company newspapers can all too easily become "good things to have" without anyone raising the question of just what effects (both overt and attitudinally) the newspaper is supposed to have on the intended audience.

Realistic Goals Are More Likely to Be Chartered

Translating public relations goals into the behavior changes of the recipients concerned has the effect of causing the public relations practitioner to be more sensible about what behavior changes are realistic. He is less likely to overstate what his public relations program can and cannot do. This is a very important function of translating public relations goals into behavior changes. There is a tendency for the public relations practitioner to become so enthusiastic about his job and his objectives that he easily loses sight of the fact that not too many other people in the world share his enthusiasm, that many of the publics that he may want to communicate with and change may not even pay any attention to his communication efforts.

Perhaps an example will illustrate this point better. Recently the author had the good fortune of participating in a small conference of U.S. Air Force Information Officers discussing the problem of informing citizens about sonic boom—the noise that is sometimes produced (and occasionally causes damage) when aircraft exceed the speed of sound. There is a great deal of misunderstanding by the general public about what causes sonic boom, why it is unavoidable in many instances, and so on. Unfortunately, many citizens have the idea that it is produced by young "hot-shot" pilots fooling around or showing off rather than a by-product of high-speed aircraft, especially military aircraft.

The work to date by information officers to explain to communities that are near air force bases and affected by sonic boom is truly outstanding in most cases. They have coined the theme "the sound of freedom" and have developed at least a portion of their public relations program around this theme and the fact that the sonic boom is an inescapable factor in maintaining an up-to-date air force. However, at one point in the discussion it became apparent that at least some of the information officers were becoming too enthusiastic about the power of their public relations program in overcoming objections to sonic boom. At that point, the author interjected into the conversation the suggestion that we take the community that was under discussion and translate it into individuals—more specifically, translate it into persons who had been very directly affected by the sonic boom. When asked to visualize an irate citizen looking at his picture window, completely shattered, or a portion of his house foundation, cracked by sonic boom, it became evident that it was unrealistic to expect him not to become upset by it merely because he had been exposed to some or all of an information program designed to "explain" the sonic boom. When this was done, it suddenly became apparent that perhaps all that could be expected from that public relations program had been attained. Even though the citizen concerned might understand sonic boom, his understanding cannot be expected to overcome his agitation about the damage to his house. Even though he may realize that it was not due to a "smart kid" and that the pilot was a responsible, mature individual, it does not obviate the fact that damage had been done.

So it is when one tries to visualize what behavior changes he expects his public relations program to produce. When a public relations program is translated into behavior changes, it sometimes becomes quite apparent that unrealistic goals (or demands on the public relations program) are being set and that one cannot expect to produce these behavior changes, as the sonic boom example illustrates.

Social Science Principles Are Easier to Relate

When a public relations problem situation is translated into the behavior changes planned or anticipated, it is easier to relate psychological or sociological principles wherever they are pertinent. If a public relations practitioner thinks of his public relations objectives in terms of what he is expecting the recipient to learn, then principles of learning are easier to relate. Likewise, if he thinks of what motivations he is attempting to induce in his recipient, the principles of motivation will make more sense to him and be more helpful in suggesting what he needs to do. Lastly, if he attempts to visualize what perceptions his recipient is likely to hold now, it is easier for him to visualize how he might go about changing these perceptions.

It is important to add here that there are no guarantees that can be extended to any problem-solving approach to render it foolproof. However, what has been put forth here is that when a public relations problem situation is couched in terms of the motivations or the perceptions that need to be changed, the *likelihood is increased* that the pertinent questions will be raised and that the social and behavioral science principles will be easier to relate to the problem situation.

Step 1C—A Summary

In Chapter 3, considerable space was devoted to the development of arguments leading to the generalization that the public relations practitioner should be viewed as an applied social and behavioral scientist. For this reason, translation of public relations problems into behavioral terms is necessary in order to be consistent with this definition. Applied social and behavioral scientists (like their nonapplied or more theoretically oriented brethren) are concerned with understanding, modifying, and predicting human behavior. It is only logical then, that they would have to translate their practical, applied problems into behavioral terms.

QUESTIONS FOR DISCUSSION

1. In this chapter, the point was made that usually a public relations practitioner is more likely to be satisfying secondary needs rather than primary needs. See if this generalization holds up by taking any public relations case you wish and noting what needs the public relations practitioner concerned was primarily dealing with. Did it turn out to be true that more often than not his actions related to some secondary need? What exceptions did you find to this generalization?

2. Translate the notion of "establishing a *favorable ratio*, so to speak, between need satisfaction and dissatisfaction" (page 155) into public relations practice. That is, try to think of examples in which a public relations practitioner tries to achieve a favorable ratio between need satisfaction and dissatisfaction. Are you satisfied that the public relations practitioner concerned probably could *not* eliminate need dissatisfaction entirely, as contended in pages 154 through 158?

3. Take our four-part formula, $N \rightarrow B \rightarrow G \rightarrow DR$, and use it to analyze some particular public relations practitioner's program of action. Be sure that you identify as best you can the behavior(s) that the public relations practitioner was presumably reinforcing. Now that you

have made this analysis, do you think the public relations program was the one best suited to reinforce the particular behaviors you have identified? What might you have done differently, and why?

4. Develop two public relations situations that illustrate (1) a situation in which a public relations practitioner did *not* understand the perceptions of his intended recipients, and (2) a situation in which a public relations practitioner apparently *did* understand the perceptions of his intended recipients. How would you summarize the consequences when one does not understand the perceptions of an intended recipient in a communication situation?

5. Take any two cases that you have used to answer previous questions. In each case, translate the presumed or apparent goals of the public relations program into behavioral terms. That is, express the public relations programs in question in terms of the changes (or maintenance) in behavior that the public relations practitioner apparently planned to produce. Now that you have made this translation into behavioral terms, are there any goals that appear unrealistic in view of what is being done to bring about the changes? Which ones (if any) appear to remain realistic, and why?

Chapter 8

THE MESSAGE STAGE IN MORE DETAIL: SEMANTIC AND ANTHROPOLOGICAL CONSIDERATIONS

INTRODUCTION

In studying the communication model to be used throughout this book, we learned that the second stage of the model is the message stage. We learned that messages can be constructed of any conceivable set of symbols that a sender wants to use and, of course, that he assumes his intended recipient understands. We also learned (Chapter 5, pages 100-104) that the public relations practitioner is at times excessively preoccupied with the message stage. An objective analysis of his daily work reveals that a considerable proportion of his energy is devoted to devising and revising messages in the forms of brochures, news releases, articles, pamphlets, and material designed for use on radio and television. In fact, one of the more common derisive epithets applied to the public relations practitioner is "word merchant." Well, let's acknowledge that the public relations practitioner is a word merchant, at least in one sense. However, the negative connotations of the term can be rendered inappropriate if the public relations practitioner has at least a minimum understanding of the science of words and their meaning, a working acquaintance with semantics and an understanding of the importance of language among human beings, and if he uses words appropriately through the proper media.

To be certain that we have this minimum understanding, let us examine some concepts borrowed from semanticists, anthropologists, and social psychologists that should enrich our understanding of the message stage and better prepare us for a more detailed analysis of its relationship to public relations practice.

LANGUAGE ACQUISITION

However much social scientists may disagree in constructing theories to account for man's behavior, on one fact they are in agreement: The ability of man to communicate by a semantic communication symbol system called "language" is unique to man. In fact, the one thing that is completely unique to human beings (as compared with infrahumans) is their language form of communication.

It would be of considerable theoretical and practical significance to know exactly how man acquired his language ability, but the fact is that we are quite in the dark on this score. We do not have a satisfactory explanation for how the ability to use a language develops in any *one* individual, let alone for all *homo sapiens*.

We do have many descriptive (as distinguished from explanatory) systems that are of at least some value in pointing out the stages through which the average individual passes on his way to language acquisition. The approach spelled out by Klineberg[1] (based on Esper[2]) is an example of such a system and consists of five stages.

1. Screaming Stage

This begins with the birth cry, which is regarded by many as a reflex activity that is instrumental in starting blood flow and oxygenation in the newborn infant. These very early cries or screams are reactions to a variety of stimuli (the most common being hunger pains) and are undifferentiated. That is, the child has not learned to relate particular cries to particular physical and emotional states.

---

[1] Otto Klineberg, *Social Psychology* (rev. ed.; New York: Holt, Rinehart & Winston, Inc., 1954), pp. 54-57. Used by permission.

[2] E. A. Esper, "Language," in C. Murchison (ed.), *Handbook of Social Psychology* (Worcester, Mass.: Clark University Press, 1935).

2. Babbling Stage

This stage normally starts toward the end of the second month of life. The babbling contains a tremendous range of sounds. Recordings have been made of the sounds that young infants make, and within the first two months all of the normal sounds of the human voice are heard. This has led some investigators to think of this period of sound production as one in which the "universal" sounds are being produced. This phenomenon is culture free, in the sense that all normal babies, regardless of their racial origins, generate the same sounds. The differentiation of sounds, which is a function of the particular culture of which the child is a member, comes later in life. Incidentally, this confirms the fact that any child could learn any language with equal facility.

3. Sound Imitation

This period in language development emerges during the second six months of life. Essentially, the child engages in repeating the sounds that he hears. The most common explanatory principle that has been employed to account for this stage has been a modification of the concept of classical conditioning as put forth by Pavlov.[3] Pavlov had developed an explanation for why his dogs learned to salivate when he sounded a bell as part of his experimental procedure. At first, Pavlov showed a hungry dog a piece of meat and, at the same time, sounded a bell. The dog salivated at the sight of the meat, as is normal for it to do. After repeated trials of seeing the meat and hearing the bell at the same time, the dog eventually learned to salivate at the sound of the bell alone. This principle of the conditioned reflex (that is, the normal reflex of salivation to meat, becoming "attached to" or produced by the bell) is often diagramed as follows:

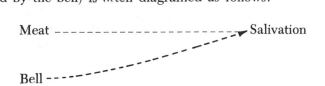

Eventually, this gives way to

Bell alone ----------------------►Salivation

---

[3] I. P. Pavlov, *Conditioned Reflexes* (London: Oxford University Press, 1927).

This principle of conditioned reflex has been used to explain all sorts of learning phenomena, and it is used in language acquisition as well. Following the model above, some sort of organic condition within a child (*e.g.*, hunger for food) causes him to make a sound. At the same time he makes the sound, he *hears* the sound he makes. Following the diagram we made for the conditioned reflex of Pavlov's dogs, it would look something like this:

S_1 (organic condition—
    in this case hunger) ------------------------→ R_1
                                      (a sound is made)

S_2 (Hearing the sound takes place at the same time)

Eventually, this gives way to

S_2 (Hearing a parent make some sound—*e.g.* "say da da")

            --------------→ R_1 (Producing the
            ←--------------   sound "da da")

4. Verbal Understanding

This phase of language acquisition emerges toward the beginning of the latter part of the first year of life. In this phase, the child begins to understand the meaning of certain words. For example, the child is playing in the tub—hitting the water. The parent says, "That's a boy —you *splash* the water." Eventually, the child learns what "splash" means and will splash the water on verbal suggestion from the parent.

5. Verbal Utterance

This final stage is language acquisition as we know it best in the adult but which is quite evident in children as young as two years old. This is language ability where an active, understood vocabulary is used to control one's environment.

LANGUAGE AND ENVIRONMENT CONTROL

Perhaps the most useful way of thinking about language (in spite of the fact that our understanding of how language acquisition takes place is limited) is to view it as man's unique tool with which he controls his environment. Starting from the earliest cry (screaming stage) we can observe man's use of sound (and, later, language) to control his environment. In an amazingly short period of time, the young infant learns how to use his cries to make the whole household stand at attention. In fact, with indulgent, overprotective parents, a child's control of his environment through the use of sounds (as distinct from a language) can be so complete his language development may be retarded. A child of overly anxious parents can have his every wish catered to merely by making a simple cry. Such parents interpret the single sounds for the child, and he does not have to use a language to make his desires known. In such a situation, language acquisition can be delayed by as much as several years.

Viewing language as instrumental to the individual in controlling his environment has permitted the use of learning theory to account for language acquisition. The reader will recall that in Chapter 7 a simple formula, N→B→G→DR, was developed as a model to account for learning that takes place in both man and animal. The application of this model to language goes something like this:

1. At first only random sounds are made—the babbling stage that was discussed earlier.
2. At the same time that these random sounds are being produced, there exist certain *needs* (the N in our formula) within an organism.
3. Certain sounds tend to be more successful in achieving certain *goals* (the G in our formula) because, of course, of the particular culture the child is growing up in. To put it another way, sounds appropriate for the English language serve to reach certain goals because the parents speak English. These sounds would not be appropriate for the German language.
4. This means that certain sounds become instrumental in satisfying certain needs, and precisely as any other behavior is acquired, this particular form of behavior (*i.e.*, *verbal* behavior) becomes learned. Learned because it is need reducing just as any other, nonverbal behavior might be need reducing.

5. To summarize: Our learning model, that served as a reasonably good "fit" in accounting for the nonverbal behavior of an individual, now becomes useful as an aid to understanding the acquisition of verbal behavior.

When learning theory is applied to language acquisition, it becomes clear why the behavioral scientist views language as an instrument that man uses for controlling his environment.

In adults, control of the environment through language reaches a most refined level. In fact, modern man lives most successfully (or perhaps we should say *adjusts* most successfully) when he uses language to control the behavior of others rather than resorting to other means. Let us examine this point a bit more fully.

When a man loses his temper and punches a fellow worker in the nose—instead of uttering an insult or a brilliant retort—he is temporarily giving up verbal control of others in favor of physical control. The man who does, in fact, resort to physical violence (in place of verbal "violence") generally loses out. He more often causes more problems than he solves, and at the same time he appears childish in the eyes of his peers. (In fact, the use of the term *childlike* in such a situation is a rather accurate description of what is going on. In such a situation, one is reverting to what might have been appropriate in childhood—indeed, for the male child even required—but is not deemed appropriate problem-solving behavior for an adult.)

One other example is called for at this time. The whole system of therapy administered by a clinical psychologist or psychiatrist to a patient is a very sophisticated example of the use of language to control behavior. When the therapist encourages his patient to talk, one objective is that by listening to his own utterances, the patient will be helped to understand himself better. Hopefully, understanding himself more fully (and viewing himself more objectively) will enable him to change his behavior. Or, from the point of view of this present discussion, he will thus be better able to control his behavior by replacing neurotic behavior patterns with more constructive and "normal" behavior patterns in his responses to his environment.

MESSAGES, MEANINGS, AND THE PROCESS OF ABSTRACTION

In our presentation of the topic of perception (Chapter 7, pages 168-176), one of the generalizations we made was that perceptions are functionally selective. That is, we observed that individuals perceive the world around them as a function of their needs, temporary mood states, and previous experiences in addition to what is "out there" to be perceived. This permitted us to imply that reality for any one individual is *not* determined by the particular environmental context in which he finds himself at any one time, but rather, is a function of the *interaction* of that individual with his environment. The combination of something out there to be perceived and the unique characteristics of the particular perceiver enable us to account for any one individual's interpretation of reality.

This is precisely the approach that we must take to any particular language employed as a message. That is, the principles of perception presented in Chapter 7 as applicable to other portions of human behavior are equally applicable to understanding the way a language system functions among human beings. Let's go into a little bit of detail and see how the principles of perception interrelate with how semanticists have suggested that we think about language and the meaning that is communicated through a particular language system.

The Arbitrariness of It All

In the process of communicating with another human being, we use some sort of a *code*. This is why in Chapter 4 we spoke of a sender as *encoding* a message—*i.e.*, translating the message he wants to communicate into a particular code system that the recipient can decode (make sense out of) and thereby understand the sender. The particular code we use and whether it consists of marks of graphite on a piece of paper, puffs of smoke, or some arrangement of piles of stones along a trail is of no consequence. The particular code we employ is perfectly arbitrary; the only requirement that we must, of course, meet is that the individual with whom we wish to communicate understands this code. The word *understanding* implies that the recipient of our message is able to (1) make sense out of what we are trying to say to him by our code and (2) that the meaning that he derives from the code be the *same* (or close enough for practical purposes) meaning that we intended for him to extract. The two words *meaning* and *intention* are key words in an understanding of the message stage in the communication process. To successfully communicate means not that our recipient derive *some* meaning out of our code, but that he derive the meaning that we intended.[4]

---

[4] An appropriate illustration can be derived from Upton Sinclair's book, *The Jungle*. In this volume, the meaning the author intended to communicate concerned the undesirable working and living conditions of the individuals associated with the meat-packing industry. One of the unexpected side effects of this book was the agitation on the part of the citizens to "do something" about the unsani-

Granted that any particular code that we employ may be arbitrary, how does it function to enable us to communicate what we are thinking and feeling to others? The answer lies in learning. We *learn* the particular codes that the culture in which we are born uses. Likewise, we *learn* the particular meanings that certain codes are supposed to convey. The only trouble with this statement—and it is accurate—is that all of the individual differences that take place in learning apply here as well. This fact accounts for all of the difficulties we have in communicating successfully, even in the simplest situations. Individual differences in learning mean that we all attach slightly (or greatly, depending on the situation) different meanings to the codes that we have learned. In a great many situations, these slightly different meanings are of no consequence; in others, they are of the first magnitude. The meaning that we perceive in a sentence consisting of symbols arranged according to the rules of some particular code is *not inherent* in the code itself. For precisely the same reasons that the meaning we attach to the behavior of a friend or the meaning we attach to the behavior of a crowd of individuals depends on how we perceive our friend or the crowd, so it is that *the meaning of a message is dependent on how we perceive the message.* In and of itself, the message is nothing. It is akin to sound waves moving through the atmosphere. Until these waves impinge upon a mechanism suitable for making some use of them (say, for example, the organ of Corti in the ear coupled with the rest of the nervous system, so that the interpretation is made that the sound is Bach), the waves are just waves. Likewise, words are just words until they are heard by an individual, with all of his individual prejudices, previous experiences, need states, and so on, who interprets them. It is this process of interpretation that is required for a message to have any meaning. *Successful communication means that you have succeeded in inducing your recipient to interpret your message in the way in which you intended for him to do.* If only communications in real life were as simple as stating what successful communications is!

This brings us to the process of abstraction—at least as it is applied to language in general and language codes in particular. Once again, let's examine other forms of behavior before looking at how this thinking applies to language. When discussing the topic of perception, we noted that all of us organize the world in a meaningful way and that this organization could be thought of as consisting of *figure* and *ground.* The term figure referred to that which we were paying atten-

---

tary way that meat was being handled before it reached the dinner tables of the nation. This was not the meaning the author intended for his audience (i.e., recipients) to derive from his message.

tion to at any particular moment, while the background consisted of everything else that we *might* have attended to (*i.e.*, perceived) but did not for a variety of reasons. In effect, what we were describing at that time was the process of *abstraction*. That is, it is humanly impossible (and the impossibility holds for all subhuman organisms as well) for anyone to attend to everything going on in his environment at any given instant in time. For one thing, there is too much to attend to. Another, of course, is the role that such things as different needs and moods play. There is also the fact that our receptors (*i.e.* eyes, ears) are constructed such that they will respond to only certain portions of the total energy presented. (Suppose, for example, that our hearing *started* at around 16,000 cycles per second rather than beginning to end there. Our sound world would be entirely different. We would not hear things that we take so much for granted now (*e.g.*, music), and we would hear a host of new sounds that we never heard before. Lastly, there is the efficiency of the process of abstracting. Attending to only the essentials of what is going on around us enables us to cope much more successfully with our environment than if we were attending to every detail of what we were being exposed to.

Hayakawa illustrates this last function of abstraction when he writes:

> This process of abstracting, of leaving characteristics out, is an indispensable convenience. To illustrate by still another example, suppose that we live in an isolated village of four families, each owning a house. A's house is referred to as *maga*; B's house is *biyo*; C's is *kata*, and D's is *pelel*. This is quite satisfactory for ordinary purposes of communication in the village, unless a discussion arises about building a new house—a spare one, let us say. We cannot refer to the projected house by any one of the four words we have for the existing houses, since each of these has too specific a meaning. We must find a *general* term, at a higher level of abstraction, that means "something that has certain characteristics in common with *maga*, *biyo*, *kata*, and *pelel*, and yet is not A's, B's, C's, or D's." Since this is much too complicated to say each time, an *abbreviation* must be invented. Let us say we choose the noise, *house*. Out of such needs do our words come— they are a form of shorthand. The invention of a new abstraction is a great step forward, since it *makes discussion possible*—as, in this case, not only the discussion of a fifth house, but of all future houses we may build or see in our travels or dream about.[5]

---

[5] From *Language in Thought and Action*, by S. I. Hayakawa. Copyright 1949, by Harcourt, Brace & World, Inc. All passages from the book reprinted with permission of Harcourt, Brace & World, Inc. (While we have borrowed our material on semantics from the 1949 edition of this work, readers would definitely profit from the 2d ed., 1964, which includes such material as the addition of more semantic exercises in the "Applications" at the end of each chapter.)

All of the above reasons account for the fact that there is never a
1 : 1 relationship between what exists "out there" to be perceived and
what any given individual will perceive. In short, we abstract, and one
dictionary meaning of the word describes this process rather well—
"to take away; remove."[6]

This process of abstraction extends to our language as well. When
we agree to let a particular noise—let's say the word "chair"—stand for
an object upon which we can sit, one that has four legs, a portion that
rises up to support the back, and so on, the process of abstraction is
taking place. For one thing, in the case of the chair, our inadequate
senses do not permit us to "see" that the chair is not "solid," but rather
it is made up of extremely small units of matter in motion. For another,
we do not attend to all of the possible nuances of differences that could
be discerned in chairs if we really tried. A chair is a chair and we let
it go at that. And so it is for any object in the real world to which we
attach a particular word.

Hayakawa has brought out this process of abstraction applied to
language with his concept of the *abstraction ladder*[7] (Figure 16, page
193).

Let's examine Figure 16 in some detail. The starting point is the so-
called *process level.* At this level we have a cow, a living, ever-changing
organism, with an almost infinite number of characteristics to which
one could respond. We could analyze this organism at the atomic level,
at the physiological level, or at any other level (or combination of
levels) that we might choose. The point is that the few characteristics
that we do pay attention to (that is, *abstract* from the total possible)
define what we mean by the word *cow.* What's more, these characteristics scratch only the surface with respect to what *could or might
have been used.* To put it another way, what the abstraction ladder
reveals is that *before* we have even attempted to attach any verbal
label to what we see, a tremendous amount of abstracting has already
taken place. Then, at the very simplest of *verbal* levels of abstraction,
we leave out even more characteristics. As Hayakawa writes,

> . . . The word "Bessie" (cow_1) is the lowest *verbal* level of abstraction,
> leaving out further characteristics—the differences between Bessie today
> and Bessie tomorrow—and selecting only the similarities.[8]

---

[6] *Webster's New World Dictionary of the American Language* (College ed.;
Cleveland: The World Publishing Company, 1954).

[7] Hayakawa, p. 169.

[8] *Ibid.,* p. 167.

ABSTRACTION LADDER

Start reading from the bottom *up*

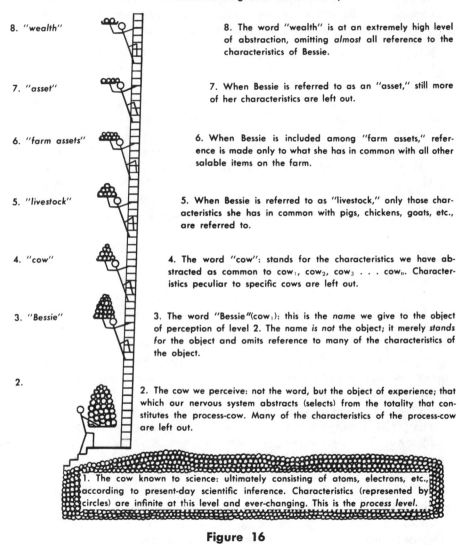

8. *"wealth"*

8. The word "wealth" is at an extremely high level of abstraction, omitting *almost* all reference to the characteristics of Bessie.

7. *"asset"*

7. When Bessie is referred to as an "asset," still more of her characteristics are left out.

6. *"farm assets"*

6. When Bessie is included among "farm assets," reference is made only to what she has in common with all other salable items on the farm.

5. *"livestock"*

5. When Bessie is referred to as "livestock," only those characteristics she has in common with pigs, chickens, goats, etc., are referred to.

4. *"cow"*

4. The word "cow": stands for the characteristics we have abstracted as common to cow_1, cow_2, cow_3 . . . cow_n. Characteristics peculiar to specific cows are left out.

3. *"Bessie"*

3. The word "Bessie" (cow_1): this is the *name* we give to the object of perception of level 2. The name *is not* the object; it merely *stands for* the object and omits reference to many of the characteristics of the object.

2.

2. The cow we perceive: not the word, but the object of experience; that which our nervous system abstracts (selects) from the totality that constitutes the process-cow. Many of the characteristics of the process-cow are left out.

1. The cow known to science: ultimately consisting of atoms, electrons, etc., according to present-day scientific inference. Characteristics (represented by circles) are infinite at this level and ever-changing. This is the *process level*.

Figure 16

In the same paragraph, Hayakawa goes on to illustrate the process of abstraction as one continues to go up the abstraction ladder, writing:

. . . The word "cow" selects only the similarities between Bessie (cow_1), Daisy (cow_2), Rosie (cow_3), and so on, and therefore leaves out still more about Bessie. The word "livestock" selects or abstracts only the features that Bessie has in common with pigs, chickens, goats and sheep. The term "farm asset" abstracts only the features Bessie has in common with barns, fences, livestock, furniture, generating plants and tractors, and is therefore on a very high level of abstraction.

Now we see how the process of abstraction—described earlier as being something that every living organism engages in with respect to his environment—also carries over to language. We also see more clearly the truth of the statement that the abstraction process is of almost incalculable aid in using our language as an aid to cope with our environment. However, this abstraction process in language is not without its hazards. If we do not clearly understand how this process applies to our use of language, we can commit grave errors in the use of language and the thinking that goes along with it. Of all people, the public relations practitioner needs to be aware of the pitfalls inherent in the abstraction process employed in language usage.

Extensional and Intensional Meanings

In order to better understand how the process of abstraction can be misleading, we need to introduce two terms that are commonly employed by semanticists: *extensional* meaning and *intensional* meaning. Extensional meanings are those that we can experience directly. Extensional meanings are sounds that we make that stand for something in the real world. In fact, the direct relationship between words and extensional meaning is such that *extensional meanings cannot be expressed in words.* Thus, when asked to give the extensional meaning of the noise "car," all one needs to do is to point to a car. The word *car* stands for that which you are pointing at, and more words are really not helpful. The meaning of the word *car* is complete by merely pointing or, as is sometimes said, by *denoting* an object in the real world.

Intensional meanings are those that must be suggested in someone else. The intensional meaning of a word cannot be given by merely pointing to the real world, because intensional meanings are not related to "point-at-able" phenomena like cars, boats or houses. Thus, the word *spirit* has a lot of intensional meaning for anyone using the term, and perhaps to the one listening as well. However, the word *spirit* has no external referent to which the user of the term can point.[9]

---

[9] It should be noted that the fact that the intensional meaning cannot be pointed to does not necessarily mean that there is no spirit. It merely means that the semanticist is reminding us that we cannot feel, handle, manipulate, and otherwise

Noises that we make can also have *both* intensional and extensional meaning. The word *democracy* is a good example. To be sure, there are many intensional meanings to this high-level, abstract term, meanings that one might have going on inside his head and for which he makes many other noises in order to connote what democracy means to him. At the same time, one could put his hand over his mouth (*i.e.*, not try to define with additional words) and point to an individual going into a booth at election time, closing the curtains, pulling levers that correspond to the names of particular candidates, opening the curtain when finished, and walking out. This could be *a* definition of the word democracy. Immediately the reader may be thinking to himself, "Oh, but there is much more to democracy than that." That is certainly true. In terms of the abstraction ladder concept that we examined earlier, the word *democracy* is a very high-level word, one that has undergone a number of abstractions. For this reason the *process level*, for which the word democracy presumably stands, could be made up of many, many demonstrable phenomena that could define (at least partially) the word democracy.

Find the Referent!

By now the reader is undoubtedly aware of the fact that in communicating with others the likelihood of confusion taking place in the communication process is *greatest* with words that have only *intensional* meaning. The reason: There is no real world to which both parties can turn for agreement. This is why whole books have been written on the subject of how many angels can dance on the head of a pin. Since there was nothing to be pointed to in the real world that could (or would) produce agreement, the authors in question could go on and on and on, using words and words and words to talk about what they presumably understood (intensional meanings) about the topic.

The likelihood of confusion is *least* when someone is communicating with words that have extensional meaning. If one person is talking about his swimming pool and makes the statement that it is thirty-five feet long, and his friend who is listening (and looking at the pool at the same time) sees clearly (*i.e.*, believes) that it is only twenty-five

---

measure spirit. Consequently, to communicate the meaning of the word *spirit*, we need to use other words to give the intensional meaning that we have within us and are trying to induce in our listener. This is why we use the word *connote* with respect to intensional meaning rather than *denote*, which is possible with extensional meaning.

feet long, something can be done to remedy the possible inaccuracy in such a situation. A tape measure can be used and the question settled as to which person is right or whether they are both wrong. With extensional meanings, there is the opportunity to use some objective aids to get at what the sender is attempting to communicate. The word *opportunity* was used intentionally by the author because there is no guarantee that individuals will use the objective reference to reality to help settle disputes or to obtain a clearer understanding of a message. Indeed, many times people refuse to look at the tape measure (or any other aid) because they are so sure that their interpretation of reality is the correct one.

Because words can have either or both extensional and intensional meaning, the semanticist admonishes, "Find the referent!" That is, in a communication situation, where words are being tossed around and confusion is likely to abound, the semanticist recommends that one ask himself, "What is the topic under discussion? What is being referred to?" This means that for any word (or words) being used, the recipient of these words must ask himself, "What type of meaning is being communicated—extensional or intensional? Is there something in the real world to which this word refers, or is it only in the mind of the sender?" This leads us to a basic rule of thumb for sorting out the meaning of words: In order to achieve some sort of agreement about the definition (*i.e.*, the meaning) of a word, we need to go *down* the abstraction ladder. We need to get down to the process level and return to "Bessie," so to speak. To return to the example contained in the abstraction ladder (Figure 16, page 193), in order to know what someone is talking about when he uses the word *assets*, we need to push hard to make the sender go down the abstraction ladder to find out if he means *that* Bessie or if all of the other cows on his farm are also included in his thinking. The speaker may not have cows in mind at all when using this word. Without going down the ladder, one can't be sure.

If one remains on the same level of abstraction or even goes *up* the abstraction ladder, then confusion will persist, and establishing the meaning or definition of a word will not be possible. Hayakawa calls this "chasing oneself in verbal circles," and he illustrates the futility of remaining on the same level (or higher) of abstraction (or going to a higher one) when trying to communicate when he writes,

"What do you mean by *democracy*?"
"Democracy means the preservation of human rights."
"What do you mean by *rights*?"
"By rights I mean those privileges God grants to all of us—I mean man's inherent privileges."

"Such as?"

"Liberty, for example."

"What do you mean by *liberty*?"

"Religious and political freedom."

"And what does that mean?"

"Religious and political freedom is what we have when we do things the democratic way."[10]

From this example, we can readily see that no progress is being made to communicate what the sender means by the word *democracy*. In fact, all that has happened by remaining on the same level of abstraction (or going higher in certain instances) is that more words are introduced which, in themselves, are loaded with other unknown meanings because at no time did the sender "point out the referent." He never communicated successfully what he meant by democracy.

While this illustration is fresh in our minds and to emphasize further the importance of this dictum of finding the referent, let us go through the same process that Hayakawa did, but with an example that is more directly applicable to public relations.

"It's obvious that this company has poor community relations."

"What do you mean by *poor community relations*?"

"By poor community relations I mean that the management of this organization has not attained enough visibility in their community."

"What do you mean by *visibility*?"

"I mean that because of poor visibility the community has not recognized that this company is really an excellent corporate citizen."

"What do you mean by a *corporate citizen*?"

"A corporate citizen is a company that lives up to its responsibilities to the community of which it is a part, thereby avoiding the *poor community* relations that I told you about earlier."

The art of talking in verbal circles is very common to public relations practitioners. It is so easy to think about public relations problems and then attempt to communicate this thinking without having the vaguest notion of what the referent is in the problem. In other words, not only is it possible for the recipient to be unclear about the meaning (because the answers he gets stay on the same level of abstraction or go higher), but it is equally possible for the sender to *not* know clearly what he is talking about. In fact, this is precisely why the reader may find it very easy to irritate someone with the type of questioning illustrated in the

---

10 Hayakawa, p. 173.

two examples above. When you keep pushing some people to go down the abstraction ladder, it becomes clear to you (and to them—hence the irritation and frustration), that they haven't the faintest idea what they are talking about.

At this point, the reader is reminded of a discussion that was presented earlier (Chapter 7, pages 175-181) wherein it was recommended that one of the steps at the sender stage be for the public relations practitioner to translate his public relations goals into *behavioral terms* —that is, to express his public relations goals in terms of the actual modification of behavior that he expects to accomplish through his program. That step is related to this discussion because, for the same reason that a public relations practitioner will avoid fantastic claims for the efficacy of his programs when he makes this translation into actual behavior, understanding the meaning of words is enhanced by pressing for examples for which the word is supposed to stand in the real world.

The Word and the World Are Not the Same Thing

With this discussion behind us, it is easy to lead into another concept that public relations practitioners must clearly understand. Words, as symbols, are designed to *stand* for other things. It is by mutual agreement with others that certain noises can be uttered that are supposed to stand for certain objects or processes in the real world. In fact, semanticists use the phrase *verbal map* to express this relationship between words and the things they stand for. This analogy is a useful one to keep in mind, because road maps or aerial maps only *stand for* the portion of the world they present. The maps are not the real world. *Likewise, words should never be confused with reality.* Unfortunately, all too often, this simple but profound fact is forgotten. We begin to react to the words as if they were the reality, rather than the things for which they stand.

Perhaps one reason that this trap is so easy to fall into is that such a great deal of our experiences are obtained verbally or through written language. At the same time, there is the fact that we control our environment by the use of words. Consider a simple example. A rat is trained to run a simple maze to find food. This maze (called a "T" maze) consists of a series of, say, twenty different points at which the rat must turn right or left. A normal rat can learn to run the maze without any errors after a fairly large number of trials. One reason that it takes a long time is that the rat does not possess a language (or the mentality to use one) to help out. It must make use of a confusing number of visual, olfactory, and kinesthetic cues (some of which the experimenter may be manipulating to the rat's disadvantage for some particular reason) in order to learn how to find the food at the end of the maze. For a normal human being this is an extremely simple thing. One reason is that he can make use of a language system to help out. He merely says, "right turn," "two left turns," three right turns," and so on through the pattern. One time through the maze, and he can "learn" what he has to do to find his way to the food. A second human being, who has never seen the maze, can execute it perfectly with merely the verbal code: "first turn right," "next two turns left," and so on. In other words, he can learn verbally how to proceed through the maze, just as we learn by verbal directions how to find a house that we have never seen in a part of the city we have never been in before.

With language serving as such a powerful tool in coping with our environment, it is not surprising that we sometimes forget that we have not had any *direct* experience with the knowledge that we possess. Studies of very young southern children have revealed that they have very well-developed "verbal maps" of Negroes, although they may never have seen or interacted with one in their lives. The average American citizen tends to have rather well developed attitudes toward the Russians, how the President should handle them, what sort of people they are, and so on, in spite of the fact that he has never seen a Russian, has never traveled in Russia, and, in fact, isn't exactly sure where Russia is—especially if he were trying to locate it on a map that did not have the USSR clearly demarcated.

The tendency to confuse a word with reality can creep up on us in other ways too. Suppose that as a young girl growing up, Mary always heard her parents refer to her as very "plain." In time the word can become so completely internalized—part of Mary's personality—that it can actually affect such things as her ability to get along with her peers. This can even persist in spite of the fact that as a young adult Mary is not plain but actually beautiful by someone else's standards. There are people who carry these "verbal scars" all of their lives, simply because the word has become reality for them.

The Importance of the Context in Determining Meaning

An understanding of how words as symbols have meaning for us is enhanced when we remind ourselves that the *context* in which the word takes place is the way in which we learn the meaning of a word. We all learn the meaning of words, from infancy onward, by hearing a particular noise—let's say the word *house*—used in various contexts.

Gradually we learn the various meanings of the word *house* by having heard (and experienced too!) this word in a variety of different contexts.

The role of context in defining the meaning of a word is what editors of dictionaries lean on to construct dictionaries. What they do is to collect all the different contexts in which a particular word is found. This variety of usage is gleaned from all conceivable sources—which literally means going through a vast amount of literature. Then, when all of these contexts are collected and the duplicates discarded, the task of editing and teasing out all of the nuances of meaning begins. But here is the important point of this process: The ultimate list of meanings which the editor assigns to a word is not a product of what *he* thinks, but rather it is a product of all of the distinguishable nuances of meaning that he has collected based on the various *contexts* that his search of the literature has uncovered. The dictionary writer is not a lawmaker, in the sense that he hands down what is right and wrong; rather, he is a verbal historian, collecting and codifying the meanings that he has found in the recorded usage of a particular word. This all-important role of context in determining meaning can be verified by a look at any reasonably good dictionary. For example, the author turned to a dictionary that he had at hand and opened it arbitrarily to the word *long*. This is a portion of what was found:

> *Long* 1. Measuring much from end to end in space or time; not short or brief. 2. measured from end to end; as, the *long* dimension. 3. of a specified extent in length; as, the parade was a mile *long*. 4. of greater than usual or standard length, quantity, etc.,: as, a *long* dozen, a *long* game.[11] [An additional 9 contexts were provided to give the various meanings of the word *long*.]

Clearly, the meanings of the word *long* are being provided by *examples of context*—"the *long* dimension," "the parade was a mile *long*." What is true for producers of dictionaries is, of course, true for all of us. We need the context to learn the meaning.

Verbal vs. Experiential Contexts

The context in which we learn the meanings of words first is experiential—that is, through the actual experiences and behaviors that we see and imitate at the same time that we hear the words being uttered. When the young infant hears his mother say, "Give Mommie a kiss," he more often than not is hearing the words *give* and *kiss* at the same time that he is experiencing being kissed and being held close enough

---

[11] *Webster's New World Dictionary, op. cit*, p. 863.

to his mother for kissing. In this real life context he learns at least *one* meaning of the words *mommie* and *kiss*. This type of contextual learning goes on all of the time, particularly for the young infant.

Verbal contextual learning can take place after the individual has enough command of his language to be able to read and thereby learn new words by seeing these words used with other words that he already knows. Thus a student in an introductory class on social science research methods may not have the faintest idea of the meaning of the term *probability sample*. Gradually, however, his understanding of this phrase emerges as he reads a passage in which the phrase is used in different verbal contexts.

Perhaps the most effective way to appreciate how verbal context provides meaning for a particular word is to read a deliberate nonsense word in a variety of otherwise normal sentences. Hayakawa provides two interesting illustrations of this process to communicate the meanings of the words *shrdlu* and *wanky*.

1. He was exceptionally skillful with a shrdlu.
2. He says he needs a shrdlu to shape the beams.
3. I saw Mr. Jenkins yesterday buying a new handle for his shrdlu.
4. The steel head of Jenkins' shrdlu was badly chipped.
5. Don't bother with a saw or an ax; a shrdlu will do the job faster and better.

1. He seems to be perpetually wanky.
2. Some people feel most wanky in the early morning, but I get that way just before supper.
3. If you want to get over that wanky feeling, take Johnson's Homogenized Yeast Tablets.
4. Everybody feels more or less wanky on a hot, humid day.
5. . . . the wanky, wanky bluebell . . . That droops upon its stem . . .
6. I am not cross, just wanky.[12]

As one reads these various sentences constructed around the words *shrdlu* and *wanky*, some meanings of these words begin to emerge. Precisely this type of process occurs in our language with words that are not nonsense words.

Meanings of Words Do Not Remain Constant

It is obvious from what has been said above that the meanings of words cannot remain constant. Since meaning is determined by con-

---

[12] Hayakawa, p. 65.

text, which in turn is a function of how living human beings make use of these words to cope with and control their environment, it follows that the meanings of words are going to both multiply and change. Another glance at a dictionary will quickly reveal this fact. Thus, the word *howitzer* has an "original" meaning of "a sling." However, the entry goes on to give the more modern meaning of "a short cannon with a low muzzle velocity, firing shells in a relatively high trajectory."[13] Unfortunately, many persons are not aware of the fact that word meanings change and do not realize the fallacy of thinking that words have fixed meanings. On the other hand, some people think shifting meanings of words is unfortunate and the mark of sloppy thinking.

Meaning Is in the Recipient, Not in the Word

By now, it should be clear that assigning meaning to a word is a very dynamic process and a function of the time, place, and person involved. As we pointed out earlier (page 190) *the meaning of a message is in the recipient and not in the words themselves.* In this connection, Berlo writes,

> It is the thesis . . . that meanings are not in messages, that meaning is not something which is discoverable, that words do not really mean anything at all, that dictionaries do not and cannot provide us with meanings. It will be argued that *meanings are in people*, that meanings are covert responses, contained within the human organism. Meanings are learned. They are personal, our own property. We learn meanings, we add to them, we distort them, forget them, change them. We cannot *find* them. They are *in us*, not in messages. Fortunately, we usually find other people who have meanings that are similar to ours. To the extent that people have similar meanings, they can communicate. If they have no similarities in meaning between them, they cannot communicate.

> If meanings are found in words, it would follow that any person could understand any language, any code. If the meaning is in the word, we should be able to analyze the word and find the meaning. Yet obviously we cannot. Some people have meanings for some codes, others do not.

> The elements and structure of a language do not themselves have meaning. They are only symbols, sets of symbols, cues that cause us to bring our own meanings into play, to think about them, to rearrange

---

[13] *Webster's New World Dictionary*, op. cit., p. 705.

them, etc. Communication does not consist of the transmission of meaning. Meanings are not transmittable, not transferable. Only messages are transmittable, and meanings are not in the message, they are in the message-users.[14]

This last point is of paramount importance to public relations practitioners. Many public relations practitioners become enamored with the messages they develop and transmit and oftentimes become victims of what might be called "word magic"—believing that the power lies in the word rather than realizing that, at best, the word is only a stimulus that awakens certain associations within the recipient. We will return to this point later in this chapter and in Chapters 12 through 16 wherein the recipient stage in the communication process is discussed in more detail.

Some Other Possible Confusions with Words

One common distinction between words that is sometimes lost sight of is the difference between *literal* and *metaphorical*. Literal and metaphorical distinctions are, of course, related to the extensional and intensional meanings discussed earlier. For example, we use the word *dead* in both literal and metaphorical ways. If one says, "The animal is dead," his intention is to communicate something about the physiological condition of the animal that occurs when an organism's heartbeat and respiration ceases. If, on the other hand, he says, "I'm dead," now the word *dead* is to be interpreted metaphorically—*i.e.*, he is trying to connote certain feelings that he has to the recipient—and the word takes on a meaning entirely different and more liable to confusion. Hartley and Hartley illustrate this difference between literal and metaphorical meanings when they write:

Just as the forms of symbols representing objects or events may take on other meanings, so the symbolic sounds themselves may develop additional meanings. For example, compare the word "high" in its literal and metaphorical uses: "The mountain is high," and "I'm feeling high." Much of the beginning student's difficulty with psychological terms derives from this fact. Because most nouns stand for existing objects, the student assumes that all nouns represent objects, and he looks for "objects" like "memory," "intelligence," "conscience," "adjustment," and "security." When a man loses his hat, the hat is assumed to con-

---

[14] D. K. Berlo, *The Process of Communication* (New York: Holt, Rinehart & Winston, Inc., 1960), p. 175. Used by permission.

tinue to exist in a location other than the one occupied by the man. But when a man loses his memory, what then? Does the memory continue to exist apart from the man? When afflicted with laryngitis, we say: "I have lost my voice." If someone were to ask "Where?" what would the appropriate answer be? The application of the literal concept is inappropriate. We need to distinguish between the literal and metaphorical uses of verbal symbols.[15]

Another equally important distinction that should be made with respect to messages is between the words used in an *informative* manner and an *affective* manner. Some words are used to inform, such as, "I live in a suburb outside of Boston." This statement is an informational one, and, incidentally, is open to objective verification by someone else. (Our old distinction between extensional and intensional is with us again, with informative statements being the extensional type statements). If, on the other hand, one says, "That fellow is a dirty rat," the phrase *dirty rat* is supposed to communicate or express certain feelings and hence represents the use of words as symbols in an affective manner.

> Many symbols carry affective connotations but are used without explicit recognition of their affective natures; that is, they are used for their sense rather than for their literal meaning. They express emotion and they arouse emotion, and they are often used to induce an attitude rather than to convey information. Expletives such as "pig!" "Hell!" may be frankly affective symbols. Others, tacitly affective, but often used as if they were merely informative, are words like "demagogue," "bureaucracy," and "plutocrat." Political speeches, especially those attacking the opposing party, may depend heavily on such words.[16]

The pair of words applied to a better understanding of the message stage—informative *vs.* affective—is particularly applicable to the public relations practitioner. Critics of public relations practice are constantly pointing out how the public relations practitioner modifies the meaning (or distorts the "truth") when he uses different words to say the same thing. Examples that come immediately to mind are conversions such as the following:

In the Air Force:
    "Sonic Boom" *becomes* "The Sound of Freedom."

---

[15] E. L. Hartley and R. E. Hartley, *Fundamentals of Social Psychology* (New York: Alfred A. Knopf, Inc., 1955), pp. 111-112. Passages used by permission.

[16] *Ibid.*, p. 112.

In the chemical industry:
"We Conduct Research in Chemistry" *becomes* "Better Things for Better Living Through Chemistry."

On radio and television:
A news program used in conjunction with advertising *becomes* "The news has been brought to you as a public service by XYZ Oil Company."

The Danger of the Copulative "To Be"

Korzybski long ago suggested that the process of attaching wrong meanings to words is implicated in neurosis and psychosis in human beings.[17] He pioneered in pointing out the danger of using the copulative verb "to be." Regardless of the validity of the suggested relationship between mental illness and attaching incorrect meanings to words, there is no question that careful usage of forms of the verb "to be" can facilitate communication and understanding of what one means by the use of certain words. For example, in the sentences "I am not talented" and "She is very talented," the very structure lends itself to the generalizations "I am not good at *anything*" and "She is good at *everything*." More often than not, when a person says, "I am not talented," he has one or several actual activities in mind in which he may, in fact, not have any talent. Consequently, the person who says, "I am not talented" really means:

"I took piano, clarinet, and trumpet lessons and never could learn to play all three."

"I have tried to learn to paint, but no matter how hard I try I can't seem to learn to paint."

"All the way through grammar school and high school, the subjects that I received poor grades in were math and science."

For one reason or another, playing an instrument, being able to paint, and receiving good grades in math and science courses may be very important to this hypothetical individual. As a consequence, he forgets that the following statements are also true:

---

[17] A. Korzybski, *Science and Sanity: An Introduction to Non-Aristotelian Systems and Semantics* (2nd ed.; Lancaster, Pa.: Science Press, 1941), p. 183.

"I am an excellent tennis player, and in addition I have many medals that I won for achieving first place in swimming meets."

"I have always been handy with my hands, and just last week I finished making a cabinet for my hi-fi set."

"I never received less than a 'B' in all my courses in social science, history, and literature."

The point of this example is that most of us are better at some things than others. By the same token, very few of us are good at everything we try. In addition, nearly everyone has something that he or she can do rather well. However, when someone says, "I am not talented," more often than not it is a misleading statement that tends to reinforce an incorrect appraisal of one's abilities. For this reason, Korzybski recommends that we avoid the use of certain forms of the verb "to be" and in its place be explicit with respect to the behaviors that we are talking about. Instead of saying that "Mary is bright" (which implies that Mary can do well in everything), we say rather, "Mary is very good at solving problems in physics" or "Mary nearly always gets good grades in chemistry" and so on. This keeps us on our toes and more aware of just exactly the basis on which we make the generalization, "Mary is bright."

This simple concept enables us to understand such complicated phenomena as prejudice just a little better. A prejudice is generally accompanied by the use of the verb "to be" incorrectly. We say, "Republicans are all reactionary" or "Big business is bad for the country" or "All public relations practitioners are phonies." In each instance, we have taken our observations of certain Republicans, big businesses, and public relations practitioners (more often than not, incidentally, the number in each category that we have had actual experience with is very small in proportion to the total) and have generalized to include *all* cases. It is this *over*generalization that gets us into trouble, and indiscriminate use of the copulative "to be" merely encourages sloppy thinking. It is for this reason that Korzybski suggested the use of "index numbers" to accompany our words. Thus, public relations practitioner$_1$ is not public relations practitioner$_2$; Republican$_1$ is not Republican$_2$, and so on. These index numbers force us to remember the basis on which we are lumping together all cases of a given category. Then, too, we are reminded of the fact that, in order to make this grand lumping together, we have had to *overlook* (or "forget") a lot of factors that really do not fit our generalizations.

The Relationship Between Language and Thinking

This brings us to one of the last major concepts concerning language that we will take up. The concept is this: Our language affects our thinking as much as our thinking affects our language. For centuries, writers, particularly philosophers, had written (some still do!) as if the process of thinking was an independent phenomenon that took place, rather mysteriously, within an individual. Others became aware of this by the way in which those writers talked, wrote, or otherwise behaved. That language was the major vehicle by which thought was made known to others was virtually ignored. Perhaps the most accurate way of expressing it is that language was seen as merely the means by which thinking was communicated to others. It has been only since the turn of the century that we have begun to realize that *how we think is greatly influenced by the language we possess.*

Let us take a few simple examples to illustrate this all important relationship between thinking and language.

1. The words rising *and* setting. Because from a phemonological point of view the world appears to stand still and the sun revolve around the earth, our language reflects this with the words *sunrise* and *sunset*. In other words, our language reflects the relationship, in terms of motion, that we perceive between the sun and the earth. We cannot spell out exactly how much, but it is obvious that the concept that the sun was the fixed object, and that the earth revolved around the sun, clashed with our language usage. After all, any fool could see the sun "rise" and "set." How could this foolish notion possibly be true!

2. The words beginning *and* end. Because we have in our language two rather fixed concepts, *beginning* and *end*, most of us have a difficult time comprehending the mathematician or the astronomer. Concepts such as "infinite," to which the words *beginning* and *end* are in direct conflict, are consequently not fully understood by most people. Likewise, intergalactic distances, expanding universes (most people immediately think "expanding into what?"—as if the universe was going to bounce off a wall or some other surface, like a squash ball does!) are very difficult to grasp because of what we have invested in the words *beginning* and *end*. "There has to be a beginning and end to everything"—because we have a word for it.

3. Reifying *and* anthropomorphism. Here are a pair of seventy-five-cent words that constantly reflect our tendency to make the word become real and so get in the way of reality. Words used by psychoanalysts, for example, like *id, ego,* and *super-ego*, illustrate this point

of reification nicely. Before long, the words are reified—*i.e.*, made real
—to such an extent that if we were to look inside someone, we would
actually find certain entities representing the id and the ego. In fact,
the psychoanalysts themselves write as if the id were "fighting" the
ego and trying to "sneak past" this censor. In the meantime, we have
completely lost sight of the fact that these words were supposed to be
representing processes of personality functioning.

The other word—*anthropomorphism*—is closely related to reification.
This term refers to the tendency of human beings to attribute human
motivations and feelings to infrahuman organisms, inanimate objects,
and natural phenomena. Thus, if we were to believe some people,
animals do all sorts of things because they are lonely, frightened,
happy, and so on as if these same emotional states commonly found in
humans were being experienced by the animal in question. We hear a
horticulturist slip into expressions such as "such and such plants *love*
a lot of water." Perhaps the most interesting example of this tendency
is provided by the meteorologist and his weather report that seems to
be so important to us all these days. It is quite obvious that there is
"good" weather and "bad" weather and that the meteorologist can't just
report what the weather is going to be. Rather, he has to apologize to
his audience if the weather is "bad" and share in the rejoicing if the
weather is "good." Even storms (particularly hurricanes) are given
girls' names, and the activities of storms are referred to in rather
humanlike terms such as, "You can't *trust* a hurricane."

4. Snow is snow is snow. The work of anthropologists has demonstrated the relationship between language and thinking very nicely,
and we will turn to their work for our last set of examples. Benjamin
Whorf[18] points out how people from different cultures abstract from
the world around them and how this in turn affects their language
and their thinking. The Eskimo has several words for the word snow.
He has words that mean "snow on the ground," "falling snow," "snow
packed hard like ice," and "slushy snow." In English, we have all of
these different variations summed up with one word—*snow*. Without
these different words for snow, it is likely that it would be difficult
for a non-Eskimo to make all of the fine discriminations that Eskimos
are able to make with respect to this phenomenon of weather. By way
of contrast, Whorf tells us that the Hopi have one word that covers

---

[18] B. Whorf, "Science and Linguistics," in John B. Carroll (ed.), *Language,
Thought and Reality: Selected Writings of Benjamin Lee Whorf* (Cambridge:
Journal of Technology, The M.I.T. Press, 1956, and New York: John Wiley & Sons,
Inc., 1956), pp. 207-219.

anything that flies.[19] Consequently, insect, ariplane, and aviator are all lumped together by the same word. In English, of course, we do not lump all facets of this phenomenon together in the same way. It would be difficult to discuss some aspects of modern life if our language did not allow for finer discriminations with respect to flight. One could go on and on listing examples to illustrate that language partly determines thinking, but those already given should be sufficient to substantiate this generalization. It is obvious that everyone's thinking is enhanced by at least the realization that his language is partly determining it. In the case of the public relations practitioner, where so many of his efforts end in developing some sort of message, some awareness of this process is imperative. *The public relations practitioner, of all people, must realize what he is doing with words and what his own words may be doing to him.*

QUESTIONS FOR DISCUSSION

1. One of the points made in this chapter is that language is used by human beings to control their environment. This contention could be used as a point of departure to describe the work of a public relations practitioner. Assume that you have been asked to argue that the work of the public relations practitioner is essentially that of using language to control the environment of his client or company. What would you say?

2. What relationship do you see between the contention that language acquisition depends in part on commonly experienced contexts of meaning and Figure 8 (Chapter 4, page 80), describing two extremes of overlap of experiences between a sender and a recipient? Would you say that we have touched on another way of expressing the importance of establishing a "commonness" in successful communication?

3. Take any term that is commonly associated with public relations (such as *public* or *thought leader*) and insert it into your own version of Hayakawa's abstraction ladder. For example, if you were to use the term *public*, what steps would you need to get down to the process level; and what sorts of steps might you construct going *up* the abstraction ladder from the term *public*?

---

[19] *Ibid.*

Chapter 9

THE MESSAGE STAGE IN
FURTHER DETAIL:
MAKING THE MESSAGE SERVE
PUBLIC RELATIONS GOALS

In Chapter 8, we considered some of the more important semantic and anthropological concepts pertinent to a more thorough understanding of words and language. We are now ready to turn to a series of further considerations directly applicable to the message stage. Specifically, in this chapter we will be placing emphasis on factors that enable a message to be attended to by a recipient and, in addition, increase the likelihood that the message will be understood and play a role in persuading the recipient to modify his behavior in the direction desired by the sender. Also, we will consider the question of how we can predict certain effects of the message on the recipient—*e.g.*, readability, interest—and, lastly, the importance of not placing too much emphasis on *information* to achieve our public relations goals.

To begin this chapter, we will borrow the headings that Schramm[1] suggests as general requirements for a message to arouse its intended response in a recipient. Under each heading, we will supply our own

---

[1] W. Schramm, "How Communication Works," in Wilbur Schramm (ed.), *The Process and Effects of Mass Communication* (Urbana: University of Illinois Press, 1954), p. 13. Used by permission.

discussions and illustrations of how these requirements apply to public relations practice.

GENERAL REQUIREMENTS OF A MESSAGE SO AS TO AROUSE ITS INTENDED RESPONSE

1. The Message Must Be So Designed and Delivered as to Gain the Attention of the Intended Destination

In simplest terms, what this first requirement spells out is that, in order for a message to have an effect, it must reach its intended destination. This requirement is easy to state, but fulfilling it has taxed some of the best minds in such diverse fields as advertising, government, and public relations. There are several subelements of the requirement that make it difficult to attain. First, there is the question of making the message available. In order to even hope to communicate with an individual or a group, you must be certain that you can reach that individual or group with your message. Of course, availability is only a portion of the story. Exposure is not the same thing as paying attention. In other words, you may have selected a medium that actually reaches your intended recipient—in the sense that what you want him to read is in his evening paper, for example—but insuring that he will actually pay attention to your message is another matter. A communicator must anticipate and counteract all of the competing factors that may intervene, so that the individual or group actually pays attention to his message.

Attracting attention is hard enough for any communicator to cope with, but for a great many public relations communication situations it is particularly hard. The reason: More often than not the public relations practitioner concerned does not have what might be called "built-in" motivation working for him. Let us consider two contrasting situations to illustrate this point.

An advertising man—say, one who has to sell cars,—has a lot of distractions to cope with in getting an intended recipient to pay attention to his message, not the least of which is the host of different makes and models a buyer may choose from, both foreign and domestic. However, there is one important factor that our hypothetical advertising man has in his favor that the public relations practitioner generally does not have: the fact that there are many *other forces* in society "on his side," so to speak, that make a high proportion of individuals want a certain sort of car (*e.g.*, the desire to "keep up with the Joneses"). To put it another way, the desire for a car (hence, the likelihood that the message will be attended to) is often already there.

Now let's consider a typical public relations practitioner. Besides all of the problems he *shares* with the advertising man (such as competition for attention from a host of other individuals and organizations), he has the *additional problem* of having to communicate with a recipient who is not *motivated to pay attention to what he has to say*. Who cares if the company our hypothetical public relations practitioner represents has been a good corporate citizen and has done its share in trying to solve a particular community problem? Who cares if such-and-such a nonprofit health group is making progress in finding a cure for some disease that very few persons know anything about in the first place? Who cares if some small liberal arts college has drastically revised its educational standards and is providing good solid liberal arts education for a certain number of students, but is now in critical financial straits? The list could extend for pages and pages describing, at least by thumbnail sketch, the problems involved in getting messages through to uninterested recipients. To make matters worse, in most of the problem situations that public relations practitioners find themselves there is another headache to contend with. In most instances if the recipient does pay attention, it can mean that he may have to take some responsibility on his own shoulders. Thus, if he pays attention to the call for blood or to the need to get out and vote or to serve as a volunteer in a local organization, it will mean that he will have to extend himself and get involved. It is all of these factors, and more, that make the simple task of designing a message to gain the attention of some recipient such a formidable one for the public relations practitioner. We will return to this general problem again and again. (See, for example, pages 224-231.)

2. The Message Must Get the Meaning Across

In Figure 8 (page 80), a schema was presented which symbolizes the relationship between effective communication of messages and the degree of overlap of experiences common to sender and recipient. This second requirement is a special case of that more generalized schema. Here we are spelling out the fact that the signs (*i.e.*, the particular symbols that are part of some language system) used by the communicator must be such that the recipient will derive the meaning intended by the sender. In this day and age, with increasing specialization and with technological developments appearing with frightening speed, fulfilling this second requirement presents its own unique obstacles.

Let's consider a specific example from the oil industry to make our point here. The sine qua non of this particular industry is the large number of oil wells that must be dug before one profitable oil well is found. This means that computing the cost of finding profitable wells must be based on the cost of *all* of the wells driven in any one year rather than just the costs associated with the successful wells. Add to this the fact that different wells have different depletion rates—to say nothing of competition from other companies at home and abroad— and the cost factor of staying in business is further complicated. But how does a public relations practitioner for an oil company find a basis for the common signs which will enable him to communicate with a group (say, the employees) who have no real basis for understanding such concepts as "depletion" and "low probability that a successful well will be found"?

To overcome the problem of communicating such abstract concepts, the Pure Oil Company made use of a special cardboard device developed by the American Petroleum Institute to illustrate the low probability of striking oil with any one drilling.

> . . . The device is built on the punch board principle and has 100 holes in a baseboard, over which hangs a metal plunger on a string which the viewer can use to pick what he hopes will not be a dry hole. (All except 3 holes are dry.) If he picks one of the three good wells, a white light flashes on. If he hits one of the 97 dry holes, a red light flashes on. The backboard bears basic information on the costs of drilling. The device was developed by the American Petroleum Institute's advisory committee on employee information. . . .
>
> Pure Oil uses it as a means of telling the depletion story to employees. It has been on display in the employee cafeteria for several weeks and is now in the reception lobby. It may later be loaned to schools or used at trade shows.[2]

This example is admittedly a variation of an old approach to putting across a message; however, it does illustrate our second general requirement: getting a message across. *Probability* may not be a word that means much to the average employee, but trying to make a white light appear on a board by inserting a metal plunger in a hole and seeing how many holes have to be tried before a white light appears *does* fit into the experience of the average employee. That this experi-

---

[2] *Communication Reports*, July, 1963 (Enterprise Publications, 20 North Wacker Drive, Chicago 6, Illinois), p. 1. Used by permission.

ence will be understood as one version of probability in real life is a reasonably safe interpretation to make.

EFFORTS TO PROVIDE MORE PRECISE GUIDES TO MAKE THE MESSAGE CONTAIN COMMON SIGNS

Every communicator would like to have some guide or formula to use in attaining this second requirement for a message. It would be wonderful, for example, to have guides as to what types of scenes in a film would engender in the viewer the meaning intended by the producer. A classic illustration of this problem in films is contained in the story told about a film designed to illustrate the role that the anopheles mosquito plays in spreading malaria. At certain points in the film, enlargements of the mosquito were presented, illustrating parts of the insect's body and how these parts play a role in transmitting malaria. After the film was over, discussions were held with members of the audience in order to continue the learning process and to translate some of the general principles illustrated in the film into specifics that fit the local surroundings. Only then did the officials learn that the people in the audience felt that, although the film was very interesting, it really did not apply to them because in their country *they had no monsters of the size they had seen on the screen*. Because the concept of *magnification* had no place in their culture, they took a very literal view of the mosquito that was shown in the film. *That this mosquito was really small and something that they were very familiar with, enlarged by a special technique, was an idea having no counterpart in their previous experiences.* In this instance, the film makers had not met our second general requirement of messages, and they *didn't even realize it* until it was too late. As was pointed out earlier, a guide to the use of visual presentations does not exist—at least in the detailed sense that one would like. It is also likely that it will be a considerable period of time before one will exist for such visual media as films and TV.

The Flesch Formulas

This state of affairs does *not* apply to the printed word, however. Some progress has been made in developing a guide to knowing when you are probably expressing something in written form that can be understood by your intended audience. We have in mind the work of Rudolph Flesch[3]—probably the most widely known work of its kind.

---

[3] *See*, for example, the following books written by Rudolph Flesch, all published by Harper & Row, Publishers, New York: *The Art of Plain Talk* (1946); *The Art of Readable Writing* (1949); and *The Art of Clear Thinking* (1951).

Because the public relations practitioner relies so heavily on the written word (as compared with the degree to which he utilizes radio and television, for example, to help solve his public relations problems), *it is important that he be cognizant of this representative example of one approach to making sure that the intended recipient can understand the message.*[4]

The Flesch approach to making written material more readable is to measure two important elements of readability: (1) ease of reading, and (2) human interest—the degree to which the intended recipient is motivated to read what is written. With this objective in mind, Flesch has evolved two scoring techniques that can be applied to written copy, a *reading ease* score and a *human interest* score. Each of these techniques measures a different thing in written copy, and one is just as important as another. In fact, Flesch feels that, if anything, the human interest score is more important because if a person is motivated to read what you have written, he will put up with a lot of unreadable material; however, if he is not interested, he is not likely to read it, no matter how easy it reads.[5]

Computing the reading ease score and the human interest score is actually quite simple, and after a little practice has been invested in the techniques, the scores can be readily obtained. To speed up the computation of reading ease scores, Flesch has developed a chart called the "How Easy" chart. The average number of words per sentence, the average number of syllables per one hundred words, and a ruler or some other straight edge are all that are needed to permit the reading ease score to be read directly from this special chart.[6]

After both the reading ease score and the human interest score have been obtained, tables developed by Flesch aid the interpretation of the scores. For example, in the case of the *reading ease score* (which can range from 0 to 100), there is one table that tells the user what type of magazine typically contains the reading ease score that he has computed, ranging from comics and pulp fiction through *Harper's* and

---

[4] Naturally, this approach to making your message understandable touches on only one portion of all of the factors that cause an intended recipient to perceive the message intended by the sender. Consequently, the Flesch formulas are only a part of the story. If the considerations brought into focus by the Flesch formulas are *not* met, however, no amount of attention to other important factors, such as persuasion (*see* Chapters 13 through 16) will be of value. In other words, the Flesch formulas are factors that must be kept in mind *along with many others.*

[5] Rudolph Flesch, *How to Test Readability* (New York: Harper & Row, Publishers, 1951), p. 41.

[6] *Ibid.,* p. 5.

Atlantic Monthly to scientific and professional journals. The other table translates the reading ease score into equivalent levels of education. For example, a reading ease score between 50 and 60 is roughly equivalent to the reading ability found among high school graduates.

A table is available to help interpret the *human interest score* also. This table gives a brief description of the style and the kind of magazine that contains such a style for different ranges of human interest scores (which also range from 0 to 100). For example, a human interest score between 40 to 60 is described in the table as "highly interesting" and typical of the writing found in the *New Yorker*.

We have obviously only scratched the surface when it comes to trying to measure the readability of written copy. The reader is strongly urged to read the sources cited earlier in this chapter. Because the typical public relations practitioner depends so much on the written word, it is imperative that he be fully aware of information such as this so that he can apply it to his work constantly.

The importance of constructing a written message that is appropriate to the intended recipient or audience cannot be overemphasized. For most of us, writing is a highly personal matter that reflects our own training, education, prejudices, and so on, which make it *extremely easy* to forget that the way we have written something is likely to be either too difficult or too simple for the intended audience. Generally, the tendency is to make the material too difficult for the intended reader. We forget that persons with a college education still make up approximately only one-third of the adult population of the United States.[7,8]

Hopefully, we have gone into enough detail concerning the Flesch formulas to motivate the reader to try out this system on some of

---

[7] It is useful at this point to remind ourselves of the basic assumption of literacy that the printed word makes. As George Arnstein points out in his article, "Automation—Threat and Promise" (*California Monthly*, January, 1963),

> . . . based in part on our affluence, we have been deluding ourselves into thinking that ours is a fully literate society. In fact, on the best evidence available there are more than *eleven million adult Americans who are not literate* by any meaningful sense of the word. They cannot read the label on a bottle of medicine and they can only guess that the sign at the corner says "No Left Turn." [Italics added. Passage used by permission.]

This gives the public relations practitioner, who is so dependent on the printed word for many phases of his public relations programing, something to think about!

[8] Also important, of course, is the *meaning* that workers attach to the words and what assumptions the sender is making on that score, too. *See particularly* the material based on the research conducted by the Opinion Research Corporation, Chapter 4, page 82.

his own copy, if he has not already done so, to get an appreciation of how these tools can sharpen one's ability to write more appropriately for the audience he has in mind. Flesch formulas do not exhaust the possible (and needed) measures that can be applied to written material; this is why we have included other measures besides Flesch in the following sections. Compared to the dearth of scoring formulas for other media (such as film and tape), the Flesch method is indeed a giant step forward. *If only we had equivalent measures to rate the understandability of the visual content of a TV show before it is put on the air!*

Measures Other Than the Flesch Formulas

As we indicated earlier, the Flesch approach to measuring readability is not the only approach available. There are other techniques applicable to other types of message problems that the public relations practitioner should know about. Let us consider briefly a few examples.

Content Analysis. First and foremost, there is the tool with very broad applications known as *content analysis*.[9] Simply stated, content analysis is a research technique for obtaining an objective and systematic description of a communication. Such a description enables one to draw valid inferences about various dimensions of a communication, whether manifest or latent. This research technique is particularly valuable in that it is not limited to a communication in printed form. Content analysis can be applied to radio broadcasts, to telecasts—in short, to any form of communication that one desires to study. Naturally, if the communication is by radio or TV, special procedures are needed to "translate" the message into a form more amenable to study. Thus, a radio broadcast would probably be transcribed and typed to make possible more leisurely and detailed study.

This is all of the detail that we shall present concerning content analysis at this point; we will return to this technique in more detail in Chapter 19 (pages 570-573).

In addition to content analysis, there are two other well known techniques designed to aid in the study of certain aspects of messages. They are the "cloze procedure"[10] and the "content response code."[11]

---

[9] Bernard Berelson, *Content Analysis in Communication Research* (Glencoe, Ill.: The Free Press of Glencoe, Inc., 1952).

[10] Wilson L. Taylor, " 'Cloze Procedure': A New Tool for Measuring Readability," *Journalism Quarterly*, XXX (Fall, 1953), 415-433.

[11] Roy Carter, "The Content Response Code: A Pre-testing Procedure," *Journalism Quarterly*, XXXII (Spring, 1955), 147-160.

Cloze Procedure. Let us first consider the cloze procedure briefly by quoting from some material developed by its originator, Wilson L. Taylor.

If you described Figure A you would probably report a triangle over-lapping a circle. Yet, *neither shape is wholly present.* You complete them by mentally "closing up the gaps." You can do this because circles and triangles are simple, regular, and *familiar* patterns. Also, there is enough of each shape to be recognized. Figure B's triangle is harder to 'see.' It is less complete, somewhat distorted, and becomes confused with its irregular background.

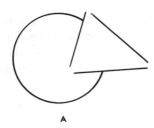

A

B

Rather than simplicity or sym-metry, sheer familiarity with the pattern made by human profile seems to explain how a person can guess that an eye is covered up by the parallelogram in Fig. C.

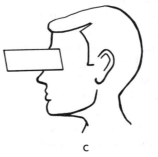

C

Altogether, success in "seeing" the incomplete patterns in Figures A, B, and C depends much upon the simplicity, regularity, and famil-iarity of the shapes themselves—and on their relative degrees of com-pleteness.

Similar qualities seem to help you guess words left out of a sen-tence. It is easy to put "loss" in "Deafness is _____ of hearing" be-cause the words and the pattern they make are simple and familiar. It is harder to guess "loss" in "_____ is _____ of hearing," or in "Anacusia is _____ of audition." Note that in "President Abraham _____ once told a _____ about a slave who . . ." you almost in-stantaneously and unconsciously fill in "Lincoln" and "story." Cloze procedure depends upon this sort of behavior.

How Cloze Procedure Operates

"Cloze" is derived from "closure," the term some psychologists use to refer to the notion that humans tend to perceive a familiar pattern as a whole even when parts of it are missing, obscured, or distorted.

The "cloze" procedure can be used to contrast the "readabilities" of printed materials. First, one "mutilates" all passages by using some systematic (mechanical) method for deleting the same number of words from each. One might count out every fifth word, or let a table of random numbers choose them. The mutilated passages are then reproduced with each deleted word replaced by a standard-sized blank, (say, 10 letter spaces long). Copies are distributed to every member of a test group. Each person is asked to guess the missing words. Every time a person fills in a missing word correctly, he scores one point. His "cloze score" for any passage is the total number or percentage of its missing words he fills in correctly.

To arrive at a cloze score for each passage, one adds together the scores that all individuals make on that passage. The passage that scores the largest total of correct "fill-ins" is considered "most readable" for the kind of population which the group represents.

Cloze procedure is *not* limited to the testing of readability. It has many other uses. But the operations just described are, with slight variations, common to virtually all its applications.[12]

It is clear from the brief description of the cloze procedure that its applications are exceedingly wide. Also, this technique, which is *not* a readability formula, may be particularly suited to certain public relations communication situations in that it gets at the *understanding* that the reader has for what the writer is trying to put across. Certainly, this particular feature of communication is at the heart of what a public relations practitioner is trying to do most of the time with his recipients, regardless of the public relations problem situation involved.

Content Response Code.[13] Still another technique, in this case designed more specifically for written communication, is the content response code (CRC). This tool is generally used to show where a

[12] Wilson L. Taylor, "Cloze Procedure," *Agrisearch*, II, No. 2 (February, 1956), 1. Used by permission.

[13] The writer is indebted to F. Earle Barcus, Associate Professor, Communication Research Division, Boston University, for permission to use his description of the content response code reported in *Recommendations for Research Related to the Communication of Gerontological Information* (a report submitted to the Gerontology Branch, U.S. Department of Health, Education, and Welfare, February, 1965) as the basis for the material included in this section.

communication will and will not produce the desired effect. It does so by pretesting the positive and negative reactions of a sample of recipients (similar, of course, to the intended recipients) to the written content of the proposed communication.

The method was developed by Roy E. Carter[14] as part of a study for the United States Information Agency. It was originally developed over a period of several months, using printed materials for distribution in the Far East and employing foreign students at the university as judges. Carter reports that with one or two persons available for tabulation work, he was able to work with groups of from twenty to forty persons. The procedures involved in the content response code are fairly simple. The highlights of the process are as follows:

1. Select a group of subjects which are representative of the audience to which the communication will ultimately be addressed.
2. Explain the purposes of the study to the subjects and assure them that their responses are anonymous. Subjects should be instructed to be totally frank in their reactions.
3. Before carrying out the CRC test, the investigator prepares master copies of the communication to be tested. He divides the text into "content units," which he marks off with a pencil and ruler in each copy. (A unit is usually a paragraph of text, but it can be less or more.) Each unit is given a serial number, and a "master sheet" for tallying subjects' responses is prepared.
4. Conduct a short training session on some unrelated materials to see that everyone understands the procedures.
5. Distribute the test materials to the subjects along with the instruction sheet. Instructions can be flexible to fit the materials to be tested.
6. Subjects are to then mark *each unit* of communication. The marking instructions are as follows: If the subject has a *positive* reaction to the unit of communication, he marks in the margin with a plus (+) sign; if he has a negative or unfavorable reaction, he marks the unit with a minus (−) sign.
7. For each unit of content, the plus and minus marks are tallied on the master sheet. The results appear as two sets of numbers for each unit (number of pluses and number of minuses).
8. Results are easily analyzed to give a "profile" as to which content units obtain the most reaction and what sort of reaction (*i.e,* positive or negative).

[14] *See* footnote 11, page 217.

9. After analysis of the responses, a follow-up procedure is used to determine *why* the subjects answered as they did. Each subject is given the original material along with his or her reactions. Then, through the use of an opaque screening apparatus, certain content units are projected on a screen and the subjects asked to comment on why they marked as they did. Responses from subjects may be made orally, or the subjects may be asked to write out what they objected to in the communication unit.

The applicability of this technique to public relations practice is quite clear. There are times when some measure of advance reaction to a publication is important enough to take the time to go through this pretesting procedure rather than "fly blind." Also, everyone who has ever written something and then given it to another individual (or several individuals) for criticism has experienced the frustration of obtaining the feedback, "It's fine" or "That's a great article" or "I don't like it," but without any details. The content response code can be employed within a public relations department or agency to insure the fact that details will be forthcoming when reactions to written material are desired.

By now we have provided enough details so that the reader has an appreciation of some of the evaluation techniques available to the message stage in the communication process. The author assumes that the Flesch approach will prove to be more *generally* applicable to established public relations practitioners and those aspiring to be practitioners. Whereas one can be certain that any public relations practitioner will have occasion to want to know something about the *readability* of the copy he proposes to use for a particular audience, this same statement is less likely to be applicable to the qualities evaluated by some of the other techniques described.

WHAT GUIDES ARE AVAILABLE FOR NONWRITTEN MESSAGES?

All of us are familiar with the saying, "One picture is worth ten thousand words." Apparently this phrase was coined by Jamison Handy while he was on the staff of the Secretary of the Interior during World War I. He was trying to persuade people to accept audiovisual training devices for various applications in war industries. As the story goes, he called his saying a "Chinese proverb" in order to give it more credibility.[15]

Chinese proverb or not, the saying goes directly to the heart of what

---

[15] Randall Harrison, "Pictorial Communication," *Search*, VI, No. 6 (1962), 1.

we all intuitively feel and believe about the role of pictures in communication. We have the feeling that it must be an ancient observation, and, therefore, it does sound like an old Chinese proverb.

For a variety of reasons—not the least of which is that so much can be communicated in pictures—we have only the vaguest of guides to offer on how to use pictures in communications. The material at the end of this section, summarizing a variety of research efforts in the area of pictorial presentation, is typical of what is available. If the reader will reflect a moment on the material presented in Chapter 7, dealing with the topic of perception, he can provide his own answers as to why an understanding of how and what a picture communicates is so sketchy at the present time. In that chapter, we learned that perception is a function of both structural and functional factors. Within the structural factors we have such things as location, isolation, and arrangement of the discrete stimuli that exists within any single picture or photograph. With such a complex array of stimuli, what can we isolate and identify as that portion of the picture which people are looking at? A consideration of the Rorschach ink blot test provides a good illustration to point out the difficulties of isolating the structural factors in any given perception. A particular card of the Rorschach series consists of an irregular configuration in black on a white background. (Some of the cards have color as well.) Typically, a person being given the Rorschach test is asked to tell what he "sees" (*i.e.*, perceives) in the picture. Research with this device has shown that literally thousands of different items (animals, people, geographical similarities, and so on) are seen in any given Rorschach card. We will, of course, ignore the question of what is normal and abnormal in the things that people see in a particular Rorschach card. The point is that the variety is tremendous for any given card. This, in turn, means that trying to predict ahead of time what a person will look at in a given visual presentation is exceedingly complex. The reasons for this extensive variety of perceptions are a function of the fact that the Rorschach card is deliberately vague or unstructured. This means that the configuration is deliberately designed so that as many things can be seen in the cards as possible. However, presenting more definite pictures does not necessarily get around the problem. Another well-known projective test— the Thematic Apperception Test—is made up of a series of more "normal" scenes: that is, people, inanimate objects, background features, and the like. However, with such stimuli as these, people still offer a wide variety of interpretations of these pictures. This means that they are seeing (once again, perceiving) different things in these pictures.

With the stimulus factors being held constant—that is, showing the same pictures to different people—the role of the functional fac-

tors—of needs, temporary mood states, and previous experiences—
are brought to the fore. The accuracy of predicting what someone
will see in a pictorial presentation varies as a result of any one or all
three of the functional factors that determine perception. When one
considers how a given segment of people can vary in their particular
needs at any moment, in their mood states, in their previous experiences, the variety of interpretations of a picture as a result of functional factors in perception is readily understandable.

Lastly, there are a variety of physiological factors to consider—such
things as visual acuity (some people have such poor vision they
just don't see the detail you included), systematic ways of viewing a
picture, and so on.

The author recently conducted a study of how people viewed a variety of advertisements covering a wide range of products and styles
of advertising. This study illustrates the difficulty in trying to predict
how people will react to a visually presented stimulus. In addition to
asking the subjects all about what they had seen in the advertisements,
a special apparatus was used to measure the eye movements of the
viewers as they scanned the ads. The author was able to tell where and
when a subject had fixated wh.: viewing the ad. A careful study of the
visual scanning patterns revealed, as expected, that no two persons
scanned the ads in a similar way. Each individual had his own unique
search pattern. In addition, however, there were a variety of factors in
the data that suggested that in each viewer a sort of "visual fingerprint"
could be detected; that is, each viewer exhibited a consistency of scanning behavior that persisted over a wide range of visual stimuli. If this
interpretation holds up with further research, it means that individual
differences in visual scanning behavior, causing each one of us to view
what we are presented in a rather fixed manner, tends to work against
the intentions of the variety of artists who have constructed a particular
visual presentation with some message in mind.[16] One could be working at cross-purposes with the others, thereby suggesting still another
variable that makes prediction of pictorial interpretation more difficult.

Armed with an appreciation of how difficult it is to predict the way
in which a message in pictorial form is likely to be reacted to, let us
look at some generalizations about the use of pictorial presentations,
based on research conducted by the Curtis Publishing Company.[17]

---

[16] Edward J. Robinson, "How an Advertisement's Size Affects Responses to It,"
Journal of Advertising Research, III, No. 4 (December, 1963), 16-24.

[17] J. B. Haskins and D. E. Stuart, "How to Increase Reader Interest in Your
Printed Material," *The Graphics Arts Monthly*, June, 1959, as quoted in Harrison,
op. cit., p. 1. Used by permission.

1. The number of illustrations in an article significantly influences the number of both male and female readers who will start the piece.

2. A large illustration and a small amount of text on an opening page is preferable to a smaller illustration and more text.

3. Even with text held constant, large illustrations are preferred to small illustrations.

4. Four-color photographs stimulate readership.

5. Vignetted pictures (with no background) are not as well liked as the same illustration with background.

6. Somewhat similarly, readers prefer 'squared up' layouts. Titled pictures and 'cookie-cutter' layouts tend to be disliked.

7. Readers prefer photographs to drawings. When artwork is used, it should be clear, realistic, and nearly photographic in quality.

8. Cartoons are immensely popular as separate features, but as illustrations they net lower readership for the article than photographs.

GENERAL REQUIREMENTS OF A MESSAGE SO AS TO AROUSE ITS INTENDED RESPONSE (Continued)

3. The Message Must Arouse Personality Needs in the Destination and Suggest Some Ways to Meet Those Needs.

This third requirement highlights the fact that senders of messages must make some assumptions about the motivations of the recipient involved. Reactions to messages are inseparable from—or, better still, are part and parcel of—the drives or needs that responding to the message will serve. The classical example, of course, is the advertiser's message. Whether directly or subtly, the advertiser attempts to make the recipient believe that doing what he recommends in his ad will satisfy some need in the recipient. The popularity of "motivation research" in recent years is nothing more than a realization that a wider range of motives than was previously suspected, with which one can align messages, are potentially usable in the market place. To put it another way: The rational motives that advertisers had been attempting to align themselves with (such as, "The product is cheaper, yet equal in quality") were not necessarily any better than emotional appeals (such as, "If you use this particular hairdressing, girls will fall all over you too").

Overemphasis on Information[18]

In recent years, a marked trend is seen among industrial and professional organizations to tell their "story" to various publics, the telling being done, of course, by their public relations practitioners. More often than not, the motivation of the public relations practitioner to tell his story stems from the fact that either (1) an incorrect version of his organization's purpose is now believed by the relevant publics or (2) for a variety of reasons *no version* is believed, simply because hardly anyone knows about the organization.[19]

In both types of change situations, it appears that great reliance has been placed by public relations practitioners on information supposedly contained in the message to bring about the desired change. By reliance on information is meant the basic assumption made by many public relations practitioners that their function is to "inform" their respective publics about their organization. This feeling is embodied in the following phrase: "If they [meaning the relevant publics] only understood us, they would like [or support] us." Seldom is the equally possible turn of events seriously considered; that is: "If they understood us, they would hate us." It is in this sense that many public relations practitioners place excessive reliance on the programs of information that they direct to their many and varied publics. One effect of this thinking is to cause the public relations practitioner concerned to overlook the third message requirement under discussion here: *A message must arouse certain needs in a potential recipient and indicate how these needs can be satisfied.* In short, the role of motivation associated with any successful communication attempt tends to be lost sight of in favor of the belief that all that needs to be done is to inform—*i.e.*, "give them the facts."

There appear to be at least *three* main reasons behind this overreliance on information.

First of all, information in the past has worked for some attitude change objectives in certain circumstances. No one will deny that providing a certain public with information is sometimes necessary or that

---

[18] For this section, the author has borrowed some material written by him and originally presented in a chapter entitled "Applying Psychology" in Howard Stephenson (ed.), *Handbook of Public Relations* (New York: McGraw-Hill Book Company, 1960), pp. 156-162. All passages from the *Handbook* used by permission.

[19] The reader will undoubtedly recognize that the two types of attitude change situations involved here are, of course, Type A and Type B. The distinction was first discussed in Chapter 2, pages 24-26. It will be useful for the reader to refer to this earlier material, since the present discussion is an extension of the thinking presented there.

it at times works to produce attitude change. Given the proper motivational context (which the public relations practitioner is either not aware of or did not produce, or both), only pertinent information is needed. However, the very fact that it does work at times has almost blinded some public relations practitioners to the limitation of merely informing a group they wish to change.

Secondly, it is quick and easy. There is comparatively little work to constructing a message and getting it to the recipients. Especially with the media at our command in these times, this is no great problem.[20]

Lastly, the field of advertising has had a powerful influence. Many people who were previously in the advertising field are now in public relations. There is no question that advertising people have been successful inasmuch as their particular goals have been met. Public relations people have borrowed heavily at times from the advertising man—particularly in the area of techniques for informing people. Advertisers have Type A change problems—*i.e.*, changing misconceptions to correct conceptions. Type B change problems are their real specialty—informing persons who were previously uninformed about a new product. Advertisers often have been quite successful with their change problems, and one of their main techniques has been to inform. The means of informing have become elaborate, but they are, nevertheless, nothing more than information techniques.

Advertising change problems, however, are not identical with the change problems faced in public relations programs. As noted earlier (when discussing message Requirement No. 1 for messages), the advertiser has culture on his side, because by the time most of us are of consumer age, we have had instilled in us motivation, or need, for many, many items sold by advertising. Hence, the job of the advertiser becomes primarily one of *directing* individuals toward one product instead of another. Motivating his publics to buy something in the first place is of secondary importance.

The energetic work of advertisers over the years contributes to—some say really constitutes—the cultural influence which provides the motivation now present in most selling situations. But regardless of how this cultural influence is produced, most of us approach the goods and services situation which concern the advertiser with a considerable number of built-in motivations. Most of us just *have* to have a new car, dress, suit, freezer, ad infinitum.

This explains, partly, why frequency of subjection to advertising

---

[20] The reader is reminded that the ease with which most practicing public relations people produce a message and then transmit it was the subject of an earlier discussion (*see* Chapter 4, pages 84-86). Everything included in that discussion concerning the "seduction" quality of the media also applies here.

results in buying a particular product. We tend to move in the direction of the product we have heard the most about. This situation, fortunately or unfortunately, *does not exist* in most public relations situations requiring attitude change.

This does not mean that information is useless—far from it. But for some situations, the message must be given an assist so that the information will be perceived and accepted. The assist can be summarized by the term *motivation*. Merely being informed generally does not produce enough of a push to cause people to change. In other situations, of course, information alone is sufficient.

To illustrate: If a fire starts in a theater, the audience needs only to be informed of it to seek safety. As a matter of fact, the problem is often just the opposite. Information in this instance may trigger off too much motivation, and a panic may result. In any case, information alone gets action.

At the other extreme, assume that you want to change the voting behavior of a certain group. If this hypothetical group is a typical cross section, probably no more than fifty per cent of the eligible voters vote. Now let us see to what extent information alone changes their behavior. Say we inform them of (1) their duty as citizens to vote, (2) how voting is an integral part of our freedoms, (3) why not voting invites loss of these freedoms, and so on. If this group is typical, mere information will make hardly any change at all in their behavior. In fact, we need only to look at the results of precisely this type of campaign around election time—particularly election for national offices. We saturate the newspapers, radio, and TV—to say nothing of billboards and the like—with information such as that listed above. And still the proportion of people voting remains remarkably constant. What's more, people who do not vote more often than not realize that they should and that it is their duty as citizens. Information had done all that it could.

In other words, there are many public relations problem situations where the information contained in the message is essentially useless as an instigator of behavior change. It is this second kind of situation that public relations practitioners find themselves running up against so often. Public relations practitioners ask whether anything can be done to help them motivate as well as inform. This question needs further discussion.

PARTICIPATION IN CHANGE ATTEMPTS

In the past two decades, numerous experiments have been performed dealing with the problem of changing behavior and attitudes. We have the well known studies by Lewin and his co-workers during

World War II, experimenting with ways of changing the meat-eating habits of people.[21] Naturally, due to wartime conditions, it was important to get people to change from the popular cuts (steaks, chops, and the like) to the less popular (kidneys and sweetbreads, for example). Lewin and his workers invited the people involved to work on the "problem" itself—how to make meat supplies go farther by a process identified by them as "group decision." The people themselves would "solve" the problem by deciding, among other things, that eating unpopular cuts of meat was one of the answers. Using this approach, Lewin found that more people changed their eating behavior and that the change lasted for a longer period of time than was the case among those people who had merely been informed of the necessity for changing meat-eating habits. This was true in spite of the fact that the change information stressed patriotism, wartime sacrifices needed, etc.

Research work in an entirely different area with entirely different change objectives has tended to generate the same conclusions. Coch and French conducted experiments with changing work procedures of workers in industry.[22] The approach which permitted the group to participate in the "problem"—what should or could be done to maintain or improve production—was superior to other ways of changing their behavior. The usual approach of calling the workers together, informing them of the change (message), giving them the reasons behind the change, and answering the questions they asked was not nearly as effective.

Some generalizations about participating. The studies cited above, along with many others,[23] permit us to make some generalizations which have application to many public relations change situations. Among them are:

   a) Attempts to change people appear to be more successful when some sort of participation on their part is possible.
   b) Participation appears to be highly related to motivation. That is, when an individual has an opportunity to participate, he seems

---

[21] K. Lewin, "Group Decision and Social Change," in *Readings in Social Psychology* (rev. ed.; New York: Holt, Rinehart & Winston, Inc., 1962), pp. 459-473.

[22] L. Coch and J. R. P. French, "Overcoming Resistance to Change," *Human Relations*, 1948, pp. 512-532.

[23] *See particularly* such studies as reported in "Acquiring Conviction Through Active Participation," in C. I. Hovland, I. L. Janis, and H. H. Kelley, *Communication and Persuasion* (New Haven, Conn.: Yale University Press, 1953), pp. 215-240.

to become more strongly motivated, especially in the direction of the topic under consideration.

c) Participation must give the individual involved the feeling that his contribution to the situation is either recognized or utilized. Situations in which an individual is asked to participate but over which he has little or no control cannot be expected to produce the same desirable results. As a matter of fact, such pseudoparticipation situations might well have a reverse effect.

d) For some types of change situations, information alone, even when carefully directed to a "captive audience," is not effective in changing behavior or attitudes. If this is true of a captive audience, how much more true may it be of a public that is merely being reached by mass media.

Participation plus information.
We have now considered three main factors:

1. A series of reasons which explain why public relations practitioners have relied on information to achieve behavior changes.
2. An argument to demonstrate why this dependence is unwarranted.
3. An area of experimentation in social psychology, the results of which point to the importance of participation on the part of the individual in attempts to change his behavior.

To complete our discussion of factors that must be kept in mind about this third requirement for a message to be effective, let us examine a public relations case in which one phase of the program, as handled by the author, reflects an attempt to induce motivation in the recipients to attend to the message rather than rely on the message content alone.

An example of supplementing the message.
A group of professional optometrists had three major public relations objectives to achieve. They desired to:

1. change the incorrect information people had concerning the profession's services to correct information because they wanted the public to be cognizant of their services;
2. make people who were totally ignorant of their existence aware of them; and
3. change the unfavorable views of other, allied professions toward them to favorable ones.

Analysis of previous communication attempts made by the public relations counsel for this group indicated that they had not considered either the motives of the recipients concerned or how they perceived the services of this professional group. They had apparently been more interested in the possibilities of transmitting their messages by radio, television, and the newspapers than in the analysis of how their communication would be perceived. In short, they had placed undue emphasis on the information contained in the various messages rather than considered how the recipients were to be *motivated* to pay attention to their messages in the first place.

A more realistic examination of the communication situation they faced suggested that a solution to some of their problems lay in the *children* of the recipients. The professional group could more effectively arouse the motivations of the recipients to take an interest in communication by directing efforts toward them *as parents*. Actually, a great service potential lay with children. Early preventive eye care for a child can avoid a great deal of corrective work for him as an adult. If communication were to be slanted in such a fashion that the relationship between the child and the profession could be emphasized, this might provide the "commonness" referred to earlier as a basis for effecting attitude change.

To achieve this, certain members of the professional association were asked to serve as a panel to appear before women's clubs. Each panel member gave a ten minute presentation of his specialty, as it applied to a phase of child care. To prepare for these talks and to make reasonably certain that the topics would be of interest to the audience, data were assembled on typical complaints that represented fairly common vision problems encountered among children.

Invariably, as the details of the case material presented unfolded, there were a number of parents in the audience to whom this case sounded "like their Johnnie." Because of this tie-in, the recipients were now much more likely to pay attention to and respond to the information contained in the presentations.

To further insure parent participation, a question period followed the presentations. This, too, helped to stimulate motivation. In this two-way flow of communication, the panel members gave direct, pertinent information on subjects of concern to members of the audience. They described informally the type of service they rendered. The women of the audience participated most actively. At the same time, they had the opportunity to see warm, friendly professional men who were responsive to their questions.

Demand for panel dates exceeded all expectations. This moved the association, on advice of public relations counsel, to broaden the presentation. Skits were written around actual visual problems and performed by the professional men. To maintain participation after this dramatic type presentation (and especially with the larger audiences that were beginning to result), techniques such as the so-called Phillips 66 method[24] were used, in which the audience huddled in groups of six to discuss a topic and then each group reported to the whole audience on its conference.

A marked awakening of interest in the work of the profession soon was apparent in the community. Other phases of the public relations program backed up the panel meetings. As a dividend, the professional men learned that their own participation is of great value in public relations.

So as not to lose sight of the fundamental point of this case presentation, let us repeat the lesson to be derived here. The messages of this professional organization required a context which would produce increased motivation of the recipients to attend to the messages. Just telling people that your profession does such and such is not enough. The public relations practitioner must also consider how he is going to motivate his recipients to pay attention to the message (and the information it contains) and to do something about what they have learned from the message. Or, to put it in terms of our third requirement of a message, the public relations practitioner must see to it that his messages arouse the needs of those to whom he is communicating. This means he must motivate as well as inform.

GENERAL REQUIREMENTS OF A MESSAGE SO AS TO AROUSE ITS INTENDED RESPONSE (Continued)

4. The Message Must Suggest a Way to Meet Those Needs Which Are Appropriate to the Group Situation in Which the Destination Finds Himself at the Time When He Is Moved to Make the Desired Response

This fourth requirement of the message emphasizes the point made in Chapter 5 (pages 106-109) to the effect that one never really communicates with a single individual, even in a face-to-face situation.

---

[24] The expression "Phillips 66 method" stems from the work of J. D. Phillips, wherein audiences are divided into groups of six, and each group discusses a given question or problem for six minutes; 6 persons for 6 minutes is shortened to 66. See J. Donald Phillips, "Report on Discussion 66," Adult Education Journal, VII (1948), 181-182.

Even with the single individual, you are communicating with him *and* the numerous reference groups of which he is a part.

We will consider further details of the importance of remembering that any individual or group is in turn a part of a larger group when we consider the recipient stage in more detail. At this point, let us add some of the principles that Dorwin Cartwright suggests must be considered when studying the problem of changing behavior and attitudes.[25] His principles, which bring change attempts and group influences together (which is what our fourth principle stated above does also) are paraphrased[26] below with additional discussion.

1. If the change attempts directed at an individual require him to deviate from the norms of his group, they are very likely to be resisted and consequently unsuccessful. Often our change objectives, viewed from the point of view of the recipient, are really asking him to differ from his group. Many change attempts within a company require some employees to act in a manner that is at variance with some of the other members of the group. Any sort of training program which involves only part of the group places special problems on the recipients of the training. The philosophy that "people ought to have the strength of character to differ from their group" does not answer the problem.

2. Group pressures within any group are strong on its members. Change attempts which are directed toward "dovetailing" with this force are much more likely to succeed than change attempts which go against the group. Furthermore, if the group can be utilized in the change efforts, success is much more likely. This often requires that some attitudes be created and then caused to be shared by the members of the group so that pressure for change comes from within rather than from without. This approach is well exemplified in the military. Creating within the group the feeling that it is a "topnotch outfit" often facilitates internal policing with respect to appearance, attention to training, etc., because now performance in these areas is part of the picture of a topnotch outfit. This same approach has been used with satisfactory results in industrial organizations that were attempting to improve their community relations. Once some employees had accepted the suggestion regarding their appearance to the community, they in turn served to police the behavior of other employees in the

---

[25] Dorwin Cartwright, *Business Week*, August 14, 1954. Used by permission.

[26] This paraphrasing originally appeared in a chapter written by the author, entitled "Applying Psychology," in Howard Stephenson (ed.), *Handbook of Public Relations* (New York: McGraw-Hill Book Company, 1960), pp. 167-168.

community. And the impression of the company in the community improved.

3. *Change attempts directed toward any group (i.e., recipients) may fail, because the group itself is a part of a larger group that is thrown out of balance by the change attempts.* Certain departments within a company may attempt to bring about changes by training their people in one way or another. This may upset the balance within the total organization. For example, that department might now become a "threat" to other departments. Thus the training might produce negative consequences for the initial change attempts. Stating it another way, a training program for the foremen in one department might result in excellent changes in these foremen, yet upset the balance of relationships with other foremen and workers in the company.

4. *Whenever change attempts are utilizing group membership as an aid to change, steps must be taken to ensure the fact that the recipient views himself as part of the group in question.* This principle is often overlooked in fund drives. Occasionally, a fund drive stresses that "as a loyal citizen you wouldn't want to let your town down in this drive." Perhaps the individual in question does not give a hang about the town. Thus, he is unaffected by the attempt to use this particular group identification as an additional force to cause him to contribute. We often make this mistake of assuming that a segment of a group identifies itself with a particular group and then attempt to use the group as a change pressure. Prior research on the make-up of the group can prevent a mishap here.

SPECIFIC CONSIDERATIONS APPLICABLE TO THE MESSAGE STAGE

Communication on a Continuum

A starting point in examining further considerations at the message stage is the realization that the communication process can also be viewed as being on a continuum ranging from face-to-face communications to mass communication. In Chapters 4 and 5 we discussed the topic of communication in great detail. The only additional concept that this continuum of communication, depicted in Figure 17,[27] raises is that of mass communication. There is no single, agreed-on definition of the term *mass communications*, but most experts do agree

---

[27] G. D. Wiebe, "Mass Communications," in E. L. Hartley and R. E. Hartley, *Fundamentals of Social Psychology* (New York: Alfred A. Knopf, Inc., 1955), p. 163. All material used by permission.

Figure 17

Communication Depicted in Terms of a V-Shaped Continuum

that it involves sizable numbers of people—in the millions—within which there is good representation of all major subgroups of a society in terms of such factors as age, education, income.[28]

This V-shaped continuum has only three points of the total continuum depicted: (1) face-to-face communications as between two individuals, (2) intermediate communications where a particular public relations public (say, employees) is being communicated with, and (3) mass communications involving millions of individuals. Obviously, there are about as many in-between points on this continuum that one might want to construct. The characteristics of this continuum that Wiebe spells out as one moves from the lower end of the V toward the top are as follows:

1. The audience per communicator becomes progressively larger. In the United States today a single mass communication may reach an audience of more than 20 million people.

2. The *nature of the message* communicated becomes less and less private or specialized, and more and more public or nontechnical. [Italics added.]

---

[28] One additional point needs to be made here. As with the term *socioeconomic class*, the word *mass* does not contain any value judgment. Thus, when social scientists use the word *mass*, they do not mean that these are people with lower social status, less education, and so on, a meaning that is sometimes attached to the word. The word merely means that a huge number of people are involved.

3. The range of difference between various communications becomes progressively narrower. (One can say anything to his best friend. But as the audience becomes larger, the communicator is subject to more and more restrictions, taboos, codes, and cautions.)

4. "Ready-made" interest on the part of the audience is less and less dependable, and purposeful interest stimulation is more and more apparent. (You may mumble an incomplete sentence, and your mother bends toward you to catch the words. She completes the meaning from her backlog of interest in and acquaintance with you, and responds to your communication. By contrast, an advertising writer or a newspaper reporter uses all of his professional skill to capture your attention and engage your interest. He works on the assumption that you are busy and no more than mildly interested.)

5. In general, the recipient of the communication has less and less immediate access to the communicator.[29]

As one thinks about these characteristics, it becomes obvious why successful communication becomes less and less likely the farther away from face-to-face communication one moves. The public relations practitioner operates at all points along the continuum, but it is probably fair to say that in a majority of the times, he finds himself operating in that portion of the continuum labeled "intermediate and special-interest communications." This point on the continuum is where the public relations practitioner is operating when he attempts to communicate with a particular public—say, stockholders or employees.

The real difficulty facing any public relations practitioner as he operates in this range of the continuum is how he is to overcome the negative effect on communicative effectiveness of the characteristics noted by Wiebe (such as, "ready-made" interest on the part of the audience is less and less dependable). Another way of expressing it is to say that the public relations practitioner attempts to operate in this middle range of the communication continuum (involving from several hundreds of people to several thousands) with some of the flavor of face-to-face communications. In fact, as we noted earlier (Chapter 5, pages 113-116), one way of looking at the company newspaper is that it is a device for overcoming the fact that there are hundreds of people involved. A company newspaper attempts to maintain (or regain) the operating characteristics of an extremely small organization where all employees know each other and see each other every day.

---

[29] Wiebe, pp. 163-164.

The Fraction of Selection as a Guide

What guides are there to help the public relations practitioner operate in the middle and upper ranges of the communication continuum? For the mass communication end of the continuum, only rough guides are available—guides that suggest essentially a way of thinking about the communication problems faced. Typical of such guides is the *Fraction of Selection* suggested by Schramm. He writes,

> What determines which offering of mass communication will be selected by any given individual? Perhaps the easiest way to put it is to say that choice is determined by the Fraction of Selection—
>
> $$\frac{\text{Expectation of reward}}{\text{Effort required}}$$
>
> You can increase the value of that fraction either by increasing the numerator or decreasing the denominator, which is to say that an individual is more likely to select a certain communication if it promises him more reward or requires less effort than comparable communications. You can see how this works in your own experience. You are much more likely to read the newspaper or magazine at hand than to walk six blocks to the news stand to buy a bigger newspaper or magazine. You are more likely to listen to a station which has a loud clear signal than to one which is faint and fading and requires constant effort from you to hear at all. But if the big game of the week is on that faint station, or if your favorite author is in the magazine at the news stand, then there is more likelihood that you will make the additional effort. If you were a member of the underground in occupied France during World War II, you probably risked your life to hear news from the forbidden Allied radio. You aren't likely to stay up until 2 a.m. simply to hear a radio program, but if by staying up that long you can find out how the Normandy invasion is coming or who has won the Presidential election—then you will probably make the extra effort just as most of the rest of us did. It is hardly necessary to point out that no two receivers may have exactly the same fraction of selection. One of them may expect more reward from Milton Berle than will the other. One of them may consider it less effort to walk six blocks to the news stand than does the other. But according to how this fraction looks to individuals in any given situation, the audience of mass communication is determined.[30]

---

[30] Schramm, pp. 19-20. Used by permission.

The ability of the public relations practitioner to "fill out" the fraction of selection—that is, make estimates of reward that might be expected on the part of the recipients in question, and to figure out how to reduce the effort required, will be enhanced by two factors: (1) experience on the job functioning as a public relations practitioner, and (2) increased understanding of the recipient.

QUESTIONS FOR DISCUSSION

1. Obtain a copy of some written material that was produced by a public relations practitioner. This may be a booklet, a company newspaper, or a stockholder report. Look this material over and make two *estimates*: (1) estimate the reading ease score and human interest score that this material would receive if analyzed by the Flesch formulas introduced in this chapter and (2) estimate the average reading level ability of the intended audience of the written material you are using.

   After you have made your two estimates, obtain a copy of Flesch's book, *How to Test Readability*, and compute the reading ease score and human interest score for a sample of this written material according to the procedures developed by Flesch and provided in this chapter. How do the two computed scores agree with your estimates? In which direction did you err, if at all? How well suited is the material for the audience that you implicitly, if not explicitly, assumed would be receiving it?

2. How does the generalization that was made in this chapter concerning the overemphasis that public relations practitioners place on "informing" people strike you? Obtain some examples that support this contention. For good measure, obtain some examples that *do not* confirm this generalization. Which examples were the easiest to find?

3. Take two of the four principles that were cited from Cartwright's work concerning changing behavior and attitudes (*e.g.*, change attempts directed toward any group may fail, because the group itself is a part of a larger group that is thereby thrown out of balance by the change attempts), and find a public relations problem situation that illustrates them. For example, you should be able to find a public relations case dealing with some aspect of

community relations that failed because of the fourth principle, given on page 231.

4. Take any one of the characteristics that Wiebe stated as true as one moves from the lower end of the V-shaped continuum depicted in Figure 17 (page 234) to the top, and express it in public relations terms. For example, how would you translate Wiebe's second characteristic (page 234) into public relations terms?

Chapter 10

THE MEDIA STAGE IN MORE DETAIL: PERSON-TO-PERSON COMMUNICATION AND SPECIALIZED AUDIENCES

The media stage is undoubtedly the most difficult to deal with when public relations is the topic of consideration. At one and the same time, the media stage receives the greatest amount of emphasis from the average public relations practitioner, yet his understanding of media usage is not nearly so complete as it should be. Most books dealing with the topic of public relations refer to the media as the "tools" of the public relations practitioner. Unfortunately, these tools appear at times to be in control of the public relations practitioner rather than the other way around.

For most people, the public relations practitioner is identified in terms of the media that he uses so constantly. It is a little wonder that the average man on the street sees little difference, if any, between a publicity agent and a public relations practitioner. They both seem to be connected with the media so closely that they appear to him to have the same function in our social system.

But perhaps we are getting ahead of ourselves, as this line of thinking is likely to lead us to a discussion of the differences among publicists, advertisers, public relations practitioners, and the like. They all are intimately associated with the media. However, before going any further in our discussion, let's use the same approach that we found appropriate to use in arriving at a definition of public relations. First, we shall examine the ways in which public relations practitioners become involved with the media by using brief cases or illustrations. In addition, we shall make use of a schema that combines the *continuum of communication* that we first considered in Chapter 9 (Figure 17, page 234) with the *variety of media* that public relations practitioners utilize to help them solve their problems (see Figure 18).

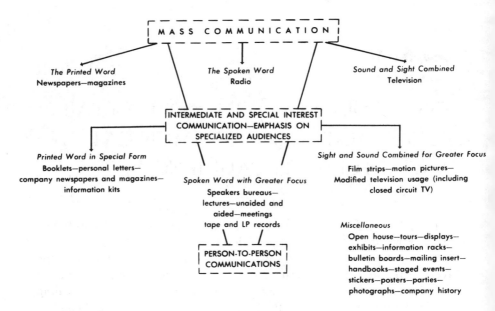

Figure 18

Communication media viewed in terms of a continuum of communications

CONTINUUM OF COMMUNICATION AND MEDIA USAGE COMBINED

Person-to-Person Communication

Let us begin our examination of Figure 18, which illustrates the ways that public relations practitioners use media, with a consideration of the person-to-person portion of the communication continuum. A great deal of the work that a public relations practitioner engages in is conducted at the person-to-person or face-to-face level. Contacting a variety of people either in person or by telephone is a standard portion of the working day of the average practitioner. The importance of personal contacts in public relations work probably cannot be overstated. However, our discussion of media will not include any attention to how the public relations practitioner operates on the person-to-person level. By definition, the media do not play much of a role here as the spoken voice usually is all that is required.

The person-to-person situation must be a starting point in our discussion of the media for another reason, however. It's this: *In public relations work, most of the other points on the continuum of communication* (Figure 18), *when translated into media terms, are used as a substitute for the person-to-person contact, which cannot be used because of size of audience, physical separation of sender and recipients, and so on.* Let's explore this point a little more fully.

In a very small organization—let us say with five to ten employees—the owner or person supervising these people is generally in intimate contact with them. He more than likely knows their likes and dislikes, how they are feeling on any given day, what their complaints are at any given time, and so on. In a situation such as this, there is usually no need for the variety of media that a public relations practitioner normally uses to keep management in touch with their workers and vice versa.[1] It is only when the organization grows too large for the direct personal contact of the supervisor or owner and the employee that the media come into play. Thus, in a large organization, we institute a company newspaper. One way of viewing this newspaper is as a substitute for certain of the communication that would take place if the organization were smaller (Chapter 5, pages 113-116). Thus, news about bowling scores, births and deaths, promotions and transfers, and a host of other similar items usually found in company newspapers are an effort to achieve a degree of fellowship among employees that would be taken for granted if their number were small enough so that they would see each other in their daily work. In fact, as we have noted earlier, a great many of the communication activities of a public relations practitioner on behalf of his organization can be seen as an effort to overcome the impersonality and breakdown in communication that so often accompanies the increase of size of any organization.

---

[1] It might be added here that this same statement applies to the other specialized subdivisions of large organizations that have emerged since the turn of the century, such as personnel departments, safety departments, and the like. When an organization is very small, the various personnel needs are taken care of directly, as are the communication needs.

The same can be said about the "official" portions of the public
relations, practitioner's communications—that is, when management's
views are communicated to the employee. When the plant magazine
or special brochures are used to communicate to the employee management's views about such things as unemployment insurance, retirement benefits, or local or national politics, these communicative efforts
are merely substitutes for what the employee would presumably already know if he saw his boss every day or at least several times a
week.[2]

To summarize this point in another way: One reason for looking at
the public relations practitioner's use of the media from the standpoint
of person-to-person communication is that, regardless of the type of
media involved, *it is a substitute for what, ideally, would have been
communicated by person-to-person contact, if some special situation—
such as size—did not obviate the personal communication level.*

*Why is the person-to-person level employed as a basis for examina-
tion of media usage?* Two important reasons are suggested here
as to why this point of view is useful when considering the utilization
of media by public relations practitioners: (1) the person-to-person,
personal communication context embodies all of the features of the
communication process (*i.e.*, maximum potential feedback, maximum
potential intelligibility) that other points on the communication continuum inevitably lack in some way, and (2) the selection of media to
use for any given public relations problem situation is guided by the
degree to which certain features of the person-to-person situation are
kept or remain relatively unaffected by certain other media.[3]

The importance of the guidance provided by this approximation to
the personal communication context is made all the more important
when one realizes that there is pitifully little research data available in
the social science research literature on the suitability of different
media for different communication objectives.[4] In short, the person-to-

---

[2] In order to make a point here, we are deliberately excluding the situation
where the boss happens to be very inarticulate (or noncommunicative for any of
a variety of other reasons) and would *not* keep his employees informed even if
he did have daily intimate contact with them. There are many times when public
relations practitioners (and personnel managers, too!) have to take steps to cope
with supervisory individuals who are unable to communicate. However, such situations are fewer in number than the more general case being argued here.

[3] As we shall see in one of our illustrations a little later, the decision to use
closed-circuit television was dictated by the degree to which this particular medium
approximated the person-to-person "warmth" that the other media lacked.

[4] One might add here that this is why the advent of television, for example, has
been such a frustrating development from the standpoint of effectiveness of media

person communication context embodies all of the features of the communication process of which we are aware and have been discussing. Other points on the communication continuum (with their particular media versions as illustrations) are special cases of the personal communication situation that the media try to emulate, approximate, or accentuate, depending on the particular media and communication situation.[5]

INTERMEDIATE AND SPECIAL INTEREST COMMUNICATION—EMPHASIS ON SPECIALIZED AUDIENCES

Returning to Figure 18 and moving up the communication continuum, we see that there are many varieties of media modifications used by public relations practitioners at this level, designed to meet the needs of communicating with specialized audiences. Let us examine a few of the media breakdowns at this point on the continuum in Figure 18 in some detail.

Printed Word in Special Form

The printed word is by far the most important medium in which the public relations practitioner works. There is no better exemplification of this modality than in what we have called the printed word in special form. This includes company newspapers, magazines, bro-

---

for certain communication objectives. However firm our intuitive feelings may be about the excessive strength (or weakness, depending on how you view the situation) that television may have for an audience—especially children—the fact is that the research data to date have been exceedingly sparse and inconclusive. We can't even determine what the effects of television are—let alone determine if they are stronger than the effects of the other media—how they can be counteracted if so desired, etc. We will return to the question of the electronic media a little later in this chapter.

[5] It is interesting to examine the instructions that one finds in many books— particularly books on public relations—on how to increase the likelihood that your news release or special article will be published in a newspaper. One of the instructions prominent on most lists is to be sure to include a "human interest" twist. This is suggested because editors are looking for things that appeal to readers, and human interest items are always "sure fire." When one examines the criteria of editors, however, he sees that they are merely reflections of what editors have *assumed* will appeal to readers. Making a newspaper contain homey items about people (which presumably makes a newspaper a substitute for face-to-face conversation with a lot of people you don't know and will never see) is one of the important ingredients in making a paper "sell." These are our person-to-person characteristics all over again, applied in a different context.

chures, pamphlets, booklets, and the tremendous number of other means by which the public relations practitioner employs the printed word for his objectives.[6] The variety of the printed word in special form is practically unlimited; however, the following three examples are representative of the total and should provide the reader with an understanding of how the public relations practitioner functions in this communication medium.

1. *Specialized booklets.* One common version of the printed word is the small booklet. One such example is from the National Retail Merchants Association and illustrates how they made use of the booklet as a natural outgrowth of the NRMA Reader's Digest Awards Program.[7] The background to the development of these booklets is as follows. In 1961, in order to help the association obtain national recognition for its function, the NRMA Reader's Digest Awards Program was developed, designed to recognize and reward retail store personnel who have performed outstanding individual acts or initiated programs or projects of community service. The booklets are a logical outgrowth and continuation of the award program in that they summarize within their covers the community service acts and programs that have received awards across the country. The booklets describe such things as the awards (*e.g.*, plaques, glass bowls, and the like) given and the categories of winners (e.g., small-store competition, large-store competition, internal competition, and so on).

2. *Personal letters.* The use of personal letters as a part of a public relations program has long been recognized as an effective form of the printed word. Letters are comparatively inexpensive (if the volume involved is small) and quick to send out. Perhaps most importantly, however, is that they are tailor made for some particular phase of a public relations program because they can be designed to pinpoint

---

[6] Whole chapters can be and have been devoted to spelling out the degree to which the public relations practitioner employs the printed word as one portion of his communicative efforts in solving public relations problems. (*See particularly* Philip Lesly [ed.], *Public Relations Handbook* [2d ed.; Englewood Cliffs, N.J.: Prentice-Hall, Inc., 1962], chaps. 7, 27, 28, and 30; and Howard Stephenson [ed.], *Handbook of Public Relations* [New York: McGraw-Hill Book Company, 1960], chaps. 7-12.) We have avoided spelling out such data for two reasons: (1) they are available from a variety of sources, the preceding two citations being only a small sample of what is available; and (2) understanding the role of media in achieving certain public relations objectives and how these media integrate with the communications continuum are more important than a recitation in detail of such things as how to write booklets and how to make them visually appealing.

[7] The author is indebted to Robert Gur-Arie, Public Relations Director, National Retail Merchants Association, 100 West 31 Street, New York 1, New York.

objectives and audiences. Our illustration here of the use of the personal letter comes from England.[8]

Massey-Ferguson was for many years a comparatively small company in terms of the size of the industrial complex of Coventry, England. The main reason for this was that they did not manufacture their own equipment (tractors and other heavy equipment) but rather subcontracted this work to another organization. Toward the end of 1959, however, the management of Massey-Ferguson purchased the manufacturing rights for their own product from their major contractor. As a result, virtually overnight the payroll jumped from between five and six hundred employees to over five thousand. With this size, Massey-Ferguson became a fairly important manufacturing unit within the life of Coventry.

This change in scope of operations prompted the public relations division of Massey-Ferguson to embark upon a multipronged community relations program designed to acquaint Coventry with the change in scope of the operation of the company. One part of the public relations program consisted of a letter (see below) which contained an offer of help, such as lay within the means of the company, to the secretaries of 180 social and philanthropic organizations which are organized to benefit the life of residents of the local community. A similar letter was sent to each of the aldermen, councillors, and principal officers of the borough and to the local press. The letter read as follows:

Dear Sir/Madam

Massey-Ferguson has recently become more closely linked with the day to day life of Coventry. It is our belief that industrial organisations today should seek to contribute not only to the economic prosperity, but also to the social activities of the communities in which they are situated.

My Company is aware that its future is closely linked with the civic life of the city and is happy and proud that this should be so. It is our hope that in this future there will be many opportunities for Massey-Ferguson to help some of the many local voluntary organisations and thus to contribute something not only to the working, but also the recreational life of Coventry.

---

[8] The author is indebted to John A. Keyser, General Public Relations Manager, Massey-Ferguson (U.K.) Ltd., Banner Lane, Coventry, England, for this personal communication.

Accordingly, we shall be glad to learn of any opportunity which may arise for co-operation with your organisation and of rendering assistance of which we may be capable.

Such opportunities may vary considerably in both type and scope. For example we may be able to provide facilities for meetings, conferences or competitions by lending buildings or land. We may also be able to lend tractors or other equipment to provide transport at local fairs, carnivals and other events, or to help local organisations with various projects. We shall also be glad to provide 16 mm. films, mostly on agricultural subjects, with or without projection equipment, or lecturers, to local clubs and societies.

We hope, therefore, that if at any time you feel that we can be of assistance to you or to the work of your organisation, you will not hesitate to call upon us.

Correspondence on such matters should be addressed to:

The General Public Relations Manager
Massey-Ferguson (United Kingdom) Limited,
Banner Lane,
Coventry.

Yours faithfully,
[signed]   John A. Keyser,
General Public Relations
Manager

The effectiveness of the personal letter, especially in a comparatively small city, is very often marked. In this case Massey-Ferguson received 132 acknowledgments, twenty-five of which were from organizations who were not recipients of the original letter but nevertheless felt that they could take the liberty to contact the company. Press coverage on the local scene has been quite favorable, and more than a score of replies were made in a similar vein from aldermen and councillors and the borough's principal officers.

In a nine-month period following the mailing of the letters, twenty-three film shows were booked. Various pieces of equipment have been loaned and two major projects of assistance undertaken. One is the loan of a large truck to serve as a mobile library for the elderly and others who are confined to their homes. The second is that of excavating a site for a swimming pool for a local school. The school concerned did not have the necessary funds nor did the local government have any such provision in its budget for such a venture.

This type of response tends to be typical of the reaction that a personal letter of this type evokes, especially when it is linked with a larger public relations program. Unlike the use of booklets as the case cited previously, awareness of the impact that the personal letters has achieved is generally rather immediate and direct so that the worthiness of the effort can be rather quickly assessed.

3. *Information kits.* Another effective version of the printed word is the information kit. We have left this to last because kits generally use just about every variation of the printed word imaginable as well as suggest how to use the spoken word and develop visual presentations. But let's back up a minute and learn what a kit is for, what it is like, before we get into the details of a specific example.

Information kits come in all sizes and shapes and for all purposes. Essentially, they consist of a compilation of materials designed to be informative and helpful to a specific audience. Press kits are one example. A public relations practitioner will assemble materials that a reporter might make use of in conjunction with a press conference. Usually press kits contain background material about the company or organization concerned, some information about key personnel, and pertinent names and addresses. Then, depending on the purpose of the press conference (*e.g.*, development of some new product, process, or the like), some details about the product or process will be included. In essence, the press kit is designed to facilitate the newsman's job of reporting upon what he has seen and heard at the press conference.

The information officer in the military has made extensive use of the information kit. In the Air Force, for example, practically every base Information Officer has at his disposal an information kit to supply to visiting officers and civilians. Such kits generally contain material describing the unique mission of that particular air base, something about the commanding officer and his staff, pictures of interesting weapons, and a history of the air base itself.

To get a better feeling for information kits and their contents, let us examine in some detail a more unique use of the information kit put out by the Public Information Department of the American Optometric Association (AOA). Typical of their information kits is their "Back to School Kit" for 1961 with the theme "School Time is Vision Examination Time."[9]

One of the main purposes behind the back-to-school kits is to assist the various local public relations committees (and individual optometrists) of local optometric associations across the country to get their message across to various publics about the services of optometry in

---

[9] Used by permission of the American Optometric Association, 4030 Chouteau Avenue, St. Louis, Missouri 63110.

the area of visual care. Like many other less well understood and
accepted professions (*i.e.*, less well understood and accepted than
medicine, for example) optometry still has a tremendous educational
job to do with respect to parents, school teachers, administrators, and
the like. (Other professions with similar educational tasks are podi-
atrists, chiropractors, psychologists, and, in still other ways, psychiatrists and dentists.) Because one of the most important visual care services that optometrists have to offer is preventive and remedial work
with children, the advent of return to school in the fall offers a natural
way to launch a concentrated public relations effort on the behalf of
optometry, in addition to laying the groundwork for consistent attention to vision throughout the school year. The back-to-school kit is
designed to stimulate the concentrated effort and to provide local
public relations committees, made up of local optometrists, with ideas
for sustained action during the school year.

Each kit is built around a particular theme. The one we are examining here was developed around "Schooltime is Vision Examination
Time." To appreciate the scope of the kit, a list of the contents is
provided:

1. General poster for bulletin boards (8½ × 11)
2. Poster for in-school use (8½ × 11)
3. 15-20 minute speech for general use (title: "Bricks Can't Replace
   Eyes")
4. Press releases
5. 1 column × 1 inch newspaper "drop-in" mats
6. Transcribed radio spots
7. Live station breaks
8. Live 20-second spots
9. Live 10- to 15-minute radio script (RS-22—"Better Vision for
   your Child")
10. Live 5-minute radio or TV script (RS-3—"Remedial Reading")
11. 60-second TV film ("Types of Parents")
12. 20-second TV film adaption ("Types of Parents")
13. Pamphlet: "Teachers Guide to Vision Problems"
14. Pamphlet: Reprint of "Your Child Must See Well to Grow Well"
15. Pamphlet: Reprint of "An Important Problem for the College
    Student"
16. Vision literature catalog
17. Report on local or state Back to School Program

Accompanying these diversified samples of materials is an eight-
page "blueprint for action" from the Public Information Department

of the AOA, directed to the optometrists themselves and suggesting how they should organize their efforts (*i.e.*, set up a general school-vision committee) and use the materials described in the kit. There are lists of groups that may be contacted and general do's and don't with respect to implementing a year-round local public relations program. Once a particular local chapter has worked out how it plans to make use of the materials that the kit provides, appropriate amounts of any of the materials (*e.g.*, one of the pamphlets or posters) may be ordered from the AOA.

One last feature of the contents of the back-to-school kit worth noting is the provision for feedback of information from the local chapter to the Public Information Division of AOA. Each kit contains a form—to be filled out by the committee chairman of the local chapter—which summarizes what public relations action the committee took. There is provision for reporting on newspaper, radio and TV coverage obtained, number of times that the various speeches provided in the kit were given, and other details such as the number of posters distributed and pamphlets given away. In addition, reporting chairmen are encouraged to describe what other activities they engaged in as part of their total public relations program and what suggestions or criticisms they have for the next year's kit. Here we see at least some effort built into the kit, so to speak, to find out how effective the kit has been from the point of view of stimulating action and distribution of materials.

To round out our description of the back-to-school kit, the five twenty-second radio spot announcements are quoted. (These spot announcements are all prepared for use by a local announcer. The task of some member of the public relations committee is to take the initiative to call attention to the availability of the spot announcements to the local radio station management.)

SYMPTOMS

ANNCR: If your child rubs his eyes, is a slow reader, does poorly in school or frequently complains, he may have a vision problem. This is not uncommon and is *not* often detected by simple school eye chart tests. The American Optometric Association and your family optometrist urge a professional vision examination at least once a year. Remember school time is vision examination time!

SLOW READERS

ANNCR: Did you know that more than half the children who are slow in learning to read have visual problems? This is serious, and yet often neither the child nor its parents know this. The

American Optometric Association and your family optometrist urge you to have a child's eyes professionally examined
at least once a year. School time is vision examination time!

PARENT'S RESPONSIBILITY

ANNCR: In preparing a child for school, what is the parent's responsibility? One of the major ones is providing the tools with
which to learn. It is estimated that 80% of all learning is
based on *vision*. That's why the American Optometric Association and your family optometrist urge you to care for
your children's sight with professional vision exams. School
time is vision examination time!

SCHOOL VISION CHECKS NOT ENOUGH

ANNCR: Children must do more than see accurately to learn easily.
They must see comfortably and efficiently as well! Simple
school vision checks are not enough to assure this. The
American Optometric Association and your family optometrist
urge you to have your children's vision *thoroughly* examined
at least once a year. School time is vision examination time!

A CHILD'S VISION CHANGES

ANNCR: Just because your child's eyes were examined last year does
not mean that your child's eyes are up to the visual requirements of school this year. As a child grows, changes occur
quickly. As a child progresses, visual requirements change
as well. The American Optometric Association and your
family optometrist recommend a professional visual examination at least once a year. School time is vision exam time![10]

Because the AOA is an association of professional people, the public relations practitioners representing them faced one problem not
too often encountered: avoiding commercialism yet achieving public
relations goals of better understanding and acceptance which result
in more people becoming patients of optometrists. As in many other
professions, there are prohibitions against direct advertising and information programs that are obviously commercial. The net result is
that designing a program for a professional association—which demands financial success in the long run as all professional associations
do—is no easy task. One way out is to use the professional man himself in a grass-roots approach that will expose him to his community

---

in a professionally acceptable way. The information kit serves this purpose reasonably well. It provides guidance for local public relations committees, which is essential because, like most professional people, optometrists do not have the slightest notion of how to structure a public relations program. It tends to assure some uniformity of the approach and of the quality of what is done by encouraging the use of prepackaged materials. Perhaps the most salutary effect of the kit is that it causes the professional man to be more conscious of the fact that, in his case particularly, there is no such thing as having all the public relations work "done for you." Instead, the realization is sometimes achieved that *the professional man himself must work at bringing about understanding and acceptance of his profession every day in a variety of ways.*

The drawbacks to kits are many, of course. One or two of the more important have to do with the motivation of the user with the difficulty of anticipating all the problems that he will encounter in order to make the "canned" material acceptable universally. With respect to the first problem, making kits available in no way assures that they will be used. In fact, they carry with them their own "seeds of destruction," so to speak, in that they require the potential user—especially when it is a professional person with a rather special self-image—to do the very thing he is most uncomfortable doing. For example, it is up to *him* to place the station break material with the local radio or TV stations. This means that he must play the role of a salesman to some extent and run the risk of being given the polite "brush-off." The news-release guide presents a slightly different problem. Although the model is there for him to follow, the typical user is, as a rule, a poor writer and knows nothing about preparing a news release, then following through and getting it to the local newspaper office. This means that, with the exception of certain special kits (perhaps a press kit), nearly as much attention must be paid to motivating and training the potential user as is paid to developing the contents of the kit in the first place.[11]

The second problem is one that faces anyone who is trying to write universally applicable material. So-called canned speeches, news releases, and radio and TV break material are bound to suffer in some

---

[11] Apropos of this last point about the need for training potential users of an information kit, the author recently designed such a training program for small groups of optometrists. The training program (only a few hours in duration and divided into two different meeting times) produced much more effective use of information kits, such as has been discussed above, and also tended to spark more independent public relations actions as well.

context because they do not fit. Two steps can be taken to avoid this problem as much as possible. One is to encourage your user to use his own creativity to modify the material whenever appropriate. He should not be led to believe that the material is perfect or inviolate. Another is to obtain personally as much experience with the various contexts in which your material is to be used as possible. This provides the individual producing the kit with a better perspective with which to develop useful materials.

The ultimate question, how effective information kits are, is a difficult one to answer. They share with booklets and other written material the difficulty of determining just what good they have done. Information from the *user* of the kit is, of course, valuable, as well as his estimate of how widespread has been the dissemination of the material suggested in the kits. With respect to the specific kit we have been discussing, there is always the haunting question of how often making people aware of vision problems causes them to wind up in the office of an *ophthalmologist* rather than of an *optometrist*. In either case, the prospective patient benefits because he is paying attention to something very precious that most of us tend to take for granted and overlook—our vision. However, if the former professional man is visited too much because of the public relations program of the latter, it is not what was intended in the first place, to say the least!

Spoken Word with Greater Focus

As one turns to the use of the spoken word to communicate with specialized audiences, a wide range of specific variations present themselves. Essentially, however, the use of the spoken word with greater focus breaks down into two major subcategories: *aided* and *unaided*— that is, with or without electronic augmentation of the voice in some way. *Unaided spoken word usage* includes, of course, all meetings, lectures, or assemblies of any kind before which a verbal presentation is made to an audience of some sort. (The people in the audience are necessarily limited to a small number in view of the use of the unaided voice.) One of the most typical uses of unaided oral presentations from a public relations standpoint is when some fairly high-ranking official of an organization meets with selected groups of employees to announce some new development within the organization. Generally, this verbal announcement is followed closely by additional meetings and discussions and specifically prepared printed materials. In order for unaided oral presentations to be of some value as part of an over-all public relations program, they need to be carefully planned. There are many details that can be overlooked and, therefore, detract from the success of such a meeting. Seeing to it that there is adequate and comfortable seating, refreshments as appropriate, verbal material that is carefully prepared and presented in a fresh, spontaneous manner, and visual aids to help put across the messages intended are only a few of the details that must be taken care of by the public relations practitioner concerned.

Speakers' bureaus represent special cases of the spoken word used for greater focus.[12] Speakers' bureaus come in all sizes and degrees of complexity, but essentially they consist of individuals, carefully selected by a public relations practitioner, who are used to communicate certain portions of a public relations program. Industrial use of speakers' bureaus consists of having certain management people available to speak to all sorts of groups that traditionally are in need of speakers, such as Rotary, Kiwanis, P.T.A., and the like. All of the details noted in the section devoted to meetings apply to speakers' bureaus, plus a few that are peculiar to the bureaus. Items that need particular attention are (1) how to make known the availability of speakers, (2) coordinating requests for speakers, (3) integrating what is said by the different speakers so that the lectures contribute to the over-all public relations program of the company, and (4) avoiding conflicting policy statements by the speakers. These are but a few of the additional headaches that speakers' bureaus can cause for the public relations practitioner, although it is an acknowledged technique for communicating certain messages to certain types of publics. An interesting military utilization of the speakers' bureau technique is exemplified by the Strategic Air Command's use of flight crews as their speakers. One or two officers of a crew will be made available to a particular club or organization. In addition to a presentation about the mission of SAC and some of the details of the life as a SAC officer, the speakers bring along various pieces of flight equipment such as crash helmets, oxygen masks, emergency survival equipment and the like to liven up their presentations and add realism to what they have to say.

Aided spoken word usage includes situations where mechanical or electronic aids are used to augment the voice of the speaker. As a rule, this is done to reach an audience too large to be assembled in one room

---

[12] We are, of course, excluding situations wherein members of the speakers' bureau are before large audiences that require the use of electronic aids. (See discussion devoted to *aided* spoken messages.)

or too scattered physically even if it is not particularly large.[13] The use of aids to the spoken word as used here implies a much smaller and more homogeneous audience than that of radio or TV, and hence this particular form of voice transmission is included in the specialized audience portion of the communication continuum. The following example illustrates the use of aid to the spoken voice:

Because IBM feels that its benefit programs are important, any changes in the benefit plans are announced by the chairman of the board, Thomas J. Watson, Jr. On such occasions Watson's voice goes over a national telephone network to all IBM plants and offices throughout the country, and reaches the employees through a public address system. If a facility does not have a public address system, a temporary installation is made for the occasion.

Telephone communication of benefit plan changes was introduced over ten years ago, after the company had become so large that the then-chairman, Thomas J. Watson, Sr., couldn't visit all plants in the course of the year.

Announcements are made during working hours, and talks last from five to ten minutes. Word is passed that the chairman will speak the day before the talk, so that work can be arranged in such a way that everyone can hear.

Is it worth the cost? IBM thinks so. The company feels that the personal announcement by the top man is a practical demonstration of the company's genuine concern with the welfare of its employees. One proof of the fact that employees value the opportunity of hearing Watson's announcement: During one presentation, transmission in a part of one building was accidentally cut off. So much disappointment was expressed by the employees who didn't get to hear the announcement that supervisors in the area brought it to the attention of top management, and the program was repeated for that group.

Printed follow-up is fast. As soon as Watson begins to speak, his words are also transmitted by teletype throughout the country, and a printed form of the announcement is put on the bulletin boards. Company newspapers and magazines will carry the story within about two weeks,

---

[13] The reader should note that the use of radio is *not* included in the category of aided spoken word usage. The distinction is in terms of the audience involved. The use of radio implies a very large, heterogeneous audience. Aided spoken word usage implies a comparatively small and homogeneous audience. This is one of the reasons why radio usage was inserted at the mass communication (and, hence, mass audience) point on our communication continuum.

and new pages for the loose-leaf employee handbook follow along within a few months.[14]

There is no question that the efforts associated with the utilization of the human voice (either unaided or aided) as part of the over-all public relations program of an organization are generally worth the trouble. There are times and places where there is no substitute for the spoken word in this form. However, perhaps the greatest difficulty that the public relations practitioner faces in using the spoken word to focus on certain objectives is the unevenness of quality among the speakers. Individual differences being what they are, there are bound to be some people who are completely at home on the speakers' platform (either aided or unaided) and as a consequence do an effective job. On the other hand, listening to a poor speaker is perhaps one of the most uncomfortable and agonizing experiences to have to sit through, and the effectiveness of a poor speaker is, of course, open to question. It is comparatively easy for the public relations practitioner to edit poor copy; suggestions to improve written material can be made comparatively easily, and re-writing is also a reasonably simple task. Also, it is not particularly difficult to sort out the people who can write from those who cannot, and, lastly, there are seldom situations where a poor writer (especially if he is an executive) *has* to write. He can just skip over that weakness. *With speaking, the public relations practitioner faces a different situation.* It is not an easy matter to improve a poor speaker. You can't do the speaking for him; there are no such things as "ghost speakers" as there are ghost writers. Then, too, there are times when the person in question is *expected* to make a verbal presentation, and avoiding the issue can be awkward. All of these factors and more make the utilization of the spoken word for specialized audiences both an opportunity and a headache for the public relations practitioner.

Tapes and Long-Playing Records[15]

Although the use of tapes and long-playing (LP) records has not received much attention from public relations practitioners, the development of new equipment and recording processes now makes it

---

[14] *Communication Reports*, April, 1963 (Enterprise Publications, 20 North Wacker Drive, Chicago 6, Illinois), p. 1. All passages from *Communication Reports* used by permission.

[15] The author is indebted to Sidney A. Dimond, President, Creative Associates, Inc., and former professor at Boston University School of Public Communication, for the examples of tape and long-playing records described in this section.

possible for the perceptive public relations practitioner to use, as part of his over-all program, the medium of the spoken word on tape and LP records. In fact, this particular version of the spoken word could in time prove to be one of the most effective techniques available to the public relations practitioner to reach specialized audiences.

The virtue of tape is that it *always* says the same thing in the *same way*. The public relations practitioner has the assurance that his message was phrased and stated just as he planned it to be. (Compare this with the speakers' bureau situation, wherein considerable variation is found in how something is expressed.) Also, properly handled and reproduced, a tape never wears out. It can be used over and over again, enabling the cost of the preparation to be spread over a large number of presentations. Tapes require no special handling or storing. In addition, they are inexpensive to mail. Once you have a master tape prepared, there are numerous organizations that can quickly and efficiently duplicate it to produce as many copies as you may need and at a cost which is frequently less than what you would have to pay for the tape itself.

An example of the use of tape in a public relations program is the work done for the American Alumni Council (AAC), an association of fund raisers. The tape prepared served a training function for the AAC in that it contained information about fund raising. To make the tape even more effective the advice was given by the voices of fund-raising pioneers. Various colleges and universities have availed themselves of this tape to train new fund raisers as they are recruited.

An interesting variation of the use of tape was employed by the Massachusetts Institute of Technology during their Second Century Fund-Raising Campaign. A tape recording was played over telephone lines hooked into some one hundred hotel auditoriums in the United States and Canada where MIT alumni were gathered. The tape consisted of a résumé of voices and sounds of the campus. The use of the actual sounds and voices did much to make the message more interesting and, presumably, more effective. As a precaution, a copy of the tape was sent to each of the local groups in case the quality of the telephone transmission was not satisfactory.

LP records have essentially the same advantages mentioned above for tapes with perhaps the exception of wear. Records do wear out eventually; however, for all practical purposes this possibility is not much of a consideration because the average LP record of today can be played a great many times. An example of the use of LP records in the area of fund raising is the work that the University of New Hampshire Alumni Association recently had done for them. A seven-inch LP record entitled "Some UNH Songs and Sounds" was prepared. The record contained familiar sounds from the UNH campus, and the purpose of the record was to bring into the homes of each of the alumni (the records were sent free to all alumni) a "package of nostalgia." There was a very low-keyed request for support that went along with the record (*no* solicitation appeared on the record jacket, however) to the effect that "the Alumni Association hoped the record would re-create some fond moments on campus." The enclosed note further indicated that "if you're not now supporting the University of New Hampshire Alumni Fund, your consideration would be appreciated."

One of the most interesting and advantageous features of LP records, from the standpoint of the public relations practitioner, is provided by the new, thin plastic LP record which can even be bound into the pages of a magazine! (H. H. Scott, manufacturers of high fidelity equipment, recently did produce an LP record which was bound into the pages of a national magazine.) Another advantage of these records is that printing in several colors can be placed directly upon the record itself, thus giving both an audio and a visual approach. Another advantage, although this may change should the use of this technique become more widespread than it is now, is that people are quite reluctant to throw away one of these records—at least, until they have heard what is on it.

LP records of this kind are being used more and more to present, in dramatic form, messages of all sorts—particularly such things as reports to stockholders and municipal reports. An insurance company in Worcester, Massachusetts, recently bound into its printed annual report to stockholders an explanation of the previous year's growth in the voice of the company's president.

One particularly interesting example is the use that citizens of Ypsilanti, Michigan, made of this technique recently. They had produced for them a record which tells the story of Ypsilanti, entitled "The Sounds of Your City." Over five thousand copies were pressed for community-wide distribution. With the record, citizens could hear the sound of the gavel and roll call at a city council meeting; sirens and fire bells in the report on fire and police services. An air hammer and construction noises were woven into the narrative describing public works and the department responsible for such activities.

The jacket for the record was as important as the disc itself. On it was printed the income-and-cost chart (a dollar bill divided appropriately), a list of city accomplishments, plans for the future, and the names of city officials and various board chairmen. Even telephone numbers of the various city departments were included.

Municipal officials developed a preliminary tape recording with help from personnel of a local radio station. This tape was turned over to a public relations firm which wrote the narrative bridges, recorded the sound effects, and added the musical background. Boy Scouts were used to deliver the LP records to homes.

From our brief treatment of the use of tapes and LP records, it should be apparent that these two approaches offer tremendous potential to the public relations practitioner. Not only can either of these approaches stand alone, but they can potentially be used to *supplement* other approaches—such as films, speakers' bureaus, exhibits, or open houses. It would appear that the only limitation of these two forms of the spoken word is the creative ability of the public relations practitioner employing them.

Sight and Sound Combined for Greater Focus

Specialized uses of closed circuit television and specially prepared motion picture films constitute comparatively exotic (and expensive, at times) means of furthering certain public relations goals. As a result, these particular variations of the media are beyond the reach of most public relations practitioners in terms of finances and are generally used only by the larger corporations, more affluent associations, and government agencies at the state and federal levels. Film strips (which are also included in this category in Figure 18) are another matter; they are considerably less expensive but no less complicated to develop and integrate with public relations objectives. Let us examine each of these illustrations of sight and sound combined for greater focus in more detail.

1. *Film strips.* Silent and sound film strips are probably most often used by public relations practitioners in supplementing talks given to specialized audiences, although in some circumstances film strips are produced and distributed to interested parties to be used by teachers or other persons working with groups of individuals. An example of the latter is the film strip "Money at Work in the Steel Industry," developed by the Education Department of Hill & Knowlton, Inc., for the American Iron and Steel Institute.[16] This silent, color film strip, consisting of more than forty frames and a series of discussion frames as well, is supplied free to interested teachers. A booklet is sent

---

[16] Used by permission of Albert L. Ayars, Director, Education Department, Hill & Knowlton, Inc., Public Relations Counsel, 150 East 42 Street, New York, New York 10017.

along with the film strip itself. This particular film strip constitutes a part of a comprehensive, long-range public relations program of the Iron and Steel Institute. By this technique, along with a variety of other approaches, the Institute hopes to build a better understanding of corporate financing (in this case, how money is used and stressing the importance of profits to keep businesses going) among school children in America today, children who are potential future employees, stockholders, and members of the voting public on issues pertaining to private enterprise.

Film strips are often within the means of many public relations practitioners because they can be produced for as little as one to two thousand dollars. This dollar range, prorated over hundreds or thousands of viewers, represents a per-viewer cost that is very reasonable. Nevertheless, a film strip represents a sizable undertaking. In addition to the creativity that any communication effort requires, the problems associated with selecting "still" shots to put across visually what one wishes to communicate and at the same time integrating the visual material with the written captions that accompany each (or most) of the frames in a strip are formidable. Any public relations practitioner who has developed one or more film strips as part of his over-all public relations program can testify to the fact that he has spent many man-hours on the project.

As noted earlier, film strips are most often used to supplement and reinforce material that is being presented verbally. In addition to this use, film strips are also particularly suited to provide information, to help teach skills, to focus group attention, and to develop interest in further pursuit of topics.[17] Any one or a combination of these uses are of importance to public relations practitioners.

2. *Motion pictures.* The use of motion picture films for public relations purposes is rather widespread in spite of the costs involved. In fact, industrial use of films is way ahead of their use in educational institutions. The Educational Policies Commission of the National Education Association estimated that as of 1956 approximately seven times as much money was spent by business and industry on 16mm film production, distribution, and the like than was spent in all schools and colleges.[18]

The following excerpt illustrates the way in which films are used by public relations practitioners. Of particular interest is the fact that

---

[17] J. W. Brown, R. B. Lewis, and F. F. Harcleroad, *A-V Instruction Materials and Method* (New York: McGraw-Hill Book Company, 1959), pp. 140-141.

[18] *Ibid.*, chap 8.

the film served as a major means of integrating a broader public relations program.

"Let's face it" has become a watchword at Crouse-Hinds Company, Syracuse, New York, as a result of a program designed to create greater cost and profit consciousness among employees.

The program itself was called "Let's Face It" after the film which was a featured part of the campaign. The producer of the film is American Economic Foundation, 51 East 42nd St., New York, N.Y. Only the first part of the two-part film was used at Crouse-Hinds.

The specific purposes of the program as described by Ellen Van Dusen, Communications and Personnel Manager, were:
  —Broaden employee understanding of the cost of doing business by using the film.
  —Provide the opportunity to highlight Crouse-Hinds costs on a basis presented in the film.
  —Orient employees to the need for keeping costs down to remain competitive.
  —Lay the groundwork needed for conducting profit improvement programs planned for the future.

The first announcement of the program was made in the employee magazine. Curiosity was created by spreading the formula $MMW = NR + HE \times T$ around the plant on stair risers. The formula (which means: Man's Material Welfare equals Natural Resources plus Energy times Tools) was explained in the film.

In groups of 30, employees were shown the film and given a chance to participate in a discussion which was led by one of the group of 17 supervisors who had been prepared to handle the program. Groups were made up of employees from the same department wherever possible in order to encourage discussion among friends. As part of the presentation, charts showing the actual cost situation at Crouse-Hinds were used. Immediately before the program and also on the day following, the employees were surveyed anonymously about attitudes on key points such as costs, profits, job security, etc., so that any shift in employee opinion could be determined. Printed handouts before and after the meeting were also used. Articles in the employee magazine featuring employee interviews provided an additional follow-up.

Five sessions a day during five days of each week were held until the whole employee group of 2,200 had been reached. The total cost of the program came to about $10,000 in time away from the job, another $1,000 for materials.

Mrs. Van Dusen summed up the result of the program this way: "It was a tremendous undertaking; however, it was worth it, because we know we changed opinions about the need for a profitable business, raised the level of employee understanding, and stimulated thinking and questioning. 'Let's face it' became a popular phrase."[19]

When one examines how public relations practitioners use films, what stands out is the educational flavor of the films they employ. In our illustration above, the educational objectives of Mrs. Van Dusen and Crouse-Hinds Company are very apparent. They were concerned with the economic education of their employees at two levels: general and specific. They were interested in having their employees understand the economic facts of life that all companies must face (the general information) as well as how these economic facts applied specifically to Crouse-Hinds and their employees. Implicit in the whole effort is the assumption that, if an employee understands such things as the need for profits, what factors contribute and detract from profits, and, most importantly, how the individual employee actually *contributes* to the profit-making potential of a company, this understanding will engender more desirable behaviors on the part of the employee. He will be likely to become more productive. He will realize that when he "cheats" the company (no matter how—by low output, tardiness, or in other ways), in the long run he cheats himself. In fact, this assumption is very much akin to a basic assumption that educators make about all students: The more educated an individual is, the more likely he is going to be a responsible, mature citizen. Translating this thought to the Crouse-Hinds situation, one would say that the more educated, economically speaking, a Crouse-Hinds employee is, the better employee he is going to be.

Because of the strong educational character of films (and film strips, for that matter), it is useful to list what educators specializing in the audio-visual area have said about the educational advantages claimed for them and about what should be done to supplement their use to make them maximally effective.

With respect to advantages of films, the following are some of those claimed:

(1) *films combine "sight in motion" with various sounds* to act upon two senses at a time, (2) *films compel attention* through the use of motion and directed sight in a semi-darkened room, (3) *films can help to overcome important intellectual barriers to learning.* For example, they

---

[19] *Communication Reports,* May, 1963 (Enterprise Publications, 20 North Wacker Drive, Chicago 6, Illinois), pp. 1-2.

are efficient idea communicators which depend very little upon reading skills. Students who find difficulty in "experiencing" such complicated concepts as those involved in "electric current" or "nuclear fission" may be helped by a well-paced, clearly presented sound film on the subject.[20] Students who lack interest in a topic may be drawn to it by a moving, dramatic, colorful film presentation, . . . and (4) *films provide "common" experiences*. They bridge background differences for members of the same group. For example, a film may use a dramatic situation to set up a problem for class discussion. Communication between members of the group is usually improved when references apply to film problems all have experienced. . . .[21]

In the advantages of films cited above, the reader should substitute the word *public* for the word *student*. Thus, in the public relations application of films, although most of the time we have an educational objective, we still do not think of our publics as students. Be that as it may, however, it is interesting to relate these claimed advantages to our Crouse-Hinds example. Certainly in their intent to communicate economic concepts such as profits and capital and their special formula, $MMW = NR + HE \times T$), they were capitalizing on advantage No. 3, namely, that films can help to overcome important intellectual barriers to learning. Instead of "electric current," they were trying to portray "profit and loss." Both can be equally difficult to understand because they are not directly observable phenomena. Trying to communicate about profit and loss and other economic concepts is like trying to tell someone what a circular stairway looks like with your hands tied behind your back.

Advantage No. 4 is particularly applicable to the Crouse-Hinds example. If there is one thing that we can be certain of it is that any given group of employees will have widely differing views about economic concepts. Thus, from the standpoint of both the company and the employees, the film undoubtedly helped to provide "common" experiences before any group discussions were fruitfully held. In this case, information about economic concepts helped to provide a "commonness" both among employees and between employees and the company.

From the standpoint of how to use films, there are a number of

---

[20] For further discussion of the use of film reader units and teaching skills, see Robert Leetsma, "The Film Reader Program," *Elementary English*, XXX (February, 1956), 97-101.

[21] Brown, Lewis, and Harcleroad, p. 162. All passages from *A-V Instruction Materials and Method* used by permission of McGraw-Hill Book Company.

guides that research in this area has provided us. First, there are the more obvious admonishments[22] such as the following:

1. Know thoroughly the film that you are going to use and the subject matter contained therein. This means that you (*i.e.,* "you," the public relations practitioner and his associates) should view the film carefully before use. More than one viewing will be needed, because you will "see" (remember what we said in our section on perception) different things in the film each time you view it.

2. Also part of your homework is thinking through the physical arrangements you require, such as where the film is to be viewed and who is to handle the projector. There is nothing worse than to have minor details (such as the projector's not working) upset the viewing of a film.

3. Another part of your preshowing homework is thinking through how you are going to provide for participation of your audience after the viewing. Showing a film without providing for audience participation—such as discussion of the material after its presentation—is an exceedingly poor use of film. (Remember here how the Crouse-Hinds people carefully arranged for group discussion after each showing, based on the film and led by trained supervisors.)

4. Lastly, it is always valuable to arrange for follow-up material—usually in printed form—to be provided the audience after viewing.

Less obvious guides to film use are provided by studies conducted by The Pennsylvania University researchers for the U.S. Navy between the years 1947 and 1956. Some of these guides are listed here:

1. Good films can be used as the sole means for teaching some kinds of factual material and performance skills. Where the instructional situation makes this advisable, take advantage of this possibility.

2. Learning from film showings can be increased by repeated showings, pre-testing, or post-testing with knowledge of results given to the students. Learning is also increased by introducing the film, stating the purpose and importance of the showing and how it relates to their training.

3. Ability to learn from films improves with practice in learning from

---

[22] Additional discussion of this topic may be found *ibid.*

films. Trainees will learn more if printed study guides are used before and after viewing.

4. Note-taking should not be encouraged during the average film showing because it interferes with attention and, hence, with learning.

5. Film viewing sessions of informational material can extend to at least one hour without reduction in training effectiveness. (Some evidence from other studies contradicts this finding, especially for young children.)

6. Do not assume that learning has occured as a result of showing a film. Evaluate the effect of a film by giving a test.

7. It is important for students to know ahead of time what special terminology or nomenclature must be learned.

8. The sound tract often covers the important material to be learned in an informational film.

9. The more films one sees in a study situation, the more he learns from other films.

10. After testing students on film content, the correct answers should be explained. This can improve their learning.[23]

Once again, the reader should substitute the word *public* or *audience* for the word *student*.

These generalizations are borrowed from a book that is viewing films from an educational point of view. Our use of them rests on the contention that the public relations practitioner has an educational objective as well, although it is not always referred to in this manner in practice.

Each one of these generalizations has implications for a public relations practitioner who plans to use a film. However, certain of them appear worthy of additional comment. For example, generalization No. 6 is particularly interesting. It says that one cannot assume anything about the effectiveness of a film without really testing to find out what it has communicated to the viewers. All too often, public relations practitioners equate *exposure* with successful persuasion or informing, and this is not always the case. It is interesting to note that in Crouse-Hinds' use of the film on economics they introduced an attitude test *before* they showed the film and held the discussions, and *then* repeated this type of testing. In this way they were making sure what the effects of the film and discussion were rather than assuming that because the employees saw the film, the desired effects were attained.

This invalidity of assuming the effects of a film on the audience viewing it is precisely the reason that a public relations practitioner must

---

[23] *Ibid.*, pp. 173-174.

take such measures as frequency of showing and tallies of audience size with a grain of salt. All that these figures tell one is that a certain number of people saw a film in a given number of showings. They do not even hint of what may have been the impact of these films. Film showings and audience numbers have this trait in common with the newspaper and magazine clippings that public relations practitioners are so fond of showing and quoting. Valuable as these measures are, all they tell us is that people had an *opportunity* to view certain material, not that they, in fact, *did* view the material or were affected by it.

Generalization No. 2 highlights the fact that the film alone is not nearly so effective as using the film *along with other steps* such as testing, providing knowledge of how the participants learned following the viewing, preparing the viewer with a well-developed rationale for why he is being exposed to the film, and so on. To put it another way, as valuable as films may be, they need to be supplemented to obtain the full value from their usage.

Earlier, we alluded to the high cost of films as tending to place this particular media variation out of the reach of many public relations practitioner's budgets. Cutlip and Center (basing their remarks on a report developed by the Association of National Advertisers, Inc.) write:

> Keeping pace with its expanded use, the number of firms producing sponsored films has mushroomed in the past 20 years. It is estimated that there are 1200 such firms. The breadth and quality of service these firms offer varies greatly. Sponsors should use care in selecting a film producer. Costs of production likewise vary greatly. The A.N.A survey of business films found that costs of 157 films studied ranged from $1,732 to $426,000. The median cost was $25,800. Translated into costs-per-viewer, A.N.A. found that nearly 87 million viewers saw 46 films for an average of 26 minutes at an average cost for production and distribution of each film of $87,264. This communication was achieved at a cost of 4.6 cents per person. Showing nine of these films on TV brought the cost per viewer down to 1.6 cents for those films.[24]

Undoubtedly, the costs of films have continued to rise, thus emphasizing that film making is a step a public relations practitioner must weigh carefully before allocating his budget for such a purpose. No hard and fast rules can be given, and each case must be weighed individually. However, one particularly noteworthy consideration (after

---

[24] Scott M. Cutlip and Allen H. Center, "*Effective Public Relations* (3rd ed.; Englewood Cliffs, N.J.: Prentice-Hall, Inc., 1964), pp. 166-167. Used by permission.

such important details as "Is what we have to say suitable for film?" "Is our message durable enough to be 'frozen' on film?" and the like) is whether one will be able to insure that all of the accompanying details to film showing—such as creating proper motivation, having trained people available for postviewing discussion—will be competently handled. In other words, for a film to be eligible in the "specialized audiences" portion of the continuum of communication (as contrasted with the "mass communication" portion), it must be handled in a way that insures its reaching that specialized audience under reasonably favorable viewing conditions. Let us illustrate this point more fully. A few years ago, the author was consultant to a professional organization which was planning to develop a film to tell the story of their profession. The main medium for showing this planned film, however, was to be television, in order to reach a wider audience. In this instance, the film would no longer be a means of communication that would fall at the specialized audience portion of the communication continuum; rather, it would become a mass media communication technique. Under these circumstances, one could *not* assume the usual audience motivation, for example, that can normally be made when films are shown to smaller, more select groups. For this reason, it appeared to the author that this film could not possibly achieve the communication objectives desired. The objective they had (*i.e.*, to have the audience become interested in knowing more about their profession) was not attainable through the mass media. To return to the point made just before our example, in certain circumstances films can be placed at the "specialized audience" portion of the communication continuum. At other times, because of the conditions of viewing, films are closer to the mass media range of the continuum. The author would argue that *most* of the communication objectives of a public relations practitioner are *not* attainable by utilization of the mass media. The reason for this statement is simple: Mass media conditions generally do not permit the public relations practitioner to engender the degree of motivation among the recipients that is usually required for most public relations objectives. As we noted in Chapter 9 (page 235), the closer one is to the mass media end of the continuum, the less one can assume *ready-made interest on the part of the audience.* Without motivation to attend to a communication, most public relations objectives are practically doomed. Thus, if a film is to operate primarily at the mass media portion of the communication continuum, then the author suggests that serious doubts may be raised about such a venture. It probably will not contribute to solving the problem of the public relations practitioner concerned, anyway. We will return to this point in Chapter 11 (pages 300-302).

Modified Television Usage.   This is a phrase designed to cover any usage of television that renders it an example of the use of sound and sight for a specialized audience. The example of modified television usage that immediately comes to mind is, of course, closed-circuit television. However, this particular form of media is comparatively rare for the public relations practitioner because of the costs involved. In addition to costs, there is the problem of the arrangements necessary to make close-circuit viewing possible.

One interesting variation of the utilization of television that qualifies it as an example of modified television usage is described below. It also illustrates how the high costs of closed-circuit television were circumvented by one organization.

. . . Northrop Corporation, Beverly Hills, California, has used television as a means of "introducing" its company president to its 25,000 employees.

During the summer, Mr. Collins, company president, had been absent from his office for several months. Part of this absence was caused by illness and convalescence. It was felt, therefore, that it would be desirable for company personnel to see him in person and thus be assured, without mention of the illness, that he was back at his desk in vigorous health and leading the company as usual.

A closed-circuit television hookup was considered, but this proved unwieldy and expensive. It was finally decided to purchase time on a principal local television station outside of regular broadcasting hours— in this case 8:00 A.M. on a Saturday morning. It was felt that since no regularly scheduled programs are on the air at that time, this would have the effect of furnishing virtually a private channel.

Before the broadcast, plant papers were used to alert company personnel. Stuffers were also placed in pay envelopes and distributed the day before the broadcast.

A professional announcer was used to introduce Mr. Collins, who talked for thirty minutes: The program was terminated with the regular station sign-off. The station did not resume broadcasting until later in the morning.

The total cost was roughly $1,000. The reaction was exactly what was hoped for and the whole event considered highly successful. Kinescopes were also prepared and sent to outlying facilities in Florida and Texas, which were, of course, outside the normal viewing area.

Another factor that made television look good in this case was the company, for several years, had addressed occasional communications to company personnel in the form of a letter signed by the president. Since employment had gone as high as 25,000, the cost of sending these letters had been a considerable cost item.[25]

Besides illustrating the use of television to reach a specialized audience, this example is particularly applicable to points that were made at the beginning of this chapter: The various media are *special cases* of the person-to-person situation in communications, and selection of media is made (implicitly or explicitly) with interpersonal needs in mind. Here we see at least two major considerations that led the public relations practitioners concerned to see if they could figure out a way that television, in a modified form, could be used. One was the question of communicating about the health of the president. The fact that he could be seen by the employees obviated the need to say that he was healthy and able to direct the company effectively. No mention had to be made of this rather delicate point, because the appearance of the man plus how he performed showed his audience that he was once again well.

The other point had to do with the reputation for the personal touch that the president had in the past shown the employees through personal letters. The television presentation done especially for them tended to maintain the tradition of direct concern on the part of the president for his employees.

Closed-circuit television, or modifications such as those illustrated by the Northrop Company, are not likely to become widely used by public relations practitioners for some time to come. However, technological advances being what they are, this means of communication may rapidly become cheaper. Public relations practitioners must watch the development of this media carefully as it offers a potentially wide range of applications once the problems of costs and physical arrangements are overcome.

QUESTIONS FOR DISCUSSION

1. In this chapter, the contention is made that one way of viewing the media stage (other than face-to-face communication as one form of media) is "as a substitute for the person-to-person contact, which

---

[25] *Communication Reports*, July, 1963 (Enterprise Publications, 20 North Wacker Drive, Chicago 6, Illinois), pp. 2-3.

cannot be used [by the public relations practitioner] because of size of audience, physical separation of sender and recipients, and so on." Obtain some public relations examples that support this contention—that is, as far as you can determine that face-to-face considerations were either implicitly or explicitly behind the selection of the media used. Also, obtain some public relations examples that apparently do *not* support this generalization. Once again, which type of examples were easiest to obtain?

2. With the list of contents of the back-to-school kit as your guide (page 248), develop a list of contents for an *information kit* of your own, designed to supplement an over-all public relations program for some hypothetical public relations problem situation that you have devised. In your own kit, did you find that you were able to make use of the various forms of the media—*i.e.*, print, sound, and sound and sight combined? If you were not able to use all of the forms of the media, why was this so?

3. In this chapter, the point is taken that public relations practitioners have not made much use of tapes and long-playing records. Why do you think this is so? Do you suppose the "print heritage" (that is, the fact that many public relations practitioners came from previous jobs in the print media) of many public relations practitioners has contributed to this? What uses of tapes and long-playing records can you develop and for what kinds of problem situations?

Chapter 11

THE MEDIA STAGE IN FURTHER DETAIL: RELATIONSHIP TO MASS COMMUNICATION

In Chapter 10 we examined the media stage from the standpoint of relating our continuum of communication notion (Chapter 9, page 234) to media usage for public relations purposes. In this context we argued that the qualities found in face-to-face communication situations serve as a basic guide to media selection or usage in situations where we are unable to face the recipient directly. Following this, we concentrated on media usage with what we called the specialized audience portion of the communication continuum.

We are now ready to extend our examination of the use of the media with the large-scale audiences: that is, situations where we are attempting to communicate with a great many people, such as is implied when we speak of *mass* communication and the *mass* media. We will examine mass communication from the standpoint of our three media breakdowns introduced in Figure 18: The Printed Word, The Spoken Word, and Sound and Sight Combined.

MASS COMMUNICATION

The Printed Word

This portion of the communication continuum represents the "stamping ground" for a great many public relations practitioners. The printed word in some mass media outlet has become almost the *sine qua non* of the public relations profession. Newspapers come to mind first, of course, since the public relations practitioner has become exceedingly proficient in harnessing this form of the mass media for his professional purposes. An exhaustive treatment of how the public relations practitioner employs the newspaper is beyond the scope of this chapter. However, a reasonable appreciation of the utilization of the printed word in mass media form can be obtained by considering the following topics: (1) the assumption of the mass audience; (2) press relations— personal and impersonal components; (3) paid *vs.* unpaid newspaper space; (4) unpaid space—the "trademark" of the public relations practitioner; and (5) a word about magazines.

THE ASSUMPTION OF THE MASS AUDIENCE

Newspapers are, of course, one of the oldest and most familiar forms of mass media. There are approximately seventeen hundred daily newspapers with total circulation in the tens of millions. In addition, thousands of weekly and semiweekly newspapers add substantially to the flood of newsprint that is absorbed by the public. We have become so strongly attached to our newspapers that "missing the newspaper" because of strikes or natural phenomena has a serious impact upon many of us.[1] Consequently, there is no question of the importance of the newspaper in the lives of literate persons, and there is really no need to belabor the point with statistics concerning how widespread newspapers are and how many readers, individually or collectively, they are able to claim. What is of importance is the question of *mass audiences* that any mass media imply and the extent to which a public relations practitioner is really concerned with a mass audience. This is the first time that this issue has arisen in our consideration of media because prior to this we were talking about either person-to-person communication or communication with specialized audiences. How-

---

[1] *See*, for example, Bernard Berelson, "What 'Missing the Newspaper' Means," in Wilbur Schramm (ed.), *The Process and Effects of Mass Communication* (Urbana: University of Illinois Press, 1954), pp. 36-47.

ever, whenever any form of the mass media is considered from the standpoint of transmitting what a public relations practitioner wants to have said, the question of an audience becomes a critical one. To whom is the public relations practitioner directing his message and what permits him the assumption that he does, in fact, have a mass audience? Because of these questions, our starting point in a discussion of newspapers is, "Why are we using the newspapers as a means of solving our public relations problems?" It has been the author's experience that this question is not well answered by many public relations practitioners. They have not really thought the question through. Rather, they have been led into newspaper usage by several factors, some of which we have considered briefly before (see Chapter 4, pages 84-86).[2]

First, there is the question of the professional training and occupational backgrounds of many public relations practitioners. Because a great many of them are former newspapermen, magazine writers, and other people who dealt with some phase of the printed word, it is natural for them to turn to the printed word—particularly its use in mass media—to help solve their public relations problems. What is more natural for a former newspaperman than to get material into a newspaper for his client![3]

A second force is that the exhilaration of seeing your own material in print creates a tremendous sense of euphoria. Writing is hard work that requires training and skill, and the products of this effort and skill

---

[2] It should be added here that many of the points questioning the use of newspapers as mass media apply to radio and television as well. This will become evident when we touch on radio and television usage in a mass communication context later in this chapter.

[3] It is interesting to note in this connection that when an assortment of public relations practitioners are questioned about the essential educational and experiential qualifications needed to be a success in public relations, the replies tend to reflect closely the previous occupational experiences of the respondents. Thus, former newspapermen tell you that there is no substitute for the experience of working on a newspaper. Someone who has *not* had a journalism background is very likely to tell you that journalism is *not* a prerequisite, but will stress his previous experiences whether they be in economics, education, or what have you. In addition, the nonjournalist is likely to tell you that you can always hire someone to do your writing for you! There is no question that a public relations practitioner must be able to write and write well. But whether he should gain this experience from a job on a newspaper is another matter. The safest thing that can be said at this point is that the precise formula for producing a well-rounded public relations practitioner is still in evolution. Also equally clear is the fact that not any existing fields of endeavor—of which journalism is, of course, one—hold the key to success, especially when one keeps in mind how public relations is undoubtedly going to be practiced in the future.

set a man apart and give him something of which he can be proud. One is even tempted to borrow from learning theorists to account for this well entrenched behavior. Seeing your material in print can serve as a reinforcement (*i.e.*, it relates to your success in serving a client) for your writing efforts. However, the reinforcements are not always forthcoming; that is, one can never be sure just what articles will be accepted. This means that the reinforcements are uncertain and unpredictable. Learning theorists have found that animals trained according to random reinforcement schedules (*i.e.*, the animals have no way of figuring out when they will be reinforced) develop responses that are the most difficult to extinguish (*i.e.*, to "unlearn" or "forget"). For this reason, the learning theorist would suggest that the nature of the reinforcement in writing for newspapers is precisely the form that should make the response of writing the most difficult to stop. Maybe this is why it is often futile to get some public relations practitioners to at least question why they are writing material for the mass media.

A third factor is that writing—in any form—creates a tangible by-product that one can show for all of his time, effort, and money. Unlike most other endeavors in life, the public relations practitioner is very often hard pressed to show "what good he has been doing." A book full of clippings dealing with the client in a variety of ways and in a host of daily and weekly newspapers becomes proof in itself that the public relations practitioner has done his job. In many ways, this has become a substitute for research data in any other form. Two other factors are very closely related to this force: the demands of the client and the influence of advertising measures such as circulation figures, cost per reader indices, and the like. Thus, the public relations practitioner, even if he tries to downgrade the importance of clippings and attempts to equate public relations success with the column inch, finds many clients (or superiors in his own organization) demanding such measures from him. It is hard to reverse a process that has become well entrenched and is waved conspicuously by competitors! The influences of advertising measures are also closely related, because it is an easy step to reason that if an *advertisement* in a paper could claim such and such a potential audience, why not apply the same reasoning to a potential audience for an *article* placed in a newspaper? In this way we can come to regard a particular newspaper as a "good" outlet because it has a very large readership, without paying any attention to the fact that readership claims that may apply to an advertisement may not apply to an article.

A fourth force that can be discerned, and which also contributes to many public relations practitioners' faith in newspapers, is that so often the public relations practitioner is dealing with objectives which are very hard, indeed, sometimes impossible, to measure. Whereas the advertiser always had purchasing behavior to use as a measure of effectiveness, such is not the case in many public relations situations. Such objectives as providing one company with a fine reputation for basic research, another as a good place to work, still another as a responsible "corporate citizen," and in another instance overcoming the negative effects of being a "big corporation" are very difficult objectives to measure. Who can say whether you have achieved these objectives or not? This, in turn, means that it is very difficult to question the value of newspaper coverage. In other words, *it is just as difficult to demonstrate that a whole lot of newspaper clippings are not effective and worth the effort as it is to demonstrate that they are!*

A fifth force can best be described with the phrase *thought leaders.* Public relations practitioners have long believed in the effectiveness of reaching thought leaders (or any other phrase one may wish to use to characterize influential and powerful people in a given community). Such people generally read newspapers avidly and carefully; hence it follows that adequate newspaper coverage on behalf of your client or company means that you are undoubtedly reaching these thought leaders. Because these people are influential, one's public relations cause is furthered. A comparatively recent concept from the social science literature known as the "two-step flow" hypothesis—the flow of ideas or information from the originator of the information to the recipients of the information—lends some support to this notion.[4] The two-step flow suggests that influential thought leaders are contacted through the mass media (because they read more and are more motivated to "pay attention" to what is going on around them) and that they in turn influence people who look up to them and respect their views on various matters. Thus, an old rule of thumb in public relations practice receives some support from social scientists.[5]

---

[4] Paul F. Lazarsfeld, Bernard Berelson, and Hazel Gaudet, *The People's Choice* (2d ed.; New York: Columbia University Press, 1948), p. 151; *see also* Elihu Katz, "The Two-Step Flow of Communication," in Wilbur Schramm (ed.), *Mass Communication* (Urbana: University of Illinois Press, 1960), pp. 346-365.

[5] More recent thinking on this question of transmission of information or ideas suggests that both concepts (*i.e.,* "thought leaders" and "two-step flow") need more refinement and additional empirical support. There appears to be solid evidence that there is no such thing as a thought leader in the sense of an individual who is looked to for guidance in all matters, but, rather, that individuals who play influential roles in shaping the thinking of others vary with the topic in question. For financial matters, it might be one person; for world series bets, it might be another; and so on. The two-step flow hypothesis requires this same modification in thinking (and, indeed, is receiving it from researchers in this area) as well as the realization that it is a gross oversimplification of a very complicated process.

A sixth factor that must not be overlooked is that some perfectly wonderful copy (from a public relations practitioner's point of view) can be placed in a newspaper (or lots of newspapers) free! (In fact, the "free" part of much of what the public relations practitioner wants to get into print has become a bone of contention between some public relations practitioners and newspapermen, not to mention advertising people.) Consequently, the fact that widespread newspaper exposure of certain information can be attained with little or no cost to the public relations practitioner (ignoring for the moment the cost of maintaining a public relations staff or consulting organization capable of placing the material) is no small factor in causing such approaches to solving public relations problems to continue to be used.

Lastly, we should not forget that material successfully placed in newspapers (or other mass media such as magazines) sometimes works! The definition of success varies, of course, from situation to situation, but there are numerous available examples illustrating that many people read a particular release or series of releases; that a lot of reaction was obtained from the reading public in terms of letters of inquiry, attendance at open houses and new business locations; that certain material placed in newspapers was picked up by other writers and rewritten in various forms, then appeared in various types of mass media across the country. Naturally, when a certain approach seems to do the job, it is not surprising that it becomes firmly entrenched as a modus operandi.

There are undoubtedly other factors that make the use of the newspaper such a popular and well accepted mode of operation for the public relations practitioner. The reader has probably thought of others he would like to suggest. It is important to emphasize a point at this time: The author does not for one minute mean to imply that the use of the newspaper as a means of reaching mass audiences should not be used by public relations practitioners. This would be nonsense to suggest because there is sufficient evidence to support its use. However, of all of the means of approaching public relations problems, the newspaper has evolved into one of the most traditional techniques employed by the public relations practitioner. For all of the reasons discussed above, it has become very entrenched and almost unquestioned. The rationale for looking more fully into some of the reasons for this entrenchment is that it is the contention of the author that *a closer examination of the appropriateness of all mass media usage must be made by public relations practitioners.* The focus should not be on newspaper usage alone. There are reasons for believing that the uniqueness of public relations problems have not been fully realized, even by public relations practitioners. There has been too much unquestioned use of mass media techniques patterned after advertising reasoning or logic. It appears that for many public relations attitude and behavior changes desired by a public relations practitioner, the mass media are entirely inadequate. It is exceedingly difficult to engender motivation, emotional commitment, and personal involvement through material printed in the mass media. It is time that the peculiar problems of the public relations practitioner be more fully appreciated, and communications techniques reflect this fact. We will return to this point later in this chapter.

Press Relations—Personal and Impersonal Components

Because the daily work of many public relations practitioners requires a high degree of interaction with the press, personal contacts with newspaper people from the lowliest reporter to editors and publishers is naturally desirable. However, the public relations practitioner must never try to take advantage of his personal relations to further press relations; nothing can more quickly finish his effectiveness for an organization. People connected with newspapers regard their independence to print what they see fit as a most precious right. Any suggestion of an infringement of that right on the part of a public relations practitioner trying to get preferential treatment will almost invariably be rejected, and the public relations practitioner concerned will be immediately downgraded in their estimation. The only profit that a public relations practitioner can safely make from his personal contacts among newspaper people is to use those contacts to learn the idiosyncrasies of the various individuals, then to let that knowledge serve as his guide in determining what kind of material to present to them. This must be the extent of his use of personal contacts.

Impersonal factors, reflecting the skill of the public relations practitioner as an upright, ethical communicator and representative of an organization, are another matter. The public relations practitioner should try to capitalize on these as much as he possibly can. The public relations practitioner must realize that the job of the editor is to fill his paper with material that he thinks his reader would (and also should) want to read. One of the most often repeated guides here is that what is submitted must be news. That is, it should be fresh, interesting, of some importance in the daily affairs of people, and so on. This means that no matter how interesting a promotion, a speech, an innovation, or what have you may be to a particular organization, the question is: Will it be of general interest or importance? Here is where the "impersonal" factors (that is, things that are not dependent on your interpersonal relations with the newspaper representative) play a role. The public relations practitioner is expected to know thoroughly the make-up of the newspaper with which he is dealing. He must know if the paper is large enough to have separate sports editors, women's editors, financial editors. If so, he must plan to direct his material to the appropriate editor. He must gradually build his reputation for accuracy, so that in time newspaper people come to have faith in what he writes. In fact, the higher the degree to which he can build his reputation for being an authority in a particular area, so much the better for his relations with the press. On this point, Marston writes:

> Editors also usually welcome knowing about the availability of helpful authorities in news related to their fields. Frequently a man handling public relations news releases for an oil company or a chemical firm knows (and should know) more about oil or chemicals than the business or perhaps even the science editor of a newspaper.
>
> One public relations man for a French oil company has not only become an expert in his field but has also assembled a great library of facts and pictures about world petroleum production and processing. When an oil crisis breaks out in the Sahara or in Iran or in Venezuela, reporters for many French newspapers call upon him first for factual material.[6]

This quotation really summarizes the spirit of what we are trying to communicate here about the impersonal factors in press relations as contrasted with personal ones. It is naturally helpful to be on a first-name basis with newspaper people of all levels and types of newspapers. However, there is absolutely no substitute for the ability of a public relations practitioner to write clearly, crisply, and accurately. There are no substitutes for his knowledge of what a newspaper is looking for; how it is constituted organizationally; what its policies are with respect to submissions, time deadlines, accompanying photographs; and the like. Lastly, the reputation for being an expert in whatever field (*i.e.*, organization) you represent as a public relations practitioner is of prime importance.

One final point. The volume of material received by a newspaper, particularly the large, prestige papers, is staggering. The competition for that precious newspaper space is enormous, with most editors receiving enough material to write whole books and only enough space to absorb a standard short story. Add to this the unpredictable flow of world and local events—wars, floods, disasters. At any time, these unpredictable events can come along—a good example is miners trapped by a cave-in hundreds of feet below the surface—and "all bets are off."

---

[6] J. E. Marston, *The Nature of Public Relations* (New York: McGraw-Hill Book Company, 1963), pp. 126-127. Used by permission.

What might have been printed is now pushed out of the way by columns or pages of material (including pictures) dealing with this unforeseen disaster or noteworthy event. To top it off, you have the day-to-day changes in the editors, how they feel one day, how something "strikes" them, what their views are concerning what will interest people, and so forth. All of this adds up to the unpredictableness of getting material printed in a newspaper. You just can't be sure. But what is even more important—and this is a cardinal rule that public relations practitioners must observe—is that you *must accept* this unpredictableness without protest. The worst thing a public relations practitioner can do is to try to argue with an editor or to complain that something he sent in was not printed. Trying to beg, borrow, or steal space in a newspaper is out. It can't be done, and the public relations practitioner who does not try grows in the esteem of newspaper people. The reasoning behind this important "don't" is reflected in what one city editor, who was fed up with the amateur public relations practitioner, wrote:

> Please, mister, if that's a handout in your hand just give it to me. That's all there is to it. If we can use it, I'll ask a reporter to re-write it. If we can't use it, I'll throw it away. Don't hold it under my nose and read it to me with your finger tracing every line. I can read. . . . And don't suggest that we have a little talk about it. I haven't got time for conferences. . . . No use standing there. There are 16 more press agents waiting to see me.[7]

This quote, is, of course, an exaggeration, but it does put across the point about not complaining about getting material in a paper. Likewise, the identification of the individual trying to submit material for the paper as a press agent may be rejected by some who insist that they are more than press agents and that the editor does not understand the difference between a press agent and a public relations practitioner. Lastly, a lot of material is *not* rewritten (some papers have come to have *too much faith* in the public relations practitioner). However, it is the spirit of the quote that must be heeded by all people who call themselves public relations practitioners.

Paid *vs.* Unpaid Newspaper Space

Our definition of public relations (developed in Chapters 1 and 2 and explicitly stated in Chapter 3) is a detailed statement which spells

---

[7] Scott M. Cutlip and Allen H. Center, *Effective Public Relations* (3rd ed.; Englewood Cliffs, N.J.: Prentice-Hall, Inc., 1964), p. 308. Used by permission.

out what a public relations practitioner is, what he stands for, and what he does in his daily work. One additional way of comparing a public relations practitioner with other types of communicators is in terms of how and what they place in newspapers and whether what is placed is paid for or is free.

The distinction between paid and unpaid space in a newspaper tends to distinguish advertising people from public relations practitioners. The ad people, naturally, are the ones who tend to pay for what they place with a newspaper. The paid-unpaid distinction does not always distinguish between public relations practitioner and publicist, however. Two suggestions are offered here to help keep clear the differences among various categories of communicators. One is the distinction of the media phase of the total communication process as a *means to an end* or *an end in itself*. Usually, the public relations practitioner's placement of material in some form of the mass media is only one part of a many-faceted effort to solve some particular public relations problems. This means that, in general, a public relations practitioner will have many other details to attend to as part of his over-all problem-solving efforts. For the advertising man, the publicity man, or any other title that one might generate to designate an individual who is preoccupied with getting material in print, the placement of the material, the design of the material, and a host of other details associated with media placement become much more of ends in themselves. Other than the fact that he may have to suffer the consequence if his ads do not sell his client's products, the work of the advertising man (and the publicist) is largely completed when the media placement has been achieved successfully. Such is not the case with the public relations practitioner.

A second suggestion to help distinguish the various occupational groups concerned with placement of material in the mass media is embodied in Figure 19, entitled "Media Placement Continuum." In Figure 19 we see that at one extreme of our media placement continuum (left-hand end) is "Straight Advertising." Here is a direct effort on behalf of a product (or cause) of an organization for which the newspaper space (or other mass media) is paid for. (This is why this end of the continuum is labeled "Direct Gain to Organization.") The type of communicator is nearly always an advertising man. The benefits to the organization ultimately paying for this advertising are direct, generally in terms of increased sales of some product or service.

At the other end of the continuum, we find the "Public Service Material." In this instance, an organization (usually a profit-making one) places material in newspapers or magazines which is of some general

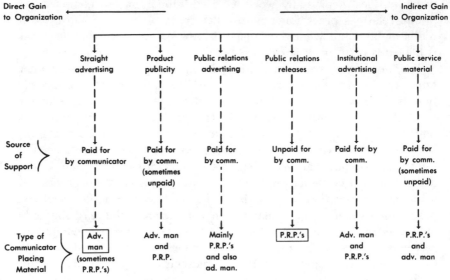

Figure 19

Media Placement Continuum

value (usually to a fairly large segment of society) but does not generate any direct gain or return to the organization paying for the space. Perhaps one of the best examples of this type of public service material is New York Life Insurance Company's career guidance series. In this series, NYL has engaged an outstanding individual in a certain career field (say, for example, engineering or nursing) to describe briefly the career in question, the qualifications necessary to enter the career, the work done, benefits to be obtained, and so on. In addition to the material contained in the magazine, there is material that the company will supply on request. This type of material tends to be developed (at least, the idea for such a series) by a public relations practitioner, but there are instances of advertising people doing this type of work as well (see Figure 20,[8] pages 281-284). Public service material, like institutional advertising, is not designed to sell either an organization or its products and services directly. Rather, it is intended to perform a public service

---

[8] Reprinted through the courtesy of the New York Life Insurance Company, copyright owner. For the past two years, this particular advertising series has been run in scholastic magazines only.

SHOULD YOUR CHILD GO INTO PUBLIC RELATIONS?*
by John W. Hill
Chairman of the Board, Hill and Knowlton, Inc., Public Relations Counsel
as told to Jhan Robbins

Thirty-three years ago when I left my job as a journalist and entered the field of public relations, there were only a handful of people in the entire country who thought of public relations as a career. Today it is a lively, creative, fast-growing profession, employing about 100,000 people. Several thousand companies, both large and small, have their own public relations departments. There are more than 1,500 public relations agencies. In addition, public relations people are active in government agencies, trade unions, church organizations, educational institutions, medical research groups, philanthropic and cultural campaigns.

What Is Public Relations?

Since public relations is a relatively young profession, it is difficult to define. Public relations bears family resemblance to journalism and teaching, for it aims to inform; to the law in that it often counsels and advises clients on public attitudes and represents them before the bar of public opinion; and even to the dramatic and graphic arts in meeting the need to present and portray facts to the public in an effective, imaginative way.

Responsible public relations practice hews to standards of ethics equal to those of other professions. There is no lasting way to impart a sweet aroma to a smelly situation. No company or organization can long persuade public opinion that it is acting in the public interest when it is not. Public relations has no hidden power to manipulate the public mind. The only lasting power public relations has is the power of truth. Anyone who attempts to advance a cause by public misinformation, trickery or deception is courting an eventual setback.

What Does a Public Relations Man Do?

I find that some of our young people have the idea that public relations men spend all their time hanging over tables at expensive restaurants, drifting from one party to the next and slapping influential people on the back. The fact is that the range of activities in public relations today is exceedingly broad —and few of these activities are frivolous.

Public relations people may be called on to deal with the public opinion aspects of almost any corporate or association problem from a plant opening to a plant closing, a merger or taxation matters; with problems of health, air or stream pollution, labor relations, overseas relations, gaining public understanding of needed or pending legislation, introducing new products—in fact, almost any facet of our daily lives.

* Since 1953, New York Life has been presenting advertisements like this to help parents and their children plan for the future. This particular message appears in *The Saturday Evening Post*, Nov. 5; *Look*, Dec. 20; *Life*, Nov. 28; *Scholastic*, Dec. 7. It is reproduced here because of the special interest it may hold for readers of this publication. As noted below, this article is available in booklet form without charge. Quantity reprints can be requested by interested companies, schools, professional groups, and other organizations. *Compton Advertising, Inc.*, New York Life—Ad No. 19-013B, *Public Relations Journal—November*, 1960, 9-20-60.

Figure 20

There are as many ways for the public relations man to convey his client's message as there are channels, or media, of communication. In news releases, magazines, company publications, booklets, brochures and annual reports, he employs the medium of the written word. He may use radio, television or the public platform, either speaking himself or preparing material for others to deliver. In the area of visual aids he uses films of all kinds, displays, posters, signs.

Each of these public relations efforts involves skills and techniques all its own, and so there is a tendency among public relations people to specialize. The extent of this specialization depends largely on the size of the public relations agency or the department within an organization. The large agency or department may employ individuals who do nothing but write press releases, booklets, or speeches; or make information available to editors and broadcasters; or plan special events.

At the other extreme, there is a large number of public relations men who operate alone, or nearly so, as one-man agencies or small departments. They do all the jobs or as many as possible themselves, resorting when they can or must to outside counsel for extra help. I started as a one-man agency myself in Cleveland in 1927.

While skills in the communication arts are important in public relations, the ability to advise on what and when—or even whether—to communicate, is even more important. This calls for good judgment and, of course, experience. The responsibility for public relations policy decisions rests with top management of an organization. The public relations man can influence policy to the extent that he has won the confidence of management.

What Qualities Are Needed to Succeed?

Since the aim of public relations is to inform and convince, the good public relations person has a talent for both understanding and telling. He enjoys explaining things to others and, like a good debater, wants to persuade. The public relations man thus tends to have an aptitude for expression. He is likely to be a good writer or speaker. Choosing the right word at the right time is of real importance to him, for he is sensitive to people's responses.

The good public relations man has curiosity and thoroughness, too. To convince others, he must himself know; and to know, he has to dig. Thus, the good public relations man has factual knowledge, but he knows people, too—how and why they react, when and how to present his message. He must be equally concerned with the big program and the small detail.

College Training Desirable

At least four years of college in a liberal arts program are desirable, with post-graduate courses whenever possible. Studies should emphasize history, economics, public affairs, modern languages and other social sciences. The student who aims for public relations will probably want to join the staff of the school newspaper or magazine. He will benefit from student government activities and from arguing on the school debating team.

Courses in public relations are offered at a number of our institutions of higher learning. Courses in law, business administration and corporate management are valuable.

How to Get a Start

I continue to believe that working in the editorial department of a newspaper provides excellent training for public relations. In a newspaper office, objectivity, clarity and brevity are taught side by side with the human touch. Increasingly, however, young people are preferring to learn their skills on the job, either in the public relations department of a company or with the consulting firms. This manner of starting doubtless will become more popular as corporate public relations departments grow in size and public relations firms become more numerous.

Job classifications, duties and compensation in public relations vary widely from place to place. In a small organization, the public relations novice may be hired for general usefulness around the shop; in a larger agency or department he or she may be assigned immediately to assist in one of the specialized fields. Compensation for the public relations trainee compares favorably with that in other beginning professional jobs, ranging roughly from $4,500 to $7,500.

As in any field, aptitude, experience and opportunity will ordinarily determine an individual's rate of rise. A skilled public relations person with ten years in the business—sometimes less—may earn between $10,000 and $20,000 a year.

Advantages and Disadvantages

As in every walk of life, frustrations are not uncommon in public relations. Excellent programs, the result of many hours of hard work, are sometimes endlessly delayed or suddenly abandoned. Progress may come by leaps and bounds or by slow, painstaking steps. Teamwork is at a premium; individual recognition may be difficult to come by. Working hours, especially during emergencies, are long and often unpredictable.

The disadvantages are more than offset, however, by the frequent appearance of the unexpected challenge. Good public relations people are always on their toes. They share the excitement that comes from dealing with timely and important problems. There is frequently an opportunity to instruct, to inform, to offer useful service. The profession is not burdened by the shadows of outmoded ideas or prejudices. Opportunities for women are excellent. Many hold top positions.

If I were asked to sum up the qualifications of the ideal public relations person, I would say, first of all, that he would display a flair for clear expression. Second, he would have a solid education, especially in the liberal arts. But to reach the top levels in public relations he will need much more— he will need superior qualities of mind and character—intelligence, judgment, objectivity, curiosity, imagination and above all integrity.

What About the Future?

In the United States and other free countries of the world, public opinion is the controlling force.

The need is unmistakable for an informed public opinion to insure sound judgments on the complex problems of today and tomorrow affecting the lives of individuals and the fate of the economy. And, so long as this need exists, there will be the need for public relations skills to help groups in government, business and many other fields to inform the public and to debate their views.

which, hopefully, will at the same time produce more positive attitudes toward the organization sponsoring it. For this reason, public service material is placed at the right-hand end of the media placement continuum where only indirect gains to the organization are involved.

"Institutional Advertising" is placed alongside public service material because it, too, belongs at the "indirect gain to the organization" end of the continuum. Perhaps the best examples of institutional advertising are the ads that associations place in the mass media. Thus, no one trucking company is named when an ad highlighting the contribution that the trucking industry makes to the maintenance of our nations' roads is placed in a large circulation magazine or newspaper. Likewise, when the Iron and Steel Institute places an ad dealing with the need for profits or the desirability of tax reductions, no one steel company is mentioned. For this reason, it is almost impossible to trace the effects of institutional advertising back to any one company or even to the industry as a whole. The *belief* that this material does some good, in lieu of direct proof, is one of the major motivations for continuing to place such advertisements. As noted in Figure 19, institutional advertising is a place where there is considerable overlapping of the public relations practitioner with the advertising man. Usually, when the public relations practitioner is involved, his role is that of generating the idea of the ad series and structuring how it fits in with other portions of his organization's public relations activities. The actual development of an ad is sometimes farmed out to an agency, or in some circumstances, is done by the public relations practitioner.

A comparable position in media placement on the continuum, but on the left-hand end rather than the right, is "Product Publicity." Product publicity, as the phrase implies, is designed to promote a particular product or service of an organization. The only justification for making a distinction between product publicity and straight advertising is in terms of the blend of paid and unpaid publicity. Straight advertising is a clear-cut situation where paid advertising is designed to sell products. Product publicity campaigns have the same objective —i.e., sales—but, the methods vary from paid ads to press conferences, with just as many efforts designed to obtain free publicity as to obtain paid publicity. A typical program may be to have a press conference in connection with the development of a brand-new product. If the conference is successful, there may be a considerable amount of publicity emerging from this one step alone. Concurrent with this may be efforts to place articles in trade magazines and to encourage specialized articles in certain portions of the paper such as the financial or trade sections. At the same time, a series of paid ads in a variety of outlets may be underway. Product publicity is a creative blend of paid and unpaid efforts with a single purpose: widespread acceptance of a particular product which will end in sales. Here, too, there is a mixture of the types of communicators who do this sort of work.

"Public Relations Advertising" is still another distinction made along our media placement continuum. The distinction between public relations advertising and either straight advertising or product publicity is that there may be involved some larger, over-all theme or concept which the public relations practitioner is trying to make more widespread and accepted. An excellent example of public relations advertising can be derived from the Esso Research and Engineering Company case (Chapter 2). In that case was raised the question of how the public relations practitioners at Esso could make their company's reputation for basic research commensurate with the actual volume conducted. One step which was taken was to develop a series of public relations advertisements designed to reach a very specialized audience: research-minded and research-capable readers in industry and academics. To achieve this, the ads were published in *Chemical and Engineering News*. Each ad consisted of a handsome, intriguing color photograph depicting some aspect of a current research project at Esso Research and Engineering. The copy accompanying the picture gave a brief but highly technical description of the project, along with identifying the research scientists or engineers involved. (See Figure 21, a reproduction of an advertisement dealing with "cationic polymeriza-

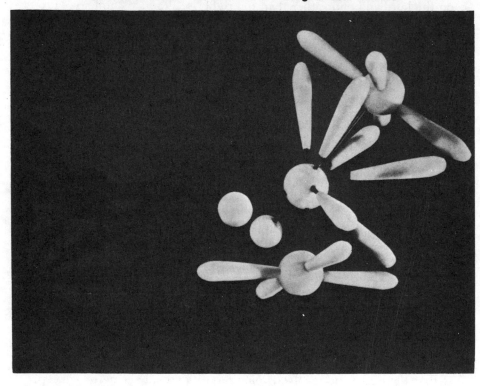

Figure 21

An example of sophisticated advertising that dovetails with public relations objectives

tion of isobutene at low temperatures" that was run in the April 16, 1962, issue of *Chemical and Engineering News*.[9])

After reading the copy in Figure 21, it is clear that this is not advertising in the usual sense. What is being communicated (via a paid advertisement) is a much more sophisticated message to the effect that (1) Esso Research and Engineering personnel are doing basic, significant research work in the physical sciences, particularly chemistry; and (2) this is the product of competent, highly trained scientists and engineers doing research work in which they are interested. More subtle portions of the message are such things as: (1) Esso Research and Engineering Company provides an excellent environment for research; (2) Esso Research and Engineering permits a man to pursue significant research work if he is capable of doing it and is *not* doing applied research exclusively; (3) Esso Research and Engineering might be a place where I would like to work; or (4) Esso Research and Engineering might be a place to which to guide my next talented young Ph.D. in chemistry.

Such an array of communication objectives, designed to reach a small but significant audience, could not be achieved on a regular enough basis by unpaid public relations release. Rather, they called for an outlet that permitted public relations practitioners to have explicit control over content and audience designation. In addition, to attain these communication objectives, the basic messages needed to be repeated in a number of creative and interesting ways.

The last media placement example is entitled "Public Relations Releases." This is the placement category that really required this whole continuum to be developed and discussed as it has been in the last few pages. This category has become the one most often associated with public relations practitioners. This is as it should be, because this category is the only one that belongs to the public relations practitioner almost exclusively and is, by definition, unpaid space. Into this category falls all of the attempts of a public relations practitioner to obtain newspaper space for his organization. It includes such things as having the company president's speech noted and the event at which he spoke given some attention. Plant expansion, relocation, additions, branches, and the like are typical of things that public relations practitioners use to try to garner newspaper space. Literally anything and everything that the public relations practitioner thinks is news (and where the newspaper editor agrees with him) finds its way into this media place-

---

[9] Published here by permission of the Public Relations Division, Esso Research and Engineering Company and of *Chemical and Engineering News*.

ment category. To repeat, this category is almost the exclusive domain of the public relations practitioner, and it is here where the least overlap with other communicators occurs.

Looking again at Figure 19 as a whole, two concluding observations are worth noting. One is that the only media placement category that is uniformly unpaid is the public relations releases category. All of the other categories are either always paid for or are at least occasionally paid for. A second observation is that, whereas the advertising man (or the publicist or any other occupational term one might want to use) functions in *some* of the media placement categories, the public relations practitioner is the *only* one that ranges across the entire continuum. This fact certainly contributes to the confusion as to just what a public relations practitioner is or does. On the other hand, it supports the position taken in this book that the public relations practitioner may use any means of transmitting a message as long as it is consistent with over-all public relations program planning.

UNPAID SPACE—
    "TRADEMARK" OF THE PUBLIC RELATIONS PRACTITIONER

As noted earlier, obtaining unpaid space is in a sense the "trademark" of the public relations practitioner. It is a portion of public relations work that has caused the most confusion, too, for it contributes to the inability of individuals to discern between a public relations practitioner and all other types of communicators. At this point, we need to direct attention to some additional features associated with obtaining this free space.

The news release.   The most common technique designed to obtain free newspaper coverage is the news release. A news release consists of written material that the public relations practitioner sends to the newspaper because he feels that it has the necessary ingredients—*i.e.,* newsworthiness—to be published. The guiding rules of thumb about news releases are that they should be brief, devoid of wordiness, and to the point. The majority of practitioners follow the classic guide to newspaper format by seeing to it that the *who, what, where, when, why,* and *how* are included in the first sentence or so. After accomplishing the summary sentences, the news release should go into the details. News releases, as originally submitted, are generally longer than what will finally be printed in the paper (with the exception of small dailies and weeklies). This is due primarily to the value of providing background material for the newspaper. Then, too, the amount of material to be printed always exceeds the space any paper has to allot, hence the need for pruning and cutting. Even though some of the details of the news release are not printed, it is helpful to the newspaperman to give him some background so that he can make an intelligent rewrite of the news release.

The press conference.   One technique that represents the blitzkrieg approach to obtaining newspaper coverage is the press conference. If handled right, and if the public relations practitioner in question really has something to say, the press conference is undoubtedly one of the quickest and most effective ways of obtaining newspaper coverage. One of the most frequent usages of the press conference is in connection with product publicity, and the following description of a press conference held by the Connecticut Chemical Research Corporation and reported by the *Public Relations Board Newsletter* illustrates the technique nicely:

Recently, at the Waldorf-Astoria Hotel in New York City, the *Connecticut Chemical Research Corporation*, of Bridgeport, held what we believe was a most impressive press conference.

One of the world's leading packagers of products in "Aerosol" pressurized containers, Conn-Chem had long recognized the limitations of the field. Without going into technicalities, "Aerosols" demand the use of refrigerant gases which, by nature, were suitable for only about 10 per cent of products in liquid, cream or powder form.

During almost two years of research, Conn-Chem developed a concept of using non-refrigerant gases as propellents, thereby *making pressurized packaging possible* for all liquid, cream, and powder products. They call the new concept "Polysols," *a truly revolutionary advancement in the packaging trade.*

Since this was a process of interest to many fields, from cosmetics and health to paint, *almost 200 publications were invited to the press conference.* The invitations were not formal or austere. They were simply personal letters from the president of the company in which he described, in a clear, yet intriguing way, what the conference was about—but did not give away the specific points to be unveiled.

Of the 200 invited, *132 "RSVP'd" they would come!!!* Actually, 140 people showed up, representing magazines all the way from READER'S DIGEST to the EXPORTER'S JOURNAL and newspapers from the WALL STREET JOURNAL to WOMEN'S WEAR DAILY. There were even *three* journalists from LIFE!

After the customary drinks and hors d'oeuvres, everyone was shepherded into a small auditorium for a 10-minute talk on the technical aspects by Conn-Chem's chief chemist. The president A. O. Samuels followed up with a discussion of the marketing and merchandising implications.

Finally came a *10-minute demonstration*—hair literally squirted off a man's arm, mouth wash sprayed into throats by the touch of a button, even antibiotics jet propelled smoothly onto cuts.

Each person at the conference was given a press kit containing stories on the development and *product applications* of the process, a history of "Aerosols," and a history of Connecticut Chemical Research Corporation.

All publications present indicated extreme interest in the new concept—probably because they were informed how news of it would apply to their own particular editorial needs.

The lesson is simple but clear—a press conference must be planned from the standpoint of the press. Is it necessary? Do you have a genuine story to tell? Is this the best possible way of arousing editorial interest in your product or idea?

Obviously, this conference *answered "yes"* to all three questions. As the PRB NEWSLETTER goes to press two weeks after the party, 15 publications had already carried important stories, 23 more have definitely scheduled coverage and 46 others—many of them monthly publications—indicate they are seriously considering features on the new process.[10]

From this description of a press conference, it is clear that if the venture is successful, the sponsoring public relations practitioner and his organization can expect considerable free space in newspapers, magazines, and the like. In fact, press conferences are often not restricted to any one category of mass media. When appropriate, magazine, radio, and TV representatives are invited as well as newspaper reporters. Equally clear is the fact that press conferences represent a lot of hard work and smooth execution to make them a success. First there are the questions of what is to be said, how it is to be presented, and what techniques can be used to dramatize the presentations. Then there are questions of physical arrangements, refreshment if any,[11] who is to be invited and why, the press kit and its contents, and follow-up after the conference. A press conference can be a bewildering combination of petty details and major decisions all wrapped up in one. When it works, however, it is well worth the effort!

A WORD ABOUT MAGAZINES

During our examination of the newspaper as a mass media category, magazines inevitably came into the picture from time to time. This was particularly true in our example of the press conference to which

---

[10] *The Public Relations Board Newsletter*, June, 1956 (The Public Relations Board, Chicago, Illinois). Used by permission.

[11] There are some who feel that refreshments—particularly liquor—have no place at a press conference. Persons holding this view feel that refreshments belong at press "parties," as distinguished from press conferences.

many magazine representatives were invited and attended. Likewise, when we considered Figure 19 depicting our media placement continuum, it was equally clear that magazines could be and are used along with newspapers in some of the particular media placement categories. Although the use of magazines by public relations practitioners as a mass media outlet is not nearly so extensive as the use of newspapers, this is definitely a mistake. It appears that many public relations practitioners avoid magazines due to certain misconceptions they have about this medium and their unfamiliarity with how to place material in them. Let's look at some of the highlights of placing material in magazines.

Recognizing the uniqueness of magazines. A starting point is the realization that the preparation of an article for a magazine calls for a much different process than preparing one for a newspaper. For one thing, magazines are much more "individualistic" in the sense that they tend, over time, to develop a rather unique style in terms of writing and content, and this, in turn, tends to appeal to a more homogeneous audience than a newspaper attracts. For this reason, different classification schemes have been evolved to break down various magazines into the type of audience they primarily but, of course, not exclusively, appeal to.

The general placement formula for magazine stories is to develop an idea with either a detailed outline or some sample material. Next, a check with the editor of the intended magazine is important. Unlike newspaper editors, who have hourly or at least daily deadlines to meet, magazine editors have more time to think about patterns of articles that are going to appear in any one issue. For this reason, magazine editors generally appreciate the opportunity to react to the article idea, and then, if they like it, suggest changes or modifications so that it will fit the magazine better. Thus, for example, in a women's or home magazine, the editor may be planning a whole issue devoted to remodeling of old homes or installing do-it-yourself swimming pools. With advance notice of what a public relations practitioner might want to develop (assuming that the outline submitted overlaps with the theme planned for the magazine), the editor is able to shape the material more appropriately.

Magazine articles as an outlet for some phase of a public relations program deserve careful thought. Although they do not offer the opportunity of repetition of messages or, in most cases, as heterogeneous an audience as newspapers, they do afford the public relations practitioner a medium that permits certain ideas to be presented in depth and an audience that is much more likely to read what the public relations practitioner has written.

The Spoken Word

The use of radio as a mass communication medium has not been utilized by public relations practitioners nearly so much as the printed word, although it has been used more, perhaps, than television. A glance at some of the current books on public relations quickly reflects this in the generally short treatment given of radio and TV. Although an excellent case can be made for its use, radio has not been used extensively by public relation practitioners for two main reasons:

1. The medium, with its emphasis on immediacy and its major drawback of inability to hold an audience (the slightest distraction and a recipient is lost), does not lend itself to public relations objectives. This is particularly true for manufacturing or other commercial organizations. In other words, radio fits the advertiser's objectives far better than the public relations practitioner's. The reader can appreciate this fact very easily by considering once again the four cases that we presented in Chapter 2. If each one of those cases is examined from the point of view of what role radio could play in helping to solve the problems involved, it becomes clear that the answer probably would be "not much."[12] This is generally the conclusion arrived at in most public relations problem-solving situations.

2. The second reason is that paid time on radio is rather expensive and generally beyond the budget of most public relations practitioners. For the cost that would be involved in using radio, several versions of the printed word could be employed. This, coupled with the fact that it is often difficult to demonstrate the impact of radio on public relations problems, tends to preclude its use.

The fact that radio does not fit a public relations practitioner's needs as readily as the newspaper does not mean, however, that he should overlook this medium. Leonard L. Knott expressed nicely both the obstacles to radio usage and that these obstacles should be overcome when he wrote:

---

[12] An exception to this generalization might be Case No. 4 (Chapter 2, pages 18-22), dealing with how to induce a more widespread acceptance and use of seat belts by the motor-going public. Because of the noncommercial status of the National Safety Council, it is in a very strong position to use public service time on networks and local stations for the "cause" of seat belt use. (See particularly the section on public service time later in this chapter.)

Too few Public Relations people have learned to use radio and television well. Since most of them *gravitated to their present positions from newspaper offices*, they are better informed about newspaper practices than they are about radio or television. Because they know and understand newspapers better, they are inclined to put the emphasis on that medium and simply adapt their newspaper releases for radio. That isn't good enough.

There are as many, or more ways to approach radio and television as there are to approach publications. The successful Public Relations person *must study these media and learn their requirements*, just as he must study newspapers or magazines. And *he must develop the techniques to serve these media*, realizing that radio stations have wastebaskets as large and as accommodating as those of newspaper editors. [Italics added.][13]

USE OF RADIO FOR PUBLIC RELATIONS PURPOSES

Unpaid Radio Time

There is a parallel here between radio and newspaper usage by public relations practitioners in that the largest use of radio by the public relations practitioner is probably through approaches that result in free radio time. This means that considerable creativeness must be used to come up with program ideas that will fit and be accepted by those responsible for developing programs. There are many discussion programs, extended news programs, variety shows, quasi-educational shows and the like that are constantly looking for material. If the public relations practitioner is able to come up with an idea of how his organization's interests can be made to coincide with the interests of the program producer, he may be lucky and obtain free radio time. Some of the major categories of free radio time follow.

1. News broadcasts. One of the most obvious outlets for public relations practitioners is the many news broadcasts on radio. Here the public relations practitioner is viewing radio as an extension of his efforts to reach mass audiences, and his approach and rationale are exactly the same as in the case of newspapers. It is important, however, for the public relations practitioner to make his efforts to place material specialized for this particular medium on news broadcasts. Radio releases cannot be merely warmed over or slightly modified newspaper

---

[13] Leonard L. Knott, *The PR in Profit: A Guide to Successful Public Relations in Canada* (Toronto, Ont.: McClelland & Stewart, Ltd., 1955), p. 121. All passages from *The PR in Profit* used by permission.

releases. Writing for radio is writing for *listening* rather than *reading*. Radio releases have to be even more to the point and devoid of wordiness than newspaper releases. Earlier, we noted the tremendous ratio of news *to be* printed as compared with news that *can be* printed in any given issue of a newspaper. In radio, the reduction factor is even greater. Thousands and thousands of words have to be compressed into several hundred, which is all that a few minutes on radio can permit. A radio news item must always be terse, to the point, and greatly simplified so that it can be understood immediately by the listener. In radio news, the *what* and *who* of the classical format of newspaper reporting are of great import. In addition, the recital on the air of the specific names of individuals normally mentioned in a newspaper release is avoided as being too time consuming and not worthy of radio time.

2. Fitting existing programs. There are generally a large number of programs on any given local station that can be utilized for public relations purposes. We have in mind here such programs as home and food hours, various women's programs, and forum programs, which are constantly in need of material to make up their shows. If handled properly, these programs can become outlets for free radio time.

The cardinal rule for placing material on these programs is to always assume the point of view of the person in charge of the show. The public relations practitioner should study the show, observing what types of material have been used in the past. If the program appears suitable for his needs, the next step is to come up with a program idea and then follow this idea through with at least an outline of what might be done. Only after this "homework" has been done should the public relations practitioner approach the individual producing the show. (There is a definite similarity between preparing material for radio shows and developing material for magazine articles, as the reader may have already observed.)

If all of these steps are followed, and the idea is a good one, the odds in favor of successful placement on a radio show are rather good. The public relations practitioner must appreciate the special difficulties under which the person working in radio operates and how this, in turn, requires different procedures for the placement of material. Knott brings this point out nicely when he writes:

> On the air the personal appearance takes the place of the newspaper interview. The radio producer, however, must be more cautious in his selection of people to be interviewed. Unlike the editor, he cannot edit the interview once it has been completed. A newspaper reporter

can write his story in such a way as to leave out objectionable remarks, and, a fact for which many business and association executives should be thankful, he can even dress up the interviewed person's grammar. He is thus able to protect the person interviewed from the public ridicule or public ill-will.

An airwaves interview does not have this advantage. Once a person has spoken on a live show, his words have been carried to his radio audience and cannot be recalled. The same, of course, is true of interviews on TV.[14]

To illustrate the fact that existing radio shows may coincide with certain objectives of a public relations practitioner in solving his particular public relations program, let us consider the example of the "conversation" show. We shall briefly describe this kind of show and some of the materials that were made to "fit."[15]

The widespread popularity of the so-called conversation format on radio has resulted in excellent opportunities for public relations goals to be achieved via existing programs. Conducted by what the radio industry calls a "yakker" (a talkative personality who chats about a variety of topics with experts in the studio and with listeners on the phone), the conversation format includes dozens of featured programs from coast to coast.

The conversation shows in the Boston area are typical of programs elsewhere. For example, WBZ has "Contact!"; WEEI has "Conversation Piece" and "Night Line," and WNAC features "The Haywood Vincent Show" and "Mary's Mail," a discussion program especially slanted toward women.

Within a short period of time there appeared on these programs the following:

1. A florist (from a chain of florists) talking about problems in the garden and how to overcome them.

2. The president of a large Boston travel agency discussing problems in traveling and how to avoid them.

3. A representative of a large local lumber yard discussing how to make things at home in the best do-it-yourself tradition.

4. A representative of a brokerage house when the question of how to invest wisely was the focus of the program.

---

[14] *Ibid.*, pp. 119-120.

[15] The author is indebted to Sidney A. Dimond, President, Creative Associates, Inc., Boston, for the examples concerning radio usage cited here.

   5. A boat manufacturer discussing the fine art of sailing and how to
      do it safely.

   In each instance, the information provided by the guest was of
comparatively widespread interest to the listening audience and was
useful and educational, making it worthwhile to all parties concerned:
the broadcasting station, the radio audience, and the commercial companies which provided the free talent.

   3. Public service time.   Under Federal Communications Commission
(FCC) regulations, all radio (and, of course, TV) stations devote a
certain portion of their time to public service broadcasting. The theory
here is that the FCC operates on behalf of each of us and that the air
through which the stations broadcast is the property of all of us.

   The exact amount of public service broadcasting expected from any
given station has never been determined, although there have been
many hearings on the subject. The "rule of thumb" allegedly used by
the FCC in reviewing applications for renewals of licenses is that
approximately 15% of the total programing of a typical broadcast day
should be devoted to public service material.

   Precisely what constitutes public service also has never been clearly
defined by FCC. However, news, news commentaries, social problem
documentaries, and religious broadcasting obviously would qualify.

   In examining the broadcasting records of a station or the projected programing of an applicant for a license, the FCC usually takes
an over-all look in an effort to determine the *intent* of the broadcaster.
If the intent of the broadcaster is to "serve the public interest, convenience, and necessity," he generally has no problem. So far as the writer
is aware, no American radio station has ever had its license revoked
because of failure to live up to its public service broadcasting responsibilities.

   As one would expect, the noncommercial organizations—such as professional associations and educational institutions—can most readily
qualify for public service time. To illustrate two types of material that
qualify for public service time, let us look at some ten-second radio
(and TV) station breaks provided by the American Optometric Association (the reader may find it useful to refer to page 248 of Chapter 10,
where this material is listed being part of the back-to-school kit).

   The American Optometric Association says that most children who have
   vision problems do not realize it. Be safe with a professional examination. Station _____ reminds you schooltime is vision exam time!

Reading, writing, arithmetic! Diversified school activities require all-around good vision. The American Optometric Association urges yearly professional vision examinations for school children. This is station
_____.

Important message to parents and teachers! Watch for symptoms of vision difficulty in children. The American Optometric Association reminds you "Schooltime is vision examination time." This is station
_____.

A child must see well to learn well. 80% of learning is seeing. The American Optometric Association reminds you "Schooltime is vision examination time." This is station _____.

Prepare your child for school with a vision examination. The American Optometric Association reminds you that "Schooltime is vision examination time." This is station _____.

Did you know that half the children who are slow in reading have visual problems? The American Optometric Association recommends vision examinations at least once a year. This is station _____.[16]

Still other examples of how public relations objectives can be made to coincide with the public service time provision applicable to radio are as follows:

1. A five-minute tape-recorded program sponsored by Associated Industries of Massachusetts and called "Industry Reports" was distributed to approximately thirty radio stations in Massachusetts. The main objective of these five-minute tapes is to give the public additional information on the value of industry to the state. This, in turn, contributes to causing various industries to view Massachusetts in a favorable light as a locale in which to establish their businesses. Some of the programs featured only a narrator with a short message; others utilized the actual sounds and employee voices of a given industry. The stations tended to use the programs in prime public service time.
2. The Massachusetts Council of Churches makes available to a considerable number of radio stations throughout the country a tape service and/or manuscripts for a weekly series called "The Churchman Views the News." Radio stations generally have

[16] Used by permission of the American Optometric Association, 4030 Chouteau Avenue, St. Louis 10, Missouri.

neither the staff nor the time to read religious publications to dis-
till information of this kind, but they are extremely happy to help
fill their public service time with such programing when it is
professionally prepared in script form or a tape is sent to them.

3. The University of New Hampshire Alumni Association as a part
   of a recent fund drive sent to all its alumni *and* all radio and TV
   stations in New Hampshire an LP record entitled "Some Sounds
   and Songs of UNH." The songs, performed by the University of
   New Hampshire Men's Glee Club, were featured on various disc
   jockey shows; many of the sounds have been used on the air with
   ad libbed comments; and some of the music on the LP record was
   used to introduce other UNH public service programs which are
   normally taped and sent to stations as part of the regular public
   relations program of the university. Many persons associated
   with the Alumni Association fund drive felt that the special LP
   record played a major role in doubling the number of con-
   tributors and increasing substantially the amount of money given
   in just one year.

4. Perhaps one of the most active groups in making use of public
   service time is the National Safety Council. They supply stations
   with a steady stream of materials which are used constantly.
   One of the most widely known practices of NSC is their providing
   of predictions of the number of deaths and injuries in automobile
   accidents during holiday weekends and then providing the news
   media with a running total during the course of those weekends.

As one would expect, it is more difficult for commercial organizations
to qualify for public service time. In addition to qualifying, there is
the problem of making the public service time "fit" the long-range
public relations program. However, both of these stringent requirements can be met with some ingenuity as the illustration below shows.

Most large metropolitan communities in the United States have
rather horrendous traffic problems. More and more expressways and
highways slash across the countryside and into the big cities, pouring
into them additional thousands of cars for which there is no room—
particularly for parking. At the same time this is happening, railroads,
bus lines, and other forms of mass transportation are either going
bankrupt or are cutting back on service and facilities.

Taking advantage of this situation in Boston, the Jenney Gasoline
Company built an entire advertising campaign, which is paid for,
around the theme, "Balanced Transportation." This theme was put

forth as the only answer to transportation chaos. Jenney ran full-page newspaper ads and hundreds of radio spot announcements pleading with citizens to demand subsidy or other assistance through legislative action on behalf of public transportation.

The idea of a gasoline company paying for ads which urged people to stay off the highways, to ride the trains and subways, created intense public interest and curiosity. As a result of this campaign, Jenney Gasoline representatives were invited to appear on numerous radio and TV shows, and the Jenney Gasoline action became the discussion focus of numerous radio discussion programs. Although the author does not have specific data to support his contention, Jenney probably created far more good will with the free time—a by-product of the paid time— than the original paid time was able to accomplish.

Paid Radio Time

When one is prepared to pay for his radio time, most of what was discussed under the heading "Unpaid Radio Time" does not apply. When you are footing the bill, you have only yourself, as public relations practitioner, and your organization to please. You are free to turn your entire energies to such questions as what type of program will be effective in contributing to what phase of a public relations program. The cost can be rather substantial, so that the natural advantages of radio—such as speed of contact with an audience, the fact that audiences can be engaged in other activities such as housework or driving to or from work—must be made the most of. Following are some illustrations of the use of paid radio time for public relations purposes.

1. A recent strike of the drivers of trucks used to haul new cars to dealers throughout the Eastern Seaboard resulted in a serious sales and public relations problem for the automobile manufacturers and distributors involved. People who wanted to buy new cars in many cases just couldn't get delivery because there was no way to get the new cars in sufficient quantity to the outlets. After the strike ended, a number of automobile companies, notably General Motors (for Buick and Oldsmobile), bought a considerable number of radio spots to thank the public for its patience and announce that cars were now being rushed as rapidly as possible to dealers.
2. During employee strikes which have grounded aircraft, airlines have frequently run radio spots apologizing to the public for the inconvenience and promising even better service at the end of

the strike. One airline, Eastern, buys radio time on numerous
stations from coast to coast to give up-to-the-minute information
on arrivals and departures.

3. The makers of Carlings beer and ale recently launched an advertising campaign selling not only its product but also The Heritage
Trail, a highway network which passes some fifteen hundred tour-
ist attractions in New England. Apparently the purpose of the
campaign, besides increasing sales, is to identify Carlings increasingly as a good New England corporate citizen.

Sound and Sight Combined—Television

Television has still eluded full and effective use by the public relations practitioner, much as it has for certain other occupational groups
in our society, such as educators. Many educators feel that the potential
television offers them to achieve certain educational objectives is tremendous, but that they are far from realizing this potential. The same
thing can be said of the relationship between public relations practitioners and television. Intuitively, at least, where one has the opportunity to include sight as well as sound, there is a feeling that the
ultimate applications of TV to solving public relations problems should
be extensive. This utilization, however, has hardly begun to take place.
Just how far it will go is still anyone's guess.

Perhaps one reason that TV has the power to make many persons
feel that it has tremendous potential is that it appears to be so revolutionary, even to us jaded moderns who are getting to the point that
nothing new could surprise us. One reason for the air of expectancy
associated with television is that it appears to be a potential high-
water mark of the principle that every change in communication has
an effect on the entire society.[17] If print had effects, and assuredly it
did, one can hardly imagine how extensive the effects of television can
be. The only trouble is that we have not been able to identify these
effects as yet; indeed, we are not agreed as to what these effects *might*
be.

Another reason for the implicit assumption that TV *must* have
strong effects is that when comparisons are made between TV and
other media—particularly print—TV appears to have certain qualities

---

[17] *See*, for example, Harold A. Innis, *Empire and Communication* (Oxford, England: Clarendon Press, 1950); or Harold A. Innis, *The Bias of Communications*
(Toronto, Ont.: University of Toronto Press, 1951).

that make it particularly compelling. Seldes comes to essentially this
conclusion when he compares print with electronics.[18]

Print	Electronics
—Requires the ability to read	—No special training required
—Usually experienced individually and in silence	—Usually experienced in company and with sound
—Taken in small quantities	—Taken in large quantities
—Relatively slow diffusion	—Very rapid diffusion
—Can be reread and checked	—Generally not available for re-observation
—Relatively inexpensive to produce but costly to the consumer	—Very expensive to produce but relatively cheap for the consumer
—Created for minorities of varying sizes	—Planned for major audiences

Such factors as "no special training required" and "very rapid diffusion" make one feel immediately that television is bound to have a
profound effect on us all. Add to this such ingredients as bouncing the
signal off of satellites, which permits worldwide, instantaneous live
broadcasting, and one really has a potent communication tool in his
hand. Under these conditions, we have the potential to communicate
with tremendous segments of our own society (and the societies of
others) who do not have enough formal education to read and write
or, if they do, possess this ability at grade-school levels. These people,
through the "magic" of television, can be persuaded, propagandized,
illuminatcd, dcluded, and so on, but without the benefit of an education to assess what they are being exposed to. Is it any wonder that
great minds, from all walks of life and professions, have at some time
wrung their hands or thrown up their arms over either the potential
dangers and misuses or benefits and advantages of television.

Just as we have very little evidence of the effectiveness of this relatively new communication medium in areas such as education and
delinquency, so it is that we do not have much evidence of the effec-

[18] Gilbert Seldes, *The New Mass Media: Challenge to a Free Society* (Washington, D.C.: American Association of University Women, 1957), pp. 10-11. All
passages from *The New Mass Media* used by permission of Gilbert Seldes.

tiveness of TV (used on a mass-media–mass-audience basis) in helping to solve public relations problems. TV is used by public relations practitioners probably the least of all of the means of communicating that we have considered thus far. The classification scheme that proved useful in presenting the use of radio (pages 293-300) for public relations purposes fits television equally well and will be repeated here.

Usage of TV for Public Relations Purposes

Unpaid TV Time

As in the case of radio, perhaps the most regular use that is made of TV for public relations purposes is through the acquisition of unpaid TV time. In general, the public relations practitioner is really at a disadvantage in knowing how to make use of television, how to strike that happy combination of being of service to those who are responsible for TV programing, and at the same time achieve his own public relations goals. For many practitioners, the television industry came into being long after they were committed to a career in public relations. The observations made by Knott concerning the public relations practitioners' use of radio and TV, quoted earlier in this chapter (page 293), appear to apply particularly to television. The same old obstacle faces the public relations practitioner in TV as it did in radio and, to a lesser extent, in the newspaper: knowing what the person in charge of programing needs and can use. Many public relations practitioners are very inept at visualizing a TV show and even less skilled at coming up with really good ideas for TV programing. In spite of the fact that he does not utilize television nearly so much as some claim he could, the use of television for public relations purposes can be demonstrated by the following illustrations.

1. News broadcasts. As with both radio and the newspapers, one broadcasting activity that presents a natural outlet for public relations purposes is TV news broadcasting. In preparing news releases for television, the public relations practitioner has to contend with writing for the ear instead of for the eye (as in newspaper releases), as was brought out earlier when we discussed news releases for radio. However, on top of that, the public relations practitioner needs to know how to take advantage of the *visual* capacity of TV and supply (or induce the TV station to obtain) good, usable still photographs or motion pictures to use in the news broadcast. Knowing what and how to supply the TV station with visual materials to go with his copy is somewhat of an Achilles heel to the public relations practitioner.

2. Fitting existing programs. The variety of TV programing into which a public relations practitioner may fit some of his own material is at least as extensive as in radio. The technique of placement is essentially the same as in the case of radio: a creative idea that helps the TV program director, properly "packaged," and enthusiastically communicated by the public relations practitioner. There is one other hurdle worthy of mention with respect to TV. At times either the public relations practitioner or his client is necessarily a part of the show and being a TV "performer" takes some understanding of how a television show is put together. Not only does TV share with radio the problem that once something is said, it cannot be edited or changed (see Knott's remarks again, page 294-295), thus causing the producer to be cautious about whom he allows on the program; in TV there is also the problem of how the person *behaves,* his mannerisms, his gestures, and so on. Personal idiosyncrasies that would make hardly any difference on radio can make quite a difference on television. As the TV political debates between Kennedy and Nixon brought out, the *appearance* and *personal performance* of the individual are equally or more important than what he has to say, in terms of the over-all impact on the audience. These factors have to be weighed by the public relations practitioner as he develops ideas for utilization of television for his purposes.

To give the reader a feeling for the unexpected that illustrates the above point, the following is an incident that occurred on Boston's Channel Four (WBZ-TV) a few years ago:

Polly Huse, a white-haired hostess of many New England radio shows, was hired by WBZ-TV as its home economy expert. She had a long run on many Channel Four TV programs. One of these was "Domestic Diary," a morning, Monday thru Friday daytime strip (the usual interviews, demonstrations, kitchen sequences were shown). During one of her table-top demonstrations, she removed a large pressure cooker from the studio range, brought it to the display table, and opened it before allowing the pressure to diminish. It could have been a serious accident, fortunately . . . it wasn't. But it did possibly lessen Polly's prestige for a short period and threw water and beans on one of her distinguished guests. The beans burst, covered Polly, grey hair to midriff apron, the kitchen walls, and traversed the width of the studio. When Polly completed her segment of Boston-baked, regained her composure, introduced her guest . . . a transition was made from kitchen area to living room setting . . . as Polly entered the scene, her guest was busy picking pea-beans from her hair, shoulders, suit, et al. They laughed, chatted and the program continued. We were happy no one was injured.

. . . In addition to the danger of the top of the pan, the beans were hot and travelled like fragments of a burst mortar shell.[19]

All of the problems notwithstanding, TV is used. The following examples should bear out this contention.[20]

1. In the early 1950's, there was a show entitled "Lady of the Book-shelf," which enjoyed a very long run. Wonder Books (distributed by Curtis Publishing Company) were given exposure on the program. The Wonder Books were used in their entirety, with the narrator reading the story while the book illustrations were scanned by TV camera close-ups. In addition, from time to time the Curtis representative would arrange for the appearance of authors, illustrators, and other personages identified with a magazine story.
2. A poetry-writing bus driver from the Grey Lines Sight-Seeing Company made a guest appearance on one of the live segments of "Boston Movietime," an early feature film offered on Channel Four in Boston. He read his original poems to promote a printed collection of his works, and, of course, Grey Lines was given mention on the program, which was one that received quite high ratings.
3. "Swan Boat," a morning hour variety program on WBZ-TV, offers still another example of free use of TV time. A trainer in charge of animals from Benson's Animal Farm in New Hampshire (entry by admission fee) appeared as a guest on the program. The station benefited from the entertainment value of the guest and his animal exhibits while Benson's received considerable exposure over TV.

3. *Public service time.*   Along with radio, TV is bound by the FCC to provide public service time. Once again, noncommercial organizations have a pronounced "edge" in obtaining TV time for their public relations purposes.

Because of the wording of the FCC regulations concerning public service time, it is quite difficult for a commercial organization to qualify for this sort of exposure on TV as was also noted in the case of radio.

---

[19] This example is kindly provided by personal communication from Iran Berlow, Assistant Professor, Division of Broadcasting and Film, School of Public Communication, Boston University.

[20] These examples are kindly supplied by Iran Berlow (*see* footnote 19).

Usually the methods have to be indirect and very often in cooperation with some nonprofit group or association. An example that fits this stringent category follows.[21]

The Connecticut Mutual Life Insurance Company provided TV stations with a package including eighteen slides and a 14.5-minute script with a pictorial storyboard. The content emphasized mental health and the need for family understanding for those suffering from mental illness. The only mention of the organization supplying these materials was in giving the address to which viewers could write for additional information. The material provided by Conneticut Mutual could be used as a single program, or portions of it could be used within other appropriate programs.

Paid Television Time

Paid television time for public relations purposes is perhaps the smallest category of mass media used by public relations practitioners. The overriding consideration is, of course, the cost. In Seldes's comparison of printed to electronic media, one of the characteristics of the electronic media—particularly television—stressed is the high cost of *producing* what is eventually *consumed* by the recipient at a comparatively lower cost. Even with the advent of paid television, this state of affairs is not likely to change, because it would be even more difficult (if not impossible) to develop a paid television program for public relations purposes and interest an audience in paying for it. Most people in the field of public relations are quite uncertain as to what the future will hold with respect to their use of this medium. The public relations practitioner of the future will have to keep a watchful eye on this medium and be alert for any changes that would imply more widespread usage.

The major means by which paid television time is utilized to further an over-all public relations objective is to sponsor what hopefully will become a popular TV show. With the TV show as an inducement to the viewer, brief periods at the beginning, the middle, and end of the program are relied on to get across one's public relations message. Perhaps the best-known users of this sort of paid TV time are the large oil, chemical, and electrical companies. Almost all of these companies have adopted general themes (such as "Progress Is Our Most Important Product" and "Better Things for Better Living Through Chemistry") and have used these themes as a general "umbrella" under which a host of particular messages can be communicated. Currently, partly

---

[21] This example is kindly supplied by Iran Berlow (*see* footnote 19).

because opinion attitude surveys have indicated that *science* and *research* are concepts that have a positive halo associated with them, almost every organization that can possibly talk legitimately about the research it conducts has jumped upon the research theme bandwagon. With research as a theme, the brief periods normally given over to straight advertising can be devoted to reasonably interesting individual subtopics, subsumed under a larger public relations advertising theme (see Figure 19, page 280).

A Word about Educational Television

A much less frequently employed version of television usage in public relations is educational television. Educational television, in terms of numbers of stations and hours of broadcasting, is growing every year, although it is nowhere near the volume that many educators had hoped for at this stage in its development. By its very nature, educational television has a comparatively small, rather homogeneous (in terms of education, income, and reasons for viewing) audience for its various programs. For this reason, under certain conditions it may be consistent with the long-range plans of larger industrial organizations to be identified with educational television by developing programs that educational television stations might use. However, it is doubtful whether commercial support of educational television for public relations purposes (as distinct from the philanthropic or "good citizenship" aspects behind this type of activity) will ever be very extensive. On the television program itself, the credits are usually limited to a mere mention that the program is paid for or produced by such and such a company. That is all the company identification permitted. In fact, the secondary mentions of educational television activities—i.e., in news releases, stockholder reports, and the like—are far greater sources of attention than the program itself. Because the public relations practitioner has to demonstrate the economic value of his various public relations activities as does any other functioning unit within an organization, educational television expenditures would appear very difficult to justify, and this state of affair would appear to hold for the foreseeable future.

Miscellaneous Media Usage Examples

The last section of Figure 18 (Chapter 10, page 240), depicting communication media viewed in terms of a continuum of communication, is the miscellaneous, or wastepaper basket, category. In a box in the lower right-hand corner of that figure we have listed a number of other means of communication that public relations practitioners characteristically use. The reader could undoubtedly develop an additional list of miscellaneous categories of his own. Some of the items listed are rather difficult to classify in the scheme we have developed. One example is the use of *exhibits*. The Time-Life Exhibit Center is a good case in point.[22] During a one-year period, this exhibit area (occupying an area 102 by 58 by 32 feet and involving telephones, a receptionist, and written materials of all descriptions) was used to feature ten different themes. Some of the themes were (1) "Since Time Began," consisting of a display of 193 photographs spotlighting world events that had transpired since *Time* magazine was first published in 1923; (2) "Eisenstaedt," an exhibit of the top pictures of this world-renowned photographer (incidentally, this exhibit was timed to coincide with the completion of one million Leica cameras, and Mr. Eisenstaedt was presented the first camera of the second million); and (3) "Name the Newsmakers," where sixty unidentified pictures from *Time*, *Life* and *Sports Illustrated* were displayed and the public invited to identify them. The persons correctly identifying all sixty were granted the honor of having their own photos taken and mounted in simulated magazine covers.

These exhibits were viewed by enough people that we would have to place the very heterogeneous audience reached somewhere between the *specialized audiences* and *mass communication* portion of our continuum. On the other hand, the follow-ups that such displays engender —newspaper articles and radio and TV coverage—extend the range of impact of the exhibit into the mass media portion of the communication continuum.

The open house technique, or plant tour, is an example of another communication technique that puts a bit of a strain on classification systems. The open houses that are conducted by the Air Force on Independence Day offer a good example. Air Force bases across the country open their gates to the general public, and the people are allowed to inspect, climb over, and otherwise enjoy themselves with a lot of interesting Air Force equipment. Collectively, the audience for this one communication technique (designed to acquaint the general public with the Air Force that they support through their tax money) places the open-house approach on the mass communication portion of our continuum. On the other hand, for any single individual who

----

[22] The information about the exhibit is borrowed from a case entitled "The Exhibit—A Valuable Public Relations Tool," *Public Relations News*, XVII, No. 51 (December 25, 1961). Used by permission.

slides into the seat of a B-52 bomber or tries on some of the equipment that a modern-day pilot wears in flight or talks with a real live combat pilot, the experience is at the person-to-person end of the communication continuum.

The object of this brief discussion concerning our miscellaneous category of communication media techniques that can be utilized by public relations practitioners is to highlight one main point: Whatever approach is used by a public relations practitioner to communicate with a particular audience, an analysis must be made along the lines suggested in this chapter. The public relations practitioner must have a clear-cut appreciation of what portion(s) of the communication continuum he is, in fact, employing to reach his intended audience. Then he must relate this to his communication objectives, being certain that the technique and desired impact are consistent with one another. That is, he must have a look at the *person-to-person characteristics* of the *communication* that he desires (assuming that an actual person-to-person communication technique is not involved) *and how well these characteristics are being approximated by the communication technique(s) he is employing.* There are times when mass communication techniques (with their particular limitations) are acceptable for a public relations practitioner, and there are times when they are not. The public relations practitioner, of all persons, must be cognizant of the degree of agreement between his communication objectives and the communication media being employed.

IN CONCLUSION: THE LURE OF NUMBERS AND MASS COMMUNICATION TECHNIQUES IN MEDIA USAGE

In Chapter 5 (pages 100-104), during an analysis of the communication model as a whole, the point was made that one stage of the communication process may be stressed to the exclusion of another. This point is worth repeating at the close of this chapter as a means of summarizing the media stage from the standpoint of public relations. First, the generalization itself: Public relations practitioners tend to favor the media stage (with the message stage a close second) in the sense that if one were to measure the amount of time and energy devoted to the four stages of the communication process (sender, message, media, recipient), the media stage along with the message stage would represent all or nearly all of many public relations practitioners' working time. This means that the considerations introduced in the sender stage (Chapters 6 and 7) and the ideas to be presented in the recipient stage

(Chapters 12-16) receive comparatively little attention. If there is one fact that we can be sure of it is that *all* stages in the communication process need to be functioning effectively for successful communication to take place. This brings us to our first observation: The typical public relations practitioner must become aware of this tendency to stress the media stage and avoid becoming caught up in the crush of "making like a communicator." The sheer physical act of writing a plant newspaper, sending out news releases, writing brochures, and all of the other hundred and one media-based activities that a public relations practitioner can get caught up in can become an end in itself. The average public relations practitioner can, with clear conscience, make the protest that he does not have time for all of this sender stage nonsense, that he doesn't have time for the research activities that will be discussed in Part 3 of this book. The point is that the public relations practitioner must *make* time to arrive at a perspective so that the daily crush of communicating (in terms of implementing the *mechanics*) does not rob him of the opportunity of seeing the communication process as a whole, rather than only viewing one stage. The author finds it useful to think of this in terms of the *lure of numbers*. If one bulletin board does not do the trick, maybe several will. If one news release is good, then fifty would be fifty times better. A media outlet that "reaches thousands" of individuals must be better than another outlet that reaches only hundreds or even fewer.

Part of this lure of numbers stems from a confusion between public relations and advertising. The advertiser has solved many of his problems by widespread use of the mass media and vigorous exploitation of the principle of reaching large numbers of individuals. However, more often than not the public relations practitioner is confronted with the problem of *inducing involvement* on the part of the recipient with which he wishes to communicate. The recipient's mere awareness of the existence of an organization or his merely being informed as to the goods and services that a particular organization has to offer is seldom enough for the public relations practitioner. Consider the public relations practitioner who represents one of the hundreds of health and welfare organizations across our country (including hospitals and various institutions). His job, too, is that of *inducing involvement* of his intended recipients to donate free time, to become ego-involved enough to care what happens to people who suffer from this or that disease so that research money can be raised, to pay attention so that the bona-fide organization is supported and the phony ones are got rid of.

The list of public relations practitioners could be extended to include those who are trying to induce an interest in good government, in conservation, in peace, in civil defense, in fighting crime, in combating juvenile deliquency, in overcoming general citizen apathy regardless of the issue. In each instance, the public relations practitioner is confronted with inducing involvement to the extent that the recipient of his communication efforts is willing to assume his rightful share of the responsibility of solving the particular problem(s) at hand.[23]

The reader may by now be taking refuge in the fact that all of the examples cited thus far are from public relations practitioners representing nonprofit organizations: universities, health and welfare organizations, and the like. Thus far, this is true. However, an equally strong case can be made that profit-making organizations more often than not are trying to solve problems that require inducing involvement and the assuming of responsibility by the recipient. Let's consider several examples.

Internal publics.   The public relations practitioner of a typical commercial organization is charged with (among other things) the responsibility of building employee loyalty. Ideally, we would like the employee to realize that he is *part* of the organization in the sense that if he steals, he is in the long run stealing from himself; if he does not do an honest day's work for his pay, he is adversely affecting his own future; if he does not contribute *in some manner* to solving such things as the problems of automation, competition from foreign countries, or absenteeism, that one day his company may not be able to solve them either—to his detriment. (We would particularly like for employees who *belong to unions* to share this feeling of responsibility in coping with problems that their companies face.) We would like the employee to realize that his behavior, both on the job and off, directly affects his organization's ability to stay in business and compete. Ideally, we would like employees to have some understanding of our economic

---

[23] One is reminded of a point that Seldes makes about the reduction of "noise" in communication (*i.e.*, any factor that contributes to unintelligibility), thereby making the "address adapted to the listener." In this connection, Seldes goes on to say:

> So we can say that one of the consequences of the revolution in communication is an increase in noise level. Another is that the obstacle of the noise level can be overcome by simplification, repetition, "training" the listener, or "raising the voice" of the broadcaster. *All of these devices tend to reduce the complexity and the meaningfulness of what is communicated.* [Seldes, *op. cit.*, p. 15.]

Unfortunately, the problems that the public relations practitioner confronts are such that he cannot tolerate a reduction in complexity and the meaningfulness of what he wants to communicate. If anything, just the opposite is true: He eventually needs to present messages that are more complicated and that require more thought and involvement from the recipient.

system so they can think clearly about what position they will take with respect to corporate profits, public *vs.* private ownership, taxation, governmental controls of business, "big business," and a host of other topics. Ideally, we would like employees to appreciate the need for continuing their education throughout their lives rather than just when they are young, because the implications of automation are such that employees need to be continually aware of the danger of becoming obsolescent.

In each one of the employee relationship areas, the public relations practitioner faces a job just as difficult (if not more difficult) as the representative of a nonprofit organization does. Making progress in helping management attain these communication objectives is going to tax considerably the abilities of the public relations practitioners of the future.

External Publics.   When we consider the *external* publics of a profit-making organization, we find the public relations practitioner facing equally difficult tasks. For one thing, there is the community (or communities) within which the company is located to be considered. Supply of good employees, fair tax rates, services from the community—are all dependent on maintaining positive relations with the citizens and particularly with the elected representatives of the community. This extends on up to state and federal levels of government, with each increase in government level implying a more profound potential effect on the company. To top it off, for many organizations the vista that they need to maintain to stay in business includes the rest of the world. The implications of relationships with emerging countries and with the older, established manufacturing economies are immense. The role of international public relations in the future is going to be increasingly important and difficult.

In short, the public relations practitioner representing profit-making organizations has his share of public relations problems to solve—problems that require him to induce involvement on the part of the recipients he is trying to reach, and that, in turn, require the recipients to assume enough responsibility toward the organization so that those problems are solved or avoided.

It seems that what is called for is a basic re-evaluation of the function of the public relations practitioner. This re-evaluation should carefully weigh the question of whether assumptions (generally implied ones) made about the media stage need to be reconsidered. It is appropriate here to re-assert the point made earlier that public relations practitioners are *always concerned with behavior and attitude change* in their work, that when a public relations practitioner is successful in solving his problems, usually some fairly pronounced behavior and attitude changes have to take place. If this contention is true, then the public relations practitioner, as a communicator, does *not* face the same tasks as other communicators, notably advertisers and journalists. This means that the use of the media by a public relations practitioner perforce needs to be different than its use by advertisers and journalists. Here is precisely where the "rub" comes in, because the public relations practitioner has *not*, generally speaking, approached his communication problems in a way fundamentally different than other communicators have. When one looks at the activities of many public relations practitioners (note particularly the case cited in Chapter 5, pages 100-104), it becomes evident that their use of the media is barely distinguishable from the use of the media by other communicators, notably advertisers. Extensive use of the mass media, preoccupation with reaching large audiences, and reliance on repetition are seen over and over again in their programs. If one accepts what was said earlier in this section—that public relations practitioners have the involvement of the recipient and his willingness to accept responsibility as their communication tasks—then the public relations practitioner cannot place his reliance on the media as other communicators can. This is most notable in the use made of the mass media. If you will return to Figure 18 and examine again the relationship between media usage and the continuum of communication, you will readily see that *the portion of the communication continuum that poses the greatest difficulty for the public relations practitioner is the mass media portion.* He has the greatest difficulty tracing just what "good" the newspapers do for him. It is highly questionable that placing news releases successfully for a client in fact has anything to do with solving the public relations problems faced by the client. To be sure, the officers of a company may feel good about seeing their pictures in the newspapers, and this, in turn, may make the public relations practitioner appear "successful" in their eyes, but the ultimate answer to just what all of this newspaper publicity did to solve the types of problems sketched out earlier is very definitely open to debate. What is true of the newspaper is applicable to radio and television alike. To have a fifteen-minute documentary describing some professional association or to be successful in gaining a fairly large proportion of a TV or radio news broadcast may again, as in the case of the newspaper, make clients (or bosses) happy, but whether they contribute much to public relations problem solving is another matter.

It should be added quickly at this point that the public relations practitioner is not all to blame. For one thing, the universities that teach public relations have been comparatively quiescent, on the whole, with respect to leadership in public relations research. That is, they have not taken the lead in conducting necessary research to help the public relations practitioner understand how to use the mass media most effectively or how to supplement the mass media with other communication techniques so that the weaknesses of the mass media in "fitting" public relations problems can be overcome.[24] Public relations departments at the university level have the same responsibility as do other disciplines taught at the university level, namely, leading their field in research activities as do chemistry, physics, and biology departments across the country. Until this responsibility is met, progress in solving many public relations problems is going to be very slow, because no field looks to its practitioners for research or theoretical break-throughs.

It must be admitted, also, that the present state of development of measurement and theory in the social and behavioral sciences as a whole leaves much to be desired. For this reason, an applied field such as public relations cannot hope to make the same progress as other applied fields such as engineering and medicine.

The time has come for both sides, the public relations practitioner and the academician, to submit media usage to the closest scrutiny. The public relations practitioner must ask himself what he assumes the various mass media do for him and his public relations problems in *behavioral terms*. Precisely what does he assume that the publicity in newspapers, radio, and television does to change behavior and attitudes? More importantly, besides examining what he *assumes* the mass media do, he must ask himself what evidence he has that his assumptions are warranted.

The academician in fields related to public relations must do research on many fronts. But particularly, from the point of view of our discussion here, the academician needs to develop communication techniques to supplement the mass media in precisely the area that the mass media are the weakest: as vehicles which induce involvement and motivation to pay attention to the sender of the message. The academician must concentrate on what differences, if any, exist between communicating about a tangible product or object and about intangible things such as ideas, causes, and responsibilities. The academician should turn his

---

[24] There is the other side of the coin to be considered here, too, of course. The public relations practitioners as a group are not completely behind the idea of public relations training and research at the university level. Partly because of this, they are not supporting research in public relations at that level. The two reasons go hand in hand, and it is difficult to say which comes first or who is to blame, because they both contribute to what could be called a circular process.

attention to what the author likes to call "time-future" communications, a phrase that denotes the situation where one is trying to get someone to do something *now* about a crisis that is several years away. Public relations practitioners are so often faced with "time-future" communication situations. Conservation of natural resources, disease preventive measures, citizen involvement, planned suburban growth, planned economic growth, concern about population growth—are all examples of where the recipient of the communication needs to do something *now* about problems that *can* be put off for some time without immediately visible consequences.

What are the implications of what we have said thus far? In the opinion of the author, there are several that the public relations practitioner of the future must consider:

1. There must be re-examination of the total communication process as it applies to solving a public relations problem. The public relations practitioner must ask himself if he has become preoccupied with the message and media stages to the exclusion of the other stages of communication. Part and parcel with this assessment is facing squarely the question of whether the problem-solving efforts he has been using are more appropriate to other communicators (notably the advertiser with his emphasis on numbers, repetition, and the mass media) and not really suited for public relations problems. In other words, in line with the point made earlier that the public relations practitioner is concerned with inducing involvement in his recipients and a willingness on their part to assume some degree of responsibility toward the problems, the public relations practitioner must be alert to how he utilizes the media. This media usage must be consistent with his unique communication problems at all times.

2. Secondly, the public relations practitioner must re-examine the role of the mass media with respect to their effectiveness in helping to solve public relations problems. As we noted earlier when we first considered the continuum of communications (Chapter 9, pages 234-235), the mass audience (*i.e.,* the recipients of our mass media efforts) is notoriously uninterested in becoming involved in the problems they share and should face. As we noted then, "ready-made" interest becomes less and less dependable, the larger the audience. We must be certain that we have not become confused between our function as public relations practitioners and the functions of other communicators. For *them,* the mass media may serve admirably; for *us,* it may play a much more

limited role. We need to devote some attention to *supplements* to the mass media. By supplements is meant techniques to involve the recipient more and thereby increase the likelihood that he will be motivated to pay attention to the sender—*i.e.*, the public relations practitioner.

3. As a direct consequence of consideration No. 2, we must take a hard look at the thick clipping book, filled with evidence that we have been hard at work at the media stage. We must be prepared to *reject the column inch as the measure of effectiveness of a public relations program*. In its place, we must evolve our own, perhaps unique, measures of public relations effectiveness. We must generate our own kinds of feedback and the measures of this feedback. (We will consider this topic more fully in Part 3 when we take up research as it relates to public relations.)

4. We must be cognizant of the fact that communication dealing with ideas, attitudes, and efforts to produce the involvement of the recipient *may* pose different problems to solve than communication about goods and services. To put it another way, communicating involvement in a social problem or being a loyal member of a company may require different communication techniques than communicating about a new model car or brand of cigarettes.

5. We must expend much more effort on the two more neglected stages of the communication model—sender and recipient—so that our communication efforts are more balanced and effective.

QUESTIONS FOR DISCUSSION

1. Early in this chapter, the admonishment is put forth that the public relations practitioner needs to examine carefully the assumption that the print form of the mass media (particularly newspapers) is suitable for his public relations problem-solving efforts for any given problem. In this connection, gather as many news clippings as you can obtain that are a part of a public relations program, that is, developed by a public relations practitioner and placed in a newspaper as part of his over-all public relations practitioner program. After you have obtained the clippings, examine them from the point of view of their appropriateness and probable effectiveness for the given public relations problem they were supposed to solve (or help solve). What do you find? How many clippings do you find

that stand up under this type of analysis? Are you always able to make the connection between a clipping and the purpose that this news release is supposed to accomplish?

2. If someone asked you to explain the point made in this chapter that unpaid newspaper space is the "trademark" of the public relations practitioner, what would you say? Do you agree with this generalization? What evidence can you suggest (in addition to what is in this chapter) to support this contention?

3. We have suggested in this chapter that the public relations practitioner is not "at home" with the radio and television media. What reasons (besides those considered in this chapter) would you suggest to support this contention? Do you find it more difficult to think of examples of the utilization of radio and TV for public relations purposes than of the newspaper?

4. Because of our belief that the public relations practitioner is more often than not faced with the problem of producing involvement on the part of the recipient he is trying to reach, in the face of the recipient's lack of motivation to pay attention to the sender in the first place, we have argued that the mass media (particularly the common use of the news release) are not particularly appropriate for the public relations practitioner. For this reason we also said that a key concern of the public relations practitioner should be how he is going to *supplement* his use of the mass media. With respect to this general assertion, try to obtain evidence that (1) supports and (2) refutes the points made. Is there more evidence for or against our assertions in this area? How do our assertions fit into what was quoted from Wiebe in Chapter 9, pages 234-235?

Chapter 12

THE RECIPIENT STAGE IN MORE DETAIL: CONCEPT OF ATTITUDE

Toward the beginning of this volume, we pointed out that in one sense the recipient stage represents the whole point of communication in that it is the recipient's behavior and attitudes one is attempting to modify and change in some manner. Social communication is always purposive, and, more often than not, the purpose of a communication, regardless of the sender, is to have some impact on a recipient.

The basic objective behind this and the next four chapters is to provide the reader with additional concepts that have been found to be useful in understanding the recipient and, therefore, in better predicting his reactions to a particular communication effort. These concepts have been deliberately selected so as to represent a key *psychological* concept, two useful *sociological* concepts, and two concepts that are overlapping—that is, used freely by psychologists and sociologists alike.

The concept we have selected to represent the psychological approach to understanding human behavior is that of *attitude*. Our pair of concepts representing the sociological point of view (Chapter 13) are *formal* and *informal* structure. Lastly, our overlapping pair of concepts are *role and status* (Chapter 14). In addition to selecting these concepts to represent major points of view in understanding human behavior, we have also selected those that appear to be most fruitful for the public relations practitioner as well. Let us turn first to a consideration of the two main points of view—the psychological and the sociological—that we will be addressing ourselves to in these three chapters.

COMPARISON OF PSYCHOLOGICAL AND SOCIOLOGICAL APPROACHES TO UNDERSTANDING HUMAN BEHAVIOR

The Psychological Approach

Obviously, both psychologists and sociologists are concerned with understanding human behavior. But how are they different in their approaches to this understanding? First, let us look at their basic units of analysis and see what we can learn from this.

Taking the psychologist first, his unit of analysis is the single individual. Although he may work with more than one individual in a given experiment or in a field survey, his focus is on individual reactions to whatever stimulus or stimuli that he may introduce to the individual. Consider again for a moment the work of Lewin that we touched upon in Chapter 4 (pages 61-62) when we discussed the use of models to better understand the world around us. In that context, we saw one example of Lewin's efforts to conceptualize what is going on inside an individual. Lewin was trying to spell out the "life space" of an individual who was interested in becoming a physician. Here we see typified the psychological approach to understanding human behavior in that the processes within one individual are the focus of attention, and the efforts at model building or even theory building are directed toward understanding the single individual. From such study or conceptualizing, generalizations are made, meaning that certain "principles" or "explanations" of behavior that are used to account for *one* person's behavior, are extended to all other people. Thus, Lewin believed that what he was postulating as the dynamics of behavior for one person could be applied to other persons as well.

The point of this brief excursion concerning Lewin is not to focus on his models or theories. The point of importance to us is that Lewin is a good example of the *psychological* approach in the sense that the basic unit of analysis is the *single individual*. This "individual approach" argues that individuals are the ones who are happy or sad. Individuals are the only "reality" that we have to deal with. They argue that, strictly speaking, there is no such thing as a group. *Group* is merely a word that describes more than one individual.

Perhaps one additional example will help to make this point about the individual as the basic unit of analysis more clear. Consider the question of prejudice. We see prejudices manifested all around us: prejudices toward race, religion, and color. We also encounter prejudices toward inanimate objects, so that some people are prejudiced toward certain types of art, manufactured objects, and parts of the country. Suppose you were interested in studying prejudice: how prejudices form, how they can be changed, and the like. How would you go about it? Consider the question of prejudice against minority groups, for example. A psychologist, Frenkel-Brunswik, was interested in prejudice against minority groups and the relationship between prejudice and personality. After many years of study, Frenkel-Brunswik and her co-workers generated the concept of an *authoritarian* personality. One of the distinguishing characteristics they ascribed to the authoritarian personality is that such people are much more likely to be prejudiced against minority groups.[1] With this concept of authoritarian personality, we see certain social phenomena, in this case prejudice of one individual toward another, explained in terms of the *individual personality of the persons in question.* To repeat, a concept such as the authoritarian personality as it applies to an understanding of prejudice could come about only if the *individual* is your basic unit of analysis.

The Sociological Approach

This brings us to the sociological approach to understanding human behavior. Essentially, the sociologist argues that an understanding of group functioning cannot be derived satisfactorily from laws that describe individual behavior. It is not that the sociologist denies that individual factors (such as one's motivation, perception, and the like) are not important. Rather, he argues that certain outcomes, such as war or depression, occur in spite of the fact that nearly everyone involved would rather not have a war or a depression. He argues that there are certain processes to be understood about *groups* of people and about the effects of groups on the behavior of the individual that can be understood only by utilizing the *group* as the unit of study.

The group as a unit of study is very often misunderstood by the average person because he is so used to thinking in individual terms. When he hears or reads that the group is the unit of study, it puzzles him.

---

[1] In fact, they evolved a set of traits or an identifying syndrome of the authoritarian personality which includes, besides prejudice and intolerance toward some minority groups, such things as heavy stress on conventional behavior, extreme deference to superior authority, rigidity of thought process, and close conformity to group norms.

Lundberg, Schrag, and Larsen address themselves to this unfamiliarity when they write:

> When it is announced that the next unit of study will be "group behavior," students sometimes raise this question: *"Is the group real; can it be studied as such?"* Some people who raise this question think of the *individual* as the only reality to be studied. To them, groups, institutions, societies, or any organized *patterns* of human experience are not "real." It is claimed that they are nothing more than the sum of traits and actions which actually exist only in separate individuals. This view overlooks the fact that the individual is himself a most dramatic example of group behavior—billions of cells and organs working together in a highly coordinated and synchronized manner. It further overlooks the fact that when individual parts become organized into wholes, new characteristics may emerge which are not observable in the separate parts alone. This point may be illustrated by reference to a football team.
>
> Can the "teamwork" of a football team be explained by observing the individual players separately? The answer would seem to be that the members must be joined in a *structure of relations* before the property of teamwork emerges. In a like manner, the distinctive characteristics of water cannot be observed in hydrogen or oxygen separately. Only the interaction of the elements in certain proportions (H_2O) and under certain conditions produces the substance called water. As to the "reality" of the part or whole, it is clear that when we go to a football game we may observe with equal reality one player, one team, the game, or the crowd. It may be noted, too, that while the group factor of teamwork varies with the quality of individual players, the team continues to function with substitutions of individual players. That is, a team, like many organized groups, has duration and extent beyond that of any of its members and cannot properly be considered a simple sum of its members.
>
> The "group behavior" of a team is mapped out in plays that are rehearsed in practice sessions. Each member learns a role. The success of the team is dependent upon the successful fulfillment of each role. When one man misses an assignment, team play may go wrong. Something called "morale" or "team spirit" also seems to make a difference. Various forms of team leadership also emerge. The official captain who consults the referee may or may not be the quarterback who calls the plays, who in turn, may or may not be the team's inspirational leader. In addition, it is known that when the organizational structure of the team is varied, as from a T-formation to a single wing, the behavior patterns change in a predictable way.[2]

---

[2] G. A. Lundberg, C. C. Schrag, and O. N. Larsen, *Sociology* (New York: Harper & Row, Publishers, 1954), pp. 394-395. All passages from *Sociology* used by permission.

And a little later, the authors go on to say:

> The behavior of human beings may be studied profitably and realistically on many levels. Sciences have arisen to study events at atomic, molecular, cellular, organismic, and social levels because certain questions can be answered only on each appropriate level. The organization and behavior of a community of ants, for example, cannot entirely be accounted for by a study of a thousand or ten thousand *individual* ants. To answer questions about the ant community, how it moves on a foray, how it circumvents physical obstacles, how it retreats at night, one must study the community. The same is true of all group behavior. When we have questions about human group situations, be they teams, clubs, families, audiences, crowds, or publics, we must at some point turn to the observation of human groups as groups.[3]

A rather classical example of the sociological approach to understanding human behavior, where the *group* is the unit of analysis, is found in the study of rumor transmission in the married housing units at Massachusetts Institute of Technology.[4]

This study was designed to reveal, among other things, the effect of the arrangement of housing units, with common pathways and certain access and egress points, on friendship ties and patterns of rumor transmission. To summarize briefly one portion of the study, the researchers found that they could predict friendship ties and spread of rumors (rumors that the researchers had deliberately planted and traced) on the basis of *the physical separation of families* in different apartments, with distances of only a comparatively few feet significant. On the basis of the data collected, all that the researchers had to know about an individual (or a family) was how far away he lived from other individuals or families in order to predict successfully whether these people would likely be friends or strangers. The point to be stressed here is that, in this type of study, the *individual* motives, interests, and personality characteristics were *not* considered.[5] In this study, the units of analysis were certain physical measurements applied to the group as a whole. The authors of the study would not deny for a minute that differences existed among these individuals or that other analyses of

---

[3] *Ibid.*, p. 395.

[4] Leon Festinger, Stanley Schachter, and Kurt Back, *Social Pressures in Informal Groups* (New York: Harper & Row, Publishers, 1950).

[5] It should be pointed out, however, that the fact that the people involved were all students at M.I.T., married, of roughly the same age, and, more than likely, from similar socioeconomic backgrounds was undoubtedly important. Whether the same results would have been obtained if a very heterogeneous group had lived in the housing area is uncertain, a question which the authors raised themselves.

these data could be made with the individual differences taken into account. The point is that certain intelligent observations can be made of the relationship between the physical environment within which a person lives and how he interrelates with other persons, all *without considering the individual as such* but, rather, concentrating on the group as the unit of interest.[6]

This example illustrates the sociological approach, which is less commonly understood by most people than the individual approach with which they are more familiar. For purposes of contrasting the two major approaches to understanding human behavior, the extreme positions of the psychological and sociological approaches have been outlined. In practice, the extreme positions are not adhered to in a strict sense; rather, psychologists and sociologists borrow from one another and use *both* approaches in order to better understand human behavior. In fact, some of the most useful concepts, both for theoretical and applied social scientists, are concepts that are shared by the psychologist and sociologist.

A PSYCHOLOGICAL CONCEPT: ATTITUDE

The concept of attitude is unquestionably one of the most popular in psychology. Along with the popularity has come confusion, as many different meanings and uses of the term *attitude* have arisen. So as not to add to the confusion, let us begin our discussion of the concept of attitude by defining what we mean by this term.

For a more formal definition, let us borrow the one developed by Krech and Crutchfield. They define an attitude as follows:

> An enduring organization of perceptual, motivational, emotional, and adaptive processes centering on some object in the person's world. Attitudes may be positive or negative, that is the person may be favorably disposed or unfavorably disposed toward the object.[7]

---

[6] One further point is worth mentioning here. Although we have argued that the majority of the work reported in *Social Pressures in Informal Groups* (*cf.* footnote 4) is sociological in nature, it is interesting to note that two of its authors, Festinger and Schachter, are psychologists. This item of information helps to reinforce the point we are making here concerning the psychological *vs.* sociological approach to understanding human behavior. We are talking about *methods* or *conceptual approach*, not the researchers themselves. A psychologist is able to "cross over" and utilize the approach of the sociologist, and the reverse is obviously equally possible.

[7] David Krech and R. S. Crutchfield, *Elements of Psychology* (New York: Alfred A. Knopf, Inc., 1958), p. 692. Used by permission.

Let's go over this definition part by part to be sure that we understand this concept. First, the word *enduring*. From this word, one can see that an individual's attitude is something that is relatively permanent. Our attitudes toward minority groups, political parties, and the like are things that took a long time to develop, as a rule, and are likely to remain the same for a long period of time. (This enduring quality is the very thing that can be so disconcerting to a public relations practitioner at times. He is almost invariably faced with the job of changing attitudes, and he quickly comes to learn how difficult this sometimes can be.)

Next, the remainder of the first sentence, "organization of perceptual, motivational, emotional, and adaptive processes centering on some object in the person's world." Packed into these words is a lot that we need to tease out. For one thing, it should be clear that an attitude is organized with respect to some event or object in the world of the individual. Having an attitude implies an object of that attitude. It can be another person, a product, a political idea—anything can be the object of an attitude as long as it exists for the individual concerned. Secondly, it should be clear that an attitude is a *composite* of how a person perceives, what motivates him to perceive, and what emotional involvement accompanies this perception. This means that an attitude is a synthesis of a large portion of any one individual's personality. To put it another way, an attitude is a unifying phenomenon that represents many aspects of any one individual's personality "in action," so to speak.

A less obvious point in this definition is in the phrase "in the person's world." What that phrase tells us is that attitudes are intimately related to what exists for the individual and that this is not necessarily the same as what exists in the world for others. As a practical matter, this means that not every possible object or event in the world necessarily exists for all persons. As real as the European Common Market may be as a fact and a phenomenon of the 1960's, the Common Market just does not exist for large numbers of individuals. They may really have no attitudes toward the Common Market.[8] (See once again Chapter 7, pages 168-176.)

---

[8] This point creates major problems for opinion-attitude survey work. Many persons who have no attitudes toward the Common Market, who are completely uninformed about just what it is and what it will mean for the participating nations, may, nevertheless, express their views on the pros and cons of the Common Market if quizzed in an interview. Because a person answers a question does not necessarily mean that he has an attitude toward the subject under discussion. This point will come up again when we talk about the inferential nature of attitudes.

The last sentence in the definition tells us that an attitude reflects the disposition that one feels toward some person, object, or event in the world. This disposition can range from strongly positive (that is, the person, if very favorably disposed, likes what he sees or hears) to strongly negative, with many degrees of the positive or negative in between. In fact, one of the most useful properties of attitudes is that we are able to ascertain how negatively or positively an individual is disposed toward something. With this information, we are often able to predict better how he is likely to behave.

So much for a more detailed examination of our borrowed definition. Let's examine a few more properties of attitudes that must be clearly understood so that we as public relations practitioners can intelligently make use of this concept.

Attitudes Are Inferred

We should be clear from the beginning that one never "sees" or measures an attitude directly. An attitude is not something that can be found inside an individual, like his stomach or kidneys; neither is it something that he possesses in the same sense that he owns a car or a house. Mason Haire summed up a way to consider attitudes when he wrote:

> We should not think of him as "having" an attitude, but rather as having organized the world in a certain way. In this sense, the word "attitude" should not be used as a noun, but rather as an adverb that modifies the verb "to see." An attitude is a way of seeing things. To attack it as "his" attitude is to miss the meaning of the organization of the other person's perception of the world. Instead, we must try to see the way in which he sees things and then help him to see other things there.[9]

An attitude is an inferred phenomenon. It is a concept that is, in effect, describing an *implied* process that occurs in a given individual for a variety of reasons. All that we have to go by is the behavior that we observe. On the basis of this behavior, we *infer* the fact that an individual has such and such a positive (or negative) attitude. Let us consider this inferential process for a moment. We met an individual for the first time, say at a cocktail party. In the process of discussing a wide range of topics, we gradually collect bits of verbal behavior

---

[9] Mason Haire, *Psychology in Management* (2d ed.; New York: McGraw-Hill Book Company, 1964), pp. 106-107. Used by permission.

along with observing various gestures, facial expressions, and the like. On the basis of these verbal and nonverbal behaviors, we gradually begin to *infer* that this individual is probably quite interested in sports and has very definite positive attitudes in this area. We come to categorize this individual politically and infer that he has very positive attitudes toward the Democratic party and quite negative ones toward the Republican party. And so the process goes—observing, listening, inferring. (Incidentally, for the moment we will ignore completely whether these inferences are correct or incorrect. Obviously, some people are very poor at inferring attitudes on the basis of the behavior to which they are exposed, while others are quite good.) This means that at no time is an attitude "visible"; rather, we observe behaviors that we infer are a *function* of (or reflect the presence of) a particular attitude.

This point about attitudes being inferred is very important because it is so easy to reify concepts in the social sciences, particularly in psychology. Essentially reification consists of treating a concept as if it were a thing, something that could be seen and handled. Perhaps the classical examples of reification come from the psychoanalytically oriented psychologists and psychiatrists and the way in which they write and think about such concepts as the *ego, super-ego,* and *id.* These concepts were originally constructed to understand better certain processes of an individual's personality. In this way, these concepts are precisely like the concept of attitude. The concept of attitude is supposed to enable us to understand some aspects of human behavior more effectively. However, people have come to write and think about the ego, id, and super-ego as if they were actual entities (sometimes called homoculi—*i.e.,* little men—by critics of this approach) at war with one another. Some writers have visualized the ego as having to "defend" itself (with the help of the super-ego) against the socially unacceptable drives contained in the id. These people write in such a way that it makes one expect that, if he were to open up the head of an individual, he would find the ego, id, and super-ego. The fact is, of course, that there is no such thing as an ego, for example, within an individual. It is merely a word that stands for certain processes that are assumed to take place within an individual. As long as we remember that it is a term that stands for certain processes, and if, at the same time, it *does* enable us to understand and predict human behavior better than if we did not have this concept, fine. This is exactly why concepts are developed: to help us understand certain phenomena more readily. If, however, we forget that it is merely a term that stands for a process and begin to believe that it is an entity (hence the word *reify*, to make real) that exists within an individual, then we can make serious errors and the value of the concept is lost.

So it is with the public relations practitioner and the concept of attitude. It is a way of thinking about human behavior that has proved useful in understanding and predicting certain aspects of behavior. It is a word that stands for certain assumed processes (*i.e.*, perceptual, motivational, and so on) that are going on within an individual. These processes are assumed to modify how a person organizes the world around him—*i.e.*, certain attitudes are related to certain ways of reacting to events going on in the world. To go beyond this and attribute to the word *attitude* any additional meanings is to destroy the usefulness of the concept as well as to be incorrect concerning what actually exists within an individual.

The value of realizing that the word *attitude* refers to a process and is not a thing or an entity within an individual is implied in the passage that we quoted from Mason Haire. When he suggests that we think of an attitude as an adverb that modifies the verb *to see*, he is stressing the *process* aspect of the concept of attitude. When he says that we should not think of attitude as a noun, he is saying that we should not reify the word *attitude* and try and make a thing out of it. This subtle point is extremely important to the public relations practitioner, because he must always remember that his task, with respect to attitude change, contains two important steps: (1) to understand how the intended recipient sees something and (2) armed with this understanding, begin to think how it might be possible to cause him to see it in a different manner. With this distinction clear in his mind, the public relations practitioner is much less likely to approach his recipient as if he had an "incorrect" attitude—*i.e.*, some *thing* (the process of reification again) that has to be got rid of as one might get rid of a malfunctioning appendix. Rather, he will begin to concentrate on what *modifiers* (previous experiences, previous training, ethnic factors, reference group factors, and so on) probably cause his recipient to see things in a particular way. The task is one of adding new modifiers or reducing the effectiveness of certain old modifiers so as to alter the perceptions of his intended recipients. There is no surgery available to the public relations practitioner to remove the attitude. It never existed in that sense in the first place. We will return to this point again a little later when we consider a case illustrating the problem of attitude change.

Opinion vs. Attitude

One concept very closely related to that of attitude is *opinion*. Many writers distinguish between opinion and attitude and argue that there is a need to make such a distinction. By the same token, there are writers that use the two terms almost interchangeably or in such a fashion that it is difficult to verbalize just how the two concepts are really different. For example, Hartley and Hartley write,

> Attitudes are commonly differentiated from opinions although they are equally commonly confused with opinions. It scarcely seems helpful to consider opinion as merely the "verbalization of an attitude." Opinion is a fact of a different psychological order; it differs in its functional relation to behavior. It comes into being just when, and to the extent that, attitudes are not adequate to enable the individual or the group to cope with a situation. Many situations are problematical in that they involve new and strange objects or new combinations or arrangements of familiar objects, as in the old illustration of the cow in the parlor. These problem situations require that participants "take thought," that they try to find out what the situation portends, what will happen if this or that course of action is followed. In this process of assessing the situation, participants draw upon past experience, bringing to bear attitudes that seem to be relevant; but they cannot rely, except tentatively, upon these attitudes to carry them through the situation. With a greater or lesser degree of rationality, a definition of the situation, a conception of the kind of action appropriate to it, will be worked out; it is just such a definition that seems to be referred to, on both the practical and the scholarly level, as *opinion*. It involves, or is based in part upon, attitudes; but it is not, therefore, synonymous with attitude. It is always concerned with doubtful elements in the situation, with conflicts and uncertainties, with problems or "issues," and is, therefore, a more rational construct.[10]

From such a discussion, the reader can appreciate that it is not easy to verbalize how attitudes differ from opinions. In addition, other writers use the terms in the same sentence, such as the following from Krech and Crutchfield,

> The most extensive measurement of attitudes occurs in *public opinion* polls and surveys. [Italics added.]
>
> . . . . .
>
> In public opinion research our interest is ordinarily not in the attitudes of a single person, but in the attitudes of specified population of people.[11]

---

[10] E. L. Hartley and R. E. Hartley, *Fundamentals of Social Psychology* (New York: Alfred A. Knopf, Inc., 1955), p. 657. All passages from *Fundamentals of Social Psychology* used by permission.

[11] Krech and Crutchfield, pp. 682-683.

How, if at all, should the public relations practitioner regard the distinction between these two concepts? Our suggestion is that we do not try to distinguish between them from the standpoint that attitudes are "predispositions" to act, whereas, opinions are only the "intellectual" components of attitudes. *Rather, it appears most useful to regard attitudes (learned as a function of growing up and living in a particular culture) as short-cut labels (that are inferred) for ways of reacting to the world around us.* The term *opinion* is best described by remembering the most common context out of which the term *opinion* arises— survey work. Opinions are the verbal utterances that we obtain from people when we ask them questions, or in a typical conversation. That is, while we obtain opinions from individuals in formal survey work, we also do the very same thing in our everyday conversations with friends and acquaintances. On the basis of the replies, we infer certain attitudes in exactly the same way we infer attitudes from the way they behave nonverbally.

Naturally the process of inferring attitude from verbal behavior (i.e., *opinions*) is just as risky as inferring attitudes from any other sort of behavior. Some of the more common reasons why our inferences can be wrong are that people often say things that they do not mean or say things that are not related to their attitudes. Another reason is that any verbal expression can, in fact, be the reflection of a number of attitudes, and the difficulty is to sort all of this out from what one says.

No one is more aware of the dangers of inferring attitudes from opinions than are the social scientists who specialize in survey work designed to measure, as accurately as possible, public opinion on certain issues. They are fully cognizant of the fact that people can even give opinions about phenomena that do not exist. Thus, for purposes of control, in many surveys purely fictitious names of people, companies, products, and places are included only to find respondents who will render opinions about these fictitious items during an interview. Likewise, survey experts realize only too well that people are untruthful and even that many who have every intention to be truthful are somehow inaccurate. Experimental work has indicated that certain proportions (which vary from situation to situation, of course) of individuals give wrong answers in response to even simple questions such as their age, occupation, income, purchases, and voting behavior.

In spite of these difficulties in using opinions for purposes of inferring attitudes, survey work is still a valuable tool for the social scientist and applied individual alike. There are many pitfalls in the whole process of inferring attitudes from any sort of behavior, be it verbal or nonverbal, and any individual utilizing opinions for this purpose must be aware of them.

Some Properties of the Concept of Attitude

RELATIONSHIP TO BEHAVIOR

The fact that any one individual is more likely than not to behave tomorrow as he did yesterday is testimony to the fact that regularity or consistency of behavior is the rule rather than the exception. Because of this consistency, we are able to go one step further and relate what a person *says* with what he actually *does*. Or, in terms of our section here, we are able to relate attitudes (*i.e.*, statements about feelings toward a variety of topics from which we infer attitudes) to subsequent behavior. Stouffer expresses this point when he writes,

> I suppose the main reason why anybody thinks there is or can be a social science is that all around us in our everyday behavior we see not only how necessary prediction is, but also how successful it is. True, we take most of the successful predictions for granted. Our very living from hour to hour is based on it. . . . While we drive a car down the street only a few blocks we may make a score of predictions about what other drivers will do—and we are hardly conscious of any of these predictions until one of them fails and we have a smashup or a near miss. Indeed, all human living is possible only because a large part of our daily activities permit us to make successful predictions. . . .
>
> Of course, nobody dreams of a science of human behavior which seeks to predict each private thought any more than one dreams of a science of hydraulics which would predict the location and duration of each little eddy in a Mississippi River flood. But a science of human nature or of social relations must be based on the solid fact that there are regularities in man's behavior which do admit of actuarial prediction.[12]

The fact that there is a fairly reliable relationship between attitudes and behavior is of vital importance to the public relations practitioner. What makes it even more important is that in the past two decades excellent progress has been made in reducing the amount of time (and number of people) required to obtain accurate attitude measurement of a representative sample of people. To understand just how important the above statements are to the applied individual, consider for a moment where we would be if we could not use measures of attitudes as a short cut to predicting behavior. Suppose, for the sake of argu-

---

[12] S. A. Stouffer, "Basic Social Science Research," in N. C. Meier and H. W. Saunders (eds.), *The Polls and Public Opinion* (New York: Holt, Rinehart & Winston, Inc., 1949), pp. 11-13. Used by permission.

ment, that we needed a thorough series of clinical-type tests and prolonged interviews of individuals before we could predict their behavior. That is, suppose the applied individual needed to proceed as a
clinical psychologist working with a patient. For all practical purposes,
this state of affairs would mean that none of the applied fields—business, journalism, public relations, advertising, to name a few—could
utilize social science as an adjunct to their efforts in predicting behavior. Clinical methods would be too costly and slow for the applied
individual. Happily, such is not the case. With proper safeguards, we
are able to use attitude measurement as a short cut to predicting behavior. A short cut in the sense that we obtain our information (i.e.,
responses to questions designed to permit interpretations concerning
attitudes which, in turn, permit us to predict subsequent behavior)
about the individual relatively quickly and then utilize this information to make predictions.

To round out this point concerning the utilization of attitude measures as a means of predicting behavior, let us examine a series of
studies in which this relationship between attitude and behavior was
the major instrument used by the researcher to predict behavior.

1. *Attitude measures to predict voting behavior.* Perhaps the most
widely known use of attitude measurement as a means of predicting
behavior is in the area of politics. The political opinion poll has become
part and parcel of the world of politics, and most politicians would not
be without poll results to help guide their behavior. Many jokes are
made about the accuracy of political polls, and in this area particularly
the professionals at work still must cope with people who doubt the
accuracy of the polls. Probably two reasons contribute most to causing
some people to still doubt the accuracy of political polls. One is the
fact that large errors in predicting the winning candidate have been
made in the past (and may, of course, be made in the future), and, as
in any other field, mistakes are sometimes hard to live down.[13] The
classical error that many people point to is *The Literary Digest* poll
of 1936 where the prediction was made that Landon would win the
election against Roosevelt. The fact was, of course, that Roosevelt won
by a landslide and the *Digest* was wrong by about nineteen percentage

---

[13] The persistent, widespread notion that anyone can predict the weather better
than a meteorologist stems partly from the fact that the meteorologists still sometimes predict the weather incorrectly. The fact that the proportion of times that
they are correct is increasing and now exceeds the ability of the average person
with only hunch or his corns to guide him is still hard to communicate. The old
stereotype of the weatherman who is always wrong is hard to live down, and
hence the popularity of the jokes about the inaccuracy of his predictions.

points. There was a good reason for this error, however, and no professional today would make the same mistake. *The Literary Digest* poll was based on returns obtained from people who had telephones—that is, on a sample of people whose names were obtained from telephone books. The trouble with this approach was that in 1936 the people who had telephones were very likely to be in a different income bracket from people who did not. Consequently, the survey could not obtain the views of a sample of the millions of people who did not have telephones. Mistakes like this are hard to live down.

The other reason that the accuracy of political polls (and all polls for that matter, as this factor applies to all types of surveys) is doubted is that most people are not aware of the great strides that have been made in scientific sampling procedures. Today it is possible to draw a sample of only fifteen hundred persons and have it be representative of the entire United States. This point was brought out with statistical evidence in an answer that George Gallup gave to the question, "Is such a sample [fifteen hundred persons] representative of the entire population?" His reply follows.

Yes. When a sample is drawn properly it should contain approximately the same proportions of old persons and young—the educated and uneducated—rich and poor—farmers, unskilled workers, skilled laborers—Catholics and Protestants, etc.—as exist in the population. *And the various regions of the country should be properly represented.*

Here, for example, is a comparison of a recent Gallup Poll sample with the latest available estimates of the U.S. Census:

	GALLUP Dec., 1959 %	U.S. CENSUS Estimate %
East	29.3	30.3
Midwest	31.2	29.9
South	25.3	25.6
West	14.2	14.2
Men	47.6	47.4
Women	52.4	52.6
White	88.5	89.0
Non-white	11.5	11.0
21-34 yrs.	28.3	29.0
35-49 yrs.	34.0	32.8
50 yrs. & older	37.7	38.2

The Gallup Poll samples the adult civilian, non-institutional population. Recent census data are not available for a directly comparable population in all instances, but provide close approximations to the population sampled by The Gallup Poll.[14]

It is clear from these data that the representativeness of a sample of people, from the standpoint of how well they agree with the population at large in such characteristics as age, sex, region of the country, and so on, is pretty hard to refute. This agreement between sample data and total population has been demonstrated again and again, and the agreement in figures noted above is the rule rather than the exception. Of course, these data do not throw any light on how representative the attitudes between the sample and the total population would be on certain questions. There are many factors that can make the attitudes sampled not representative of the total population. However, if handled correctly, the survey can sample attitudes as accurately as other characteristics, such as age and sex, are sampled.

With these two main considerations out of the way, let us return to our main concern here: Can attitude measures be used to predict political behavior? The answer is: most assuredly. The accuracy in this connection is remarkable, considering all of the factors that could introduce error into the prediction. Once again we borrow from Dr. Gallup for our data:

ACCURACY RECORD OF THE GALLUP POLL[15]
(Since 1948)

Popular vote in elections	Gallup Poll Results		Election Returns		Deviation of poll
1950 Congressional	51%	Dem.	50.3%	Dem.	0.7%
1952 Presidential	51%	Eisen.	55.4%	Eisen.	4.4%
1954 Congressional	51.5%	Dem.	52.7%	Dem.	1.2%
1956 Presidential	59.5%	Dem.	57.8%	Dem.	1.7%
1958 Congressional	57%	Dem.	56.5%	Dem.	0.5%
Average deviation for these five elections					1.7%

It is clear from these data that the accuracy of prediction of the Gallup Poll (prototype of many other scientifically conducted polls) is remarkably high. In the same article from which these data were

---

[14] Taken from "How a Public Poll Is Conducted," by George Gallup, Director, The American Institute of Public Opinion (Princeton, New Jersey: The Institute, 1960). All material used by permission.

[15] *Ibid.*

taken, the point was made that the average deviation for seven elections from 1936 through 1948 was 3.9%. This means that progress is
still being made in polling accuracy, and it could be that in the future
the margin of error between prediction based on an attitude poll and
fact (e.g., what happens in an election) may become even smaller.

Let us examine the implication of this accuracy in a little more detail.
The accuracy of prediction of these polls means that we can reliably
estimate one facet of behavior of some sixty million people, based on a
random sample of approximately fifteen hundred of those sixty million.
To put it another way, scientific sampling procedures have evolved
to such an extent that only .000025 of the total voting population needs
to be interviewed in order to make reliable estimates of the total group!
The practical significance of this sampling accuracy is tremendous. It
means that for the applied individual to utilize polling for certain of
his applied problems is both economically feasible and scientifically
defensible. Our example here is in terms of voting behavior, and there
may be comparatively few times that the public relations practitioner
would like to predict how a certain public with which he is concerned
is likely to vote on a certain issue. (There are times, of course, when he
is vitally interested in a "voting-like" outcome of behavior. Perhaps the
best example of this is the way stockholders are likely to vote in a
proxy fight or employees are likely to vote concerning joining a union.)
The principle, however, is easily applied to other situations with which
a public relations practitioner may be more often concerned. Two
examples that come quickly to mind follow. A company plans to relo-
cate in a different community, far enough away from the present one
so that the question of how many employees are likely to leave the
company because of the relocation is a vital question. Here we are
interested in the attitudes of the employee toward the plant relocation
and just what he is going to do about it. The second example is the
measuring of employees' reactions to their company publications, such
as the plant newspaper or monthly magazine. Now we are interested
in employees' attitudes toward the newspaper and magazine and why
they hold them. Armed with this information, a public relations practitioner can develop a more widely read and accepted publication.

It is clear that there are many times when the public relations practitioner is faced with the question of predicting how a certain public
is likely to react under certain conditions. One extremely useful device
that has been evolved to help out in such cases is the opinion-attitude
poll. In such polling situations, attitudes are inferred from the replies
to the questions asked, and on the basis of these inferences predictions
are made. Such procedures have become invaluable tools to many prac-

titioners. They must be utilized as fully as is practicable by the public relations practitioner.

2. Attitude measures to predict consumer behavior or to pretest advertising. Perhaps the most avid users of attitude measures to predict behavior have been marketing and advertising people; in fact, some of their work represents the most sophisticated examples of the use of attitude measurement for applied use. The general pattern of attitude measurement that they employ is to predict the behavior of the potential consumer toward an advertisement of a particular product. It may be predicting how the consumer will react to the introduction of a new brand of cigarettes. Or, it may be predicting how a new toilet soap will be accepted. Or, in contrast to the last two examples, it may be an effort to find out what characteristics of a product are objectionable to the consumer so that changes can be made in the product to make it more acceptable. Regardless of the specific example, the use made of the attitude measures obtained is generally to predict some aspect of the consumer behavior of individuals. To illustrate the use of attitude measures to pretest advertising, we will borrow a case from a book developed by the National Industrial Conference Board, Inc.

CASE NO. 6

INFORMATION SOUGHT: Truck users' opinions about truck manufacturers
RESEARCH METHOD: Rating-scale questions asked in a mail questionnaire
COMPANY: An industrial truck manufacturer

The advertising agency for an industrial truck manufacturer made a survey of the attitudes of customers and prospects toward this company and four major competitors. One purpose of the survey was to uncover strong points of the client's reputation that could be emphasized and weak points that could be corrected in future advertising.

PRETESTING PROCEDURE

The attitude survey was conducted by mail.* A one-page questionnaire was sent to a random sample of 2,262 names taken from a list of 12,000 lift-truck users in or near a large industrial market area. The list was compiled and kept up to date by sales representatives of the company.

The questionnaire asked the respondent to rate the five truck manufacturers on seven attributes: salesman service, size of product line, application engineering, financing, repair service, parts availability, and

---

* There were, in addition, a few semistructured individual interviews.

economy of operation. Each one of these attributes was amplified by means of an illustrative question or two. For example, these questions were used to describe salesman service: "Do their salesmen keep you informed? Do their salesmen show continued interest in your problems?"

There were five numbers to choose from in rating each company on each attribute. Number one was the highest rating, five the lowest, in these scales. The respondent made each rating by circling the appropriate number. A question mark was provided for him to circle if he didn't know how a given company rated on the attribute in question.

The respondent was asked also to indicate the make of trucks that he was currently using.

To analyze the results and evaluate the companies' relative stature, a rating index was computed for each company on each attribute. The step-by-step process in this computation was as follows:

1. Weighting inversely, so that "very high" became a score of 5; "high" became 4; "average" 3; "low" 2; and "very low" 1.
2. Counting the number of people who had circled each number.
3. Multiplying the number of people circling each number by its proper weight.
4. Totaling the weighted scores.
5. Dividing the total by the highest possible score (five times the total number of respondents rating the company on the attribute).

The question-mark ratings were given no weight in this analysis.

The agency also divided the repondents into three groups and calculated rating indices for each group. The groups were: users of the client company's trucks only; users of the other brands only; and users of both the client's make and other makes.

Twenty-eight per cent of the recipients completed and returned the questionnaire.

APPRAISAL

The company believes that the questions asked in this study evoked a useful profile of its stature in the market place as opposed to that of its competitors. These profiles in turn suggested: (1) ideas that need consideration in future advertising, and (2) areas in which material changes in the product or its distribution might be made.

The "don't know" answers in the study measured the degree of the respondent's familiarity or unfamiliarity with the five companies and with factors significant in the sale of lift trucks. This is a most important measure, according to the company management, because it established the effectiveness of the company's communications (or the lack of communications) with its market. The company believes that it is likely that if a respondent has no opinion concerning a company, he also knows very little about that company. Therefore, the company regards such responses as warnings that its communication efforts have not been achieving their basic objectives.[16]

3. *Attitude measures to guide development of public relations programs.* Although the use of attitude measures to guide the development of public relations programs is not yet nearly so widespread among public relations practitioners as among advertisers, such research is being used increasingly in this respect. To illustrate how public relations practitioners do make use of opinion-attitude surveys, let us examine briefly the work that was done by The Borden Company.

THE BORDEN COMPANY, Van Wert, Ohio
EMPLOYEE AND COMMUNITY ATTITUDES STUDY[17]

The Borden Company is America's second largest dairy concern, operating some three hundred plants and distributing products throughout the United States. One of its cheese factories is located in Van Wert, Ohio, a Midwestern city of over ten thousand population.

Borden had operated a plant in Van Wert for many years. However, in the years immediately prior to 1947 (the point at which our story begins), this particular facility had undergone rapid expansion of its work force. With nearly four hundred employees—and the title of "the largest cheese factory in the world"—acute growing pains were being felt, the prominent symptoms of which were high turnover and reports of employee dissatisfaction. The plant management was concerned about these problems and what to do about them.

At the same time that the Van Wert plant problems were about due for some remedial action, the company's Public Relations Division faced the not uncommon problem of demonstrating to skeptics that public relations programs could produce desired results. The director of Public Relations was at that very time examining the various plant locations of Borden's farflung operations in the hope of finding a "typical" community in which a pilot public relations program, designed to ascertain the effectiveness of public relations, might be established.

The director of Public Relations talked over the idea of using Van Wert as a pilot plant with various Borden executives and with the

---

16 Harry D. Wolfe, J. K. Brown, Stephen H. Greenberg, and G. Clark Thompson, *Pretesting Advertising* (New York: National Industrial Conference Board, Inc., 1963), Case No. 6, Business Policy Study No. 109, pp. 83-84. Used by permission.

17 Used by permission of Milton Fairman, Vice President, The Borden Company.

superintendent of the Van Wert plant. The Public Relations Department people said,

> If the Cheese Division will cooperate in a pilot plant operation to the extent of underwriting opinion surveys before and after a program . . . if it will give its active support to the work . . . we will provide trained public relations people necessary to do the job.

The Cheese Division officials, along with the management of the Van Wert plant, agreed to the proposal. Briefly, the plan proposed called for four steps: (1) a "before" opinion-attitude survey to ascertain employee and community attitudes toward the company; (2) the development of a public relations program designed to change unfavorable opinion and to correct causes of friction among employees as ascertained by the survey; (3) the execution of the public relations program for a two-year period; and (4) a second, or "after" survey, to ascertain the effectiveness of the two-year-old public relations program.

The study itself was designed to provide information on how Borden's Van Wert employees felt about their company on a wide range of issues and how the residents of Van Wert felt toward the Borden Company on an equally wide range of issues. In order to insure the proper context in which to analyze the reactions of the community toward Borden's, the study was designed to include five other local employers so that comparisons could be made among the six local organizations, one of which, of course, was Borden's. This tended to avoid pinpointing the sponsor of the survey as Borden's in the minds of the respondents. In all, nine hundred personal interviews were conducted in both the "before" and "after" studies. Seven hundred interviews were obtained from the townspeople of Van Wert. One hundred interviews were obtained from the nearly four hundred Borden employees and a like number of Company X employees (a leading local competitor with an excellent reputation for employee relations policies).

As was expected, the data obtained in the before study was not too favorable toward Borden's Van Wert plant, particularly in comparison with Company X, specially selected for comparison purposes. In response to such questions as "Which of these companies do you feel contributes most to making Van Wert a good city to live and work in?" and "Does your company supply you with various types of information such as: (a) company activities elsewhere, (b) information about products, (c) annual report of operations, (d) company paper or magazine, or (e) bulletin boards on premises?" the Van Wert operation often came out quite poorly. Clearly, remedial action was called for.

Space limitations prohibit us from going into details concerning the public relations program that was developed and implemented in the face of these data obtained in the 1947 "before" survey. We can, however, indicate the activities in brief form.

With respect to *internal* public relations programing, the following were implemented: (1) plant tours for employees, (2) a special employee publication, (3) distribution of the annual report, (4) centralized personnel records, (5) indoctrination program for new employees, (6) a Borden Management Club for Van Wert administrative personnel, and (7) a community relations checklist of activities to engage in regularly for the Van Wert administrative people.

The *external* public relations measures consisted of the following: (1) plant visits by local groups encouraged and arranged, (2) institutional-type ads were run in the local paper frequently, (3) the Midwest public relations office of Borden's arranged special promotional programs when appropriate, (4) a magazine, the *Dairy Digest*, was developed and was sent to all milk producers, (5) both producers and haulers were publicized in the employee publication, (6) a speakers' bureau was developed, (7) an illustrated talk on the plant was developed and made available to the speakers' bureau, (8) locally made cheese was vigorously promoted through groceries and restaurants, (9) many Borden products were demonstrated in local stores, and (10) special publicity was devoted to the amount of local disbursements made by the Van Wert plant.

The "after" survey, based on the same number of respondents consisting of community residents and Borden and Company X employees, was conducted two years later, in 1949. Over-all, the two-year public relations program had been quite effective in improving the standing of the Van Wert operation with employees and community alike. Again, we are limited by space in terms of the amount of detail we can present concerning this case. One major observation can be put forth, however: In comparing the two general objectives of the Van Wert project—*i.e.*, improving the image of Borden's in the community and making Borden employees happier with and prouder of their company—it appears that the first objective had been attained more successfully than the second. That is, the image of Borden's in the community, its acceptance by the citizens of Van Wert, and the realization that Borden's is taking a responsible position in the community had been rather satisfactorily attained. There is still room for improvement, but one can be pleased with this amount of progress in two years. It is in the second area—the employee attitudes area— that less progress had been made, and this is to be expected. On the basis of much that we have considered thus far, we know that it is much more difficult to change the attitudes of individuals who know you best. This suggests that the public relations practitioner himself needs to be very clear about the limitations of certain "standard" public relations program elements—such as forming a management club—in modifying employee attitudes. It is in the area of internal relations that the standard approaches are least likely to be effective; it is here where the creativity of the public relations practitioner is put to the test to devise programs to modify attitudes that are much more "tailor made," so to speak.

4. *A word of warning about the relationship between attitudes and behavior.* The reader should remember that the relationship between attitudes and behavior is never perfect. The fact that attitudes have been used successfully to predict behavior in many, many instances does not obviate the fact that there are also many times when this process fails. Perhaps the simplest way of explaining why attitudes and behavior are not perfectly related is to say that there are many factors which determine a person's behavior and that his attitudes are only a part of the causal picture. Let us take a simple example to illustrate this point.

Suppose that on the basis of prolonged discussion with an individual, we feel that it is safe to conclude that he has rather strong attitudes against segregation—to take an example from a topic with which there is considerable concern today. Let us say for the sake of argument that this same individual participated in the civil rights march on Washington, D.C., in August, 1963, and has done considerable work to bring about desegregation in his own neighborhood. On the basis of these behaviors, one would be permitted to make the generalization that the individual in question had definite antisegregation views. It is perfectly possible, however, that he might also be the type who is quite submissive or passive, particularly in the presence of authority figures (*e.g.*, bosses, parents). With such personality traits, he might not say a word or exhibit any other opposing behavior in the presence of an authority figure who is openly attacking the Negro and denouncing the desegregation movement. In such an instance, our predictions about what our hypothetical individual might do, on the basis of our knowledge of his attitudes toward segregation, could be quite wrong. The reason is simple: His attitudes toward segregation would not be the only factors that would play a role in how he might behave around certain people in particular social situations.

To summarize this section on the use of attitudes as predictors of behavior, what we have been saying is that many factors are involved in producing certain behavior. An individual's attitudes are only part of the picture. Other factors, such as group pressure and personality variables (as in the illustration cited), are but two of a host of variables that could affect how a person will behave. For this reason, the relationship between attitudes and behavior will always be less than a 1 : 1 relationship. From a practical point of view, this means that the public relations practitioner must be cautious in using attitude measures to predict behavior. On the other hand, in proper circumstances, attitude measures as a means of predicting behavior are one of the most powerful tools that the public relations practitioner has in his repertoire to cope with public relations problems. The whole question is one of intelligent use of this short cut to predicting human behavior.

Relationship to Learning

A second property of attitudes worth highlighting is that attitudes are a learned phenomenon. People are not born with attitudes; rather, they learn or acquire certain attitudes as a function of growing up in a particular cultural environment. In the language of the learning theory that we discussed briefly in Chapter 7, attitudes fall in the category of secondary needs in the sense that whatever motive power or contribution that an attitude may make to bringing about certain behavior, it does it in the sense of a secondary need, or learned need.

To some, the obviousness of this statement about attitudes being learned may be so strong as to question why this point needs to be made. The reader may recall that as an introduction to the topic of motivation the point was made that all behavior was caused. This, too, seemed to be an obvious statement. However, we were able then to demonstrate that there are many instances when people react to the behavior of others as if there were no cause for that behavior. The same analogy applies here. It seems obvious to state that attitudes are learned, yet without much difficulty we can begin to find instances where people behave as if attitudes were inborn or unlearned. Let us consider some examples to make this point more clear.

Consider the way that management can come to view the attitudes of workers, particularly rank and file, unskilled, minority group (e.g., Negro) workers, who come predominantly from the lower-class ranks (as distinct from middle-class or upper–middle-class ranks in the case of management). Many management people approach the question of dealing with these employees as if their attitudes toward work were inborn. They come to think of what they call "shiftlessness," "lack of ambition," and the like as attitudes toward work that are essentially inborn or unlearned. By contrast, they think of their own traits—stressing "ambition," "getting ahead," and "making something of yourself"—as an individual achievement. In fact, these two different attitudes toward work—ambition on the one hand and shiftlessness on the other—are learned responses that both categories of persons have developed as a function of living in a particular environment. As elementary as the statement that attitudes are learned may have seemed, this is one of many, many situations where the persons operating within this context behave toward each other as if the attitudes were inborn. In this instance, the attitudes are primarily a function of the socioeconomic class in which one originates.[18]

Perhaps the area where the greatest confusion exists about the origin and effect of attitudes lies in personality development and our everyday assessment of one another's behavior. As we learned in our section on motivation of human beings, by far the greatest proportion of our motives are learned and are a function of the cultural environment in which we live. The same statement, of course, applies to attitudes. One of the factors that makes each one of us unique is our attitudes. The combination of unique needs coupled with the equally unique "package" of attitudes is the very stuff of which personality is made. In the give and take that occurs among human beings, it is the process of one person's way of seeing things (Mason Haire's definition of an attitude) interacting with another person's way of seeing the same thing. But in this interaction, we react to one another as if these attitudes were not learned, as if they were in some unexplained way inborn. It is probably because some of our most enduring and strong attitudes are formed by our parents (or parental surrogates) that attitudes can seem to be inborn. Our reactions to fear or stress, to social situations, or to life in general are in great part molded during our early, formative years. Consequently, just as it has taken us so long to realize that we *learn to see* (and that it is not an inborn ability), so it is that now we must realize that we also learn to react to the world around us. These reactions or ways of viewing the world can be summed up with the word *attitude*.

Why is it so important for us to realize that attitudes are learned? What difference does it make to the public relations practitioner? The

---

[18] This particular point concerning the attitudes of one socioeconomic class toward another and how these attitudes can be viewed by one class as being inborn in the other is, of course, an old idea. In this connection, we are reminded of Allison Davis, in his chapter, "The Motivation of the Underprivileged Worker," (in William F. Whyte [ed.], *Industry and Society* [New York: McGraw-Hill Book Company, 1946], pp. 84-106), who made this point long ago.

difference is likely to come out in the ways in which he deals with and communicates with other individuals. *If, almost without realizing it, a public relations practitioner believes certain behaviors that he observes in another person are inborn, then he is less likely to be able to find ways of enabling the individual to see things differently.* If one is convinced that he is up against an inborn attitude, it will not occur to him that there might be ways of modifying the attitude.

Concerning this point there might be some value in drawing an analogy to another type of inborn *vs.* learned confusion that took place in industry. Early in the twentieth century, industrial psychology books contained chapters on such topics as "Influence of Heredity upon Achievement," and "Family Inheritance."[19] The flavor of the writing contained in such chapters was that characteristics of desirable employees were, by and large, due to inborn causes. The solution for the employer was obvious: hire only those employees with the desirable traits or characteristics. With this approach to understanding human behavior, it is obvious that employee training programs, management training programs, human relations courses, and the like were not likely to be implemented by management. How could they? If one believes that these behaviors are not learned, then there is not much sense in instituting a course to teach these behaviors. It was only in later years, when the industrial psychologist began to place greater stress on what was learned rather than what was inborn, that the climate for the concept of on-the-job training and management training programs came into existence. To continue the analogy, the "climate" necessary for the proper understanding of attitudes is to realize that they are acquired by the individual as a function of living in a particular cultural environment.

RELATIONSHIP TO PERSONALITY

We have already introduced the notion that attitudes and personality are intimately related, in the sense that one of the factors enabling us to distinguish one personality from another is each individual's unique "package" of attitudes.

One of the observations that can be made most readily about any individual (particularly from his early 20's on) is the enduring quality of personality—the sameness of personality—day after day after day. All things being equal, the best prediction that one can make about the

---

[19] H. L. Hollingsworth and A. T. Poffenberger, *Applied Psychology* (New York: Appleton-Century-Crofts, 1917).

personality make-up of an individual is that it will remain remarkably constant. This is due partly to his attitude patterns. Many of our most important attitudes toward religion, sex, minority groups, and so on are formed early in life and remain remarkably unchanged throughout our lives. For this reason, many psychologists utilize attitudes as a way of understanding how the individual attaches meaning to his environment. The reader will recall that in our section on perception the statement was made that there was no such thing as withholding interpretation and attachment of meaning to events going on around us. How one perceives his environment will be partly a function of his attitudes. If one has a strong prejudice against certain minority groups or religious groups, these attitudes will help to shape a lot of different and specific behaviors. These enduring attitudes can serve as anchor points which enable the individual to make sense out of his world. Regardless of how shortsighted or unwarranted an outsider might think these views are, it would be overlooking an essential quality of attitudes to forget that they provide a way of unifying or organizing an individual's reactions to the world in which he lives. An intense anti-Jewish attitude can manifest itself in business, in social contacts, in the clubs we join, in what we read, and in the selection of behavior that we admire and applaud in others. In summary, the different patterns of attitudes that we all possess go a long way in determining our personality structure, how we perceive others, and how others perceive us.

RESISTANCE TO CHANGE

Linking attitudes with enduring personality traits has undoubtedly caused the reader to anticipate the next point to be made about attitudes: They are remarkably resistant to change! One of the discouraging facts of life that all public relations practitioners (or anyone else, for that matter) must face is that it is extremely difficult to change people's attitudes, especially through the means that a public relations practitioner generally has at his disposal—some version of the mass media. But we are getting ahead of ourselves. Let's back up a bit and see why it is that attitudes can be so difficult to change.

Avoidance or withdrawal. One reason that attitudes can be difficult to change is that individuals engage in a variety of practices that, in effect, *insulate* them from factors that might change their attitudes. One insulating factor is just simple avoidance or withdrawal. Thus, an individual who objects to classical music practically never lets himself become exposed to this type of music. He avoids concerts, and is very selective of the radio stations to which he listens, and can therefore hardly ever be exposed to anything that might cause him to re-evaluate his attitudes toward this type of music. This generalization can be extended to literally all sorts of experiences, but the principle is the same: One way to avoid conflicting views is just not to expose yourself to them!

This avoidance tendency that we all have to a greater or lesser extent represents one of the most exasperating and formidable hurdles that *any* communicator has, especially the public relations practitioner. A great deal of what a religious leader has to say never reaches the very people that he wishes to influence most—those who never go to church. The target audience of anyone interested in a strong, active, democratic form of government consists of the very individuals who never vote, who never support a political candidate, and who never take any action whatsoever as a private citizen, such as writing congressmen or some equivalent participant action.

Perhaps without his fully realizing it, many of the things that a public relations practitioner does to solve his public relations problems consist of trying to overcome this form of insulation. A number of the practices that we take so much for granted and identify as "standard" components of a typical public relations program are, in effect, efforts to break through this insulation of a particular public. A plant tour or open house, (either when it is first tried, or a thousand tours later) represents an effort to involve certain individuals who might never pay any attention to that particular company under normal circumstances. A company publication designed with the worker's family in mind (and perhaps mailed directly to the home) is also an example of an effort to reach an audience that heretofore had not been reached. And lastly, the public relations practitioner responsible for developing an inexpensive but high quality record of the "sounds of the campus," sent to alumni, represents an effort to be different in order to reach certain individuals who had avoided (and thereby insulated themselves from) the previous attempts to garner alumni support and interest.

Perceptual selectivity. Another closely related form of insulation is one that psychologists often call *perceptual selectivity.* We learned earlier (Chapter 7) that perceptions are functionally selective, meaning that we select and attend to some features of the environment around us and avoid others. It means that what we read, what we listen to, the programs we watch on TV, the social circles in which we travel, all tend to be subjected to a *filtering* process. Such filtering, employed by each one of us, means that we attend to only what we want to hear and see, and thus avoid being exposed to contrary views. This filtering process can be employed so that one does not have to withdraw himself physically from any particular activity or event with which he does not agree. Filtering, selecting out certain portions of the experience and ignoring or "forgetting" other portions, accomplishes the same purpose.

With this selectivity we can emphasize the philanthropic behavior of a well-known businessman and ignore the fact that the money which enables him to be generous has come from cheating and taking advantage of others in shrewd business deals. Likewise, we can be charmed by the polite behavior of a host who travels in the best country club set and "forget" the fact that this same individual is extremely and actively prejudiced toward a number of minority groups. It should also be added that this perceptual selectivity is not always undesirable, as these two examples imply. At times this selectivity is a positive and desirable process as well. For example, most of us tend to ignore certain traits of close friends and loved ones which are quite offensive in someone that we do not like. In such instances, we are "accentuating the positive," to borrow a phrase from a popular song of a few years ago, and filtering out what is less desirable.

Whether the filtering is desirable or undesirable, the fact is that this form of attitude preservation is another difficult process within individuals with which a public relations practitioner has to deal. The reason that the perceptual selectivity is so difficult to cope with is that it is so easy to filter out what one does not want to see or hear. If the public relations practitioner is trying to reach the recipient with some particular message, especially one that he does not want to receive, the filtering process can take place readily and the communication effort fail to "reach" the intended recipient.

Recognition of the powerful role that perceptual selectivity plays is generally implicit in most treatments of persuasion through propaganda.[20] For example, most guides to how to be more effective in persuasive efforts contain such items as (1) be sure that you appeal to the needs (*i.e.*, the motives or drives) of your respondent; (2) be sure to use arguments that fit, as much as possible, the existing attitudes of your recipient; and (3) be sure that you take into consideration the needs of the group(s) with which your intended recipient identifies and belongs. All three of these "guides for the propagandist" can be reinterpreted in terms of the perceptual selectivity process under discus-

[20] The reader will perhaps recall that, in Chapter 9, when we were discussing the overemphasis on information associated with the message stage, the point was made that one of the really difficult tasks facing the public relations practitioner is to motivate his recipient to pay attention to what he has to say. One reason for the need to motivate is to overcome the perceptual selectivity that we are discussing in this section.

sion. These guides are assuming that if you dovetail with the motives of your recipient and his reference groups (guides 1 and 3) and understand what his existing attitudes or prejudices are (guide 2), then you are *least likely* to have your messages filtered out. Or, to put it another way, you will be more likely to get the opportunity to have an impact upon your intended recipient. Selective perception has the effect of not letting your point of view (as a sender) see the light of day, so to speak.

As in the case of withdrawal or physical avoidance, the public relations practitioner has long been devising methods to cope with selective perception, once again sometimes without even realizing what he has been doing. In proxy fights, each side attempts to persuade stockholders that it will be able to manage the corporation more effectively than the other and in the long run produce the greater profits. Implicit in this approach is the assumption that the typical stockholder is motivated to make money so that communication designed to dovetail with this motivation will be responded to most strongly and at the same time will be subjected to less filtering or selective perception.

By the same token, those responsible for dealing with employees are quick to stress that the desire for money plays less of a motivating role than is often assumed and can cause a communicator to overlook the employee's desire to be informed. An implicit assumption behind any employee newspaper or magazine is that the employee is motivated to learn something about the company and its plans and policies. Consequently, the content of an employee publication places some of its hopes on "getting by" the filtering process by writing stories that have the interest of the employee in mind, stories that will make the employee feel he is a part of the organization and that management cares enough about his being informed to take the trouble to communicate.

It might be mentioned here that the ability of publc relations practitioners to bypass the filtering processes and in fact have an effect on his intended recipient is sometimes blown up all out of proportion to the truth of the matter. It is the public relations practitioner of Machiavellian character with powerful tools of unsuspected dimensions whom we read about from time to time. This potential to control people is one of the most objected-to features of the public relations practitioner. The fact of the matter is that the power to persuade is far less than most practicing public relations practitioners would like. If we had only a fraction of the power attributed to us, we would be quite successful indeed. The fact is that we are still very much in the dark about how to change attitudes to the degree that we would like and to the degree some problems call for. If we were more powerful, we would not have such problems as voter apathy, lack of interest in international affairs, lack of interest in combating juvenile delinquency, in alcoholism, and in a host of other problems, all of which require a change in people's attitudes and behavior.

An interesting reflection of the power that is sometimes attributed to the public relations practitioner is reflected partly by a very cleverly written booklet, produced by the AFL-CIO, called "Look Out." The booklet is designed to warn employees that management will try to persuade them by using devices to bypass the filtering that we have been talking about.

1. *Look Out for Love Letters* from the boss. . . . For the very first time since you began to work for the company, the boss may start sending letters to your home. From these letters, designed to be read by both you and your family, you will learn for the first time how "deeply concerned" he is about your welfare. . . .

Did you know that the boss has always maintained an "open door" policy? Did you know that any time you had a grievance or felt any dissatisfaction about wages, hours, or any other part of your working conditions, all you had to do was pay him a little visit to talk it over? Well, if you haven't been aware of all this, the love letters will make it clear to you.

2. *Look Out for Rumors* spread by foremen and supervisors. You may hear that raises are coming, "if only that union doesn't get in." You'll hear that the boss knows whom he can "trust" and who is a "union sympathizer." You will hear that those who are backing the union have always been troublemakers who have never carried their share of the work. . . .

3. *Look Out for Special Meetings Called by the Boss.* The best name for these meetings is "captive audience meetings." They'll be held on company time and will feature a homey chat from the boss himself. It may be the first time he's ever felt moved to call you together that way—at his expense—but he'll do it now, because he feels that it is so important that you know the "facts of life" or "understand" his problems. He'll remind you of all he and the company have done for you and your community; he'll tell you that you and the company are partners in a great enterprise and that you will make progress together. But he'll sadly inform you that there won't be any more "togetherness" if you decide to join that "outside" union.

He may read from a printed statement to be sure that he doesn't get too excited—say what he really means, and thus violate the law. If you listen to the words of the speech carefully, you will realize that he isn't

actually saying that he will fire anyone, or close down the company if
the union wins, but you and your fellow workers won't have any trouble
getting his "message."[21]

Self-perpetuation.   A third form of insulation that tends to maintain attitudes is the reinforcement that the individual contributes to
his own attitude structure. Each new experience, because of the selectivity process (aided by the avoidance noted earlier), is likely to make
one's attitudes even stronger. A person who believes that Jews are
shrewd and not to be trusted in business dealings is likely to select
out of his experiences with Jews the factors that tend to strengthen
his attitudes against them. In this way, each one of us is more likely
than not to continue to add to the strength of an attitude over time.

Another part of this self-perpetuation is that every event that occurs
in the world around us needs to be interpreted. One thing we are sure
of is that "facts do *not* speak for themselves." A fact or, in other words,
an event taking place in the world around us does not dictate how it
shall be interpreted. Rather, it is the individual perceiver who interprets what goes on around him. This "making sense out of the world"
is the process that we discussed in our section on perception. This
"making sense" means that we reinterpret events to be consistent with
our attitudes. At times, this "making sense" literally means that we
twist reality around to fit what we believe to be reality. Sometimes this
reinterpretation is or borders on the pathological, it is so extreme. Most
of the time, it is far less extreme, and the modification that we make of
the experiences we have is much more slight. Extreme or slight, however, the effect is a self-perpetuation of the attitudes that we have.

Perhaps some illustrations may make this more concrete. Take the
paranoid personality as an example of the extreme reinterpretation of
the environment. Characteristically, the paranoid individual is suspi-
cious of nearly everyone about him. He tends to have delusions (the
specifics of which will vary from individual to individual, of course)
that someone or something (or both) is "out to get him." Suppose a
paranoid is walking down the street. He looks behind him and he sees
someone "following him." He turns the corner and this person turns the
corner. He crosses the street and this same person crosses the street.
After a few more events such as this, the paranoid might go running
into the police station yelling that someone is going to kill him. In

---

[21] Quoted in William L. Safire, *The Relations Explosion* (New York: The Macmillan Company, 1963), pp. 171-172. (NOTE. The quote in Safire's book is taken
from an AFL-CIO booklet entitled "Look Out." No further information is provided, such as date and origin of publication.) Used by permission.

talking with such an individual, it might be almost impossible to point out that the person who was "following him" happened to be an individual that was going to the same department store the paranoid was going to. The "sinister" individual "stalking his quarry" was, in fact, a perfect stranger, and the affair was merely a coincidence.

This admittedly extreme example of reinterpretation of events to which an individual is subjected illustrates the process that we are talking about here: Events can be reinterpreted to fit existing attitude structures and thereby contribute to their strength.

A less extreme example of this reinterpretation is illustrated in the work of Cooper and Jahoda on how prejudiced people can evade communications directed toward them and thereby perpetuate their prejudiced attitudes.

Mr. Biggott Interprets Propaganda

Cooper and Jahoda, at the Bureau of Applied Social Research of Columbia University, undertook to answer the question of what happens to a prejudiced person when he is involuntarily confronted with anti-prejudice propaganda.

In these studies prejudiced people were presented with a series of cartoons lampooning a character named "Mr. Biggott," who was depicted as holding the same prejudices as the subject. The producers of the cartoon assumed that the prejudiced person would perceive that Mr. Biggott's ideas were similar to his own; that Mr. Biggott was an absurd character; and that therefore, the subject would reject or at least begin to question his own prejudices in order to avoid identifying himself with the absurd Mr. Biggott. But the study showed quite different results from what the cartoonist had hoped for.

In one cartoon Mr. Biggott is shown lying in a hospital bed and saying to the doctor that he wants only "sixth-generation American blood" for his blood transfusion. This cartoon was shown to anti-Semitic subjects and then they were interviewed and asked what they thought of Mr. Biggott and his attitudes. One of the subjects said that obviously Mr. Biggott was a socially inferior person, and that one who was *only a sixth-generation American* had no right to pretensions! In this way the point of the cartoon was reinterpreted to deal with snobbishness rather than with prejudice, and thus the subject's own absurd racial prejudices remained unaffected by the absurd Mr. Biggott.[22]

Both of these examples, an extreme one and a less extreme example,

[22] E. Cooper and M. Jahoda, "The Evasion of Propaganda: How Prejudiced People Respond to Anti-Prejudice Propaganda," *Journal of Psychology*, XXIII, 15-25, as quoted in Krech and Crutchfield, *op. cit.*, p. 680. Used by permission.

illustrate the self-perpetuation process that all attitudes can undergo. Naturally, not all attitudes are insulated to the degree that these examples illustrate; however, the two degrees of extremeness were selected to illustrate the process. To a lesser extent, this reinterpretation of the world around us, resulting in self-perpetuation of attitudes, is going on all the time. Hence, the inclusion of this factor as another form of the insulation of attitudes to change.

This third insulating factor, along with the others already discussed, can also operate counter to the communication objectives of the public relations practitioner. To some extent, the average public relations practitioner has been less well equipped to cope with this factor than with the other two. The communication techniques intuitively devised by public relations practitioners to reach certain publics happen to cope with the insulating factor we discussed first (avoidance or withdrawal) better than this last one. The reason is probably that to cope with self-perpetuation one needs to know the attitudes of the recipient and have some data on just how he reinterprets experiences common to both the public relations practitioner (as sender) and the recipient. Just as the researchers in the Mr. Biggott example cited above were surprised to find that the resistance to propaganda against racial prejudice took a different turn than they had expected, so it is that time and time again a public relations practitioner's communication efforts are reacted to differently than he had planned. The trouble is that many public relations practitioners never do any research and find out what has happened to their communication efforts. This third insulating factor highlights the importance of knowing how your intended recipient views things *before* efforts are made to change his attitudes.

SOME CONCEPTS RELATED TO ATTITUDE

A number of concepts closely related to the concept of attitudes are to be found in the social science literature. Now that we have examined the concept of attitude in some detail, let us turn to these related concepts.

Attitude and "Frame of Reference"

One concept related to the concept of attitude is *frame of reference*. This concept is also related to the distinction in Gestalt psychology of figure and ground, which we first encountered in our examination of perception.

Frame of reference is defined slightly differently by different writers, but the following is more or less typical.

It is a psychological truism that stimuli do not have an absolute stimulating value. The stimulus is perceived and responded to in relation to other stimuli to which it is functionally related, whether these other stimuli are present in physical fact or have been experienced in the past. For example, a line may be experienced as either horizontal or vertical, depending on its relationship to the position of other stimuli in the stimulus field. If the visual stimulus field is slated by the use of a mirror, the object slanted in the same direction appears vertical, indicating that the position of the object is perceived in its relation to the field as a whole.

The shifts in meaning that accompany changes in the context of words have direct parallels in laboratory studies of judgment. In psycho-physical experiments requiring the judgment of lifted weights as "light," "heavy," and so on, it was found that the judgment of the weight of any one unit in the series was a function of the whole series. A unit that might be judged "light" in a heavy series was judged "heavy" in a light series.[23]

.   .   .   .   .   .

Social attitudes are often thought of as a frame of reference structuring the social field. The reader will remember that we use the term frame of reference "to denote the functionally related factors (both present and past) which operate at the moment to determine the particular properties of a psychological phenomenon (perception, judgment, affectivity, etc.)." . . . This general definition, originally offered by Sherif and Cantril, has been modified through loose usage in the field of attitude study so that "frame of reference" has largely come to be identified with the general structuring that the individual tends to impose on a social field.

The "frame of reference" is used, therefore, on the one hand to refer to an orientation of the individual, to those tendencies which cause him to structure his perceptions of a situation in a particular way; and on the other hand, it is also used to describe his general structuring of a situation, the context he provides for a particular observation. This dual use of the term represents its application in both attitude and opinion study. The attitudinal frame of reference is inferred from the expressed frames of reference.[24]

It should be clear to the reader by now why the concept of frame of

---

[23] Hartley and Hartley, pp. 124-125.
[24] *Ibid.*, p. 661.

reference was brought up in connection with the concept of attitude. The main reason is that the public relations practitioner should be aware that many people use the concept of frame of reference almost interchangeably with the concept of attitude. Thus, some people will say that such and such an individual interpreted things as he did because he had a certain frame of reference with respect to politics or to labor relations. In so doing, this usage is almost exactly the same as another individual who says that the behavior of a particular individual in a certain situation was due to his attitude toward politics or labor relations. In both instances, the two concepts—attitude and frame of reference—are supposedly employed to make the behavior of a single individual or a group of individuals more understandable. When the concept of frame of reference is used in this way, it takes on most, if not all, of the same properties of the concept of attitude. That is, such things as being an inferred concept, learned by the individual as a function of growing up in a particular culture, and so on.

Perhaps the main point to be stressed about these overlapping concepts is that either one requires the public relations practitioner to be careful of how the terms are used. Both concepts *can* be useful to help the public relations practitioner better · nderstand the behavior of the recipient. For them to be helpful, however, care must be taken to be as precise as possible concerning what behavior is being used to infer the existence of either concept with respect to a recipient.

Attitude and Stereotype

When we were learning introductory concepts in the area of perception, a fundamental point was made that the world in which we all live is organized by each one of us in a different way and in a meaningful way. Certain aspects of the world around us may be reacted to (and summarized) in a comparatively rigid and oversimplified way. Examples are the rather common, everyday generalizations such as fat people are jolly and professors are impractical and are not able to handle ordinary, daily problems in life. To such perceptions, we sometimes apply the concept of *stereotype*. Krech and Crutchfield define stereotype as follows:

> Stereotype may refer to two related phenomena. As a sociological and statistical concept it refers to a belief or attitude which is widespread in a society (e.g., the belief that blondes are less intellectual than brunettes.) As a psychological concept it refers to a belief or attitude

which is oversimplified in content, in which the unique attributes of the object are not observed, and which is resistant to change.[25]

It is obvious from this definition why we must consider the concept of stereotype in a discussion of attitude. (The word *belief* is included in the definition and is used, under certain conditions, as synonymous with the word *attitude*.) The public relations practitioner must be prepared to encounter this overlap and understand that a stereotype is generally seen as an attitude that a person (or group) holds, the main characteristics of which are that it is rather rigidly held and usually is not based on factors that can be objectively agreed on by unbiased observers.

The feature of bias in a stereotype is probably the most characteristic aspect of this concept. Normally, when we use the word *stereotype*, we do so to connote the unfavorable (or, at least, incorrect) attitudes that an individual or group possesses toward some other person or thing. The public relations practitioner should keep in mind, however, that the word itself is like the word *propaganda*. When we use the word *propaganda*, we normally do so in a negative context or sense. However, the word itself merely refers to the efforts of one individual or group to influence another individual or group. Propaganda can be correctly applied to the efforts of a teacher to inform his class, although we usually do not think of the term in this context. So it is with the word stereotype. As a concept, it merely refers to the fact that certain portions of our world are organized in such a way so as to be less responsive to the "facts" of that world (*i.e.*, less responsive to characteristics that might be agreed on by more than one independent observer). Hence, stereotypes are not good or bad; they are generally just inaccurate perceptions or attitudes based on inaccurate information.[26]

---

[25] Krech and Crutchfield, p. 694.

[26] In this context, the word *prejudice* also comes to mind and is related to this discussion. *Prejudice* is another word for describing the way an individual has organized some aspect of the world around him. Thus, an individual prejudiced against Negroes generally believes certain things about Negroes that are untrue. It is just as easy to be prejudiced toward events in the world about which society may not be upset. An individual may hold very definite prejudices about sports (*i.e.*, hold views that are, in fact, inaccurate), about certain products, medicines, foods, and the like. In spite of this, however, we tend to stress the negative aspects when we use the word *prejudice*, as is being brought out with the concept of stereotype.

THE CONCEPT OF ATTITUDE—A SUMMARY

By now we have devoted a considerable number of words to the concept of attitude. Before going on in Chapter 13 to sociological concepts that are useful to the public relations practitioner, let us summarize what we have said thus far:

1. The concept of attitude was presented as one that is very useful to the psychologist in helping him understand human behavior. As a concept, it reflects the emphasis on the dynamics of a single individual as a means of understanding all individuals. This, we noted, was the unique approach of the psychologist, as contrasted with the sociologist.

2. We noted that attitudes are inferred and that we never view an attitude directly. For this reason, the process of inferring attitudes must be used with caution, and the public relations practitioner must be continually aware of this fact so that incorrect inferences can be avoided.

3. A number of properties of attitudes were discussed, but perhaps the most important one was the relationship between attitude and behavior. Considerable time was devoted to this relationship with illustrations from a variety of sources of how attitude measures have been used to predict behavior. Although the point was stressed that there is no simple relationship between attitude and behavior, the generalization was made that this property of attitude was a most useful one to the public relations practitioner. In fact, it is this property of attitude that guided the author to select this particular concept for elaboration as an illustration of a psychological concept used to understand human behavior.

4. The dilemma of resistance to change—another outstanding property of attitudes—was also examined in some detail. Particular emphasis was placed on the various "insulating" processes that can occur to make attitudes difficult to change.

5. Lastly, the relationship of the concept of attitude to a number of other very common concepts, such as stereotype, for example, was examined.

With this brief summary we are now ready to examine concepts that are illustrative of the sociological approach to understanding human behavior and are extremely useful to the public relations practitioner.

QUESTIONS FOR DISCUSSION

1. From whatever sources you have available to you, make a list of all of the psychological and sociological concepts (such as attitude, stereotype, reference groups, etc.) that you can find which have some bearing on public relations problems and/or practice.

   Which list is longer, the psychological concept list or the sociological concept list? Which type of concept did you have more difficulty with in terms of relating it to public relations practice? After having developed your list, are you in agreement with the contention made on pages 318-322 that sociological-type concepts are less well understood and used by people in general and by public relations practitioners in particular?

2. With one or two friends or acquaintances in mind, make a list of some of the attitudes that you have inferred they have. For each attitude listed, indicate the basis on which you have made this inference. In other words, what behavior did you use to infer the presence of a given attitude?

   Now that you have your list, how justified do you feel about the inferences you have made? Are all of the inferences equally well supported by observable behavior on which they are presumably based? Are there any attitudes in your list for which you had difficulty identifying the behavior upon which they are based?

3. Obtain one or two examples of relationships between attitudes and behavior along the lines of the examples provided in pages 329-340. That is, obtain your own illustration(s) of how attitudes were used to understand or predict behavior in some applied situation. Were examples easy or difficult to find? Did you find many examples of the use of attitude measures to deal more effectively with a public relations problem? Were the warnings listed on pages 339-340, with respect to the use of attitudes as a measure of or predictor of behavior, adhered to in your examples?

4. Which "resistance to change" category (with respect to changing attitudes) do you think a public relations practitioner encounters most often? Why? Which one do you think is the most difficult to cope with in public relations problem situations? Why?

Chapter 13

THE RECIPIENT STAGE IN FURTHER DETAIL: CONCEPTS OF FORMAL AND INFORMAL STRUCTURE

INTRODUCTION

In Chapter 12 the distinction between the psychological and the sociological approaches to understanding human behavior was introduced and examples of each examined. Following this, an illustration of the psychological approach to understanding behavior, the concept of attitude, was examined in some detail. All the way through this presentation, the relationship or usefulness of the concept of attitude to public relations was pointed out.

We are now ready to examine the sociological approach in more detail, utilizing the pair of concepts known as *formal* and *informal* structure. As in the case of the concept of attitude, we have selected these two related concepts with two main purposes in mind: (1) they illustrate rather well the sociological approach to understanding human behavior, and (2) they are concepts which are quite useful to the public relations practitioner in his efforts to understand the recipient more adequately.

FORMAL AND INFORMAL STRUCTURE

A simple but fundamental observation that can be made of individuals interacting with one another is that in certain circumstances these relationships are rather carefully defined and controlled, whereas in other circumstances they are much looser and, on the surface at least, are not as completely defined and controlled. Sociologists distinguish between these two broadly different ways of interacting with two concepts: *formal* and *informal structure.*

Quite simply, the term *formal structure* refers to the explicit system of rules and regulations that govern the behaviors, goals, powers, and responsibilities of individuals functioning within a particular organization. This definition means that when the sociologist turns his attention to the formal structure of an organization, he is interested in how the organization conducts its work and achieves its goals regardless of whether the work and goals are in a profit-making context or a non-profit-making one. In short, the concept of formal organization is applicable to *any* organization. All that is required are people working together in some organizational set-up.

By contrast, *informal structure* refers to all of the rules and regulations *that are not explicit,* but implicit. That is, informal structure refers to all of the almost countless ways in which formal structure is modified when put into actual practice. Informal structure includes all of the friendship ties, cliques, and "in-group" *vs.* "out-group" relationships that inevitably build up within any formal organization. The word *implicit* was used here because seldom, if ever, can one find the informal relationships spelled out on paper or readily articulated by any member of the organization. The concept of informal structure takes cognizance of the fact that people, being human, never function according to some static organization chart, but rather that modifications are constantly taking place. Informal structure recognizes the dynamic, ever-changing nature of individuals interacting together, be it in a family, a factory, or a fraternal organization.

For purposes of study and analysis of human behavior, it is useful to make a distinction between formal and informal structure within an organization. However, it should be remembered that the two categories shade imperceptibly one into the other because the two types of structure distinctions are describing different behavioral aspects of the same people. To express it another way, the individual who appears as the president or plant manager on the formal organizational chart is also a part of the web of friendship ties, cliques, and the like that go to make up the informal organization. This point is nicely demonstrated by Figure 22.[1]

In Figure 22, we see in the upper portion a "idealized" or "typical" organizational chart describing the formal organization of a factory. In the lower portion of the figure is a "sociogram" (*i.e.*, a diagram depicting the interactions among individuals in a group) which illustrates the contacts among the persons who occupy the boxes of the formal organization chart. In the sociogram we see that certain people eat lunch together (*e.g.*, top management and managers and superintendent), while other groupings of individuals (*e.g.*, clerical office workers) lunch together, are in the same car pool, and join one another for recreational purposes. Figure 22 helps to keep clear the fact that the concepts of formal and informal structure applied to organizations provide a means of analyzing the things that people have to do and ought to do (the formal structure) with what people actually and eventually do (the informal structure). In some instances, there is much discrepancy between the two; in others, very little; and in still other cases, the actual behavior lies somewhere in between.

Some Additional Properties of Formal Structure[2]

Organization charts are based on two assumptions or ideas with respect to administrating groups of people: *rationality* and *discipline*. Rationality comes into the organization chart because the very existence of a chart implies that there are some ways that are better than others to administer an organization such that its goals are attained. Thus, having a certain number of top management slots (depicted by the boxes in the organizational chart) with responsibilities for sales, accounting, manufacturing, and such assumes that this is more efficient than having other organizational breakdowns. To be sure, in many instances those responsible for making organizational changes have empirical evidence (*e.g.*, profits take a marked drop; sales are off; internal frictions and problems resulting in turnover increase) to guide them in their decisions as to how or how not to develop an organization.

---

[1] Delbert C. Miller and William H. Form, *Industrial Sociology* (New York: Harper & Row, Publishers, 1951), p. 151. Copyright 1951 by Harper & Brothers. All material reprinted by permission of Harper & Row, Publishers.

[2] This section and the next, dealing with additional properties of informal structure, are adapted from Leonard Broom and Philip Selznick, *Sociology* (New York: Harper & Row, Publishers, 1963), pp. 218-230. Copyright © 1955, 1958, 1963 by Harper & Row, Publishers. Reprinted with their permission.

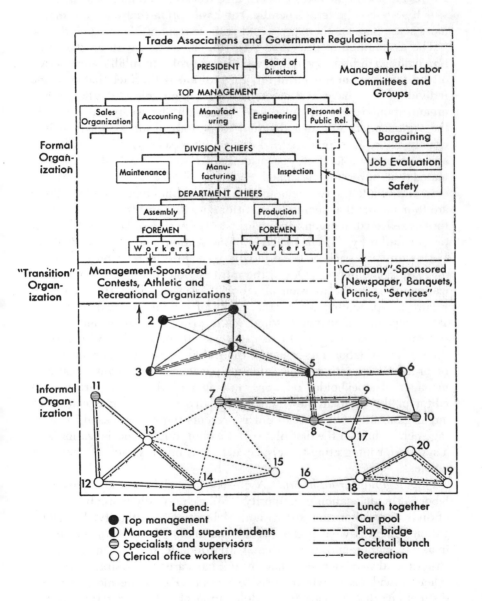

Figure 22

The Formal and Informal Structure of Management

However, seldom, if ever, is there any research conducted to find out which system is better. Generally, the *assumption* that one way makes more sense than another is enough for those responsible for such things.

The assumption of discipline arises in connection with an organization chart as different people have different roles to fulfill as a function of the jobs they are given to do. In addition is the fact that any one individual may have a number of overlapping roles to fulfill in the organization. Hence the everyday expression "he wears two hats" in the organization. For an individual to perform a job assigned to him exactly as he is supposed to do it requires self-discipline. Like the assumption of rationality, self-discipline is something that is approximated but never fully attained.

In addition to the two assumptions of rationality and discipline, there are four factors that should be mentioned with respect to formal structure as reflected in organization charts: (1) division of labor, (2) delegation of authority, (3) channeled communication, and (4) coordination. Let us examine each of these factors in a little more detail.

1. Division of labor.   One of the most obvious features of any organization chart is the division of labor that every chart represents. In Figure 22 (page 359) we see that some of the larger breakdowns are sales, accounting, manufacturing, engineering, personnel, and public relations. Within each of these categories there is, of course, further subdivision of labor. For example, the public relations department may be broken down into subunits such as manager of community relations, manager of stockholder relations, manager of the news bureau, and editor of the company newspaper. This division of labor is central to any organization chart because it represents the major reason for having such a chart in the first place: the assumption of specialization and a system for integrating these specializations into a smoothly operating whole.

2. Delegation of authority.   A closely related feature of division of labor is the delegation of authority. In fact, no really workable system of division of labor can exist without delegation of authority. This delegation system is what highlights the *hierarchy of authority* that exists in any formal organization system. Consequently, formal organizational structure always defines what individuals are responsible for what other individuals or who reports to whom. One of the most common distinctions that is made in the delegation of authority is the one between *line* and *staff*. The *line* organization describes those who are presumably charged with the responsibility of getting the work done. Of course, the larger the organization the longer the line of authority, but the principle is the same: The succeeding members of the line organization are there to help the top man achieve the goals of the organization regardless of what those goals may be. The *staff* organization consists of the many specialists who are essential to making an organization function but who are not directly connected with production. For example, those responsible for personnel, research, and maintaining financial records are staff personnel who are responsible to some particular segment of the line organization in any formal organizational structure.

3. *Channeled communication.* This aspect of the formal structure of an organization perhaps best illustrates the two assumptions of rationality and discipline discussed earlier. Every formal organizational chart has built into it an assumed communication system, generally referred to as "through channels." Of all of the discrepancies between the "ideal" and the "actual," the greatest number probably belong in this particular element of formal structure. Therefore, as nearly everyone knows, although certain persons are supposed to be communicated with for certain problems or operating situations, this feature of a formal organizational chart is ignored most often. This is probably the reason that the communication patterns (and malfunctions) represent one of the most frequently studied aspects of formal organizations.[3]

---

[3] Apropos of this generalization is the following:

The individual employee who obstructs the flow of communication for personal reasons is an important cause of internal communication problems in large organizations, according to Opinion Research Corporation, Princeton, N.J. . . .

In a gathering of the findings on corporate communications problems in 17 companies, the following types of personal obstruction were found:

"Gate Keeping": The second in command in an organizational unit frequently serves as a filter through which communications must pass before they reach the person in charge. Although the system frequently is effective, it may result in a situation in which the "gate keeper" only communicates to his superior what he thinks he wants to hear. In such cases the head of the unit may operate with a distorted view of reality.

Information as a Status Symbol: Managers and other supervisory personnel have been found to scrupulously guard "top secret" information, since sharing it with subordinates would in effect raise them to equal status. In other cases, a superior may release just enough information to enhance his importance, but not enough to communicate effectively.

Withholding Information for Personal Advantage: This has been found to occur when two rivals are competing for a higher job and keep information to themselves because of what they perceive to be the positive effect on their reputation or the negative effect on the rival's reputation.

Unapproachability: Because of temperament, ignorance, or inadvertence, a manager may behave in such a way as to discourage subordinates from approaching him. In other cases a manager may be available to employees but insists on talking rather than listening, thereby inhibiting upward communication flow.

Buck Passing: This often is related to the desire of a manager to make himself and his department look good, even at the expense of others. Such a situation typically occurs when management undertakes to reduce costs and asks

Regardless of the difficulties in *prescribing* communication, another function of a formal organization chart is that it spells out the routes that communications are supposed to take within a given organization.[4]

4. Coordination. A fourth property of the concept of formal structure is coordination. We saw earlier that an organization chart reflects the division of labor and its inevitable specialization within an organization. For the benefits of specialization to materialize, there must also be provision within a formal organization for coordination so that there is unity of purpose and the various units within an organization are able to function as an integrated whole. This is what is implied with the category of coordination. There must be, at every administrative level within an organization, people who weigh recommendations from subordinates and decide what should be done next. They must resolve the conflicts that are inevitable when people are brought together. Lastly, they must establish policies that will serve as guide lines to behavior of the individuals within an organization.

One further point should be brought out at this time, and it is associated with the word *bureaucracy.* In our everyday language (and this is also reflected in dictionary definitions), we tend to use *bureaucracy* to refer to much of what has been described earlier under the heading of *formal structure.* In this sense, certain connotations of the two terms are overlapping and, in certain circumstances, might be used interchangeably. However, social scientists do not define bureaucracy in negative terms—or positive, for that matter. That is, the word is not used to de-

---

the co-operation of all departments. Instead, a manager may cover up his departmental deficiencies and suggest deficiencies in areas outside his province.

Departmental Rivalry: This may result from differences between department heads, from the barriers that increasing specialization of departments may produce, or for other reasons. No matter what the cause, communication is impaired.

Used by permission of *Communications Reports,* August, 1963 (Enterprise Publications, 20 North Wacker Drive, Chicago, Illinois 60606), pp. 2-3.

[4] Perhaps the most common exceptions to the *prescribed* communication patterns are those modifications in the communication process that occur when a subordinate is communicating with his superior. In order for an organization to function smoothly and efficiently, we expect the subordinate at whatever level to inform his superior about the problem situations as they arise so that the superior can be prepared to act. Also, he is then in a better position to report to his own superior. What all too often happens is that the subordinate *filters out* the unpleasant information (and tries to correct the problem himself) and tends to stress the pleasant or positive information. One result of such filtering is that the farther one goes up the organizational chart, the more removed he may become from the problems that actually exist. This filtering process can actually make a top level officer a "prisoner" of such incomplete information. In some situations, if other means of obtaining this information are not provided, serious problems can develop within the organization and top people can be dangerously ignorant of the extent of the difficulties.

scribe any undesirable features of formal systems that can occur, such as rigidity in handling problems or the unnecessary "red tape" or paperwork that can develop.

Normally, social scientists reserve the term *bureaucracy* to embrace the functioning of *administrative officials* (and excluding nonsupervisory workers and members of trade unions) within an organization. This means that from the point of view of the social scientist, *all* features of administrative personnel in action would be included under this heading, embracing what might be desirable as well as undesirable behaviors. One further point: Formal structure normally covers the behavior of all of the individuals within an organization. The word *bureaucracy*—from the standpoint of the social scientist—narrows the focus to administrative people, as was noted earlier.

This is not to say, of course, that social scientists are unaware of or insensitive to the lack of initiative, the inefficiencies, and the like that *can* occur in any organization. An understanding of formal structure and the study of formal structure include both positive and negative by-products that occur when individuals—particularly large numbers of individuals—group together in organizations, regardless of their nature.[5]

Some Additional Properties of Informal Structure

As can be readily understood, the rules or dictates that are embodied in formal structure cannot begin to account for all of the patterns of behavior that can be observed within any organization. One could not account for all of the behavior patterns that he would observe in a given organization by referring to the formal structure—or organizational chart—of a company, a welfare agency, a governmental department, or a university. There are patterns of behavior that develop because of the interaction of many different personalities and work situations. There are many problem situations for which there is no formal solution or provision for action. Some problems are persistent and constantly recurring; still others are the "one of a kind" variety. The problems that must be faced and handled account for the additional properties of informal structure that should be considered at this time. They are (1) impersonality of the formal system, (2) lag of the formal

---

[5] At this point, the reader is encouraged to read C. Northcote Parkinson's delightful book, *Parkinson's Law,* if he has not already done so. This volume contains one of the most incisive yet humorous discussions of the negative features of bureaucracies or formal organizational structures that are possible (and do occur) after many years.

system, (3) generality of the formal system, and (4) personal problems and interests.

1. Impersonality of the formal system. Formal organization charts provide for the system of rules and prescribed roles or behaviors of the individuals who eventually become a part of the formal structure. However, we are now well aware that to make the system or organization work, the impersonality of the formal structure must be replaced by the warmth and understanding that is a part of the informal structure. We try to learn something about the likes and the dislikes of the people who fill a particular "box" in an organization chart. Wherever possible, we use the personal, face-to-face approach to overcome the feeling that this is a "big, impersonal organization" where people are just payroll numbers instead of individuals. Experiences from organizations in action, with very carefully spelled out organizational charts—the military is the best example of this—have taught us that.efforts must constantly be made by supervisory people to overcome the impersonal effects of large units of men in the army, navy or what have you. Such vital but difficult to measure aspects of military outfits, identified by words and phrases such as "morale" or "pride in one's outfit," were attained only in units that had leadership which was aware of the impersonal characteristic of formal organizational structure and sensitive to the need for supplementing that formal structure with personal contacts and considerations.

2. Lag of the formal system. Most of us are well aware of the fact that with any system of rules or codes of behavior there can be a lag between the establishment of the rules and the conditions in the organization that these rules are supposed to help regulate. For this reason, we know that no organization functions just exactly as it is supposed to on paper. An illustration of this type of lag can be found in the area of employee training. Many times, according to the organizational chart, a certain person is supposed to take care of breaking in a new employee. For a variety of reasons, it may in practice be someone else: The person designated did not want the work and managed to pawn it off on someone else; or perhaps the person designated to do the breaking in happened to be a very poor instructor and whoever it was who assumed the responsibility was much better at on-the-job training.

Perhaps, in some instances, the lag between the rules and what is actually taking place is considerable; in others, it is slight. In some instances, the lag can be a symptom of malfunction, as in the case of the person who did not want to be bothered with the training. In other instances—as when a more suitable person took over the training function —the lag reflects a rather creative or responsible reaction to a particular problem situation. Lag between the formal rules and what is happening in practice does not necessarily mean that something is wrong with the functioning of the organization. A more useful way of thinking about lag is to realize that at different times, and in different portions of the formal structure, there may be a *difference* between what is supposed to be happening and what is actually happening. In any event, this difference or lag reflects still another way, and another reason why, the formal structure cannot account for all of the patterns of behavior seen within an organization.

3. *Generality of the formal systems.*   This property of formal systems merely reflects the fact that no set of rules can be constructed so as to anticipate every problem situation. As a matter of course, the rules are generally expressed in broader terms in order to allow for individual variation in executing them. In fact, there is much to be said for the inadvisability of restricting the action of an individual—particularly the supervisory person—by spelling out in excessive detail exactly how any one rule is to be applied. Regardless of the reasons why formal systems do not "fit" all problem situations, the fact is that it remains for the informal structure of an organization to "bridge the gap," so to speak, between the formal rules and the application of these rules to organizations made up of living, ever-changing individuals.

4. *Personal problems and interests.*   Such factors as lag of the formal system and generality of the formal system have highlighted the fact that there cannot be any 1 : 1 relationship between the formal structure of an organization and the patterns of behavior that can be observed in it. This statement would be true even if we could assume (and, of course, we can't) that everyone in a given organization was preoccupied with attaining the organization's goals. This fourth property of informal structure is an acknowledgment of the fact that everyone fills his particular formal niche in an organization in a different way. This fourth factor allows for the personal variations that are bound to happen in interpreting organizational goals and responsibilities. The formal organizational structure covers *categories* of individuals—such as presidents, foremen, typists, and so on—whereas the informal structure allows for the individual variations that take place when particular *individuals* fulfill the roles of the categories allowed for in a formal organizational chart.

FORMAL AND INFORMAL STRUCTURE—A SUMMARY

To pull together what we have said about the concepts of formal and informal structure thus far, we have developed a series of six generalizations. They are as follows:

1. Any organization has functions that can be identified and "put on paper," so to speak. One of the most commonly used set of functions for this purpose is the so-called organization chart which details the hierarchy of authority in terms of what department has charge of what other department and what individual reports to what other individual.

2. This organization chart also identifies the formal communication channels within a given organization. Thus, an examination of a chart for a particular organization will give an individual a feeling for how communication flows from top to bottom within that organization.

3. These organizational functions that can be identified are a part of the definition of the *formal structure* of an organization: that is, the explicit system of rules and regulations that govern the behaviors, goals, powers, and responsibilities of individuals within a given organization.

4. The *informal structure* of an organization embraces all of the governing forces such as cliques and friendship ties that are not explicit but implicit within a given organization. Informal structure includes all of the modifications of the formal structure that inevitably occur and are necessary to understand in order to comprehend how the organization functions in day-to-day situations; it includes all of those factors that account for the differences between how the functioning of an organization is described on paper and how it really works.

5. Four of the most common aspects of the functioning of an organization that are presumably taken into account by descriptions of the *formal structure* are (1) division of labor, (2) delegation of authority, (3) channeled communication, and (4) coordination.

6. The four aspects of group functioning most commonly handled by the *informal structure* are (1) impersonality of the formal system, (2) lag of the formal system, (3) generality of the formal system, and (4) personal problems and interests.

APPLICATION OF FORMAL AND INFORMAL STRUCTURE TO PUBLIC RELATIONS

Perhaps one of the most useful ways to illustrate the value of the concepts of informal and formal structure to public relations practice is to emphasize the relationship between these concepts and communication. To do this, let's begin by returning to Figure 22 (page 359) depicting a typical social organization of management. With this figure before us, and the property of formal structure which we called "channeled communication" (see pages 361-362), we can identify certain prescribed communication channels that link the various levels of authority in an organization. Thus, the division chief in the inspection department would channel any communication he wants directed to the workers through some particular department chief and perhaps several different foreman. This would be the *prescribed* communication route of the formal structure of the organization as reflected by the organization chart.

We know, however, that communication within an organization seldom follows the prescribed pathways. One reason is that the informal structure within the organization, depicted in Figure 22, may serve to "short circuit," in a sense, the prescribed communication pathways. Thus, one of the workers may have a friend who is in turn a friend of the division chief in the inspection department. Through this informal channel, this worker (and some of his friends) may learn about what the division chief intends to communicate to the workers before the department chiefs and foremen learn about it. This is merely one rather common sense example of how the prescribed communication patterns may be altered by the informal communication pathways.

At this point, perhaps the reader feels that what has been said thus far is rather obvious and almost simple minded. However, we are using this relationship between formal and informal structure and communication as a step to a second example which is not so obvious and which escaped notice by administrative people and social scientists for some time. *This second example deals with how communication patterns going up the formal structure are different from those going down.* Let us borrow a passage from Miller and Form's book to illustrate this point.

The Relation of Communication and Segmentation

Communication is basic to the understanding of human relations in a work plant whether it is large or small. In a large plant the many segmented parts tend to multiply the difficulties of securing clear and accurate communication.

Theoretically the line is supposed to carry all communication, orders going down and reports going up. Orders are never supposed to flow up the line, and reports about the "big boys" are not supposed to go down the line. Apart from orders and reports, a third type of communication, though acknowledged, is often neglected. It may be called "peer" communication, because it is horizontal in nature. When equals or peers consult and advise with each other, there are no orders or reports in the strict sense. Peer communication is important because it provides an excellent index to the process of segmentation and integration. For example, the fact that foremen of two departments frequently consult with one another and are friendly, whereas they rarely consult or have social contacts with other foremen, provides a clue to the relative integration or segmentation of the departments of the work plant.

Segmentation of groups does not occur accidentally. It develops naturally in the manner that communication travels up and down the line. The very nature of the man-boss linkage affects the accuracy, speed, and content of communication.* Obviously, the more levels communication must travel, the less complete and accurate it will be. A superior is only kidding himself if he thinks he has comprehensive knowledge of what is going on as close as two levels below him. He is largely dependent for what knowledge he does have on what the intervening supervisors want to tell him. Supervisors presumably report all the information which their bosses need to make decisions. This ideal is seldom achieved, however. More frequently bosses do not get the important information; indeed, irrelevant details often clutter their desks, making efficient administration an impossibility.

Distortion up the line

Gardner points out that each supervisor wants to have a good record for himself and for his department. In his efforts to make a good impression the communication he sends up the line is distorted. There is the tendency to give the boss what he wants to hear, namely, that "operations are going according to plan." Also, subordinates are likely to "cover up" when things do not so move.** This is done in the hope that the job will soon be straightened out and the boss won't find out what the situation really is.

Thus, each responsibile person up and down the line acts as a *sieve* or *filter*. Orders going down the line should be concise, accurate, and complete. In the process of interpretation, and making orders increasingly specific, errors or omissions sometimes intrude themselves. Orders may be issued too late; they may be incomplete, inaccurate, or ambiguous. Sometimes information which should not be released is accidentally circulated. Thus communication going down the line can become as distorted and filtered as information traveling in the reverse direction.

---

* Gardner, Burleigh B., *Human Relations in Industry*, Richard D. Irwin, Inc., 1945, chapter 2, "The Line of Authority and Communication," for an excellent discussion of this problem.

** *Ibid.*, pp. 25-28.

From these observations it is apparent that formal communication does not travel evenly, freely, and accurately from each section to all other sections of the work plant. There may be little or no interchange of information between some departments of the organization. The isolation may be the result of previous friction, physical segregation, or other factors.

On the other hand, there may be frequent, rapid, and accurate communication between two or more sections of the organization. Or communication may travel rapidly, but it may be inaccurate or antagonistic in content. The communication flow among the segments of an organization may be accurately charted. It should be recorded in terms of its source, frequency, duration, direction, intensity, and content. Such a diagram for a particular plant would be of invaluable aid in examining its problems.

Even with such a diagram, however, all problems would not be solved. Some writers have asserted that if there is free and open communication in a work plant people will understand each other and problems will be automatically solved. Although many problems may be reduced by good communication, all of them cannot be erased, for several reasons. First, it is impossible for any group to anticipate all the information another wants. Even if this were possible, some would not regard it as desirable. To withhold information is sometimes as vital as to release it. Yet withholding communication may arouse resentment in other groups. Even when there is no restraint on releasing facts, people will interpret them differently and act upon them differently. This is especially important when different segments of an organization do not share the same values. Further, when groups do not want to cooperate, free communication between them does not necessarily reduce the friction. In fact, *it may increase it.* In the following sections we shall demonstrate how organizations develop internal ruptures which increase rather than decrease the friction within them.

Time Segmentation

Sometimes segmentation develops within organizations because of the difficulty in synchronizing activities. Strains develop particularly in an industry which has two or more shifts.*** In the first place, the "regular shift" regards itself as the most important shift. Most of the staff is present during the day. Problems of the regular shift are met and solved, with the expectation that the following shift will merely follow precedent. The regular shift is frequently regarded as the big money-maker; the others as secondary. They keep the plant going and, by doing so, keep costs down. The members of the second and third shift,

---

*** Paul and Faith Pigors, "Human Aspects of Multiple Shift Operations," Publications in Social Science, Series 2, No. 13, Massachusetts Institute of Technology, 1944.

however, do not regard themselves as secondary. They are quick to feel slights and insults.

All too frequently, there is little or no face-to-face communication up and down the line between the people in the various shifts. The sum total of communication is often no more than hastily scribbled "memos" pointing out the difficulties of the last shift and setting the quotas for the next shift. Rarely is there social or recreational contact between shifts. Obviously, this incomplete and impersonal communication is the source of irritation.

On paper little distinction is made between the shifts. They are all part of the organization. Theoretically, each shift's performance should dovetail neatly into the others'. Since the interdependence of the shifts is real, anything that interferes with the fulfillment of expectations is a source of frustration. Problems between the shifts cannot be as adequately met as those arising within a shift, for the physical presence of people is often needed to meet problems on the spot.

Since no shift has complete dominance and advantage over the other, each shift can make the life of the next miserable. When poor relations develop between shifts, the irritations are cumulative. Each shift tries to outdo the other in inconveniences it can concoct for the other. The causes for intershift tensions may appear petty and unimportant to outsiders. To the workers themselves these irritations seem to mount to obsessive proportions. The ravings of a foreman in a tube-making department of a New York factory demonstrate this obsession:

> We're in a hell of a fix tonight. Everything's gone wrong from the first minute. But what can you expect from Krieger and his bunch. Krieger scribbled me a note to keep on making ⅜" tubing. His men as usual stopped the machines with the whistle, leaving the stock inside of the machines. Naturally we thought they was making ⅜". So for two hours we've been making half-inch. We're supposed to turn out thirty thousand feet of ⅜" tonight, but we'll never make it. . . . I'll catch hell for not checking the dies first. So we looked for the dies in the cabinet. The cabinet was locked and Krieger had the keys. So while I send Charles to get the keys I ask the men to clean up the machines and sweep up. I get lip from them because they claim that Krieger's men always leave them the dirty work. 'Course my boys ain't angels exactly. Krieger blowed off the other night on account of my men put so much grease on the stock that it was almost impossible to handle. I tell you, half of this trouble wouldn't happen if the chief took an interest in this department and in this shift. I usually see him leaving as I come in, taking off like a bat out of hell, to play golf or something.

Similar problems of time segmentation occur within a shift, especially when work teams are dependent on other teams for supply of materials. When one group in an interrelated work flow organization fails to meet a time schedule, total production is affected.[6, 7]

This quote was included to stress the fact that the public relations practitioner must contend with many organizational subtleties when trying to communicate. The public relations practitioner must realize that his role (in this case, we are stressing his function as the one responsible for certain internal communications, let us say in the form of a company newspaper) must be placed in the *context* of the total organization and the effects of his actions visualized in this manner. Let us consider one small point in the material quoted and then relate this to the public relations practitioner in order to make our point clear.

We learned above that communication *patterns and content* are different as a function of whether they are going *up* or *down* the formal organizational structure. We also saw how these communication patterns were affected by the informal organizational structure. The company newspaper, produced by the public relations practitioner, becomes still another part of the complex jigsaw puzzle of communication. If, in addition, we assume that the public relations practitioner is attempting to use the newspaper as a means of keeping workers *informed* (particularly with an eye of overcoming the "time segmentation" effects that we noted earlier) and, to complicate matters, the newspaper contains information that is *not normally communicated down*

---

[6] Miller and Form, pp. 162-165.

[7] One is reminded at this point of two fundamental questions that Elton Mayo raised in his book, *The Human Problems of an Industrial Civilization* (2nd ed.; Boston: Division of Research, Graduate School of Business Administration, Harvard University, 1946). In chapter 5 of that volume, Mayo asks:

(a) Is some experience, which might be described as an experience of personal futility, a common incident of industrial organization for work? and
(b) Does life in a modern industrial city in some unrealized way predispose workers to obsessive responses?

He partly answers these questions by the following (*op. cit.*, p. 116):

Human collaboration in work, in primitive and developed societies, has always depended for its perpetuation upon the evolution of a nonlogical social code which regulates the relations between persons and their attitudes to one another. Insistence upon a merely economic logic of production—especially if the logic is frequently changed—interferes with the development of such a code and consequently gives rise in the group to a sense of human defeat. This human defeat results in the formation of a social code at a lower level and in opposition to the economic logic. *One of its symptoms is "restriction."* In its devious road to this enlightenment, the research division had *learned something of the personal exasperation caused by a continual experience of incomprehension and futility.* It had also learned how serious a consequence such experience carries for industry and for the individual. [Italics added. Used by permission.]

the organizational structure, it is entirely possible that the public relations practitioner may make matters worse rather than better within his
organization. His intentions may be laudable, but the net effects deplor-
able. What is even worse, it may not occur to him that he is complicat-
ing the communication networks in the fashion described above.

One reason that it might not occur to him is that most public relations practitioners do not have the sociological background to make this
type of analysis. This is more or less obvious. What is not so obvious
is, as this discussion highlights, an almost basic *modus operandi* of the
typical public relations practitioner: *that is, to keep his various publics
informed*. Implicit behind this drive to keep others informed is the
notion that if people understand you (*i.e.*, are in communication contact with you) they will be more likely to like you or accept you. The
public relations practitioner seldom considers the possibility that once
recipients understand you they will *dislike* you. Or, in the terms of our
quote from Miller and Form, seldom does the public relations practitioner seriously consider the possibility that communication may *produce frictions rather than reduce or alleviate them*.

Still another point that might be made is that very often a company
newspaper attempts to achieve a degree of acceptance and intimacy
with its readers that borders on being accepted as part of the informal
communication channels. For example, by including items in the newspaper about employees, their promotions, running features on "the
employee of the month," and the like, the newspaper, in effect, is
attempting to achieve a type of communication that is normally reserved for informal channels. At the same time, however, the paper
very often tries to voice the point of view of management by including
articles devoted to certain "issues" (*e.g.*, company position on automation, Medicare, and the like). In this role the newspaper is much closer
to the formal communication structure in that the reader knows that
this is "management talking."

Lastly, there are times, as we noted earlier, when some portions of
the newspaper tend to run counter to the "normal" communication
content "down" and "up" the formal structure. If the newspaper attempts to keep the workers fully informed about such things as a
proposed merger, plant relocation, or plant expansion, the newspaper
may, in fact, be communicating more than the individual representatives of management normally communicate themselves. That is, in
some respects the newspaper can become more "enlightening" from the
standpoint of keeping employees informed than management itself.
It is in this way that, as a vehicle of management communication to

its employees, the newspaper may introduce more content into the "downward" communications than might ordinarily be there.

All of these examples of the various communication functions that a company newspaper may take on are presented here to emphasize the fact that a public relations practitioner *is never just putting out a company newspaper.* He is entering into the complex communication networks that are a part of formal and informal structure, and he needs to analyze his newspaper from this standpoint. He must be aware of the degree to which he is altering the communication "status quo" in his organization and must anticipate as best as he possibly can what the effects of this change in communication equilibrium will be.

QUESTIONS FOR DISCUSSION

1. Take any one or two of the cases that you have used to answer previous discussion questions. Look at these cases with the concepts of formal and informal structure in mind. From what you have been told in the case(s), how detailed a formal structure are you able to make? Are you able to make any inferences concerning the informal structure of the organization(s) in question? Are the public relations problems involved in these cases in any way related to malfunctioning of some aspect of the formal structure—e.g., the lines of communication or the lines of authority not being clear? Are you able to make any guesses as to whether the public relations practitioner concerned is even cognizant of the concepts of formal and informal structure and how they might apply to his problem situation?

2. One of the additional properties of the concepts of formal structure discussed in this chapter was entitled "channeled communication." What relationship do you see between the internal communication activities of a public relations practitioner and this notion of channeled communication? Can you visualize any times when the activities of a public relations practitioner might clash or be in conflict with what is implied by this additional property of formal structures?

3. What relationship do you see between the internal communication activities of a public relations practitioner and the four additional properties of the informal structure discussed in pages 363-365? Would it be fair to say that the activities of a public relations prac-

titioner (as reflected in the company newspaper and/or magazine and orientation and informational booklets) assist in overcoming such things as the "impersonality of the formal system" and the "lag in the formal system"?

4. What relationship do you see between the "distortion up the line" discussed by Miller and Form and the concept of feedback, first introduced in Chapter 4? Do you think that a public relations practitioner can help to reduce the distortion "up the line" by his internal public relations program? If your answer is yes, give one or two examples of how you visualize the public relations practitioner helping out. If your answer is no, elaborate on why you do not think that the public relations practitioner can or should (or both) reduce the distortion up the line.

Chapter 14

THE RECIPIENT STAGE IN
FURTHER DETAIL:
CONCEPTS OF ROLE AND STATUS

INTRODUCTION

In this chapter, we are going to extend our analysis of the recipient stage by taking a pair of concepts that are used extensively by psychologists and sociologists alike. In Chapter 12, we emphasized the psychological approach by examining the concept of attitude. In the previous chapter, we stressed the sociological approach by our analyses of the concepts of formal and informal structure. There are some concepts, however, that have been used so extensively by both categories of scientist that they really do not belong exclusively to one discipline or the other. Two such concepts are *role* and *status*. For this reason, it is not inaccurate to consider them as "overlapping" concepts. At the same time, however, they share with the other concepts that we have considered thus far the property of being extremely useful to public relations practitioners.

ROLE AND STATUS DEFINED

Role and status are highly interdependent concepts, and it is best to introduce them together. In its simplest terms, the concept of role

highlights the fact that all of us are expected to behave in different
ways in different circumstances. We shall employ the definition of
social role as put forth by Krech and Crutchfield:

> A pattern of behavior characteristics of an individual occupying a
> given niche in society, or fulfilling a specified function. The same in-
> dividual may display many roles. For example, a person may be ex-
> pected to behave in one manner vis a vis his children (the role of a
> father), in another manner in his job (the role of a worker), and in still
> another manner in the office of the doctor (the role of the patient).[1]

The concept of status is already partly covered in the definition of
role in the phrase "occupying a given niche in society, or fulfilling a
specified function." What the concept of status emphasizes is that all
of us occupy different authority positions within the social structure of
which we are a part. English and English define status in the following
manner:

> ". . . the position accorded, formally or informally, to a person in his
> own group; the acceptance and honor accorded to a person. While
> office or class usually confer status, they do not always do so. Status
> is always dependent upon the others in a group or community, and
> is partly a matter of how others directly perceive an individual.[2]

From these two definitions, it is obvious that role and status are interdependent terms and each derives its meaning from the other; each
is, in effect, nonexistent without the other. Also, as in the case of attitudes, we learn our appropriate roles as a function of the various status
positions in which we find ourselves.

WHY ARE THE ROLE AND STATUS CONCEPTS USEFUL TO BOTH FIELDS?

The concepts of role and status (both initially *sociological* concepts)
help the sociologist bridge the gap between the *individual* and *society*.
That is, as we learned earlier, the approach of the sociologist to understanding human behavior is through studying the *group* as the unit
of analysis. We noted, too, that in general the behavior of any single

---

[1] D. Krech and R. S. Crutchfield, *Elements of Psychology* (New York: Alfred A.
Knopf, Inc., 1958), p. 693. Used by permission.

[2] H. B. English and A. C. English, *A Comprehensive Dictionary of Psychological
and Psychoanalytical Terms* (New York: Longmans, Green & Co., Inc. [David
McKay Company, Inc.], 1958), p. 552. Used by permission of David McKay Company, Inc.

individual is overlooked or not emphasized in a sociological study.

In spite of this emphasis on the group as the basic unit of analysis, the sociologist is fully aware of the fact that there are individual differences among people; that the analysis of group behavior might be made more precise *if* we could also take into account individual differences. By making use of the concepts of both role and status, the sociologist has been able to take into account, more effectively, the fact that individual differences do exist. Hence, when a sociologist studies an organization—let us say a company, as in the case of an industrial sociologist—he is able to describe that organization more fully and more accurately by utilizing the concepts of role and status. They afford him a way of including the individual while still studying and emphasizing the total organization. Let us consider a classical example of a sociological study that was enriched by the use of the concepts of role and status.

The Yankee City Study[3]

The Yankee City study came about for a number of reasons, but one key reason was that it was a one-industry town (shoe manufacturing) and a very stable community in which there had been few strikes and no successful ones. Also, over a period of years, the efforts of unions to organize the workers had met essentially with failure. Yet in a comparatively short period of time, unions *did* make substantial inroads, and all of the factories of this one industry went out on strike and did so successfully. Why? What changes had taken place within this community and within this industry that could account for this? Why was the union able to make such inroads in a setting where they had previously experienced failure?

The researchers felt that in order to understand the changes that had taken place they first needed some historical perspective. Out of this extensive analysis the following emerged:

1. The process of making shoes could be broken down into *five* main factors: tools, skills, materials, distribution, and location. (We will illustrate below how these factors were employed to analyze the changes that had taken place sociologically over the years in the production of shoes.)

---

[3] The material in this section is based on the chapter, "The Factory in the Community," by W. Lloyd Warner and J. O. Low, in William F. Whyte (ed.), *Industry and Society* (New York: McGraw-Hill Book Company, 1946), pp. 21-45. Used by permission.

2. Major phases or periods of shoe manufacturing were noted over the years, and these stages were related to the five factors listed above.

3. With these two modes of analysis, the following picture emerged:

   a) At one time, the manufacturing of shoes (before the turn of the century) was a family affair. In this context, the individual worker had control over *all five* of the factors important to producing shoes. That is, the shoes were made by a highly skilled craftsman (skill factor). This craftsman worked with his own *tools*, in his own *home* (location factor), had control over acquisition of the *materials* out of which the shoes were made, and also handled the *distribution* of the finished product.

   b) Through a series of social changes (including the industrial revolution), this state of affairs gave way, around the turn of the century, to a central factory in which the worker performed certain skilled tasks. This was prior to the full impact of shoemaking machinery that was ultimately to have such a severe impact on the worker. With this central factory system, the worker no longer had control over the *distribution* of the shoes (*i.e.*, how they were sold) the acquisition of *materials* (the company took care of supplying him with the leather and other materials), the *location* of his work (now he had to go where management elected to erect a factory), and his *tools* (he used the tools and machinery supplied by the company). The only factor that the worker still had within his control was the *skill* that he possessed to use certain tools and certain machines in order to transform leather into shoes.

4. This leads us to a first main point. Prior to extensive mechanization within shoe factories and in spite of the fact that far-reaching changes had taken place in the manufacture of shoes (along the lines described briefly above), the *skills* of the worker were very important and served to distinguish one category of worker from another. There was a definite social system that was dependent on the skills possessed by a worker. Thus, for example, a young man who had not learned the many facets of the skills involved in making shoes was paid less and had less prestige in the factory; and, on top of that, his community standing tended to be related to his factory standing. By contrast, an older man who was a highly skilled worker earned more, had more prestige within the

plant, and his standard of living within the community reflected his status within the factory.

5. To translate what we have said into the concepts of role and status: The sociologists were able to discern a definite *status* hierarchy within a shoe factory in the years prior to widespread mechanization within factories and the period of time during which the strikes took place. This status system was largely a function of the work skills which the individual worker possessed. Also, there were rather clearly defined *roles* within each of these statuses. That is, a helper—a young, untrained, and unskilled worker—had definite duties to perform and a certain relationship with respect to the senior and highly skilled workers.

6. During the years immediately prior to the inroads made by unions and the resulting strikes (*i.e.*, prior to the depression years, during which the strikes took place), the sociologists found that with the advent of mass production methods, whereupon the machines played an increasingly important role in the making of shoes and the skill of the worker became unimportant, the *social system built around skills crumbled.* The importance of the older, senior man changed drastically. The younger man, better able to keep up with the machine, was, in effect, in more demand than the older man who had the skills but perhaps not the stamina to operate his machine all day long. With this change came the change in the status of the older worker in relation to the younger. In this limited way, the younger man was more valuable than the older. In fact, being older was now a liability rather than an asset. This meant that the last factor, *skill,* joined the other four in the sense that it was no longer under the control of the individual worker.[4]

To summarize at this point, one of the major factors apparently contributing to the change in disposition of the workers towards strikes and unionism was the fact that their roles and statuses had changed so drastically. The social system that had maintained an orderly relationship among workers underwent a revolutionary change in a comparatively short period of time. Belonging to a union, *with its emphasis*

---

[4] It should also be pointed out that Warner and Low identified other factors of importance, such as that factories had changed from local family ownership to absentee ownership. This particular factor naturally accounted for the tendency of the worker to become interested in unionization. We are focusing our attention, however, on factors that help to bring out for the reader how the sociologists made use of the concepts of role and status in their analysis of the changing work conditions for the individuals in that shoe manufacturing community.

on a seniority system (which can be interpreted as a substitute status system for one built upon skills), was a way of restoring order and evolving a social system to take the place of one that machinery had destroyed.

There is, of course, far more that went into the analysis of what happened in this community, and there were other variables that had an effect, on the workers' change of heart. However, enough of this study has been related to enable readers to understand how the concepts of *role* (in this case applied to the changes that workers' roles underwent as a function of skill acquisition and loss) and *status* (how the standing and respect of an individual were defined by his factory skill ability) aided the sociologist to better understand what had happened in this community. To return to the point made earlier, the concepts of role and status *helped the sociologist bridge the gap between the individual and society.*[5]

There are, of course, other ways in which sociologists make use of the concepts of role and status. The Yankee City study should be sufficient to illustrate some of the sociological uses that can be made of these concepts. Let us now turn to some examples of uses that psychologists make of these same two concepts.

Active Participation vs. Attitude Change

Using the concept of role by the psychologist is demonstrated by the research work of Janis and King on the relationship between active verbal participation on the part of an individual and the degree to which his attitude toward the topic he presents is influenced by this participation.[6] Let us examine their work in some detail.

---

[5] At the risk of redundancy, it should also be noted how this study is an example of the sociological approach. Here we see sociologists attempting to understand what had happened in a community in order to account for a drastic change in behavior, yet at no time is there a discussion of *individual* dynamics—that is, how any *single* individual was motivated, how he perceived the changes, etc. The entire analysis was made through concepts that did not require this type of analysis. The emphasis was on groups of individuals. In fact, the concepts of role and status came the closest to a consideration of the individual, and even here the individual was viewed in an impersonal sense. That is, no attention was paid to any *particular* individual and his view of his changed role and status; rather, it was a synthesis of all role and status changes that were treated.

[6] The material presented in this section is based on Chap. 7, "Acquiring Conviction Through Active Participation," in C. I. Hovland, I. L. Janis, and H. H. Kelley, *Communication and Persuasion* (New Haven, Conn.: Yale University Press, 1953), pp. 215-240. All material from *Communication and Persuasion* used by permission.

In their first experiment, Janis and King devised a study to determine what effect role playing had on producing increased acceptance of a communication by the individual participating in the role playing.[7] In essence, what Janis and King wanted to do was to compare the degree of attitude change—after being exposed to a particular communication—within two groups of subjects: the *active participants* (those subjects who had been "induced" to take an active role in the study, in this case by *giving* the communication in question rather than just listening to it) and the *passive controls* (those individuals who did not actively participate, but who merely listened to the communication). To make this comparison experimentally, the authors did the following:

1. All students used in the study participated as subects in a general opinion survey approximately four weeks before the study itself. This was the *precommunication* measure that was to be compared with a *postcommunication* measure taken after the study was completed.
2. The students were divided up so that each individual served as an *active participant* in one of the communications used and as a *passive control* in the other two communications used. In this manner, all of the students experienced both types of involvement in the study.
3. All of the students were told that they were involved in a *speaking test*. This provided the rationale for producing both the active participant (*i.e.*, the one giving the speech which he thought was being rated for speaking effectiveness) and the passive control (*i.e.*, the others listening to the speaker and rating his speaking ability).
4. Each active participant was asked to give an informal talk based

---

[7] *Role playing* is a phrase that describes any situation in which an individual is asked to behave as if he were someone else. One of the oldest uses of this technique is in clinical psychology. As part of a diagnostic or therapeutic program, a patient is asked to act out a play in which he assumes the role of father or uncle or other family member. From the patient's role playing of another member of the family and his acting as if he *were* that family member, the psychologist often learns something about his relationship with his father or uncle, and, perhaps more importantly, the patient himself learns something about his attitudes toward his family.

Many variations have been developed from this clinical use of role playing. For example, industrial training programs make liberal use of this technique. If you want to teach group discussion leadership skills, the best thing to do is to have the trainee *assume the role* of a superior in some particular setting (supplied by the trainer) and lead a group discussion designed to solve some particular problem.

on a prepared outline supplied by the experimenters. The active participant was told that he should assume the role of a "sincere advocate" of the point of view in his prepared outline. So as to control for selective attention effects, no participant was told what his topic would be until his turn to speak arose.

5. At the end of each communication presentation, the subjects were asked to complete a questionnaire that asked for their ratings of each speaker's performance and "their answers to a series of questions concerning their interest in, and opinions on, the various topics covered." This latter measure provided the *post-communication measure* which the experimenters needed. By comparing it with the precommunication measure (see step 1) the effect of the communication could be ascertained, depending on whether the student was a participant or a passive control.

The three communications used were concerned with widely different topics. The arguments provided in each communication were logical and relevant but strongly biased, tending to stress evidence for only one side of the issue presented. The particular communications follow:

. . . Communication A predicted that as a result of television and other recent developments, "movie attendance will be hit so hard that *two out of every three* movie theaters will have to go out of business during the next three years." Communication B took the position that "within two years, the total meat supply available to the civilian population in this country will decline to the point where there will be only *50 per cent* of the amount that is currently available." Communication C argued that "a completely effective cure for the common cold will be discovered very soon—probably within the next year or so."[8]

The results of this experiment can be summarized as follows:

1. In communication A and B the active participants were more influenced than the passive controls.
2. In communication C both groups showed about the same amount of opinion change.

Because of the discrepancy of the findings between communication A and B as compared with C, the researchers made further analyses of the data to see if some explanation for the different findings for

---

[8] Hovland, Janis, and Kelley, pp. 219-220.

communication C could be found. They found two factors that might account for the discrepancy:

1. For some reason the active participants in the communication C situation followed the outline provided by the experimenters more closely. They ad-libbed less and did not seem to be able to insert their own examples or additional arguments. The authors characterized this group as engaging in *less improvisation*.
2. The communication C situation tended to be more difficult for the active participants. They tended to stumble more in their presentation and were more ill at ease or tense. In addition, after the experiment they complained more about their assignment. Lastly, they seemed to be less satisfied with their performance as active participants.

Because satisfaction with one's own performance now emerged as a possible additional variable—along with the factor of *improvisation*—the authors went on to conduct a second study to test the following:

a. whether the main findings on the gain from role playing [*i.e.*, increase in attitude change] would be confirmed when a much more familiar and more ego-involving topic is used, and

b. whether either *improvisation* or *satisfaction* is critical in producing participation effects. [Italics added.][9]

Essentially the same type of study was designed. The persuasive communication used in this second study dealt with the question of military service for college students.

. . . It contained arguments in support of two main conclusions: 1) that over 90 *per cent* of college students will be drafted within one year after their graduation, and 2) that the length of military service required of the majority of college students will be at least *three* years, i.e., one or more years longer than the current official requirement.[10]

Utilizing role playing as a means of getting at active participation once again, and introducing factors that would require a high degree of improvisation and no improvisation and, lastly, obtaining measures of satisfaction with one's performance, the second study revealed the following:

1. As observed in the first study, those individuals who were active

---

[9] *Ibid.*, p. 223.
[10] *Ibid.*

participants demonstrated opinion change in the direction advocated by the communication greater than those who were passive.

2. The variable of improvisation—*i.e.*, having to participate under
   "stress" (presenting the communication without an outline shortly
   after having read it)—tended to induce a greater opinion change
   within an individual than those not required to improvise.

3. The factor of satisfaction, however, did *not* induce significant
   amounts of opinion change. As the authors point out: ". . . the
   subjects who received favorable ratings from the experimenter
   on their improvised talks had manifested a relatively high degree
   of satisfaction in their self-ratings, but showed approximately the
   same amount of opinion change as those who received unfavorable ratings or no ratings."[11]

On the basis of the two studies combined, the authors conclude that
active participation is a factor in helping to modify the attitudes of the
participant in the direction of the argument presented and that an
important "mediating" or facilitating mechanism accompanying the
active participation appears to be the variable of improvisation—*i.e.*,
allowing for even greater personal involvement in the task of presenting
a persuasive communication.

To return now to the main point of introducing this experiment, we
see here a very interesting use of the concept of role by psychologists
interested in one aspect of the effect of communication on attitude
change. As we will learn a little later in this chapter, all of us assume
a number of different roles which are appropriate for different social
situations. The experiments by Janis and King use this property of
roles—*i.e.*, that we can assume different roles at different times—to explore the relationship, if any, with attitude change. By so doing, they
have opened up an important area of study: the various psychological
mechanisms or dynamics that are involved in opinion change. Let us
now examine some research work that illustrates how psychologists
have made use of the concept of *status*.

The Use of Status to Pinpoint Intended Recipients

Perhaps one of the oldest working assumptions that the public relations practitioner uses in his daily work is that influential persons (*i.e.*,
in the context of our discussion here, people who enjoy higher status
within their particular social environment) can be extremely important

---

[11] *Ibid.*, p. 225.

in communicating to a wider audience. The most common term used among public relations practitioners is the phrase "thought leaders." (See again Chapter 11, page 274.) In practice, public relations practitioners often contact thought leaders in a given community in order to inform or persuade them, generally with two assumptions in mind: (1) that these thought leaders will, in turn, communicate to their particular circle of friends and thus widen the total number of people that the public relations practitioner is able to reach with his message, and (2) that it is too costly, and perhaps pointless, to try to reach the entire population; therefore, the wisest expenditure of time and energy is to try to influence the thought leaders.[12] One of the weaknesses in the way in which public relations practitioners have utilized this concept is that they have implicitly, if not explicitly, assumed the thought-leader concept to be a rather static one. That is, thought leaders, generally made up of clergy, lawyers, physicians, and elected officials among others, are considered as thought leaders regardless of the subject matter or topic under consideration. One particular thread of research in this area, designed to more effectively identify, define, and pinpoint "thought leaders," illustrates the utilization of the concept of status by psychologists. Let us examine this work briefly.

"The Initiators": A Special Case of Status Groupings[13]

Researchers at the Opinion Research Corporation were interested in making some progress in better defining who a thought leader is and how he could be more readily identified and thereby communicated with. They realized, too, that the older notion of thought leader was a rather static concept. In addition, the ORC people had done some research which suggested that people tend to respect a given person's opinion in one area, but not necessarily in another. Thus, they might well listen to a prominent businessman on such topics as automation and productivity and raising living standards, but would not pay much attention to him on such topics as how to cope with foreign

---

[12] This working assumption of the public relations practitioner is not without a counterpart in the social sciences. In the area of communication, one of the most widely known concepts of communication flow is the "two-step flow of communication," which suggests that ideas flow from the media—newspapers, radio, etc.—to *opinion leaders*, and from them to the less well read and informed segments of the population. (See again Chapter 11, particularly footnote 5.)

[13] The material in this section is based on a report entitled *The Initiators*, XVIII, No. 12 (December, 1960), a research report published by the Opinion Research Corporation. All material from *The Initiators* used by permission.

competition, balancing the federal budget, and a more equitable system of taxation.

Also, the ORC people were well aware that other difficulties existed when one tried to work with these so-called thought leaders. For one thing, they were often rather difficult to reach—*e.g.*, physicians, other professionals, and busy businessmen. For another, they were not often very interested in most of the messages that *did* reach them. Lastly, very often thought leaders were not in frequent contact with the very groups in which they might be expected to have some influence. Thus, a local physician, dentist, or college professor might be so wrapped up in his own work that he had not taken the time to join local groups. Although one *might* regard him as being more credible on certain topics, the fact was that no one knew about him.

In addition to these difficulties, the ORC people were convinced about a number of points that are related to the general concept of thought leader. Some of the more important are:

1. It is impossible for an organization to be in touch with everybody. (They were directing their attention to profit-making organizations.) Some sort of selective process of communication must take place, and these people, if selected properly, would, in turn, disseminate the message from an organization more widely.
2. "Image-building" is a concept of proven utility to management and must be pursued vigorously by companies all of the time.[14]
3. The right groups of individuals with which to communicate are bombarded with communications of all sorts at all times; therefore, identification of the groups most important to an organization is of utmost concern.

---

[14] ORC's definition of "image" is best understood from the following excerpt from their report:

> As complex entities, corporations affect their human surroundings in many complex ways. Until recently, it did not seem possible to gain a meaningful way of pulling together into a common pattern all the different strands of corporate activity, ranging from product sales and advertising to institutional promotion in such diverse fields as financial and community relations.
>
> The concept of Corporate Image has provided the needed landscape portrait of the over-all effect of corporate activities on various publics, together with profiled detail revealing how each of these major activity areas contributes to the over-all portrait in people's minds.
>
> The concept of Corporate Image may be defined as a kind of "summing up" of how people perceive and react to companies—to their products, personnel, policies and prospects. Its importance stems from the fact that, whether they wish it or not, large companies do significantly affect their social environment and are in their turn affected by the images they create in the public mind. [*The Initiators*, p. 1.]

Perhaps the most telling point about the need for identifying the various thought-leader groups more precisely came from research data. For example, ORC researchers found that:

Many professional people may be costly to reach because they don't give much attention to the media that carry management's messages.

Say they give relatively little time to . . .	Those in Professional Positions
Reading business or professional journals	52%
Reading weekly news magazine	52
Reading general magazines like *Life*, *Post*, etc.	46
Watching television	34
Reading daily newspapers	16

Stockholders are often thought to be a group with management-oriented interests, yet large majorities are not active idea propagators in areas that concern corporations.

Not likely to talk about . . .	Owners of Stock in U.S. Corporations
Labor union matters	75%
Government policies	66
Political affairs	61
National problems	58
Business conditions	50
World affairs	50
Community problems	47

The actual influence sphere of many presumed influentials is limited, because they have not linked themselves to groups organized for social action.

	Not Active in Any Political, Business, Labor Service, Social or Other Organization or Association
College graduates	20%
Professionals	23
Income $10,000-15,000	27
Executives	33
Entrepreneurs	39

On the basis of data such as the above, and convinced of the importance of communicating with the right groups for purposes of corporate image-building, ORC embarked on research designed to determine the groups that were most important to corporations for image-building. A summary of this research is, in effect, a thumbnail sketch of the concept of *initiators*.

As a starting point, the ORC researchers developed a way of identifying the "right groups," those most important to developing a corporate image. This consisted of a number of steps:

First is establishing a criterion for judging a group's priority

Second is selecting out of the infinite possibilities those groups that appear profitable to evaluate. (There is no theoretical limit to the number of characteristics that can be used to identify "groups." The beginning of such a list might be found in the adjectives that can be applied to human beings.)

Third is evaluating the various groups against the established criterion.

Fourth is examining the interconnectedness of High-Priority Groups to isolate those whose members are most likely (a) to belong to, and (b) to influence other High-Priority Group members.

The analysis is complex, and admittedly only one of many possible lines of attack. But the attempt is to provide an objective evaluation that will isolate those groups offering the maximum opportunity for the pyramiding of influence.[15]

Out of this analysis emerged an "initiator scale." This concept is based on analysis of three questions which were asked of the respondents used in this ORC research effort. To analyze the replies to these three questions, a scoring system was developed whereby points are assigned to such *free time* activities as reading daily newspapers, business and professional journals, traveling, attending plays and ballet, and reading books. In addition, this scoring system reflects the degree of participation of the person in political affairs, community and national work, church and religious groups, civic or local associations, and business and/or union associations. The end result is a *public affairs score* ranging from zero to seven, with zero representing the lowest and seven the highest initiator score.

A person with a score of six or seven is one who does a lot of reading, is involved in organizational activities, and is concerned with national and world affairs. Conversely, a person with a score of zero or one is

---

[15] *The Initiators*, p. 16.

comparatively inactive in organizational concerns and is not widely read.[16]

The ORC research reveals that persons defined as initiators (*i.e.*, as scored on a series of questions along the lines described above) tend to be concentrated in groups thought to be influential in our society. Also, initiators tend to be found throughout our society—in large cities and small towns, in all of the major religious denominations, in all of the age groups from twenty-one to seventy plus that one might want to make. In short, initiators are found everywhere and in addition, as we noted earlier, are well read, active in many groups, travel a lot, and so on. On the basis of these data, the ORC researchers conclude that the initiator is an excellent "target" audience for corporate image-building communication efforts. In addition, they suggest that the initiator may well be a worthwhile target audience for a number of purposes besides corporate image building.

We could spend much more time on this interesting concept of the initiator. The point is that this type of work represents another way of classifying an individual for purposes of better understanding his probable beliefs and attitudes and how he might react to certain communications. As such, this work joins a long list of experimental efforts to assign individuals to certain *status groups* (such as the old, standard measures of income, education, and occupation) which in turn becomes a sort of short-cut classification system that presumably aids one's ability to measure and predict behavior. For example, the most common uses of such classification systems or status-defining categories is to relate these status systems to the attitudes of individuals. Thus, we tend to find that persons with large incomes have different attitudes toward certain social phenomena, such as social security and old-age assistance programs, than do those with very low incomes. Likewise, we know that highly educated persons have different preferences in the mass media—particularly radio and TV—than those with very little education. In each case the objective is the same: to make use of a classification system that will enable us to understand human behavior more adequately to be more effective in predicting reaction to communication.

The *initiator scale* represents a more refined effort to classify individuals, but the purpose is the same as we have just stated. Hopefully, persons identified by means of the initiator scale will be communicated with more effectively (we have a means of identifying them now) and

---

[16] This initiator scale is based on a self-administered questionnaire used to create the initiative scales and to identify this most important group, the initiators.

will have a greater impact on other people. How do we know this? The research cited earlier tells us this should be so. The person with a high initiator score reads more, travels more, and is more active in various groups. For this reason, we have more confidence that money spent on communication designed to reach the initiator will in turn reach a wider secondary audience and with greater impact than before.

To sum up at this point, the initiator concept was introduced here because it illustrates a special case of the concept of status and how a team of sociologists and psychologists at ORC employed this thinking to sharpen corporate communication.

SOME ADDITIONAL PROPERTIES OF ROLE AND STATUS

Now that we have had an opportunity to examine a number of ways in which psychologists and sociologists use the concepts of role and status, let us turn to a discussion of some additional properties of these concepts.

Role

A social concept. The concept of role is almost unique from the standpoint of being so dependent on a social system for its existence. By this is meant that the concept of any one role is completely dependent on the existence of other roles. The role of father is senseless without the role of son or daughter. The role of president or foreman is entirely dependent on the existence of a vice president and workers. In fact, the role of a hermit would make no sense if we did not have the rest of society for the hermit to remain apart from. In short, the concept of role is a completely social one; in fact, in the sense that we use the term, it is a concept unique to human beings. For example, the ability of an individual to evolve the concept of "me" or "I" as different from "you" or "them" requires an order of intelligence and communication by symbols that is found only in man. Most of the phenomena associated with the concept of role could not be applied meaningfully to animals.

A multidimensional concept. A second important property of the concept of role is that we all assume multiple roles. There is no such thing as an individual having only one role in his society. This point

Figure 23

Multiple Roles Assumed by a Typical Member of Our Society

is nicely brought out in Figure 23[17], which illustrates some of the many possible roles that an adult male may fill in our society today.

From Figure 23 it is easy to see that the business of being an adult in our society, or in any society, for that matter, is a highly complicated affair. A tremendous amount of social learning must take place within all of us for us to be able to learn what behavior is appropriate for what role and when. In fact, all of us see another individual in only

---

[17] Reproduced by permission from G. A. Lundberg, C. C. Schrag, and O. N. Larsen, *Sociology* (New York: Harper & Row, Publishers, 1954), p. 245. Copyright 1954 by Harper & Brothers. Reprinted by permission of Harper & Row, Publishers.

some of the many possible roles that that individual may assume. Most parents are completely ignorant of the roles that their children assume when they are at school or among their friends at a party. One of the oddest feelings that one can experience is to see someone he knows well in a completely different role. The rare occasion when parents might run into their college-age son among his friends—and let's add that the offspring is quite drunk—affords those parents a completely different glimpse of their child. They just "do not know him," and this is quite literally true in the sense that they have never seen him in that particular role situation before.

The same is true when, on a rare occasion, a child is able to see his dad at work or with *his* own age group at a party. Once again the phenomenon is the same: The child just does not "recognize" the father, behaviorally speaking, of course. At home, Dad might be a big wheel and demand deferential treatment. At work, he may occupy the lowest rung in the organization with a role that requires him to be quite deferential to all those around him.

There are a number of reasons why it is important for a public relations practitioner to be aware of the multiple role behavior that all of us engage in. One important point that multiple role membership highlights is that the assumptions made about the communication appropriate to each role situation may have to vary. That is, communicating with Joiner J. Jones (the individual depicted in Figure 23) when he is assuming the role of father may require quite different tactics compared with communicating with Mr. Jones as a college alumnus or member of the Chamber of Commerce. In short, the public relations practitioner must be sure that he understands *what role his recipient may be assuming* at any one time in order to determine effectively what assumptions about communication he can safely make.[18]

The inevitability of role conflict. Because multiple role demands are inescapable, it follows that role conflicts are likewise inevitable. It is impossible for an individual to avoid always the conflict that arises because one role demands such and such behavior that may be at odds with the demands of another role. In our contemporary society there

---

[18] At this juncture, the reader may recall a closely related point that was made in Chapter 5 in the discussion of reference and membership groups. At that time, we pointed out that an individual may be a member of a particular town or neighborhood but *not* identify himself with that town or neighborhood in the sense that he does not really care much about what happens to either locale. We brought out that if the public relations practitioner assumes physical membership as being the same as psychological membership (or identification), errors in judgment can result. When thinking about an intended recipient, incorrect role identification can be just as bad as incorrect group identification.

are two role conflicts that we often read about, both of which apply primarily to men. One is the conflict between *career* (and the role demands of devotion to work) and the *family*, particularly the children. In job situations the more successful the male is in one role (say, the job) the worse he is in the other. This is particularly true if the type of work that he does requires him to travel extensively and thereby to be away from home a lot. The other commonly encountered role conflict is between job and religion; what might be appropriate in certain circumstances for business reasons (leading to financial success and power) may be inconsistent with being a practicing believer of a religious faith.

Regardless of the example, the fact is that the demands put on all of us by the various role expectancies of a given society are a source of conflict. Some clinical psychologists feel that role conflicts are a source of a great deal of abnormal behavior or maladjustment among some individuals.

Status

Overlap with role. Probably the first point to be made about the concept of status is that it shares most of the properties of role since they are such highly interrelated concepts. Thus, as in the case of role, status is a uniquely social concept. The status of "superior" (organizationally speaking) makes no sense without the status of "subordinate." Likewise, because we have many different roles in life, we also have different statuses. Perhaps the best illustration of multiple status may be found in fraternal orders. In certain circumstances, the leader of a fraternal order may be in a comparatively low status hierarchy of his company while the company president is one of the rank and file members of the fraternal order. In effect, the status of the individual may be completely altered by the particular social situation in which he finds himself.

Ascribed vs. achieved status. Another characteristic of the concept of status is the distinction between *ascribed* and *achieved* status. *Ascribed status* is a term referring to the status distinctions that are independent of the behaviors of an individual. Thus, the sex of an individual has status implications (which vary as a function of the society into which the individual is born) over which, of course, he has no control. The kinship ties into which an individual is born is another example of ascribed status. If an individual is born into a family with wealth or into one with royalty or "built-in" leadership, such as the chief or ruling family of a particular tribe, then he has some status

merely as a function of being born into that family. Then there are
some ascribed status positions that are not as static or fixed as sex and
kinship ties. One such example is age. At different ages in our lives,
we assume different status positions. Here again, in common with the
other ascribed status examples cited earlier, age is another variable
over which we have no control, yet it has definite implications for our
status position in the society in which we live. To summarize, ascribed
status includes all of those factors that place us in a particular status
position over which we have little or no control and which we generally find almost impossible to change.

By contrast, *achieved status* is a term that embraces all of the ways
in which our status is changed or affected by the behavior we exhibit.
If we are ambitious and achieve great wealth or write prolifically and
well or prove to be an outstanding leader, regardless of whether it be
politically, militarily, or industrially, then our status can be changed.
In fact, sociologists very often distinguish between what they call
caste and *open-class societies*.[19] By these terms, they account for the
fact that in caste societies (for example, India) there are very fixed
social strata with a minimum of interaction between the strata, severe
prohibitions against intermarriage, and practically no social mobility
—*i.e.*, movement from one social stratum to another. By contrast, the
United States is comparatively open-class in that there are fewer re-
straints placed on intermarriage and social mobility.

Most public relations practitioners are implicitly, if not explicitly,
aware of the distinction between ascribed and achieved status, and
generally the things that they do or do not do in their public relations
work reflect this awareness. However, with rapid changes in our
society (and in the societies of the rest of the world) brought about by
incredibly fast advances in technology, ever-expanding standards of
living, and increasing numbers of individuals going to college, the
need for understanding the concept of status (including both ascribed
and achieved) is increasing. In the United States, the upward social
mobility, changing rapidly all of the time, is a phenomenon that bears
examination by public relations practitioners. This is brought out by
Broom and Selznick when they write:

Since the 1870's there has been an enormous shift in the occupational structure: farming and the extractive industries have shrunk;
manufacturing and mechanical industries are beginning to contract with

---

19 L. Broom and P. Selznick, *Sociology* (3rd ed.; New York: Harper & Row,
Publishers, 1963), pp. 206-207.

the use of automatic machinery; the public service, business, clerical, and professional occupations are expanding. The lower status occupations have diminished, and the higher status occupations have increased both relatively and in absolute numbers.

The transition from blue-collar to white-collar work can be taken as a rough index of upward occupational movement. Considering only transfers between these two very broad categories and disregarding vertical mobility within each one, changes in the national economy between 1870 and 1930 produced a very marked upward shift in the center of occupational gravity. . . . Some 9,000,000 persons who were white-collar workers in 1930 would have been engaged in manual labor if the occupational distribution of 1870 had persisted. On the average, about 150,000 workers per year ascended from blue-collar to white-collar jobs.*

Although the effects of mass immigration upon upward mobility have diminished (and have even been reversed at times with the immigration of professionals), differential birth rates have contributed to upward mobility. Lower fertility in the higher occupational and income brackets creates a vacuum in the upper strata, and this is filled by individuals from the lower strata.[20]

If we relate what we have learned earlier about all of the factors that determine how a person will perceive, learn, and be motivated, it is clear that in a society with a rather high degree of social mobility there will be a comparatively rapid change in the value systems and attitudes of people who are comparatively new arrivals to a particular social strata as compared with those who have been there for some time. This has profound implications for one who is responsible for communicating with such individuals as the public relations practitioner often finds himself having to do.

Perhaps the importance of the public relations practitioner having some awareness of the concept of status can best be demonstrated by an example that has implications for the financial public relations of an organization. The example comes from Peter F. Drucker's book, *America's Next Twenty Years.*[21]

---

* 2d paragraph taken from Elbridge Sibley, "Some Demographic Clues to Stratification," *American Sociological Review,* 7 (1942), 322-30.

[20] Broom and Selznick, pp. 213-214. From *Sociology.* Copyright © 1955, 1958, 1963 by Harper & Row, Publishers. Reprinted with their permission.

[21] Peter F. Drucker, *America's Next Twenty Years* (New York: Harper & Row, Publishers, 1955). Copyright © 1955 by Peter F. Drucker. All passages used by permission of Harper & Row, Publishers.

Drucker points out that today in the great majority of the one thousand companies listed on the New York Stock Exchange, the only large stockholders are institutional trustees. In only one quarter of these companies do the members of the founding family or the present management own effective control of the company. The institutional trustees are investment trusts, pension funds, and banks. In making this point he says:

> By and large, these enormous holdings have been acquired in the past ten years. The pension funds only got going after World War II; there were about two thousand then, there are twenty thousand now. Ten years ago both investment trusts and bank-managed personal trusts were still insignificant. The shift of the center of security buying since then represents an unprecedented democratization of business ownership, *for the real owners of these holdings are small people, the middle class and the workers.* It also represents an unprecedented concentration of legal ownership, for the number of fiduciary managers is fairly small.[22] [Italics added.]

Drucker goes on to tell how the general public *and even the financial world* is not particularly aware of this shift in financial control. In addition, he notes that seldom is there mention of this fact on the financial pages. Immediately following this point, however, he presents two paragraphs that make this shift in financial control illustrative of the change in social structure and upward social mobility (this time, because of a social phenomena such as pension funds rather than the actions of any given set of individuals):

> Anonymity, however, is exactly what our new masters prefer. The fiduciary managers are as unlike the old Lords of Creation as they could possibly be. *They run heavily to Ph.D. degrees and Phi Beta Kappa keys. Their incomes generally are modest, usually much less than those of executives in the companies whose stock they manage. . . .*
> It is unlikely that the public at large has even heard the names of men like Clarance Stanley of GM, Wallace Dunkel of the Bankers Trust Company's pension fund department, or Merrill Griswold of Massachusetts Investors Trust. Even in the financial community they are barely known; when the Fulbright Committee investigated the stock market in 1955 none of them was called to testify. Yet they are the "New Tycoons." In financial importance and the impact of their decisions on the economy, they—and the other managers of large investors—represent more power than the tycoons of yesteryear ever dreamed of possessing. They could easily match resources with a

----
22 *Ibid.*, pp. 35-36.

Rockefeller or a Carnegie, the most lordly of the "old" tycoons whose names are still, half a century after their heyday, household words throughout the world. The Sears, Roebuck pension fund owns 26 per cent of the stock of the world's largest merchandising business; the General Motors pension fund has almost $100 million of new money to invest every year; and the Massachusetts Investors Trust, largest of them all, has a "cool billion" in assets.[23] [Italics added.]

When this change in the economic structure is coupled with the upward social mobility possible in our society, we have a fascinating example of how changes in the status structure—and the socioeconomic and psychological make-up of individuals filling these various strata in society—have profound implications for anyone wishing to communicate with such individuals. Consider the public relations practitioner who is responsible for the announcements and the various other communication details associated with a new stock issue of his company's stock or even that the company is now "going public." If he does not realize that the make-up of his intended recipients (*i.e.*, the financial officers of various trusts who are a ready market for purchase of stock if it is worthy of purchase) has changed drastically over the past few years, he could badly misjudge how to communicate with them. As we have repeated at various times throughout this book, a communicator must know the make-up of his intended audience, those who are to be the recipients of his communications. Upward social mobility, along with other concepts from sociology, may play a role in enabling him to understand the thinking of his recipients more accurately. For one thing, if the make-up of such financial officers leans heavily toward the Ph.D. degree and Phi Beta Kappa key holders, their intelligence level and comprehension ability of audience will be quite different from what it was just a few short years ago when such people were not in these positions.[24]

THE CONCEPTS OF ATTITUDE, FORMAL AND INFORMAL STRUCTURE, ROLE AND STATUS: A SUMMARY AND LOOKING AHEAD

In this and the two preceding chapters, we have attempted to do a number of things to further our understanding of the recipient in the

---

[23] *Ibid.*, pp. 36-37.

[24] At this point, the reader will find it useful to review what was said in Chapter 6, particularly with respect to reading difficulty levels and the types of materials that would interest different recipients.

communication model. As a starting point, we distinguished between psychological and sociological approaches to understanding the recipient. Following this we examined one concept each from psychology and sociology—attitude and formal and informal structure—as well as two overlapping concepts—role and status. In addition to presenting these concepts in enough detail so that they would be understandable and usable to the reader, an attempt was made to illustrate how these concepts are applicable to public relations practice and how they can guide the thinking of the public relations practitioner as he faces his daily problems.

With this material as background, we are now able to extend our analysis of larger scale efforts to understand the recipient. Specifically, we shall now examine such concepts as *cognitive dissonance, diffusion theory*, and a number of terms that one hears and reads about constantly, such as *public opinion* and *persuasion*, which properly, in the opinion of the author, should be considered when one is trying to understand the recipient in order to communicate more effectively.

QUESTIONS FOR DISCUSSION

1. List three or four examples of problem situations where one could argue that it would be useful for the public relations practitioner concerned to be cognizant of the concepts of role and status. If possible, include with your examples concrete predictions or estimates of the *type of error(s)* that a public relations practitioner *without* this knowledge might make.

2. Develop one or two examples of how a public relations practitioner might make use of the concept of *The Initiators*. That is, assume that a public relations practitioner had obtained measures of a given number of recipients with respect to their "initiator" score. In what ways would the public relations practitioner be helped with this particular knowledge?

3. Try to develop one or two examples of how a public relations practitioner might make use of the findings obtained by Janis and King —e.g., that those individuals who were active participants demonstrated greater opinion change in the direction advocated by the communication than those who were passive. Did you find that it was difficult to relate these findings to public relations practice? Why or why not?

Chapter 15

THE RECIPIENT STAGE IN FURTHER DETAIL: COGNITIVE DISSONANCE AND DIFFUSION OF INNOVATION

INTRODUCTION

In Chapters 12 through 14, we launched into detailed examination of the recipient stage in the communication process with consideration of the differences between the psychological and sociological approaches to understanding human behavior. We learned that one fundamental difference is that the psychologist tends to use primarily the *individual* as his unit of analysis whereas the sociologist uses the *group* as his unit of analysis. With this distinction elaborated on, we then examined representative concepts from these two distinct points of view: from the psychological, we considered the concept of attitude; from the sociological, we examined the concepts of formal and informal organizational structure. To make the point that psychologists and sociologists are constantly making use of one another's work, we examined a pair of overlapping concepts—role and status—that are used by both disciplines.

All of these concepts have added something to our ability to understand the recipient. Hopefully, the point is also clear that the public relations practitioner can make frequent use of these concepts to perform his work as a public relations practitioner more intelligently.

In our more extended analysis of the recipient in the preceding three chapters, *we considered concepts that are comparatively narrow in their scope with respect to understanding human behavior.* That is, such concepts as attitude, role and status, and formal and informal structure are applicable to only *some* behaviors exhibited by individuals. There are many different sorts of other behaviors that these concepts do not encompass in the sense that they do not help us to better understand or predict such behavior. *For this reason, we shall continue our detailed analysis of the recipient in this chapter, with our focus on more extensive concepts—concepts that are designed to account for a great deal of behavior.*

Two such comparatively all-inclusive concepts that exemplify more elaborate theorizing in both psychology and sociology and at the same time are particularly pertinent to the public relations practitioner are (1) a theory of cognitive dissonance and (2) a theory of the diffusion and adoption of innovations.

A THEORY OF COGNITIVE DISSONANCE[1]

As a starting point in his book on cognitive dissonance, Festinger points out a basic generalization that can be made about an individual's behavior: He attempts to maintain internal consistency; that is, his beliefs and attitudes are consistent with each other, at least from *his* point of view. Implicit behind this notion of consistency is the assumption that consistency is somehow psychologically comforting, that maintaining a consistent set of beliefs, attitudes, and accompanying behavior is rewarding or motivating and is something that appeals to most individuals.

An equally obvious observation, according to Festinger, is that for a variety of reasons one cannot always achieve this consistency. In addition, it appears safe to assume that *inconsistency* is psychologically uncomfortable—that is, something that an individual wishes to avoid. With these two points established, Festinger writes:

> The basic hypotheses, the ramifications and implications of which will be explored in the remainder of this book, can now be stated.

---

[1] The material for this section is adapted from Leon Festinger, *A Theory of Cognitive Dissonance* (Stanford, Calif.: Stanford University Press, 1962), Chap. 1. All material borrowed from *A Theory of Cognitive Dissonance* used with the permission of the publishers, Stanford University Press. Copyright © 1957 by Leon Festinger. For those readers who are intrigued by the concept of cognitive dissonance the author suggests that they examine two other related books: J. W. Brehm and A. R. Cohen, *Explorations in Cognitive Dissonance* (New York: John Wiley & Sons, Inc., 1962) and L. Festinger, *Conflict, Decision and Dissonance* (Stanford, Calif.: Stanford University Press, 1964).

First, I will replace the word "inconsistency" with a term which has less of a logical connotation, namely, *dissonance*. I will likewise replace the word "consistency" with a more neutral term, namely, *consonance*. A more formal definition of these terms will be given shortly; for the moment, let us try to get along with the implicit meaning they have acquired as a result of the preceding discussion.

The basic hypotheses I wish to state are as follows:

1. The existence of dissonance, being psychologically uncomfortable, will motivate the person to try to reduce the dissonance and achieve consonance.

2. When dissonance is present, in addition to trying to reduce it, the person will actively avoid situations and information which would likely increase the dissonance.

Before proceeding to develop this theory of dissonance and the pressures to reduce it, it would be well to clarify the nature of dissonance, what kind of concept it is, and where the theory concerning it will lead. The two hypotheses stated above provide a good starting point for this clarification. While they refer here specifically to dissonance, they are in fact very general hypotheses. In place of "dissonance" one can substitute other notions similar in nature, such as "hunger," "frustration," or "disequilibrium," and the hypotheses would still make perfectly good sense.

In short, I am proposing that dissonance, that is, the existence of nonfitting relations among cognitions, is a motivating factor in its own right. By the term cognition, here and in the remainder of the book, I mean any knowledge, opinion, or belief about the environment, about oneself, or about one's behavior. Cognitive dissonance can be seen as an antecedent condition which leads to activity oriented toward dissonance reduction just as hunger leads to activity oriented toward hunger reduction. It is a very different motivation from what psychologists are used to dealing with, but as we shall see, nonetheless powerful.[2, 3]

To round out this very cursory introduction to the theory of cognitive dissonance, we need to quote a few more paragraphs.

---

[2] *Ibid.*, pp. 2-3.

[3] It may be useful at this point to remind the reader of the discussion that preceded the examination of various concepts from both the psychological and the sociological literature in Chapter 12. From what little we have seen of dissonance theory thus far, it is clear that the *basic unit is the individual* (*i.e.*, the dissonance or consonance of his cognitions, which in turn proves to be a source of motivation of behavior). These processes going on within *one* individual are assumed to be true of *all* individuals. Hence, it is an *individually* oriented theory which presumably permits one to predict the behavior of *many individuals*. This theory of cognitive dissonance obviously fits into the category of psychological concepts, as distinct from sociological concepts.

The terms "dissonance" and "consonance" refer to relations which exist between pairs of "elements." It is consequently necessary, before proceeding to define these relations, to define the elements themselves as well as we can.

These elements refer to what has been called cognition, that is, the things a person knows about himself, about his behavior, and about his surroundings. These elements, then, are "knowledges," if I may coin the plural form of the word. Some of these elements represent knowledge about oneself: what one does, what one feels, what one wants or desires, what one is, and the like. Other elements of knowledge concern the world in which one lives: what is where, what leads to what, what things are satisfying or painful or inconsequential, or important, etc.

It is clear that the term "knowledge" has been used to include things to which the word does not ordinarily refer—for example, opinions. A person does not hold an opinion unless he thinks it is correct, and so, psychologically, it is not different from a "knowledge." The same is true of beliefs, values, or attitudes, which function as "knowledges" for our purposes. This is not to imply that there are no important distinctions to be made among these various terms. Indeed, some such distinctions will be made later on. But for the definitions here, these are all "elements of cognition," and relations of consonance and dissonance can hold between pairs of these elements.[4]

Cognitive Dissonance Applied to Advertising Readership

One area in which the use of cognitive dissonance theory can be illustrated is in decision making. According to the theory, dissonance is an unavoidable consequence of making a decision. The *amount of post-decision dissonance* is hypothesized by Festinger to be dependent on the following:

1. The importance of the decision.
2. The relative attractiveness of the unchosen alternative to the chosen one.
3. The degree of overlap of cognitive elements corresponding to the alternatives.[5]

An individual who has just made a purchase is one who has gone through some sort of decision-making process leading to an eventual

---

[4] Festinger, pp. 9-10.

[5] *Ibid.*, p. 47.

choice. In keeping with the theory of dissonance, an individual who has made a particular decision to purchase a particular item should have some cognitive elements that are dissonant with the decision that he made. Also in keeping with the theory, there should be some observable efforts to reduce the uncomfortableness associated with this dissonance. Here is where advertising readership comes in: Reading advertisements devoted to the product just purchased should provide information that is consonant or consistent with the individual's thinking about the purchase; reading competing advertisements should do just the opposite. Therefore, according to dissonance theory, an individual who has recently purchased a particular product, providing the purchase is an important one to him, should tend to read ads about the product purchased and avoid reading ads about the product not purchased.

Ehrlich, Guttman, Schonbach, and Mills designed and executed a research study to test the implications of dissonance theory.[6] The study focused on the purchase of a new car, because this is usually an important decision to most people. The purchase of a new car is generally the largest dollar purchase that most people make, second only to the purchase of a home. Specifically, the authors theorized the following about the relationship between the decision to purchase and advertisement readership:

1. New car owners would read many more ads about the car they just bought than about other cars.
2. New car owners would tend to avoid reading ads about cars they considered but did not purchase.
3. Comparable owners of old cars should show little or no discrimination in their advertising reading since their dissonance would largely have been eliminated or at least stabilized. Furthermore, new car ads which emphasize all the attractive features of the latest model would hardly reduce the dissonance which may still exist in the owner of a car which is two years old.[7]

The following data was obtained by personal interview with sixty-five adult males in the Minneapolis area, about four to six weeks after the purchase of a new automobile. A second group of sixty-five adult males were interviewed, all of whom owned cars three or more years

[6] D. Ehrlich, I. Guttman, P. Schonbach, and J. Mills, "Post-Decision Exposure to Relevant Information," *Journal of Abnormal and Social Psychology*, LIV (1957), 98-102, as quoted in Festinger, pp. 50-54.

[7] Festinger, pp. 50-51.

old. These interviewees were roughly comparable to the new-car purchasers in that they were selected from neighborhoods similar to those in which the new-car purchasers lived. The rationale provided for all interviewees was that the study was devoted to ascertaining what newspapers and magazines people read regularly. In that context, the interview was devoted largely to showing the subject each automobile ad that appeared in the magazines and newspapers that the respondent said he read regularly. After having been shown the ad, the respondent was asked whether or not he had noticed the ad, and if it had been noticed, whether he had read some or all of it. At the end of the interview, the respondent was asked the different makes of cars that he had seriously considered before making his final purchase. The results of the study are as follows:

TABLE 1[8]
READERSHIP OF "OWN CAR" AND "OTHER CAR" ADS

Ads Dealing with	Mean Per Cent of Ads Noticed by		Mean Per Cent of Ads Read by	
	New Car Owners	Old Car Owners	New Car Owners	Old Car Owners
Own Car	70	66	65	41
Considered cars	66	–	40	–
Other cars	46	–	34	–
Considered plus other cars	48	41	35	30

Festinger interprets these data as follows:

Let us first examine the data for the new car owners. It is clear that they noticed a high proportion (70 per cent) of ads that dealt with the car they just bought. It is also clear that they went on to read an extraordinarily high proportion of those "own car" ads which they had noticed. On the average, a new car owner read 65 per cent of the ads he noticed which concerned his recently purchased automobile. The comparable percentages for the readership of ads dealing with other cars, that is, cars not at all involved in the decision, were, respectively, 46 and 34. Clearly, the prediction from dissonance theory is borne out so far. In the presence of dissonance following a decision, new car owners attempt to reduce their dissonance by reading material advertising the car they just bought.

The theory, however, also has something to say about the reading of ads dealing with cars they considered but did not buy. Specifically, it

_____
[8] *Ibid.*, p. 52.

would be expected, from the theory, that they would avoid reading these ads since such material would increase their dissonance. The obtained data are not in line with this expectation. While it is true that "considered car" ads were read significantly less frequently than "own car" ads, they were read as much as (or perhaps slightly more than) "other car" ads; hence we can hardly speak of avoidance of these "considered car" ads. This inconsistency with the theoretical prediction can perhaps be understood if we realize that recent new car purchasers were still rather sensitive to car ads and were used to reading them. Undoubtedly, during the period of decision they had noticed and read ads of all the cars they were considering. This sensitivity continued, and they still noticed the ads of the cars they had considered. "Considered car" ads were noticed by new car owners almost as frequently as "own car" ads were noticed. However, they did not read them as much as they used to. There was, very likely, an attempt to avoid reading these ads which, until recently, they had perused very carefully. The existence of dissonance is, after all, only one among many determinants of behavior such as reading ads. It is not surprising that once in a while these other factors override the effects of pressure to reduce dissonance.

The higher sensitivity to car advertising among new car owners is also seen in the comparison with old car owners. New car owners noticed and read more car ads of all types than did old car owners. The big difference between the two groups lies, however, in the frequency with which they read ads of their own car. As expected, new car owners read "own car" ads much more than did old car owners, 65 per cent as compared with 41 per cent. For old car owners the data have not been presented separately for considered cars and other cars because the great majority of the old car owners did not mention any other makes they considered before making their purchase. It is interesting to note that over a period of time, old car owners tended to forget or deny that they even seriously considered other makes.[9]

Cognitive Dissonance Related to Public Relations Practice

This brief excerpt of one study generated by an interest in cognitive dissonance theory should enable the reader to have at least an appreciation of this particular theoretical approach and how it is used to predict behavior. It is interesting to note that the predictions of dissonance theory to advertising readership following a purchasing decision does not follow "common sense" lines. That is, it is not a common sense observation that an individual would be *more* interested in reading copy pertaining to his purchase *after* he has made the purchase. One

---

[9] *Ibid.*, pp. 52-54.

might just as logically have argued that following a purchase, an individual did not have to *read* about the product he possesses. Why should he? He has the product itself to experience directly. This should make copy *about* the product pale by comparison.

A second observation, more to the point, is that there could be a number of situations in which a public relations practitioner might apply these research data that we have just considered.[10] Thus, a public relations practitioner responsible for stockholder relations would seize the opportunity to communicate directly with a recent purchaser of stock of his company, particularly if the purchase were sizable. Based on the advertising study, one would predict that the new stockowner would be *more likely* to read about the company just after making his purchase than at almost any other time that the public relations practitioner would have occasion to communicate with him. This same type of reasoning would apply to the new employee, particularly in a situation in which his decision to come with the organization represents a rather major one in his life. This employee would probably be most amenable to learning all about the organization that he has joined. The reader can doubtless think of many other examples of how this finding might be translated to public relations problem situations.

It should be clear to the reader by now why cognitive dissonance theory is a much more all-inclusive approach to understanding behavior than concepts such as role and status. Cognitive dissonance theory has been extended to a very wide range of problems thus far. For example, in the basic text cited up to now (Festinger's *A Theory of Cognitive Dissonance*), data are supplied on such topics as (1) the difficulty of reversing decisions, (2) the relationship between dissonance and force compliance brought about by reward and punishment, (3) the effect of decision on future action, and (4) the reduction of dissonance through rumors. More recently, another book, Brehm and Cohen's *Explorations in Cognitive Dissonance* (see again footnote 1), has appeared which affords the reader an even wider range of examples of application of dissonance theory. In this volume, data are reported on such additional topics as (1) the motivational effects of dissonance, (2) the relationship between dissonance and the defense mechanisms, (3) the effect of choice upon dissonance arousal, and (4) the relationship between dissonance and decision processes.

---

10 This assumes, of course, that there has been no "public-relations-type" research in which dissonance theory was tested. Naturally, the public relations practitioner would prefer to have direct research results rather than extrapolations from other data.

As the public relations practitioner becomes more sophisticated in his ability to relate social science theory to public relations practice, cognitive dissonance theory may well be one area that he will want to concentrate on.

Let us now turn to an illustration of a more all-inclusive concept that reflects the sociological approach to understanding human behavior.

A THEORY OF THE DIFFUSION AND ADOPTION OF INNOVATIONS[11]

Probably most people are aware of the great number and variety of changes that are going on around them at the present time. In fact, our age is characterized as one in which the only thing of which we can be certain is that there will be exceedingly rapid changes.

Perhaps the most dramatic kind of change that can be cited is technological: new machines, new processes, new methods of doing business and handling data. In short, in the world of "things" or material processes, practically every day some new process or piece of equipment is introduced.[12]

What is not so commonly understood is that while new ideas—regardless of their type—are tumbling forth from creative minds at an ever-increasing pace, acceptance of these new ideas (or the physical equipment produced by them) and their implications are not keeping up with the pace. We still have a considerable time lag between the introduction of a new idea and acceptance and utilization of the fruits of that new idea, regardless of its type. In this connection, Roger writes,

> In spite of Americans' generally favorable attitude toward science and technology, a considerable *time lag* is required before an innovation reaches wide acceptance. This is true despite the economic benefits of the innovations studied. For instance: A 40-year time lag was found between the first success of the tunnel oven in the pottery industry and its general use (Carter and Williams, 1957). Over 14 years were required for hybrid seed corn to reach complete adoption in Iowa

---

[11] The material for this section is based largely on Everett M. Rogers, *Diffusion of Innovations* (New York: The Free Press of Glencoe, 1962). All material adapted or quoted is done so with permission of The Free Press and Everett M. Rogers. Copyright © 1962 by The Free Press of Glencoe.

[12] In the United States, $10 billion was spent on research and development in 1960, and this will increase to about $21 billion in 1970 (*Ibid.*, p. 2).

(Ryan and Gross, 1943). About 50 years elapsed after development of a new educational practice before its adoption by all public schools (Ross, 1958). Put in another way, the average American school lags 25 years behind the best practices.

Similar time gaps have been found in other studies of innovations. For example, the average U.S. farmer could support 50 other persons (rather than 27) if he adopted already developed innovations. In fact, two U.S. Department of Agriculture experts stated, "People develop and apply technology in agriculture in a way that reminds us of a slow motion game of leapfrog, in which the time between advancing leaps is months or decades" (Green and LeRay, 1960, p. 31). So while large sums are invested in developing innovations and communicating them to intended audiences, there are important time lags before these innovations reach wide-spread adoption.[13]

A number of social scientists, particularly those who are concerned with the field known as Rural Sociology, have been concerned over the years with attempting to understand how new ideas are communicated and adopted. To these individuals, interest in this area is identified under the heading of "diffusion and adoption of innovations," and this section is designed to impart to the reader an appreciation of this type of thinking.

A Starting Point: an Examination of an Innovation That Failed[14]

Before examining a theory of the diffusion and adoption of innovation, let us consider briefly a case that highlights a great many of the problems that social scientists face in attempting to better understand how new ideas are communicated and either accepted or rejected. This case illustrates the difficulty of introducing the simple act of boiling drinking water in the little town of Los Molinos, Peru.

Los Molinos is a town of some 200 families. Water is obtained by the residents from three sources: an irrigation ditch, a spring and a public well. All of the sources are generally contaminated, and the prevalence of typhoid and other waterborne diseases is high. Consequently, the public health service in Peru is vitally interested in persuading its citizens to boil their water in order to reduce the incidence of disease.

---

13 *Ibid.*, p. 2.

14 This material was adapted from *ibid.*, pp. 7-12. Rogers' version of the case was based on modification of a case presented by Edward Wellin, "Water Boiling in a Peruvian Town," in Benjamin D. Paul (ed.), *Health, Culture and Community* (New York: Russell Sage Foundation, 1955).

Intensive efforts to change the behavior of the people of Los Molinos through a local hygiene worker, supported by a physician and fifteen housewives who had already changed their behavior, essentially failed. Why did this simple behavioral change fail to take place? A more detailed examination of the people involved revealed that the change desired by the health officials was directly contrary to many strongly held cultural beliefs of the people. For one thing, germ theory was rejected because it was really not understood. How can anything so small as a microbe hurt anyone? In addition, there were too many other, more tangible problems such as hunger and poverty to worry about. Also, with large families and much to do, how could anyone be expected to have the time to collect firewood? And buying fuel was out of the question. Lastly, the health inspectors were perceived as "snoopers" or "dirt inspectors," who do nothing but cause trouble.

In addition to these perceptions held by the bulk of the residents of Los Molinos, there was the question of cultural norms concerning the use of water to be contended with. These people have a belief embracing many materials so that these materials are classified as hot or cold, and this classification is not dependent on actual temperature. For example, pork is "very cold," whereas brandy is "very hot." Uncooked water is regarded as "very cold" as well. The residents of Los Molinos believe that extremes of hot and cold should be avoided, particularly when one is ill. Thus, when one is ill *then* he drinks boiled water, but not to control the contamination; rather, it is to rid raw water of its "cold nature." Associated with this belief is the dislike of the taste of boiled water. Only boiled water flavored with sugar, cinnamon, or herbs can be tolerated. In short, the very process which the health officials wished to institute (that is, boil water) was in conflict with a distinct aversion to the taste of boiled water and, in addition, was a practice that was normally only engaged in by ill individuals. Small wonder that this practice of boiling water was rejected by healthy individuals.

The Innovation That Failed: Some Comments

This case dramatically illustrates the difficulties that a communicator faces in attempting to bring about change, in this case the relatively simple innovation of boiling water before using it for drinking or cooking purposes. We could have just as easily selected from Rogers' book a case describing the difficulty of including innovations in our own culture—there are many in this volume that describe efforts to diffuse a new idea or process in our country.[15] The case of failure to induce the citizens of Los Molinos to boil their water was selected in preference to others that might have been presented because (1) the innovation that the health authorities wanted to bring about was so simple, and (2) the many variables, both individual and societal, that are involved when one tries to diffuse an innovation are so clearly evident.

The question of simplicity of the innovation is of importance because it brings out how essential it is to remember that the desired change must be viewed from the standpoint of the recipient, *not* of the one desirous of bringing about the change, namely, the sender.[16] As we have seen illustrated time and time again, we must approach any communication problem situation with the viewpoint of the potential recipient clearly in mind. This case on the diffusion of an innovation once again brings this principle into focus very clearly.

The multiplicity of variables is of importance to us because the public relations practitioner so often tends to oversimplify the communication problem that he faces. Pertinent here is the discussion presented earlier (Chapter 9, pages 225-227) about how the public relations practitioner relies too much on "informing." In our current case, we see evidence of the attractiveness of structuring the problem of getting people to boil their drinking water as *merely* one of "informing them" about the dangers of not doing so. Implicit is the assumption that once they appreciate the dangers of *not* boiling water, they certainly will do so.[17]

Another feature of this case is how an appreciation of the *social context* (with the various unique beliefs of the people, such as "hot" and "cold" foods) is invaluable in understanding what might be the bases for resistance to an innovation. Public relations practitioners are particularly vulnerable on this point because rarely do they turn to pertinent *sociological* concepts to guide them in their problem-solving efforts. (See again the last section of Chapter 5 and Figure 14.)

---

[15] Among the many cases cited are the problems associated with bringing about the adoption of such things as sprays, driver training, and new fabrics.

[16] The reader is reminded at this point how the material on perception applies here (see Chapter 7, pages 168-176).

[17] It is interesting to note the similarity between this boiling water case and seat belt use in our own country. For many associated with bringing about a diffusion of this particular innovation, there was implicit the assumption that all that was needed was to inform the American public about the dangers of not using seat belts, then they would do so.

So much for why this case is particularly pertinent as a guide to public relations practitioners. Let us now turn to an examination of a version of diffusion theory designed to handle the complex and extensive variables that are involved in any diffusion of innovation problem situations, such as were depicted in the water boiling case.

A Paradigm of Adoption of Innovation

Let's begin our examination of diffusion theory with an explanation of Figure 24[18] (page 412), which depicts Rogers' paradigm of the adoption of an innovation by an individual within a social system. This model is developed around three major phases of an innovation: *antecedents, the adoption process itself,* and *results.*

Antecedents. By antecedents, Rogers has in mind such things as the *actor's identity* and the way in which the actor (*i.e.,* the individual in question) perceives the innovation situation. The category of "actor's identity" is the way in which the model takes into account individual differences that will, of course, exist among any segment of a society into which one may be trying to introduce an innovation. This heading includes such things as how secure or anxious the individual happens to be, what values he possesses, and his intellectual capacities.

The other subheading under antecedents in Figure 24 is *perceptions of the situation.* This portion of the model accounts for the fact that an individual perceives an innovation in a social context and that the social context involved will play an important role in how a given new idea or innovation is perceived. As Rogers writes,

> The actor's perception of the situation affects his adoption behavior. The social system's norms on innovativeness serve as incentives or restraints on his behavior. Individuals in a social system with a modern norm will act differently from the way they would where the norms are traditional. The economic constraints or incentives, and the characteristics of the unit (such as the farm, business, or school) also affect adoption behavior.[19]

Adoption process. Our first point about the adoption process is that this portion of the model attempts to account for what is happening to the *individual.* That is, diffusion is a concept of communication of an

---

[18] Rogers, p. 306. Used by permission.
[19] *Ibid.,* p. 307.

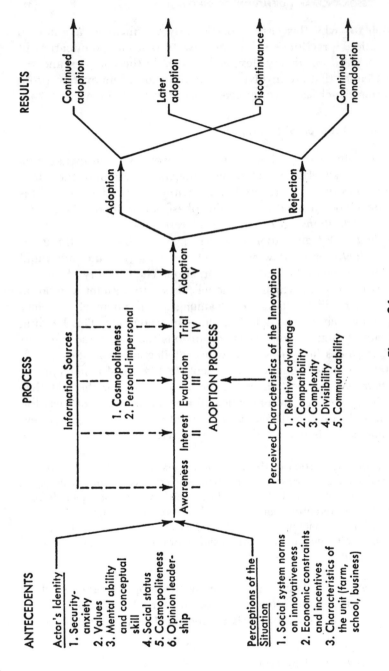

Figure 24

Paradigm of the adoption of an innovation by an individual within a social system.

idea throughout a group or segment of a particular social setting. As such, diffusion can be described in statistical terms—*i.e.*, so many people accepted a new idea and used it per unit of time passed—without any reference to what happens within the individuals who make up a group. The *adoption process* segment of the model attempts to conceptualize what goes on within the thinking of a single individual.

With this distinction in mind, the adoption process is conceptualized as undergoing the following stages: (1) awareness, (2) interest, (3) evaluation, (4) trial, and (5) adoption. These categories are probably self-explanatory to the reader. For instance, the awareness stage is that point at which the individual first hears about, or becomes cognizant of, a new idea or innovation. The trial stage, by contrast, is that point at which the individual actually tries out the new idea, process, or whatever is involved. The last stage, of course, refers to the fact that the idea or technique becomes relatively fixed as a part of the behavior repertoire of the individual.

Two other segments of the adoption process that the model encompasses are the *information sources* and the *perceived characteristics of the innovation*. Two distinctions are made of information sources—that is, the sources from which individuals receive information about the innovation. They are (1) whether the information is obtained by personal or impersonal means, and (2) whether the information comes from *outside* the social system within which the individual resides (*i.e.*, cosmopolite) or *inside* the social system within which the individual resides (*i.e.*, localite).[20] Naturally, combinations of these sources are possible as well.

The last main portion of the adoption process phase of the model in Figure 24 is the *perceived characteristics of the innovation*. These categories—*i.e.*, relative advantage, compatibility, and so on—represent an effort to classify the various major ways in which an innovation can be perceived by the individual. That is, they represent how the recipient views a particular innovation, not how the sender perceives the innovation. The first three categories are somewhat self-explanatory. The category *relative advantage* refers to how the recipient perceives the advantages of the innovation to him. *Compatibility* refers to the extent to which the innovation fits the cultural norms of the groups in which the individual resides. *Complexity* covers the degree to which a particular innovation is readily understandable or whether it is a

---

[20] To avoid confusion on the part of the reader, it should be noted that the term *localite*—the opposite of cosmopolite—does not appear in the model in Figure 24. This term is found in Rogers' book in the text accompanying the figure.

complex affair requiring considerable explanation to the recipient.

Divisibility and *communicability* are not so readily apparent. *Divisibility* refers to the degree to which an innovation can be tried out on a small scale or partial basis. To take two widely separated examples, some farm innovations, such as new feed, can be tried out on a limited basis so that the farmer does not have to make an expensive and extensive commitment. On the other hand, most automation schemes generally require rather substantial segments of an organization to be converted to an automated basis. The farm example is one of a high degree of divisibility, whereas the automation illustration depicts an innovation with a comparatively low degree of divisibility. *Communicability* essentially refers to the visibility of an innovation—that is, the degree to which one individual is able to tell or show another about a particular innovation. Rogers illustrates this category when he writes as follows:

> . . . *The communicability of an innovation, as perceived by members of a social system, affects its rate of adoption.* One illustration of this generalization is the case of pre-emergent weed-killers that are sprayed on a field before the weeds emerge from the soil. The rate of adoption of this idea has been slow by Midwestern farmers, in spite of its relative advantage, because there are no dead weeds which the farmer can show his neighbors.[21]

Results. So much for the three main segments of that portion of the model entitled *process*. The last segment of the model, *results*, is straightforward. Initially, a dichotomy is depicted—that is, the individual either adopts or rejects the innovation. Since neither adoption nor rejection are static or fixed features of an individual's behavior, the model allows for four outcomes to follow from this initial breakdown of adoption or rejection. Some of those individuals who initially adopt an innovation may continue to do so. Still others who at first adopted it are likely to discontinue the innovation. Conversely, some of those individuals who rejected the innovation adopt it later, and still others continue to reject the innovation and remain nonadopters.

Making Use of the Paradigm

The model of diffusion of innovation that we have examined briefly represents an effort to synthesize the generalizations that have been formulated by literally hundreds of research studies of the diffusion

---

[21] Rogers, p. 132.

of innovations. As a last step in our attainment of a working knowledge of this diffusion of innovation model, it will prove to be helpful if we reverse the process. That is, take one or two generalizations, consider briefly the experimental evidence on which they are based, and then relate them to the model. In this way, we should also achieve further insight as to how a model such as has been presented here can be used by a public relations practitioner in his problem-solving efforts.

1. *Our first generalization:* "*Impersonal information sources are most important at the awareness stage, and personal sources are most important at the evaluation stage in the adoption process.*"[22] Rogers reports that a great many studies have been conducted which support this generalization.[23] An illustration of the type of research study on which this generalization is based is a study done by Beal and Rogers in 1960.[24] The data are based on responses from 148 Iowa farmers regarding the adoption of 2,4-D weed spray. The authors paid particular attention to the relative importance of personal or impersonal communications to the farmer at each stage of his adoption of the weed spray. On the basis of these data, Rogers writes:

> . . . The percentage of respondents mentioning a personal information source (such as neighbors, friends, and relatives) increases from 37 per cent at the awareness stage, to 50 per cent at the interest stage, and 63 per cent at the evaluation stage; however, this percentage then decreases to 50 per cent at the trial stage. Experience with the innovation gained at the trial stage was reported as the most important information source by 95 per cent of the respondents at the adoption stage. Impersonal sources (such as farm magazines and bulletins) are more important than personal sources only at the awareness stage for 2,4-D weed spray.[25]

What this generalization highlights in our diffusion model (see Figure 24 again) is that the relationship between the hypothesized adoption process stages that an individual undergoes is related to the sources or types of communication to which he is exposed. This generalization

---

22 *Ibid.*, pp. 311-312. Generalization No. 4 in Rogers' list.

23 For example, Rogers writes:
Research studies supporting this generalization are Wilkening (1956), Copp and others (1958), Rogers and Beal (1958a), Rogers and Pitzer (1960), Beal and Rogers (1960, p. 8), Beal and Rogers (1957), Rahim (1961, p. 43), van den Ban (in press), and Wilkening (1952b, p. 16). [*Ibid.*, p. 99, n. 31.]

24 George M. Beal and Everett M. Rogers, *The Adoption of Two Farm Practices in a Central Iowa Community,* Iowa Agricultural and Home Economics Experiment Station Special Report 26 (Ames, 1960).

25 Rogers, p. 101.

suggests that there is an appropriate time for certain types of communication efforts on the part of a sender during certain phases of his efforts to persuade or change the recipient with respect to a new idea or innovation. One cannot afford the illusion that any one type of communication media *is always appropriate or best* for his communication objective. The reason that this particular example was selected is that earlier (Chapter 4, pages 84-86) the author pointed out that many public relations practitioners are inclined to make excessive use of the mass media. At that time, we examined various reasons for this over-reliance. This generalization under discussion raises another dimension that must be added to the thinking of the public relations practitioner: When are impersonal communication efforts appropriate? In effect, either through research or based on an "educated" guess, the public relations practitioner must assess at what phase (and in what proportion) his intended recipients are in the adoption process. Clearly, if the bulk of the recipients are beyond either the awareness or interest stage, *communication efforts poured into impersonal channels or outlets may be wasted.* What is needed is for the public relations practitioner to devise means by which the *personal* types of communication can be brought to bear (either directly or indirectly) on his intended recipients.[26]

2. *Two additional generalizations:* (a) *"There is little evidence that lack of knowledge about innovations actually delays their adoption"*; (b) *"Awareness occurs at a more rapid rate than does adoption."*[27]   To illustrate further the use of the paradigm introduced in Figure 24, these two generalizations are particularly appropriate because they are so closely related to typical public relations practice. Let us first examine the generalizations briefly and then turn to their relationship to public relations practice.

---

[26] This last point is very close to one made by the author in an article entitled "Research in Public Relations" (*Public Relations Journal,* January, 1961). In that article, the notion was put forth that it was time for us to turn our attention to what might be called *supplements* to the mass media. The mass media were conceded to be immensely important to the public relations practitioner, but the point was made that there are many times when the mass media do not accomplish the communication objective. Although in that article supplements to the mass media were expressed in terms of techniques that produced more personal involvement on the part of the recipient, what was said fits perfectly into the generalization now under discussion. In the context of our present discussion, *supplements to the mass media* would be efforts to achieve *personal*—as contrasted with impersonal—communication with intended recipients.

[27] Rogers, p. 312. Generalization No. 4.

Although the first generalization might have been expressed differently,[28] it relates to the so-called adoption period, that is, the duration of time required for an individual to move from awareness to adoption of an innovation. A number of researchers have reported that many persons who do *not* adopt an innovation are quite aware of its existence. For example Ryan and Gross,[29] in a study of 259 farmers and their reaction to a hybrid seed corn, found that, while *nearly all of the farmers were aware* of the new seed corn, there was a period of time when only a very small percentage had actually planted the corn. This example illustrates that merely being informed about something (*i.e.,* being made aware of its existence) is no assurance that the *motivation* to go on and make use of it will be forthcoming.

The second generalization simply points out that, for a given innovation, individuals become *aware* of the existence of a new idea, process, or product more rapidly than they *adopt* it. This generalization is illustrated by Figure 25,[30] in which the difference between the rates of awareness and adoption is illustrated by selecting a given percentage level, then looking to see how much time elapsed before that particular percentage was reached. Thus, we see that for ten per cent of the farmers to *adopt* the 2,4-D weed spray, it took 1.7 years *longer* than it did for ten per cent of the same group of farmers to become *aware* of the spray. *This is true regardless of the particular percentage of awareness vs. adoption selected: It always takes considerably longer to bring about adoption.*

Diffusion Theory Related to Public Relations Practice

The generalizations discussed in the preceding section are intimately related to public relations practice, or, at the very least, are related to assumptions with regard to practice. For one thing, many public relations practitioners function as if their whole job were to inform or, in the context of our present paradigm, to make people aware. The author argues that in most of the applied situations in which the public relations practitioner finds himself, he is *trying to get people ultimately*

---

[28] It appears to the author that this generalization might possibly be interpreted by some to mean that awareness is not an essential step in the adoption process. It is, of course. What the generalization means is that awareness is not the *only* element necessary to move an individual toward adoption of an innovation.

[29] Bryce Ryan and Neal C. Gross, "The Diffusion of Hybrid Seed Corn in Two Iowa Communities," *Rural Sociology,* VIII (1943), 15-24.

[30] Rogers, p. 109. Used by permission.

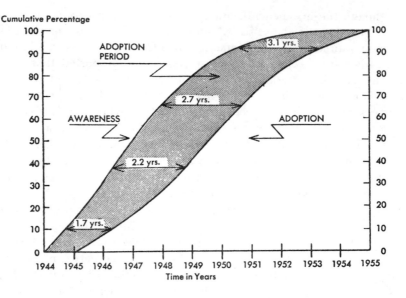

Figure 25

Adoption period for Iowa farmers adopting 2,4-D weed spray by year

The shaded area in this figure illustrates the aggregate adoption period between awareness and adoption of 2,4-D weed spray. Awareness proceeds at a more rapid rate than does adoption. This suggests that relatively later adopters have a longer average adoption period than do earlier adopters. For example, there are 1.7 years between 10 per cent awareness and 10 per cent adoption, but 3.1 years between 92 per cent awareness and 92 per cent adoption.

Source: A reanalysis of data originally gathered by Beal and Rogers (1960, p. 8). Used by permission.

to adopt a certain idea, attitude, or behavior, or all three. Trying to make employees ego-involved in their company, or citizens concerned about local, state, or national government, or a whole country conscious of fallout, water pollution, or some such problem is *not* just a matter of creating awareness. In fact, we find repeatedly that people who are inactive or nonparticipants *are* aware of the very issues about which they do nothing.[31]

Two factors appear to account for the fact that the typical public

[31] The reader is reminded again of how the discussion in this section—in fact, all of the material on diffusion theory—relates to the points made in Chapter 9, pages 210-238.

relations practitioner confuses *informing* with *adopting*. One reason is that implicitly the public relations practitioner has *equated* the two processes. That is, he often approaches his public relations problems as if to be informed were to be changed. Some readers may protest that this is not so, that many public relations practitioners know that there is a difference. The fact that some public relations practitioners do know the difference is really not the point. What is more pertinent is that, by and large, most public relations operations are *geared* for *informing*. Their usage of the mass media, their reliance on the printed and electronically transmitted word belies any claim that they "know better" concerning the difference between becoming aware and becoming an adopter. The *first stage* (*i.e.*, awareness) in what sociologists call the adoption process accounts for a tremendous proportion of public relations practice.

The second main reason for this state of affairs is that, with the exception of a comparatively limited effort to regard public relations practice in *theoretical* terms, the practically oriented man dominates the public relations scene. One who is oriented toward practice and away from theory is not likely to analyze the process of adoption of a new idea as it is illustrated in this paradigm. It seldom occurs to the man in practice to think this way or to avail himself of material compiled by others who are thinking of the diffusion process from a theoretical or analytical point of view.

It should be clear, too, from these generalizations that the public relations practitioner of the future must be better equipped to cope with bringing about the diffusion of an innovation. In the years to come, it will probably become "old hat" for the public relations practitioner to employ certain techniques to achieve awareness of a given proportion of his intended recipients. The awareness will probably be achieved by modifications or extensions of the mass media that we can only dimly imagine now. On reaching these levels (determined by rapid, efficient research techniques) he will probably use *different* techniques to facilitate the adoption process—different, that is, in the sense that the mass media usage will be supplemented by novel, sophisticated versions of face-to-face methods. In short, the public relations practitioner will follow carefully all phases of the adoption process and modify or introduce appropriate communication techniques as he goes along.

So much for our brief excursion into diffusion theory. Although we have only scratched the surface, we have examined enough of this second illustration of a more all-inclusive approach to an understanding of human behavior to give the reader a feeling for this approach. It should be clear that in this area there is much more useful information for the public relations practitioner to become acquainted with.[32]

QUESTIONS FOR DISCUSSION

1. On pages 400-407 in this chapter, the theory of cognitive dissonance was extended to public relations practice, particularly with respect to how a public relations practitioner might apply some of the findings to communicating with stockholders of a given company. Develop your own example of how the notions involved in the theory of cognitive dissonance might be applied to public relations practice. After you have developed your illustration, would you say that this theory was merely "common sense"? Or did the theory help you develop an application that might not have occurred to you otherwise?

2. Take any one of the three generalizations borrowed from Rogers concerning what we feel is now known about the diffusion of innovations and relate it to public relations practice, as you did in the above question for cognitive dissonance theory.

3. On pages 418-419, the contention is made that the typical public relations practitioner confuses *informing* with *adopting*. Using one of the cases employed in answering previous discussion questions, try to develop as much evidence *for* and *against* this assertion as you can. Which way do you find the evidence coming out?

4. On page 419, the idea is put forth that in the future public relations practitioners will employ different techniques for different phases in the over-all diffusion of innovation process. Try to develop one reasonably detailed example of how the techniques might vary as functions of the different stages of the adoption process

---

[32] One final point. From our distinction between the psychological and the sociological approaches, introduced in Chapter 12, it is clear that diffusion theory falls into the sociological category (as contrasted with cognitive dissonance, which is an illustration of the psychological approach). With the exception of the adoption process, the *group* is the unit of analysis in diffusion theory. Even when the individual is taken into consideration (*e.g.*, in identifying the stages in the adoption process), the point of departure is primarily in terms of groups of individuals. The process of adoption is, of course, recognized as an individual affair, but the model developed to understand and predict rates of adoption, etc., is based on numbers of individuals taken together—the typical sociological approach.

involved. That is, spell out, for a given public relations problem, what would be done to bring about *awareness*, how these methods would change to produce *interest*, then how different things would be done to bring about *evaluation*, then *trial*, and finally *adoption*. Did you find it difficult to generate *different* techniques to achieve the various phases of the diffusion of innovation process? Which phase of the five did you appear to be particularly well equipped to handle? If it happened to be the awareness phase, why do you think this is so?

Chapter 16

THE RECIPIENT STAGE IN FURTHER DETAIL: RECIPIENT CATEGORIZATION SYSTEMS AND THE CONCEPT OF PUBLIC OPINION

INTRODUCTION

In the preceding four chapters we have been concentrating on an analysis of the recipient stage in more detail. Thus far, we have put forth a point of view about two main approaches to understanding human behavior: the psychological and the sociological. In the context of this major distinction between approaches to dealing with human behavior, we have considered a number of concepts ranging from comparatively circumscribed or specific ones, such as attitude and role and status, to quite inclusive ones, such as cognitive dissonance and diffusion of innovations.

We have two final considerations to examine in this last chapter to be devoted to an analysis of the recipient stage in more detail. First, we must consider the various ways in which social and behavioral scientists have tried to categorize intended recipients. That is, what schemata have proved to be fruitful in grouping intended recipients (that are to be objects of communication efforts) so that their reactions

RECIPIENT CATEGORIZATION SYSTEMS 423

to communication efforts can be better predicted? In this connection, we will examine a series of categorization systems that range from some that are purely conjecture (done "by the seat of the pants," so to speak) to some that are the end result of some rather extensive experimentation.

Lastly, we will examine the concept of public opinion in some detail because this term has considerable significance to a discussion of the recipient and crops up in all sorts of social and behavioral science literature.

EFFORTS TO CATEGORIZE INTENDED RECIPIENTS OR AUDIENCES

All of us resort to categorization systems in order to deal more effectively with others. Usually these categorization systems contain generalizations or, perhaps more properly, have accompanying generalizations. For example, when we state and believe that "all fat people are jolly" and, conversely, that "all thin people are mean," these generalizations both enable us to classify people that we meet, and to then predict behavior, depending on the generalizations that accompany the categories.[1]

This tendency to categorize and then generalize on the basis of the categories is dependent on an element of truth that nearly anyone can observe for himself. Namely, that one can group individuals according to some classification scheme, then observe that predictions based on

---

[1] It is only fitting that we point out in passing that as a rule the generalizations that accompany these practical, everyday categorization systems have their limitations. What so often happens is that we can find conflicting generalizations that have grown out of our experiences. This is demonstrated by Krech, Crutchfield, and Ballachey in their illustration of the "polarity" of psychological generalizations. Their table shows how one can easily find a well known generalization that is the opposite of any other well known generalization:

If these don't work . . .	*. . . Try these*
Repeat a lie frequently enough and people will believe it.	The truth will always prevail.
Clothes make the man.	You can't make a silk purse out of a sow's ear.
Never too old to learn.	You can't teach an old dog new tricks.
Absence makes the heart grow fonder.	Out of sight, out of mind.
East is East and West is West and never the twain shall meet.	Brothers under the skin.

See D. Krech, Richard S. Crutchfield, and Egerton L. Ballachey, *Individual in Society* (New York: McGraw-Hill Book Company, 1962), p. 3. Used by permission.

this system tend to be more precise than before the grouping was made.[2]

An illustration that brings this point closer to home would be the public relations practitioner's use of the concept of the *thought leader* years made use of this classification system to isolate persons with (see Chapter 11, page 274). Public relations practitioners have for whom they should communicate in order to more effectively achieve their communication objective. The concept of thought leader is nothing more than a particular form of this tendency to form classification systems that we are now examining in more detail.

Let us pursue a more detailed examination of classification systems and how they are utilized to better understand and predict the behavior of the recipient. Specifically, let us examine (1) intuitive categorization systems and (2) various types of experimentally based classification systems.

Explicit Intuitive Groupings

One type of grouping of recipients is the more detailed yet essentially intuitive categorization system, which is usually more elaborate than the "thought leader" illustration noted above. An example of this type of system is Roper's classification scheme which brings together intuition, educated guessing, and experience based on long years of research dealing with recipients.[3] Roper generated his classification system in the context of the general problem of understanding how ideas penetrate the public as a whole in the United States. As a guide to understanding this process of penetration, he suggests that the entire American public can be broken down into *six groups* visualized as concentric circles that grow rapidly in size from the inner circle, which is extremely small, to the last, outer circle which is extremely large. Briefly the six groups are broken down as follows:

---

[2] We have already considered (Chapter 5, pages 106-108) another variation of the general concept of grouping: *reference groups*. The concept of reference groups, particularly the generalizations that we make about them (*e.g.*, primary groups to which an individual belongs exert a more powerful influence on him than secondary groups of which he is also a member), is merely another variation of this grouping tendency for purposes of better understanding and prediction. The point that the reader should keep clear is that all of the particular variations of grouping to be discussed in the forthcoming section are part and parcel of the general process of grouping individuals for more adequate description, understanding, and prediction.

[3] Based on material contained in a foreword written by Elmo Roper in E. Katz and P. F. Lazarsfeld, *Personal Influence* (New York: The Free Press of Glencoe, 1955), pp. xv-xx. All material from *Personal Influence* used by permission of The Free Press and the authors. Copyright 1955 by The Free Press, A Corporation.

1. *Great Thinkers*—Only about a half dozen are living in the world at any one time. Defined by Roper as follows: "The ground common to all Great Thinkers is that all have evolved important philosophies or major theories which at some point in history have gained wide acceptance. Among the living I would venture to name only Einstein as a Great Thinker in the field of science."[4]

   Roper goes on to point out that another characteristic of Great Thinkers is that they may be leaders in their respective fields but complete novices outside their fields of competence.

2. *Great Disciples*—About a dozen of such individuals are to be found in any one country at any one time. "They are people who do not think out great theories or philosophies, but they have a sufficient understanding and a close enough mental association with those who do to become most effective advocates and protagonists for an idea or philosophy. In the field of religion, for instance, St. Paul would be a Great Disciple."[5]

3. *Great Disseminators*—Their number ranges from about two hundred fifty to one thousand persons at any given period of time. Roper defines these individuals in this manner: "Great Disseminators are people who have an important forum—national or international—and who are respected and listened to by a number of people. The United States Senate might be an illustration of such a forum, and as widely separated as Senator Ralph Flanders and Senator Joseph McCarthy might be on many points, they are together in that both are 'Great Disseminators'—under this theory."[6]

4. *Lesser Disseminators*—This group ranges from as few as fifteen thousand to as many as fifty thousand and is defined by Roper as follows: "These people also have a forum and are listened to—but their forum is more limited. For instance, a national labor leader might have the role of a Great Disseminator, but the president of a local union would be a Lesser Disseminator—listened to, but in a more localized and more limited area. Other illustrations would be a minister in a small town, the editor of a country weekly, or a purely local news commentator."[7,8]

---

[4] *Ibid.*, pp. xvi, xvii.

[5] *Ibid.*, p. xvi.

[6] *Ibid.*, p. xvii.

[7] *Ibid.*

[8] The reader has undoubtedly noted the overlap between this particular category and the thought-leader concept discussed earlier.

5. *Participating Citizens*—This group takes a substantial jump in size, numbering between ten to twenty-five million Americans. In describing this group, Roper writes, "They vote with some regularity, contribute money or work in local and national campaigns, belong to organizations active in civic or public affairs, write letters to Congressmen and public officials, are active in discussions on current affairs and problems."[9]

6. *Politically Inert*—This group is by far the largest of all of the groups identified, totaling some seventy-five million people. By way of identifying this group, Roper says: "These are people generally who are not very much at home in the world of ideas, at least when ideas are presented to them in raw or undiluted form. They seldom are active in their communities, and they rarely speak out on any subject. They are not vocal about what they believe in. But they are extremely important."[10]

So much for this categorization system. It provides a rough guide about how to think about the recipient, particularly from the standpoint of dissemination of new ideas. There is a strong kinship among this system, the thought-leader concept developed earlier, and any other categorization system that is primarily based on intuition rather than research. One of the major limitations of any such categorization system is the problem of identifying the people that belong in the various categories. In terms of Roper's system, how does one readily identify a "Lesser Disseminator," for example. This is the type of question that the public relations practitioner must ask, because his task is reaching such people as well as the other particularly pertinent categories of individuals, the "participating citizens" and the "politically inert." In fact, one could safely generalize and say that usually the public relations practitioner—regardless of his particular problem—is interested in identifying and communicating with the last three categories of individuals noted in Roper's system.

Experimentally Based Categorization Systems

Not all categorization systems applied to intended recipients are intuitively based. There are many that result from research into specific areas: for example, *what* categories best group individuals with similar attitudes and *how* such individuals are identified.

Social scientists have used three methods in evolving categorization

---

[9] Katz and Lazarsfeld, p. xviii.
[10] *Ibid.*

systems—what sociologists call "social stratification." They are (1) the reputational approach, (2) the subjective approach, and (3) the objective approach.[11] The *reputational* approach essentially asks individuals how they would categorize others. Some researchers ask members of a community to give their understanding of what various social strata exist within that community. In addition, the respondents are asked what bases they have for their classification of people. The *subjective* approach is more direct: Individuals are asked to categorize themselves with respect to some class or stratification system. The *objective* approach covers situations in which the social scientist evolves some classification scheme and then places individuals in this scheme according to certain observable and measurable criteria.

Before we consider some examples of these three different categorization system approaches, there are two things that we should bear in mind about experimentally based categories. Aside from the fact that from time to time people object to classification systems on the grounds that we do not have a class or caste system here in America (a view that misses the point of these systems entirely), occasionally the question is raised as to which classification system is best or which system is correct. The reply is that there is no "right" or "wrong" or "best" system. In addition, in certain circumstances, individuals may fit into a number of categorization systems. Broom and Selznick address themselves to this point when they write,

> The schoolteacher is a case in point. *Objectively*, using income as a criterion, she may be in a lower stratum. She probably makes less than the zoo cook. *Reputationally*, using the criteria of service to children or place of residence, she may be placed in the middle class by members of her community. *Subjectively*, because of her association with intellectuals and her advanced training and degrees, she may place herself at a higher level. Which is her *real* class position?[12]

There is, of course, no *real* class position in the sense that there is only one ultimately correct categorization system. It depends on the system used and the purpose for which it was developed. This brings us to the second point about categorization systems: The most fruitful way of thinking about any categorization system, regardless of its type, is what *use* can be made of the system. That is, what predictions can be made on the basis of the categorization system and how accurate

---

[11] L. Broom and P. Selznick, *Sociology* (3rd ed.; New York: Harper & Row, Publishers, 1963), pp. 182-185. All material from *Sociology* used by permission.

[12] *Ibid.*, pp. 184-185.

do they prove to be? In this light, it may be that for a certain prediction situation—how many people will be voting in a forthcoming election—one system is more effective. For another—predicting certain types of consumer behavior—another categorization system is most effective.

Reputational approach example. Perhaps the most widely known and used classification system is the one that grew out of the work of W. Lloyd Warner and his associates, dating back more than two decades. On the basis of interviews conducted in several communities (a New England community called "Yankee City," a Southern town named "Old City," and a Midwestern town that had several names: "Jonesville," "Prairie City," "Hometown," and "Elmtown") *in which the investigators elicited information about how the respondents identified others in their own community*, they evolved the now-famous six social classes that have been used again and again to categorize respondents in all sorts of subsequent studies.[13] The categories that Warner and his co-workers named and described on the basis of information derived from the interviews, are as follows: upper-upper, lower-upper, upper-middle, lower-middle, upper-lower, and lower-lower. Broom and Selznick summarize and describe these categories as follows:

1. The *upper-upper* class is an aristocracy of birth and inherited wealth. The "old families" have a way of life characterized by ritual behavior and intricate codes of etiquette. Community members refer to this class as "the 400," "the aristocrats," and "the people with family and money."

2. Members of the *lower-upper* class, like the upper-uppers, live in costly homes in exclusive districts, and have similar patterns of participation, income, and occupation. They engage in such occupations as finance, industry, and the professions. But they lack the distinguished ancestry of the upper-uppers and the tradition of the upper-class behavior. Their money is too new and their achievements too recent to warrant the same prestige as the upper-uppers. In Jonesville, however, these two upper classes are combined, making only five classes in all.

3. The *upper-middle* class is composed of professionals and substantial businessmen. These respected members of the community often act as civic leaders, but they are not "society." They live in comfortable houses

---

[13] W. L. Warner and P. S. Lunt, *The Social Life of a Modern Community* (New Haven, Conn.: Yale University Press, 1941).

in the "better" residential sections. They are referred to by community members as "above average but not tops." . . .

4. The *lower-middle* class is composed of small-business men, white-collar workers, and a few skilled workmen. Their small neat houses are in the "side streets." They are proper and conservative, careful with their money, concerned about respectability, and labeled as "good common people."

5. Members of the *upper-lower* class are the "honest workmen" and the "clean poor." They are semiskilled workers in factories, service workers, and a few small tradesmen. They live in the less desirable sections and have lower incomes, but they are "respectable." They are often referred to as the "poor, but hard-working people."

6. The *lower-lower* class is not "respectable." They are the "level below the common man," live in the worst sections and are semiskilled and unskilled workers. In Yankee City they comprised the largest proportion of individuals on relief. They are regarded as immoral by the other classes and are referred to as "poor but not respectable," "the river rats," etc.[14]

Warner and his co-workers suggest that these social class distinctions are applicable to all parts of our country. Naturally, the number of the classes and the actual proportion of the total community that falls into any one class may vary slightly from community to community. Class sizes and variations that occur from community to community are illustrated in Figure 26.[15] In this figure, we see that not only do the percentages differ in each community with respect to how many people fall into a given class (e.g., lower middle class: 28% in Yankee City; 32.2% in Jonesville), but also the number of classes utilized to describe each community differs. Jonesville has only an upper class and not an upper-upper and a lower-upper class.

This classification system has had a tremendous impact on applied work in advertising, public relations, and any number of other facets of the business world; it has sharpened the grouping of and the understanding of the intended recipient so that the sender is more likely to communicate successfully with him. Today it is almost impossible to find a marketing or opinion-attitude survey that does not make use

---

[14] Broom and Selznick, pp. 190-191.

[15] *Ibid.*, p. 191. (Sources used by Broom and Selznick for Yankee City data, Warner and Lunt, *op. cit.*, p. 88; for Jonesville data, Warner *et al., Democracy in Jonesville* [New York: Harper & Row, Publishers, 1949], pp. 50, 51.)

of some version of the social stratification introduced by Warner and his co-workers. We have learned that consumer behavior and attitudes can vary markedly as a function of socioeconomic status or class.

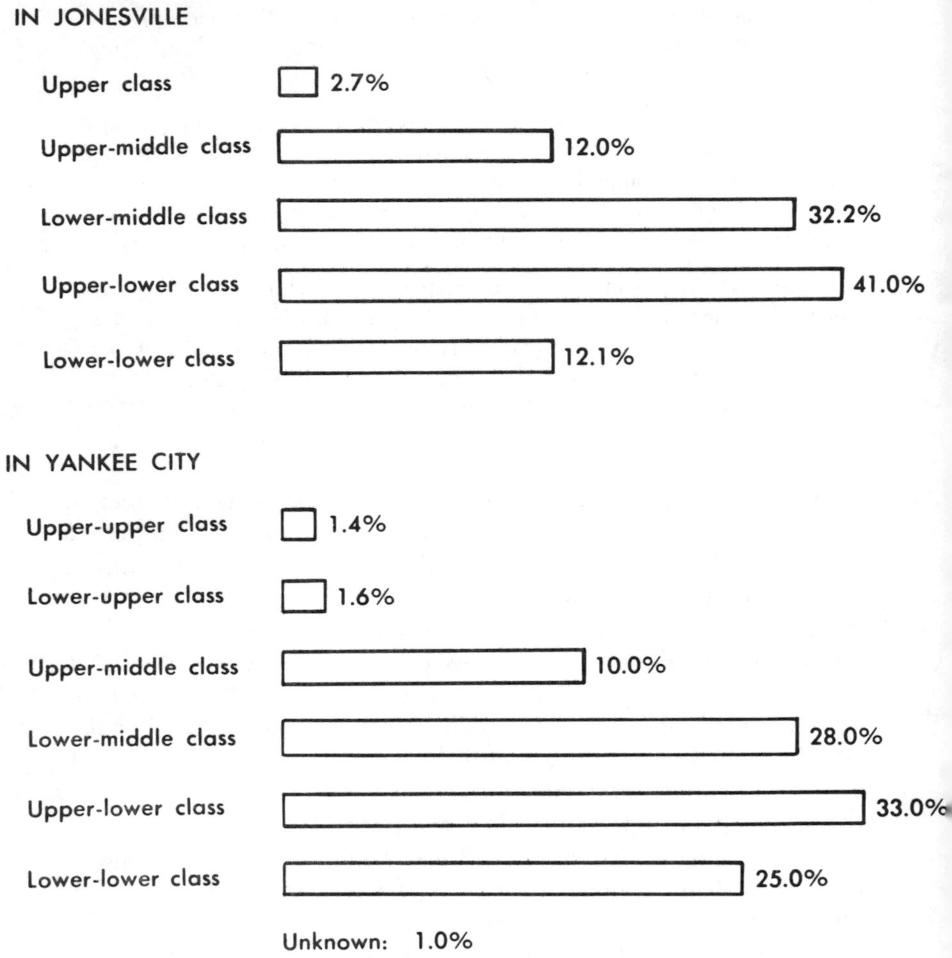

IN JONESVILLE

Upper class	2.7%
Upper-middle class	12.0%
Lower-middle class	32.2%
Upper-lower class	41.0%
Lower-lower class	12.1%

IN YANKEE CITY

Upper-upper class	1.4%
Lower-upper class	1.6%
Upper-middle class	10.0%
Lower-middle class	28.0%
Upper-lower class	33.0%
Lower-lower class	25.0%

Unknown: 1.0%

Figure 26

Size of Classes

Subjective approach example. A number of studies can be cited to illustrate the subjective approach. One of the better known is that of Centers, who studied the self class identification of 1,100 persons. In addition, he related these subjective class identifications with opinion differences these individuals held about a number of major social, economic, and political issues.[16]

The way in which Centers was able to establish the relationship between subjective class identifications and opinions on important issues was by asking questions such as the following:

Which one of these statements do you most agree with?

1. The most important job for the government is to make it certain that there are good opportunities for each person to get ahead on his own.

2. The most important job for the government is to guarantee every person a decent and steady job and standard of living.[17]

On the basis of replies to such questions, the respondents in the sample were assigned to a series of five categories ranging from ultra-conservative to ultra-radical. These classification groupings were then related to the class groupings into which each individual had placed himself.

One of the interesting findings that emerged from this work was that when the respondents were offered the opportunity to categorize themselves into "working class" as well as "lower class" (apparently few people like to think of themselves as "lower class," even if the term is supposed to describe financial status more than any other dimension). Centers obtained groupings of individuals that were more stable with respect to attitudes toward certain social and political issues of the day. He observed that certain previous studies had not been too successful in relating *self class identification* with attitudes toward social and political issues. What Centers found, among other things, was that his approach tended to break down the comparatively large middle class into a middle class and a working class. These data suggest that in certain circumstances greater communication precision is possible if the public relations practitioner is able to make a distinction between middle class and working class in a given group of intended recipients. This would certainly be true in a number of situations where a public relations practitioner is responsible for communicating with a large heterogeneous employee group.

Objective approach example. Perhaps the approach that offers the

---

[16] R. Centers, "The American Class Structure: A Psychological Analysis," in G. E. Swanson, T. M. Newcomb, and E. L. Hartley (eds.), *Readings in Social Psychology* (New York: Holt, Rinehart and Winston, Inc., 1952), pp. 299-311.

[17] *Ibid.*, p. 299.

greatest promise for the development of categorization systems is the objective approach. The reason is simple: In the objective approach, we find greater promise of evolving categories that effectively differentiate people into truly separate or distinguishable categories along some dimension of interest to the investigator. But even more important, many objective systems *offer methods for identifying the individual or individuals that belong in a particular category as well as merely categorizing them more effectively.* This point will become clearer as we consider an example of the objective approach in more detail.

Perhaps the objective approach most familiar to the reader is the one whereby the recipients are classified into age groups or income brackets ranging from low to high. The same has been done with respect to education, occupation, neighborhood, and a number of other objective criteria that can be used as measures of the recipient. With these classification systems, various correlates of the classes can be derived, such as the relationship between income and leisure time activities; between occupational status and community standing; and between education and mass media preferences. Some of these relationships have proved to be useful; however, more often that not, these categorization systems have proved to be too static to be really effective predictive devices for such dynamic behaviors as political preferences and consumer behavior. For this reason, we have selected as an example of the objective approach a concept which tries to categorize individuals in terms of a dynamic system so as to be in keeping with how people actually behave. The approach we shall consider is the one identified as the Tastemaker Concept, developed by the Opinion Research Corporation.[18]

Our starting point in understanding the rudimentary elements of tastemaker theory is the situation faced by a company that wants to market its products or services: How can it predict what products will sell in the future, and to what extent?

As the researchers at ORC point out, most of the existing efforts to classify intended consumers have been based on inadequate concepts and outmoded procedures. For example, the bulk of the consumer studies tend to break up the interviewees into categories dictated primarily by those used by the U.S. Bureau of the Census in its work. Hence, the usual marketing study classifies the respondents into the appropriate income, age, sex, number of children, occupation, and marital

---

[18] The material from this section is based on *America's Tastemakers*, Tastemaker Research Report No. 1 (April, 1959) and Tastemaker Research Report No. 2 (July, 1959) (Princeton, N.J.: Opinion Research Corporation). All material from Tastemaker Research Reports used by permission.

status categories. Superimposed on these categorization systems have been more refined schemes, such as interviewing individuals by what might be called "purchase units"—*i.e.*, if the decision to buy is primarily the result of a man and his wife, then the thing to do is to interview married couples together. Another scheme is the "life cycle" analyses; that is, distinguishing between broad periods within an individual's life—premarital; marital, with growing family; marital, with grown children; old age—and trying to correlate consumer behavior patterns with these broad periods in an individual's life. These innovations, along with the traditional categorization systems borrowed from the census people, have their limitations as effective predictive devices in marketing work. What has been particularly weak about these standard approaches is that they do not lend themselves to predicting *changes* in consumer behavior.

The limitations of these conventional means of categorizing the intended consumer for purposes of prediction is illustrated by the discussion that the ORC researchers devote to the built-in assumptions that accompany these standard measures taken of respondents. For example, they write:

> In any survey, the individual is in effect cut up into various bits and pieces. One of them is labeled "income," another "education," another "age," and so on. We then assemble all the "income" pieces in one heap, the "education" pieces in another, and so on. We then compare one aggregate with another—what is the relationship between education and income? Age and washing machine purchase? Life cycle and advertising exposure? In more sophisticated analysis, we form aggregates out of several aggregates of pieces. Combining income, education and occupation, for instance, we may get "socioeconomic status." Most market research, however, has tended to use the simpler form: income versus product usage, one variable versus another. Whether in its simpler or more complex form, this type of analysis is an invaluable tool in our research kit.
>
> From the standpoint of prediction, however, it has a serious flaw: it takes the individual apart (in certain ways), but it does not put him back together again.
>
> This has two serious consequences. First, any one of our standard groups contains a wide diversity of human beings. As our society changes, this diversity is increasing. For example, the occupational categories are almost notorious for their heterogeneity. Within the "manager-proprietor" class may be found together the President of General Electric and the proprietor of a corner fruit stand; and a 40-acre farmer is classed together with the modern farmer who may winter in Florida, live in the city, and fly to his farming operation in a Piper

Cub. Other categories are almost as badly mixed. Within the same age category we will find a grandfather and a just married; within the same metropolitan area, a swarm of Tennessee hillbillies and the intellectual community of the University of Chicago; within the same region of the country, and the same state, millions of migrant Mid-Westerners and millions of native Californians; within the same "life cycle" stage, professional men who are supporting children away at college and day laborers whose adult children are supporting them.[19]

.　.　.　.　.

To sum up, (a) we abstract from the individual certain characteristics we assume are significant or likely to be; (b) we examine the relationship between these characteristics and certain kinds of behavior in which we are interested, but not between individuals and behavior. With the results that (c) each of these characteristics may be found in such a diversity of people that predictive value is lost, and (d) we cannot isolate in our analysis those individuals whose behavior puts them in a minority today but a forerunner of the majority for the years ahead.[20]

The preceding quotes describe what the ORC researchers wanted to overcome in their own research. They also serve to give the reader an appreciation of why the ORC people felt that improved means of categorizing and identifying recipients (in this case, in their consumer role) were important. The end result of this concern was to be called the *Tastemaker Theory*.

On the basis of considerable preliminary work, the ORC researchers ascertained that three types of information obtained from an individual tended to predict his consumer behavior surprisingly well: *income*, *values*, and *mobility*. An approach that would synthesize measures of these three dimensions of an individual would, in turn, enable them to predict consumer behavior more effectively. In their own words, they introduce this synthesis with the following:

In summary, our conceptual structure has three pillars. The first of these is the most familiar, *Income*, which is always important but becomes less so as disposable income and the freedom to choose increase. We have described its role by pointing out that the first critical variable in consumer behavior is the ability to command sufficient resources to act in behalf of values in terms of goods. Thus, when we appraise the

---

[19] *America's Tastemakers*, Tastemaker Research Report No. 1 (April, 1959), p. 13.
[20] *Ibid.*, p. 14.

prospects of a given product, we are also lowering the necessary role of income, ascribing a larger role to the values with which that product is associated.

Thus, even a middle-income household can allocate its scarce resources to the purchase of a new Cadillac—if it values such an acquisition above alternative purchases. Other families, higher on the income scale, may be out of the Cadillac market not because they cannot scrape together or borrow the purchase price, but because their values dictate that such a use of their resources would be unwise. We, therefore, cannot safely predict future sales of Cadillacs solely from estimates of rising national income. With the additional increment, many families may buy boats, or improve their houses, or educate their children, or run up larger liquor bills, depending on where their values lie.

We are led inevitably to the second pillar of our structure, *the role of values* in consumer behavior. By this time we have begun to see how values fit into the picture of changing consumer behavior. We have seen, for example, that people who concentrate their energies on religious life are not as a rule people whom the marketer can rely on for product adoption leadership. By contrast people whose resources are concentrated on recreational life are likely to be among the most important bellwethers.

For our third pillar, we study those people who habitually perform the role of giving form and substance to changing patterns of values and the way they are expressed—individuals who spread and cultivate the seed of change. *For this, we utilize mobility.*

These, then, are our three tools for isolating a consumer elite with the power to forewarn us of change. Our task now is to combine them in one instrument. [Italics added.] [21]

The end result of all this work is an aproach that measures individuals on three scales: Mobility, Values, and Income (abbreviated, the MVI measure). This three-way *tastemaker identification* provides the person responsible for market research within an organization the ability to find and identify persons who are leaders. In addition, he can learn how the values of these mobile individuals will or will not be served by certain products (both old and new). Lastly, he can predict acceptance of these products and the likelihood that these people will disseminate their reaction of the product to others, thereby fostering a new trend from the standpoint of product adoption.

To show how the MVI scale works, the relationship between the

---

[21] *America's Tastemakers*, Tastemaker Research Report No. 2 (July, 1959), pp. 73-74.

MVI measures and early product adoption for seventy-five different "recent growth" products tested in the community of Ridgewood, New Jersey, is illustrated in Figure 27.[22]

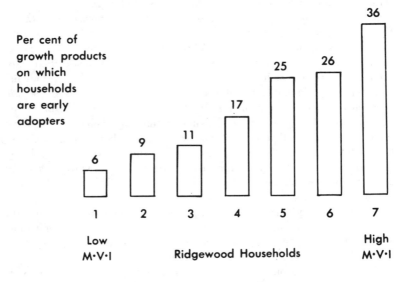

EARLY ADOPTION OF GROWTH PRODUCTS
ON THE MOBILITY • VALUE • INCOME SCALE

Figure 27

Three-way tastemaker identification system provides market research with new predictive power.

What this chart says in effect is this:

If we were to examine how new products fare with the top three MVI groups, their acceptance or rejection would provide us with a strong indication of mass behavior to come.

These top groups not only have the ability to purchase should their values be effectively served by new products, they also are in a position to (a) learn about these products earlier than others, and (b) disseminate their reaction to others.

For a particularly sensitive barometer of things to come, we would be especially concerned with Group 7—the very small group whose habits and values and actions are so critical to the formation of new trends.

To wrap up this treatment of the tastemaker concept, it may be of

---

[22] *Ibid.*, p. 76.

value to list the general scheme of how the tastemaker concept can be used with specific tailoring for particular companies and their products and/or services. The reader can grasp how the tastemaker concept is applicable to almost any sort of marketing problem by studying the steps:

a. Identify the high mobiles.

b. Determine the distribution of values among the consuming public.

c. Determine the movement of a given type of product into (and out of) the high mobile market.

d. To tighten prediction, determine what values are critical to the product's success.

e. Determine how the critical values are distributed nationally.

f. Determine what the future holds for the value pattern critical to the product's success.

g. Determine how the tastemakers for the product X group are reacting.[23]

A DISCUSSION OF CATEGORIZATION EFFORTS—IMPLICATIONS FOR PUBLIC RELATIONS PRACTICE[24]

Certainly one thing is clear by now: There are a great many systems whereby one can categorize his intended recipient more precisely and thus communicate more effectively with him, regardless of the way in which "communication effectiveness" is defined.

It should be equally clear that these categorization systems hold promise for the public relations practitioner—particularly the research derived systems. It does not take much imagination to envision that there might well be times when the public relations practitioner would like to make use of the tastemaker concept and thereby identify in a given public those who score high on the MVI scales described earlier. Certainly for some public relations objectives, these people would be those whom the public relations practitioner would wish to reach. It would likely be useful to persuade such individuals to his point of

---

[23] *Ibid.*, pp. 82-89.

[24] It should be remembered that we have hardly scratched the surface so far as itemizing all of the categorization systems that exist. However, we do have examples of systems that are characteristic of the threefold schema that we borrowed to portray experimentally based categorization systems. With the schema and the examples provided, the reader should be able to properly identify any other categorization system that he might encounter in his reading.

view, because it appears that these individuals might well serve as leaders in "ideas" as well as leaders in consumer behavior.[25]

Our purpose here is not, however, to argue for the superiority of one categorization system over another. This can be settled only by research or, at least empirically, by a public relations practitioner trying it out. Rather, our objective is to make clear the following points:

1. The public relations practitioner *does* make use of categorization systems, regardless of the fact that he may not express it in these terms. The thought-leader concept, included in our discussion, makes this quite clear.
2. Unfortunately, the public relations practitioner has *not* availed himself, on any wide scale, of the categorization systems that exist; such crude systems as thought leaders or any other "rule-of-thumb" system has been allowed to suffice.
3. From point No. 2, it follows that the public relations practitioner needs to search the literature (or a segment of the literature) for recipient categorization systems that may prove to be useful to him. Many of the larger public relations organizations (as well as the advertising agencies which also offer public relations services to their clients) maintain "research" staffs. However, instead of always gathering clippings and reading articles in a variety of sources that may prove to be of interest to a client, such a staff could devote some of its time to uncovering literature about this kind of recommended research.
4. The public relations practitioner needs to pull together much of what has already been written in this book and make use of it to define more precisely just what sort of recipients he is interested in. In other words, he needs to make a careful analysis of the motives and perceptions of his intended recipients. He needs to make a searching reappraisal of the *assumptions* that he himself has brought to his public relations problem. In short, he must be certain that he devotes as much time to thinking his problem through as he does to generating written copy and engaging in all forms of message transmission—activities that can cause one to forget that he has never really made an analysis of his intended recipients or audience.

----

[25] In this connection, one is reminded of the initiator concept (Chapter 14, pages 385-390—also an Opinion Research Corporation development—and how this particular categorization system would likewise be suitable for public relations purposes.

5. Lastly, the public relations practitioner needs to adopt the attitude that it is time that research be done to find out what categorization systems could be developed that would have direct application to public relations problems. *As we saw, the ORC researchers took a fresh look at consumer behavior; now, the same needs to be done for public relations.* The larger public relations firms can either develop an "in-house" capability to do this type of work or go to research organizations and have it done for them. The smaller practitioner needs to demand that his professional associations be concerned with sponsoring such research. What can't be done individually can often be done collectively.

MISCELLANEOUS TERMS WITH IMPLICATIONS FOR DEALING WITH RECIPIENTS

If one examines the general social science literature or goes through the index of a book on social psychology or sociology, he will find a number of terms or concepts that have application in one way or another to the recipient. In this connection, the author took one of the social psychology texts from his library and thumbed through the subject index. In this perusal, terms such as the following were noted: *anxiety, attitude formation, catharsis, conflict, group norms, intergroup relations, individual differences, norms, remembering, socialization, values.*

In one sense, this list constitutes a miscellaneous category of items that can be considered as we examine the recipient in more detail—miscellaneous in the sense that these terms do not fit into any one system or theory of psychology or sociology, and have grown rather like Topsy. Also, most of the terms listed have rather extensive literature associated with them. In general, one could overlook the need for a consideration of most of such terms on the grounds that any one book can cover only so much material. Most of them have been dismissed by the author on just such grounds. Some of them, however, are so pertinent to public relations that we must devote some time to them at this juncture.

Three key terms come to mind in this connection with two more as possible candidates for this miscellaneous category. The three main ones are (1) persuasion, (2) propaganda, and (3) public opinion. The two "candidates" for this same category are (1) education and (2) information.

What do these candidates for our miscellaneous category have in common? First, as we have already observed, they are terms that reflect a concern for the recipient stage of the communication model, to put it in the frame of reference that we have expounded in this volume. The term *persuasion* refers, of course, to efforts—regardless of their nature—to induce a certain segment of people (or a public) to believe or behave in a certain manner, the nature of the belief and the type of behavior to be consistent with the beliefs or behavior desired by the sender. The term *propaganda*, on the other hand, certainly includes everything that would normally be included under the heading of persuasion. In addition, it tends to include the "whys" behind the reason for any one person or group to be interested in propagandizing another person or group. Also, it almost inevitably gets mixed up in such additional topics as politics or government, conflicting ideologies, and the like. Regardless of how much more the term *propaganda* might include, it certainly is a term that represents preoccupation with the recipient.

It is generally in connection with propaganda that one encounters the two "candidates" for our miscellaneous category: *information* and *education*. One can hardly discuss the topic of propaganda without trying to distinguish it from information. Generally, the distinction is along the dimension of intent. Propaganda usually has attributed to it some intent or purpose, a more obvious "goal" behind the communication that is directed toward some recipient. *Information*, on the other hand, is more often than not judged to be neutral. That is, the information is merely provided and what the person does with this information and how much it influences him is seen to be a secondary consideration, if it is one at all.[26]

Education, in contrast to the other two terms, seems to be held in more reverence by most people. We really have difficulty thinking about education in propaganda terms; we would usually rather think of education as being the most neutral of all. Education is supposedly merely designed to enable people to think and to be able to cope with their environment most effectively. The relationship between education and propaganda is one that we would rather forget about in the first place.

Public opinion is, of course, another concept that illustrates the preoccupation with the recipient. Depending on how the topic is treated, one may find either generous or only passing reference to the other

---

[26] Of course, this raises the whole question of how one goes about selecting what information to provide to a given category of recipients. Obviously, just the fact of providing only some information and not all of it can be propaganda.

two key terms, *persuasion* and *propaganda*, already mentioned, as the subject of public opinion is examined. One characteristic of the term *public opinion* that differs markedly from the other two terms is that it has generally been associated with trying to measure the recipient, much more so than in the other cases discussed. Thus, public opinion, regardless of how else it may be characterized, is usually associated with large- or small-scale survey work and an effort to synthesize and quantify the opinions of the recipients.

The second characteristic that these terms have in common is that they are by nature eclectic, variously defined, and the province of different types of social scientists. All three terms are eclectic in that, in the process of discussing any one of them, a writer may draw on psychological, sociological, or anthropological theory to explain them. From the standpoint of definitions, these terms enjoy more confusion and disagreement than social science concepts usually have.

One can find almost any category of social scientist making liberal use of these terms in his writing, much as he does the concept of attitude. These terms are as much at home in books on political science and government as they are in volumes dealing with psychology and sociology.

Still another characteristic worth noting is that these topic areas have tremendous appeal to academician and applied practitioner alike. Obviously, practitioners of all sorts—business, advertising, or public relations—have certain persuasion and propaganda objectives, and hardly any practitioner category exists toward which the accusation is not directed that they are trying to "mold" public opinion in one way or another. The academician, of course, has long been interested in all three topics, and perhaps the best evidence for this statement is the voluminous literature on these three topics that academicians have generated.

A final characteristic is that each one of the terms has evolved into a major subdivision within the social sciences, each with its own books, research literature, and theoretical schemata. Indeed, there are many colleges and universities which list separate courses devoted to one or all of the three topics.

So much for some of the characteristics that these subject matter areas have in common. It is because of them that we are paying special attention to these subjects at this time. One point that has been perceived by the reader by now is that at this stage in his study of this volume he is actually equipped to discuss and consider the implications of any one of these topics. He should be able to read, with comprehension, books or research reports that go into greater detail concerning

persuasion, propaganda, or public opinion. With our approach of integrating pertinent social science subject matter—such as learning, perception, and motivation—with a communication theory model, we have
handled a great deal of the theorizing and general thinking that is
normally associated with these terms. To illustrate this contention let
us take one of the topics—public opinion—and see just how much our
approach has equipped us to handle such a subject matter area.

Public Opinion Considered in Some Detail

As the reader can appreciate, books devoted to the topic of public
opinion vary considerably with respect to what is discussed under this
heading, and how. Regardless of the variations, some of the elements
that tend to be found in most treatments of the subject are:

1. Discussion of the problem of defining public opinion.
2. Examination of how public opinion is formed.
3. Relationship between principles of human behavior and public
   opinion.
4. Characteristics or attributes of public opinion.
5. Effect of communication on public opinion and vice versa.

Naturally, our list is incomplete; however, it is sufficient for our
purposes—*i.e.*, to demonstrate that what we have covered during the
preceding twelve chapters of this book enable us to examine public
opinion intelligently. Let us take individually the five features of public
opinion that are normally discussed and see how we can treat them
in the light of our own material.

1. The problem of definition. We have certainly learned by now to
ask first what we are talking about; consequently, our starting point in
a consideration of the term *public opinion* is to ask: What is it? There
are various definitions of public opinion and much disagreement among
these definitions, but let us see what our own interpretation of the
term would be.

Taking the word *public* first, we interpret this to mean some particular segment of a grouping of individuals that have certain characteristics in common—characteristics that are of interest to us as senders
(those interested in the public opinion of the subgroups with which we
are dealing). Thus, all employees of a particular company could be a
specific example of a public. With this particular definition, any grouping of individuals—whether by neighborhood, political preference,

known opinions or attitudes, or geographical location—could be included in the definition of a public.

How about the word *opinion*? In Chapter 12 (page 328), we defined opinions as that which we obtain from individuals when we pose questions for them to answer, as in a typical survey or in an everyday conversation. From these statements—the expressions of opinions—we attempt to infer certain attitudes. In short, opinions are the verbal utterances that we obtain from people and then use in order to infer their attitudes, exactly as we attempt to infer attitudes from nonverbal behavior.

After this separate treatment of the two words, *public* and *opinion*, what happens when we put them together? One meaning that we can attach to the phrase is that public opinion is a term that summarizes the inferred attitudes of a particular segment of people. Thus, when we speak of the public opinion of a particular town or community with respect to some issue (let us say the question of fluoridation of the community's drinking water), we are referring to the various attitudes of the people in the community.

What we have learned by now can also cause us to raise several precautions. One is that the use of the phrase *public opinion* is useless or can be highly misleading to both the sender and the recipient unless two additional statements are provided: (1) a specification of the public concerned and (2) a statement of the basis we have for making the inference concerning the opinions which are presumably held by this public. Unless both additional statements are provided, it is clear that the use of the phrase becomes nothing more than a figure of speech or an expression designed to communicate authority when, in fact, the person using it has no basis for the implied authority. These two demands would avoid statements such as "Public opinion is against such a move" or "We can't do this in the face of public opinion," both of which are meaningless unless the public and the means of obtaining the opinion measurement are specified.

A second general precaution that we can raise with respect to public opinion is that the ability to *measure* public opinion limits the degree to which we can talk about or infer public opinion. From what has been said already, it is obvious that unless one has a reasonably defensible measure of opinion (perhaps based on an opinion-attitude survey or on a careful content analysis of certain publications), it is useless to use the term. Based on intuition or hunch or "common sense," a sender's ideas of the public opinion of a certain aggregate of recipients with which he is dealing can be very inaccurate, hence rendering any actions taken relative to that public quite suspect or hazardous. This is why in Chapters 6 and 7 so much time was devoted to how well the sender had analyzed his intended recipient. It is only when we have carefully delineated what we actually know about a particular group of recipients that we can hope to develop realistic objectives and the means of attaining these objectives.

There is more that we could say about defining public opinion and just what public opinion is. The point is that what we have discussed here—which is based on preceding portions of this book—squares quite well with what the experts say about how public opinion can be defined and why a definition is essential.

2. *Formation of public opinion.* As the reader can imagine, the question of what factors shape or produce public opinion is an exceedingly complex topic. Whole books have been devoted to this one feature of public opinion alone. Briefly, what can we say, based on the schema that we have developed thus far?

A reasonably good answer can be given, based on Figure 14 (Chapter 5, page 122) alone; and that is what we shall do here. Our first observation is that public opinion emerges or is formed in a social context. That is, public opinion, like any other behavior, is subject to the effects of the society in which the public and its opinions is found. Thus, public opinion is bound to be shaped—depending on the topic and the relevance—by the larger events going on in the society. Whether the nation is at war or peace; whether there is civil unrest or calm; whether there is a prosperous economic outlook or a depression.

A second, more specific factor in the formation of public opinion, which Figure 14 reminds us of, is the role of reference groups. We learned earlier that all of us belong to many, many different reference groups, all of which play some role in shaping our attitudes and behavior. In the case of the family, the effects are generally quite pronounced and long lasting. In the case of some secondary groups—our associates at work—the effect is much less strong and of shorter duration. We conclude, then, that reference group memberships play an important role in shaping public opinion.

Thirdly, we expect, based on Figure 14, the formation of public opinion to be related to the frequency, extent, effectiveness, and so on of communications directed at influencing public opinion on any one issue.

Lastly, we are aware of the fact that the various personality characteristics of any *one* recipient play a role in how that single individual reacts to a particular issue, and that this phenomenon will be true for all of the recipients in any particular public.

We could easily supply more details if we were to focus on any single public and its opinions. We have, however, hit on what are the major elements of any discussion of public opinion: namely, that the formation of public opinion is a complex product of (1) the society in which the particular public resides, (2) the reference group membership of the various members of the public involved, (3) the kind and amount of communication that has taken place in that society and has been directed to the members of that particular public, and (4) the personality factors of each and every one of the individuals that go to make up the public whose opinion we are interested in and are trying to characterize. Here, again, what we have derived from Figure 14 pertaining to factors in the formation of public opinion is consistent with expert opinion in this area.

3. *The interrelatedness of human behavior and public opinion.* It is almost superfluous to say it, but, of course, you can't have public opinion without people. Likewise, the minute people are involved, all of the elements of human behavior—motivations, perceptions, and the like —become involved in an understanding of public opinion. It is small wonder that this relationship between the principles of human behavior and public opinion occupies considerable space in most treatises on public opinion. Once again, what can we say on the basis of our approach?

Perhaps the most logical place to turn is to Chapter 7 where, in a section devoted to a more detailed examination of the potential recipients (pages 142-176), we developed ways of thinking about their motivations, learning, and perceptions.

For one thing, from our material on motivation, we can suggest that for the individuals within a given public, having a certain opinion is part and parcel of their individual needs. In certain circumstances, holding certain opinions can serve as rationalization for some individuals. In other circumstances, holding certain opinions can reflect projection on the part of individuals. Thus, collectively the motives of individuals in a public can serve to account for why those individuals cling to certain opinions.

From what we have considered about learning, we of course realize that public opinion is a learned, not inborn, phenomenon. We can undoubtedly suggest that having certain opinions serves to reinforce certain motives; hence, we must generate new learning situations and appeal to different motives in order to change public opinion.

Lastly, from our material on perception, we can suggest that public opinion—that is, the measures that we take to infer public opinion—is, in effect, a reflection of the various ways in which individuals organize the world around them. Hence, certain opinions which reflect certain attitudes are nothing more than descriptions of the perceptual world of an individual. From this we can assert that variability of opinions within a certain public is the rule rather than the exception, as each one of us perceives—*i.e.*, organizes the world—in a different way. It also follows from what we have said that different people react differently to communication attempts to modify or change their opinions. Likewise, we need not be surprised to find that, in any given public, however we define the term, there are individuals for whom the issue does not exist; some have no opinion—the issue or question just does not exist for them.

Although we have been brief, we have actually hit on the highlights of what the experts discuss when they attempt to account for the relationship between principles of human behavior and public opinion. The role of motivation, learning, and perception generally receives considerable attention.

4. Characteristics of public opinion. Most discussions of public opinion include generalizations that can be made about the phenomenon as a whole. Let us see what ones we can generate, based on our approach to understanding human behavior.

One generalization that we can make is that public opinion represents a "simplification" of complex issues. We can predict that, rather than continue to think about an issue in complicated terms with all of the ramifications that a topic rightfully deserves, people are more than likely to reduce issues to slogans which stand for or sum up a view. Although it always does injustice to the complexity of a given problem situation, such phrases as "ban the bomb," "massive retaliation," "war on poverty," and "de facto segregation" represent a simplification of larger issues which facilitate the polarization of public opinion.

A second generalization that we can make is that people are very likely to interject *personal* views or to undergo identification with other people or with problems involved in some issue. Thus, public opinion generally reflects the degree to which individuals have identified with an issue, and the most logical or likely thing for them to do is to couch the issue in personal terms. To state the generalization in opposite terms—if individuals are *not* able to identify with the issue in question and if they are *not* able to interject personal views, then they are very likely not to become involved at all.

A check of the literature on public opinion reveals that simplification and personification are only two of the many characteristics that are discussed by the experts. They generally include the material that we have derived as well as such other characteristics as consistency-inconsistency of public opinion and rational-emotional bases on which public opinion is based.

5. *The effect of communication on public opinion and vice versa.* A little thought on the subject is all that is needed to realize that public opinion is affected in some manner by communication, and that the reverse is also true. Obviously, this relationship between communication and public opinion is a topic to which serious consideration is given in the literature. What, briefly, does our schema suggest that might be said in this connection?

A brief review is in order once again. In Chapter 5 (pages 92-98) we discussed the concept of feedback in some detail. We noted particularly that what a sender does affects a recipient and vice versa; each serves as feedback to the other. That aspect of our thinking causes us to predict that public opinion affecting communication is just as likely an occurrence as communication affecting public opinion. That is, we are not surprised to find that what a sender communicates can be, to some degree, shaped or modified by what he perceives to be the opinions of the recipients—that is, their "public opinion." Thus, certain content may be omitted from a message, certain issues included or avoided, all because the sender is being influenced by what he perceives the recipient to believe.[27]

There is another place in our previous discussions that can cause us to visualize communication and public opinion as a two-way street. (see Chapter 6, pages 139-140). At that time, we noted that all communicators are affected to some extent by their perceptions of what the recipients are like: their stereotypes, prejudices, and so on. These perceptions have some effect on how the communicator will communicate with the recipient. This is what is embodied in the notion that public opinion affects communication.

Naturally, we can predict that communication will have an effect on public opinion. The schema and theories considered thus far, however, will cause us to add many provisos to that generalization because we realize that all communications will not have the same effect. We can predict that, all things being equal, the more personal the communication (*e.g.*, person-to-person), the more effect it may have on shaping the opinions of the recipient. Likewise, we can be quick to point out that the *content* of the communication plays an important role, too. Thus, if the subject matter under consideration deals with

---

[27] This would account for why, during national political campaigns, speeches directed to one area of the country (say, for example, the South) would be different in content from speeches directed to another area (say, the North).

religious issues, we expect less change in public opinion than is likely if it is devoted to less emotionally charged areas, such as the latest clothing styles and popular tunes.

We can go on making more and more precise generalizations about what we can predict about the effect of communication on public opinion. Likewise, we can be much more explicit in predicting what effect public opinion can have on certain communications given by certain senders. If we look at the literature on this particular feature of public opinion, we will find discussions similar to those presented here, indicating once again that our schema permits us to have much to say about public opinion.

Public Opinion—A Summing Up

In this brief discourse on public opinion, we have tried to accomplish one main purpose: to illustrate that by now, with the preceding twelve chapters of this book under our belt, so to speak, we are equipped to examine a wide range of topics that may be encountered in the social science literature, but perhaps labeled differently than we have labeled them in this volume.

To support this contention, five common considerations, normally found in most treatments of public opinion, were considered. A brief comparison was made between how we can discuss these points and how these topics are handled in the public opinion literature. Although this exercise was necessarily brief, we found that by using our schema we tend to raise the same considerations and make similar observations and generalizations as those found in other literature sources.

Although it is beyond the scope of this book, the reader is encouraged to do the same with the topics of persuasion and propaganda. He will find that, armed with our communication model and all of the psychological and sociological principles that we have imbedded in the model, he can discuss these other topics in a quite sophisticated manner.[28] If the reader were to do this as an intellectual exercise, he probably would discover two main points. (1) Although there are many concepts or theories which are supposed to enable one to understand human behavior more effectively, the one thing that you can always be sure of is the behavior itself. Thus, although concepts may come and go, *the behavior that they were supposed to make more intelligible*

---

[28] It probably has occurred to the reader that we could have done the same thing we have done here at the other stages of the communication. For example, we could have considered such concepts as "set" and "stereotypes" as they pertain to the sender stage.

remains with us and demands explanation; (2) our limited schema, designed to enable us to understand human behavior more effectively, is now reasonably extensive, with wider application than might first be suspected.

THE INFLUENCE OF THE RECIPIENT UPON THE SENDER

There are at least two places in previous chapters where we have touched on the influence of the recipient on the sender that should be recalled here. The first is in Chapter 4 (pages 71-77) and in Chapter 5 (pages 92-98), where the concept of feedback as it pertained to both the sender and recipient stages was discussed in detail. This concept was also included in our model as depicted in Figure 14 (Chapter 5, page 122).

In both of these places the influence of the recipient on the sender was discussed. The emphases then, however, were more on how the sender had to take the recipient into account—*i.e.*, consider his motivations, perceptions, and so on—in order to understand how to approach him and how to deal with him. The point of departure earlier was that when the recipient was taken into consideration, the sender would have a greater impact on him. The feature that we must now dwell on is *how the recipient shapes the behavior of the sender*, sometimes without the sender even being aware of it.

To begin our examination of the effect of the recipient on the sender, let us read some of what Bernard Berelson has to say on this topic. He raises this subject in the context of the effect of public opinion on communication, but he is discussing exactly the same thing we are here.

> This problem is usually neglected in analyses of the relationship because it is not so obvious as the other and perhaps it is more difficult to study. [The "other" to which Berelson refers is the effect of communication on public opinion.] The problem deals with the extent to which, and the ways in which, communication content is determined to harmonize with the actual or presumed opinions of the actual or potential audience. It is clear that one factor, among others, that conditions what the media of communications say on social and political issues is the desire or expectation of the readers-listeners-seers to be told certain things and not others. The reporter or commentator or editor or producer may know or may think he knows "what his public wants" on a given issue, and to the extent that such knowledge affects what he communicates, to that extent public opinion becomes a determinant of communications. This aspect of the relationship between

communication and public opinion is not always admitted, or even recognized, because of the immorality of suggesting that anything but "truth" or "justice" contributes to the character of communication content.* However, everyone knows that communication channels of various public opinion sets limits upon the nature of what is typically communicated.

This determination (or really, partial determination, since this is of course not the only factor responsible for communication content any more than communication content is the only factor responsible for public opinion) can operate in two ways, once the communication channel (newspaper, magazine, political writer, radio commentator, and so forth) has attracted to itself a distinguishable audience. The two ways are themselves interrelated and can coexist. First, it can operate through conscious and deliberate and calculated manipulation of the content in order to coincide with the dominant audience opinion. Sometimes this operates by rule of thumb, as when someone on the production line in the communication process decides that "our public won't take this, or won't like it." Sometimes it operates through elaborate machinery organized precisely for the purpose, as when thousands of research dollars and hours are spent in finding out what kinds of people the audience is composed of and what kinds of opinions they hold on controversial issues. Whether the decision to conform to audience predispositions is taken on the front line or in the front office is for the moment immaterial; so is the question of why it happens, e.g. the desire or need for constant and large audiences for economic reasons. The important point is that overt consideration of audience opinion does (help to) shape the social and political content of the mass media. Everyone recalls the story of the foreign correspondent who cabled a thoroughgoing analysis of a relatively obscure Hungarian crisis to the home office only to be told: "We do not think it advisable to print it because it does not reflect Midwestern opinion on this point."**

The other method by which public opinion can affect communications is implicit, through the sincere and more or less nonconscious correspondence of ideology between producers and consumers. The two groups often see the world through the same colored glasses. The correspondence is achieved through a two-way process: the audience selects the communications which it finds most congenial and the producers select people with "the right viewpoint" to prepare communications for other people with "the right viewpoint." Although this latter

---

* However, some circles frankly acknowledge the power of the public to participate thus indirectly in the construction of communication content. This position is usually rationalized in terms of the presumed democratic ethic in which "the public is entitled to what it wants."

** Leo Rosten, The Washington Correspondents (New York: Harcourt Brace, 1937), p. 231.

process also occurs through deliberate decision,*** it also happens through the most laudable and honest motives that people of the same general persuasion as their audience are found in influential positions in particular communication agencies. This is all the more true in specialized enterprises like trade papers or magazines like *Fortune* or *The Nation*. In such cases, producers react to new issues and events like the modal members of their audience; and their communications fit audience predispositions, not through a process of tailoring, but through correspondence in outlook. "The daily re-election of the editor" serves to make the editor quite sensitive to the wishes of the electors. Here again the economic necessity to hold an audience and the political desire to do so are relevant factors, as well as the "correctness" of outlook. The point is that the nature of one's audience places certain limits upon what one can say to it—and still have an audience. The need of the audience is not only to be informed but also to be satisfied, and the latter is sometimes evaluated more highly than the former.

It is important to take account of this direction in the flow of influence between communication and public opinion in order to appreciate the reciprocal nature of that influence, i.e., to recognize that it is not all a one-way process. It is also important to note that the total effect of this reciprocal process is probably to stabilize and "conservatize" opinion since ideologies are constantly in process of reinforcement thereby. The over-all picture, then, is that of like begetting like begetting like.[29]

Support for the contention that the audience influences the sender or communicator can be garnered from a number of sources. For one thing, the concept is not a new one. Besides such social scientists as Hartley and Hartley, with their concept of "the image of the other"[30] (and they, in turn, acknowledge that their phrase means essentially what George H. Mead meant by his concept of "the other"[31]), the notion that the audience influences the communicative process can be found in the writings of a number of other social scientists. For example, over two decades ago, Florian Znaniecki put forth what he called his "social circle" theory.[32] In this concept, he articulates the basic

*** See Rosten for examples.

[29] Bernard Berelson, "Communication and Public Opinion," in Wilbur Schramm (ed.), *The Process and Effects of Mass Communication* (Urbana: University of Illinois Press, 1954), pp. 343-345. Used by permission.

[30] E. L. Hartley and R. E. Hartley, *Fundamentals of Social Psychology* (New York: Alfred A. Knopf, Inc., 1955), pp. 39-41.

[31] G. H. Mead, *Mind, Self and Society* (Chicago: University of Chicago Press, 1934).

[32] F. Znaniecki, *The Social Role of the Man of Knowledge* (New York: Columbia University Press, 1940), pp. 14-15.

notion that is embodied in social role theory, namely, that one role—such as mother—presupposes and is entirely dependent on the existence of another role—such as daughter or son. The social circle concept emphasizes the circular nature of all of our roles and how one role is dependent on another. This is very close to the meaning that we are discussing here, namely, that the audience can influence the communication and, in turn, the sender initiating the communication.

There is also research data to support the fact that the audience influences the communicator (although there is less of this type than of research which attempts to spell out how communication influences the recipient—i.e., public opinion). Gitter reflects these data when he writes,

> Znaniecki's seminal theorizing has been elaborated by Ithiel de Sola Pool and provided with an empirical validation by a study conducted by Zimmerman and Bauer.* This study is based upon the hypothesis of the authors, later validated by their data, that not only does an audience play a significant part in influencing the way in which a person prepares his messages to others, but that in fact it induces him to play the role that it expects of him. The playing of a particular role will in turn influence his subsequent attitudes and recollections of his communication. It would seem likely, therefore, "that the groups which a person carries around in his head as potential prospective audiences may be a significant factor in the way in which he perceives, organizes and uses new information."** The authors clearly demonstrate the crucial role that an audience, real or imaginary, plays in a person's conscious organization of his communicative behavior.[33]

From a theoretical and research point of view, it is clear that the recipient has an effect upon a sender, whether we are talking about two individuals in a face-to-face situation or a public relations practitioner (representing a group) communicating with a particular public. What implications does this have for the public relations practitioner?

There appear to be both *general* and *specific* implications, and this time let us reverse the usual order in which we consider things and take up some specifics first. The sender is particularly vulnerable to

---

* C. Zimmerman and R. A. Bauer, "The Effect of an Audience upon What Is Remembered," *Readings in Social Psychology*, ed. E. E. Maccoby, T. M. Newcomb, and E. L. Hartley (3rd ed.; New York: Holt, Rinehart & Winston, Inc., 1958), pp. 65-72.

** *Ibid.*, p. 66.

---

[33] A. George Gitter, "Hypocrisy as a Way of Life" (unpublished manuscript), Vol. II, 212-213. Used by permission.

the effects of the recipient in the case of associations. The public relations practitioner who works for an association, regardless of the type, is continually in danger of being influenced by the very audience that he is supposed to keep enlightened, informed, and otherwise on its toes. This is, of course, what Berelson was getting at in the material quoted earlier. This is such an important point, it is worth repeating a small portion of the long quote once again.

> The other method by which public opinion can affect communications is implicit, *through the sincere and more or less nonconscious correspondence of ideology between producers and consumers.* The two groups often see the world through the same colored glasses. The correspondence is achieved through a two-way process: the audience selects the communications which it finds most congenial and the producers select people with "the right viewpoint" to prepare communications for other people with "the right viewpoint." *Although this latter process also occurs through deliberate decision, it also happens through the most laudable and honest motives that people of the same general persuasion as their audience are found in influential positions in particular communication agencies.* [Italics added.][34]

There are two phrases in the above material which fit the association public relations man (and the practitioner in any similar public relations position) squarely. One is, "and the producers select people with 'the right viewpoint' to prepare communications for other people with 'the right viewpoint.'" Translated, this phrase means that associations often hire public relations practitioners who have "the right viewpoint" about the causes and objectives that the association is trying to promote, so that when the public relations practitioner communicates to the rest of the association, he will do so in a manner that is acceptable to the association.

The other phrase is "people of the same general persuasion as their audience are found in influential positions in particular communication agencies." Translated into our frame of reference, this means that public relations practitioners, who can certainly be found in influential positions at times, tend to share views similar to their audiences—the audience for whom they presumably work and whom they are supposed to guide.

Let us quickly assert that, by and large, this relationship between the public relations practitioner and his association (*i.e.*, his audience in the sense of our discussion here) is certainly understandable and defensible. It would be inconceivable to have in the position of the

---

[34] Berelson, p. 344.

public relations practitioner someone who was hostile to the aims and objectives of a given association. This overlap of sympathies and viewpoints is, of course, essential. What is involved here is the question of *degree*. That is what this section on the possible influence of the audience on the sender is focusing on—the situation where the overlap has gone too far, where the public relations practitioner is so imbued with the views and objectives of his audience that he cannot examine their behaviors (or planned behaviors) with any semblance of objectivity. When the public relations practitioner has lost his ability to function as a professional and tell his audience from time to time about realities that are unpleasant but nevertheless valid observations about themselves, his effectiveness for that organization is seriously impaired. The public relations practitioner must never lose his ability to take a stand or educate his association to a fact that is unpopular but, in his best judgment, right. Whenever a public relations practitioner is *not* able to function objectively with respect to his association, then the influence of the audience on the recipient has gone beyond the necessary degree of sympathy with objectives and, as a consequence, makes the position of the public relations practitioner untenable and his service to his association questionable.

One last point should be made about this problem of the degree of overlap of viewpoint between the public relations practitioner and the association he represents. Perhaps the most distressing feature of the influence that an audience can have on the public relations practitioner in these circumstances is that the practitioner can be almost completely unconscious or unaware of the degree to which he is being influenced. It requires conscious, sustained efforts to overcome this phenomenon to even a small degree, and no one, of course, can ever completely free himself of this type of influence. However, the degree of improvement that is possible by conscious effort to retain a semblance of objectivity, and the salutary effect that this improved perspective can engender for the public relations practitioner, makes the effort very worthwhile.

A second, *specific* manifestation of influence of the audience on the public relations practitioner can be seen in cases wherein the public relations practitioner (almost always as a part of a public relations consulting firm) directs the activities of an institute, association, or committee developed to further the objectives of some particular subgroup within our society. Many of these groups are guided almost exclusively by one or more public relations practitioners associated with the public relations firm that handles the institute as an account, and these practitioners shape policy (generally with the guidance of an advisory committee made up of representatives from the group concerned) and are usually responsible for all communication efforts on behalf of the group. There are many, many examples of such institutes, or their equivalents that employ slightly different wordings in their titles, that are run primarily by public relations firms. Below is a partial list of public relations firms and the trade associations that they counsel.[35]

Hill and Knowlton, Inc.
  American Iron and Steel Institute
  Licensed Beverage Industries
  Savings Banks Association of New York State
  The Tobacco Institute, Inc.
Carl Byoir & Associates, Inc.
  The Tire Council of America
  Glass Container Manufacturers Institute
Dudley-Anderson-Yutzy
  Corn Products Manufacturing Industries
T. J. Ross and Associates, Inc.
  The Shipping Association
Selvage & Lee, Inc.
  American Committee for Flags of Necessity
Farley Manning Associates, Inc.
  Paper Cup & Container Institute
John Moynahan & Co., Inc.
  Bourbon Institute

The usual pattern of relationship between an institute and the public relations firm responsible for its functioning and direction is characterized by the following: (1) close, intense relationship between the public relations practitioners involved and individuals representing the particular industry in question; (2) the presence of executives on the public relations firm's roster who are extremely knowledgeable about the industry that the institute represents; (3) intimate *physical* relationship between the public relations firm and the institute (very often the institute's offices are in the same building and perhaps even on the same floor as the public relations firm representing it; (4) the relationship between the public relation's firm and the institute is

---

[35] The author is indebted to Albert L. Ayars, formerly Director, Education Department, Hill & Knowlton, Inc., and now Superintendent of Schools, Spokane, Washington, for the list of public relations firms and the organizations they represent. Naturally, such a list is only partial, and the affiliations are subject to change at any time. Used by permission.

seldom, if ever, publicized. In all likelihood, the average citizen is completely unaware of the relationship between institutes and public relations firms.

The point of all of this is that precisely in the same way that a public relations practitioner representing an association can become influenced by the members of the association itself, the institute audience can begin to influence the public relations practitioner. If anything, because of the consulting-firm–client relationship, the danger of being influenced by the audience is even greater in view of the understandable motivation of any consulting firm to maintain a favorable client relationship.

One further point must be made. *The reader should not infer from the two specific examples cited—i.e. associations and institutes—that either or both types of organizations in our society are undesirable, dishonest, incapable of objectivity, or any other unsalutary interpretation that could be made.* In and of themselves, associations and institutes are merely instrumentalities for furthering the self-interests (and, in many instances, the public interests) of certain groups within our society. As such, they are one manifestation of democracy in action. In this sense, they are much like the word *propaganda*, which, we learned earlier, is neutral in character, and whether we label propaganda good or bad depends on particular circumstances and our viewpoints in the matter. So it is with associations and institutes. As such, they are neither good nor bad. The labeling of any one association or institute as good or bad depends on a variety of factors and requires the collection of considerable amounts of data before any intelligent decision can be arrived at concerning its worthiness. The same is true of individual public relations practitioners who function either as employees (which is more often the case in associations) or as consultants (which is more generally true in institutes). What is important to remember is that these specific examples of public relations efforts in action happen to represent particularly good situations in which the public relations practitioner (as sender) can potentially find himself becoming unduly influenced by the audience to whom and for whom he is communicating (*i.e.*, the association members or affiliated institute organizations).

To take up the *general* implication of what we have been talking about here in this section we need to return to Chapters 6 and 7 where we were examining the sender in more detail. Early in Chapter 6 (page 126), the point was made that the beginning point in a more detailed analysis of the sender stage is *self-analysis*. That is, the public relations practitioner has to analyze and understand his own motives, goals, degree of overlap (or lack of it) of his motives with that of his intended recipient, and so on *before* he can proceed to do anything else in tackling a particular public relations problem.

What we have been discussing in this section of Chapter 16 is, in effect, another aspect of this self-analysis, the discussion of which had to be delayed until now. The fact is, however, that another element of the self-analysis step introduced in Chapter 6 is for the public relations practitioner to make a searching analysis of the extent to which he has become influenced by the very organizations that he is supposed to help. This particular aspect of the self-analysis process will prove to be one of the most difficult mandates for the public relations practitioner to live up to; many never manage to accomplish this desirable but elusive goal.

PART 2—A POSTSCRIPT

With the completion of this chapter, our detailed analysis of the communication model, introduced in Chapters 4 and 5, is complete. All four stages—sender, message, media, and recipient—have been examined in considerable depth. Although we could easily lengthen this book by a factor or two, the reader is now reasonably well equipped to follow through on most of what was called the public relations process in Figure 11, Chapter 5 (page 96)—equipped, that is, to function in all of the steps described in that figure, with the exception of Step 4, which is "Evaluation of the effectiveness of the public relations problem; research done to obtain necessary feedback." To be able to fulfill the demands of Step 4, the public relations practitioner needs a reasonably thorough grounding in social and behavioral science research—one of the most effective means by which the public relations practitioner is able to obtain reliable knowledge by which to judge the effectiveness of his public relations program.

That is the objective of the next and final section of this book. Part 3 is devoted to an introduction of social and behavioral science research and its relationship to public relations practice.

QUESTIONS FOR DISCUSSION

1. Develop two or three examples of how public relations practitioners have made use of explicit intuitive groupings (such as the one cited

from Roper) in their dealings with intended recipients. In your examples, how would you characterize the *value* of these intuitive groupings for the public relations practitioner? That is, what evidence do you have that these intuitive groupings helped the public relations practitioner to understand his audience better, helped him to shape communication intended for his audience more effectively, etc?

2. Try to find one example of the use of an *objective* categorization system by a public relations practitioner. Did you have difficulty finding such an example? If you did, why do you think that so few examples exist?

3. Take the Tastemaker Concept as developed by the Opinion Research Corporation and give one or two examples of how such a concept might be modified for use in public relations work. Do you think that such a categorization system would be more helpful to a public relations practitioner than the intuitive categorization example that you developed to answer question No. 1? If you *do* think it is more helpful, why do you think so? If it is *not* more helpful in your opinion, why do you feel this way?

4. Try to find at least one illustration wherein the audience or recipient influenced the sender, where the sender was a public relations practitioner. Do you have any evidence for inferring that the public relations practitioner concerned was *aware* of the influence that the recipients had on him?

5. In our discussion of the influence of the audience or recipient on the sender, we implied that it is more difficult for an individual to be aware of this influence that to be conscious of the possible influence that he (as sender) may have on a given audience or group of recipients. Do you agree with this generalization? If you do, try to generate some evidence to support your thinking. If you do *not* agree, develop some data to support your notion that such influence is not more subtle.

Part 3

SOCIAL AND BEHAVIORAL SCIENCE RESEARCH METHODS AND THEIR RELATIONSHIP TO PUBLIC RELATIONS

Repeatedly, in a variety of contexts, we have argued that the public relations practitioner of the future will have to know something about social and behavioral science research methodology in order to progress toward the right-hand end of the problem-solving continuum introduced in Chapter 3 (page 48).

In later chapters, we pointed out that the public relations practitioner needs badly to arrange for feedback of information in order to guide intelligently his public relations programing and changes in programing. One of the most effective means of obtaining feedback of information is through research such as the opinion-attitude survey.

We argued that the public relations practitioner needs to assume the point of view of the "image of the other," meaning that he needs to understand how the recipient perceives him in any given communication situation. Once again, research is useful in that through it we are able to learn more about the recipient and, in so doing, learn how to deal with him more effectively.

Lastly, in almost every previous chapter, we have either explicitly or implicitly stressed the need for the public relations practitioner to understand the related social and behavioral sciences so that he can apply this knowledge to his problems wherever it is appropriate. In fact, we defined the public relations practitioner as an applied social and behavioral scientist. This means that the public relations practitioner of the future will increase his study of pertinent social and behavioral science journals and books to keep abreast with developments in these fields. To do this intelligently, he needs to know something about social and behavioral science research methodology.

Part 3, consisting of four chapters, is designed to cover this fundamental knowledge. These chapters are intended to impart the minimum knowledge that a public relations practitioner needs to have. They are written from the point of view of the practitioner and the practitioner-to-be who are *not* interested in research as an end in itself, but who *need to know something about research* so as to pursue the solving of their problems more effectively. Hopefully, in these last four chapters a happy balance has been achieved between presenting social and behavioral science methods in a rigorous and accurate manner while avoiding undue jargon and obscurity. This is a discussion of research for the *practitioner*, not for the researcher himself.

Chapter 17

SCIENTIFIC RESEARCH:
A POINT OF VIEW AND THE FIRST
THREE STEPS IN THE
RESEARCH PROCESS

INTRODUCTION

Since World War II, a virtual revolution has taken place in a variety of applied fields in which communication plays a vital role: advertising, radio, TV, magazines, newspapers, and business management. This revolution can be summed up with the word *research*.

In advertising, for example, research is used in all sorts of contexts—choosing a brand name or a label color, selecting or evaluating a potential market, or measuring the impact of this copy slant or that. The importance of research to advertising was emphasized at the annual meetings of the Advertising Research Foundation in 1959 when it was stated that "research will be the most important aspect of advertising for the next decade."

The role of research in the press media is gradually increasing. Newspapers often check out such things as reader attitudes toward editorial impact or the acceptance of this comic strip or that women's page feature. Radio and TV programs, for better or for worse, are to a large extent dependent for their existence on their Hooper, Neilsen or Trendex Trend ratings. The magazine people made famous the continuous reader study.

Business management's use of research has become too broad in scope to present in any detail in this brief introduction. To summarize, however, research plays a role in marketing, in the selection and placement of personnel, in the choice of new business sites, and in evaluating profit potentials. In short, a wide range of business decisions are becoming linked with research results and their interpretations. There is the feeling that the old "flying by the seat of the pants" is very definitely on the way out. We find computers used to simulate problem-solving procedures that one would need to use to solve problems on the job. Mathematics is being applied to all phases of business. In the field of purchasing, for example, the purchasing agent who does his buying "intuitively" is being replaced by the purchasing agent who employs sophisticated mathematical tools to assist him in arriving at his purchasing decisions.[1]

The point being made here is a simple but important one: Almost any applied field that one can name is becoming increasingly rigorous in execution, with practitioners in these applied fields relying more and more on a variety of related sciences (with their varied techniques) to help attain this rigor in performance.

Public relations practice must not be an exception to this trend. This is why in Chapter 3, when introducing the *Problem-Solving Continuum* (page 48), the thesis was developed that the public relations practitioner had to move *away* from the "fly by the seat of the pants" school *toward* the "best obtainable evidence" school. As we will endeavor to illustrate in some detail in these chapters, research is the way by which the public relations practitioner can achieve the scientifically derived knowledge stage described in the problem-solving continuum. The future of public relations as an accepted discipline in our society depends on the degree to which public relations practice becomes more rigorous. Part of this rigor is derived from knowing more about what impact public relations programs have after their execution. Research, broadly defined, is the means of finding out about this impact.

PERSPECTIVE FOR THESE CHAPTERS

Before getting into the details of the research process, let us generate a perspective for these chapters, because research, unlike the topics considered in the other chapters, is comparatively unknown to the present or prospective public relations practitioner.

---

[1] *See* Chapter 3, pages 44-45.

1. Our main objective is to convey an understanding or appreciation of the research process which, hopefully, will ultimately lead to the reader's positive attitude toward research and its role in public relations practice. The reason for using such words as *understanding* and *appreciation* is because it is just not possible to produce a researcher in the space of four chapters. In fact, it can't be done in the space of a whole book. The ability to do research is a complicated process that is made up of information, specific skills, the opportunity to practice or employ these information and skills, and, above all, actual experience. For these reasons, it is doubtful that research can ever be taught by books alone.

   However, at this stage in the development of public relations practice, it is not so important that a public relations practitioner be a researcher as it is that he approach his problem solving with the attitudes and methods of a researcher. As we shall learn presently, our definition of research—the seeking of reliable knowledge—leaves room for all sorts of steps to improve one's knowledge, steps that, when taken, lead the practitioner toward the right-hand end of our problem-solving continuum (Figure 2, page 48). However, the key to this process lies in one's attitudes toward research and how reliable knowledge is obtained.

2. A second reason for our more modest goals of coverage of the relationship between research and public relations is that reaching the right-hand end of the problem-solving continuum is going to take time. For any applied field to become more rigorous in its execution is a slow process; for the field of public relations, with its welter of activities, complexity of problems, types of practitioners, and variety of definitions of subject matter, the process of moving toward the right-hand end of the continuum will undoubtedly take more time.

   There is also the fact that it is not yet clear just what kind of research will prove to be most effective to the public relations practitioner. At present, there appears to be little question that the single most used type of research employed to help solve public relations problems is the opinion-attitude survey. Whether this state of affairs is because the opinion-attitude survey is, in fact, the public relations practitioner's most valuable research tool or whether it is because both the practitioner and the researcher have not fully exploited the full range of possibilities is a moot question. Also appropriate here is the point that has been made several times earlier in this book: Much more work needs to be conducted by the researcher with interests in public relations before a definitive picture of exact relationship between social and behavioral science research and public relations practice can be sketched.

3. In keeping with the points made in (2), we shall try to accomplish two things in our treatment of research: (a) to consider research in broad terms so that the reader will appreciate the similarity of the research process in all of the sciences, regardless of the content of the research; and (b) to focus on research as it applies to human behavior, particularly field or survey research, as contrasted with laboratory research involving human beings.

    The reason for our broad approach to research is that it is essential for the reader to understand what is often called the "unity of science." One meaning of this term, especially as it pertains to research, is that the means (and the reasons behind these means) by which reliable knowledge is obtained in all of the sciences are fundamentally the same. Thus, in conducting research, the chemist goes by the same rules as the biologist, who in turn goes by the same rules as the psychologist. The differences among these disciplines is in terms of the *content* or *subject matter* studied. The same research rules apply to all of these fields.

    The rationale for our focus on research as it applies to human behavior is, of course, self-evident. With the exception of the few times that insights to human behavior are afforded by what we learn from comparative research (*i.e.*, research with infrahuman organisms), obviously the public relations practitioner is concerned only with human beings.

4. We shall try to provide the reader with material which will enable him to read research reports or excerpts of research reports with more understanding. To this end, we shall present such things as a schema that provides a context into which to place a variety of specific measuring devices, particularly those commonly found in surveys. Also, we shall discuss certain research techniques that have become particularly popular over the past few years (*e.g.*, projective techniques) and how these techniques relate to certain topics that one hears a lot about, for example, motivation research. In short, the purpose is to provide the reader with a frame of reference so that he can intelligently examine almost any example of research that he may encounter.

5. Lastly, the presentation of research will be made from the perspective that there are all sorts of ways by which to obtain reli-

able knowledge, and that scientific research is only one of them. In this context, we shall examine approaches to reliable knowledge that are potentially useful to the public relations practitioner but cannot be classified as scientific research.

AN INVESTIGATIVE CONTINUUM

In ordinary conversation, the term *research* is used quite loosely to embrace a wide range of activities. Characteristically, a public relations practitioner may say of some particular public relations problem that he has "done some research on that problem." It has been the experience of the author that until further details are known, one cannot be sure just what the public relations practitioner concerned had done. Some mean that they telephoned a few people or did some background reading; others mean that they called in a survey research organization and had a full-blown attitude survey conducted. Unfortunately, the term *research* embraces both extremes in everyday practice.

Because of the confusion that obviously can be generated by such looseness, we begin our discussion of research with some definitions and a way of thinking about obtaining reliable knowledge. In this connection, let us examine Figure 28. At one end of this investigative continuum (which could also be called a continuum of reliable knowledge), we see the word *intuition*; at the other end, the term *scientific research*

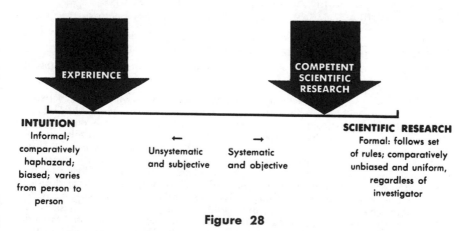

Figure 28

Investigative continuum depicting the extremes of intuition and scientific research

is found. Oftentimes this phrase is shortened to the word *research*. What this continuum is designed to highlight is that methods by which we go about seeking reliable knowledge range from sheer intuition on the one hand to scientific research on the other. Also, as we will shortly see in a little more detail, there are in-between steps—steps that are more reliable than pure intuition, yet are not rigorous enough to be classified as scientific research.

The intuitive end of the continuum embraces all of the efforts that an individual makes to obtain reliable knowledge which, in fact, may *not* be reliable. When an individual makes a decision which is based on information that is no more reliable than that depicted by the intuitive end of the continuum, he is, in effect, "flying by the seat of the pants." Call this end of the continuum what you like—educated guessing, hunch, or what have you—but the observation remains the same. The individual operating at this point on the continuum is basing his decisions on knowledge that is not very reliable.[2]

As was noted earlier, the term *research* really stands for the longer expression "scientific research." Research is one means of investigating a particular problem for the purpose of better understanding the problem in question. In order for any investigation to qualify as scientific research, the investigator must follow certain rules. It is by close adherence to rules that scientific research has become distinguished from all other ways of investigating problems and obtaining reliable knowledge. In one sense, these four chapters are devoted to giving the reader an appreciation of how much is involved when problems are investigated according to the rules of scientific research.

The in-between steps are more difficult to discuss because there are so many in-between steps and because establishing just where they fall along the continuum—short of one extreme or the other—is difficult to establish. We will return to a discussion of the in-between steps in

---

[2] The reader has undoubtedly observed the close relationship existing between this continuum and the problem-solving continuum introduced in Chapter 3, page 48 (Figure 2). In that continuum, we distinguished between individualistic knowledge and scientifically derived knowledge. One end of the problem-solving continuum we called the "fly by the seat of the pants" school and the other the "best obtainable evidence" school. In the context of our present discussion, when an individual is basing his decision to act on intuition, he is, in effect, flying by the seat of his pants. Because intuitive knowledge is not very reliable, the decision may not be very reliable either. Conversely, when an individual is operating at the best obtainable knowledge end of the continuum, he is basing his decisions on the most reliable knowledge that he can obtain. This is knowledge obtained through scientific research. We shall touch on these points in different ways later in this chapter.

more detail later; for now, however, let us look at one example. Take the case of a public relations practitioner who does a lot of reading about his client: its products, market analyses, stockholder reports. In addition, this same public relations practitioner talks to a number of individuals within the organization about its strengths and weaknesses, its goals, and its competition. Obviously, after all of this work (which is typical of the activities that a public relations practitioner engages in regardless of what else he might do to better solve his problems), we cannot say that the public relations practitioner is operating at the purely intuitive end of the investigative continuum. He has moved from the extreme left-hand end of the continuum depicted in Figure 28 toward the right-hand end, and here is the difficulty: just *how much* he has moved is impossible to state. Probably the best way to characterize this stage of affairs is with the word *experience*. This is why an arbitrarily selected point near the intuitive end of the continuum has been labeled *experience*. This is to convey the point that experience *does* make a contribution to obtaining reliable knowledge. The only trouble is that experience is so personal and variable that it is difficult to assess the contribution.[3]

We are now ready to turn our attention to another feature of Figure 28. That is the point toward the other extreme of the continuum labeled *competent scientific research*. This point is added to draw attention to the fact that there is no such thing as the perfect scientific experiment. There is probably no experiment ever conducted that did not contain some flaw or error; consequently, the information obtained is something less than perfect and, therefore, the knowledge is diminished by that amount. Admittedly, for a great many carefully conceived and executed experiments the amount of error is so small that the limita-

---

[3] The reader has probably viewed a TV program during which a successful businessman or representative of some other occupation was interviewed and, during the course of the interview, was asked to give "the secret of his success." As a rule, such an inquiry is followed by a series of inconsequential replies filled with sayings like "the early bird catches the worm" and "keep your eye on the ball." The reason that the man who *is* a success has so much difficulty telling *why* he is successful is that he really doesn't know. He tries to dip into his experiences to show 'how they served in aiding him to make good decisions, excluding, for the moment, those that were good decisions because of sheer luck. The point on our investigative continuum labeled "experience," about which we are now talking, places us in the same position as our hypothetical businessman on television. We know that experience contributes to reliable knowledge; for this reason, we have been compelled to include it on our continuum. A more detailed explanation will have to wait until we are able to pinpoint more precisely how experience contributes to the acquisition of reliable knowledge.

tions introduced into the reliable knowledge derived is practically negligible. The factors that make a given piece of scientific research less than perfect might be called "modifiers of reliable knowledge." Among these modifiers are such things as the training and integrity of the researcher and the nature of the problem to be researched. Consequently, while the position that we have labeled *competent scientific research* is quite close to the right-hand end of the continuum, it is not the same as the extreme end of the continuum. This is a theoretical point, but an important one.

One last comment. From Figure 28 it is clear that there is no hard and fast dividing line between what is scientific research and what is not scientific research. That is, *there is no magic point at which a person begins to obtain 100% reliable knowledge and before which he obtained zero reliable knowledge.* Rather, the point on the continuum labeled *scientific research* depicts an ideal or theoretical state of affairs. In practice, we make approximations of this end (and of the other end, for that matter). Thus, when we execute a scientific research project, following all of the rules and implementing all of the necessary controls, we are as close to the right-hand end of the continuum as it is humanly possible to be. This continuum also highlights the fact that there is *no one* way of obtaining reliable knowledge. There are as many ways of attempting to obtain reliable knowledge as human beings can conceive or develop. Experience has taught us, however, that the approach called "scientific research" is the most reliable that man has developed thus far. There are times or conditions that prohibit the use of the scientific research approach. In these circumstances, we do the best we can with the realization that we have less confidence in the knowledge obtained.

If these points are granted, it must also be granted that there are a number of efforts *that may not qualify as scientific research* but which, nevertheless, are more reliable than sheer intuition or blind guessing. In the remainder of this chapter and in the next two chapters, we will devote most of our attention to detailing what makes a study a scientific research effort at obtaining reliable knowledge. In Chapter 20 we will spend time discussing the in-between or less-than-perfect efforts at obtaining reliable knowledge. They embrace what *some* public relations practitioners now do and include things that *all* public relations practitioners should do in appropriate situations along with using scientific research whenever it is feasible and possible to do so. In fact, it is this in-between portion of the continuum that represents the greatest opportunity for the "do-it-yourself" approach to reliable knowledge.

SCIENTIFIC RESEARCH IN MORE DETAIL

Research vs. Everyday Living

One of the most common thoughts that people have about research is that it is done by "someone else." This someone else is very often depicted as wearing a white coat and working in a laboratory. Such stereotypes have contributed greatly to the tendency to make research something very different and foreign to most people and, what is worse, foreign to people who should be more conversant with it.

There is no advantage in pretending that research is not a highly specialized and sophisticated endeavor. Nevertheless, there is considerable overlap between what scientists do that is labeled research and what we all do in our everyday lives. An improved understanding of this overlap should contribute to a better over-all understanding of research.

To demonstrate the overlap, let us take a hypothetical example of a public relations practitioner arising in the morning and wondering what the weather is going to be like for that day. For our purposes, let us assume that he does not pay attention to the weatherman's report. What is he likely to do? He may look out the window, quickly make an observation of the skies, and apparently very simply come to a decision to wear a raincoat and rubbers. To bring out the overlap between research and everyday life, let us delve a little deeper into this apparently simple behavior.

For our starting point, we ask, "Why does he look out the window and look at the sky?" Asking this slightly ridiculous-sounding question enables us to bring out several very important aspects of research that are hidden in it. They are:

1. *Our public relations practitioner has at least an idea of what problem he is trying to solve.* That is, he wants to be able to tell what the weather is going to be for the coming day. As simple as this sounds, it is not always an easy goal to know exactly what it is you want to solve.
2. *Our public relations practitioner knows what information he needs to solve his problems.* He knows that he must have some information about the present cloud cover (or lack of it); what it "looks like" outside—threatening, dark, and so forth.
3. *Our public relations practitioner knows where to look for his*

information. Half the battle in solving any problem is knowing where to go to obtain the necessary information. In our illustration, we must not overlook the fact that the public relations practitioner knew that he had to look outside and observe the sky and the general environment. Because this step is so simple and obvious in this instance, it should not mask the fact that knowing where to look for the pertinent information to solve a problem is of paramount importance.

With this step of the over-all process still in mind, our next question may run something like this: "What led our public relations practitioner to the conclusion that he had better dress for rainy weather?" (assuming, for purposes of our illustration, that this is the conclusion he comes to.) This question helps us to bring out some other hidden processes in this apparently simple bit of behavior.

4. *Our public relations practitioner applied some of his previous experiences to the present problem.* He related the information that he had obtained on the outcome of similar days in the past to this particular day.
5. *With the past and present before him he came to a decision.* In short, he decided to dress for rainy weather.

This examination of a typical, everyday act in the life of a hypothetical person serves to highlight our central theme. It's this: *Much of what we do in our everyday life has its counterpart in the research process.* Naturally, not all of the important elements of research can be brought out in such a simple example. However, a surprisingly high percentage of the research processes can be found in everyday life.

This raises still another question: "Why is there so much overlap between the processes we associate with research and everyday behavior?" The reason is this: In order to be able to exist from day to day, we need knowledge about the world around us—reliable knowledge. We do surprisingly well in spite of the fact that we have our biases and that we make our mistakes. Reliable knowledge is also the goal of the research scientist. In keeping with this objective, he has developed a set of rules for obtaining reliable knowledge. When we put the two together—everyday life and the work of the research scientist—we see the overlap. It is our contention that by keeping the overlap in mind the novice can facilitate his learning about scientific research. All of the aspects listed above are so important that they are part of the formal research process as described in most volumes dealing with research.

The suggestion to use everyday experiences as an aid to understanding research is not so farfetched as it may seem. Tate, in his book on statistics, illustrates this kind of reasoning applied to statistics. In his chapter on statistical inference, he discusses the concept of "levels of significance"—points at which we accept the hypotheses we are testing as valid. He writes:

> It is interesting to note that the five per cent level of significance *roughly checks with our intuitive reaction* to the working of chance in the following situation. Suppose someone hands us a coin, asking us to flip it several times, without examining the coin. Suppose now that on the first three flips we observe heads. The probability of this sequence, if the coin is unbiased, is $\frac{1}{2} \times \frac{1}{2} \times \frac{1}{2}$ or about .12. Although at this point we would tend to have some doubt about the fairness of the coin, few of us would be ready to conclude that the coin is unfair. Now suppose that we observe heads on the fourth and fifth flips. The probability of the 4-head sequence is $\frac{1}{16}$ or about .06, that of the 5-head sequence $\frac{1}{32}$ or about .03. Most of us would begin to have quite serious doubt about the fairness of the coin after the 4-head sequence, and our doubt would sharply increase with the 5-head sequence. In other words, in this situation, we *intuitively* tend to reject the notion that chance is a reasonable explanation of happenings characterized by probability figures in the .03-.06 neighborhood. [Italics added.][4]

With this example from statistics we see another case of overlap between everyday life and that which we broadly categorize as scientific.

One additional point should be made: *The intimate relationship between everyday life and research should be kept in mind by the novice in research so that he does not become discouraged in his quest for acquisition of knowledge concerning the research process; at the same time, he must take care not to lull himself into the trap of thinking that research is just common sense and not worthy of serious and deliberate study.*

What Is Research

Our hypothetical situation involving a public relations practitioner has served to give us *some* feeling as to just what research is all about.

---

[4] Merle W. Tate, *Statistics in Education* (New York: The Macmillan Company, 1955), p. 382. Used by permission.

In addition, we defined some of the terms we will be encountering when we discuss the investigative continuum depicted in Figure 28.

Let us turn now to a more detailed treatment of the question, "What is research?" As a starting point, let us state that research represents a systematic attempt to attain reliable knowledge. Reliable knowledge means simply an understanding of the world in as accurate a manner as possible. Understanding that enables one to better cope with his environment. Reliable knowledge in this sense is the general goal of the scientist.

Benton J. Underwood expresses the research goals of a scientist in a way we agree with:

> The purpose of the methods of sciences is to achieve a description and understanding of nature (the universe). By description I mean the definition, cataloguing or classification of events, objects, and phenomena which define nature, and the statement of empirical relationships associated with these events, objects, and phenomena. By understanding I mean the reduction to the smallest possible number of general laws which would account for the various specific facts. The descriptive part of science is concerned with research per se; what I have called understanding is usually achieved through theory.[5]

With such a definition under our belts, we may ask, "What groups of people seek reliable knowledge and "understanding of nature?" When some thought is given to this matter, we see that *everyone* is interested in acquiring reliable knowledge. Scientists want reliable knowledge, to be sure. But so do businessmen, clergymen, educators, and, yes, public relations practitioners! Everyone needs reliable knowledge in order to exist in this world of ours.

What, then, you may ask, is all this fuss about research and learning how to understand it? If research and everyday living have considerable overlap and all individuals need reliable knowledge, aren't we, in effect, all scientists?

The answer lies in *how* reliable knowledge is attained. Businessmen, clergymen, and public relations practitioners are constantly seeking reliable knowledge. When they go about obtaining this knowledge according to a set of rules, *then* we say that they have acquired scientific knowledge. *The thing that sets the scientist apart from all others is how he goes about obtaining his knowledge.*

---

[5] From *Psychological Research*, p. 1, by Benton J. Underwood. Copyright © 1957 by Appleton-Century-Crofts, Inc. Reprinted by permission of Appleton-Century-Crofts.

The "how" is according to a set of rules. These rules are sometimes known as the "scientific method" or the "research process." Our major objective in this portion of the book is to learn more about the scientific method and to start applying it to the field of public relations.

Assumptions Behind Research

One thing that we can be fairly certain of is that assumptions color how we look at anything. If we assume that the world is hostile, somehow more people in the world appear hostile to us. If we start a task with the assumption that we can't do the job, very often we wind up failing. In short, what we assume colors how we will perceive and how we will interpret.

So it is with a new subject. We want to ask ourselves what has been assumed. This same reasoning must be applied to a study of the scientific method. What are the more important assumptions that lie behind the research process and go to make up the scientific method? The following are a few that public relations practitioners, as those who apply much of the knowledge of the social sciences, should know.

1. *Assumption concerning the stability of nature.* This assumption has been called different things by different writers, but what is meant is that events going on around us are assumed to be stable and repeatable, lending a degree of permanence which makes a given subject matter amenable to study.

This assumption is not inconsistent with the fact that the subject matter may be highly complex or difficult to measure. This assumption does imply, however, that even such highly complex social phenomena such as rumor transmission, propaganda and persuasion, and even the behavior of large aggregates of individuals is stable enough for study.

To be sure, the behavior of individuals or groups of individuals causes us at times to wonder about the assumption of stability. Anyone who has tried to study scientifically the behavior of a single individual, let alone a group, certainly will have his doubts. However, even in the case of rapid social change we have a basic, necessary assumption that the social events are stable enough to be studied. Individuals are different, but there are uniformities. Groups, too, behave differently, but there are uniformities.

If this assumption were not feasible to make, it would not only cast doubt on the work of the scientist; it would cast doubt also on anyone attempting to understand anything. This would include all of us as individuals or as representatives of various professions. It would even include the practical and hard-headed businessman who believes so strongly in experience and common sense. To say that experience and common sense are useful guides to future behavior is to say that there is enough permanence in human behavior to be able to make such predictions.

2. *Assumption concerning causality in nature.* Closely associated with the assumption of permanence in nature is the assumption that there is a finite set of causes for a particular event or occurrence in nature. That is, something happens because of the action or presence of something else.

As a practical matter, this assumption does not relate everything in nature to everything else. Thus, we would seriously question that the length of a person's arms is related to whether he will successfully complete a college course. On the other hand, the assumption of causality states that there is a reason for everything that happens, no matter how complex and obscure the reason may be at any particular time.

It is worth noting that this second assumption concerning human behavior is firmly entrenched in the thinking of the average person. This is especially true when it comes to the behavior of others. Listen to almost any conversation and you will hear people using phrases such as "The reason he did it was . . . ," "I know why she acted that way," and so on. We are always looking for or supplying a reason for the behavior of others. As a matter of fact, one of the deficiencies of a person untrained in the social and behavioral sciences is his readiness to attribute certain causes to behavior he sees. More often than not he attributes the behavior to the wrong causes.

3. *Assumption concerning the uniformity of all sciences.* This assumption states that the rules governing the scientific method are essentially the same for all sciences. The physicist is no different from the sociologist; the difference lies in the subject to be studied and the various techniques that are suitable for study in the one area as against the other. In the final analysis, whether one qualifies as having done "scientific research" *is a function of his adherence to the same common rules of scientific method; it is not dependent on the subject matter of the research.*

Let us see how this third assumption relates to public relations. Most public relations practice proceeds as if public relations need not be conducted scientifically. Or worse, that it can never be scientific. The bias of the author is that, however far off we may be from a more rigorous practice of public relations, the goal is to be as scientific as possible at all times. Our third assumption is intimately related to this point of view. As we learned in Chapter 3 (page 49), regardless of how imprecise the practice of public relations is today, theoretically it can become much more rigorous. Public relations practitioners *can* have a scientific basis for their decision making and the steps that they take to solve public relations problems. These generalizations could not have been made were we not able to make the assumption concerning the uniformity of all sciences. If we could not make the assertion that being scientific is a matter of method and measurement and of approach to understanding and obtaining reliable knowledge, then we could *not* argue that public relations practice can become rigorous. Public relations, along with any other discipline which presents particularly difficult problems to understand and experiment with (and this would, of course, cause us to include all of the social sciences), would remain imprecise or toward the left-hand (*i.e.*, the individualistic) end of our problem-solving continuum.

Research—A First Summary

Up to now, we have attempted to introduce the concept of research and how it is the best method thus far known to man as a means of obtaining reliable knowledge. In this vein, we introduced an investigative continuum with two extremes: the intuitive and the scientific research ends. Two additional points on the continuum were examined: the experience and competent scientific research points. On the basis of this continuum, we developed the following generalizations:

1. Research, simply defined, is a means of obtaining reliable knowledge.
2. There are all sorts of means by which we go about obtaining reliable knowledge. Experience has taught us that scientific research is, as yet, the most reliable method.
3. All of us need reliable knowledge in order to cope with our environment. In this sense, the scientist and the average individual share the same need. The difference between the scientist and the average individual (or nonscientist) lies in how each goes about obtaining the reliable knowledge that he seeks.
4. There are times when we are not able to obtain our reliable knowledge with scientific research. That is, we must operate at other points along our investigative continuum, particularly toward the left-hand (intuitive) end. This does *not* mean that such knowledge is worthless. Far from it. It merely means that the closer one operates at the left-hand end of the investigative continuum the more that he must take his knowledge with a grain of salt. The likelihood of error is greater.

In addition, the relationship between our investigative continuum and the problem-solving continuum introduced in Chapter 3 was discussed. It was pointed out that operating at the individualistic end of the problem-solving continuum is, in effect, operating with knowledge obtained by methods appropriate to the left-hand end of the investigative continuum. Conversely, operating at the scientifically derived knowledge end of the problem-solving continuum was tantamount to obtaining knowledge through the scientific research end of the investigative continuum.

Lastly, some of the assumptions involved in the scientific method were discussed. In our discussion of these assumptions, one of the main points brought out was that the validity of the argument that public relations practice can become precise and based on knowledge obtained by scientific research is intimately related to these assumptions concerning science.

Let us now examine in some detail the research process itself.

THE RESEARCH PROCESS

Earlier we stated that the major factor that distinguished the scientist from all other types of people seeking reliable knowledge was *how* he went about acquiring his knowledge. This "how," we said, proceeded according to a set of rules.

In books on research, this procedure is generally referred to as the research process or scientific method. Like any other process, it consists of different components that can be distinguished and discussed separately. When any total process is broken down into parts for discussion, a certain order is imposed. We will be examining the research process according to a particular logical sequence. It should be pointed out here, however, that in practice scientists do not *necessarily* proceed step by step in the fashion described. They may skip around. Unexpected developments or unanticipated insights may play havoc with orderliness in procedure. This is true in any ideal theoretical procedure as compared to practice. The thing to appreciate here is that scientists, being human, do not necessarily follow the rules in the same way. Equally important to note, however, is that *eventually they do touch all the bases outlined below*. This is what makes them scientists.

Laboratory Research vs. Other Research

Before examining the research process in some detail, a comparison between laboratory research and all other research should be made.

If there is one word that epitomizes research, it is probably the word *control*. The scientist is vitally interested in controlling for all of the factors involved in any particular test situation. For example, in a psychological experiment, one needs to control for the environmental conditions surrounding the experiment, certain characteristics of the subjects that are used, and the test materials or test situation presented to the subjects. The more that the scientist is able to control, the better his chances are to find out what factors caused a particular phenomenon to occur.

In the physical sciences, we can see that, to control the various factors, it is generally more convenient to conduct the experiment on a somewhat reduced scale and to bring it indoors. An experiment indoors is an experiment in a laboratory. Before long, *experiment* and *laboratory* come to be virtually synonymous, because in our everyday language when we refer to someone who works in a laboratory, it is almost automatically assumed that he does experimental work.

In the nineteenth century, psychologists began to turn to experiments to further their understanding of human behavior rather than depending on speculation and "common sense" as they had in the past. It is only natural that they tried to ~ulate the actions of physical scientists and set up laboratories in which to do their experiments. After all, the physical scientists had had spectacular results in furthering knowledge in their fields; hopefully, the social scientists could do likewise. Also, psychologists had to be as concerned about controlling for all of the relevant factors in their experiments as any other scientist.

In the laboratory context, whether you are doing a psychological experiment or one in physics, the step-by-step procedures that you follow tend to be highlighted. Even persons completely unacquainted with research associate standardized procedures with laboratory experimentation. Unwittingly, the reader may make an unnecessary assumption concerning the steps in the research process—that you need to have a laboratory, or something close to it, to do research. In short, laboratories, research, and the necessary steps in the research process all appear to go together naturally. The fact is, of course, that they do go together, but what may not be so apparent to the reader is that a laboratory is not the. *only* place where research can take place. *Research is essentially a process and, as long as this process is followed, can take place in any context.*

Perhaps a continuation of our comparison of research in the physical sciences with psychology can serve to illustrate this point. As indicated earlier, psychological research started out "in the lab." However, as the range of human behavior to be understood increased, the psychologist was very often forced out of the laboratory. There were several factors that brought this about. For example, for some research objectives—say, research on the behavior of small groups of people— the laboratory conditions often distort the behavior of the group so that the behavior of the group in a laboratory is different. So different, in fact, that one can not reliably generalize from results obtained in the laboratory relative to outside situations.

These differences in behavior can be brought on by such things as the unfamiliar surroundings of the laboratory, the realization that someone is "studying" you, or the artificiality of the situation (*i.e.*, the rationale supplied by the experimenter) that brought the group to be studied together. These and many other factors can serve to distort or somehow change everyday behavior when we try to bring it into the laboratory for study.

In other instances, the laboratory conditions just cannot duplicate the actual situation closely enough: for example, studying the behavior of a child at home or in school or playing with his peers at the playground. Almost innumerable examples such as this can be provided. The point is that the psychologist (and all other social and behavioral scientists, too, of course) sometimes have to go outside the lab.

Going outside the lab, however, doe not permit freedom from controlling all the pertinent factors in an experiment. In fact, it generally makes it that much more difficult. It does not relieve the scientist from the necessity of following the research process in every detail. The only thing that differs is *how* the research steps are modified by the researcher to fit the research problems outside the laboratory.

As we go into detail about the research steps, the reader should bear in mind that the thing that makes a particular research effort qualify as a scientific research endeavor is *how* it is conducted. *Where* it is conducted is beside the point.

THE NINE BASIC STEPS IN THE RESEARCH PROCESS

As we see it, the nine basic steps in the research process are (1) statement of the problem; (2) deciding on a manageable portion of the problem; (3) establishing definitions; (4) literature search; (5) developing hypotheses; (6) deciding on the study design; (7) obtaining the data; (8) analysis of data; and (9) implications and generalizations. Before analyzing these steps, let us clarify a number of points.

1. This list of nine steps is not the only way in which the steps in basic research can be stated, nor does any listing necessarily have

to contain nine steps. Someone else may break up the research process into eight steps, or ten steps. The reader should not construe this to mean that there is no agreement among scientists as to what constitutes the research process. All that it means is that some points may be considered by some as subheadings under a different set of main headings. Eventually, all discussions of the research process touch on and discuss the same main elements of the research process.

2. The *order* of the nine basic research steps is also somewhat arbitrary. For instance, some persons may want to put the literature search in a different place in the sequence; someone else may argue that establishing definitions should come after developing hypotheses.

3. The reader should not confuse an orderly presentation of the research process with what actually happens in real life. Scientists do not, as a rule, go from Step 1 to Step 2, then to Step 3, and so on as they conduct their research. A multitude of factors may cause them to have to take the steps in different order in different research projects. The point is that somewhere along the line all the steps are fulfilled. There is a similarity between this point and how a chemist describes a chemical process or a physiologist describes a physiological process. A scientist discusses the research process in an order that facilitates his attempt to communicate with his reader. The way in which the process takes place in "real life" may be quite unlike the schema presented in printed form.

4. Although we will be concentrating on the research process as it applies to human behavior, *the reader should not lose sight of the fact that these steps apply equally well to other sciences.* That is, all scientists must be able to state their problems (Step 1), establish definitions (Step 3), and decide on the study design (Step 6). This is the unity of science concept once again. If the reader will keep this point clearly in mind, he will be able to avoid the confusion that complicated measurement devices or complicated research designs introduce to a given experiment. Behind the complexity are the same requirements that all scientists must meet. This point will become particularly clear when we discuss such topics as motivation research a little later. Behind all of the confusion that exists with the unfortunate term, *motivation research,* lies the simple fact that it refers primarily to a comparatively novel way of obtaining responses (Step 7) from individuals. However novel the particular measurement

technique may be, it still must live up to the requirements that
the scientific process places on *all* measurement techniques, regardless of their nature.

5. In spite of the fact that these research steps apply to all of the
sciences, our emphasis will be that of the social and behavioral
scientist. We will be stressing the point of view of the researcher
who is doing research on human behavior. This will be particularly true with Steps 6 and 7.

6. Lastly, two points of view are suggested to the reader concerning
the steps in the research process taken as a whole:

    a) One is that, hopefully, after all of the steps have been dis-
    cussed, a better understanding of research will be reached.
    Hence, one way of viewing this description of the research
    process is that it is a means of learning something about
    research.

    b) A second, entirely different use that can be made of the
    steps of the research process is to apply each of these steps
    to public relations practice directly. Each step in the research
    process has some features ssociated with it that make it
    immediately useful to the public relations practitioner. Let
    us elaborate this point a bit. Take Step 3, establishing defini-
    tions, for example. As we will see in more detail later, it is
    essential that a public relations practitioner constantly *define*
    what it is he is talking about, trying to solve, or hoping to
    communicate. A researcher knows that he cannot successfully
    conduct his research if he cannot define all of the terms or
    concepts that he uses in conducting and describing it. Un-
    fortunately, many public relations practitioners spend a lot
    of time working on a public relations problem only to find,
    when they are pressed, that they cannot really define what
    they mean by "better public relations." They have difficulty
    identifying the factors that contribute to better public rela-
    tions. So it is with some of the other steps in the research
    process. They suggest things that a public relations practi-
    tioner can put into action immediately in his own work. We
    will be returning to this point again and again because it is
    pertinent to our discussion of the various steps in the re-
    search process.

With these points behind us, let us examine the nine basic steps in
the research process in some detail.

TATEMENT OF THE PROBLEM*

The first step in the research process consists of clearly stating what it is you want to study. This may appear to the reader as stating the obvious. Yet experience has demonstrated time and time again that being able to state what it is you want to study—i.e., the problem—can be difficult. Several factors operate to make this first step more difficult than it might appear.

Multiplicity of Problems

One factor that makes it difficult to state the problem clearly is that normally any practical working situation contains *many* problems, all highly interrelated with one another. For example, suppose a public relations man is interested in improving the over-all public relations of a hospital of which he is director of public relations. Let us also assume that he has started by discussing the current status with his staff in order to figure out what problem or problems they have to face and cope with. (This would be the equivalent of the researcher assessing the state of knowledge of a given field in order to figure out what research problem deserves study next.)

To begin with, he finds himself confronted with the typical group discussion that can accompany an examination of a problem. To one staff person, it is "obvious" that their problem lies in the lack of communication among the hospital staff. To another staff person, it is "equally obvious" that the problem lies in not having proper communication with the community which the hospital serves. Other persons may have additional views in which they believe very strongly. In a practical situation, trying to sort the most important problems from all of the problems that *could* be studied can become more formidable than it appears at a first glance. What is true of the practitioner is also true of the scientist. For him to sort out a problem to be studied from all of the problems that *could* be studied is usually a rather difficult task.

Inability to State a Problem

Another factor that often arises is that the persons involved are not able to identify any problem clearly enough for study. Or, equally frustrating, not all situations lend themselves to the formulation of research problems that are practical to study. This is particularly true in public relations work. Selltiz *et al.*[6] tell of an educational institution that brought a large number of men and women from all walks of life together each summer for a "summer workshop." Social scientists were invited to this conference for the express purpose of advising this group on how to assess the value of the summer workshops. The outcome of this analysis was the discovery that the workshop effects they wished to measure would not be assessable short of a twenty-year research program. It was an undertaking that neither the institution concerned nor the social science advisers could envision as feasible at the moment.

Another illustration of this second difficulty associated with stating a problem lies in institutional-type advertising often used by public relations practitioners. Although important to know, the impact of this particular portion of one's over-all public relations program is exceedingly difficult to assess. One of the main reasons for this is simply that it is often so difficult to state what effects (behaviorally speaking) one expects from this feature of an over-all public relations effort.

Once again we see the public relations practitioner and the scientist facing the same difficulties with respect to research. At times, both are unable to state the problem, or the problems they are interested in are so formidable that it appears impractical to try to study them.

Assumptions Get in the Way

Perhaps the most subtle stumbling blocks to a clear formulation of a problem for scientist and practitioner alike are the assumptions all of us bring to our problem areas. We feel that we "know" our audience well enough that we do not need to study the effects of our communication to them. Likewise, we "know" that the public will accept our organization if we just have the chance to tell them our story. To make matters worse, there are many assumptions of which we are unaware. In other words, the explicit and implicit assumptions that we bring to any problem area—be we scientist, public relations practitioner, or housewife—affect strongly how we structure what needs to be done next.

Let us pursue this point just a bit further. Take the case of a scientist doing research on the causes of cancer and how he can counteract these causes. If he approaches his work assuming that some sort of chemical changes taking place within the body are likely the locus of the causes

---

[6] C. Selltiz, M. Jahoda, M. Deutsch, and W. Cook, *Research Methods in Social Relations* (rev. ed.; New York: Holt, Rinehart & Winston, Inc., 1959), pp. 31-33.

that he is seeking, the way in which he identifies the next research problem to be worked on will be influenced heavily by this assumption. If, on the other hand, a researcher brings to the task the assumption that a virus causes cancer, then the way in which that particular worker states the problem will be entirely different. What is true of the scientist concerning the assumptions he brings to his task is, of course, equally true of the public relations practitioner.[7]

STEP 2: DECIDING ON A MANAGEABLE PORTION OF THE PROBLEM

As a rule, the next step following a clear statement of a problem is selecting a manageable portion to study. The key word in this second step is the word *manageable*. The researcher has to face all sorts of realities with respect to what he wants to do. He has limitations imposed on him in terms of time, financial resources, research facilities, and manpower, to mention some of the more obvious. Also part of this translation of a problem to be studied into manageable portions is the question of establishing a hierarchy or priority of what is to be done. Inevitably, there are so many aspects of any problem that one has to decide what will be studied first, what will follow the initial effort, and so on.

Most public relations problem situations are usually of such scope that not all of the parts of any one problem can be studied at one time. This, as a rule, implies for the public relations practitioner a priority listing of manageable units taken one at a time, or however quickly manpower and finances and facilities will permit.

Returning to the hypothetical hospital public relations director referred to earlier, let us see how Steps 1 and 2 of the research process go together. Let us assume that the problem that he and his staff agreed on was that special efforts had to be made to improve the support for and understanding of the hospital on the part of the local community. By means of their discussion, the public relations staff of the hospital had narrowed down the "over-all public relations problems" of the hospital to an examination of community relations. Within this they had selected as their problem *an examination of the local*

---

[7] In this connection, it will be useful for the reader to review what we had to say about the importance of the sender undertaking a self-analysis as one of the steps in solving his communication problems (Chapter 6, pages 125-141). The material on pages 132-134 dealing with the effects of assumptions on problem-solving efforts is particularly applicable to our present discussion.

community's understanding of the goals of the hospital. Step 1 of the research process had been achieved.

Ascertaining the understanding of the hospital's goals by the local community still embraces more than any one study can cover. Step 2 —deciding upon a manageable portion of the problem—is still called for.

An illustration of Step 2 would be to decide to first study the hospital volunteers. Here is a group of individuals from the local community who have far greater contact with the hospital than the average person in the community. It is logical to assume that they have a good understanding of the hospital's goals and problems. If the efforts of the public relations department have been successful, evidence of this success will be readily evident among the hospital volunteers. By the same token, insights as to why the public relations department's efforts have *not* been successful will also be readily recognized because the hospital volunteers are more likely to have the interests of the hospital at heart than are other members of the community and are, therefore, more likely to be particularly cooperative in providing feedback to the public relations department.[8]

On the basis of this reasoning, a logical, manageable portion of the over-all problem is a study of the hospital volunteers to see what understanding they, as a group, possess. Obviously, if such a study reveals that they have a poor understanding of hospital objectives and problems, it is safe to assume that the general community possesses even less understanding.[9]

If this final study demonstrates that the hospital volunteers are poorly informed of the goals or objectives of the hospital, several "next steps" are obviously called for: (1) a check on present orientation programs for the hospital volunteer, (2) a revision of the orientation program, and (3) a similar study pointed toward the general community. But we are getting ahead of ourselves because now we are describing further steps within this particular problem area. The point to return to and highlight is that by narrowing down their efforts to a study of

---

[8] A closely related assumption to the rationale behind this focus on hospital volunteers is that the volunteers represent one of the best communication outlets to the local community. If they have a good understanding of hospital problems and objectives, they can be a good source for communicating these facts to the local community. On the other hand, if they have a poor understanding of hospital problems and objectives, they can impede communication or, conceivably, make things worse.

[9] It should be noted, however, that if the volunteers should prove to have excellent understanding of the objectives of the hospital, it still is a moot point as to what understanding the rest of the community has. Another decision would have to be made as to whether a similar study should be extended to the entire community.

the hospital volunteers, the public relations department takes the second step in the research process—*deciding on a manageable portion of the problem.*

STEP 3: ESTABLISHING DEFINITIONS

As we learned in Chapters 6 through 9, in our daily life we are constantly organizing the world about us and establishing relationships between one event and another. This organizing is done in a manner that semanticists describe under the heading "abstraction." To repeat some of what we said earlier, abstraction is the process of paying attention to only a portion of the possible events that we could attend to in the world about us. For example, in reacting to another person we respond to only a few of his many aspects to which we could conceivably pay attention. We cannot possibly pay attention to all of the different gestures, statements, and movements that go to make up the behavior of another individual. As a result, we pay attention to only *some* of his behavior.

Sometimes we pay attention to things that annoy us. We focus so completely on these annoying factors in another person that we can't see anything good in him. The so-called first impressions that one has on meeting someone for the first time serves as an excellent illustration of the process of abstracting. Of all of the things that we could pay attention to, we generally focus on an amazingly few factors. The handshake or the way one does or does not "look us in the eye" can often be concentrated on to the exclusion of all other behavior.

In addition to abstracting, we also *organize* the abstracted parts of the total process into certain categories. These organized categories are normally given labels. Thus the words *Girl Scout* stand for a great many abstractions which go together and add up to a particular category of person. These words act as a short cut for us by including a number of events under one general heading. In thinking of or communicating to others about Girl Scouts, we use the single term as a kind of shorthand notation to stand for all the meanings and separate observations that make up the category of persons that qualify for the heading Girl Scouts.

The Term "Concept"

This aspect of the process of abstraction is identified by the word *concept.* A concept, according to English and English, is an "idea that represents a number of individual instances, all of which have something in common. 'Dog' is a general concept; it represents any dog, or dogs in general."[10] As stated in this definition, the process of abstraction involves two steps: (1) perceiving selectively—that is, isolating some portion of the stimulus field from the rest of the field, and (2) assembling a set of selected perceptions which have some common characteristics. The abstracting and organizing described earlier with respect to the term *Girl Scout* is the process of concept formation. "Girl Scout" is a concept which sums up Girl Scouts in general.

It is interesting to note in this connection that present preoccupation about the "image" of an organization—particularly the "corporate image"—on the part of many persons is an illustration of concept formation. A favorable corporate image means nothing more than that people possess *concepts* which sum up the corporation in a positive light rather than a negative one.

Concepts Vary in Closeness to What They Represent

Some concepts have a close relationship to the objects or events they represent. Thus, for example, the meaning of the word (or concept) *chair* is demonstrated quite nicely by pointing to a particular chair. Chairs in general, represented by the plural of the word, can be demonstrated by pointing to a group of chairs. The fact that the word *chair* stands for the "idea that represents a number of individual instances" is particularly well demonstrated when one thinks of a group of chairs of assorted shapes and sizes. No matter how much they vary they all fit the category chair. So it is with the term *Girl Scout*. Girls can come in all sizes and shapes and still fit the category Girl Scout.

Other concepts are not so easily identified or related to what they stand for. The concept "personal assets" serves as a good illustration. Personal assets can include such items as chairs or furniture in general; however, personal assets also include one's home, clothes—a whole host of possessions. Hence, when you use the phrase *personal assets* it takes a bit more doing to communicate what you mean.

With a concept like "personal assets" it is still, however, relatively easy to relate the concept to what it stands for. With concepts like "morale," "good public relations," "public acceptance," we have a much more difficult job in communicating the meaning of the terms. A great many factors may stand for or produce good public relations.

---

[10] H. B. English and A. C. English, *A Comprehensive Dictionary of Psychological and Psychoanalytical Terms* (New York: Longmans, Green & Co., Inc. [David McKay Co., Inc.], 1958), p. 105.

In casual conversation with someone you may use the phrase *good public relations*. The person to whom you are communicating may think of many particular examples, none of which you may have in mind. What is worse, you yourself may not be quite sure of exactly what you mean by the term. How often, when asked for a definition of public relations, have you found yourself fumbling for words and examples?[11]

Concepts can be thought of as varying along a continuum from denotative to connotative or extensional to intensional (Chapter 8, pages 194-195). Figure 29 illustrates this way of thinking about con-

Readily defined;
point-at-able;
meaning easily
communicated to
others; objective
in character.
  Examples:
    "girl scout"
    "chair"

Difficult to define,
not open to view
or "point-at-able."
Meaning not easily
communicated to
others; subjective
in character.
  Examples:
    "public acceptance"
    "morale"

Figure 29

A Concept Continuum

cepts. The left-hand end of the continuum represents our first illustrations dealing with the concepts "chair" and "Girl Scout." Any concept that is readily definable—very often just by pointing at the object to be defined—falls at this end of the continuum. The distinct advantage of dealing with such concepts is that communication is possible. Accuracy in communication is also possible since the person communicating knows what he is talking about and so does the person receiving

---

[11] The reader has undoubtedly observed by now that in the past few paragraphs we have been discussing—with slightly different emphases—material that was first introduced in Chapter 8 (pages 189-194). At that time, we examined Hayakawa's abstraction ladder and what the semanticists mean by extensional and intensional meaning.

the communication. In terms of Hayakawa's abstraction ladder, we are able to come down the ladder successfully.

The right-hand end of the continuum in Figure 29 represents just the opposite situation. Here is where concepts such as "public acceptance," "good public relations," and "morale" belong. Such concepts are characteristically much more difficult (or practically impossible) to define. Unlike "chairs" and "Girl Scouts," such concepts as "public acceptance" and "morale" cannot be readily pointed at. You have to use other words in your attempt to communicate what you mean, and this is where the trouble begins. They are such abstract concepts that they can stand for a great many things. "Good public relations" is a perfect case in point. The phrase is used constantly by public relations people and others, yet even the most cursory examination reveals that few people can define clearly what they mean. No wonder, then, with concepts at this end of the continuum so much confusion in communication occurs.

Confusion in everyday communication is one thing; confusion in research is another. In research it is imperative that one be able to define the term he is using. This brings us to the main point of introducing the concept continuum. Public relations people in general and those wishing to do research in particular need to be *constantly conscious of the concept continuum*. They must develop an awareness of what type of concepts they are using in their daily language. Can they be clearly defined, or do they have vague, highly personal meanings? As communicators, public relations practitioners must constantly strive to use concepts toward the left-hand end of the continuum. To the extent that they do, they will be more effective communicators.

The Relationship Between Concept Formation and Establishing Definitions

With this background we are able to examine intelligently the third step in the research process—establishing definitions. Every research study is bound to have a lot of concepts necessary to the research and necessary in order to communicate about it afterward. These concepts must be defined, however, so that the researcher (and others) knows precisely what he is doing when it comes to later steps in the research process, such as deciding how to collect the necessary data, analyze it, and interpret the results.

To illustrate this third step in a public relations context, let us assume that an organization is interested in knowing more about how well they have achieved public acceptance, the concept that is going to be involved in this research. (As pointed out previously, it is a concept that is toward the right-hand end of the continuum presented in Figure 29. This is because the meaning of public acceptance is not readily pointed at.)

To be able to do any meaningful research, we must first define the term *public acceptance*. To illustrate, let us consider public acceptance as "good" or "adequate" if the general population understands the objectives of the XYZ health organization. This general definition equates public acceptance with public understanding. Here we are arbitrarily defining understanding as being equivalent to acceptance.

Obviously, what we have done thus far is not enough. What will constitute "good or adequate understanding of objectives"? Defining the last word in the phrase is not too difficult. It merely means that the investigator must write out the explicit objectives of the organization about which the public relations department has been communicating. Defining the rest of the phrase—"good or adequate understanding"—requires a little more elaboration. One way of defining "good or adequate understanding" can be in terms of how correctly a person identifies the organization's objectives. A survey can accomplish this; if a person correctly identifies a certain number of the objectives of an organization, it will be taken as "adequate understanding." This, of course, takes care of only the single respondent in the survey. To get around this problem, we can define "adequate understanding on the part of the total community" as a given percentage of the total sample of respondents who correctly identified a certain number of the organization's objectives. These two additional steps allow us to communicate to another individual what *we* mean by "adequate understanding" both for the single individual and the community as a whole.

To put it another way, in the above illustration the definition of good public acceptance is in terms of a respondent's "score" on an opinion-attitude survey *and* in terms of the performance of a certain percentage of the total number of individuals interviewed. By these refinements we have narrowed our definition down to a very specific one for both individuals and groups.

Obviously, this is only one way of defining public acceptance. The reader can undoubtedly generate many more. To illustrate this point more fully, let us take another example. Public acceptance could be defined in terms of the *volume* and *type* of letters received by an organization from the public over some specified period of time—say, two years. One could define "adequate acceptance" in terms of an *increase* in the number of letters received and their favorable content. An increase in the percentage of favorable letters received could define what we mean by community acceptance. An increase in the percentage of unfavorable letters can be taken as an indication of a decrease in acceptance by the community. Obviously, an arbitrary in-between point could be used as a measure of "no change" in public acceptance, meaning that the organization has neither improved its position nor has lost ground with respect to its public acceptance.

As the reader has probably anticipated, we would also have to arrive at some definitions of what we would regard as unfavorable and favorable letters. Different methods could be used, depending on the circumstances. For example, a word or sentence count could be made breaking the letter up into positive, negative, and neutral ("in-between") words or sentences.

As pointed out earlier, this is not the only way nor the best way to define public acceptance. One could, for example, quarrel with this definition on the grounds that it is possible to understand the objectives of an organization without accepting it. Likewise, we have overlooked other related difficulties that would have to be coped with (and about which we are unable to go into detail here) for purposes of making our point about definitions. For example, there is the question of making provision for the bias inherent in using as data only letters from persons that are interested enough to write. Some way of accounting for the person who did not write would, of course, be in order. Also, there is the question of the validity of our definition: How well does it, in fact, represent public acceptance? Could there be some factors of which we are unaware that would make measures of positive and negative words and sentences not a valid representation of public acceptance?[12]

The point worth repeating here is that there are always pros and cons of *any* definition for *any* concept. In spite of disagreement, with concepts defined carefully one can communicate and, sometimes for the first time, we realize what someone else means. Even finding out that we disagree is progress! At least we know what the other person is talking about.

Two additional thoughts should be presented here. (1) How one defines a concept is, in a sense, arbitrary. Naturally, a definition reflects the experience that the definer has had in working with a specific research problem. However, *arbitrariness does not mean the same thing as unreasonableness.* Public understanding (measured by test questions in a survey) as a definition of public acceptance is arbitrary

---

[12] Consider, for example, the farfetched but possible increase in unfavorable letters as the result of a campaign conducted by a single letter writer using pseudonyms. In this case, our definition would not be a valid representation of public acceptance.

in the sense that it can be defined in many other ways. However, the definition is defensible and is in keeping with research that has been done in public relations and psychology. (2) With this effort in establishing a definition, some precision in thinking has been produced. Also, accurate communication concerning this public relations problem area is now more likely. A step forward has been made in taking a very vague concept, such as public acceptance, and making its meaning more precise. In keeping with our concept continuum (Figure 29), we have moved toward the left-hand end.

A Word About Operational Definitions

Up to now, we have avoided the term *operational definitions*. There is no question that most readers would not have understood this term had we used it to start our discussion of definitions. However, when one defines public acceptance in terms of public understanding and then obtains a measure of that understanding by means of a test built into a survey questionnaire, this is the process of defining a term in an operational fashion. That is, the *operations* of asking individuals certain questions about an organization, scoring these answers as either right or wrong, establishing a "passing" and "failing" score, and then defining understanding in terms of a high score (and the converse in terms of a low score) is what is meant by an operational definition. The operations or behaviors that one would go through to test people defines what is meant by understanding and, therefore, acceptance.

Consider another example—the concept "measurement." When we use a yardstick to measure the length and width of a table, we are operationally defining length and width measurements. The width measurement is defined by the operation of placing a yardstick along one edge of the table's width and determining how many yardstick lengths (and fractions thereof) are required to span it. We add up the amount and report the width in feet and inches. We say that the table is five feet, four inches wide. This is an operational definition of the width of the table.

Let's consider one last example of an operational definition. Consider the concept "hunger." Suppose that a psychologist wants to show the relationship between how hungry an animal is and how strongly he will strive for food. That is, how hungry does an animal have to be to put up with a mild electric shock in order to reach the food. Among other things, the psychologist has to define hunger. He must be able to communicate to other scientists how he was able to determine how hungry the animal was in each of the different test situations. If one stops to think about it, how would you determine just how hungry an animal is—certainly you just can't ask it.[13]

One way around this difficulty has been to define hunger in terms of the number of hours since the last feeding. That is, to speak of an animal as "one hour hungry" or "five hours hungry." In this way, we have avoided trying to "get inside" the animal to figure out how he feels and have, instead, defined hunger in terms of the operations involved in feeding the animal. To be sure, there are difficulties or weaknesses in this definition (it does not overcome the fact that one animal is not as hungry after five hours as another), but at least the research *can* communicate what he means by hunger, and another researcher can duplicate what he has done to see if he gets the same results. Just in passing, it does serve as a rather good measure of hunger, although it is arbitrary, and the reader can probably think of other ways of operationally defining the concept of hunger.

QUESTIONS FOR DISCUSSION

1. With Figure 28 (page 465) in mind, give an example of a public relations practitioner who is operating at the intuitive end of the investigative continuum. Also, develop an example of the practitioner at the opposite end, the scientific research end. Was it equally easy to find examples of a public relations practitioner operating at the scientific research end as it was to find illustrations of the practitioner at the opposite end?

2. Assume that you have been asked to support the contention that there is considerable overlap between obtaining reliable knowledge in everyday life and obtaining reliable knowledge through scientific research. What arguments would you put forth? What examples can you give to support the contention of overlap?

3. Develop one or two examples that illustrate the asumptions that lie behind research discussed on page 474—how we assume stability in nature or causality in nature. Assume the role of someone

---

[13] At first blush, it might appear that if the psychologist had worked with human subjects, he would not have such a big problem. After all, he could just *ask* a man how hungry he is. However, as one thinks about asking people how hungry they are, it becomes apparent that this would not be so simple. People would use so many different words to communicate how they feel, to say nothing of the fact that each would feel differently because none of us becomes hungry at exactly the same time or to exactly the same degree.

trying to explain how assumption No. 3 permits one to argue that public relations can, *theoretically, at least,* become more rigorous in practice.

4. Take each of the difficulties of stating a problem (listed in Step 1 in the research process) and translate it into public relations terms. For example, illustrate how the public relations practitioner is faced with the difficulty of stating his problem because he has so many problems to cope with.

5. Take any one of the cases you have used for previous discussion questions and define a few of the terms that were used by you to identify the problem or problems involved. Try to express at least one of the definitions in operational terms.

Now that you have done this, can you think of any other instances where concepts used by a public relations practitioner have been operationally defined? If you have difficulty finding examples of operational definitions in public relations writing, why do you suppose that this is so? Do you think that the precision of communication concerning what the public practitioner had in mind or planned to do to solve his problem suffered in any way because of a lack of operational definitions?

Chapter 18

SCIENTIFIC RESEARCH CONTINUED: THE NEXT THREE STEPS IN THE RESEARCH PROCESS

INTRODUCTION

In the preceding chapter, we established a point of view, or way of thinking, about scientific research. In addition, we considered in detail the first three steps of the research process, thus launching us in our consideration of the relationship between research and public relations.

In this chapter, we are going to extend our examination of the reserach process to the next three steps, which are the literature search, developing hypotheses, and deciding on the study design. With these three steps, we will extend our examination of the research process into areas that nonresearchers tend to think of when they imagine what scientists do in their everyday work. As before, we shall pay particularly close attention to translating what we take up into public relations terms or problem situations so as to continue to relate research to public relations practice.

STEP 4: THE LITERATURE SEARCH

Man is a highly inquisitive being. His tremendous impact on the earth, in spite of his comparatively short history, attests to this. From a research point of view, it is seldom that you are the first person who is curious about the answers to a particular problem. Either someone else has been seeking exactly the same information or what they have done is close enough that you cannot intelligently conduct your research without taking it into account.

This adds up to Step 4 in the research process: the literature search. Any competent investigator examines the knowledge that is related to his area of research before going ahead on his own problem. By literature search we mean, of course, looking through all related written material—books and articles to be found in any library, either public or personal. It also includes communicating with other people to seek whatever information may be pertinent to your problem. Some very practical benefits can be forthcoming from a literature search.

What You Seek May Already Be Known

The information you seek may already be known; what you are planning to do, someone else may already have done. Obviously, this can be an extensive saving to you in time and money if it should prove to be true. Someone else may have experimented with certain new techniques in fund raising and have data to compare with the more "tried and true" methods. Admittedly, in the social and behavioral sciences in general and in public relations in particular, such a perfect "find" is not very likely. This is because many problem situations are unique to the particular public relations situation. Also, in the area of public relations, "explanatory principles" usually have very strict limitations when it comes to generalizing from the results. There are so many factors affecting any public relations phenomenon that seldom can you generalize from one situation to another with any great degree of confidence.

Incidentally, two previous discussions are particularly pertinent here: definitions and the process of abstracting. The importance of defining our terms becomes very obvious when we engage in a literature search to find out what others have done in an area in which we are interested. If we are not clear about what we have in mind and if we read about the work of someone else who has not been careful in his definitions, the whole effort can become a joke. Take our example of working in the area of public acceptance. If you were to read an article in which the writer never made clear how he defined and measured public acceptance, you would not be able to relate his work to yours. You would not be able to take advantage of this prior work nor add anything to it by your own efforts.

The process of abstracting relates to the literature search in this manner. If a public relations practitioner cannot put his problem into more abstract terms—that is, take the question of public acceptance and translate it into meaningful terms like "amount of understanding of objectives" or "attitudes toward the worthwhileness of his organization"—a literature search may prove to be useless. It is not very likely that you will find a study done by an organization exactly like yours and dealing with precisely the same problem areas in which you are interested. You *may*, however, find research that deals with *changing attitudes, imparting information more effectively,* or *measuring the impact of copy written in a certain style.* If you are able to abstract the essence of your problem area (that is, translate it into some communication and/or psychological concepts), then it is likely you will find a number of research articles that may prove to be helpful.

You Can Learn from the Work of Others

A much more likely occurrence is that, in spite of the fact that what you seek may not be known, enough related work may exist so that you can benefit from the mistakes or findings of someone else. If nothing else, you may find out what "won't work." You may uncover a valuable suggestion for measuring or obtaining the information you seek. In short, you may be able to do what man has always done—build on or benefit from knowledge obtained from others.

The notion of searching the literature is, after all, a very simple, fundamental idea. We could have presented this step in fewer words. The reason we have elaborated somewhat on Step 4 in the research process is that to many action-oriented people taking the time to make a literature search appears to be a backward step. The author is well aware that if a public relations practitioner were to spend a few hours in a library it might be regarded as killing time. His superior might wonder what he was doing and when was he going to "get to work." Nothing could be farther from the truth.

Another observation is related to this fourth step. Because the practice of public relations has not moved in the direction of the "best obtainable evidence" end of the continuum (Chapter 3, Figure 2), and too few public relations practitioners function as applied social and behavioral scientists, they have not adopted the attitude and approach of the scientist in solving their problems. This means that they do not normally think of searching the literature because, for one reason, they are not equipped to understand the social and behavioral science literature. To make matters worse, this attitude has had the effect of making the public relations literature that does exist not too helpful. In other words, there is a circular action here involving the public relations practitioner who does not regard the literature step as an important one, the lack of literature, and the lack of the ability to read profitably the related literature. The author is well aware that it is going to take time to break out of this circular process, and that action on a variety of fronts—both in academic circles and in applied settings—will all contribute to remedying this unfortunate situation.

STEP 5: DEVELOPING HYPOTHESES

Undoubtedly each one of us at some time or another in his life has used the expression "I wonder what would happen if I . . ." The end of that sentence always contains action of some sort. Thus, you ask yourself what would happen if you turned that dial, added in that particular number, or asked that particular question. The completion of the sentence "I wonder what would happen if . . ." usually implies action of some sort and is often helpful but not always correct.

The point of interest here is that asking the question "I wonder what would happen if . . ." usually occurs when there is a problem to be faced. It is a *problem*-solving step that we all take in our everyday lives. What is even more interesting is that this form of "wondering" very often helps us solve the problem facing us.

This thinking out loud about the possible outcomes of certain actions is known in science by a different heading, namely *hypothesis formation*. The scientist takes this very same procedure which helps to solve everyday problems and uses it to help him to solve scientific problems. This aid, the development of hypotheses, is the fifth step in the research process. Let us examine it in some detail.

What Is a Hypothesis?

In simple terms, *a hypothesis is a statement of an assumed relationship*, a statement that one phenomenon or occurrence is somehow related to another phenomenon or occurrence. For example, one may hypothesize that the financial support of the general public for any or all health and welfare organizations is inadequate due to the fact that we do not, in training our children to become responsible adults, teach them meaning of voluntary support of these organizations. We train our youth to earn money, to be competitive, to want many material acquisitions, to live, to hate; but nowhere do we really pay attention to teaching that certain institutions in our society are voluntarily supported, as distinct from other types of support (*e.g.*, through state and federal taxes). What may be even more significant, we do not impart an understanding of *why* or *how* voluntary support might be preferable to governmental support in certain circumstances.

The foregoing hypothesis makes an assertion that public apathy to the appeals for support generated by health and welfare organizations stems mainly (or partly, depending on how you state the hypothesis) from certain inadequacies in the training our society provides for its youngsters.

Our illustrative hypothesis has suggested a relationship between the difficulty of obtaining money from the public and an assumed state of affairs with respect to the type of childhood training *most* of the public received.

Let us extend this example one step further in the interest of clarity. Earlier, it was noted that a hypothesis is a more formal statement of a very common everyday practice summed up in the phrase "I wonder what would happen if . . ." With our hypothesis now stated, we are saying something like this: "*I wonder what would happen to the amount of financial support given by the public if a greater percentage of the public received some training in childhood about the difference between voluntary and governmental support of our type of organization, in our particular form of government.*" The answer to the question, following the phrasing of the hypothesis, is that *public support would increase if this particular childhood training came to pass.* This is an illustration of stating a hypothesis in the context of one of the constant problems in any health and welfare organization—fund raising.

A point worth noting here is that probably all hypotheses are abstract in character in that the relationship assumed is not directly "seen" or "experienced." It goes beyond present experience to some extent. For example, the hypothesis concerning the relationship between voluntary giving and childhood training goes beyond any experiences we can point to directly. You can't walk up to an individual who donates generously and determine readily if he had the type of childhood training referred to. It is a subtle and complex combination of a whole host of previous experiences expressed in abstract, yet definable terms.

One last point should be brought out to communicate the meaning of the term *hypothesis* more adequately. Previously, we stressed the importance of stating our research problem both in general and specific terms, and we noted the importance of defining the concepts that are to be employed in the research effort. Now that we have taken up a definition of the term *hypothesis,* it can be seen readily that a hypothesis is probably one of the most useful ways of succinctly stating the essentials of a research problem. If we are interested in doing research on the relationship between childhood training and adult giving, we would be another step along the way with our hypothesis. Assuming that we have accepted our hypothesis, we are able to focus our attention on the next steps in the research process. *In short, a hypothesis is an extremely efficient, shorthand way of expressing the essence of a problem area.*

A Hypothesis Cannot Be Escaped

In other books written on research, some strong points of view can be found concerning the function of hypotheses. Some writers claim that research is not possible without first formulating hypotheses, while others take a more moderate view, holding forth the idea that research progress is possible without first formulating hypotheses.

Perhaps a more useful point of departure concerning the role of hypotheses in research is the suggestion that in practice one cannot really escape hypotheses formulation. Whether one realizes it or not, whenever an attempt is made to state a problem and embark on research, hypothesizing takes place. In thinking about a research problem, one is guided by certain hypotheses. This may take place with or without the person being aware of the process. Certain relationships (or hypotheses) are rejected because the investigator, on the basis of his experience, concludes that they are not true. Other relationships (or hypotheses) are considered more carefully because past experience and the knowledge of other research results dictate that they are feasible. In short, since hypotheses are statements of relationships, wittingly or unwittingly they creep into the formulation of a research problem.

Since you can't escape from hypothesis formulation, it is much more desirable to make hypothesis formulation a definite part of your problem-solving efforts; there are benefits to be derived from hypothesizing.

Making Hypotheses Work for You

If the argument that hypothesis formation can't be avoided is accepted, the logical question arises—"How can hypotheses be made to help?" The answer is that there are several advantages in making hypothesis development explicit instead of implicit. Two of the more important follow.

Hypothesis development helps to organize pertinent thinking. A hypothesis serves to organize one's thinking in a problem area. Let us consider our previous example dealing with the problem of giving financial support. If giving as an adult is hypothesized as being related to certain training as a child, immediately this helps one bring to bear other experimental data or general knowledge of the problem area. One is more likely to sort out the pertinent studies of early childhood experiences and their adult manifestations, more likely to move in the right direction when it comes to searching the literature for information bearing on the problems to be studied.[1]

Hypothesis development improves the design of studies. As we shall discuss soon, another important step in the research process is the design of experiments. Research designs are the plans an investigator makes for such things as the execution of experiments or surveys or the procedures for collecting data. The point is that developing hypotheses often highlights methods or procedures in the design of studies that might otherwise be overlooked.

For example, in the illustration used earlier about a study of public acceptance, one might generate the hypothesis that the more a person understands the objectives of an organization, the more positive his attitudes will be toward the organization.

This hypothesis highlights the importance of how we measure "understanding" and "positive attitudes." Previously, it was suggested that one way of defining understanding might be in terms of the number of the hospital's objectives an individual is able to correctly identify in a survey. How the particular individual is questioned and what methods we use to "score" the answers of the respondent are pointedly brought out by this hypothesis that suggests that understanding of and attitudes toward an organization are positively related. With a hypothesis such as this, it would be more difficult to overlook details about how understanding is going to be measured in a survey.

"Proving" Hypotheses

One final word that should be included here concerns "proving" hypotheses. Popular use of the word *prove* generally carries with it a

---

[1] It should be recognized that it is entirely possible to state a hypothesis that later proves to be incorrect, that will, with hindsight, be seen to have been misleading and not helpful. However, this type of error would happen anyway, because it merely reflects the potential weakness of any investigator. He may be doing a research project that does not answer the questions he wants answered. Making your hypotheses explicit does not increase the likelihood of being wrong.

degree of finality or "ultimate truth" that can be misleading. Nothing is final, nor do we obtain ultimate truths through research work. Hence, proof in that sense just doesn't happen in research work.

Instead, it is more useful to think in terms of *substantiating* a hypothesis and to keep in mind that *whenever you substantiate a hypothesis, it is a matter of degree.*

The mode of analysis for substantiating (or not substantiating) a particular hypothesis or relationship is in terms of departure from chance. We pose the same basic question of any data that we have: "Could the findings be due to chance factors alone?"

The research that went into the Salk polio vaccine can serve as an excellent and rather dramatic example. As the persons connected with the testing of the vaccine compiled their data, they, too, had the same basic question to answer. Could their results be explained by chance, or did the vaccine really work? Were the number of polio cases reduced significantly as compared with previous years when there was no vaccine? If the number of cases of polio was reduced enough that we cannot say that the results are due to chance, then the value of the vaccine is demonstrated. Or, to put it into our terms, the hypothesis that Salk polio vaccine does reduce the likelihood of contracting polio is substantiated: It was not chance; it was the vaccine.

If the reader wishes to continue the use of the word *prove*, he should keep in mind that all that proving means is that an experimenter is able to make a statement about the role chance did or did not play in obtaining the results from any experimental effort.

STEP 6: DECIDING ON THE STUDY DESIGN

Research design is the "how" of experimentation. By this stage in the research process the experimenter knows what is is going to do, he has settled on his problem, and now it remains for him to plan how he is going to execute his experiment or survey or what have you. *The study design is a detailed plan of execution covering all phases or stages of the total study.*

Be Sure That Your Study Tests What You Want It to Test

The reason that one goes to all of the work of doing a study is to provide information which has bearing on a particular problem. Consequently, one of the main purposes of a study design is to insure the fact that the findings attained have bearing on the problem.

For example, in our discussion of hypotheses formation, a hypothesis was formulated that suggested a relationship between a certain type of childhood training and adult support of various health and welfare agencies. The hypothesis further stated that the type of childhood training deemed important was teaching that imparted an understanding of voluntary support of certain organizations in our society. With this hypothesis in mind, let us see how the study design would be developed to insure that the experiment, when executed, would yield the necessary information.

CAREFUL ATTENTION MUST BE GIVEN TO THE INDEPENDENT VARIABLE

In the language of the researcher, the type of childhood training referred to in the hypothesis above is known as the *independent* or *experimental variable.* The independent variable is the variable (or factor) the functioning of which research is supposed to make more understandable. Or, to put it as Kerlinger has,

> . . . An *independent variable* is the *presumed* cause of the *dependent* variable, the *presumed* effect. The independent variable is the antecedent; the dependent variable is the consequent. Whenever we say "If A, then B," whenever we have an implication, A implies B, we have an independent variable (A) and a dependent variable (B). . . .[2]

In the Salk polio vaccine situation mentioned earlier, the vaccine itself constitutes the independent or experimental variable. This substance is what the researchers wanted to know more about, particularly its possible role as an agent in helping to prevent an individual from contracting polio.

Understanding the terminology of independent variable (and other terminology to be introduced later in this section) may be made clearer if we pause for a moment and examine the simple, classical "cause and effect" model that is often employed to guide the thinking of the behavioral scientist. This classic model is usually depicted as follows:

$$S \rightarrow O \rightarrow R$$

where S = stimulus, O = organism, and R = response. The simplest interpretation of the above model is that a stimulus impinges on an organism, interacts in a complex way with the various "inner" motivating factors of the organism itself, and results in a response or behavior. The response or behavior is caused by a combination of the stimulus

---

[2] Fred N. Kerlinger, *Foundations of Behavioral Research* (New York: Holt, Rinehart & Winston, Inc., 1964), p. 39. All material used by permission.

interacting with the organism. Hence, the notion that this is a "cause and effect" model. When we have identified the stimuli both internal and external to the organism, we have identified the causes of certain behavior.

It is likely that no single stimulus produces a response and, likewise, that an organism does not react with just one response, but rather with multiple responses. Hence, the more correct form of the model is as follows:

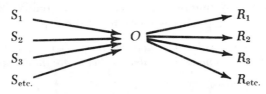

The interpretation of our second schema is simply that, more typically, there are many different stimuli impinging on an individual (or organism) which results in complex responses or behavior.

To relate this model to the terminology of "independent variable" introduced earlier, all that we need to do is label one of the S's in our schema above. Let us assume that S_1 now stands for "childhood training concerning health and welfare organizations." It is a factor that may operate to cause some individuals to respond differently—in this case, to support health and welfare organizations financially (R_1). R_1, then, stands for the behavior of supporting an organization financially. The whole purpose of the experiment is to ascertain whether S_1 (special childhood training) does operate to induce R_1 (greater giving).

Our model also has bearing on the term *hypothesis*. Our earlier hypothesis stated that there is assumed a relationship between childhood training and adult giving. In the symbols of the model we have presented, what we have hypothesized is that S_1 *does* interact with the organism (or individual), O, in such a way to produce financial giving, R_1.

> *Decisions as to what constitutes childhood training in voluntary giving will have to be made. In short, the researcher must decide what to measure.*

Childhood training in voluntary giving can conceivably occur in many ways. Consequently, we must make a decision as to *what* we will measure. We must make up our minds as to what will or will not qualify as childhood training in voluntary giving.

Let us consider a few of the many items of information that can qualify as the "what." One item may be specific times that our respondents can remember when their parents had taken the time to explain the difference between voluntary and nonvoluntary organizations in our society. Another could be the times that their parents explained to them what organizations they themselves supported and why. Still another item could be the times that their parents began to suggest that they give to voluntary organizations from their own allowance, much in the same manner that many parents introduce the idea of thrift and saving money by starting bank accounts for their children. Clearly, any number of measures can qualify, and our first step constitutes deciding what is going to be the experimental variable.

Decisions must be made about how the researcher is going to determine what childhood training his subjects (who are now adults) had as children.

There is, of course, more than one way of getting at this information. Depending on the circumstances, the researcher may accept the *memory* of his subjects. He will probably take the additional precaution, of course, of requiring his subjects to cite specific examples of their childhood experiences that they think are illustrations of teaching about voluntary organizations. The experimenter will then take the illustrations given and decide how to classify them. Those that qualify as examples of training will be tallied alongside the name of the individual. Those that do not qualify will be ignored. This will be done with all of the subjects to be tested.

On the other hand, the investigator may want to take the more rigorous (and limiting) approach of comparing what his subjects remember with what their parents remember. Working independently with both the individual and his parents, we can argue that, if they agree, we have greater certainty concerning the reliability of their recall of what happened many years ago.

At this juncture, the particular *way* in which the early childhood experiences of the individuals to be studied are ascertained is not important. What *is* important is that the reader understand that it is during the study design phase of the research process (*i.e.*, Step 6) that one decides how to identify and measure the independent variable.

Decisions must be made concerning the gradations of the independent variable.

Unless the researcher has only a twofold classification of "had acceptable childhood experiences" and "did not have acceptable childhood experiences," some attention must be given to gradation or degrees of the independent variable to be manipulated. For example, it may be feasible to have *four* categories of experience: high, medium, low, and none. Then decisions have to be made as to what will constitute a high degree of childhood training, what will constitute a medium degree of training, and so on.

To illustrate, it may be that for a person to qualify for the high degree category, he must be able to recall at least twenty different instances of childhood training. A low-degree respondent may be one who had five or fewer instances of childhood training. This approach of *counting* the number of instances enables the experimenter to determine *gradations* (or degrees) of the experimental variable in the group he is testing.

Translating what we have said into our $S = R$ model, *gradations* of the experimental variable means that we have some increments in S_1 (childhood experiences) that we will be able to relate to increments in R_1 (variation in agency support as an adult). We *may* find that a little S_1 produces a little R_1. Or, we may find that a little S_1 produces no discernible R_1 and that it takes a lot of S_1 to produce a little R_1.

The ability to identify gradations of the experimental variable can often be very important. For example, with just the twofold breakdown of "had acceptable childhood experiences" and "did not have acceptable childhood experiences," a great deal of information may be lost. We are not able to tell, for example, whether just a little training produces results, or whether we need to have a lot of training to produce any results. This can have very practical implications. If just a little training produces satisfactory results, it makes the goal of widespread training a more realistic objective for the public relations practitioner. If, however, only a great deal of training produces the type of adult who supports voluntary health and welfare organizations, it becomes another matter entirely. It might be completely unrealistic to expect that extensive training can come to pass.

Careful Attention Must Be Given the Dependent Variable

We must apply the same series of considerations to what will constitute the *effects* (or results) of the independent variable in operation. These effects are referred to in scientific terminology as the *dependent variable* and were included in our discussion earlier concerning a definition of the independent variable. As noted in our cause and effect model, the experimenter refers to this under the heading of the response or R_1. As in the case of the independent variable, our first question with respect to the dependent variable is *what* adult behavior are we going to consider as being the *result* of this particular childhood training.

Returning to our hypothesis for a moment, we see that explicit in the statement of the hypothesis is that the result will be *greater support* of health and welfare organizations. That is, persons who receive childhood training are assumed to be the persons who will give greater support to such organizations as adults.

Greater support, however, like childhood training, needs to be specified much more closely. What adult behavior are we going to consider as being the result of this particular childhood training? Will it be the act of giving money to a voluntary organization? Will it be the act of serving as a volunteer worker? Will it be both? As part of the study design, we must decide ahead of time what responses we are going to measure and relate in some manner to the independent variable.

Secondly, as in the case of the independent variable, *how* are we going to measure what we have agreed on? Will it be just the frequency or number of acts of giving? Will it be the amount of time a person volunteers? Will we attempt to weight some giving and some volunteer work as more important than other giving and other instances of volunteering? Here, too, we must decide ahead of time how we are going to measure the responses.

Lastly, as with the independent variable, what will be the gradations of measurement that we apply to the responses (the dependent variable)? If we agree on financial giving as the response we are going to measure, what will be the gradation of giving? Will we measure the number of times a person gives and ignore the amount? Will the amount one gives determine the gradations? Will we use some sort of formula taking into consideration the giver's ability to contribute?

We have not gone into the same amount of detail with respect to the response as we did with examining some considerations of the independent variable. This is not because the response (or dependent variable) is not every bit as important as the independent variable. The limitations of space require that we merely point out that *the same considerations that were made with respect to the independent variable apply to the dependent variable as well.* Considerations of *what* and *how* and all of the other details must be taken up with respect to the response and included as a part of the study design. We need to plan both carefully.

A Brief Summary

Thus far in our discussion of the design of studies we have:

a)   discussed the meaning of the term independent or experimental variable;

b)   discussed the meaning of the term dependent variable (in behavioral terms, the response);

c)   examined briefly the simple cause and effect model of the behavioral scientist: $S \rightarrow O \rightarrow R$;

d)   indicated the relationship between the cause and effect model
and the terminology of the independent variable and the dependent variable. We have learned that the experimental (or independent) variable is what the researcher manipulates to determine its relationship to some dependent variable. In the context
of behavior, the independent variable is the S (or stimulus) and
the dependent variable is the R (or response);

e)   noted, with respect to the independent variable, that the researcher must ask himself *what* is going to constitute the experimental variable, *how* is it to be measured, and in what *gradations* or *degrees*; and

f)   discussed the same considerations of what, how, and in what
gradations or degrees with respect to the dependent (or response)
variable.

A Word About Different Types of Research[3]

Ex Post Facto *Research*

Thus far in our presentation of Step 6—deciding on the study design—we have attempted to consider some of the more important
factors in study designs in a rather general sense without emphasizing
any particular type of study, other than to couch the examples and
terminology in human behavior terms. Although our purpose is to continue to discuss the design of research studies in more general terms, it
may be useful at this point to introduce briefly some of the more common types of research that exist: (1) *ex post facto* research; (2) laboratory experiments, field experiments, and field studies; and (3) survey
research.

In *ex post facto* research, the phenomenon that an investigator is
interested in has already occurred and his interest is in sorting out independent variables thought to account for the dependent variables
that he has already observed. Thus, one may be interested in the
causes of juvenile delinquency and for this reason study samples of
youths that are and are not delinquents, attempting to sort out variables (such as broken homes, slum conditions) that seem to be more

---

[3] In this section, we follow the categories put forth by Kerlinger, *op. cit.*, pp.
359-408.

prevalent within the delinquent groups as compared with the non-delinquent groups. This particular study approach is very common. Although the major weaknesses of *ex post facto* studies are the inability of the researcher to control and manipulate independent variables and to obtain the proper samples for study, there are many times when he has no other alternative. Sometimes he can't control the variables that he wishes to study for a variety of reasons. In the face of such a condition, an *ex post facto* study is the only action open to the researcher. In fact, it is useful at this point to bring out that different study approaches have different strengths and weaknesses. The thing for the public relations practitioner to keep in mind is that researchers use what they can for given circumstances, and the interpretation of their results is dependent on what methods they have been able to employ.

One variation of *ex post facto* studies is correlational studies. That is, an investigator attempts to correlate one phenomenon with another to see if these phenomena are related to one another. As we shall learn in more detail later, correlational studies are *ex post facto* in nature in that one cannot say, on the basis of a correlational study alone, that one particular variable singled out for study causes another variable to occur. As with all *ex post facto* studies, correlational studies must be interpreted with extreme care because it is very easy to come up with a very plausible but completely erroneous explanation of the phenomena observed.

Laboratory Experiments, Field Experiments, and Field Studies

Laboratory experiments. As we learned in Chapter 17 (pages 476-478), laboratory experiments have a paramount virtue in that the controls that the experimenter is able to exert over his experiment are greatest in such settings. Thus, the independent variables can be introduced and manipulated, and unwanted variables excluded. Likewise, the dependent variables can be measured. As a consequence, the classical cause and effect model, which, in a sense, can be thought of as the basic point of departure for all study efforts, is achieved most closely. Social and, particularly, behavioral scientists have attempted to conduct laboratory experiments on phenomena in which they are interested for some time now with considerable success, in spite of the enormous complexity of human and infrahuman behavior.

As with any other approach, there are drawbacks to the laboratory experiment. Thus, laboratory experiments, at times, are limited to extremely artificial "part" behaviors—that is, only a small segment of the total behavior of a given organism may be under study, and the relationship of this part to the whole is sometimes difficult to ascertain. Also, there is the question of the artificiality of the laboratory situation, and one is never quite certain what will happen in "real life." Lastly, the temptation to generalize from the laboratory to outside the laboratory can be great, and sometimes the care necessary in making interpretations is overlooked.

In spite of these limitations, the laboratory experiment is the most precise approach that we have to control for variables for the purpose of obtaining reliable knowledge and is consequently the type of research approach used most often to test hypothesized relationships between variables, to test predictions, and to refine theories.

Field experiments. Field experiments are conducted precisely because of the "artificial" limitation of the laboratory approach discussed above. Thus, one does a field experiment when he wishes to extend a study interest into a setting that is closer to "real life," where the setting is more like the everyday, dynamic behavior that all of us are a part of and would like to understand more effectively.

The difference between a field experiment and a laboratory experiment is one of degree. Thus, everything that we said about the laboratory experiment applies, except that in the field the controls the experimenter has over all facets of his study *may* be less precise. To put it another way, the danger of "contamination" (whether we are speaking of the independent variable, the dependent variable, or any other feature of the total study) is greater.

In compensation for the likelihood of contamination that the field experiment offers, this approach has several distinct advantages. If carefully done (that is, tightly controlled, as in the laboratory experiment), the field experiment has the advantage of dealing with variables as they are found to be in natural settings, the independent and dependent variables are manipulated and measured in complex and dynamic social situations, and solutions to practical problems can be obtained while broad hypotheses concerning human behavior are being tested.

In short, unlike a laboratory experiment where the investigator may be trying to ascertain the relationship between the effects of electric shock on the ability of subjects to remember verbally presented poetry, the field experiment may be trying to establish the effects of certain systems of introducing a new method of work to employees to ascertain which approach is more effective in overcoming resistance to change.

Once again, it may be worthwhile to repeat that there is really no such thing as the "best" approach to obtaining reliable knowledge.

Rather, there are different approaches with different advantages and disadvantages. This point is particularly noteworthy when one contrasts the laboratory experiment with the field experiment. Some people tend to exaggerate the importance of "real life" studies, so they dismiss the laboratory experiment because it is too artificial and not practical enough. Obviously, from what we have said thus far, such a view is not warranted.

Field studies. Field studies can be viewed as a special case of *ex post facto* studies that are directed at finding out more about the relationships of psychological and sociological variables in actual social situations. Thus, field studies may include such things as investigations of school systems to find out how a teacher perceives her role and how this factor is related to her effectiveness as a teacher; studies of industrial organizations to ascertain how communication patterns are affected by various formal organizational plans; or studies of how racially nonintegrated communities react when racial integration is brought about within the public school system.

As Katz has pointed out, field studies can be either *exploratory* or *hypothesis-testing*.[4] In an exploratory study one is merely looking for significant variables or relationships between variables that lay the groundwork for more systematic and precise follow-up studies. In other words, exploratory field studies very often lead to field experiments or even laboratory experiments.

Hypothesis-testing field studies are quite similar to exploratory ones, with the exception that some tentative hypothesis may lie behind the field study. For example, we may have a tentative hypothesis that the discipline, comradeship, and special learning experiences of scouting may be related to school adjustment and ability of a boy to function successfully in school. With this tentative hypothesis in mind, we could conduct a field study involving boys in a certain number of schools to see whether there was any substance to this hypothesized relationship between being a Boy Scout and being better adjusted socially and a more effective student.

The reader is obviously aware of the relationship of field study and the field experiments and laboratory experiments. By and large, field studies have as their major disadvantage the looseness with which variables are controlled for and/or measured. In this respect, field studies are the least precise of the three. On the other hand, field studies offer the advantages of realism and the exciting possibility that some fruitful hypothesis or study area may be uncovered.

---

[4] L. Festinger and D. Katz, *Research Methods in the Behavioral Sciences* (New York: Holt, Rinehart & Winston, Inc., 1953), pp. 75-83.

Survey Research

Although from one point of view survey research can be thought of as a special case of the field experiment or the field study, this particular approach to obtaining reliable knowledge has become so extensive that it is probably fruitful to consider it as a separate type of research.

With respect to the notion about survey research as a "special case," it has probably already occurred to the reader how this might be so. That is, in the process of doing a field experiment, one may well make use of personal interviews to obtain the information necessary to find out how communication patterns within a given organization are affected by different organizational plans. The personal interviews can be used to establish what each individual had heard within an organization and from what source he obtained his information. In this manner, the technique of the personal interview, a key variation of the survey approach, can be used to achieve a given field study objective.

Taking surveys as a separate type of research, we can make the following distinctions within this approach: personal interviews, mail questionnaires, telephone interviews, and panels.

The personal interview.   Probably the most powerful and versatile variation is the personal interview. Subjects can be questioned in considerable depth, thus enabling the investigator to obtain a great deal of information about an individual's attitudes as well as his factual knowledge for an almost unlimited range of topics. In addition, the personal interview coupled with modern sample survey techniques can enable a researcher to achieve remarkable results in generalizing from a sample to a larger population.

Mail questionnaires.   These are essentially interviews put on paper and sent to an individual in lieu of talking with him directly. There are many situations where personal interviews are virtually impossible (*e.g.*, the persons to be interviewed are scattered throughout a given country, precluding the cost of interviewing them personally). In certain circumstances, sending them a mail questionnaire will achieve the desired results quite satisfactorily. Naturally, there are many times when this variation of survey work is not successful because of such defects as lack of response on the part of certain individuals and the inability to determine with any precision how this "response bias" might affect the results of the mail survey.

Telephone interviews.   Speed and low cost are the obvious advantages of telephone interviews. A great many individuals can be interviewed by telephone in a short period of time. Once again, in certain circumstances such an approach is a satisfactory method of obtaining information. Equally obvious is the fact that telephone interviews offer unusually difficult obstacles to the interviewer in terms of obtaining cooperation to be interviewed in the first place, establishing the necessary rapport with the respondent to insure some measure of accuracy in the answers given, and obtaining detailed information or information in depth.

The panel technique. A selected sample of respondents who are willing to be interviewed repeatedly during a specified period of time ranging from a matter of days or weeks up to one or two years constitutes the panel used in this technique. It offers the researcher the advantage of being able to study changes in the behavior and attitudes of the persons on the panel over a period of time as a function of almost anything that he wishes to study: world events, advertising campaigns, product usage, or any other sort of variable. As with any approach, there are weaknesses. There is the problem of the panel member being aware of events to which he has been exposed, thereby enabling him to "second guess" the researcher as to how he should react. Or there is the simple fact that knowing he is going to be interviewed again in the near future may cause him to be overly sensitive or insensitive, depending on the circumstances. In short, knowing that he is part of a "study" can have unwanted effects.

From this extremely brief account of some of the variations of survey research, the reader can appreciate why this approach has become so widespread in usage today. In any given year thousands and thousands of survey research projects are carried out under both commercial and noncommercial auspices for every conceivable information seeking purpose.

Types of Research: A Summing Up

We began this section illustrating to the reader that an exceedingly wide range of types of research exist and are used in the quest for reliable knowledge in the social and behavioral sciences. It is useful to conclude this section with two important generalizations:

1. Every type of research has both advantages and disadvantages. As a consequence, it is useless to ask which type is best. Rather, the question of which type to use must be answered in terms of such things as the problem to be solved, the resources available to the researcher, and the present status or "state of the art" with respect to the measurement precision that is possible. What is best to use is answered in terms of what the problem to be solved requires.

2. No matter what type of research an investigator may use, he still must consider the various factors that we have introduced thus far and will take up immediately following this section. *In other words, regardless of approach, the researcher must be clear about his independent variables and dependent variables and how well he is able to measure and manipulate them. And, conversely, he must be aware of when he is not able to identify his independent and dependent variables and measure them well.*

CAREFUL ATTENTION MUST BE PAID TO THE EXTRANEOUS OR RELATED VARIABLES

Seldom, if ever, does any one event or phenomenon take place in an isolated fashion. What is nearly always the case is that many highly related events are happening all at once. This is especially true in the complex human behavior that occurs in public relations.

In the language of the experimenter, what this means is that whenever any phenomenon is being studied, there are many variables involved beyond the experimental variable. In our illustration, a person has many more experiences and training opportunities than merely those we have classified as "does or does not have childhood experiences and training with respect to voluntary organizations." Normally, scientists call these variables *extraneous* or *related variables.*

An understanding of what must be done with related variables can best be achieved by returning for a moment to the problem area that we are using as an example. Adult giving to voluntary organizations can be a function of many things. In our hypothesis, one factor is assumed to be important enough to make a major contribution—the childhood training one receives with respect to voluntary organizations. However, people give to voluntary organizations for many other reasons besides the type of training they may or may not have received in this area. In order to be able to assess the role, if any, that' this particular childhood training contributes, we must *control* for (or remove the effect of) the related variables.

Returning once again to our cause and effect model, the reader will recall that we noted in real life there are always many S's and multiple R's in response to these S's. Relating that observation to the present discussion, *extraneous* or *related variables* are some of the other S's—that is, S_2, S_3, S_4, etc. Certain of these other S's have an effect on the response (R_1—*i.e.*, adult giving) that we have singled out to relate to our S_1 as stated in our hypothesis. Adult giving is a function of more than some childhood education obtained from one's parents concerning nonprofit organizations.

In order to determine the effect of our experimental variable, we must control for the possible effect of related variables. The meaning of the word *control* is probably best communicated by substitution of "to isolate or otherwise exclude, so that the dependent variable is brought about only by the independent variable." To remain with our example, we need to isolate the relationship between certain childhood training and adult giving and exclude, as best we can, all other variables that influence adult giving.

Control of related variables means that we handle them in such a way that they do not contribute to the behavior we are measuring. We are, in a sense, trying to isolate all the other factors that contribute to adult giving and "hold these constant," so to speak. What one must do to control these related variables is another factor that the research design must take into consideration.

How to Identify Related Variables

Which variables qualify as related variables cannot be spelled out in cookbook fashion. The accuracy with which related variables are identified and controlled is a function of the knowledge of the experimenter. This knowledge is a mixture of such things as training, personal experience, awareness of related literature of the subject, and educated guesses.

Take our present illustration. It is obvious that a great many factors other than childhood training with respect to voluntary organizations will or will not determine the extent to which an individual supports a voluntary organization. One may support a voluntary organization because of social pressure, especially if the giving is done at one's place of work. It is harder to turn down a request for funds from a fellow worker than from a stranger at your door. On the other hand, one may give because of a very definite personal benefit derived in the past from the organization concerned. The list could be extended greatly, and an equally lengthy list of reasons a person does *not* contribute—besides not having received appropriate childhood training—could be compiled.

All that can be said at this point about identifying related variables is that the experimenter must (in a sense, arbitrarily) decide what factors he thinks are related variables.

For example, it was noted that having benefited personally from a health and welfare organization is a variable that may be considered as related. This means that if a person has benefited personally *and* also had the childhood training as defined earlier, we could not tell which was determining the giving behavior (assuming for the moment that our hypothesis is true). It also means that if a person had only the personal experience and did *not* have the childhood training, his behavior could *confuse* the issue. It is contamination of results along the lines of the above examples that point to the need of controlling related variables.

Variables that are truly unrelated, of course, do not cause us any trouble. Thus, we might reason that such variables as age (within broad limits), sex, and occupation, to name but a few, may not be related to the experimental variable. Being unrelated means that we do not have to pay any attention to such differences among our subjects and that for a given study they can be ignored.

There is nothing to prevent an experimenter from making a wrong decision about what are related variables. If he should overlook or misjudge a variable that proves to be related, his study is in error to the extent that the variable deemed unrelated is in fact related. Sometimes the researcher is able to detect the error himself as the experiment progresses or as he analyzes his data. In other instances, it is not discovered until some other experimenter, working in the same area, treats this previously unsuspected variable as a related variable and discovers that it does have some effect on the response being measured. In short, there is no magic to this feature of the design of experiments. Unlike some other steps of research design (such as sampling, where there are many guide lines to help the researcher), when it comes to deciding on and controlling for related variables, there are no cut and dried formulas to turn to. However, an adequate review of the pertinent literature beforehand helps to reduce the possibility of overlooking relevant extraneous variables.

How Related Variables Are Controlled For

A detailed discussion of how related variables are controlled for is beyond the scope of this book. However, for purposes of obtaining appreciation of this phase of the research process let us examine briefly three main methods that are employed to achieve control over variables.

One approach is that of *excluding* the variable so that it cannot have an effect on the response under study. For example, if education were thought to be related—let us say that the more highly educated person is more likely to give support to nonprofit organizations regardless of what other factors might cause him to give—then we might exclude from our experiment *all* persons with a lot of formal education. We might include in the group to be studied only those with less than college education.

To take a completely different example, suppose that in a study of the effect of drugs on certain behavior we had reason to suspect that excessive weight was a related variable that had to be controlled.

In our study we should *exclude* overweight persons and thereby control for that particular unwanted effect in our study.

A second approach is that of *including* the related variable deliberately (in a known amount or degree) so that its contribution to the experiment can be taken into account when analyzing the results. In this sense, the related variable becomes a constant. That is, it is contributing to the response in a particular manner that is consistent and known, and hence this constant value can be subtracted or parceled out of the study when it comes time to analyze the results. A simple example of this is age. Suppose in a study of vision we have reason to know, on the basis of other studies, that persons over forty years of age react visually to certain stimuli (such as an eye chart, a flash of light, or whatever might be manipulated by the experimenter) in a certain way. Let us say their visual reaction time is slower. With this knowledge, we could include persons over forty, and when it came time to analyze the results, take this contribution of age to reaction time into account. In this way we are controlling the variable by deliberately introducing rather than excluding it.

A third approach is that of taking a comparatively large number of people for study and assigning them to our treatment groups on a random basis. (We will consider the question of sampling and random sampling in a little more detail shortly.) Explaining how random assignment of subjects (or anything that is to be studied) helps to control related variables is not so simple to comprehend as the other two types of control already discussed. To explain this form of control, let us assume that we were going to do an experiment to determine whether one form of teaching mathematics is superior to an approach now employed in a given school system. Let us call this experimental approach "System A" and the group taught by this system, "Class A." In order to be able to compare System A with the old teaching approach, we have to have another group taught mathematics according to the standard approach. This we will call "Class B." With this simple design, there are a number of obvious controls that we will introduce. One is to rotate the teachers to control for the teaching *ability* of the instructor in order to be able to separate this from the effectiveness of the teaching *approach*.

However, let us consider one or two related variables that an experimenter might also think of that are *not* so readily controlled. For example, how about the fact that some parents take a lot of interest in their children and work with them frequently when they do their homework. Let us also make the reasonable assumption that such parental help could manifest itself in affording the child a better grasp of mathematics and, ultimately, better grades in school. If it should work out that Class A has *more* children in it who receive help from their parents than Class B, then this variable *may* contribute enough to the ability of the kids to make it appear that the *teaching approach of System A is superior*, when, in fact, it was no better and no worse than the old approach. Such a variable—that is, parental help—could be reasoned to be important, but it is not so easy to control such a variable.

A second variable that offers control difficulties might be motivation—that is, the motivation of the child to study his mathematics. Once again, suppose that *more* highly motivated children happened to be in Class A than in Class B. Once again, the method might *appear* to be more effective when in fact it is not.

One could go on and on thinking of variables that are important and can interfere with the ability of the researcher to determine the effects of his experimental variable. Undoubtedly the reader has thought of variables that should be considered. Let us now see how random selection can be used as a control.

Returning to our two basic groups—Classes A and B—how are we going to assign the students to these two groups? If we assign them randomly—that is, without bias—this step can serve as a control over such hard-to-control factors as were described above. The reason: Because of random assignment, we can be assured that whatever variable is operating—such as extra parental help or more than average motivation—will be distributed evenly within the two groups, thus nullifying its effect on the response that we are measuring. Consequently, even though we are not able to control the variable *directly*, such as by excluding it, we can do so *indirectly* by the technique of randomly assigning our subjects to their particular groups, normally called *treatment* groups.[5]

The examples given only scratch the surface of controls in experiments. Depending on the experiment, controls can be achieved by such things as surgery, use of drugs, electrical and mechanical manipulations, and psychological testing. Regardless of the particular type of control or controls used, the objective is always the same: *to*

---

[5] The term *treatment* reflects the fact that different groups in an experiment are handled in different ways. Thus, in our example above, Class A was to be taught mathematics by a new technique; this group was to be treated in a certain way. Class B was to be taught by the old method; this group was to be treated in a different way. We could have developed a third class to be taught one half of the course by the new method and one half by the old. If combinations of the two methods had made sense, these could have been included in the design of the experiment. Regardless of the number of treatment groups, the assignment of persons to these groups would be the same, in order to control for certain unwanted related variables.

*be able to get rid of (or introduce in a standardized manner) the un-
wanted extraneous or related variables and thereby determine the
effect of the independent variable being studied.* Figure 30, developed
by McGuigan, serves as an excellent summarization of what we said
about extraneous or related variables.[6]

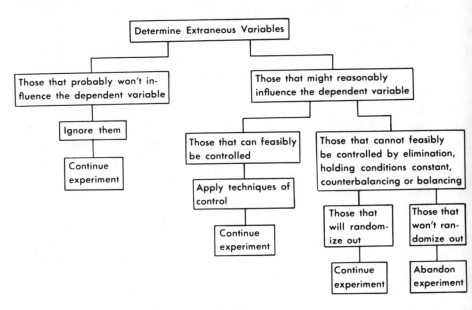

Figure 30

An over-all diagram of steps to be followed in considering
extraneous variables

CAREFUL ATTENTION MUST BE PAID TO SAMPLING

Seldom are experiments done to ascertain if such-and-such is true
of only the individuals included in the study. As a rule, the researcher
is interested in generalizing beyond the limits of his own particular
study. Thus, when we study the voting preferences of a certain number of people, we are interested in being able to make statements that
apply to all voting people. If we study *some* of the employees of a
particular company, we are usually interested in talking about (*i.e.*,
characterizing) *all* of the employees of that company. Any time we
study only a portion of a total phenomenon—be it persons, places, or
things—we are sampling, and sampling procedures are among the
most powerful tools that a researcher has today.

---

[6] Frank J. McGuigan, *Experimental Psychology: A Methodological Approach*
(Englewood Cliffs, N.J.: Prentice-Hall, Inc., 1960), p. 117. Used by permission.

Some Definitions

A particular set of scores or observations, measurements or people, events, or objects is known as a *sample*. A sample is a part, usually a small one, of all of the possible, but not obtained, scores or observations or measurements. The term *population* or *universe* is used to refer to the larger, complete set of possible measurements. Thus, any sample is a part of a larger population.

For example, all of the Girl Scouts in the United States could be considered a particular population. Any number of Girl Scouts selected for study from this population would be a sample of Girl Scouts.

The *main use* of samples is to learn something that can be generalized to the total population. To do this, a sample must be *representative* of the population. For a sample to be representative of a population, it must be a *random sample*. A random sample is one that is selected in such a fashion that each element, score, or observation has either an equal or a specifiable opportunity to be selected. If this condition is satisfied, we can generalize about the total population and, through certain statistical techniques, estimate the likely degree of error in our estimates.

The way in which a sample *stands for* or is *representative* of a population is a *matter of degree*. Some samples will be highly representative of a given population, while others will differ widely.

If any sort of bias is introduced in the way in which a sample is selected, then the sample will be nonrepresentative. The greater the bias, the less representative the sample.

When we obtain a *random sample*, we have a sample that is obtained *without* bias. That is, we have removed from the selection process all sources of bias that would affect the representativeness of our sample. There is one source of error that remains, however. That one remaining source is *chance*. A chance event is one that has an unpredictable (thus, no known) cause. A chance event is one which occurs randomly, and this is why we speak of a random sample as one which has no bias, that is, no *cause* other than the factors which cause it to behave randomly.

Although chance events, taken singly, are unpredictable, if we take a *large number* of chance events, we *can* make predictions. This is why we were careful earlier to define chance events as those without any *known* cause. This is not the same thing as saying *no* cause. A chance event is one which has some causes, but we do not know what they are. But if you take a large number of these chance events and study them, the combined effects *can* be predicted. This is known as the study of *probability* and is a part of that special branch of mathematics known as *statistics*.

Authors always run the risk of inaccuracies in making simplified presentations of complex subject matter. From our discussion of the desirability of random samples, it is possible that the reader has concluded that there are really only two categories of error in a sample: sampling error and, in the case of a nonrandom sample, certain unknown inherent biases that produce error. There is another source of error that the experimenter must always cope with: *errors that crop up because of mistakes made by the researcher himself or his assistants in recording data, making measurements,* and so on. In short, errors that crop up because researchers and their colleagues are human. Deming makes this point when he suggests that the following triangle of errors be kept in mind:

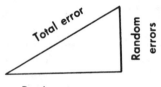

Persistent errors

In connection with this triangle, Deming writes:

> . . . One leg of the triangle represents persistence. The other leg represents the random errors, which include the sampling variation. The hypotenuse is the sum of the uncertainties, or the total error. When the non-sampling errors are large, it is uneconomical and ineffective to waste funds on a big sample, as a big sample will decrease the sampling error but leave the total error about the same. One must face the fact that the *overall usefulness and reliability of a survey may actually be enhanced by cutting down on the size of sample* and using the money so saved to reduce the nonsampling errors. *In the sampling of records, this might mean tracing and correcting wrong and missing information. In a survey of human populations, this might mean more time and money on the questionnaire, hiring fewer and better interviewers, providing better training and better supervision in the field, and making more recalls on people not at home on a previous call.* [Italics added for the last two sentences.][7]

In this excerpt from Deming, we may translate *persistent errors* to mean the same thing as *nonsampling errors*. What this triangle brings out is that there are all sorts of errors that can be made in the execution of an experiment (nonsampling or persistent errors) that

---

[7] W. Edwards Deming, *Sample Design in Business Research* (New York: John Wiley & Sons, Inc., 1960), pp. 61-62. Used by permission.

will affect the accuracy of predictions of data based on samples. Of course, these same sorts of errors will persist even if the entire population is studied! In fact, one of the advantages of sampling is that the likelihood of nonsampling errors is *greater* if one tries to study an entire population, simply because there are that many more chances for error to occur. By and large, these nonsampling errors are known. That is, we *know* that we must check for accuracy when people are asked to take measurements or readings. We *know* that we must take pains to train interviewers and check out questionnaires very carefully. We *know* that in spite of our carefulness we must double check our data and run "spot checks" all of the time in order to weed out these nonsampling errors. However, in our discussion of errors we will be focusing on errors *due to bias* introduced by nonrandom selection of samples. *This type of error we are not able to anticipate and correct because we do not know what it is.* Or, if we find out (as in the case of the Literary Digest Poll situation), we are not able to do anything about it. To put it another way, errors due to nonrandom sampling can be avoided by using random samples. Thus, our total error is reduced. The errors that have a nonsampling basis (carelessness, misplaced data, incorrectly tabulated data, or, in short, all human errors) must be constantly combated by the researcher. However, there is no comparatively simple step that he can take to rid himself of such errors as in the case of errors due to nonrandom sampling.

Now let us return to what we said about a random sample being a selection process that removes all bias and leaves only chance as the source of error. Because statisticians have evolved very precise estimates of *errors inherent* in samples *because of chance*, a randomly selected sample is one in which the experimenter can *estimate* the error in his predictions. This error is commonly known as *sampling error*. Thus, although he cannot remove this last source of error by resorting to a randomly selected sample, at least he can estimate what it is. This is almost as good as removing it entirely.

If an experimenter uses a sample that is *not* randomly selected, *he is subject to biases over which he has no control.* That is, a sample selected nonrandomly will contain errors *other* than sampling errors. Unfortunately, the statistician cannot help the researcher estimate errors due to bias.

In view of the fact that sampling error can be estimated and all other errors due to biased sampling cannot, it should be clear to the reader why the researcher prefers to work with randomly selected samples. With nonrandom samples he is faced with errors that are unknown to him. With random samples he knows what his sampling error will be. Therefore, we say that random samples offer us the most *representative* estimates of a given population and, in addition, because of probability theory we can estimate the contribution of that one additional error, sampling error.

Because we have just pointed out that the statistician is *not* able to help the researcher predict errors due to biased sampling, naturally we cannot give examples of how to predict errors due to nonrandom sampling. We have pointed out that they can be large, as in the case of the Literary Digest Poll of 1936 which predicted that Landon was going to defeat Roosevelt (see Chapter 12, pages 330-334). We can, however, provide the reader an example of how the error to be expected in a random sample was estimated and how much this estimate actually differed from the known population values. Let us use an example from Slonim's book, *Sampling in a Nutshell*. Slonim discusses how to determine what size samples a researcher would need to estimate average military pay of Air Force personnel in various pay categories—that is, base pay, crew flying pay, and so on. After he has illustrated how sample size increases as the demands for precision increase, he presents a table that illustrates how accurately his estimates of pay were when compared with the actual pay based on the entire population of Air Force personnel. He writes:[8]

> It may be of interest to our readers to review the results of an actual test of the precision of some simple random sample estimates, as shown in the table below. In this case, the actual figures were known, and random numbers were used to draw the simple random samples in each of the military grades listed. The sample sizes shown are those that our sampling theory stated would yield us estimates of average base pay in each grade that were in error by not more than 2 per cent in 99 out of 100 samples.

Grade	Approximate Total No. in Each Grade	Size of Sample	Actual Percentage Error in Sample Estimate of Average Base Pay
M/Sgt	50,000	68	−1.3%
T/Sgt	60,000	81	+1.2
S/Sgt	120,000	157	−1.1
A/1C	150,000	190	+1.0
A/2C	210,000	218	−0.4
A/3C	160,000	175	+0.1
A/B	50,000	74	−1.6
Total	800,000	963	−0.2

[8] Morris J. Slonim, *Sampling in a Nutshell* (New York: Simon and Schuster, Inc., 1960), p. 76. Copyright © 1960, by Morris James Slonim. All passages reprinted by permission of Simon and Schuster, Inc.

As Slonim pointed out, the estimate of error provided by statistical knowledge was that the estimates of average military pay would not be wrong by more than ±2%. The results indicate that they were even better than that, with the greatest error being in the Airman Basic (A/B) category, where the estimate based on the sample was wrong by only −16%. Slonim's example illustrates the remarkable power of the use of samples *if* the samples are properly selected. We will return to this feature of sampling in a slightly different manner when we consider briefly the question of how large samples have to be.

Let us return to one or two more points that should be made with respect to the concept of population. A researcher has the prerogative to define any population as he wishes. That is, he may say that he is interested in studying the learning ability of persons with crossed eyes and flat feet, all over six feet tall and left-handed to boot. *All* such persons in existence who fit those particular characteristics would then make up the *population* of individuals so described. Then, this same researcher would select a *sample* from this admittedly rather unusual *population* of individuals to determine their learning ability. In this sense, defining a population is arbitrary.

Aside from the obvious fact that it helps the researcher to know whom or what he is going to study, the requirement of defining the population to be involved in any study serves one other important function worth noting here. *It determines the limits of the generalizations that the researcher may make.* That is, if a sample is derived from a population made up of only *males*, then the researcher may not say that what he has discovered to be true in his sample of males is true of *females*. If he has studied only *children*, then his generalizations are limited to children and cannot be extended to *adults*. The reader should note one point in this connection: The researcher is permitted to *speculate* (or hypothesize, if you will) that what he has found to be true of males will prove to be true of females, or that what he has found to be true of children will prove to be true of adults. In fact, the process of controlled speculation is the very stuff of which science and research are made. One study gives an individual insights that lead him on to the next study. However, aside from the value of speculation, the researcher is limited strictly to generalizations that involve the population from which he has derived his sample. This is the beauty of representative sampling. It permits one to study only a few representatives of a given population and yet be able to make amazingly accurate statements about the entire population. However, the moment one begins to *overgeneralize*—that is, begins to make statements that apply to populations that one *did not* sample (unless they are carefully labeled as speculations)—then a serious error may be made. In fact, one of the simplest things that a public relations practitioner can do with any research study that he reads is to compare the sample, the population, and the generalizations. If all three do not agree (*i.e.*, if, for example, the sample obtained does not permit a researcher to generalize to a given population, but yet he does), the public relations practitioner should raise a danger signal and re-evaluate his acceptance of the study—the chances are strong that errors of generalization have been made.

One final point. All that has been said concerning sampling thus far applies equally to *anything* that might be studied by man. We can define a population of nuts and bolts (perhaps the production of nuts and bolts of one factory in a week) and then take a sample of that population of nuts and bolts for purposes of a quality control study. The limits of our generalization are the nuts and bolts of that given factory for that given period of time.[9]

In a like manner, our population can be all the hurricanes during a particular time period, all the corn raised by a particular farmer, or all of the relatives of a given pair of white rats for a certain number of generations. The population can be anything we wish to generalize to, and the sample for us to study is selected from this population so that we may make our generalizations.

Why Do We Use Samples?

There are several reasons why we use samples. One is that seldom, if ever, is it possible or practical to study the entire population. In the example of Girl Scouts used earlier, it would be practically impossible to study all of the Girl Scouts in the United States. We must content ourselves with a sample.

A second reason is that in many instances a proper study of an item spoils it or destroys it; hence, if the entire population were studied, this would be self-defeating. Consider a company that manufactures an item that must be tested for its ability to take stress or strain. If *every item* coming off the assembly line were tested for its breaking point,

---

[9] If the researcher had no reason to believe that the particular production time period he selected as his definition of the population of nuts and bolts manufactured by a given concern differed in any way from any other time period of production, he could then generalize from his sample to all of the nuts and bolts produced by that factory with that given equipment and design specifications. On the other hand, if certain periods of time during the year (or over the years) did make a difference, then the researcher would have to define his population differently and sample differently to take these differences in time periods into account.

the entire production would be destroyed, which is, of course, out of the question. Here, too, we must work with a sample.

Perhaps the most convincing reason of all for using samples is that a properly obtained sample will provide information so accurate that there is *very little increase in accuracy to be obtained by studying the entire universe.* To put it another way, once the researcher has established the level of precision or accuracy he needs in his study, this requirement shapes the size of sample that he will need. Obtaining more and more cases or items beyond a certain point, thereby enlarging the sample, the costs, and the likelihood of human errors, adds *very little* to what the researcher already knows. In sampling, as in many other situations, the so-called law of diminishing returns sets in and does so quickly. The curve in Figure 31 depicts this point. What

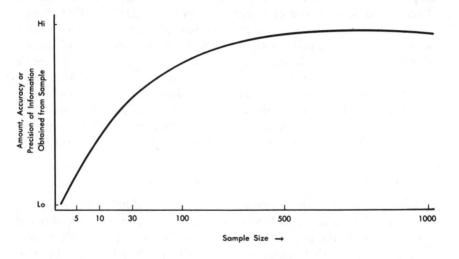

Figure 31

Relationship between sample size and precision or accuracy of knowledge obtained

it illustrates is that the amount of information one derives from a study of a sample or the precision with which predictions can be made based on sample information (such as average income of a given population) increases sharply at first, while the sample sizes are comparatively small. However, as sample size increases, the increase in precision or amount of information obtained begins to level off markedly. Hence, the information to be derived from a sample of 1,000 is not much more accurate than was obtained from a sample of 500. Twice as many cases in the sample is likely not to be worth the extra time and money, to say nothing of increasing the likelihood of what Deming called "persistent errors." Twice as many cases when the increase in sample size is from 10 to 20 or 50 to 100 is another matter, however. Here the increase in precision is more marked and generally worth the extra effort and money, assuming, of course, that the researcher needs greater precision in the first place. We will introduce further material that should add some clarity to the point we are trying to make here when, in the next section, we discuss the question of the size of samples that are needed in research.

Once again we are simplifying in order to make a point. Naturally, there are many factors that enter into sampling. Studies in which the population concerned is the entire eligible voting populace of the United States are based on samples of between 2,000 and 3,000 persons. These sample sizes have gone beyond our illustrative curve, which stopped at 1,000. In such cases, other sampling considerations dictate that the sample size must be larger. The principle of rapidly diminishing returns as sample size increases still holds, however. Even so, it is interesting to note that with sample sizes of between only 2,000 and 3,000 we are able to predict, with remarkable accuracy, certain behaviors of a population of over sixty million. The effectiveness of small numbers, properly sampled, is supported by such studies.

Misunderstanding About the Size of Samples

Perhaps one of the most common misunderstandings about sampling lies in the size of the sample necessary for a given study, as compared with the size of the population. For many people, it goes against common sense to say that comparatively small samples of a large population can be accurate. It appears more logical or intuitively correct to argue that the larger the population, the larger the sample ought to be. The truth is that the main factor in determining the "error" in a sample depends primarily on the *variability inherent in the population* and only secondarily on the ratio of sample size to the total population. For a given degree of variability within a particular population, a sample of 200 is almost as precise when the total population is 200,000 as when the population is 2,000 or 20,000.

Interestingly enough, when it comes to the area of sampling, common sense and intuition must be employed very carefully. This point is demonstrated very effectively by what Slonim calls the "Birthday Paradox." In this connection, he writes:

Readers may find it diverting or even profitable to learn about the "Birthday Paradox." This concerns itself with the odds that at least two persons in a group of 30 have the same birthday. The uninitiated layman usually estimates (following some celeritous cerebrations), that the odds are around 11 to 1 against the occurrence of such an event. His reasoning is along the following lines: There are 365 possible birthdays and only 30 people; hence the probability is 30 in 365, or approximately 1 in 12, of a match in birthdays. Actually, the odds are better than 2 to 1 that at least two of the thirty people will have the same birthday.

In order to check the theoretical odds in an actual case, the author selected, at random, page 188 in the *Air Force Register* of January 1, 1958, and tested the first ten groups of 30 names. Nine of the ten had at least two officers with the same birthday. If a large number of groups of 30 each were examined, approximately 7 out of 10 would have at least two persons with the same birthday. The dubious reader can check these odds by sampling several different groups of 30 people from such publications as *Who's Who, Men of Science*, etc.

Experience, as well as mathematics, in this instance discloses the error in one's intuitive feeling that the occurrence of multiple birthdays in a group of 30 people is rare. One way to explain the rationale of this apparent paradox is as follows. Picture the 30 people lined up in a row. Number One states his birthday. The remaining 29 then compare their birthdays with his. If there are no matches, Number Two then announces his birthday. The remaining 28 now have a second chance to compare their natal dates with that of Number Two. If, again, none match up, one or more of the remaining 27 may still duplicate Number Three's birthday. So on down to Number Twenty-nine, whose birthday may still be the same as Number Thirty's. Each of the 30, therefore, has 29 separate chances of matching his birthday with another's.

Another way to explain the variation between the average person's intuitive guess and the true probability was stated very aptly by Professor Jerome Cornfield of Johns Hopkins University. He said, in effect, that the average person sees the problem as "What are the odds that any one of the other 29 has the same birthday as *mine*?" whereas he more properly should ask, "What are the odds that any one of the 30 has the same birthday as *any other one of the 30*?"

The formula for computing the probability (denoted by "p") in this problem is:

$$p = 1 - \frac{\overbrace{365 \times 364 \times \ldots \times 336}^{30 \text{ terms}}}{\underbrace{365 \times 365 \times \ldots \times 365}_{30 \text{ terms}}}$$

As one might expect, the odds in favor of multiple birthdays drop as the number of people decreases. For 23 people it is about a 50-50 bet. On the other hand, the odds rise sharply as the size of the group increases. Now that there are fifty states in the Union, and 100 U.S. Senators, the skeptical reader might like to use the same formula (but with 100 terms in each part of the fraction) to calculate the odds that at least one Senator has the same birthday as some other Senator. The odds (and we hope you didn't take 3 to 1 against) are more than *3,000,000 to 1* that at least two of our senior solons can split the same birthday cake![10]

To return to our discussion of how common misunderstandings are about the size of samples necessary to make reliable predictions, the following quote from "How a Public Opinion Poll Is Conducted" is appropriate:

> A widely held misconception is that accuracy is merely a function of the *number* of persons included in a survey. Amazingly enough, simple facts about the laws of probability are virtually unknown to many educated people in high positions in government and business. Actually the "average," or "probable error," for a pure random sample of only 500 cases is only *two* percentage points.
> The poll that made the greatest error in polling history—the Literary Digest poll of 1936, which had an error of 19 percentage points—was based upon a final return of 2,375,000 mail ballots . . .[11]

The *size* is not the important factor; it is *what type* of sample you have. If it is a true random sample, remarkable results can be obtained with surprisingly small numbers.

To further illustrate the point that sample size bears comparatively little relationship to the absolute size of the sample, let us borrow another passage from Slonim's book:

> As an example of sample size requirements in an actual situation we have selected the project (referred to earlier) in which the purpose was to obtain estimates of average military pay of Air Force personnel for selected elements of pay (e.g., base pay, crew flying pay, subsistence allowance, etc.).
> The following table shows the size of simple random sample required to estimate the average base pay of Airmen 2nd Class (A/2C) with an error of less than 2 per cent in 99 out of 100 samples:

---

[10] Slonim, pp. 9-11.

[11] George Gallup, "How a Public Opinion Poll Is Conducted" (Princeton, N.J.: American Institute of Public Opinion, 1960), p. 1, col. 3. Used by permission.

Total Number of A/2C (Size of Universe)	Size of Sample Needed for 98% Precision or Better, 99 Samples in 100	
	Number of A/2C in Sample	Sample Size as % of Universe
200	105	52.5
500	152	30.4
1,000	179	17.9
2,000	197	9.8
5,000	209	4.2
10,000	213	2.1
20,000	216	1.1
50,000	217	0.4
100,000	217	0.2

One of the most important facts of life in sampling is illustrated clearly in the little table above. *It may appear paradoxical to many of our readers and incredible to a few, but the fact is that as the universe increases in size the sample size remains remarkably constant.* In turn, this means that the per cent of universe to be sampled declines considerably. It is because of this gratifying state of affairs that very often a miniscule sample can be used to obtain rather precise results for a king-size universe. [Italics added.][12]

A Word About Achieving "Randomness"

The word *random* has been used several times. Earlier the term was defined as a method of selection that was "without bias." There is considerable misunderstanding about how a random sample is selected and, in fact, about the concept of randomness itself.

Selecting a sample without bias—*i.e.*, randomly—is not always a simple thing to do. Insuring that every person or item (or whatever is being sampled) in a population to be sampled has an equal opportunity to be selected is very often difficult. The people or items may be spread over large geographical regions. It may be very difficult just to obtain a complete list of the population. For example, when one wants to sample an entire city, the problem of making a list of all of the individuals of the whole city would be a costly, if not impossible, thing to do. In the face of such situations, there are various techniques—*e.g.*, area sampling—to overcome such problems. It is beyond the scope of this book to go into these techniques. The point to be left

---

[12] Slonim, pp. 73-74.

with the reader is that *regardless of the name given to the sampling technique, it is mainly designed to allow the potential of being sampled to every unit or item or person in the entire population concerned.*

To select a sample randomly requires that we institute special procedures in order to insure that we achieve random selection. Many public relations practitioners have the mistaken notion that if one looks in a telephone book and takes a series of names, seemingly without any basis for selection—that is, without any pattern of selection in mind—random selection has been achieved. Nothing could be further from the truth. This aspect of random selection is illustrated in the following excerpt:

> "Randomness" refers to a set of events in which one event has no predictable effect on the next. Games of chance involve events of this kind, provided they are honestly run. Knowledge of the outcome of one throw of a die, one turn of a wheel, or one toss of the coin in no way aids in our prediction of what the next throw, turn, or toss will reveal. "Randomness," in other words, refers to events which are independent and unrelated to one another. *Independence* is a crucial condition of randomness. Thus, when a scientist wishes to create a *random sample*, he must not only be certain that he draws his sample in such a way that each item in the sample is drawn *independently* of every other item but also that each item has an *equal likelihood* of appearing in the sample. Otherwise, he cannot claim to have met the conditions of randomness. (See Box 22.)

The concept of randomness has a very particular definition and it differs markedly from the everyday definition that is often given for that term. Hence, when a person says that he selected this or that list of persons *randomly* or that he jotted down some *random thoughts*, it should be clear from our discussion that it is a misuse of the term *random*—at least from the standpoint of statistics and research—unless some guide was employed to achieve random selection.

It should be equally clear that whenever a researcher wishes to select a random sample, he does so by resorting to some sort of aid in order to keep his own biases out of the selection process. The most commonly used aid is that of a table of random numbers which is employed as a guide as to what units to select from a given population.

It has been the author's experience that even though an individual may understand the concept of randomness and accept the fact that some sort of aid to selecting a random sample must be employed, because such devices as a "table of random numbers" are not frequently encountered, his grasp of random selection is incomplete. The public

BOX 22

Random Thoughts Are Impossible*

". . . nothing is so alien to the human mind as the idea of random-ness. It is true that we can conceive of randomness in a negative way as devoid of pattern or form. And we can think of sequence that appears to lack system, and therefore has an unpredictable character, the unpredictability being due either to the limitations of the human mind or to the intrinsic nature of the material. But we ourselves cannot perceive, think, decide, or act in a random manner. When we construct so-called randomizers, mechanical or electronic, or when we prepare series of numbers which we believe are random in the above sense, we do so by withdrawing our mental participation from the randomizing process. The moment we intervene we introduce an element of pattern. Try to utter or write down a series of numbers or words 'at random;' you will find that the resulting series is not random at all but marked by certain patterns or meaningful linkages between the items. A sequence of choices made by the youngest child who can understand speech invariably has a pattern. Even if he merely has to decide in which hand a sweet is hidden, his suc-cessive selections of right or left hand will reveal a pattern of preferences which is characteristic of children of his age in the particular circumstances of the experiment. There will of course be variation from child to child, but the choices will never be random."[13]

---

* J. Cohen, *Chance, Skill and Luck* (New York: Harmondsworth: Penguin Books, 1960).

relations practitioner frequently must make selections of samples from larger populations, but he does not do it randomly because he does not know how to make a simple random selection of a population by means of a table of random numbers. For these reasons, the following excerpt illustrating the use of a table of random numbers has been included.

PROCEDURE A. THE SIMPLE RANDOM SAMPLE

1. *Selection by a table of random numbers.* A table of random num-bers is simply a list of digits generated by some mechanical mixing and

---

[13] Kenneth R. Hammond and James E. Householder, *Introduction to the Statis-tical Method* (New York: Alfred A. Knopf, Inc., 1962), pp. 238-239. Textual ex-tract used by permission of Alfred A. Knopf, Inc.; Box 22 used by permission of Penguin Books, Ltd.

drawing procedure (or by computers programed for random selection),
so that each digit has an equal chance of coming up on each draw. For
purposes of illustration, a table of 300 digits has been provided in
Table 1. Its use is a simple matter and may be adapted for many sampling problems.

Table 1. A Short Table of Random Numbers[A]

Columns

Rows	1–5	6–10	11–15	16–20
1	69646	90312	78612	16226
2	73399	81179	95187	23079
3	16198	72047	61633	09005
4	65695	03685	46983	71608
5	01347	05357	39655	58816
6	71911	76315	70232	55220
7	91425	65220	35977	80393
8	99256	76783	24094	23600
9	18661	12968	66351	60111
10	33211	97675	46427	11911
11	65605	93505	64129	54327
12	86085	61911	90089	43839
13	94626	59218	31003	97933
14	39080	18210	03809	79751
15	38385	01695	60797	01636

[A] Reprinted from the RAND Corporation, A Million Random Digits, Glencoe,
Illinois: The Free Press, 1955, p. 77, with the permission of the RAND Corporation.

    a. Assign a number to each element in the population (each num-
ber should be associated with only one element). For example, if
there are 100 cases, number them 1 to 100.

    b. Beginning anywhere in the table and proceeding in any pre-
determined direction, select numbers until the desired sample
size has been drawn. (It makes no difference whether rows or
columns are used, where the starting point is, whether one goes
from top to bottom, bottom to top, or in serpentine fashion. The
only requirement is that the starting point be determined by
chance and the procedure specified before looking at the table.)

ILLUSTRATION: Suppose that a sample of ten cases must be drawn from
a population of 100. This means that two digits are required (00 being
used for 100, 01 for number 1, etc.). As the first case, select any two
adjacent digits, then move on (in the predetermined direction) to the
next two adjacent digits for the second case, and so on. For example,
if we begin with the upper left-hand two columns, the first number
between 00 and 99 is 69, so the 69th case would be in the sample.
Proceeding down, the 73rd and the 16th are the next two cases ob-

tained. Proceed until ten cases have been selected. If you come to a number already selected, simply skip it and continue on to the next two digits.[14]

CORRELATIONAL VS. EXPERIMENTAL STUDIES

With the help of our simple S-R model we are prepared to examine another dimension of research: the difference between *correlational* studies (a special case of *ex post facto* studies—see pages 507-508) and *experimental* studies including laboratory and field experiments. Let's take the *experimental* studies first. The classical approach to obtaining reliable knowledge is for an experimenter to *isolate* some particular S_1 (*i.e.*, independent variable) and manipulate it. At the same time this stimulus is being varied, the researcher attempts to hold constant the effects of *all other variables* that would confound, in any way, the effects of the S_1 in which he is interested. (This is the notion of *controls* discussed on pages 513-518.) Exactly in the same sense that the researcher has isolated a particular stimulus, he also isolates a particular *response* (R_1) to be measured (dependent variable). *With the stimulus isolated, along with the response identified, and all other conditions remaining constant or under control, we have described, in simple terms, a classical experimental design.* By this approach, a researcher is able to identify the relationship between a given stimulus and a given response. Or, to express it in the parlance of everyday life, he should be able to identify the *cause* of a particular response if he carries out his experiment.

At this point the reader can insert all sorts of specific S's and R's that might be related causally. The S's can range from drugs to electric shock or social situations, such as panic or cooperation. A researcher may want to ascertain what effects certain drugs produce, how behavior can be modified by electric shock, or how perceiving panic among a group or sharing in cooperative ventures with other individuals affects the behavior of a given individual.

There are a great many difficulties that confront anyone wishing to identify the cause of a given phenomenon along the lines described in the preceding paragraph. These difficulties can be thought of as the steps or prerequisites to conducting an experiment. One of these prerequisites that we want to single out at this time is manipulation of the S's, because it enables us to explain what is meant by a correla-

---

[14] From *Sociological Research II: Exercises and Manual*, p. 171, by Matilda White Riley, © 1963 by Harcourt, Brace & World, Inc., and reprinted with their permission.

tional study. Then we can contrast the two—*i.e.*, the experimental and the correlational—which, of course, is our purpose in this subsection. This step is embodied in the term *manipulation*.

One of the things that an experimenter must do is manipulate or vary the stimulus condition so as to ascertain its effect on a response (or outcome) of some sort. To stick with an example mentioned earlier, if the experiment is designed to determine the effects of a drug, the researcher must be able to introduce *some amount of a drug* within an individual (more likely a group of individuals) and contrast this with *no drug*. This is the very least that he must do. However, seldom, if ever, is such a simple manipulation sufficient. More than likely he will want to be able to give *varying amounts* of a drug to different experimental groups, in addition to no amount of the drug. The reason for the need to be able to manipulate the S is simple: If it is not varied at all, then the effects of this S cannot be isolated, at least not in any useful manner.

We now come to the notion of a correlational study. There are many, many times when an experimenter is *not* able to vary the stimulus conditions in which he is interested. Take the meteorologist as an illustration of this statement. As yet, he is not able to vary such things as the amount and type of cloud cover, amount of moisture in the air, or the velocity and direction of air flow in the upper atmosphere, just to mention a few examples. The same is true of the astronomer. He is not able to vary the movements of stars and planets according to some experimental plan, nor is he able to vary the movement of the earth so as to treat the earth itself as a stimulus condition for some other reactions that he might like to observe in the universe.

We do not need to limit ourselves to the physical scientists, of course. The economist would like to relate large-scale economic developments to their presumed causes. How does he go about getting at least *some* insight into the causes of a depression? He is not able to manipulate certain business conditions of whole countries (or portions of a country) in order to see what happens to the general economy of that country. Even if he could do it with one country, there is the unfortunate fact (for the research-oriented economist) that the economic state of one country is not entirely independent of the economic conditions of a whole host of other countries.

Consider the sociologist. He would like to study the effects of panic on large aggregates of individuals, such as in the case of earthquakes or fires. Certainly he is not able to induce earthquakes of any degree of severity in order to study their effects. Even if he *could* vary panics, perhaps by engaging the services of a pyromaniac, certainly this would not be tolerated by society.[15]

We could go on with almost endless examples of situations in which an experimenter is not able to manipulate the stimulus that he wishes to study. One way out of such a situation is to resort to a *correlational* study. The term *correlation* means to co-relate, and this is exactly what the researcher attempts to do. He tries to see how one variable (or set of variables) co-relates (*i.e.*, correlates) with another variable (or set of variables). Take a simple example, but one which is gaining more attention all the time these days: college entrance exams. To establish cut-off scores (that is, scores below which an applicant is rejected), we first give our tests to a large number of applicants, and then follow their careers through college. After doing this for a number of years, we are able to establish the correlation between our entrance exams and college success. (College success defined, for example, in terms of grades obtained and whether the individual eventually graduates). If the correlation is a high, positive one—that is, if a high scorer on the college exams almost invariably receives high grades and nearly always graduates—then we can make use of the college exams as a selection device for admitting candidates to college.[16]

How has our correlational study differed from the experimental one that we described earlier? For one thing, we did not manipulate any variables with respect to the subjects (*i.e.*, college applicants) in any

---

[15] What we are touching on here are the controls that society places on the experimenter both in terms of *what* he will be permitted to study and *how*. Some of the controls are more or less political in nature. Imagine what would happen if a researcher were to apply for a grant to study what system of government, communist or democratic, has what advantages and disadvantages with respect to accomplishing the national goals of a country. Other controls are more moral in nature, such as frowning on a study of tape recordings of what actually goes on when a jury deliberates a verdict in a trial, or a study of the types of incompatibility of husbands and wives when the husbands happen to be Presidents of the United States. Also, there are the activities of the antivivisectionists in their crusade against the use of animals, particularly dogs and cats, in research. Society controls the actions of the experimenter, regardless of the field, in many, many ways. In general, the physical sciences are comparatively unhampered in this respect; the biological and social sciences have the greatest number of constraints placed on them.

[16] In order to understand the process of correlation, we do not have to go into computation or distinguish among the types of correlation that one can obtain, or go into a number of other important technical details associated with the proper use of correlation. The reader is reminded, however, that this is only a superficial examination of this concept and has just enough depth to illustrate the difference between a correlational study and a causal study.

way. We merely measured them by a tool that we had, a college entrance exam, which gave us one sort of measure. In other words, we did not manipulate any stimulus conditions. We merely gave the candidates the college entrance exam and scored their performance. Likewise, we did not control for any other variables that might be operating at the time that individuals were taking the exam, nor did we try to isolate our stimulus. Lastly, we subjected our individuals to a gross and complex stimulus situation. The test itself, the test conditions, the persons administering the test, the type of day—*all* of these things were operating.

What are we able to say as a function of this type of study? First, let us assume that we obtained a very high, positive correlation between the college entrance exam score and college success. This would mean that the higher the exam score, the more certain we can be that an individual will successfully complete college. And *this* would mean that we could, with confidence, require candidates to take the exam and either admit or reject them on the basis of their scores. Now comes the sixty-four–dollar question: Can we make any causal statements on the basis of this study? Can we say that high college entrance exam scores *cause* an individual to be successful in college? The answer is *no*. In fact, we are not able to make any causal statements whenever we conduct a correlational type study. All we know is that one *co-relates* with the other. A large amount of one variable is correlated with a large amount of another. We cannot say why or how this correlation takes place.

Some individuals find such statements hard to accept at times. The reason is that, like so many correlational studies, the two things correlated (i.e., college entrance exam scores and successful completion of college) seem so obviously related in some way. Good performance on an exam seems logically to go along with good performance in college. After all, from one point of view, a college career is nothing but one series of exams after another. It is not that there is *no* relationship between what a college entrance exam taps and what a college career brings out in someone. Intelligence, hard work, and the ability to function under stress, to name but a few, are probably involved in both instances. The point is that in a correlational study the researcher had no basis for knowing these relationships. The study was not designed to unearth causes in the first place, as was in the case of the classical experimental design described earlier.

Perhaps a slightly facetious example, still devoted to college entrance exams, can make for clarity. Suppose, instead of a college entrance exam, we now required that every candidate have his big toes measured to the nearest millimeter. Suppose too, as in the case of the college entrance exam, we measured the big toes of thousands of individuals and also kept track of their performance in college. Lastly, grant one more assumption. Suppose that this study revealed a very high positive correlation between big toes and college success. That is, very clearly, those with big toes went on to outstanding college careers. What would we be justified in doing with these data? The answer: *Exactly the same thing that we did with the conventional college entrance exam!* The reason is simple. Even though in this contrived example we do *not* have the feeling that the data makes sense—that is, we do not see how big toes and college success go together—the fact is that we would have to make the same interpretation. In both instances, all that we have really demonstrated is that one factor correlates with another. In neither instance have we been able to determine any causes.

The error of attributing cause to correlational data is very common. It is done by individuals who are otherwise very bright and competent. In almost any daily newspaper or radio and TV account of the news, one can spot causal statements being made on the basis of correlational data. Let's consider two examples. Back in 1955, when President Eisenhower had his first serious illness, it was observed that the stock market took a downward dip. Following his second illness in 1956, the same thing happened. A most common interpretation of these data by commentators at that time was that *President Eisenhower's illness caused the stock market to drop.* On the basis of these data, one cannot make such a statement. It is not that anyone would doubt the assertion that there is probably a relationship between the health of a President and the stockmarket; the point is that correlational data (*i.e.,* observing the relationship between a condition of health and activity in the stockmarket) do not permit such interpretations.

Another example of misuse of correlational data is seen in the work of the psychoanalyst. His patient tells him of certain problems that he now has—fears, anxieties, ways in which he is functioning inadequately. In the process of exploring the previous experiences of that same individual, the therapist learns of certain childhood experiences that the patient had. Now we have variable or variables A (the childhood experiences) and variable B (the present, undesirable behavior). The therapist has observed similar correlated behaviors in other patients and, in addition, his colleagues have reported the same type of observations in the professional literature. Before long, the statement is made that certain childhood experiences *cause* certain behaviors in adulthood. Once again, it is not that one doubts the relationship between early experiences of an organism and adult behavior (in fact, we have many experimental studies conducted under controlled conditions with animals that have illustrated that some of the most subtle early experiences are related to certain adult behavior); the point is the way in which the therapist obtained his behavior was through correlation. No matter how strongly we may feel that the two are causally related, on the basis of such data we cannot make such statements.

The reader can doubtless supply several examples of his own. In almost any situation where some sort of frequency tally is kept and related to some other frequency record, the danger of imputing cause is there. We relate more cars with greater horsepower per car to more accidents, and out comes the conclusion that greater horsepower is the *cause* of more accidents. We observe more colds in the winter than in the summer, and soon we are talking about certain features of winter (rain, cold) *causing* colds. Once again, it is not that certain things correlated do not also have a potential causal relationship. The point is that, on the basis of the correlational data alone, we are not *able* to say. We would have to devise experiments, along the line discussed earlier in order to get at causes; to get at what S's cause what R's.

We are now able to contrast an experiment with a correlational study. In the former, certain S's are isolated and manipulated so that their relationships with certain R's can be ascertained. The whole point of the experiment is *to be able to make causal statements*. In correlational studies, we co-relate the presence of one variable with another. In such instances, all that we need to do is *measure* and *count* variable A and variable B. By a statistical technique known as correlation, we are able to arrive at a statement of the degree to which these two variables are correlated. If the variables are highly correlated, then we can use this correlation to predict events or to make decisions of all sorts. Or we can use the fact of high correlation as an insight and proceed to develop an experimental study to determine how and why variable A and B are correlated.

It may have occurred to the reader by now that the correlational method is inextricably involved in everyday living. We meet a few people in our life with such and such a personality and find that those people are the kind we can trust or like to be with. Gradually, we build up sort of implicit correlational data relating personality with certain outcomes. Before long, we use this information to predict how we will like subsequent people who have similar personalities. The only trouble is we do not realize that we have only correlational data. *We believe that we know why this or that person can be trusted.*

We observe that clouds are correlated (we may use the term *associated*) with rain. That is, in the past, nearly every time that it has been cloudy, it has rained. In time, we use such observations (in a sense clouds are "variable A") to predict the outcome of the weather (that is, "variable B"). In fact, the correlational approach is evident everywhere in our daily lives. One thing that our appreciation of the research process can do is teach us to use correlational data more wisely and understand the limits of such data.

Let us now summarize why we have paid special attention to a distinction between experiments and correlational studies:

1. The ability to denote cause, that is, to be able to say what phenomena cause what other phenomena, is the prime reason for the existence of research. Therefore, we need to clarify what sorts of studies lead to causal statements as contrasted to what ones lead to valuable insights but not causal statements.

2. One of the most powerful tools available to the scientist *is* the process of correlation. As noted earlier, there are so many situations where we are unable to do experiments that tell us about causes. Correlational studies provide valuable *insights* as to where to look for causes. Sometimes they provide a way of figuring out how to overcome the obstacles to doing experiments. The history of mankind is replete with observations that were originally based on correlational data which later paved the way for causal experiments. Work in the area of vitamins, X-ray, and antibiotics, to name but a few, went through phases in which correlational data was either accidentally observed or deliberately obtained.

3. Consistent with the statement of the *power* of the correlational approach, hopefully, the reader appreciates how much useful work can be done *long before* we are able to sort out causes. Even though it is somewhat fashionable today to be critical of psychological tests, for example, the fact is that a large number of practical predictions can be made successfully on the basis of tests. Consider the success in World War II of being able to predict, with rather high precision, the number of pilots that would be forthcoming from every hundred men sent to preflight school, and these predictions were made for some eighteen months to two years in the future. We are still unable to identify such fundamental items of information as "What is thinking?" "How do people solve problems?" "What do we mean by intelligence?" and a host of other unanswered problems. In spite of these gaps, we are still able to make useful predictions through correctional techniques.

4. Lastly, and perhaps most importantly, in the area of public relations, nearly all of our information is of a correlational nature. What's more, for some time to come a large proportion of the research that will be done in the area of public relations will be based on correlation. Let us take the hypothesis that we developed during our discussion of the role of hypothesis formation in the research process. We hypothesized that certain childhood experiences (some teaching about nonprofit organizations) would be related to certain adult behavior (greater financial support of nonprofit organizations). For certain public relations practitioners, information bearing on this hypothesis would be very valuable. Two main routes of study suggest themselves. One would be to take different groups of children, induce this sort of training through such things as the cooperation of their parents or building it into school curricula, and then observe the outcome many years later, when the children had matured to adults. (Naturally, a variety of controls would have to be built into such a design.) The trouble with this approach is that we would have to wait for years and years to learn the outcome of this childhood training.

A second approach would be to take a large sample of adults, obtain the information about the type of education they received in this area, and correlate this with the way in which they, as adults, do or do not support nonprofit organizations. This second study would not permit us to say that the early childhood experiences *caused* adult giving, but, if the correlation were high enough, it would be sufficient grounds for the public relations practitioner to take action. He could seek out the adults with such education on the grounds that it would be more rewarding to approach this special group rather than the "general public." For long-range planning, he could develop steps that would lead to more widespread education of this sort among children on the grounds that greater support for his organization will be forthcoming in the future.

Regardless of what sorts of subsequent actions are taken, the reader can appreciate that probably most of the time, the public relations practitioner, because of his applied interests and the constraints of having to face problems as they exist *now*, will find correlational research data with their quickly obtained results most fruitful for him. Incidentally, there is a very good parallel between the public relations practitioner and the practicing therapist. The therapist has patients to help. He needs to act on the best evidence that he can obtain *now*. He can't turn people away and say, "Wait a few years until some experimental type studies are done to confirm what we have obtained through correlation research." Rather, he uses the data he has. So it has to be with the public relations practitioner. The point of our extended discussion of the differences between the two approaches is that the public relations practitioner (like any other practitioner) needs to know the limitations of his data.

SUMMARY

Obviously, research studies, regardless of their type, require extensive planning in order to be executed properly. The plan is the experimental or research or study design. Assuming that all of the above details concerning the study design are employed, one can be reasonably certain that the hypotheses to be tested will in fact be tested, and that when all the data are collected, the necessary material for intelligent analysis will be available. We are now ready to turn to some of the highlights of data collection (Step 7) as well as the last two steps in the research process.

QUESTIONS FOR DISCUSSION

1. Take any one of the cases you used to answer previous discussion questions and apply to it what was said in this chapter about the literature search. That is, see if you can find any material in the various public relations publications or social and behavioral science literature that either told you what you needed to know for your public relations problem situation or gave you some insights or "tips" on how to better cope with it. Which type of information did you find more readily? (That is, did you find any information that told you exactly what you needed to do to solve your problem? Or did you find information that was helpful but far from solving your problem?)
2. Take still another public relations case that you used for answering previous discussion questions and translate the pertinent portions of the case into hypotheses. That is, spell out in hypothesis form your assumption regarding the problem or problems you face in the case, your hypotheses of what you might do to solve the case,

and your hypotheses concerning *why* what you plan to do to solve the case will work. Did you experience any difficulty in expressing the different aspects of the case in hypothesis form? If you did, why do you think this was true? If you did not, why did this translating into hypotheses prove to be comparatively easy for you?

3. Take any experiment that you may have read about in either a physical science course (*e.g.*, chemistry or physics) or a social or behavioral science course (*e.g.*, sociology or psychology) and identify the independent and dependent variables involved in it. Also, identify some of the extraneous variables that were controlled for, and point out *how* they were controlled for.

4. Drawing from any sources you wish, obtain *at least two* examples on each of the different types of research that were spelled out in pages 507 through 512. Because human behavior is more pertinent to the interests of the public relations practitioner (or practitioner-to-be), be sure that all of your examples of research are based on studies of human behavior.

5. Develop one or two examples of your own of correlational data in which the individual reporting correlational data talked or wrote as if he had the data necessary to talk about *causality*. It might be a good idea to review what we had to say about this topic on pages 533-541 before you develop your examples. Just in passing, did you have any reason to believe that the individual in question realized that there was a difference? That is, that correlational studies are not the same thing as experimental type studies?

6. Just to be certain that you understand this chapter's discussion of sampling, try to explain to a friend or relative who knows nothing about sampling, the terms *sample, population*, and the like. Also, explain why sample size is not dependent on the size of the population from which it is selected.

7. While the concepts of sampling are still fresh in your mind, try to find two studies based on probability and nonprobability samples. Also, examine the generalizations made by the author of the reports and come to your own conclusion as to whether he has or has not overgeneralized.

Chapter 19

SCIENTIFIC RESEARCH CONCLUDED: THE LAST THREE STEPS IN THE RESEARCH PROCESS

INTRODUCTION

In the preceding chapter, we considered Steps 4, 5, and 6 in the research process. In so doing, we covered the literature search, the step wherein the researcher checks to see if what he seeks may already be known or whether he can benefit from the efforts of others in his own work. We took up the reasons for expressing research objectives in terms of hypotheses and how doing so helps to crystallize research objectives and to point up assumptions that the scientist brings to his work. Lastly, we considered the necessity of deciding on the study design and all that this step entails so that the researcher knows what he is going to do and is certain that his research efforts will shed light on his problem area.

In this chapter, we will examine the last three steps in the research process: obtaining the data, analysis of the data, and implications and generalizations. Step 7 covers the intricacies of obtaining the data that the researcher has decided he needs on the basis of considerations involved in Steps 1 through 6. Our emphasis will be on data collection as it applies to human beings. Step 8, in a sense, represents the "pay-off" of all of the previous steps, because it is at this point that the researcher experiences the excitement of making sense out of his data and translating it into a form that is meaningful to him. The reliable knowledge that he has been seeking all along may become apparent at this point. Step 9 reflects the fact that there must always be a point at which the implications of the data are spelled out. What have we found? Where do we go from here? If the study is an applied one or has applied implications, how may the data be used by a practitioner? Also, we learn at this juncture that research is a never-ending process. Regardless of how fruitful the research effort has been in bringing some reliable knowledge to a given problem area, almost invariably new problems are uncovered or new areas of ignorance are exposed, and the whole process begins all over again.

STEP 7: OBTAINING THE DATA

At this stage in the experimental process, a researcher has pretty well structured what he is going to do and why. In order to fulfill the six previous research steps, he has stated a manageable problem, generated hypotheses to be tested, defined his terms, and planned the design of the entire experiment. Step 7 consists of obtaining the measurements that he needs to move the study one step closer to completion.

The phrase "obtaining the measurements that he needs" bears further examination as, from one point of view, a scientific experiment reduces to the collection of certain measurements under certain conditions. No matter how complicated the experiment and elaborate the equipment, the ultimate purpose is to obtain measures of one sort or another. The measures may be of conditions in outer space, where the focus is on the amount of lethal radiation that exists. The measures may be of a physiological nature where changes in blood-sugar level as a function of variations in diet are of interest. Or the measures may be of the amount of aggression that working on a difficult and frustrating task engenders within a single individual or among individuals in a group. In each instance the "pay-off," so to speak, lies in the measures that the researcher is able to obtain. In the three examples cited above, which vary drastically in terms of the equipment necessary to obtain them, the thing that they have in common is that when the data collection phase is completed, the researcher will have obtained the measurements which he needs.

Although all of the research steps that we have discussed or will discuss are the same for all sciences, it is Step 7, or, more properly, the end results of Step 7, that best illustrates the unity of science. Returning to the three examples of data collection cited in the preceding paragraph, we might have difficulty discerning which experiment was involved if we were to look only at the measurements. In each instance, the data might be nothing more than a series of numbers (or percentages) arranged in a table that might not readily reveal *which* experiment was involved. We would have to know what units the numbers referred to, whether they represented measures of radiation, blood sugar, or frustration, in order to be certain of which experiment was involved.

We are stressing the unity of science in introducing Step 7 in the research process because, in the opinion of the author, it is the data collection phase of experimentation that has contributed the greatest amount of confusion to the beginner's understanding of research. Because a whole roomful of tubes and heat sources and flasks are necessary to collect data that has bearing on some chemical process, the uninitiated can lose sight of the fact that the chemist is following the same rules that apply to someone doing an opinion-attitude survey or a learning experiment based on the behavior of the white rat. The means required to obtain data in chemistry experiments appear so different from those required when animal or human behavior is involved that somehow the experimental work appears to be *different*. Nothing could be further from the truth. The only differences are in subject matter and paraphernalia. These differences become most apparent at the data collection phase. To get at the subject matter for one experiment, a huge rocket is required to place a strange-looking measuring device in position to obtain the necessary readings. In other instances, configurations on paper (projective devices such as the Rorschach ink blot test or the Thematic Apperception Test) are used to get "in position" to obtain the necessary measures. The rules of the game apply equally to both sets of measurements. The fact that they *appear* drastically different is misleading, and in that sense, an artifice.

Consistent with the perspective that we maintained throughout the preceding two chapters—*i.e.*, illustrating the basic steps of the research process with human beings in mind—we will discuss data collection as it applies to people. Because our primary interest is public relations and the reliable information that the public relations practitioner requires, we will stress data collection techniques that are most helpful to the public relations practitioner: variations of data collection found in the broad category of opinion-attitude survey work. Although the complex behavior of human beings imparts a unique character to data collection when research with human beings is undertaken, the reader should bear in mind that *the form the collection takes must not mask the fact that this step is basic to all research*. We resort to questionnaires and interviews because they are among the best ways we know of to obtain certain information from humans. The questionnaire becomes the survey specialists' "equivalent" of the test tube and the flask so common to the chemist.

Understanding Data Collection as It Applies to Human Beings

The very simplest data collection that we can undertake, regardless of the research problem under consideration, is simple observation. Paying attention to what is going on around us is a fundamental data collection technique, common to both scientist and layman. This is sometimes referred to as *unstructured* observation. Unstructured observation can be exceedingly valuable, and the history of mankind is filled with wonderful insights that have been obtained through keen observation. In fact, valuable portions of many experiments are the direct result of simple observation.

Simple observation is not enough, however, for the scientist. There are times when he needs to systematize his observations. He needs to plan ahead and anticipate what he wants to observe and how he is going to measure and record his observations. There are many situations for which direct observation by the unaided eye is insufficient. There are times when instruments (usually nothing more than specialized extensions of one or more of the unaided senses in the simple observation situation) are needed to be able to record more, faster, or with greater objectivity.

To help visualize the data collection phase of research, Figure 32 has been constructed. Let us examine the contents of this figure in some detail.

In the column headed *Major Elements of Data Collection*, we first see the entry "The Measuring Device." This calls attention to the fact that to obtain data we need some sort of measurement device. (This is in addition to the researcher himself, who, after all, is probably the most complicated data collection device imaginable.) *Naturally, anything that can help us to obtain a measurement would qualify for this entry in our schema*. Typical measurement devices are mail questionnaires, projective-type tests such as the Rorschach ink blot test, or specially constructed devices such as The Semantic Differential to measure the meanings of words or phrases.

MAJOR ELEMENTS OF DATA COLLECTION	Continuum STRUCTURED———UNSTRUCTURED
The Measuring Device Itself	$A_1, A_2, A_3, \ldots A_n \ldots B_1, B_2, B_3, \ldots\ldots B_n$
The Measurement Situation	$C_1, C_2, C_3, \ldots C_n \ldots D_1, D_2, D_3, \ldots\ldots D_n$
The Response of the Subject (to the measuring device in a given situation)	$E_1, E_2, E_3, \ldots E_n \ldots F_1, F_2, F_3, \ldots\ldots F_n$
The Subject Matter Inherent in the Measuring Device	$G_1, G_2, G_3, \ldots G_n \ldots H_1, H_2, H_3, \ldots\ldots H_n$

Figure 32

Major Elements of Data Collection

Reading across the schema, we see that measurement devices can range along a continuum from structured to unstructured. Some measurement devices are comparatively structured (A_1, A_2, and so on).[1]

---

[1] A word about the various letters included in this schema (Figure 32). Later in our presentation, we shall want to consider various examples of data collection situations and put forth what combination of measuring device, measurement situation, and so on they represent. Hence, the need for letters to be able to characterize a measurement situation. The multiple letters for each entry are designed to highlight where on the continuum—structured to unstructured—these elements of data collection lie. The way that these letters should be read is that A_1 and A_2 represent a measuring device that is comparatively highly structured; A_3 or some other value closer to A_n is less structured. This shades over into the unstructured portion of the figure, depicted by B_1 through B_n, meaning that measuring devices range from comparatively unstructured to highly unstructured. This represents the difference between a sentence completion item in an interview, which is an example of a moderately unstructured measuring device, and the Rorschach ink blot test, an example of a comparatively highly unstructured measuring device. The reason: the Rorschach potentially permits a wider range of responses on the part of the respondent than the sentence completion technique. Both are far

This means that some of them provide the respondent very little lee-way. Typical of this portion of the continuum is the mail questionnaire that contains several questions, each with three or four possible replies, *one* of which the respondent is to circle as being the closest to his view of the subject presented in the question. The unstructured end of the continuum (B_1, B_2, B_3 . . . B_N) is exemplified by questions such as those requiring the respondent to complete an incomplete sentence. This is known as the sentence completion technique. Thus, in an interview the respondent may be asked a number of sentence-completion questions. The following is typical:

INTERVIEWER ASKS:
"The first thing I think of when I receive a telegram is _____."

RESPONDENT REPLIES WITH:
"Bad news."

COMPLETE SENTENCE NOW READS:
"The first thing I think of when I receive a telegram is bad news."

In this type of question, the respondent has much wider latitude with respect to his response. The number of possible words or phrases that can be supplied in order to complete the sentence is very large, certainly far greater than the three or four choices in the typical multiple choice question.

The second element in the data collection column of Figure 32 is "The Measurement Situation." This entry calls attention to the fact that also the conditions in which measurements are taken can be comparatively structured or unstructured. Consider the following two situations and how they differ in the degree to which the measurement situation is structured or unstructured. Take the case in which a sociologist is using the approach called "participant observation" to better understand the behavior of gangs. The term *participant observation* simply means that, for certain field research, the researcher becomes a member of the group under study in order to be able to take measurements without disturbing the group's natural functioning, and by so doing creates an unstructured measurement situation. In many such experiments, the subjects have no idea that they are being observed and

---

less structured than a multiple-choice question in a mail questionnaire. What has been said about the meaning of letters A_1, A_2, B_1, B_n, and so on applies to the other combinations of letters C through H. The only difference, of course, is that these letters apply to different elements of the data collection stage with respect to being structured or unstructured.

measured. Often, rather detailed observation schedules are filled out as soon as the sociologist is able to get to his room or some other place away from the gang. Such a measurement situation would be characterized by the D_n end of the continuum. Contrast this with an experiment in which the effects of communication patterns—that is, the channels of communication that are or are not available to individual A with respect to individual B and all of the other individuals in the experiment—on problem-solving efficiency in small groups is under consideration. In these small group studies, the subjects are quite conscious of being a part of an experiment and, consequently, are in a measurement situation that is comparatively structured (that is, toward the C_1, C_2 end of the continuum).

This brings us to the third element in data collection: the "Response of the Subject." In certain experimental conditions and with certain measuring devices, the latitude of a subject's response is quite limited. In the case of certain reflex measurements, such as the knee jerk, visual reaction to light, or motor reaction to heat, the responses of the subject are very limited. There is little, if any, allowance for personality, intellectual, or training differences among subjects. Consequently, the response of the subject is bound to be comparatively structured (E_1, E_2 portion of the continuum). By contrast, in any situation where the full range of an individual's intellectual capacities are permitted, then the responses can be comparatively wide and unstructured (F_n portion of the continuum). I.Q. tests or measures of the problem-solving ability of an individual offer response variability that is immensely larger than in the case of certain simple, autonomic nervous system responses.

The last element to distinguish in our data collection schema is labeled "The Subject Matter Inherent in the Measuring Device." The subject matter adds another potential range of structuredness or unstructuredness, in addition to the characteristics of the measurement device itself. For example, in a mail questionnaire, in addition to the *style* of the question (that is, whether it is a multiple choice question or one that is "open-ended"), there are the restrictions imposed by the subject matter of the questions. If they are what the surveyors call *demographic* questions having to do with age, income, occupation, and the like, then the subject matter involved in the measurement is quite structured because the respondent fits into these various vital statistics in a certain way. There is little, if any, variation regardless of how the question is worded and how the respondent is instructed to reply (G_1, G_2 end of the continuum). At the other end of the continuum, the unstructured end, we may have questions that deal with attitudes of an

individual toward politics, religion, or some other topic that permits for
wide variety of response. Such subject matter permits the large differences that exist among individuals with respect to knowledge, previous
experience, and training to come into play. Under these conditions,
the subject matter permits a much more unstructured reply because
individual differences become substantial when topics such as politics
or religion are involved (H_3 . . . H_n portion of the continuum).

Data Collection and the Concepts of Reliability and Validity

With the examination of Figure 32 behind us, we are able to take
up two important concepts of data collection and at the same time
illustrate how the schema presented in the figure can be helpful to the
public relations practitioner when he examines various research reports. These concepts are *reliability* and *validity*. Briefly, reliability,
when applied to a measuring device, means that if repeated measures
are made of the same phenomenon with a given device, essentially the
same measurement value will result. Thus, if you measure a table with
a ruler and find it to be four feet, six inches long, reliability means
that if you were to measure the table again, you would obtain the same
measurement: four feet, six inches.[2] In such conditions, you have a
measurement (or a measuring device) that is highly reliable because
the measure obtained the second time is the same as it was the first
time.

The question of reliability is applicable to *any measurement device*,
and it is important that the measurement device be as highly reliable
as possible. Consider an I.Q. test as another illustration. If we were to
conclude, on the basis of some particular I.Q. test, that an individual
at age 10 had an I.Q. of 100, and then on retesting a few months later
found the I.Q. was 140, our measurement device, the I.Q. test, would
not be very reliable. It would be akin to the carpenter building a house
with a rule that has shifting foot marks, so that one time he measured a
board the rule would read five feet and another time eight feet. The
results would be serious for housebuilding. The thing is, we can see
when our carpenter's rule is unreliable because the house looks crazy
and all misshapen; with an I.Q. test, we cannot so easily see the errors
due to the low reliability in our measuring instrument.

---

[2] For purposes of making our point, we are ignoring factors discussed earlier,
such as sampling error and persistent errors (Chapter 18, pages 520-521), which
would, of course, cause successive measures of the same thing to vary to some
extent and thereby affect the reliability of the measurement device.

The term *validity* means: Does the measurement device measure what it claims to measure? To take a simple example, a weighing machine presumably measures weight. To the extent it does, it is a valid measuring device for weight. A simple thermometer presumably provides a measure of the changes in temperature during the day or night. To the extent it does, it is a valid measuring device because it provides the measure claimed for it: temperature measurement.

There are many measurement situations that are not so simple or clear-cut. Consider the many personality tests that are on the market. What about their validity? As in the case of reliability, all measuring devices have to "pass the test" concerning validity. How do we know that a particular test measures personality? In other words, how do we know that a given personality test is valid? Naturally, many other equally difficult situations could be suggested. Anytime someone purports to measure such things as leadership, morale, or cooperativeness, the question of validity can be a difficult one to live up to.

Now, let us relate what we have learned about reliability and validity to our schema as developed in Figure 32, page 547. *All things being equal, the more unstructured something is, the greater the likelihood that the two major requirements of measurement, reliability and validity will not be met.* With our schema at hand the public relations practitioner has a guide in the analysis of any particular research report he encounters. If the elements of the data collection phase of the research are all (or primarily) at the unstructured end of the continuum, caution should be taken with respect to the results of the study. This is particularly true of the motivation research studies that are so in vogue today.

Consider a study that makes use of the so-called modified projective technique approach in which the respondent is handed a picture with some figures in it and is asked to respond to it in a given way. For example, the picture reproduced in Figure 33 was administered as part of an interview which was trying to get at an individual's attitudes toward science and scientists. On being shown the picture, the respondent was asked, "What do you think the scientist said that would be such front page news?"[3] In terms of our schema, the *measuring device*, in this instance, is comparatively unstructured. That is, there is an

---

[3] Edward J. Robinson and Otto Lerbinger, "Public Conceptions of Science and Research: A Comparison of Esso Research and Engineering Company with Other Companies," a study conducted by New England Consultants, Inc., for Esso Research and Engineering Company, 1959. Figure 33 appeared in the original study as Drawing E, Appendix B. Used by permission of Esso Research and Engineering Company.

exceedingly wide range of responses which can be made to that particular combination of visual and verbal stimulus situation. In this circumstance, demonstrating that such a measurement device is both reliable and valid would be more difficult than it would be for a direct question which tested the respondent's knowledge about some particular aspect of science. In such studies, the public relations practitioner should be on the alert for ways in which the researcher has attempted to come to grips with the increased difficulty of determining validity and reliability of such a measuring device.

One further point. Although our schema suggests increased caution whenever elements of the data collection device become more and

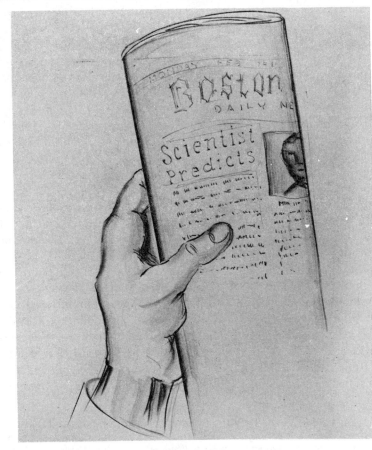

Figure 33

An example of the modified projective technique used to elicit attitudes toward science and scientists

more unstructured, the reader should not carry this admonishment to extremes. It does *not* mean that all studies employing projective-type measures are worthless. By the same token, it does not mean that data collection devices that are comparatively structured have no difficulties, either. It means merely that all measuring devices must live up to the requirements imposed by the concepts of reliability and validity and that research studies must be examined from this point of view along with all of the other requirements of sound scientific research.

The Interview: Basic Tool of the Social and Behavioral Sciences

Now, having closely examined Figure 32, which directed our attention to the major elements of data collection, we are reasonably well equipped to assess most of the data collection devices that we are likely to encounter in the social and behavioral sciences. In our brief look at a motivation research study, we saw that we were readily able to classify that particular example of a measurement device and generate the precautions that we would employ in translating the data based on such an approach. We also have a basis for understanding the importance of the concepts of reliability and validity. As practicing public relations practitioners, we know the importance of asking, "Is the measurement device employed in this study reliable? And is it valid?" and "What basis do we have for answering *yes* to both of these questions?"

To round out our examination of Step 7 in the research process, we will consider the interview because it is one of the most basic tools of data collection that we have. Modifications of this tool can be found in a remarkably high percentage of social and behavioral science studies.

To begin with, the term *interview* is being used here in the broadest possible sense, embracing all situations where one individual interacts with another, either face to face or in special cases of face-to-face contact as in the case of the mail questionnaire. Defined in this way, this data collection technique is not limited to opinion-attitude surveys. Before we go on with our analysis of the interview, let us turn to Figure 34, which was designed to present a way of thinking about this particular form of data collection.

Central to Figure 34 is the interview. We have located this box at the top and middle of our schema. Some forms of data collection in the social and behavioral sciences do not go beyond this point. Consider the therapist working with a mentally ill patient. A major portion

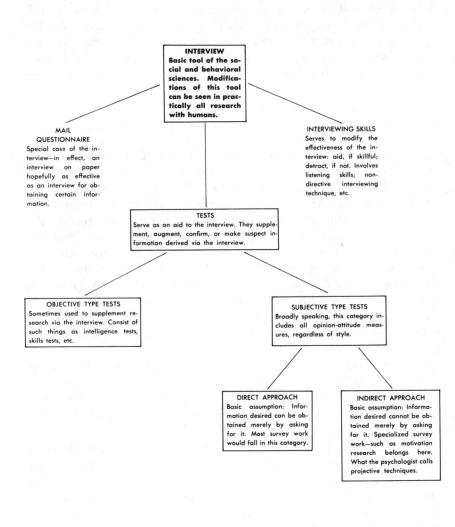

Figure 34

The interview: the basic tool for obtaining data in the social
and behavioral sciences

of the information with which he works in treating his patient is based on prolonged interview sessions. He makes his interpretations based on the verbal utterances of his patient.

Off to the right of the interview box, we have placed another box headed "Interviewing Skills." This is included to stress the fact that data obtained by the interview are no better than the interviewer's skills permit. In the therapy situation mentioned above, if the therapist is not a skilled listener, capable of eliciting information from his patient in as unbiased a manner as possible, the therapy sessions may prove to be very sterile; the therapist may not learn much or he may bias the information he obtains. By the same token, an opinion-attitude survey is no better than the interviewers who are out in the field interviewing a sample of respondents. If care has not been paid to the training of these interviewers, the measurements obtained—that is, the by-products of the interviews—can be worthless. Or worse, they can be worthless because of unskilled interviewers, and *nobody will know it!* This is the risk that a person or organization takes whenever he "buys" research. He is at the mercy of the integrity and skill of the research organization employed.[4]

The box labeled "Mail Questionnaire," at the left of the interview box, reminds us that the mail questionnaire study is a special case of the interview. *A mail questionnaire is nothing more than an interview on paper.* Hopefully, it will elicit the same information that would have been obtained had a team of interviewers been used instead of the postal department. We could, incidentally, devote a small book to this one box alone since this particular version of the interview has become so important in today's research, particularly in the commercial world.

Directly under the interview box is a box labeled "Tests." This entry is included in our schema because seldom do we rely on *only* the simple interview to obtain our measures of other individuals. In a clinical situation, the therapist quite often gives his patient a whole battery of tests ranging from comparatively straightforward I.Q. measures to all sorts of personality tests. Tests, regardless of their nature, serve as an aid to the interviewer to augment, confirm, or make suspect the measurements he obtains by interview.

The use of tests to supplement the interview is so extensive that we can make a further breakdown of them into *Objective* and *Subjective*

---

[4] It is only fair to point out that no one is more aware of what has been said than the commercial opinion-attitude researcher. The reputable, established commercial research firms are continually working at ridding the surveys that they do of errors, of which the training level of the corps of interviewers used is but one of the many, many possible sources.

Tests. This has been done by the addition of two more boxes under the one labeled "Tests." Let us consider the objective tests first. Objective tests consist of intelligence tests in many forms—aptitude tests, various skills tests, and others. Very often in a research project an objective test is given to the respondent to increase knowledge about him. This type of test is categorized as objective because how a person replies is not so much a function of his attitudes as it is a function of the knowledge he possesses.

To illustrate the way in which an objective test may supplement a research project, let us consider the following hypothetical situation. Assume that a researcher is interested in determining what relationship, if any, exists between being a volunteer worker and intelligence. In such a research situation, the subjects would need to be given some sort of an intelligence test. The results of this testing could then be related to whether the subject is or ever was in volunteer work. In this way, data could be obtained that would throw some light on whether intelligence plays any role in the likelihood of an individual's becoming a volunteer worker.

To repeat what was said earlier about objective tests, the main criterion to use to determine whether a given test designed to supplement the interview is objective is in terms of how the performance of the respondent is going to be rated or "scored." If there are some objective, "agreed-on-by-others" criteria, then the test is objective. Thus, in an I.Q. test there are answers to the questions that are either right or wrong. Whether an answer is right or wrong is *not* a function of what the one scoring the test thinks but is rather a matter of objective criteria that can be pointed to as a guide to what is right and wrong. Admittedly, in situations that are related to public relations, the use of objective tests to supplement the interview is comparatively rare. However, there are times when they are employed, and an understanding of the interview as a data collection technique requires our consideration of this adjunct to interviewing.

The other variation of tests that should be considered is entitled "Subjective Tests." This category includes opinion-attitude measures of all sorts. At first, one may feel that the *Interview* box is the place where opinion-attitude measures or survey work should be entered, but little reflection will reveal that such is not the case. *In a survey, we now have a special case of the interview* in much the same sense that the mail questionnaire had to be considered separately. A survey is usually a highly structured and focused data collection technique that is a substantial departure from the interview by the therapist or from the everyday contacts that we all have with friends, acquaintances, and strangers. For one thing, the *objectives* have been narrowed considerably, hence the reason for using the term *focused* above. In a political survey, we are after only certain information about particular candidates and for particular situations, generally a forthcoming election. In addition, because we are sampling certain populations however they are defined, *it is essential that each respondent be asked the same questions in as nearly the same manner, sequence, and so on as possible*. It is in this sense that our interview with a given respondent now takes on the character of a *test*. That is, we are trying to get at certain knowledge that the respondent has or trying to establish that he does *not* possess the knowledge.

The "test" is not an objective one, as a rule. That is, in a survey where we are interested in getting at a voter's preferences for a slate of candidates and the *reasons* for his choices, there is no right or wrong answer. Or, if in a marketing survey we are trying to obtain consumer likes and dislikes about a product or an anticipated product, once again there is no such thing as a right or wrong attitude. Indeed, he may be wrong. That is, he may believe things about a given product that are, in fact, wrong. The important thing is *what* he believes; hence the notion that this is a *subjective* affair. And because we more or less quiz the individual—that is, ask him *why* he believes such and such—we are also *testing* the individual in a limited sense.[5]

The two main subcategories of subjective tests are usually referred to as the "Direct" and "Indirect Approaches." The direct approaches are so named because the mode of obtaining the data is one wherein the individual is asked directly about what he thinks of a particular issue or question. If you want to know his voting preferences, *you ask him*. If you want to know what brand of cigarettes he smokes and why, *you ask him*. The essence of the direct approach is that the researcher has no reason to suspect he will not receive the answers he desires if the questioning is done skillfully and politely and at the convenience of the respondent. This basic assumption can be met for a wide range of information-seeking situations. Consequently, it is prob-

---

[5] It is worth noting, in this connection, that one of the problems surveyors must contend with is to make the respondent feel that he is *not* being tested or that he is *not* giving stupid answers. Because of the "testing" nature of a survey, it is so very easy to put the respondent on the defensive that the need for skilled interviews cannot be too strongly stressed. A respondent who is defensive will answer questions quite differently than he would if he were not defensive. If you have unskilled interviewers who are not sensitive to this possibility (and who, therefore, do not report any interview that is suspect in this connection), they can turn in their interview data and the researcher may never know that error has crept into his study.

ably fair to say that by far the greater number of opinion-attitude surveys fall into this subcategory of subjective tests.

The "Indirect Approach" requires quite a bit more discussion than the direct approach. As one might anticipate, this approach is so named *because we are not able to assume that we can ask the person directly for the information we desire.* This particular approach is the one that includes the so-called motivation research techniques that have received considerable attention in the past few years. The term that psychologists use is *projective technique,* and we must consider this subcategory of measurement (which is another special case of the interview) more fully.

Projective Techniques: Indirect Approach to Data Collection

The limitations of direct interviewing and the questionnaire became apparent sooner in clinical work than in industrial work. Some personal experiences or information about family and friends that the clinical psychologist needed could not be obtained directly. The patient was evasive or refused to answer. Moreover, there were instances where the patient could not supply the information. Some of the desired information was "unconscious" to the patient. No amount of direct questioning would do any good because certain experiences or feelings could not be verbalized. For these reasons, attention was turned very early to developing *indirect* methods of obtaining data, the word *indirect* meaning that the respondent was unaware of the data that he supplied the clinician.

The best known indirect methods of data collection are called "projective" methods. The classic technique in this area is the Rorschach test. This test was constructed by literally placing some ink on sheets of paper, then folding the papers to cause the ink to blot. This process produced varied nondescript dark figures on a white background and could be interpreted in various ways. Almost as famous is the Thematic Apperception Test, commonly known as the T.A.T. Unlike the Rorschach test, it consists of a series of cards depicting persons, places, and things. The subject is asked to tell a story about what he sees in the pictures—how the individuals in the pictures feel what led up to the events depicted, and the like.

One basic assumption underlies all indirect methods, including projective tests. The more vague and unstructured a situation, the more an individual is likely to "read into" the situation. The "reading into" we call projection.

To illustrate, let us consider a simple cloud formation viewed by two people. To one it "obviously" looks like a man's face. To another, it "obviously" is an animal. As a rule, a cloud formation can be anything a person wants it to be. It is highly unstructured and permits a wide range of interpretations. As with cloud formations, so it is with the Rorschach and T.A.T. tests. They are so constructed that almost anything can be "seen" in them. (Consider again Figure 33 on page 552.)

Indirect techniques tend to reveal something about the individual's personality and/or motivations. In addition, they are essentially uncontrollable from the standpoint of the individual. Projective tests are stimulus situations to which a person must react. However, how one reacts is more a function of the individual than the particular projective device used.

Not all indirect methods take the same form. Other common versions are word association tests, sentence completion tests, picture drawing tests, and doll play tests. In the word association test, the individual is given a list of words one by one. He is asked to respond to each word with the word that first comes to his mind. In the sentence completion test, the individual is read a series of incomplete sentences. The subject is required to finish each sentence with one or several words. In picture tests, the individual is asked to draw a figure of a man or a woman or something else. In doll play tests the subject, generally a child, is given a set of dolls. The dolls usually represent adults found in a child's world—father, mother, and so on. The subject is encouraged to play with them or show how these "dolls" would act in various social circumstances.

In each of the above versions of indirect methods, the end result is the same. By responding to an essentially unstructured situation, the individual reveals something about himself. As a consequence, we learn something more about his motivations.

It is important to stop at this point and relate the projective technique approach to what we learned about perception in Chapter 7 (pages 168-176). In an attempt to understand how an individual perceives, we discussed the concepts of structural and functional factors and how these two factors acting together determine a given perception. In short, $S \times F = P$: *structural factors* times *functional factors* equals *perception*. During the discussion of structural and functional factors, we defined these terms so that the structural factors embraced all events *external* to the individual, and the functional factors included all events *inside* the individual. Relating this concept to the notion of projective techniques, we see that to have an effective projective device, we must *reduce* the structural factors so that *no one interpretation is possible*, or, to put it another way, to make the structural component so *unstructured* that it contributes *very little* to the ultimate perception that the individual has. Hence, with the *S* factors reduced, the *F* factors come to the fore. Hence, in a Rorschach test (see Figure 35[6] for a figure which is similar to a Rorschach ink

Figure 35

A Rorschach Ink Blot

blot but not one of the actual test set) the structural factors—that is, the configuration of black and shades of gray on a white background—are such that almost anything can be "seen" in the card. Under such conditions, when an individual reports that he sees a certain animal or person or geographical location or object, the "cause" for this perception lies mainly within the individual. The determinants of meaning in a projective test lie primarily within the individual and presumably reflect certain personality characteristics. In fact, in the case of the T.A.T. referred to earlier, one of the cards

---

[6] Clifford T. Morgan, *Introduction to Psychology* (2d ed.; New York: McGraw-Hill Book Company, 1961), p. 481. Figure used by permission.

is a perfectly blank, all-white card. This is practically the ultimate in unstructuredness in that the story that one tells about a card that is perfectly blank *has* to be purely a function of that individual and his own primary and secondary needs.

As one would anticipate, the degree to which a given indirect (or projective—the two terms are very often used interchangeably) data collection technique *reduces* the structural factors in order to bring the functional factors to play varies from situation to situation. Earlier we considered the sentence completion technique. This technique is comparatively unstructured as compared, for example, to a question such as "Which of the two presidential candidates do you plan to vote for in November?" Thus, how a person fills in the incomplete sentence, "The first thing I think of when I receive a telegram is_____," can be quite varied. These replies can often prove to be very revealing, especially if about twenty such incomplete sentences are read rapidly, one after the other, and the individual is required to answer quickly. On the other hand, the approach is comparatively structured (that is, compared with the Rorschach test) in that the replies will tend to be focused on something to do with telegrams, communication, or related topics.

By contrast, the figure similar to one of the Rorschach cards (Figure 35) is quite unstructured. Unlike the sentence completion, the card offers no structure to guide one's response. Such things as *what* one sees in the card, *where* in the card one sees it, and *how much* one sees and reports are purely a function of the individual. There is nothing in the card to direct the individual or suggest that he reply in one way and not another.

All indirect approaches can be examined with respect to the degree that whatever serves as the structural factor in the technique is structured or unstructured. By keeping what we learned about determinants of meaning in mind, the public relations practitioner can assess any particular version of the indirect (or modified projective) approach to determine just how indirect or projective in nature that technique happens to be. We will return to this point a little later when we consider an example of motivation research employed in consumer survey work.

As noted earlier, the limitations of direct data collection became apparent sooner in clinical work than in industrial work. Opinion-attitude surveys and market potential studies, among others, have long been accepted by industry. However, they were at first conducted primarily by the direct methods outlined earlier; they leaned heavily on the simple interview and questionnaire. In time, the inadequacy or, more accurately, the limitations of direct methods became apparent. Just as the clinician had, the industrially oriented social scientist found that not all information is available by direct approaches. As a result, the tools of the clinician gradually came into use for industrial work. This is a comparatively recent development, however, in spite of a lot of early pioneer work. Today the pendulum has swung to the other extreme. Now we find the indirect methods applied to almost every type of study, including, of course, public relations problems.

Let us stop to summarize what has been said thus far.

1. Data collection approaches, embracing variations of the interview, can be seen to fall into two main categories: direct methods and indirect methods.
2. For many years the direct interview and the mail questionnaire were almost the exclusive forms of data collection in industrial type work.
3. In clinical work, and later in industrial work, the need for indirect methods of data collection became apparent.
4. This need ushered in the projective techniques—techniques that present a vague or unstructured stimulus situation to an individual. This permits the individual's personality to come to the fore and determine responses.
5. In spite of the pioneer work of some individuals, widespread acceptance and utilization of indirect techniques in data collection have only occurred in the past decade or so.

MOTIVATION RESEARCH—OLD TECHNIQUE, NEW EMPHASIS

In the past few years, the indirect approach of data collection has experienced almost unparalleled popularity for industrial use. The idea that one might more adequately understand the behavior of others, be it consumer behavior, personnel behavior, or political behavior, has proved to be very appealing. The reader will recognize the more popular term for this move toward the indirect data collection approach—*motivation research*. As we shall see, motivation research is a popular phrase that embraces what we discussed earlier as indirect or projective methods of data collection.

Any discussion of the topic of motivation research needs to be prefaced with some remarks about the term itself. Strictly speaking, most investigators in this area are not interested in what motivates people as an end in itself. Rather, they are interested in finding out such things as what types of advertising approaches or product packaging can be expected to appeal to people. This is in marked distinction, for example, to the psychologist's interest in motivation research in the academic setting; for him, understanding motivation is an end in itself, and applied possibilities of the knowledge are not considered or are definitely secondary.

In addition to the applied *vs.* theoretical distinction, two additional misconceptions about motivation research have tended to stand out and need to be commented on. These two misconceptions are:

1. Motivation research is something "brand new," a new step forward in the application of social science knowledge to applied problems.
2. Motivation research is more or less inherently "bad" or negative in character.

Let us consider these two misconceptions in order.

Motivation research—new or old? What is motivation research? First of all, it is definitely not new. Stripped of its sensationalism, the term refers to two processes that social and behavioral scientists have been employing for some time. One process is that of attempting to understand more adequately what makes people behave as they do. The current modification of this ancient preoccupation is that we are turning our attention to behavior that has industrial or economic significance. What do people respond to in an advertisement? How can we anticipate their preferences in purchases? How can we modify or influence their purchasing behavior?

The other process that is not new is obtaining information in a systematic fashion. The social or behavioral scientist, in contrast to the layman, obtains his information concerning human behavior in a systematic fashion. Careful attention is paid to how the data are collected; considerable time is devoted to the design and employment of measuring tools; there is constant vigil concerning how objective the data collection process has been. The social or behavioral scientist also pays close attention to his sample. What are the limits of his generalizations? Are the findings statistically significant? All this and more become routine in systematic data collection.

Motivation research, reduced to its simplest terms, is a process of trying to understand more about human behavior in a systematic fashion—precisely what the social scientist has been doing for years. The newness that exists lies in the popular application of social science techniques to problems of an industrial nature.

Motivation research—"good" or "bad"? Motivation research has often been depicted as essentially evil or wrong—that is, that anyone using motivation research is *ipso facto* doing something wrong or coming close to it. It is our thesis that motivation research is neutral. Motivation research defined as a process of obtaining information about human behavior is a *procedure* or a *technique*, and, as such, it is neither negative nor positive, good nor bad. The only legitimate question to ask is "What are the uses made of the information derived through motivation research techniques?" This is not to say that motivation research data have not been misused and that the applications of motivation research results are not a serious question that public relations practitioners must face. However, it is important that we be clear that the potential fault does not lie in the process, but rather in the use made of the results of the process in action.

An example of motivation research in action. The current heightened interest in motivation research warrants a brief presentation of an illustration. As Harry Henry has pointed out,[7] one can hardly avoid mentioning one of the classics in the field done by Mason Haire.[8] Mason Haire was interested in understanding women's attitudes toward instant coffee. On the basis of some preliminary work, he was convinced that he had not obtained all the data he needed. He felt that an understanding of some of the factors that determined the purchase of instant coffee still eluded him.

As a result, he developed two typical shopping lists containing such items as a pound of butter, a dozen eggs, and so on. On one list, he included the item "a pound of ground coffee." On the other list, identical in all other respects, he substituted for ground coffee a "jar of instant coffee." Next, he asked two groups of women to describe the "personality" of the woman who would have such a shopping list, one group having the list with the ground coffee, the other the list with the instant coffee. The results: the women with the instant coffee on their list evidenced a pronounced tendency to describe the woman as "a poor planner," "not a good housewife," "tending to be lazy," and the like. These personality characteristics were voiced considerably less frequently with the shopping list that contained ground coffee.[9]

In terms of our previous discussion, we can see that by asking the women to describe the personality of these hypothetical women on the basis of the shopping lists, Haire had, in effect, reduced the contribution that the list could make to eventual interpretation. The shopping lists provided no specific clues or statements as to personality.

[7] Harry Henry, *Motivation Research* (New York: Frederick Ungar Publishing Co., Inc., 1958).

[8] Mason Haire, "Projective Techniques in Market Research," *Journal of Marketing*, 1950.

[9] *Ibid.*, pp. 649-656.

Consequently, the structural factors of this situation had been reduced, and this allowed the functional factors within various women
to come into play. In effect, the women were projecting into the situation; and, without their being aware of it, they were revealing their
own attitudes—attitudes that partly explained the motives for buying
or not buying instant coffee in preference to ground coffee.

The additional information that Haire elicited by this particular
data collection technique was that the use of instant coffee was not
unrelated to the over-all perceptions that one had about being a
housewife. If the use of instant coffee (with its emphasis upon speed,
and the implication that one did not need any skill as a housewife
to use it) is perceived as something that a poor housewife would use,
then naturally one would reject the use of instant coffee. This is a
rather complicated feeling to verbalize, even if one were aware that
it existed; consequently, if directly asked about the use of instant
coffee, a respondent would be much more likely to give an answer
such as, "It doesn't have the flavor of ground coffee." For a respondent
to reply by saying, "My self-image as a housewife is diminished by
using such a product because it makes me feel less needed in the
kitchen," requires a lot of insight and a degree of rapport that is not
often achieved in the usual market survey.

The list of insights derived from this approach to industrial or
marketing problems is lengthy. We find certain researchers reporting
that people have distinctively negative connotations associated with
prunes. They tend to equate them with laxatives, old age, and death.
Others report that people feel very insecure about wine, especially in
talking about it. The topic is psychologically overwhelming because of
the different vintages and the proper kinds to serve with different
foods. With all of its weaknesses, motivation research has been helpful in answering specific questions pertaining to business in a very
wide range of contexts.

Obtaining the Data: A Summary

It should be readily apparent that there are numerous data collection techniques for the study of human behavior. We have had to
limit our presentation to highlights that communicate the scope of
the techniques rather than the details of any one technique. This
section should equip the reader with enough background to be able to
recognize and understand the various techniques as they are encountered.

One concluding point should be made. Human behavior is so complex and so difficult to measure that the social scientist has had to

resort to a multitude of techniques to obtain the data desired. One result has been that the reliability and validity of many techniques are low at best. That is, the tools do not always obtain the same results when used at different times, and the tools do not always measure what they purport to measure. The techniques that came under the heading of motivation research are particularly open to this criticism. There are many persons using motivation research techniques in such a fashion that one would think the usual requirements applied to all data collection methods do not apply to motivation research. Nothing could be further from the truth. All of the requirements for sound data collection, particularly such things as reliability and validity, are applicable to *all* techniques for data collection. There are no exceptions to the rules in scientific research.

STEP EIGHT: ANALYSIS OF DATA

In the total research process, it is at this stage that one begins to near the "pay off" for the whole effort. At this point, the researcher has presumably followed all of the other steps outlined so far and has before him the "raw data," as the experimenter calls it. It is in the analysis of the raw data that one of the real thrills of research may occur, because it is at this stage in the research process that the researcher may have found some answers to a perplexing problem or thrown some light on a cherished hypothesis.

The term *raw data* can cover any type of information that the researcher set out to collect. Consequently, raw data can be a pile of answered mail questionnaires; it can be the transcribed statements of a group of individuals interviewed face-to-face. In short, the raw data can be literally anything that the researcher set out to attain.

To illustrate, if the study of the relationship between childhood training with respect to volunteer organizations and adult giving had been carried through all of the previous stages in the research process, the raw data might consist of a series of transcribed interviews. What remains to be done is to analyze these data to see whether the hypotheses put forward before the study started are substantiated. As with all of the other phases of the research process, there is more than one way of proceeding, but the following steps are illustrative.

General Orientation and Assessment

A good way to start in the analysis phase is to take stock of the data you have on hand. If your data happen to be based on interviews, check them for completeness and be sure that you have all the interviews you think you have. Be sure that all of the answers are complete and there are no "gaps" in your data.[10] If it is numerical data of various types—test scores, ages, years of experience, and the like—group them and check their accuracy and completeness.

Following this, take the time to review your study objectives. What were you trying to find out? Why was the research instituted? This may seem like a rather simple-minded recommendation, but it would not be the first time that an investigator has become so wrapped up in various details of the execution of a research project that he has to some extent lost sight of the over-all objectives of his research. A more practical reason for review of objectives, of course, is that it will help to shape the way in which the data are tabulated and analyzed.

Any data that one collects can potentially be grouped into different units depending upon the objectives of the experimenter. Naturally, some data—*e.g.*, transcribed depth interviews—offer greater lattitude in this respect than other data. Since the data that one can obtain can conceivably be anything that is worth collecting, we cannot hope to discuss Step 8 (*i.e.*, analysis of data) so as to cover all possible variations. However, our approach to this topic will be to emphasize the *process* of data analysis so the reader can apply what he reads here to any data that he encounters.

The Need to Quantify

The basic starting point in the process of data analysis is to realize that the fundamental objective is to summarize observations, numerical readings, replies to questions, and so on in such a way that some sense can be made out of the *whole*. To do this, we must quantify, no matter how crudely.

Many persons who would not begin to regard themselves as researchers tend to resist the notion that quantification is necessary in order to communicate the essentials of anything. Consider a journalist attempting to report on a political convention. He will build his report

---

[10] In any well-managed survey, the interview returns would have been checked for completeness and accuracy as they were being conducted. However, there is still room for error, and this last check is another effort to counteract error. Also, the mere process of double checking the data helps give the researcher a feeling for what he is dealing with. Many times the researcher has turned the management of the field portion of a study to an assistant who sees to it that the interviews are conducted, the answers to the questions correctly and legibly recorded, and so forth. Hence, the researcher in charge may have been away from the study, and this last double checking gives him a chance to become familiar with its details once again.

around issues, personalities, or whatever else appears to make sense and reflect what is going on at the convention. In so doing, he inevitably will use adjectives that reflect the need to quantify. He may say that "most" of the delegates are for a given issue; he may say that "over half" of the planks in the platform have been contested. And so the process goes, and if the copy written by the journalist is analyzed carefully, again and again terms that represent efforts to quantify (and, of course, to summarize at the same time) will appear. The following phrases are typical of what can be found: "nearly all," "hardly any of the individuals," "not more than one in a hundred," "probably two out of three," "the group was unanimous." The point of this reference to a fictional reporter at a convention is that *even here* the need to quantify can be clearly discerned. In fact, the reader is asked to observe more closely his discussions with others during the next day or so in order to either substantiate or refute this claim for himself. *You can't communicate with someone else without resorting to quantification however crude and however devoid of supporting data your generalizations happen to be.* In fact, you should find that the tendency to quantify increases the more that one is trying to persuade or defend a point. As a discussion gets more and more heated, the statistical references increase—"I'll bet 9 out of 10 persons," "Not one in a hundred would do such a thing," and so on.[11]

The reason for trying to demonstrate this need to quantify *in everyday life* is that when it comes to analysis of data, quantification really sums up the whole point of data analysis. If your data happen to be numerical in the first place, then the quantification is already done for you. All that you need to do is to place these numbers in *various meaningful orders* (such as tables and graphs), and you are well on your way to making sense out of your data. Or you may compute certain statistics to aid in your characterization of all of the data. For example, one of the most commonly used statistics is the mean—hence you might well compute the mean age, mean income, and so on of your group.

Let's pursue this point with a simple example. Suppose you are interested in comparing the customers a bank has with data from the latest census for the area the bank serves. Let us also suppose that

---

[11] It is interesting to note that very often the bases for cited statistics are nonexistent. That is, the person who uses the expression "Not one in a hundred would do such a thing" has no evidence to support such a contention. More often than not, the person who resorts to statistics without evidence to back them up does so unwittingly. The deliberate falsification of statistics is comparatively rare, but it does happen, of course.

you are interested in such things as occupation, income, and age, to sort out three specific sorts of data. It will be a simple matter to tabulate all of the checking accounts, savings accounts, and loan accounts, broken down in terms of age, income, and occupation. It will also be comparatively easy to obtain this same information from the census data for your area. For such a simple study, making sense out of the data means placing the various data into some sort of numerical categories and summarizing them, either by tables or curves or both. You will then be ready to make comparisons between the bank's customers and the census data. It will be easy to determine if the bank has proportionately more customers from the "over 10,000 a year" category than the "under 10,000." It will be simple to compare the representation of the various occupational groups among the bank customers, and whether some are overrepresented and others underrepresented, with the census figures. The point is that because the data are already in numerical form (or in a form that is easily translated into frequencies, percentages, means, or totals) analysis of the data will be simple and direct. Likewise, you will be able to *make sense* out of the data rather quickly and easily.

For contrast, suppose your data consists of transcribed interviews obtained from respondents in a survey. (The data could also be the written replies to a questionnaire, reports by individuals who have been observing individuals or groups, and so on.) Let us assume that the transcribed interviews are verbatim accounts of what each respondent had to say during the interview. *Here, establishing analysis units is an entirely different problem.* When one has hundreds of interview protocols staring him in the face, analysis is quite another matter. How does one go about making sense out of thousands of words that are obtained in answer to a certain set of questions that were part of an opinion-attitude survey? In such situations, quantification is *not* provided, nor is it immediately apparent how to proceed. For example, a few years ago the writer conducted a survey which was designed to ascertain how advertisers viewed public relations practitioners, how much they knew about the work that a public relations practitioner does, and their views about public relations practitioners themselves (see Chapter 1). The following questions are illustrative of those asked:

When you hear the expression "public relations," what comes to your mind?

Would you please describe your impression of the typical (or "average") public relations man?

In your opinion, what would you say are the main activities of a public relations man?

Would you recommend a career in public relations for your son or daughter? If yes, why; If no, why not?

As the reader can well imagine, such questions tended to provoke long and rather complicated answers. As a consequence, the number of words obtained from *just one respondent* was sizable. When the same set of questions are asked of nearly a hundred respondents, the data to be analyzed become staggering. However, just as in any other type of study, eventually the researcher *must* be able to arrive at some sort of quantification, however crude, in order to make sense out of the data himself and to be able to communicate these data with their interpretations to others.

Providing the answers as to how this is done in any detail is beyond the province of this volume. However, in such cases the technique of *content analysis* is usually used to analyze the protocols (or articles, or books, or radio and TV programs, or anything else that is in a form that needs to be systematized so that it can be analyzed). In essence, content analysis is an approach which compresses the longer, often rather diffuse and complicated replies into categories which reflect what the person had to say or the views he expressed on a given subject (See Chapter 9, page 217). This approach can be applied to almost anything that requires "compression." Along this vein, Budd and Thorp write:

> The techniques of content analysis may be applied to study of the contents of any book, magazine, newspaper, individual story or article, motion picture, news broadcast, or a series or combination of any of these. It has been applied not only to printed mass media, but to private correspondence, written records of psychoanalytic interviews, radio and television newscasts (and total broadcast content), and photographs. Content analysis may be as simple as counting the number of editorials one newspaper carries during a selected time period, or it may be as sophisticated and complex as the investigator's knowledge and imagination allow.
>
> *Cases in point:* The Peterson-Thorp study of editorials in weekly newspapers* used simple counting (and simple classification)—number of editorials, number of issues with editorials, total number of editorials; mere counting, followed by percentaging, provided all the necessary

---

* Wilbur Peterson and Robert Thorp, "Weeklies' Editorial Effort Less than 30 Years Ago," *Journalism Quarterly*, Vol. 39, No. 1 (1962), 53-56.

information. At the other extreme, Bomberger's analysis of magazines**
involved the retesting of a social theory, and utilized an electronic
computer and some fairly sophisticated statistical techniques. The result was not only one kind of description of content, but also a useful
prediction tool.[12]

It may be helpful to the reader to go one step farther and provide
a little more information concerning categories, because translating
the material to be studied—regardless of its nature—into categories is
the essence of content analysis. In this connection, Budd and Thorpe
write,

> Categories are used in content analysis to describe as objectively as
> possible the contents of newspapers, magazines, radio and television
> broadcasts, or of any other medium of communication, whether it be
> visual or oral. Categories are compartments (whose boundaries have
> been explicitly defined) into which units of content of various types are
> placed. Categories are the classes into which material is grouped for
> the purpose of analysis.[13]

. . . . .

The following examples of category definitions (in this case subject
matter categories) were taken from Budd's study of the New Zealand
and Australian press.* The study was designed to analyze U.S. news
published by daily newspapers in those two countries:

> *Diplomacy and Foreign Relations.* All news of diplomatic and gov-
> ernmental relations between the United States and any other nation,
> including U.S. activities in the United Nations; news concerning in-
> volvement of any political personage, government agency or otherwise
> *official* representative of the United States with any other political
> figure from any other nation, including social activities and state visits,
> will be included in this category.

** Russell Bomberger, "An Analytical Comparison of Scope-Depth Balance with Popularity of General Circulation Weekly Magazines in the United
States, 1947-1960," Ph.D. Dissertation, State University of Iowa, 1962.

* Richard W. Budd, "A Study of News Concerning the United States in
Four Australian and Four New Zealand Metropolitan Newspapers," CMA
thesis, 1961, State University of Iowa.

---

[12] Richard W. Budd and Robert K. Thorp, *An Introduction to Content Analysis*
(Iowa City: State University of Iowa Journalism School, 1963), p. 1. All passages
used by permission of Mass Communications Research Bureau, State University
of Iowa.

[13] *Ibid.*, p. 10.

Prominent Individuals. All items in which prominent citizens of the
United States and their personal activities are featured. Includes enter-
tainers, persons of wealth and other persons of notoriety. This category
excludes political figures and their activities as they will be accounted
for in Category I (*Diplomacy and Foreign Relations*) or Category II
(*Internal Governmental Affairs and Politics*), but includes dependents
of political personages involved in non-governmental or non-political
activities.

In the Budd study, the definition of the category *Prominent Individuals*
was expanded after the analysis started. A story concerning a vacation
trip by a prominent American politician's wife did not fit the definition
of either Category I or II, and distortion would have resulted had the
article been assigned to either. It was decided to place the item in the
category of *Prominent Individuals* and expand the definition to account
for the decision, as well as provide for further such occurrences.[14]

With the above examples, perhaps the reader can better visualize
what categories can look like. It should be obvious that once material
has been categorized, it is, in effect, counted, and the researcher is
then able to make further manipulations of his data. He can describe
his data in terms of frequencies, percentages, means, departures from
means, curves—and he can even apply various tests of statistical significance. All this becomes possible once he is able to translate his
data into manipulatable form. For much raw data, the best tool available to us at the present time is *content analysis.*

Obviously, the foregoing examples cannot possibly cover all of the
forms in which data can be found. The examples selected were merely
two points on a continuum, one end being numerical in nature and
hence already quantified; the other being in prose form and a long way
from being quantified. The point to be left with the reader is that
before any intelligent use and interpretation can be made of any data,
analysis units must be decided on. Once this has been done, the larger,
usually difficult to comprehend, original data can be "translated" into
smaller, more intelligible analysis units.

We have only scratched the surface with respect to content analysis.
There are many other considerations that we did not even touch, such
as: *What* sample of material are you going to content analyze, or are
you going to analyze the entire population? How is the *direction* of
the content going to be treated (*e.g.,* is the material positive or negative

---

[14] *Ibid.,* p. 11.

in character, friendly or hostile, or what not)? Lastly, there is the requirement of all measurement or analysis techniques—are they valid and reliable? Applied to our discussion, is our particular method of content analysis reliable and valid?

A Brief Look at the Use of Statistics

One powerful aid to understanding data is to have it appropriately described. Thus, statistics can be used to describe how the data are grouped around a particular central measure ("measures of central tendency") such as a mean (*i.e.*, arithmetic mean). Knowing the mean donation, the mean hours of work for a given occupational classification, or the mean span of life for men or women, one can get an idea of how the data are grouped. Another important category of descriptive statistics the statistician calls "measures of dispersion," that is, measures that tell us something about how scores or values are scattered or distributed around a particular measure of central tendency, such as a mean. Let us consider one common measure of dispersion —the "range." The range is the simplest measure of dispersion and is defined as the distance between the highest and lowest value in a distribution. With this single value in conjunction with a mean score, one immediately has a better picture of the data. Consider two different towns with the same average contribution figure—*i.e.*, a mean of $20. One town, however, may have a range of $99 (donations of $1 to $100), while the other may have a range of only $38 ($2 to $40). With the range values combined with the same mean value, we now have a more complete picture of donations in the two towns. For example, we may wonder if the town with the wider range can potentially have more $100 donations, or if there are only one or two individuals capable of giving that much. In the town where the top donation was $40, is $40 the limit? Are the people in that town "poorer" than in the other town? Naturally, more study must be made to answer these questions. The point to be stressed here is how much more understanding a person has of the data when he has translated them into *measures of central tendency and dispersion*.

As powerful as descriptive statistics can be in enabling a researcher to understand his data, they fall short of desired objectives standing alone. It is fortunate that in addition to *description*, other statistical tools are available to aid the investigator to *determine the significance of his data*.

Invariably one of the objectives of a research project is being able to state that one group is significantly different from another group along some lines. Or it may be a comparison of individuals. In some way, the researcher is interested in stating a difference between the experimental group and the control group. Our hypothesis concerning the role of childhood training with respect to understanding voluntary organizations and supporting such organizations as adults is a perfect case in point. Assuming for a moment that all of the very difficult problems of such a study could be overcome, it is conceivable that the time would come when we would be comparing the "voluntary giving" of two groups of people—one group that had received training as children and another that had not. At this point, we would like to have a procedure that would enable us to state, with a specified degree of confidence, whether the voluntary giving was different. That is, do the people who received training give more as adults than the people who did not?

What we are attempting to ascertain here, of course, is whether the difference between the two groups could be attributed to chance alone or whether certain childhood training actually makes a difference. Statistics comes into play here as a tool in helping to determine whether the differences in total giving by the group that received training in childhood as compared with the group that *did not* receive this childhood training could be expected by chance alone. If we can rule out chance by statistical techniques—that is, conclude that the differences between our two groups are such that the training received apparently has contributed to the results we obtained—then we can begin to understand what role the experimental variable (*i.e.*, childhood training) played. This is, of course, the major objective of the research in the first place.

Any more detail on statistics is, of course, well beyond the scope of this book. It should be understood that statistical techniques are available that will enable the researcher to make statements about the significance of the differences obtained in the data. The power of such aid cannot be too strongly stated. The public relations practitioner, regardless of the fact that he may never pursue research sufficiently to make statistical analyses himself, should remember that such tools are available. If it is data that he has obtained himself and it meets all of the minimum requirements of the research process described thus far, he should, at the very least, see to it that someone competent in statistical methods makes such an analysis for him. A personal, intuitive analysis of data is unforgivable in the light of the statistical tools that are available at the present time.

STEP 9: NOTING IMPLICATIONS AND MAKING GENERALIZATIONS

The Difference Between the Findings and Implications

There is an old saying that has been around for years to the effect that "facts speak for themselves." Nothing could be further from the truth. "Facts" need to be interpreted and implications drawn from them. What is even more to the point, we even need someone to determine what will be considered a fact.

So it is with experiments or studies of any type. The data that one has painstakingly collected and analyzed do not "speak for themselves." There will always be someone needed who will note the implications or make interpretations based on the data. This, along with generalizing, constitutes the last step in the research process. Concerning this last step in the research process, two important points should be kept in mind:

1. *An experiment or study seldom, if ever, can be interpreted in only one way.* The implications that can be derived from a study can often point to several different consequences or suggestions for next steps. This statement highlights one of the commonly misunderstood features of research work, that research results can be a substitute for decision making. To be sure, research can clarify issues or reveal information not previously known; however, *the source for noting the implications for further action resides in the experimenter* and *not in the research.*

To illustrate, let us consider again the hypothesis about the relationship between a certain type of childhood training and adult giving. Let us assume that this study was conducted following all of the research steps so far outlined. Let us also assume that the statistical tools used enabled us to conclude that there was a very significant relationship between childhood training and adult giving. In terms of our hypothesis, those people who as children received training about voluntary organizations are much more likely to give to such organizations as adults than those who did not receive training. This would constitute a major conclusion (or "fact") derived from the research. (It is worth noting once more that it required someone to marshal the data in a certain way to be able to arrive at this "fact." The facts did not "speak for themselves.")

However clear this conclusion may be, *it does not provide the ex-*

perimenter with the implications of this finding. Even more to the point, it does not tell our public relations practitioner what to do next. Should we now devise a way of learning who all of the people who have had this particular type of training are, then seek them out at fund-raising time? Conversely, should we avoid spending too much time with people who have not had this training in the interests of efficient fund raising? Should we be thinking about long-range programs that will help develop this type of training in today's children, so that fund raising in the future will be more certain? One could go on and on developing implications of this one finding. In spite of the fact that one small part of the total picture has been clarified—and the value of this, of course, should not be underestimated—the implications are varied and the research does not help us here. We still need decision making based on the best estimates of the experimenter.

One should not be discouraged by this feature of research. Many times research results enable one to uncover implications that were never suspected before. This is the "enlarging the vistas" effect of research. Also, new studies are suggested by the implications derived from the preceding one, and little by little a problem area that was once completely confusing becomes more intelligible.

2. Generalizations made on the basis of data obtained are both desirable and a source of danger. Seldom are studies done to determine if something is true of just the sample group being studied. More often than not, the researcher is interested in making statements which presumably apply to the total population. On the basis of the sample, he is attempting to describe the total population.

The ability to generalize and accurately characterize the total population is an extremely powerful by-product of research. However, generalizing can be a two-edged sword. If you have not gone beyond the legitimate limits of your data, then you have helped yourself and others in further work. If, on the other hand, overgeneralizing occurs, then the incorrect characterization of the general population can impede further work.

Consequently, as useful and necessary as generalizing may be, it should not be done without bearing a few things in mind. Generalizations should be limited to populations having the same characteristics as the sample studied. If the sample were made up of children or adults or persons with college training, you should limit your generalizations to populations of children or adults or persons with college training. Generalizing beyond the characteristics of one's sample is always risky.

Whenever generalizations are made, the data on which they are based should be provided. This means providing details of the sample used, the characteristics of the persons sampled, and so on, so that the reader of the research report may be able to assess for himself the legitimacy of the generalizations made. Generalizations can be made (and interpreted by others) only with the data on which they are based clearly at hand.

The Never-Ending Nature of Research

By now the reader is undoubtedly aware that a discussion of implications and generalizations, the last step in the research process, can't help but start the whole process over again. In thinking through the implications for action especially, one immediately begins asking questions which very often cannot be answered—questions that suggest further research. The answers to some questions raise other questions, and the whole process starts over again—and so it is that the whole process of research is never-ending. It is this research process repeated over and over again that has enlarged mankind's knowledge thus far. We have no reason to suspect that the future will be any different.

And that is how it must begin to be for public relations. Research on some problems will point to the urgent need for research on others. Let us return to an illustration used earlier to highlight this point. When presenting an explanation of deriving implications, we assumed for illustrative purposes that the research on childhood training and adult giving had been completed. We then discussed how this finding (assumed to be in the affirmative) pointed to several implications. One possible implication was would we now devise ways of encouraging childhood training in voluntary organizations? This particular implication might be dismissed as being too long range. "We can't wait that long," might be the reply. However, this implication triggers off another idea which in turn suggests a rather intriguing research problem. Perhaps training children now produces results that do take too long; but would such a public relations program, directed at children (with an honest intent for improving the future), at the same time communicate to their parents in such a way to increase the parents' present giving *regardless of their own previous training?* Immediately this suggests a research problem which, if it also turned out in the affirmative, in turn would suggest a very dynamic approach to a very old problem in the support of health and welfare organizations.

We would be remiss if we did not stress the fact that although research is never-ending, *the by-products along the way can prove to be exciting and useful to the practitioner.* The public relations practitioner *must* begin to benefit from such by-products by devoting increasing time, energy, and funds toward research in public relations.

QUESTIONS FOR DISCUSSION

1. Try to obtain a research study that was conducted to help a public relations practitioner solve a problem situation that he faced. In all likelihood, the research that you will find will be an attitude survey of some sort. (If you can't find a study that was done to help further some public relations objectives, any research study such as is normally reported in the social and behavioral science journals will do).

   With the research study in hand, make use of Figure 32 to estimate how structured the measuring device(s) used in the study is (are). Similarly, make an estimate as to how structured the responses of the subject are.

2. Suppose that you were trying to explain the terms reliability and validity to someone; what would you say? Also, explain the statement "All measurement devices have the same requirements regarding reliability and validity regardless of the type of measurement device involved."

3. Suppose someone asked you to explain the statement that a sentence-completion question is more structured than the Rorschach test. What would you say? In giving your explanation, did you find yourself referring to concepts introduced when we considered the topic of perception in Chapter 7?

4. One of the assertions made in this chapter was that the interview is the basic tool of the social and behavioral sciences. Go through a half dozen issues of a few of the professional journals pertinent to public relations (such as the *Journal of Experimental Social Psychology, Public Opinion Quarterly, Journalism Quarterly*, and *Audio-Visual Communication Review*) and note what data collection techniques were used in the various research studies reported. Relate these data collection techniques to the schema developed in Figure 34. What proportion of the studies were based on the interview or a version thereof? How many studies did you find that you could *not* relate to Figure 34?

5. What is your understanding of the projective techniques (motivation research), and how does this particular approach to data collection relate to the distinction between indirect and direct data

collection methods? How do the projective techniques relate to the formula $S \times R = P$ (*structural* times *functional factors* equal *perception*).

6. Explain your understanding of the terms *measures of central tendency* and *measures of dispersion*. Try to develop a half dozen examples or situations wherein a public relations practitioner either explicitly (that is, through actual computation) or implicitly (that is, through the use of adjectives or adverbs) makes use of either measure.

7. Another assertion that was made in this chapter was that the need to quantify is very compelling, not only in research work, but also in everyday life. For the next day or so, try to make a frequency count of this need to quantify in yourself and others. That is, try to note the times and the reasons that you found yourself or someone else expressing quantitatively, either with numbers or adjectives and adverbs. Did you find that the number of times that quantification was resorted to was quite frequent? How many times did the speaker have any basis for his quantification? (That is, did he have any data to back up his figures or adjectives or were they without foundation?)

8. On the basis of what was presented here on content analysis (and also in Chapter 9, page 217), try to develop two or three applications of content analysis to public relations practice. Also, indicate how you visualize the data obtained through this technique can help a practitioner in his public relations work.

Chapter 20

THE "IN-BETWEEN" STEPS TO RELIABLE KNOWLEDGE: DO-IT-YOURSELF EFFORTS

INTRODUCTION

In the first few pages of Chapter 17 we developed the notion that scientific research represented one of the most useful methods of obtaining reliable knowledge known to man (see particularly Figure 28, page 465). We also put forth the concept that one obtains reliable knowledge by degrees; that is, there is no magic point on the continuum depicted in Figure 28 at which an individual suddenly reaches nearly 100% reliable knowledge. By the same token, this implied that useful, reasonably reliable knowledge can be obtained by operating at other portions of our continuum. Specifically, we discussed that portion of the continuum that can represent what is meant by "experience."

Now that we have discussed the research process more fully and know what scientific research consists of, we are prepared to examine portions of the *left-hand end* of the continuum that also have some value to the public relations practitioner. *Whenever possible the public relations practitioner should strive for information based on scientific research, for the simple reason it is more reliable.* (This includes having the research done for him or learning about the results of research done by someone else which are applicable to his problems.) The author is fully aware of the fact that there are many practical situations that rule out being able to operate at the scientific research end of the investigative continuum. This raises the question of what a public relations practitioner can do when he cannot operate at the extreme right-hand end of the continuum, and this last chapter is devoted to a consideration of this dilemma.[1]

THE INVESTIGATIVE CONTINUUM EXPANDED

Figure 36 is our point of departure. It consists of the same information that is in Figure 28, with the addition of some categories of efforts to obtain reliable knowledge toward the left-hand end of the continuum. We will argue that these steps, *none of which can conceivably qualify as scientific research*, are valuable to the public relations practitioner. In fact, they help him to make his daily work as a public relations practitioner just that much more precise. In addition, they happen to be things that the public relations practitioner can put into practice right away, *hence the notion that they are do-it-yourself steps toward reliable knowledge.*

One further point. Although we have of necessity depicted these do-it-yourself steps in the left-hand portion of the continuum and in a particular order, the reader should bear in mind the arbitrariness of our interpretation. That is, one could argue for a different positioning or a different order, thus highlighting the fact that we cannot at this time make such a literal translation of the steps into the investigative

---

[1] There are parallels to this dilemma in almost any field. For example, the clinical psychologist is confronted with the problem of working with mentally ill patients and "doing something" to help them. There are many points in the total analysis and therapy process at which he realizes that his decisions about what to do and how to do it are far from being based on scientific research. In fact, he must operate a great deal of the time at the intuitive end of the continuum. However, being a practitioner means that he must act with the information that he has at hand and do the best he can. The experimental psychologist, working in a laboratory, may eschew the approach of the clinical psychologist. He does not have patients who need immediate attention and consequently may be more preoccupied with the scientific research end of the continuum and not make use of any knowledge until it has become thoroughly tested. So it is in almost any field of endeavor—the practitioner and the researcher behind the practitioner having different working environments. The importance of bringing this out here is that there is nothing to be gained by taking the position of one or the other. The practitioner must continually strive toward the right-hand end of the continuum. When he must use information obtained by means other than scientific research, he must apply this information with even more than the usual caution. The task of the researcher is, in that sense, more uncomplicated; he needs merely to continue to push back the "frontiers" of knowledge.

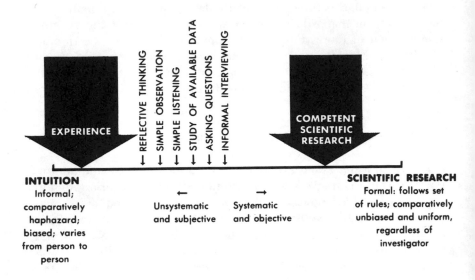

Figure 36

Investigative continuum depicting the extremes of intuition
and scientific research along with several between stages

continuum. The important point is the realization of the *relative position* of these efforts at obtaining reliable knowledge, as compared with
scientific research.[2]

Reflective Thinking

About the simplest, yet a surprisingly neglected, step that one can
take to move toward the right-hand end of the continuum is to engage
in "reflective thinking." This category is nothing more elaborate than

---

[2] The idea of suggesting that there are means of obtaining reliable knowledge
other than through scientific research has, of course, been suggested by others.
For example, Fred P. Frutchy ("Evaluation, What Is It?" in Darcie Byrn [ed.],
Evaluation in Extension [Washington, D.C.: Division of Extension and Training,
Federal Extension Service, United States Department of Agriculture, no date]) de-
votes considerable space to the following scale that he calls "degrees of evaluation":

Casual everyday evaluations	Self-checking evaluations	Do-it-yourself evaluations	Extension studies	Scientific research

sitting back in a quiet place once in a while and rethinking what one is doing and why. Another way of expressing the processes that should go on at this point on our continuum is to say that the public relations practitioner should apply the first five steps of the research process to his day-to-day work to aid his reflective thinking. Steps 1 and 2 would cause the public relations practitioner to evaluate once again just what his problems are and whether he is tackling problems that can be solved, or is he taking on more than he can possibly handle?

Step 3 (establishing definitions) directs the public relations practitioner's attention once again to definitions and has him ask himself, "On a closer look, have I really defined what I mean by *community relations*?" "Have I really thought through—in terms of the behavior of individuals—what I mean by the expression '*poor stockholder relations*'?" "Have I thought about the changes in behavior that I would expect (and how I would become aware of them) if, and when, my stockholder relations '*improved*'?"

Step 4 (the literature search), couched in reflective thinking terms, asks the questions, "Have I done all that I can to learn what others might have done in situations similar to mine? Have I taken the trouble to find out if there are related sources of information that may be helpful to me in solving my particular problems?" When one speaks of considering the literature as part of the process of reflective thinking, obviously there is the question of considering the public relations publications—in both book and journal forms. There is also the question of considering related literature. The author was making this point in a talk he gave a couple of years ago, and in preparation for this presentation, scanned the latest edition of *Public Opinion Quarterly* from the point of view of just how a public relations practitioner might react to the content. It will be useful to "go through" that journal here, as it was done at that earlier presentation:

. . . *The first article*, "Reflections of Data Sources in Opinion Research," is by John Riley, Jr. At first glance it might appear that this article is too technical or academic in nature. However, upon a closer look, it turns out that this article is an exciting example of what I was arguing for earlier; namely, that the files of organizations very often contain data in a form that proves to be very useful. In this article, Riley gives several concrete examples to support this point.

The next two articles, dealing with some of the important contributions of the late Samuel A. Stouffer to social research, would probably not be of interest to the applied practitioner.

The fourth and fifth articles, dealing with the utilization of television in political campaigns, and the whole question of the effect of campaign debates upon the voter, we would have to score "applicable for some." We have noted, increasingly, that politicians are turning to professional communicators to serve as consultants to them in their campaigns, and certain public relations practitioners who are serving in this capacity will find some ideas, background information, and data in these two articles.

The sixth article entitled, "American Subculture: The Negro's Paradox," by Duane Lockard, is another example of an article which would have to be placed in the "applicable for some" category. Many segments of our society, and this certainly includes American business, are beginning to realize that they have not understood the Negro, and are gradually coming to appreciate that their communicative efforts need to reflect an understanding of this very important, increasingly assertive, subculture of America.

The next three articles, although provocative and thoughtful, probably would not be of particular interest to the practitioner.

The tenth article is by Harold Mendelsohn and is entitled, "Measuring the Process of Communications Effect." This article is very pertinent for all public relations practitioners as it gets to the very heart of a fundamental question that is always facing the practitioner: what effect has his communication program had. In this article, Mendelsohn describes a technique that he and his co-workers are developing called the *active response scale* which, briefly, is a technique for measuring three types of response to a communication:

1. A *rudimentary response*, which is defined as the ability of an individual to recall a communication.

2. An *emotional response*, measured by recall, and defined as to whether a recipient responds emotionally to a communication by such things as a feeling of friendliness toward the source of the communication.

3. An *active response*, determined by recall, emotional reaction, and such things as whether or not the recipient feels that he has learned something about the idea, product, or service discussed in the communication.

The article then goes on to briefly describe the utilization of the active response scale in a number of practical situations, such as (1) examining the appropriateness of humor in advertising and (2) the use of the practical vs. romantic appeal in communications directed toward female consumers.

In the "living research" section, which is a report of research or findings that are a part of a larger study to be reported later, we see a total of four articles. Of the four, the last one is definitely useful to the public relations practitioner. It is "Methods of Measuring Opinion

Leadership," by Everett M. Rogers and David G. Cartano. This is certainly an area that public relations practitioners are constantly concerned with—that of finding out who the opinion leaders are in any particular public. The authors report upon a technique for identifying the opinion leaders that appears to have held up well in exploratory research done thus far.

In the balance of this issue of *The Public Opinion Quarterly*, devoted to news, book reports, etc., there is information useful to the public relations practitioner. In one section, a report is made of the proceedings of the Seventeenth Conference on Public Opinion Research held in May of 1962. Just a few of the titles of papers described briefly in this section give you an indication of their value: "An Application of Learning Theory to TV Copy Testing," by Herbert E. Krugman; "Metropolitan Growth and Motivations for Charitable Giving," by Paul N. Borsky; "Computer Simulation as an Aid to Media Selection," by James Tyson.

Let's see what our "score" is with respect to this recent issue of *The Public Opinion Quarterly* as it relates to the public relations practitioner.

The Major Articles

Of the major articles, two of them are definitely useful to a wide variety of public relations practitioners. Three articles would be valuable for certain practitioners who have specialized in such things as guiding political campaigns and specialized communications to minority groups.

The Minor Articles

Of the four minor articles, one is definitely useful to a wide spectrum of public relations practitioners.

The Miscellaneous Features

Even in the balance of the issue, there are parts—such as the report of papers given at the previous annual conference—that would be of value to public relations practitioners.

Considering the fact that this is a *related* source—that is, a source that is not designed to serve public relations practitioners in the first place—we find that a surprisingly high percentage of the articles have relevance for the public relations practitioner.[3]

Step 5 in the research process (developing hypotheses) relates to the recommendation concerning reflective thinking; bringing hypotheses

---

[3] Edward J. Robinson, "Research: The Fountainhead of Public Relations," unpublished speech given at the General Sessions of Advancing Public Relations Practice, Fifteenth Annual Conference of the Public Relations Society of America, Boston, November 12-14, 1962. Based on *The Public Opinion Quarterly*, XXVI, No. 3 (Fall, 1962).

out into the open helps us become aware of our assumptions. From time to time, the public relations practitioner must ask himself, "What am I assuming to be true?" Immediately on the heels of this question comes a closely related question: "How do I know that what I have assumed is true—what evidence do I have to support the assumptions that I have been making?"

All of the first five steps are involved in the deceptively simple admonishment described here as *reflective thinking*. As the reader can readily observe, there is nothing herein that the typical public relations practitioner could not apply to his own work immediately. This is not to imply that all of the steps involved in this do-it-yourself category are easy; in fact, some of them are very difficult to achieve. But they can be done, and the public relations practitioner who does will be much farther along toward the right-hand end of our investigative continuum than the one who does not.

Simple Observation

The second step toward the right-hand end of our continuum (Figure 36) we have categorized as simple observation. As the title implies, it means nothing more than observing more closely what goes on around you. From what we have learned about perception, we can readily understand why such a simple process can be helpful. All of us fall into what might be described as "perceptual ruts" in the sense that some things are figure and others are ground, and we literally do not "see" a large portion of what is going on. Consequently, we must make an effort to be able to observe that which has become familiar.

In practice, the notion of simple observation suggests that the public relations practitioner take deliberate steps to view his own work situation or problem situation from the view of another person, try to see how it would appear to him if he could assume the role of a newcomer to the problem situation once again. Perhaps another way of expressing this idea is to say that it represents an effort of "planned naïveté" in the sense that one tries to view a situation through the eyes of someone not so close to the problem situation. This fresh perspective is exactly the reason we try to involve others in our problem-solving efforts. Oftentimes someone who is not so involved in a problem can generate insights that someone close to the problem cannot see.

How does one go about achieving planned naïveté? There is no simple guide to this except to say that it must be a conscious effort.

The less that one is aware of the fact that he is trying to "see" what is going on around him, the more likely he is to fall back in his old ruts —the perceptual ruts referred to earlier. Perhaps a simple example will illustrate the process. An Information Officer of an Air Force base was reviewing the status of the relationship between his base and the adjacent community. One of the factors that he was speculating about was the role that treatment received by visitors to the base played in the over-all "community relations" of the base. In order to gain a closer perspective of how the base probably appeared to the visitor, he went through completely the steps that a visitor had to go through to do business with one of the units on the base. It was only after deliberately going through this experience and observing what procedures had to be followed and from listening to comments made by fellow visitors that this Information Officer could view the visiting procedures in a new light. This effort at planned naïveté proved to be quite fruitful in highlighting unnecessary annoyances that one who did not have to enter the base by the same procedures would never be aware of or would not normally "see."

Naturally, the particular procedures one adopts to achieve this ability to see things in a new light will vary from situation to situation. They all have one element in common however; namely, a planned effort to try to observe more clearly what has faded into the background, perceptually speaking.

Simple Listening

This third category of methods of obtaining reliable information may come as a surprise to some readers. Listening to others is something we do so much of in our daily lives that it probably is one of the main reasons we assume that we do it well. *The fact is that most of us listen very badly.* Nichols and Stevens bring this out when they write:

> A person who frequently makes public speeches soon becomes deeply impressed with an important fact: People in general do not know how to listen. They may come to hear you speak, but they are not necessarily good listeners. *The burden of making people listen has always been thrown almost entirely upon the speaker.* He is given many suggestions for carrying this burden. He may even be advised to perform acrobatics or tell off-color jokes. At any rate, the speaker soon learns that he must engage in an everlasting courtship of his listeners if he wants to be heard.
>
> This recognition of poor listening doesn't confine itself to the field of formal speech. Many businessmen, for example, prefer to bury

themselves in paper work rather than depend upon transmitting information from mouth to ear.

A while ago a friend of mine overheard two businessmen talking in the waiting room of the Madison, Wisconsin, airport. The men were discussing a purchase order that was urgently needed from their home office in Chicago.

"Did you let John know how to prepare the order and exactly where to send it?" asked one of the men.

"Yes, this morning," said the other man.

"How? Did you wire him?"

"No, by telephone."

"Good Lord, no!" The man groaned. "Don't ever depend on John getting anything straight verbally. You've got to get it into writing for him, so it will stare him in the face. You better get a wire off right now. Say that you're sending it to confirm your phone conversation."

Such fear of oral communication has caused some companies to set up policies that almost prohibit business from taking place through word-of-mouth. One New York City firm provides every desk with a printed memo pad on the top of which are these bold black letters: Don't say it! Write it!

Poor listening is one failing that most people recognize and admit in themselves. When I travel around the country giving speeches on the subject of listening, I find that people readily confess to being poor listeners. Indeed, their confessions are usually open and cheerful. I frequently hear such admissions as these:

"I can sit and look at a person and never hear a word he says."

"My wife is always giving me the devil because I don't pay attention to what she says."

At the same time, I have met few people who really feel that their poor listening habits are an asset. They give lip service to the need for good listening, but they seldom give a moment's thought to what could be done about it.

Behind all of these personal feelings there's a real basis of fact. [Italics added.][4]

Clearly, the art of listening is at a low ebb in our society today. What makes this generalization all the more our concern is there is evidence that we spend more time presumably listening than we do reading or speaking. In this connection the same authors write,

---

[4] Ralph G. Nichols and Leonard A. Stevens, *Are You Listening?* (New York: McGraw-Hill Book Company, 1957), pp. 3-5. All material from *Are You Listening?* used by permission.

More recently Dr. Donald E. Bird of Stephens College in Missouri made a personal communications survey for the American Dietetic Association. He mailed questionnaires to dieticians in hospitals all over the country and in U.S. territories. The questionnaires were answered and returned by 110 dieticians located in 47 states, Hawaii and the District of Columbia. In one part of the questionnaire, Dr. Bird asked the dieticians to rate reading, writing, speaking and listening in order of their importance on the job. The results:

Reading	4%
Writing	11%
Speaking	22%
Listening	63%

The 110 dieticians estimated that they spent about three times as much time listening on their jobs as they did reading.

From other kinds of studies, there's plenty of evidence to indicate that people are more influenced by what they hear than by what they read.

Several studies have shown that in political elections people receive their information mostly from what they hear. The Survey Research Center of the University of Michigan studied the mediums through which voters received the most political information in the 1952 elections. The researchers found that 27 per cent of the information came from newspapers and magazines, while 58 per cent came from radio and television.

Columbia University's Bureau of Applied Social Research has made impressive surveys to find how people reach their decisions for voting. The results from two of these surveys have already been published. In a study of the 1940 Presidential election the bureau's research workers asked voters in Erie County, Pennsylvania, whether they considered newspapers or radio to be their most important source of information for making their voting decisions. Of those asked, 38 percent said the radio was their most important source, while 23 percent gave the credit to newspapers.

In its work on voting, the Columbia Bureau found that "personal influence" was probably the most important factor in determining the decisions of voters. Most of this influence results from what voters hear among their families, fellow workers, neighbors, friends—and even what they overhear in public places.[5]

It would appear to be safe to generalize to public relations practitioners with respect to their ability to listen. This is the reason that

[5] *Ibid.*, pp. 7-9.

simple listening has been listed as still another way in which reliable information can be obtained, if it is done more effectively. Although it is beyond the scope of this book to go into details as to how one's poor listening skills can be improved, we can paraphrase the six bad habits of listening which Nichols and Stevens list and make some progress in the direction of improving our listening skills.[6]

1. Faking Attention. Apparently all of us at one time or another go to considerable lengths to convince the person speaking to us that we are paying attention. We do this in spite of the fact that it requires energy on our part to appear to be listening and paying attention while, in fact, we are not. Unfortunately, this can become a rather frequent behavior, and the admonition is rather simple: Don't waste your energy *appearing to listen;* actually pay attention to what the speaker is saying.

2. I-get-the-facts listening. This particular bad habit might be considered as the listening version of getting lost in comparatively unimportant details. Some listeners make up their minds to try to remember all of the "facts" that the speaker is reciting: names, dates, places, titles. In so doing, the listener loses sight of the *ideas* that the speaker is trying to communicate. There appears to be evidence that the opposite process—*i.e.,* focusing on the main ideas that the listener is trying to put across—will aid in the remembering of the facts.

3. Avoiding difficult listening. Being a good listener is work—for some, hard work. Because it is so much easier to "tune the speaker out" when the listening gets tough, few of us develop the attitude to work hard at listening and understand what is being said. As a consequence, we obtain very little practice at "hard listening"—that is, trying to follow difficult material—and when the time comes when we must listen to a difficult presentation, we are usually quite unprepared.

4. Premature dismissal of a subject as uninteresting. This is our old friend, selective perception, at work here, applied to audible material. If something does not appear to be interesting to us, we tend to ignore it. What's more, we often equate interest with value: what is of interest to us is deemed valuable; that which is uninteresting is not valuable. Obviously, no one is so clairvoyant that he can tell in advance what information will prove to be valuable to him in the future. Consequently, the criterion of interest should be used somewhat sparingly.

5. Criticizing delivery and physical appearance. When we considered the topic of perception, we noted that a total perception can

---

[6] *Ibid.,* pp. 104-112.

be affected by how we perceive certain "parts"—*parts* in this sense referring to various smaller portions of the total that one might attend to. In this way we were able to explain how first impressions (based on "part" perceptions of a person's manner, dress, gestures, and the like) can heavily influence subsequent feelings toward an individual: if your first impressions are favorable, your over-all reaction to an individual is likely to be favorable; if the first impressions are unfavorable, your over-all reaction is likely to be unfavorable. This fifth bad habit of listening is this part *vs.* whole in perception applied to what someone is saying to you. If a person is talking with you and you object to some feature of his dress or you are annoyed by some mannerism or speech habit, it is possible to focus so much on these small details that you literally do not hear what he has to say. Thus, the *part perception* in this instance would be the mannerism that you object to, and the *whole* is the message that he is trying to impart. The guide to better listening here is quite obvious: ignore the little things that might be annoying and pay attention to what the person is saying. These "pet peeves" are nothing more than a form of prejudice anyway; you are convinced that a person with these minor annoyances is not worth listening to, and you let this prejudice stand in the way of effective listening. There are many times that someone has something to say that is worth listening to, even though he may *appear* unworthy of attention.

6. *Yielding easily to distractions.* It is surprising how culturally accepted it has become to yield to distractions whenever we are listening to someone speak. This is true whether we are talking with someone face to face or listening to a lecture. The slightest noise, the most insignificant change in the total context in which the listening is taking place, and our attention shifts immediately to the source of the distraction. Naturally, when this happens, comprehension of what the speaker says drops sharply. This willingness to be distracted is so pronounced that one is tempted to become rather clinically oriented and suggest that listening has become such a chore for many of us that we are almost desperate in our attempts to find an excuse to not have to listen! Obviously, the converse—that is, making a determined effort *not* to be distracted—is still another simple way in which we can improve our listening ability.

Study of Available Data

Many times material that would serve to provide a public relations practitioner reliable knowledge—that is, more reliable than the extreme left-hand end of the continuum depicted in Figure 36—is available to the public relations practitioner in his own organization. For example, it may lie in his files of letters that have accumulated over the years from various publics. It may lie in various personal documents, newspaper and magazine clippings, or articles; in short, it may exist in almost any conceivable form. What is required is that the public relations practitioner *recognize* this possibility of reliable information that he may have overlooked because it is so close to him. Let us consider several examples in order to make this category of reliable information available to the public relations practitioner more understandable.

Underwood, in his book on research, refers to this source of information under the heading, "Natural variation with statistical control." Here he points out that

> In this method of research, no active stimulus manipulation is involved. Record keeping is a fetish of our social order, both in governmental institutions and private institutions. It, therefore, becomes theoretically possible to go back to records of individuals and try to find factors which are related to differences in behavior which have been noted. There are at least two different ways by which this has been worked out. First, different individuals may have actually been treated differently in some way. The investigator now attempts to search the records to see if the behavior differed as a consequence of the treatments. Secondly, differences in behavior of individuals may have been noted, and the investigator goes back to the records to see if there is one or more factors which might account for the differences in behavior.[7]

Later on in the same section he gives several examples of what we are here calling "study of available data." One of the studies cited is of a sociological nature. The investigator was interested in whether participation in a Boy Scout program contributed to a young boy's better community adjustment. His procedure was to go back to the records and divide them into two groups, one with several years of Scout work and the other with little or no Scout experience. With this breakdown, the comparison of community adjustment between the two groups was possible, and the investigator could obtain at least a tentative answer to his question about the role of Scouting experience in relationship to better community adjustment.

---

[7] From *Psychological Research*, p. 39, by Benton J. Underwood. Copyright © 1957 by Appleton-Century-Crofts, Inc. Reprinted by permission of Appleton-Century-Crofts.

Let's take an example from still another problem situation. A former student of the author was working with a local chapter of the Muscular Dystrophy Foundation. They were desirous of obtaining information about the degree to which individuals in various special publics as well as the "general public" understood their foundation, its work, and its needs and objectives. As is usually the case with such foundations, their information needs far outstripped their means to pay for the research required to supply answers to these needs. One of the author's recommendations about how to cope with this problem is another example of this fourth category of efforts to obtain reliable knowledge short of a formal research project. It turned out that this organization had in its files a considerable number of letters written by people from all walks of life and for a variety of reasons. A content analysis was made of these letters, and out of it came some very valuable data which suggested a number of useful hypotheses. For one thing, they were able to learn some of the misconceptions that individuals have about this disease and something about just what these misconceptions were. They were able to also learn more about the correct notions that these people had about muscular dystrophy. In addition, they learned more about the lay terms—synonyms, in effect—that persons used with respect to the disease. In short, a considerable amount of usable information was obtained from material that had been in their own files all along.

One final example. The author was associated with a study for a bank, the officials of which were interested in how well they were known in the community; how their reputation of being a good place to do business compared with other banks and lending institutions in the community. They were also interested in learning more about what kinds of people they were attracting to the bank and why and, if possible, about what kinds of people they were *not* attracting and why. As a starting point in this work, we used the files that the bank already had on hand for the various categories of services, such things as checking accounts, loan accounts, and savings accounts. From the information on file for each of these accounts, we were able to make an analysis of the existing customers in terms of factors such as income, age, occupation, and location of residence. With this information summarized, comparing it with the latest census data for the same area was an easy step. With this comparison we were able to make a number of observations, all of which were useful as tentative hypotheses to be checked with the survey work which was to follow. For example, we were able to raise questions such as why the bank was underrepresented when it came to customers having annual incomes of

$5,000 to $7,000 and customers of a certain nationality, in spite of the fact that this particular nationality was one of the most numerous in the region. In short, these data, which had been there all along waiting to be summarized and interpreted, proved to be an excellent source of information which served usefully to guide the direction that the ultimate community-wide survey was to take.

A particularly apropos article that supports the usefulness of available data is one written by John W. Riley, Jr. In his article, Riley demonstrates convincingly the usefulness of already available data. Among the many examples that he cites is the following:

> Let me allude to a study of family roles and their related attitudes, which will illustrate this possible extension of scope without commensurate expense. Various studies, such as those of Bales and Strodtbeck, had shown that small groups tend to develop two types of leader—an instrumental leader, who gets the group task done, and an expressive leader, who looks after the social-emotional problems of the group. The researcher in this case (Morris Zelditch)* wanted to know whether this is also true of the family—whether there is some inherent tendency within the family so that, no matter where the family is, there is typically an instrumental leader (the husband) and an expressive leader (the wife). Obviously, such a universal hypothesis requires data about a wide variety of societies and cultures. The collection of new data would require not only very large financing but also considerable time and an array of anthropological skills. Accordingly, the research was done—relatively quickly and inexpensively—*from existing materials*, in the following way.
>
> From lists of societies for which ethnographers had reported relevant data on the family the researcher drew a sample of fifty-six of these societies. He then proceeded, systematically, to reanalyze the data, working in an American library. The method enabled him to code each society according to its predominant family structure, and then to count the number of societies in which his hypothesis was supported. The report shows that the data do appear to support the hypothesis, *and serves as a good illustration of the use of available materials to extend at a minimal cost the geographical scope—hence, the generality—of research findings.* [Italics added.][8]

---

* Morris Zelditch, "Role Differentiation in the Nuclear Family: A Comparative Study," in Talcott Parsons and Robert F. Bales, eds., *Family, Socialization and Interaction Process* (Glencoe, Free Press, 1955).

---

[8] John W. Riley, Jr., "Reflections on Data Sources in Public Opinion," *Public Opinion Quarterly*, XXVI, No. 3 (Fall, 1962), 319. Used by permission.

This brief quote is included to illustrate how the study of available data is invaluable to the professional researcher and is not to be interpreted as a technique not normally utilized by scientists and employed only by practitioners who are in a hurry.

Obviously, one could go on and on giving examples of using data that is already at hand. This particular approach happens to be one of the most useful approaches, short of a full-blown research project, one may employ. It is a technique that scientists use all of the time. The only trouble is that no matter how many examples one might give, there are still so many other forms that "available data" can take that there is no such thing as providing a cookbook guide on how to recognize opportunities that will offer themselves in this area. "Study of available data" is a very broad category and, conceivably, literally anything can fill the bill and prove to be useful. The main thing to be stressed is that the reader *should adopt the attitude of being on the lookout for such data.* He should always ask himself if he has exhausted all of the possible sources of available data that he has access to. This means the public relations practitioner should familiarize himself with the files and various collections of material that any organization is likely to amass over time. More often than not, whenever an illustration of the use of available data comes to light, it is because someone took the trouble to look around the organization with a fine-tooth comb with the attitude that useful information and reliable information can be extracted from the most unlikely places if a little time and effort and creativity are expended.

Asking Questions

This next category on our investigative continuum is one that the typical public relations practitioner is more likely to employ in his everyday work, although he may not necessarily be aware of it. Asking questions consists essentially of the process of *almost unconsciously beginning to ask questions* that may have bearing on the problem one may be working on at the time, of all of those individuals encountered in a typical work day. A simple example should make this process more clear.

When the author first became a consultant to the optometric group referred to in Chapter 9 (pages 229-231) he automatically adopted the practice of asking questions. Since one of the general objectives of the optometric group was to cause more specialized publics (such as teachers and nurses) and the "general public" (in this instance, everyone who might need vision care) to be more aware of the services that optometrists offer, the question that came immediately to mind was, "What do both the specialized and general publics know now about optometrists and their services?" At first, the writer asked friends, acquaintances, and colleagues questions such as "What is an optometrist?" "What are the differences among an optometrist, an ophthalmologist, and an optician?" "What services can one render that another cannot?" After asking such questions of about twenty-five or thirty persons, the writer then began to seek out certain categories of individuals of whom to ask the same questions. Specifically, these questions were asked of a handful of grade school and high school teachers, school nurses, dentists, and physicians. These particular groups were singled out because there was strong reason to believe that they were definitely "gatekeepers" in the sense that they played an important role in directing persons needing vision care to eye specialists.[9]

What good did such questioning prove to be? First, it was clear that people were very *unclear* about the differences among these three categories of vision-care specialties. Second, regardless of how much formal education the individual possessed or how widely read he happened to be, this general lack of specific knowledge tended to hold true. Formal education and generally above-average intelligence did not seem to make much difference. Third, even those who knew the differences among the three occupational categories had a very shallow fund of knowledge; they quickly told all that they knew about the occupations.

From this process of asking questions, at least one or two definite points began to be clear. There was certainly no need to find out what the "general public" (presumably a cross-section of the United States) knew about these three occupational categories and how they differed. If generally intelligent and well educated persons along with persons who have specialties related to vision care were rather vague or shallow in their knowledge, certainly the less educated individual in a quite unrelated occupational category would know far less.[10]

---

[9] It should be mentioned that such questioning took comparatively little time and was done in a most casual way (over coffee or lunch) so the respondent did not feel that he was being quizzed. Nevertheless, very definite trends began to be apparent as the number of individuals questioned increased and the type of person questioned became more specific.

[10] The reader has undoubtedly recognized that, to be able to come to such a conclusion about the "general public," the data had to come out in this fashion. Had, for example, this biased sample of more highly educated individuals and persons in related occupational categories been quite articulate about the difference among optometrists, ophthalmologists, and opticians, then one could *not* be sure that the general public would be uninformed. Even though it still might be a safe guess, one could not be nearly so certain as in the case where the more highly educated were poorly informed.

Too, the importance of the persons described as "gatekeepers" became immediately apparent. Those nurses and schoolteachers who were aware of the differences tended, in general, to be more likely to be selective in their recommendations as to where to refer children for vision care. Thus, they would direct a child with a definite infection or physical malfunction to an ophthalmologist. On the other hand, if the child appeared to evidence a reading difficulty or needed merely a refractive correction of some sort, then the optometrist might be included in the referral process. In other words, a tentative hypothesis suggested itself: the more sensitive the position that the person enjoyed with respect to referral, the more the role played by knowledge balanced the referrals between the optometrist and the ophthalmologist. On the other hand, if the person in a position to make more referrals was *uninformed*, then the optometrist tended to be excluded in the referral patterns.

Certainly all of the above information had to be treated in a most tentative fashion. Nevertheless, with a comparatively small effort expended in the direction of carefully selected questions aimed at certain categories of individuals in the most casual settings, a wealth of information was derived. On the basis of this information, a number of hypotheses were generated that were extremely helpful in shaping further investigations and over-all work on this account. Perhaps the most important point that can be made concerning this illustration is that the process was almost automatic. This is as it should be with the public relations practitioner. He should learn to automatically begin to ask questions and seize upon the opportunity to do so in all settings in which he finds himself. If this approach is cultivated, considerable reliable knowledge should be forthcoming and, along with the other steps outlined, continue to enable the public relations practitioner to function ever farther toward the right-hand of the investigative continuum.

Informal Interviewing

In terms of differing from *asking questions*, this last category of do-it-yourself efforts at obtaining reliable knowledge is merely a matter of degree. If we return once again to the optometric illustration, we can show the relationship between the two categories.

After a number of individuals had been questioned, two aspects of this effort at obtaining reliable knowledge became clear: (1) certain questions proved to be more fruitful than others in eliciting information and generating discussion on the part of the respondent, and (2) certain types or categories of respondents emerged as more important to question than others. As a consequence, the author now had about a half dozen useful questions and certain categories of individuals in mind to approach with those questions. When this point is reached, then *asking questions*, as an approach to obtaining reliable knowledge, shades over into *informal interviewing. Informal interviewing consists of asking a certain number of exploratory questions of a certain set of respondents.* This, in turn, has the effect of imparting more orderliness to the knowledge-seeking process, and tentative hunches or hypotheses tend to be more readily developed concerning the problem situation as a consequence of this orderliness.

THE IN-BETWEEN STEPS: A SUMMARY

In this final chapter on research, we have attempted to reinforce, in a special way, the contention made at the beginning of Part 3: Reliable knowledge is a matter of degree. Some methods by which we seek reliable knowledge are very refined and precise, while others are crude and imprecise. In Chapters 17-19, we devoted our attention to one method of obtaining reliable knowledge that is about as refined as we know how to make it at the present time: scientific research.

Among other things in our examination of the scientific process we learned that the thing that sets scientific research apart from all other efforts to obtain reliable knowledge is that scientific research is conducted according to a set of rules. We summarized these rules under the heading, "The Nine Basic Steps in the Research Process." After we considered these nine basic steps in some detail, we had some appreciation of the research process and what is entailed when one sets out to obtain reliable knowledge through the process known as scientific research. The reader should now be able to be more critical of research reports that he will henceforth encounter and be able to read them with more understanding. Also, the reader should be better able to know *when* he needs some research and better able to speak the language of the researcher if and when such a specialist is called on to aid him in obtaining reliable knowledge.

In addition, there is one other bias that the author has hopefully communicated to the reader. It's this: The public relations practitioner must engage in a *wide variety of efforts to obtain reliable knowledge.* There are so many factors that may weigh against the use of a full-blown research project that if a public relations practitioner waited around for only such occasions to move toward the right-hand end of either the *investigative* continuum (Chapter 17, Figure 28, page 465, and Chapter 20, Figure 36, page 582), or the *problem-solving* continuum (Chapter 3, Figure 2, page 48), precision in public relations practice would be slow indeed in materializing! To be sure, the public relations practitioner should function at the right-hand end of these continua whenever possible. *However, he should seize the opportunity to function at the in-between points of these continua as well.* This is the main message behind what we have characterized in this last chapter as do-it-yourself steps at obtaining reliable knowledge. Every one of these arbitrarily placed points along the continuum depicted in Figure 36 can be criticized in terms of one or a combination of the points that we made about what distinguishes scientific research. Thus, we could criticize the examples cited in the category entitled "Study of Available Data" on the basis of inadequate samples, if for no other reason. Certainly persons who take the trouble to write letters to the Muscular Dystrophy Foundation are not necessarily representative of all individuals. Likewise, people who are a bank's customers are not necessarily representative of all of the persons who might conceivably be a bank's customers. As a result, whenever we make use of material that we have at hand, regardless of the form that it is in and irrespective of the type of analysis that we make, *we must do so with caution.* We must keep in mind that the insights or ideas that we obtain from such procedures should be treated as tentative and given the status of hypotheses—that is, ideas about relationships that need to be verified.

On the other hand, the author argues that the public relations practitioner who consistently uses these in-between steps *along with opportunities to employ scientific research whenever possible* can't help, in the long run, to be more precise and more effective than the public relations practitioner who does not. There is every reason to believe that he will be more effective than the public relations practitioner who continues to function only at the experience or intuitive portion of the continuum. Functioning at the right-hand end of the continuua described should be the goal of *all* applied individuals, and the public relations practitioner is no exception. The very existence of present-day practitioners depends on this shift in activity.

As we mentioned earlier in this book, the *function* of public relations within an organization is here to stay. Very few persons will quarrel with the need for someone to function in a manner implied in our definition of public relations in Chapter 3. However, what is not yet clear is the *training* of the individuals who will assume this function. In addition to what has been said in the preceding nineteen chapters, we would argue that an understanding of scientific research and its proper use, along with an ability to function at the *other portions* of the continuum described in this final chapter, will become a requirement of *all* public relations practitioners of the future.

QUESTIONS FOR DISCUSSION

1. Try to develop your own illustrations of how a public relations practitioner can make use of the in-between steps of *reflective thinking, simple observation,* and *simple listening.* After you have developed your own examples for each of the in-between steps, estimate to what extent public relations practitioners already do this sort of thing in their everyday work without calling it what we have in this chapter. Which of the three in-between steps do you think is most often used by the public relations practitioner? Why do you think this is so?

2. With the six bad habits of listening listed on pages 590-591 as your guide, observe your own listening behavior for the next few days and categorize it accordingly. That is, try to be more observant about your own listening and see whether you *fake attention,* or *avoid listening,* or *criticize delivery* and *physical appearance* or what have you, and come to some conclusion as to what bad habit you tend to engage in most frequently.

3. Reread the material presented on pages 591-595 again concerning the study of available data, then try to think of examples of available data that a public relations practitioner might make use of for a given public relations problem. As a point of departure, it might be a good idea to take one of the cases that you used to answer a previous discussion question.

4. Taking still another case that you used to answer a previous discussion question, try to develop examples of how you would implement the *asking questions* and *informal interviewing* information collection techniques, and, along the lines of the example given on page 595, generate some sample questions that you would begin to try out for a given public relations problem situation. After you have developed your tentative list of questions, ask them of a handful of individuals and see how fruitful they are in terms of generating insights to the problem situation you selected. After you have developed a few questions that appear to be fruitful, move into the informal interviewing phase—that is, ask the same questions in the same manner of an additional handful of individuals. After you have done this, assess the information you obtained in terms of its usefulness in helping you to think about the public relations problem situation you selected. Did you find that this approach generated some insights that you did not have before you started?

INDEX

INDEX

A

Aggregate, definition of, 108, 109
American Optometric Association, 247, 250, 296, 297
Anthropomorphism, 207, 208
Arnstein, George, 216
Attitude
  behavior, relationship to, 329-340
    consumer behavior example, 334-336
    public relations example,
    voting example, 330-333
    warning, a word of, 339-340
  change, resistance to, 343-350
    avoidance or withdrawal, because of, 343, 344
    perceptual selectivity, because of, 344-348
    self-perpetuation, because of, 348-350
  definitions of, 322-324, 328
  "frame of reference," contrasted with, 350-352
  inferred, must be, 324-326
  learning, relationship to, 340-342
  opinion, contrasted with, 326-328
  personality, relationship to, 342, 343

  psychological concepts, example of, 322-350
  reification, relationship to, 325, 326
  stereotype, contrasted with, 352, 353
  verb "to be," relationship to, 326
Authoritarian personality, 319
Ayars, Albert L., 258, 455

B

Back, Kurt, 321
Bales, Robert F., 594
Ballachey, Egerton L., 423
Barcus, F. Earle, 219
Barnard, Chester I., 135
Bauer, R. A., 452
Beal, George M., 415
Berelson, Bernard, 217, 271, 274, 449-451, 453
Berlo, D. K., 202, 203
Berlow, Iran, 303-305
"Best obtainable evidence" (See Problem Solving Continuum)
Bexton, W. H., 94
Bird, Donald E., 589
"Birthday Paradox" (See Scientific Research, Sampling)
Bomberger, Russell, 571